A New Companion to
Digital Humanities

Blackwell Companions to Literature and Culture

This series offers comprehensive, newly written surveys of key periods and movements and certain major authors, in English literary culture and history. Extensive volumes provide new perspectives and positions on contexts and on canonical and post-canonical texts, orientating the beginning student in new fields of study and providing the experienced undergraduate and new graduate with current and new directions, as pioneered and developed by leading scholars in the field.

Published Recently

A NEW COMPANION TO

DIGITAL HUMANITIES

EDITED BY

SUSAN SCHREIBMAN, RAY SIEMENS, AND JOHN UNSWORTH

WILEY Blackwell

This edition first published 2016
© 2016 John Wiley & Sons, Ltd.

Registered Office
John Wiley & Sons, Ltd, The Atrium, Southern Gate, Chichester, West Sussex, PO19 8SQ, UK

Editorial Offices
350 Main Street, Malden, MA 02148-5020, USA
9600 Garsington Road, Oxford, OX4 2DQ, UK
The Atrium, Southern Gate, Chichester, West Sussex, PO19 8SQ, UK

For details of our global editorial offices, for customer services, and for information about how to apply for permission to reuse the copyright material in this book please see our website at www.wiley.com/wiley-blackwell.

The right of Susan Schreibman, Ray Siemens, and John Unsworth to be identified as the authors of the editorial material in this work has been asserted in accordance with the UK Copyright, Designs and Patents Act 1988.

Library of Congress Cataloging-in-Publication data applied for

Hardback 9781118680599
Paperback 9781118680643

A catalog record for this book is available from the British Library.

Cover image: Zdeněk Sýkora, *Lines No. 56 (Humberto)*, 1988, oil on canvas, 200 × 200 cm. Collection of the Museum of Modern Art Olomouc, The Czech Republic. Photo Zdeněk Sodoma. © Zdeněk Sýkora - heir, Lenka Sýkorová, 2015

Set in 11/12.5pt Garamond3 by SPi Global, Pondicherry, India
Printed and bound in Malaysia by Vivar Printing Sdn Bhd

2   2017

Contents

Notes on Contributors

John Ashley Burgoyne is a lecturer in the Music Cognition Group at the University of Amsterdam and a guest researcher at the Netherlands Institute for Sound and Vision. Dr. Burgoyne led the compilation of the McGill Billboard transcriptions and the Hooked on Music project on long-term musical memorability.

Tanya E. Clement is an assistant professor in the School of Information at the University of Texas at Austin. Her primary area of research is scholarly information infrastructure. She has published widely on digital humanities and digital literacies as well as scholarly editing, modernist literature, and sound studies. Her current research projects include *High Performance Sound Technologies for Access and Scholarship* (HiPSTAS).

Owen Conlan is an assistant professor in the School of Computer Science and Statistics, Trinity College Dublin, with expertise in personalization and visualization. He has co-authored over 100 publications and has received several best-paper awards. Owen coordinated the European Commission-funded *CULTURA* project, and he is a passionate educator who teaches knowledge and data engineering.

Panos Constantopoulos is a professor in the Department of Informatics and Dean of the School of Information Sciences and Technology, Athens University of Economics and Business. He is also affiliated with the Athena Research Centre, where he heads the Digital Curation Unit. He was previously in the Department of Computer Science, University of Crete (1986–2003). From 1992 to 2003 he was head of the Information Systems Laboratory and the Centre for Cultural Informatics at the Institute of Computer Science, Foundation for Research and Technology – Hellas. His interests include digital curation and preservation, knowledge representation and conceptual modeling, ontology engineering, semantic information access, decision support and knowledge management systems, cultural informatics and digital libraries.

Costis Dallas is associate professor at the Faculty of Information, University of Toronto, where he served as Director of Museum Studies from 2012 to 2015, and assistant professor at the Department of Communication, Media and Culture, Panteion University. His current work as Research Fellow of the Digital Curation Unit, IMIS-Athena Research Centre, as chair of the DARIAH Digital Practices and Methods Observatory (DiMPO) working group, and as co-principal investigator in the CARARE, LoCloud, Europeana Cloud, and ARIADNE EU-funded projects, concerns developing a pragmatic theory of digital curation "in the wild", knowledge practices and digital infrastructures for cultural heritage and humanities scholarship, and knowledge representation of material culture.

Martin Doerr is Research Director and head of the Centre for Cultural Informatics at FORTH-ICS in Crete. He has led and participated in projects for information systems in culture and e-science. He is chair of the working group of ICOM/CIDOC which developed ISO 21127:2006, and on the editorial boards of *Applied Ontology* and the *ACM Journal on Computing and Cultural Heritage* (JOCCH).

J. Stephen Downie is a professor and the Associate Dean for Research at the Graduate School of Library and Information Science, University of Illinois, where he conducts research in music information retrieval. He was instrumental in founding both the International Society for Music Information Retrieval and the Music Information Retrieval Evaluation eXchange.

Johanna Drucker is the Breslauer Professor in the Department of Information Studies at UCLA. She has published and lectured widely on topics related to digital humanities and aesthetics, book history and design futures, historiography of the alphabet, and contemporary art. Her most recent book is *Graphesis: Visual Forms of Knowledge Production* (Harvard University Press, 2014).

Jennifer Edmond is Director of Strategic Projects in the Faculty of Arts, Humanities and Social Sciences at Trinity College Dublin. Jennifer is Coordinator of the EU-funded infrastructure project CENDARI (Collaborative EuropeaN Digital/Archival Research Infrastructure) among others. She publishes primarily on topics related to infrastructure for humanities research, interdisciplinarity and the broader impact of the digital humanities on scholarly practice.

Devon Elliott is a PhD candidate in History at Western University. His dissertation examines the technological and cultural history of stage magic.

Kathleen Fitzpatrick is Director of Scholarly Communication of the Modern Language Association and author of *Planned Obsolescence: Publishing, Technology, and the Future of the Academy* (NYU Press, 2011). She co-founded the digital scholarly network MediaCommons, where she has led a number of experiments in open peer review and other innovations in scholarly publishing.

Julia Flanders directs the Digital Scholarship Group at Northeastern University, where she is a professor of practice in the department of English and a member of the NULab for Texts, Maps, and Networks. Her research focuses on text encoding, data modeling, and data curation in digital humanities.

Neil Fraistat is Professor of English and Director of the Maryland Institute for Technology in the Humanities (MITH) at the University of Maryland. A founder and co-chair of centerNet, his most recent books include Volume 3 of *The Complete Poetry of Percy Bysshe Shelley* (Johns Hopkins University Press, 2012) and *The Cambridge Companion to Textual Scholarship* (Cambridge University Press, 2013).

Ichiro Fujinaga is an associate professor in Music Technology Area at the Schulich School of Music at McGill University. In 2003–04, he was the acting director of the Center for Interdisciplinary Research in Music Media and Technology (CIRMMT) at McGill. In 2002–3, 2009–12, and 2014–5, he was the Chair of the Music Technology Area. Before that he was a faculty member of the Computer Music Department at the Peabody Conservatory of Music of the Johns Hopkins University. Research interests include optical music recognition, music theory, machine learning, music perception, digital signal processing, genetic algorithms, and music information acquisition, preservation, and retrieval.

Alex Gil is Digital Scholarship Coordinator for the Humanities and History at Columbia. He serves as a consultant to faculty, students, and the library on the impact of technology on humanities research, pedagogy, and scholarly communications. Current projects include an open repository of syllabi for curricular research, and an aggregator for digital humanities projects worldwide. He is currently acting chair of Global Outlook::Digital Humanities (GO::DH) and the organizer of the THATCamp Caribe series.

Stefan Gradmann is a professor in the Arts department of KU Leuven (Belgium) as well as director of the University Library. He was an international advisor for the ACLS Commission on Cyberinfrastructure for the Humanities and Social Sciences, and was heavily involved in building *Europeana*, the European Digital Library. His research interests include knowledge management, digital libraries and information architectures, document management, and document lifecycle management.

Cormac Hampson works at Boxever, a personalization-based startup in Dublin, Ireland. Prior to that, he was a postdoctoral researcher in the School of Computer Science and Statistics, Trinity College Dublin. His research areas include data exploration, personalization, and digital humanities.

Lorna Hughes is a professor of Digital Humanities at Glasglow University. Her research focuses on the use of digital content, and her publications include *Digitizing Collections: Strategic Issues for the Information Manager* (Facet, 2003), *The Virtual Representation of the Past* (Ashgate, 2008), and *Evaluating and Measuring the Value, Use and Impact of Digital Collections* (Facet, 2011). She chairs the ESF Network for Digital Methods in the Arts and Humanities (NeDiMAH), and was principal investigator on a JISC-funded mass digitization initiative, *The Welsh Experience of the First World War*.

Fotis Jannidis is a professor of German literature and literary computing at the University of Würzburg. His research interests include the quantitative study of literature, especially with larger text collections, and data modeling.

Matthew L. Jockers is the Susan J. Rosowski associate professor of English and director of the Literary Lab at the University of Nebraska. Jockers specializes in large-scale text mining. His books include *Macroanalysis: Digital Methods and Literary History* (UIUC Press, 2013) and *Text Analysis with R for Students of Literature* (Springer, 2014). Jockers blogs about his research at http://www.matthewjockers.net

Christopher Johanson is assistant professor in Classics and Digital Humanities at UCLA, co-director of the Experiential Technologies Center, chair of the Humanities Virtual World Consortium, and director of RomeLab, a multidisciplinary research group that studies the interrelationship between historical phenomena and their spatial contexts.

Steven E. Jones is professor of English and Director of the Center for Textual Studies and Digital Humanities at Loyola University, Chicago. He is the author of a number of books and articles on technology and culture, digital humanities, and video games, including *The Meaning of Video Games* (Routledge, 2008), *Codename Revolution: The Nintendo Wii Platform* (with George K. Thiruvathukal; MIT Press, 2012), *The Emergence of the Digital Humanities* (Routledge, 2013), and *Roberto Busa, S.J., and The Emergence of Humanities Computing* (forthcoming, Routledge, 2016).

Finn Arne Jørgensen is associate professor of the history of technology and environment, Umeå University, Sweden. He is author of *Making a Green Machine: The Infrastructure of Beverage Container Recycling* (Rutgers University Press, 2011) and co-editor (with Dolly Jørgensen and Sara B. Pritchard) of *New Natures: Joining Environmental History with Science and Technology Studies* (University of Pittsburgh Press, 2013).

Sarah Kenderdine is a professor at the National Institute for Experimental Arts (NIEA), University of New South Wales where she leads the Laboratory for Innovation in Galleries, Libraries, Archives and Museum (iGLAM). She is also associate director of the iCinema Research Centre. She is head of Special Projects, Museum Victoria, Australia, and director of research at the Applied Laboratory for Interactive Visualization and Embodiment (ALiVE), City University of Hong Kong.

William Kilbride is Executive Director of the Digital Preservation Coalition, a membership organization which provides advocacy, workforce development, capacity building, and partnership for digital preservation. He started his career as an archaeologist in the 1990s, when our enthusiasm for new technology was not matched by the capacity to sustain the resulting data.

Matthew G. Kirschenbaum is an associate professor in the Department of English at the University of Maryland and associate director of the Maryland Institute for Technology in the Humanities. He is the author of *Track Changes: A Literary History of Word Processing* (Harvard University Press, 2016).

Kari Kraus is an Associate Professor in the College of Information Studies and the Department of English at the University of Maryland. Her research and teaching interests focus on game studies and transmedia fiction, digital preservation, and speculative design. She has written for the *New York Times* and the *Huffington Post*, and her work has appeared in venues such as *Digital Humanities Quarterly*, the *International Journal of Learning and Media*, and the *Journal of Visual Culture*. She is currently writing a book on long-term thinking and design.

Séamus Lawless is an assistant professor in the School of Computer Science and Statistics, Trinity College Dublin. His research interests are in information retrieval, information management, and digital humanities with a particular focus on adaptivity and personalization. The common focus of this research is digital content management and the application of technology to support enhanced personalized access to knowledge. He is a principal investigator in the SFI-funded CNGL Centre for Global Intelligent Content and is a senior researcher in the EU FP7 *CULTURA* project. He has published more than 50 refereed scientific papers and has been a reviewer for numerous high-impact journals and conferences.

Laura C. Mandell is director of the Initiative for Digital Humanities, Media, and Culture as well as the Advanced Research Consortium (http://www.ar-c.org) and 18thConnect.org, and she is Professor of English at Texas A&M University. She is the author of *Breaking the Book: Print Humanities in the Digital Age* (2015), *Misogynous Economies: The Business of Literature in Eighteenth-Century Britain* (University Press of Kentucky, 1999) and general editor of the *Poetess Archive*.

Willard McCarty is Professor, Digital Humanities Research Group, University of Western Sydney, Professor of Humanities Computing, King's College London, and editor of Interdisciplinary Science Reviews and of the online seminar Humanist. He is the 2013 recipient of the Roberto Busa Award. His current book project is an historical study of digital humanities, tentatively entitled Machines of Demanding Grace (Palgrave, forthcoming 2017).

Jerome McGann is the John Stewart Bryan University Professor, University of Virginia, and Visiting Research Fellow, University of California, Berkeley. His two most recent publications, both from Harvard UP, are A New Republic of Letters: Memory and Scholarship in an Age of Digital Reproduction (2014), and The Poet Edgar Allan Poe: Alien Angel (2014). Next year Harvard will publish his critical edition of Martin Delany's Blake; or The Huts of America.

Nick Montfort develops literary generators and other computational art and poetry. He has participated in dozens of literary and academic collaborations. He lives in New York City and is associate professor of digital media at MIT. He co-edited the *Electronic Literature Collection volume 1*. He wrote the books of poems #! and *Riddle & Bind* and co-wrote *2002*. The MIT Press has published four of his collaborative and individually authored books: *The New Media Reader* (2003), *Twisty Little Passages* (2005), *Racing the Beam* (2009), and most recently *10 PRINT CHR$(205.5+RND(1)); : GOTO 10* (2013), a collaboration with nine other authors.

Bethany Nowviskie directs the library-based Scholars' Lab at the University of Virginia, where she also serves as special advisor to the Provost. She is a Distinguished Presidential Fellow at the Council on Library and Information Resources (CLIR) and immediate past president of the Association for Computers and the Humanities (ACH). Her current projects include *Neatline* and the *UVa Praxis Program*.

Daniel Paul O'Donnell is professor of English at the University of Lethbridge. He is editor-in-chief of *Digital Studies/Le champ numérique* and founding chair of Global Outlook::Digital Humanities and Digital Medievalist. He is also a former chair of the Text Encoding Initiative Consortium. His research interests include the digital humanities, medieval philology, and research communication.

Dominic Oldman is Head of ResearchSpace, a project funded by the Andrew W. Mellon Foundation, and a senior member of the Collections Directorate at the British Museum. He specializes in digital historiography, epistemology, and the representation of knowledge. He is co-deputy chair of the Conceptual Reference Model Special Interest Group that is developing the ISO-compatible international standard on behalf of the Documentation Committee of the International Council of Museums.

Elena Pierazzo is professor of Italian Studies and Digital Humanities at the University of Grenoble 3 "Stendhal"; formerly she was lecturer at the Department of Digital Humanities at King's College London, where she was the coordinator of the masters' program in digital humanities. She has special expertise in Italian renaissance texts, digital editions of early modern and modern draft manuscripts, and text encoding. She Chaired the Text Encoding Initiative (TEI) between 2011–2015 and is deeply involved in the TEI user community. She co-chairs the working group on digital editions of NeDiMAH.

Andrew Prescott is professor of digital humanities at the University of Glasgow. He has worked in a number of digital humanities units in the UK, including Sheffield and King's College London, and was for 20 years a curator in the Department of Manuscripts of the British Library. He was the British Library contact on the *Electronic Beowulf* project, edited by Kevin S. Kiernan.

Todd Presner is professor of Germanic languages and comparative literature at UCLA, where he is the faculty chair of the digital humanities program. He has recently co-authored two books: *Digital_Humanities* (with Anne Burdick, Johanna Drucker, Peter Lunenfeld, and Jeffrey Schnapp; MIT Press, 2012), and *HyperCities: Thick Mapping in the Digital Humanities* (with David Shepard and Yoh Kawano; Harvard University Press, 2014).

Kenneth M. Price is Hillegass University Professor at the University of Nebraska–Lincoln and co-director of the Center for Digital Research in the Humanities. He is the author or editor of 11 books, including *Literary Studies in the Digital Age* (MLA, 2013). He is co-editor of *The Walt Whitman Archive*.

Stephen Ramsay is Susan J. Rosowski Associate University Professor of English and a Fellow at the Center for Digital Research in the Humanities, University of Nebraska–Lincoln. He is the author of *Reading Machines* (University of Illinois Press, 2011).

Scott Rettberg is Professor of Digital Culture at the University of Bergen, Norway. He was a founder of the Electronic Literature Organization and the project leader of ELMCIP. He is the author or co-author of novel-length works of electronic literature including *The Unknown*, *Kind of Blue*, *Implementation*, and others.

Geoffrey Rockwell is a professor of philosophy and humanities computing at the University of Alberta, Canada. He publishes on philosophical dialog, textual visualization and analysis, humanities computing, instructional technology, computer games and multimedia. He is currently the director of the Kule Institute for Advanced Studies and a network investigator in the GRAND Network of Centres of Excellence, studying gaming, animation, and new media. He collaborates with Stéfan Sinclair on *Voyant Tools*, and leads the *TAPoR* project (documenting text tools for humanists).

Stan Ruecker is an associate professor at the IIT Institute of Design in Chicago. His current research interests lie in the areas of humanities visualization, the future of reading, and information design. His work focuses on supporting the hermeneutic or interpretive process.

Jentery Sayers is Assistant Professor of English and Director of the Maker Lab in the Humanities at the University of Victoria, Canada. His research interests include comparative media studies and critical theories of technology. His work has appeared in *American Literature, Literature Compass, The Journal of Electronic Publishing, Computational Culture*, the *International Journal of Learning and Media*, and *e-Media Studies*, among others.

Susan Schreibman is Professor of Digital Humanities at Maynooth University and Director of An Foras Feasa, Ireland. Previously she was the founding director of the Digital Humanities Observatory, Assistant Dean for Digital Collections and Research, University of Maryland Libraries, and Assistant Director of the Maryland Institute for Technology in the Humanities. She is the founding editor of *The Letters of 1916* and *The Thomas MacGreevy Archive*, and of the peer-reviewed *Journal of the Text Encoding Initiative*. Her publications include *A Companion to Digital Humanities* (Blackwell, 2004), *A Companion to Digital Literary Studies* (Blackwell, 2008), and *Thomas MacGreevy: A Critical Reappraisal* (Bloomsbury, 2013). Professor Schreibman is the Irish representative to DARIAH, a European infrastructure in digital humanities.

Sydney J. Shep is a reader in book history at Victoria University of Wellington, New Zealand, and printer at the university's Wai-te-ata Press. In addition to running a letterpress lab, she directs a number of digital history research and pedagogy projects and teaches topics in print, communication, and culture.

David Shepard is the lead academic developer at UCLA's Center for Digital Humanities. He received his PhD in English from UCLA in 2012. His projects include *HyperCities*, *Bishamon*, and *HyperCities GeoScribe*, which received one of the inaugural Google Digital Humanities Awards. He is a co-author of *HyperCities: Thick Mapping in the Digital Humanities* (Harvard University Press, 2014) and has written articles on social media analysis.

Ray Siemens is Canada Research Chair in Humanities Computing and Distinguished Professor in the Faculty of Humanities at the University of Victoria, in English and Computer Science. He is founding editor of the electronic scholarly journal *Early Modern Literary Studies*, and his publications include *A Companion to Digital Humanities* (with Schreibman and Unsworth), *A Companion to Digital Literary Studies* (with Schreibman), *A Social Edition of the Devonshire MS*, and *Literary Studies in the Digital Age* (MLA, with Ken Price). He directs the *Implementing New Knowledge Environments* project, the Digital Humanities Summer Institute and the Electronic Textual Cultures Lab, and serves as vice president of the Canadian Federation of the Humanities and Social Sciences (for Research Dissemination), recently serving also as chair of the international Alliance of Digital Humanities Organizations' steering committee.

Stéfan Sinclair is professor in the Department of Literature, Languages and Cultures at McGill University and director of the McGill Centre for Digital Humanities. His primary area of research is in the design, development, usage, and theorization of tools for the digital humanities, especially for text analysis and visualization. He serves as the president of the Association for Computers and the Humanities (ACH). He loves to code.

C. M. Sperberg-McQueen is the founder of Black Mesa Technologies LLC, a consultancy specializing in the use of descriptive markup to help memory institutions preserve cultural heritage information. He co-edited the XML 1.0 specification, the *Guidelines* of the Text Encoding Initiative, and the XML Schema Definition Language (XSDL) 1.1 specification.

Patrik Svensson is Professor of Humanities and Information Technology at HUMlab, Umeå University. He was the director of HUMlab from 2000 to 2014. His work spans educational technology, media places, infrastructure, and the field of digital humanities. Two of his new projects engage with the place of academic events and the role of humanities centers.

Melissa Terras is director of the Centre for Digital Humanities at University College London, Professor of Digital Humanities in UCL's Department of Information Studies, and co-investigator of the award-winning *Transcribe Bentham* crowdsourcing project. Her research spans various aspects of digitization and public engagement.

William G. Thomas III is the Angle Chair in the Humanities and Professor of History at the University of Nebraska–Lincoln and a Faculty Fellow at the Center for Digital Research in the Humanities at Nebraska. He is a co-editor of *The Valley of the Shadow* and director of numerous digital projects.

William J. Turkel is a Professor of History at Western University in Canada. He works in computational history, big history, the history of science and technology, STS, physical computing, desktop fabrication and electronics. He is the author of *The Archive of Place* (UBC, 2007) and *Spark from the Deep* (Johns Hopkins, 2013).

Ted Underwood is professor of English at the University of Illinois, Urbana-Champaign. He is the author of *The Work of the Sun: Science, Literature, and Political Economy 1760–1860* (Palgrave, 2005) and *Why Literary Periods Mattered* (Stanford, 2013), and has published articles in *PMLA*, *Representations*, and *The Journal of Digital Humanities* as well as a dataset that uses machine learning to segment digitized volumes by genre. Underwood blogs about his research at http://tedunderwood.com

John Unsworth is Vice Provost, Chief Information Officer, University Librarian, and Professor of English at Brandeis University. Before coming to Brandeis University in 2012, he was Dean of the Graduate School of Library and Information Science (GSLIS) at the University of Illinois, Urbana–Champaign from 2003 to 2012. From 1993 to 2003 he served as the first director of the Institute for Advanced Technology in the Humanities, and as a faculty member in the English Department, at the University of Virginia. In 2006, he chaired the national commission that produced *Our Cultural Commonwealth*, a report on cyberinfrastructure for humanities and social science, on behalf of the American Council of Learned Societies. In August of 2013, he was appointed by President Obama to serve on the National Humanities Council.

Katherine L. Walter, professor and chair at the University of Nebraska–Lincoln (UNL) Libraries, is a founding co-director of the innovative Center for Digital Research in the Humanities (CDRH). She co-chairs centerNet's international executive council.

Claire Warwick is Pro-Vice-Chancellor: Research and Professor of Digital Humanities in the Department of English at the University of Durham, UK. Her research interests include the use of digital resources and social media in the humanities and cultural heritage; reading behaviour in physical and digital spaces; the infrastructural context of digital humanities.

Joris J. van Zundert is a researcher and developer in digital and computational humanities. He works at the Huygens Institute for the History of the Netherlands (Netherlands Royal Academy of Arts and Sciences; KNAW). His current research focuses on interactions between computer science and the humanities, and on the tensions between hermeneutics and "big data" approaches.

Preface

The first *Companion to Digital Humanities* appeared in 2004 in hardcover, and a couple of years later in paperback and free online, where it can still be found at http://www. digitalhumanities.org/companion. In the introduction to that volume, the editors (who are the same as the editors of this new work) observed that:

> This collection marks a turning point in the field of digital humanities: for the first time, a wide range of theorists and practitioners, those who have been active in the field for decades, and those recently involved, disciplinary experts, computer scientists, and library and information studies specialists, have been brought together to consider digital humanities as a discipline in its own right, as well as to reflect on how it relates to areas of traditional humanities scholarship.

It remains debatable whether digital humanities should be regarded as a "discipline in its own right," rather than a set of related methods, but it cannot be doubted, in 2015, that it is a vibrant and rapidly growing field of endeavor. In retrospect, it is clear that the decision this group of editors, prompted by their publisher, took in naming the original *Companion* changed the way we refer to this field: we stopped talking about "humanities computing" and started talking about "digital humanities." The editors of this volume and the last, in conversation with their publisher, chose this way of naming the activity represented in our collected essays in order to shift the emphasis from "computing" to "humanities." What is important today is not that we are doing work with computers, but rather that we are doing the work of the humanities, in digital form. The field is now much broader than it once was, and includes not only the computational modeling and analysis of humanities information, but also the cultural study of digital technologies, their creative possibilities, and their social impact.

Perhaps, a decade or two from now, the modifier "digital" will have come to seem pleonastic when applied to the humanities. Perhaps, as greater and greater portions of our cultural heritage are digitized or born digital, it will become unremarkable that digital methods are used to study human creations, and we will simply think of the work described in this volume as "the humanities." Meanwhile, though, the editors of this *New Companion to Digital Humanities* are pleased to present you with a thoroughly updated account of the field as it exists today.

Part I
Infrastructures

1

Between Bits and Atoms: Physical Computing and Desktop Fabrication in the Humanities

Jentery Sayers, Devon Elliott, Kari Kraus, Bethany Nowviskie, and William J. Turkel

Humanities scholars now live in a moment where it is rapidly becoming possible – as Hod Lipson and Melba Kurman suggest – for "regular people [to] rip, mix, and burn physical objects as effortlessly as they edit a digital photograph" (Lipson and Kurman, 2013:10). Lipson and Kurman describe this phenomenon in *Fabricated*, explaining how archaeologists are able to CT scan[1] cuneiforms in the field, create 3D models of them, and then send the data to a 3D printer back home, where replicas are made.

> [I]n the process [they] discovered an unexpected bonus in this cuneiform fax experiment: the CT scan captured written characters on both the inside and outside of the cuneiform. Researchers have known for centuries that many cuneiform bear written messages in their hollow insides. However until now, the only way to see the inner message has been to shatter (hence destroy) the cuneiform. One of the benefits of CT scanning and 3D printing a replica of a cuneiform is that you can cheerfully smash the printed replica to pieces to read what's written on the inside. (Lipson and Kurman, 2013:19–20)

Manifesting what Neil Gershenfeld calls "the programmability of the digital worlds we've invented" applied "to the physical world we inhabit" (Gershenfeld, 2005:17), these new kinds of objects move easily, back and forth, in the space between bits and atoms. But this full circuit through analog and digital processes is not all. Thanks to the development of embedded electronics, artifacts that are fabricated using desktop machines can also sense and respond to their environments, go online, communicate with other objects, log data, and interact with people (O'Sullivan and Igoe, 2004; Sterling, 2005; Igoe, 2011). Following Richard Sennett's dictum that "making is thinking" (Sennett, 2008:ix), we note that these "thinking," "sensing," and "talking" things offer us new ways to understand ourselves and our assumptions, as do the processes through which we make them.

A New Companion to Digital Humanities, First Edition. Edited by Susan Schreibman, Ray Siemens, and John Unsworth.

The practice of making things think, sense, and talk articulates in interesting yet murky ways with our various disciplinary pasts. For example, historians have written about the classical split between people who work with their minds and people who work with their hands, including the longstanding denigration of the latter (Long, 2004).[2] In the humanities, we have inherited the value-laden dichotomy of mind and hand, along with subsequent distinctions between hand-made and machine-made objects; between custom, craft, or bespoke production and mass production; between people who make things and people who operate the machines that make things. As we navigate our current situation, we find that a lot of these categories and values need to be significantly rethought, especially if, following Donna Haraway (1991), Sandy Stone (1996), and Katherine Hayles (1999), we resist the notion that cultural and technological processes, or human and machine thinking, can be neatly parsed. We also find that the very acts of making need to be reconfigured in light of new media, the programmability, modularity, variability, and automation of which have at once expanded production and framed it largely through computer screens and WYSIWYG interfaces (Manovich, 2001; Montfort, 2004; Kirschenbaum, 2008a).[3]

With this context in mind, physical computing and desktop fabrication techniques underscore not only the convergence of analog and digital processes but also the importance of transduction, haptics, prototyping, and surprise when conducting research with new media. Rather than acting as some nostalgic yearning for an authentic, purely analog life prior to personal computing, cyberspace, social networking, or the cloud, making things between bits and atoms thus becomes a practice deeply enmeshed in emerging technologies that intricately blend human- and machine-based manufacturing.[4] For the humanities, such making is important precisely because it encourages creative speculation and critical conjecture, which – instead of attempting to perfectly preserve or re-present culture in digital form – entail the production of fuzzy scenarios, counterfactual histories, possible worlds, and other such fabrications. Indeed, the space between bits and atoms is very much the space of "what if …"

Learning from Lego

One popular approach to introducing hands-on making in the humanities is to start with construction toys like Lego. Their suitability for learning is emphasized by Sherry Turkle, who made a study of the childhood objects that inspired people to become scientists, engineers, or designers: "Over the years, so many students have chosen [Lego bricks] as the key object on their path to science that I am able to take them as a constant to demonstrate the wide range of thinking and learning styles that constitute a scientific mindset" (Turkle, 2008:7–8). Besides being an easy and clean way to do small-scale, mechanical prototyping, Lego teaches people many useful lessons. One is what Stuart Kauffman calls the "adjacent possible," an idea recently popularized by Steven Johnson in *Where Good Ideas Come From*: "The adjacent possible is a kind of shadow future," Johnson writes, "hovering on the edges of the present state of things, a map of all the ways in which the present can reinvent itself" (Johnson, 2010:26). As new things are created, new processes are developed, existing things are recombined into new forms, and still further changes – lurking like specters alongside the present – become possible. Johnson (2010:26) uses the metaphor of a house where rooms are magically created as you open doors. Central to this metaphor is the argument that chance, not individual genius or intent, is a primary component of making and assembly. When things as well as people are physically proximate, the odds of surprise and creativity should increase. Put this way, the adjacent possible corresponds (at least in part) with a long legacy of experimental arts and humanities practices, including Stéphane Mallarmé's concrete poetry, the Surrealists' exquisite corpse, Brion Gysin's cut-ups, OuLiPo's story-making machines, Kool Herc's merry-go-round, Nicolas Bourriaud's relational aesthetics, and Critical Art Ensemble's tactical media and situational performances. Across this admittedly eclectic array of examples, the possibilities emerging from procedure, juxtaposition, conjecture, or encounter are privileged over the anticipation of continuity, certainty, concrete outcomes, or specific effects.

In the case of Lego, the original bricks had studs on the top and holes on the bottom. They stacked to form straight walls, but it was difficult to make things that were not blocky. When Lego introduced the Technic line for building more complicated mechanisms, they created a new brick that had horizontal holes in it. The Technic brick still had studs on top and holes on the bottom, so it could be stacked with regular Lego bricks as well as Technic bricks. But the horizontal holes created new possibilities: axles holding wheels or gears could be passed through them, and bricks could now be joined horizontally with pegs. In newer Technic sets, the Technic brick has been more or less abandoned in favor of the Technic beam. This piece still has the horizontal holes, but is smooth on top and bottom, and thus cannot be easily stacked with traditional Lego bricks. With each move into the adjacent possible, whole new styles of Lego construction have flourished while older styles have withered, even if the history of the Technic beam cannot be unhinged from Lego's original bricks. Consequently, attending to Legos as processes – rather than as objects conveniently frozen in time and space – affords a material understanding of how *this* becomes *that* across settings and iterations. It also implies that a given object could have always been (or could always become) something else, depending on the context, conditions, and participants involved.

It is easy to study how people make things with Lego – both fans of the toy and the company's designers – because many of them do what Chris Anderson (2012:13) calls "making in public." Plans for every kit that Lego ever released are online, along with inventories of every part in those kits. You can start with a particular widget and see every assembly in which it was used. People share plans for their own projects. Want a robotic spider? A Turing machine? A computer-controlled plotter? A replica of an ancient Greek analog computer? They are all there waiting to be assembled. A number of free, computer-aided design (CAD) packages make it easy for children and adults to draft plans that they can share with one another. There is a marketplace for new and used Lego bricks. For example, the BrickLink site lists 180 million pieces for sale around the world. If you need a particular part (or a thousand of them in a particular color), then you can find the closest or cheapest ones. Of course, what is true for construction toys like Lego is also true for the modular systems that make up most of the built world, especially when – returning to Gershenfeld (2005) for a moment – digital programmability is applied to analog artifacts. People who start designing with Lego can then apply the knowledge they gain to electronic components, mechanical parts, computer software, and other technical systems.[5] Each of these domains is based on interoperable and interchangeable parts with well-specified interfaces and has associated CAD or development software, open source proponents, and online repositories of past designs.

At the edges of Lego design, people can experiment with the "small batch production" afforded by 3D printing (Anderson, 2012:78). For example, when working with standard Lego bricks, it is difficult to make an object with threefold symmetry. But on Thingiverse (a website for sharing plans for desktop fabricated objects), it is possible to find triangular and three-sided bricks and plates (e.g., at http://www.thingiverse. com/thing:38207 or http://www.thingiverse.com/thing:13531). As Anderson notes, with desktop fabrication:

> [T]he things that are expensive in traditional manufacturing become free: 1. Variety is free: It costs no more to make every product different than to make them all the same. 2. Complexity is free: A minutely detailed product, with many fiddly little components, can be 3-D printed as cheaply as a plain block of plastic. The computer doesn't care how many calculations it has to do. 3. Flexibility is free: Changing a product after production has started just means changing the instruction code. The machines stay the same. (Anderson, 2012:86)

Of course, as we argue later in this chapter, practitioners must also consider how physical computing and desktop fabrication technologies intersect with administrative and communicative agendas, including labor issues. After all, Anderson ignores how "free" variety, complexity, and flexibility are culturally embedded and historically affiliated with planned obsolescence: the obsolescence of certain occupations and tech-nologies in manufacturing, for instance.[6] His interpretations of physical computing and fabrication technologies are also quite determinist (i.e., technology changes society), not to mention instrumentalist (i.e., technology is a value-neutral mechanism for turning input into output), without much attention to the recursive relationships between cultural practices and modular manufacturing.[7]

That said, Anderson's point about rendering traditional manufacturing accessible (at least in terms of materials and expertise) should still be taken seriously. For example, in the case of physical computing, Lego objects can be augmented with electronic sensors, microcontrollers, and actuators, allowing people with little to no knowledge of electronics to build circuits and program objects. Comparable to the do-it-yourself Heathkits of yore (Haring, 2007), the company's Mindstorms kits offer an official (and easy-to-use) path for these kinds of activities, providing an embedded computer, servo motors, and sensors for color, touch, and infrared. Kits like these also spark opportunities for humanities practitioners to think through the very media they study, rather than approaching them solely as either concepts or discursive constructs.[8] By extension, this ease of construction is quite conducive to speculative thought, to quickly building prototypes that foster discussion, experimentation, and use around a particular topic or problem. Such thinking through building, or conjecturing through prototyping, is fundamental to making things in the humanities. Borrowing for a moment from Tara McPherson in *Debates in the Digital Humanities*: "scholars must engage the vernacular digital forms that make us nervous, *authoring* in them in order to better understand them and to recreate in technological spaces the possibility of doing the work that moves us" (McPherson, 2012:154). Similarly, through small batch experimentation, we should engage physical computing and fabrication technologies precisely when they make us nervous – because we want to examine their particulars and, where necessary, change them, the practices they enable, and the cultures congealing around them. An important question, then, is what exactly *is* the stuff of physical computing and desktop fabrication.

What is Physical Computing?

According to Dan O'Sullivan and Tom Igoe, "[p]hysical computing is about creating a conversation between the physical world and the virtual world of the computer. The process of *transduction*, or the conversion of one form of energy into another, is what enables this flow" (O'Sullivan and Igoe, 2004:xix). Advances in the variety of computing technologies over the past ten years have created opportunities for people to incorporate different types of computing into their work. While personal computers are the most common computational devices used by humanities scholars for research, the proliferation of mobile computers has introduced some variability of available consumer computing platforms. That significant decrease in the physical size of computing devices is indicative of a more general shift toward smaller and distributed forms of computer design. In addition to the proliferation of mobile computers such as smartphones and tablets, there are various microcontrollers that can be embedded in artifacts. Microcontrollers are versatile computers that let signals enter a device (input), allow signals to be sent from a device (output), and have memory on which to store programming instructions for what to do with that input and output (processing) (O'Sullivan and Igoe, 2004:xx). Although microcontroller chips have been commercially available and relatively inexpensive since the 1970s, they have remained cumbersome to program. However, integrated boards that contain chips, as well as circuitry to control and regulate power, have been recently developed. Most of these boards have an integrated development environment (IDE) – software through which you write, compile, and transfer programming to the microcontroller chip – that is free to use and makes the processes of programming (in particular) and physical computing (in general) easier to accomplish.

The simplest microcontroller inputs are components such as push-button switches, but many more complex components can be used: dials or knobs, temperature or humidity sensors, proximity detectors, photocells, magnetic or capacitive sensors, and global positioning system (GPS) modules. Simple outputs include light-emitting diodes (LEDs) that indicate activity or system behaviors, and more complex outputs include speakers, motors, and liquid crystal displays. The inputs and outputs are chosen based on the desired interaction for a given physical computing project, underscoring the fact that – when designing interactions between analog and digital environments, in the space between bits and atoms – the appeal of microcontrollers is that they are small, versatile, and capable of performing dedicated tasks sensitive to the particulars of time and space. For most practitioners, they are also low-cost, and physical computing parts (including microcontrollers, sensors, and actuators) are highly conducive to reuse. Put this way, they encourage people to think critically about access, waste, obsolescence, repair, and repurposing – about "what Jonathan Sterne (2007) calls 'convivial computing.'"

Arduino has arguably become the most popular microcontroller-based platform. It began as an open-source project for artists, who wanted to lower the barrier to programming interactive artifacts and installations. Introduced in 2005, it has since gone through a number of iterations in both design and function, and various builds – all of which work with a common IDE – are available. Typically, an Arduino board is about the size of a deck of playing cards, and it has onboard memory comparable to a 1980s-era computer (meaning its overall computational processing power and memory are limited). There are easily accessible ports on the device that one can define, through software, as either inputs or outputs. There are digital and analog ports on the device, so it can negotiate both types of signals. There are also ports necessary for powering other components, as well as ports that can be used to send serial communications back and forth between devices. Arduino can be powered by batteries or plugged into an electrical outlet via common AC-DC transformers. Couple this independent power source with the onboard memory, and Arduino-driven builds can stand alone, untethered from a personal computer and integrated into infrastructure, clothing, or a specific object. Additionally, the open-source nature of Arduino has sparked the development of custom peripherals, known as shields. These modules are designed to plug, Lego-like, directly into the ports of an Arduino. They are compact and often designed for a specific function: to play audio, control motors, communicate with the Internet, recognize faces, or display information via a screen. Resonating with the original purpose of Arduino, shields lower the barrier to making interactive artifacts, letting practitioners focus on ideas and experimentation while prototyping.

To be sure, the introduction of Arduino has lowered the costs of creating custom devices that think, sense, or talk, but such reductions have extended across computing more generally. Microprocessors capable of much more computational speed and memory are available at prices comparable to Arduino and can be set up with free, Linux-based operating systems for more computationally intensive projects. The Raspberry Pi and Beagle Bone are two such computer boards that occupy the space between an Arduino-level microcontroller and a personal computer. They work as small, standalone computers, but have accessible input/output ports for custom devices and interaction. As small computers, they can also connect to the Internet, and – like Arduino – they can be used to build interactive exhibits (Turkel, 2011a), facilitate hands-on approaches to media history (Sayers *et al.*, 2013), construct electronic textiles (Buechley and Eisenberg, 2008), control autonomous vehicles, and support introductory programming courses (Ohya, 2013).

What is Desktop Fabrication?

In the spirit of speculation and conjecture, humanities practitioners can also prototype designs and fabricate objects using machine tools controlled by personal computers. These tools further blur distinctions between analog and digital materials, as physical forms are developed and edited in virtual environments expressed on computer screens.

Such design and fabrication processes are accomplished largely because hardware and software advances have lowered manufacturing costs, including costs associated with time, expertise, infrastructure, and supplies. In order to produce an object via desktop fabrication, several digital and analog components are required: a digital model (in, say, STL or OBJ format), the machine (e.g., a 3D printer or laser cutter) to manufacture it, the material (e.g., wood, plastic, or metal) in which to fabricate it, and the software (e.g., Blender, MeshLab, or ReplicatorG) to translate between analog and digital. Given the translations across these components, advances in desktop fabrication have unsurprisingly accompanied the development and proliferation of low-cost, microcontroller-based hardware (including Arduino) that transduces analog into digital and vice versa. These microcontrollers tighten the circuit of manufacturing and digital/analog convergence.

At the heart of desktop fabrication are precise, computer-controlled devices. Generally referred to as CNC (computer numeric control), these machines bridge the gap between CAD (computer-aided design) and CAM (computer-aided manufacture). They allow a digital design to be fabricated rapidly. Such a digital approach is scalable. It works on massive, industrial scales; but as smaller fabrication tools become available, it can be used on smaller scales, too. Tabletop CNC milling machines and lathes are also available for small-scale production; however, the rise of accessible 3D printing is currently driving desktop fabrication practices, hobbyist markets, and interest from non-profit and university sectors (especially libraries). 3D printing is an additive manufacturing process whereby a digital model is realized in physical form (usually PLA or ABS thermoplastic). Most consumer-level 3D printers are CNC devices with extruders, which draw plastic filament, heat it to its melting point, and output it in precisely positioned, thin beads onto a print bed. Software slices an object model into layers of uniform thickness and then generates machine-readable code (usually in the G-code programming language) that directs the motors in the printer, the temperature of the extruder, and the feed rate of the plastic. Gradually, the digital model on the screen becomes an analog object that can be held in one's hand.

A variety of 3D printer models are currently available, and the technology continues to be developed. Initiated by the RepRap project and popularized by MakerBot Industries (a commercial innovator), early desktop 3D printers incorporated microcontroller boards into their systems. Makerbot started by offering kits to assemble 3D printers, but also created Thingiverse, a site where people either upload their 3D models or download models created by others. Thingiverse is one of the few places online to acquire and openly share 3D models, and making digital 3D models has also become easier with software aimed at consumers and hobbyists. For instance, Autodesk has partnered with Makerbot and now offers a suite of tools for 3D development. Free software, such as Blender and OpenSCAD, provide other options for creating models, and Trimble's SketchUp is an accessible software package popular with designers, architects, artists, and historians. That said, not all models are born digital. 3D scanners, depth cameras, and photogrammetry can be used to quickly create models of physical objects. One of Autodesk's applications, 123D Catch, works well as an introduction to photogrammetry, and other open-source – but more complex – options exist (e.g., the Python Photogrammetry Toolbox and VisualSFM). Depth cameras, such as Microsoft's Kinect, can also be used to create 3D models, and tool chains for transducing analog objects into digital formats continue to be developed and refined. Across the humanities, these fabrication techniques are supporting research in museum studies (Waibel, 2013), design fiction (Sterling, 2009), science and technology studies (Lipson *et al.*, 2004), geospatial expression (Tanigawa, 2013), and data visualization (Staley, 2013). Their appeal cannot be attributed solely to the physical objects they output; they also afford the preservation, discovery, and circulation of replicated historical artifacts; the communication of data beyond the X and Y axes; the rapid prototyping of ideas and designs; and precision modeling that cannot be achieved by hand.

For instance, consider Cornell University's Kinematic Models for Design Digital Library (KMODDL), which is a persuasive example of how 3D modeling and desktop fabrication can be used for teaching, learning, and preserving history. KMODDL is a web-based collection of mechanical models of machine elements from the nineteenth century. Among other things, it gives people a tangible sense of how popular industry initiatives such as Thingiverse can be translated into scholarly projects. Each model is augmented by rich metadata and can be downloaded, edited (where necessary), and manufactured in situ. The models can be used in the classroom to facilitate experiential learning about the histories of technology and media. They can prompt students, instructors, and researchers to reconstruct the stuff of those histories, with an emphasis on what haptics, assembly, and speculation can teach us about the role old media and mechanisms play in the production of material culture (Elliott *et al.*, 2012). Pushing humanities research beyond only reading and writing about technologies, this hands-on approach to historical materials not only creates spaces for science and technology studies in digital humanities research; it also broadens our understanding of what can and should be digitized, to include "obsolete" or antique machines – such as those housed by our museums of science and technology – alongside literature, art, maps, film, audio, and the like.

Returning for a moment to this chapter's introduction, Lipson and Kurman (2013) show how this digitization results in more than facsimiles. It intervenes in the epistemological and phenomenological dimensions of research, affording practitioners new perspectives on history and even yielding a few surprises, such as learning what is written inside cuneiform. These perspectives and surprises are anchored in a resistance to treating media as distant and contained objects of scholarly inquiry (McPherson, 2009). And they are useful to researchers because they foster a material awareness of the mechanical processes often invisibly at work in culture.

With these particulars of physical computing and desktop fabrication in mind, we want to elaborate on their relevance and application in the humanities. Here, key questions include: how do we integrate physical computing and desktop fabrication into a longer history of criticism? How do we understand hands-on experimentation and its impulses in the humanities? What are some models that emerged prior to our current moment? Additionally, how do we communicate the function of making – of working with artifacts in the space between atoms and bits – in academic contexts? Where does it happen? How (if at all) does it enable institutional change, and in what relation to established frameworks? We answer these questions by unpacking three overlapping lines of inquiry: the design, administrative, and communicative agendas of physical computing and desktop fabrication.

Design Agenda: Design-in-Use

One particularly rich source of physical experiments in the humanities has traditionally been analytical bibliography, the study of books as material artifacts. For instance, Joseph Viscomi's *Blake and the Idea of the Book* (1993) brilliantly reverse-engineers the nineteenth-century British artist's illuminated books through hands-on experimentation involving the tools, materials, and chemicals Blake routinely used in his printmaking shop. Similarly, Peter Stallybrass and collaborators (2004) explored Renaissance writing technologies by recreating the specially treated, erasable paper bound into so-called "tables" or "table-books," which figure prominently as a metaphor for memory in Shakespeare's *Hamlet*. Perhaps more than any other literary subdomain, physical bibliography is a hands-on discipline involving specialized instruments (collators, magnifying glasses, and raking lights); instructional materials (facsimile chain-line paper and format sheets); and analytic techniques (examination and description of format, collation, typography, paper, binding, and illustrations). Book history courses frequently include not only lab exercises, but also studio exposure to bookbinding, printing, and papermaking. To study the book as a material object, then, is to make extensive use of the hands.

Closely associated with physical bibliography is the art of literary forgery. Derived from Latin *fabricare* ("to frame, construct, build") and *fabrica* ("workshop"), "forge" is etymologically related to "fabricate." While both terms denote making, constructing, and manufacturing, they also carry the additional meaning of duplication with the intent to deceive. In *Forgers and Critics: Creativity and Duplicity in Western Scholarship*, Anthony Grafton (1990:126) argues that the humanities have been "deeply indebted to forgery for its methods." These methods are forensic: they include the chemical and microscopic analysis of paper, ink, and typefaces. But they are also embodied: they are dependent on the tacit and performed knowledge of experts. For example, Viscomi's extensive training in material culture eventually led to his identification of two Blake forgeries. The plates in question were lithographs with fake embossments: "the images easily fooled the eye," he has remarked, "but not the hand" (Viscomi, in Kraus, 2003:2).

Historically, the figure of the bibliographer has often been implicated in forgery, either as a perpetrator or as an unmasker, and sometimes as both. Thomas J. Wise, the most notorious literary forger of the past two centuries, is a case in point. An avid book collector and bibliographer, Wise discovered and documented many previously undetected fakes and was himself ultimately exposed as an inveterate producer of them. He specialized in what John Carter and Graham Pollard (1934) called "creative" forgeries: pamphlet printings by renowned nineteenth-century poets that allegedly pre-date the earliest known imprints of the works. These printings are not facsimiles of extant copies; they are invented first editions made up entirely out of whole cloth. In Alan Thomas's words, they are "books which ought to have existed, but didn't" (Thomas; quoted in Drew, 2011). Part fabulist, part fabricator, part scholar, Wise left behind a legacy of over 100 bogus literary documents that exemplify the strange blend of fact and fiction at the heart of forgery.

As varied as they are, many of the undertakings described here share the common goal of using historically accurate tools, models, and materials to reconstruct history, while acknowledging what Jonathan Sterne claims in *The Audible Past*: "History is nothing but exteriorities. We make our past out of the artifacts, documents, memories, and other traces left behind" (Sterne, 2003:19). Indeed, we cannot live, see, hear, or experience the world like they did back then; we only have the physical stuff of history at our disposal (Turkel, 2011b). Nevertheless, the significance of these undertakings has less to do with their evidentiary value than with the exploratory mindset they promote – a mindset that is alive to meanings emanating (directly or not) from the materials themselves. The haptic experience of following a nineteenth-century recipe for acid-resistant ink can cognitively function as a kind of solvent that breaks up preconceptions and dissolves entrenched perspectives and ideas, without assuming that hands-on experiences are somehow immediate, romantic, or any more authentic than other modes of analysis.

Nearly every discipline has developed one or more methodologies designed to help us do this work: to unlearn what we think we know, to denaturalize perception and epistemology, to yield genuine surprise in our research. In sociology, the method is known as *infrastructural inversion*; in literary studies, *ostranenie* or *defamiliarization*; in critical theory, *symptomatics* or *deconstruction*; in human–computer interaction, *reflective design*. By drawing on elements of these techniques, making in the humanities is able to fulfill its promise as a tool for not only prototyping the past, but also envisioning a future. As the Provost of the Rhode Island School of Design, Roseanne Somerson, puts it, making can "manifest what has not existed previously – in many cases what has never even been imagined" (Somerson, 2013:28). In many ways, Somerson's remark resonates with Johnson's take on the adjacent possible. Unlearning does not end with identifying gaps or problematizing working assumptions; it responds affirmatively, with an alternative model or practice that can be enacted, tested, and examined by others.

Often the products of haptic inquiry are overlooked in the humanities because they fall below the waterline of published scholarship. Part of what Dan Cohen (2008) calls "the hidden archive," they assume tangible yet ephemeral, undocumented, and seemingly unremarkable forms that co-mingle with the notes, sketches, fragments, low-fidelity prototypes, and drafts from which a "final" scholarly work emerges. This type of making is pervasive; however, it requires a categorical shift in thinking. A good historical example is the compilation of the *Oxford English Dictionary* (OED) in the nineteenth century. Seventy years in the making, the dictionary eventually ran to 12 volumes when it was finally published in 1928. The lifeblood of the dictionary – the thing that set it apart from its predecessors – was the tissue of quotations, nearly two million in number, used to illustrate the history of every word (Brewer, 2008). The dictionary's indefatigable editor, the Scottish philologist James Murray, crowdsourced the massive project of collecting these quotations by calling on the public to supply examples they encountered in books and newspapers. The process of classifying, arranging, and making sense of the thousands of slips of paper on which the quotations were recorded is memorably described by Murray in his 1884 presidential address to the Philological Society:

> Only those who have made the experiment, know the bewilderment with which editor or sub-editor, after he has apportioned the quotations ... and furnished them with a provisional definition, spreads them out on a table or on the floor where he can obtain a general survey of the whole ... shifting them about like pieces on a chess-board, striving

to find in the fragmentary evidence of an incomplete historical record, such a sequence of meanings as may form a logical chain of development. (Murray, 1884:510–11)

Color-coded, stored in sacks and boxes, parceled out to cubby holes, and sometimes pasted into volumes (Brewer, 2008), the scraps of paper were like pieces of a jigsaw puzzle or the raw elements of a collage that are physically assembled into a larger artistic whole.

As an extended case study, the making of the OED illustrates what Ron Wakkary and Leah Maestri call *design-in-use*, a type of everyday design in which artifacts are seen as "resources for further [creative] action" (Wakkary and Maestri, 2007:163). Quotidian examples include using the back of a chair as a coat rack, or temporarily repurposing the cushion of a sofa as a table for a coffee cup. Design-in-use is characterized by use patterns that stress the affordances of objects, thus allowing them to be modified to perform new, different, or unintended functions. Although Murray eventually imposed order on the OED quotation slips by filing them into pigeonholes, they were originally stored in a variety of makeshift containers, including hampers and baby bassinets, and inscribed on a range of surfaces, such as the backs of envelopes (Murray, 2001:174). Design and use thus thoroughly converged on one another in Murray's nineteenth-century scriptorium, making them virtually indistinguishable. The porous boundary between them is a ubiquitous feature of humanities scholarship, as well as emblematic of design-in-use more generally. For instance, when we copiously annotate the margins of our novels and anthologies, we are taking advantage of the fact that – as Matthew Kirschenbaum suggests in "Bookscapes" – the pages of books are writeable as well as readable surfaces, a key affordance of the contemporary codex (Kirschenbaum, 2008b). In short, we are redesigning our books in the process of using them. Wakkary and Maestri point out that design-in-use has important implications for technology and interaction designers. They recommend designing tools, technologies, services, and artifacts that materially and structurally invite re-engineering and appropriation. One lesson for the humanities, then, might be to approach speculative prototyping, physical computing, and desktop fabrication with design-in-use in mind, creating objects, resources, and projects that beckon people to creatively refashion them.

Design-in-use has also flourished in what are often collectively called the GLAM (Galleries, Libraries, Archives, and Museums) professions. At first blush such an assertion might appear counterintuitive, notwithstanding the ready example of inter-active museum exhibits. After all, the purpose of archives and museums is to preserve and sustain our cultural heritage, not make or design it. Moreover, GLAMs are also industries in which the hand has historically been viewed with suspicion: it is under-stood as an instrument that breaks things as well as repairs them; deposits dirt and grime as well as removes it; accelerates an object's physical degradation as well as reverses it. At its most destructive, it loots and plunders culture rather than restoring and repatriating it. Indeed, it is precisely to protect them from the hands and other environmental stresses that museums enshrine artifacts in glass cases.

By the same token, nearly every successful preservation strategy, with the exception of basic environmental controls, involves some form of active intervention. In the conservation world, for example, collections care can run the gamut, from cleaning a corroded metal artifact or wiping the fingerprints from a statue to boldly reconstructing the missing parts of a painting or adding new architectural elements to a building. Consequently, the tolerance for change in historical antiquities will vary according to time and place. At one end of the spectrum is the view that restoration is the wrecking ball of history, resulting in – to quote William Morris (1877) – "a feeble and lifeless forgery." At the other end is a celebration of restoration as a "means to reestablish [an object] to a finished state, which may in fact never have actually existed at any given time" (Viollet-le-Duc, 1854; quoted in Viñas, 2004:4). Untethered from any obligation to historical fact, the latter view gives license to what has been called "radical subjectivism," a form of creative restoration that sanctions any alteration whatsoever, no matter how seemingly arbitrary or capricious (Viñas, 2004:147–50). The conservator, then, with her paints, varnishes, stabilizers, and glues, is making history, attempting to mediate between the two extreme poles of the restoration continuum. The established principle of discernibility can help: it dictates that any intervention must be visually distinct from the original and yet, paradoxically, harmoniously integrated with it. In practice this may be accomplished through a variety of means, including the application of thin, striated brush strokes known as *tratteggio*, or even by creating a recessed zone on the canvas that can function as a safe harbor for experimenting with more audacious conjectures (Grenda, 2010).

Recently, Amit Zoran and Leah Buechley (2013) have explored restoration practices within the context of desktop fabrication, using the traversal of content from the offline world to the online and back again as a framework for thinking through the principle of discernibility. Beginning with a broken ceramic bowl, they glued several fragments back together, scanned the resulting incomplete reconstruction, virtually restored the remaining parts, and finally 3D-printed a new lattice-like structure designed to hold some of the physical pieces together, while leaving gaps elsewhere that acknowledge the history of breakage and repair. The project is of interest not only for its hybridity (in which digital and analog components engender each other in a causal loop), but also for the way it offloads some (but not all) of the conjectural work of restoration onto CAD software algorithms. They write:

> In the restored bowl, the contrasts between new parts and old are emphasized by different surfaces, forms, textures and colors. The 3D-printed surface is smooth and white, while the original bowl's surface is rough and earthy in color. The new bowl respects both the qualities of the handcrafted object and those of the digitally fabricated restoration. (Zoran and Buechley, 2013:8)

In this instance, as with others involving the principle of discernibility, the different stages in the life cycle of an object are kept purposefully discrete. Each temporal plane is perceptually cordoned off from the others to prevent confusion, even as the digital and analog converge. More important, the original bowl becomes an artifact prompting further action, and – as one example among many – it enacts one of the more persuasive functions of physical computing and desktop fabrication in the humanities: to unlearn working assumptions about material culture and perception by speculating about what else a given object (as a process frozen in time) could be or might have been.

Administrative and Communicative Agendas: Makerspaces

Physical computing and desktop fabrication often flourish in a shared, collaborative space anchored in the use and reuse of shared materials. Typically referred to as makerspaces (as well as hackerspaces, maker labs, and fab labs), such spaces take design principles for collaboration seriously, not only because the frameworks for in-situ collaboration matter, but also because – as Anne Balsamo argues – the critical and creative practices at work in maker cultures are intricately tied to "the production of physical objects (i.e., through the acts of tinkering with various materials)" (Balsamo, 2009). Due to this emphasis on material production, the collaborative research conducted in makerspaces is deeply aware of the infrastructure, resources, and social conditions conducive to making. One of the key premises of makerspaces is that their infrastructure should be flexible, modular, and economical. When compared with research laboratories across many science and engineering disciplines, it should also be low-cost (e.g., between $10,000 and $100,000) and facilitate the repurposing of "obsolete" technologies, the demanufacturing of "dead" media, and the reuse of materials at hand. In fact, many makerspaces and allied organizations (e.g., Free Geek) have areas dedicated to reusable parts, supplies, and electronic waste. This messiness actually says a tremendous amount about a space's culture and research. Echoing John Law, "[i]t looks behind the official accounts of method (which are often clean and reassuring) to try to understand the often ragged ways in which knowledge is produced in research" (Law, 2004:18–19). In makerspaces, messiness also corresponds with a cultural investment in process and transduction, or the idea that how *this* becomes *that* is (even if untidy and complicated) fundamental to knowledge production. Thus, wherever possible, messiness, process, and transduction should not be masked, rendered opaque, or excised from the output of collaborative initiatives. As types of mediation, they are – to echo the recent work of Alexander Galloway, Eugene Thacker, and McKenzie Wark (2013) – basic conditions of mediation that we should take seriously in our research.[9]

By extension, the ethos and everyday of makerspaces are imbricated with questions of labor, including the labor of an increasingly casualized academic workforce. Bethany Nowviskie suggests a connection between stable employment and both the time and level of institutional connection required to engage intellectually as well as practically with the messiness of knowledge production:

> If the vast majority of our teaching faculty become contingent, what vanishing minority of those will ever transition from being passive digital tool-users to active humanities makers? Who among them will find time to feel a productive resistance in her materials? Casualized labor begets commodity toolsets, frictionless and uncritical engagement with [pre-packaged] content, and shallow practices of use. (Nowviskie, 2013)

Nowviskie's investment in active making here intersects with the argument that, through makerspaces, people can access, use, construct, and experiment with the "middle states"[10] of technological development instead of becoming recipients (or consumers) of neatly bundled, auto-magical gadgets. Through attention to this middle state – to the gradual transformation of one material into another – physical computing and fabrication in makerspaces also afford opportunities to ask who is building technologies, for whom, under what conditions and assumptions, and to what effects on social relations. In fact, many groups, including Double Union in San Francisco, Liberating Ourselves Locally in Oakland, and Dames Who Game in Toronto, are articulating social justice issues (including the representation of women and people of color in technical communities typically built on white male privilege) with making and makerspaces.[11] Similarly, Nina Belojevic (2014) argues that – as an applied approach to media studies – "circuit bending" is a compelling way to better understand the exploitation and spectral labor of videogame industries. Importantly, her work, and other work like it (Hertz, 2009), is conducted in a makerspace.

While online modes of social organization no doubt lend themselves to social justice research, the cultural climates of makerspaces and their dedication to place-based organizing, trial-and-error investigation, haptic engagement, and learning alongside others foster an inimitable kind of embodied community building, which does not always manifest through the avatar or the social network. However, in the context of the academy, a pressing challenge is feeding the work of makerspaces back into existing infrastructures and policies in order to prompt institutional change. Otherwise, makerspaces risk being perceived as "experimental" domains peripheral to "serious" research. Worse, if care is not taken to apply lessons learned in makerspaces to the remaking of their surrounding institutions, they will not realize their full administrative and communicative potential. They will fail to contribute positively to advanced thinking and policy development around critical issues such as privacy, surveillance, intellectual property, consumerism in education, data exploitation, and sustainability and the environment. As sites where humanities practitioners can engage thoughtfully with embodiment in all of its forms, makerspaces may also foster productive thinking on issues of representation, contingency, privilege, and other structural problems in academic labor. Finally, spaces for fabrication and physical computing can foreground the role of technology and design in fashioning new audiences for academic research. As digital humanities performance moves off the screen and into mobile computing, wearable technology, and augmented reality, the value of the humanities (and therefore of the institutions that host and foster humanities research) may be articulated to new publics in new ways.

In this area, Fashioning Circuits – directed by Kimberly Knight at the University of Texas, Dallas – is an inspiring example project. It expands digital humanities, with an emphasis on fashion, performance, and the manufacture of wearable technologies. Instead of digitizing historical artifacts, it prompts people, including beginners, to make their own. For Knight and her team, physical computing renders programming and electronics approachable to non-experts. When making things, participants can conjecture about alternate histories and possible futures (e.g., how political organizing could change alongside networked wearables). In this sense, Fashioning Circuits encourages scholars to prototype new technologies and designs, through which problems – not just content or processes – are modeled (Siemens and Sayers, 2015). Crucially, it also stresses the ways in which physical computing and fabrication emerged in part from a complex intersection of textiles, handicraft, class, and gendered labor that is frequently overlooked by popular histories of science and engineering (Plant, 1997). Its blend of historical and futurist frameworks draws attention to the cultural embeddedness of computing while inviting active participation in the nervousness of it all (McPherson, 2012). Given that the social, cultural, political, and ethical implications of wearables are starting to unfold, Fashioning Circuits thus becomes a kind of public humanities project, too. Similar to initiatives such as High-Low Tech, Local Autonomy Networks (Autonets), Machine Project, and the GO::DH Minimal Computing Working Group, it engages pressing political issues relevant to an array of audiences in and beyond the academy, inviting contributions across disciplines, interest areas, and degrees of expertise. In so doing, it resists the perception that maker cultures are not particularly ideological or invested in social justice (Sadowski and Manson, 2014).

As Fashioning Circuits suggests, one way to achieve a recursive relationship between makerspaces and academic institutions is to underscore why making things in the space between bits and atoms matters right now. As we have argued throughout this chapter, the ability to navigate the full circuit of manufacturing – from analog to digital and back again – fosters something historically unique: an engagement with the cultural implications and creative possibilities of making things think, sense, and talk. As Bruce Sterling (2005), William Gibson (2007), and Steven E. Jones (2013) observe, cyberspace has turned itself inside out, through what Gibson calls the "eversion" and what Sterling renders an Internet of Things. Whatever the preferred nomenclature, a full circuit of manufacturing implies that sculpture, architecture, historical artifacts, and other cultural objects can be digitized, modeled, rematerialized, and programmed with a granularity and elasticity difficult, if not impossible, to achieve prior to the emergence of physical computing and desktop fabrication.

More important, we are only beginning to comprehend the assumptions, effects, and trajectories of these technologies. A majority of them have yet to congeal around particular standards or normalizing workflows; they have not gained popular traction or been naturalized across demographics and settings; they are only now being tested by GLAM practitioners, historians, and theorists of material culture; and (like makerspaces) they are still rare in humanities research. That said, working in the space between atoms and bits routinely reminds researchers that things could have happened differently – that history, politics, aesthetics, and culture always have adjacent possibilities. In makerspaces, such possibilities are not simply imagined; they are repeatedly prototyped and tested. While, as with any technology, physical computing and desktop fabrication can be exploited and deployed for oppressive purposes (e.g., surveillance, warfare, privilege, or monopolization), they also allow scholars to build alternatives, construct what-if scenarios, and create what, until recently, they may have only conjectured.

NOTES

1 "CT scan" is short for an x-ray computed tomography scan, which produces topographic images using computer-processed x-rays.

2 For a brief history of this split, see Sayers, "Technology," in the second edition of *Keywords for American Cultural Studies* (2015), edited by Bruce Burgett and Glenn Hendler. There, he

notes that, during the culture wars of the late nineteenth century, arguments for the primacy of both science and the arts in education rendered technical work peripheral to the ideal university. Technology was either for Philistines (the populace without culture) or mechanics (the working-class industrialists who systematically applied science).

3   WYSIWYG stands for "What You See Is What You Get."

4   On the notion of maker cultures as nostalgia for analog life before cyberspace, Evgeny Morozov (2014) examines making through "[t]he lure of the technological sublime" and technophilia, accusing maker cultures since the Arts and Crafts movement of being more or less blind to institutional, political, and structural change. While many of his critiques of maker cultures (both historical and contemporary) are accurate and compelling, his argument is subtended by the logic that making romantically longs for the immediate. It also assumes that all maker cultures think technologies single-handedly determine social change. Put differently, Morozov first establishes a neat-yet-false distinction between technology and culture and then proceeds to build a self-fulfilling argument based on that distinction. Meanwhile, the actual, historical practice of maker cultures (as well as hacker cultures) is quite messy, often exhibiting recursive relationships between technology and culture, politics and media, and society and manufacturing. For some among many examples of such hacking and making, see Dick Hebdige, *Subculture: The Meaning of Style* (1979); Nick Dyer-Witheford, *Cyber-Marx: Cycles and Circuits of Struggle in High-Technology Capitalism* (1999); Andrew Ross, Hacking away at the counterculture (1990); Elizabeth Losh, Hacktivism and the humanities: programming protest in the era of the digital university (2012); and Cynthia Selfe and Gail E. Hawisher, *Literate Lives in the Information Age: Narratives of Literacy from the United States* (2004). In short, Morozov's argument substitutes what he identifies as a technological sublime (in maker cultures) with a sublime life of the mind (in intellectual cultures), without accounting for how the particulars of the former intersect with the practice of the latter. In this essay, we avoid such a split between intellectual agendas and technologies, without assuming that all maker cultures necessarily do the same.

5   For instance, see littleBits Electronics, which allows beginners to prototype with electronics in a fashion quite similar to Lego.

6   For more on the emergence of planned obsolescence, see Giles Slade, *Made to Break* (2006).

7   For a more historical take on modularity, see Tara McPherson, who writes: "We must historicize and politicize code studies. And, because digital media were born as much of the civil rights era as of the cold war era (and of course these eras are one and the same), our investigations must incorporate race from the outset, understanding and theorizing its function as a ghost in the digital machine. This does not mean that we should simply add race to our analysis in a modular way, neatly tacking it on or building digital archives of racial material, but that we must understand and theorize the deep imbrications of race and digital technology even when our objects of analysis (say UNIX or search engines) seem not to be about race at all. This will not be easy. In the writing of this essay, the logic of modularity continually threatened to take hold, leading me into detailed explorations of pipe structures in UNIX or departmental structures in the university, taking me far from the contours of race at midcentury. It is hard work to hold race and computation together in a systemic manner, but it is work that we must continue to undertake" (McPherson, 2012:153).

8   For an example application of DIY kits in a humanities context, see the Kits for Cultural History project at the Maker Lab in the Humanities at the University of Victoria.

9   In *Excommunication*, Galloway, Thacker, and Wark write: "Have we not forgotten the most basic questions? Distracted by the tumult of concern around what media do or how media are built, have we not lost the central question: *what is mediation?* In other words, has the question of 'what' been displaced by a concern with 'how'? Have the theoretical inquiries been eclipsed by the practical ones? Is it sufficient that media be understood as simply bi-directional relationships between determining apparatuses? Is it sufficient to say that a medium is always a tool for influence at a distance?" (Galloway *et al.*, 2013:9).

10 For more on the notion of "middle-state," see Mattern and Mirzoeff on "middle-state publishing" in *The New Everyday* [*TNE*], where "[c]ontributions are longer than a blog post, but shorter than a journal article; they're typically between 900 and 1500 words. Contributions represent ideas that are in-formulation, taking shape but not yet fully formed; *TNE* offers an opportunity for you to think through a project in public, and to

solicit feedback from the … community as part of the process of developing your ideas" (http://mediacommons.futureofthebook.org/tne/about).

11 For instance, on intersecting social justice with the production of games, merritt kopas (2013) writes: "One of my long-term goals is to establish a workshop space to work with youth in which we'd read written work on social systems and try to make games with the goal of telling stories about living with structural violences. I especially like the idea of working with youth for this, and trying to show that games can be used for a wide variety of purposes beyond 'fun,' and that the tools do exist to make them."

REFERENCES AND FURTHER READING

Anderson, C. 2012. *Makers: The New Industrial Revolution.* New York: Signal.

Balsamo, A. 2009. Videos and frameworks for "tinkering" in a digital age. *Spotlight on Digital Media and Learning.* http://spotlight.macfound.org/blog/entry/anne-balsamo-tinkering-videos (accessed June 20, 2015).

Belojevic, N. 2014. Circuit bending videogame consoles as a form of applied media studies. *New American Notes Online* 5. http://www.nanocrit.com/issues/5/circuit-bending-videogame-consoles-form-applied-media-studies (accessed June 20, 2015).

Borenstein, G. 2012. *Making Things See.* Sebastopol, CA: O'Reilly.

Brewer, C. 2008. Only words. *Wilson Quarterly.* http://archive.wilsonquarterly.com/essays/only-words (accessed June 20, 2015).

Buechley, L., and Eisenberg, M. 2008. The LilyPad Arduino: toward wearable engineering for everyone. *IEEE Pervasive Computing* 7 (2), 12–15.

Carter, J., and Pollard, G. 1934. *An Enquiry Into the Nature of Certain Nineteenth Century Pamphlets.* London: Constable.

Cohen, D. J. *et al* 2008. Interchange: the promise of digital history. *Journal of American History* 95 (2). http://www.journalofamericanhistory.org/issues/952/interchange (accessed June 20, 2015).

Drew, M. 2011. The rise and fall of a book collector: part 1. Pelgrane Press, February 8. http://pelgranepress.com/site/?p=3834 (accessed June 20, 2015).

Dyer-Witheford, N. 1999. *Cyber-Marx: Cycles and Circuits of Struggle in High Technology Capitalism.* Urbana: Unversity of Illinois Press.

Elliott, D., MacDougall, R., and Turkel W.J. 2012. New old things: fabrication, physical computing, and experiment in historical practice. *Canadian Journal of Communication* 37 (1), 121–8.

Galloway, A.R., Thacker, E., and Wark, M. 2013. *Excommunication: Three Inquiries in Media and Mediation.* Chicago: University of Chicago Press.

Gershenfeld, N. 2005. *Fab: The Coming Revolution on Your Desktop: From Personal Computers to Personal Fabrication.* New York: Basic Books.

Gibson, W. 2007. *Spook Country.* New York: Penguin.

Grafton, A. 1990. *Forgers and Critics: Creativity and Duplicity in Western Scholarship.* Princeton: Princeton University Press.

Grenda, M. 2010. *Tratteggio* retouch and its derivatives as an image reintegration solution in the process of restoration. *CeROArt.* http://ceroart.revues.org/1700 (accessed June 20, 2015).

Haraway, D. 1991. A cyborg manifesto: Science, technology, and socialist-feminism in the late twentieth century. In *Simians, Cyborgs, and Women: The Reinvention of Nature.* New York: Routledge, 149–81.

Haring, K. 2007. *Ham Radio's Technical Culture.* Cambridge, MA: MIT Press.

Hayles, N.K. 1999. *How We Became Posthuman: Virtual Bodies in Cybernetics, Literature, and Informatics.* Chicago: University of Chicago Press.

Hebdige, D. 1979. *Subculture: The Meaning of Style.* New York: Routledge.

Hertz, G. 2009. Methodologies of reuse in the media arts: exploring black boxes, tactics and archaeologies. PhD thesis, University of California Irvine.

Igoe, T. 2011. *Making Things Talk: Using Sensors, Networks, and the Arduino to See, Hear, and Feel Your World*, 2nd edition. Sebastopol, CA: O'Reilly.

Johnson, S. 2010. *Where Good Ideas Come From: The Natural History of Innovation.* London: Penguin.

Jones, S.E. 2013. *The Emergence of the Digital Humanities.* New York: Routledge.

Kirschenbaum, M.G. 2008a. *Mechanisms: New Media and the Forensic Imagination*. Cambridge: MIT Press.

Kirschenbaum, M.G. 2008b. Bookscapes: modeling books in electronic space. *Human–Computer Interaction Lab 25th Annual Symposium*, May 29, 1–2.

kopas, merritt. 2013. What are games good for? Videogame creation as social, artistic, and investigative practice. http://mkopas.net/files/talks/UVic2013Talk-WhatAreGamesGoodFor.pdf (Accessed June 20, 2015).

Kraus, K., ed. 2002–2003. "Once only imagined": the past, present, and future of Blake studies. An interview with Morris Eaves, Robert N. Essick, and Joseph Viscomi. Dual publication in *Romantic Circles* (2003) and *Studies in Romanticism* 41 (2), 143–99.

Law, J. 2004. *After Method: Mess in Social Science Research*. New York: Routledge.

Lipson, H., and Kurman, M. 2013. *Fabricated: The New World of 3D Printing*. Indianapolis: John Wiley & Sons, Inc.

Lipson, H., Moon, F.C., Hai, J., and Paventi, C. 2004. 3-D printing the history of mechanisms. *Journal of Mechanical Design* 127(5), 1029–33.

Long, P.O. 2004. *Openness, Secrecy, Authorship: Technical Arts and the Culture of Knowledge from Antiquity to the Renaissance*. Baltimore: Johns Hopkins University Press.

Losh, E. 2012. Hacktivism and the humanities: programming protest in the era of the digital university. In *Debates in the Digital Humanities*, ed. M.K. Gold. Minneapolis: University of Minnesota Press, 161–86.

Manovich, L. 2001. *The Language of New Media*. Cambridge, MA: MIT Press.

McPherson, T. 2009. Media studies and the digital humanities. *Cinema Journal* 48 (2), 119–23.

McPherson, T. 2012. Why are the digital humanities so white? Or thinking the histories of race and computation. In *Debates in the Digital Humanities*, ed. M.K. Gold. Minneapolis: University of Minnesota Press, 139–60.

Montfort, N. 2004. Continuous paper: the early materiality and workings of electronic literature. http://nickm.com/writing/essays/continuous_paper_mla.html (accessed June 20, 2015).

Morozov, E. 2014. Making it: pick up a spot welder and join the revolution. *The New Yorker*, January 13. http://www.newyorker.com/magazine/2014/01/13/making-it-2?currentPage=all (accessed June 20, 2015).

Morris, W. 1877. Manifesto. Society for the Protection of Ancient Buildings. http://www.spab.org.uk/what-is-spab-/the-manifesto (accessed June 20, 2015).

Murray, J. 1884. The president's address for 1884. *Transactions of the Philological Society*, 510–11.

Murray, K.M.E. 2001. *Caught in a Web of Words*. New Haven: Yale University Press.

Nowviskie, B. 2013. Resistance in the materials. http://nowviskie.org/2013/resistance-in-the-materials (accessed June 20, 2015).

Ohya, K. 2013. Programming with Arduino for digital humanities. *Journal of Digital Humanities* 2 (3). http://journalofdigitalhumanities.org/2-3/programming-with-arduino-for-digital-humanities (accessed June 20, 2015).

O'Sullivan, D., and Igoe, T. 2004. *Physical Computing: Sensing and Controlling the Physical World with Computers*. New York: Thomson.

Plant, S. 1997. *Zeroes and Ones: Digital Women and the New Technoculture*. New York: Doubleday.

Ross, A. 1990. Hacking away at the counterculture. *Postmodern Culture* 1 (1).

Sadowski, J., and Manson, P. 2014. 3-D print your way to freedom and prosperity: the hidden politics of the "maker" movement. *Al Jazeera America*. http://alj.am/1kanblT (Accessed June 20, 2015).

Sayers, J. 2014. Technology. In *Keywords for American Cultural Studies*, 2nd edition, ed. B. Burgett and G. Hendler. New York: New York University Press. http://hdl.handle.net/2333.1/rr4xh08x (accessed June 20, 2015).

Sayers, J., Boggs, J., Elliott, D., and Turkel, W.J. 2013. Made to make: expanding digital humanities through desktop fabrication. *Digital Humanities* 2013, July 18. http://dh2013.unl.edu/abstracts/ab-441.html (accessed June 20, 2015).

Selfe, C., and Hawisher, G. 2004. *Literate Lives in the Information Age: Narratives of Literacy from the United States*. Mahwah, NJ: Lawrence Erlbaum.

Sennett, R. 2008. *The Craftsman*. New Haven: Yale University Press.

Siemens, R.G., and Sayers, J. 2015. Toward problem-based modeling in the digital humanities. In *Between Humanities and the Digital*, ed. P. Svensson and D.T. Goldberg. Cambridge, MA: MIT Press.

Slade, G. 2006. *Made to Break: Technology and Obsolescence in America*. Cambridge, MA: Harvard University Press.

Somerson, R., and Hermano, M. 2013. *The Art of Critical Making*. Hoboken: John Wiley & Sons, Inc.

Staley, D. 2013. 3-D printing: data visualization. *HASTAC*. http://www.hastac.org/blogs/dstaley/2013/12/11/3-d-printing-data-visualization (accessed June 20, 2015).

Stallybrass, P., Chartier, R., Mowery J.F., and Wolfe, H. 2004. Hamlet's tables and the technologies of writing in renaissance England. *Shakespeare Quarterly* 55, 379–419.

Sterling, B. 2005. *Shaping Things*. Cambridge: MIT Press.

Sterling, B. 2009. Design fiction. *Interactions* 16 (3), 20–4.

Sterne, J. 2003. *The Audible Past*. Durham: Duke University Press.

Sterne, J. 2007. Out with the trash. In *Residual Media*, ed. C.R. Acland. Minneapolis: University of Minnesota Press, 16–31.

Stone, A.R. 1996. *The War of Desire and Technology at the Close of the Mechanical Age*. Cambridge, MA: MIT Press.

Tanigawa, K. 2013. Warping the city: Joyce in a mudbox. *Maker Lab in the Humanities*. http://maker.uvic.ca/mudbox (accessed June 20, 2015).

Turkel, W.J. 2011a. Designing interactive exhibits. http://williamjturkel.net/2011/12/17/designing-interactive-exhibits (accessed June 20, 2015).

Turkel, W.J. 2011b. Hacking history, from analog to digital and back again. *Rethinking History* 15 (2), 287–96.

Turkle, S. 2008. *Falling for Science: Objects in Mind*. Cambridge, MA: MIT Press.

Viñas, S. 2004. *Contemporary Theory of Conservation*. New York: Routledge.

Viollet-le-Duc, E. 1854. *The Foundations of Architecture*. Quoted in Viñas, S (2004). *Contemporary Theory of Conservation*. London: Routledge.

Viscomi, J. 1993. *Blake and the Idea of the Book*. Princeton: Princeton University Press.

Waibel, G. 2013. About Smithsonian X 3D. *Smithsonian X 3D*. http://3d.si.edu/about (accessed June 20, 2015).

Wakkary, R., and Maestri, L. 2007. The resourcefulness of everyday design. *Proceedings of ACM Creativity and Cognition 2007*. New York: ACM Press, 163–72.

Zoran, A., and Buechley, L. 2013. Hybrid reassemblage: an exploration of craft, digital fabrication and artifact uniqueness. *Leonardo* 46, 4–10.

2

Embodiment, Entanglement, and Immersion in Digital Cultural Heritage

Sarah Kenderdine

[T]he museum is a theater of anamorphic and autoscopic dramaturgy; a place in which it is not so easy to tell which is the spider and which the web, which the machinery and which the operator. It is a place at the center of our world, our modernity, in the image of which those worlds continue to proliferate … (Preziosi, 2007:82)

Museum visitors gaze through lenses that have been refined over many centuries. Finding "presence" (or literally "being there")[1] in virtual environments is the result of traversing the histories of technologic immersion; generations of 'orama, sensoriums, and all manner of optical devices. It is to delight in automata, to believe in magic and the phantasmagoric, and to be transported by special effects (Kenderdine and Hart, 2003). Discussion of these histories of optical devices could include everything from cave paintings, scroll paintings, interior frescoes, and church interiors through to magic lanterns, mondo nuovo, various phantasmagorias, all manner of seventeenth- to twentieth-century "toys," *cabinets des curieux*, *Wunderkammern*, the Great Exhibitions, glass houses, and winter gardens. These early museographic forms were all part of the architectonic spaces whose images and relationships excited the private/public curiosity and that opened into new worlds of knowledge (Bruno, 2002:133).

The visual cultural theorist Jonathan Crary, in his analysis of nineteenth-century ocular devices and modernity, observed that "techniques of the observer" involve an array of perceptual and spatial expansions. In *Suspensions of Perception: Attention, Spectacle, and Modern Culture* (2001) he noted that certain elements made artificial ways of seeing more successful than others. Rather than accepting the dominant history of an evolutionary narrative culminating in cinema, he shows a history of politics of the conformation of the body (that is, the sublimation of the body to the demands of the viewing apparatus). For him, the optical devices that survived were the ones that combined two

A New Companion to Digital Humanities, First Edition. Edited by Susan Schreibman, Ray Siemens, and John Unsworth.
© 2016 John Wiley & Sons, Ltd. Published 2016 by John Wiley & Sons, Ltd.

attributes: firstly, they were sufficiently phantasmagoric, meaning they possessed the capacity to create illusion and to conceal the process of production, and, secondly, those devices were the ones that had the ability to create a visual experience that presupposed the body to be immobile and passive. Yet, museum visitors today expect learning that stands up as an experience (Macdonald, 2007), and expect a physical experience enlisting all the senses (Hooper-Greenhill, 2006). The emergence of immersive and interactive visualization environments (IIVE) represents the greatest challenge to the "passive" body since the invention of the rollercoaster. These immersive architectures and their associated visual, sonic, and algorithmic techniques offer compelling means for mapping and remediating the tangible and intangible heritage encompassing embodiment, immersion, performance, and interactive narrative – in a new wave of cultural heritage visualization.

The purpose of this chapter is to examine immersive virtual environments and how they support embodiment for cultural heritage interpretation in museums – with broad implications for digital humanities research. IIVE provide innovative ways to interpret archaeological sites and materials for scholars and the public. The dynamics provided by the physical and digital parameters of IIVE present fresh ways of being and performing in space. An understanding of the embodied experience gives us a framework of analysis that can also contribute to an increasingly accurate evaluation of these experiences. The use of immersive systems is part of a growing trend to mobilize the viewer — stimulating embodied cognition through multimodal, kinesthetic, and somatic hypermedia design. Embodiment theory is an optic for exploring these issues, and the following analysis helps us extend the previous understandings of the immersive museum (Bruno, 2002; Griffiths, 2008) and the analysis of cultural heritage (Kenderdine, 2007a, 2007b, 2013a; Bonini, 2008; Forte and Bonini, 2008; Flynn, 2013).

A close reading of embodiment also helps us re-envision the applications we might want to build at the pivot of human–computer interface (HCI). As the humanities increasingly embrace digital tools, visualization, and interaction as the primary modes of communication, synergetic understandings of embodiment are increasingly relevant. New interface design progressively emphasizes embodiment, for example, through gesture control armband Myo, with the potential for the world to become an augmented information space with Google Glass, and by the personalization of virtual reality through Oculus VR.[2] Emerging technologies that encourage kinesthetic embodiment are simultaneously accompanied by shifts in critical theory that emphasize *performance*, *distributed* experience, and the *materiality* of the digital. These further break down dualisms of action | reaction and virtual | real.

Reframing Visualization

Visualization is the at the heart of some of the most pressing and persistent problems in society today. Visualization simultaneously offers pathways to new levels of cognition for researchers in the arts and sciences (Stafford, 2011), essential for research into new modalities of visualizing data in a world producing and consuming it at unprecedented rates (Keim *et al.*, 2006). Recent visualization research, however, remains largely constrained to 2D small-screen-based analysis, limiting interactive techniques to "clicking," "dragging," and "rotating" (Lee *et al.*, 2010; Speer *et al.*, 2010:9). Furthermore, the number of pixels available to the user remains a critical limiting factor in human cognition of data visualizations (Kasik *et al.*, 2009). An increasing trend towards research requiring "unlimited" screen resolution has resulted in the recent growth of gigapixel displays (e.g., HIPerSpace at Calit2). Virtual reality systems for large-scale datasets are increasingly focused on effectively representing their many levels of complexity, including next-generation immersive virtual reality systems such as StarCAVE (UC San Diego; DeFanti *et al.*, 2009), the Allosphere at UC Santa Barbara, the Advanced Visualization and Interaction Environment (AVIE) at UNSW's iCinema Research Centre, and Cave2 from the University of Illinois.[3]

Immersive Applications in Cultural Heritage Visualization

A broad range of work undertaken is used to contextualize this chapter. This research acts as a proposition for the reformulation of digital narrative and digital aesthetics through virtual embodiment – bringing cultural heritage experiences into the public domain, specifically in museums. This applied research falls into two primary areas: the reformulation of digital cultural archives, including museological collections and cultural atlases; and the re-presentation of tangible and intangible heritage. Four pioneering works will be described to illustrate the former. The latter will be explored through the *Pure Land* case studies.

Reformulation of Digital Cultural Archives

One research area that can be framed by IIVE is the reuse and re-articulation of digital archives (so-called "cultural data sculpting": see Kenderdine and Hart, 2011; Kenderdine and McKenzie, 2013). The rapid growth in participant culture embodied by Web 2.0 has seen creative production overtake basic access as the primary motive for interaction with databases, archives, and search engines by public users. Intuitive exploration of diverse bodies of data allows users to find new meanings rather than simply access the information. The structural model that has emerged from the Internet, however, exemplifies a database paradigm where accessibility and engagement is constrained to point and click techniques where each link is the node of interactivity. The possibility for more expressive potential through interactivity, and alternative modalities for exploring and representing data, can be described in a few salient examples.

   The Living Web (2002) by Christa Sommerer and Laurent Mignonneau, a CAVE-based interactive and immersive installation, was a pioneering attempt to explore the potential of the Internet as interactive and immersive data and information medium. In this installation, users immerse themselves physically, and in three dimensions, into image and sound information streamed live from the Internet. Microphones pick up the users' conversations and use them to generate and download corresponding image and sound files from the Web. Users interact with this data and explore its content in more detail. *The Living Web* presents a novel system for intuitive, immersive, and entertaining information creation and retrieval. The work not only permits multilayered interaction; it is also *a new scientific instrument for visual analysis*, with the option of comparing up to 1000 images in a scientific discussion (Sommerer *et al.*, 2002).

The interactive installation *CloudBrowsing* (2008–2009) was one of the first works to be developed and shown in ZKM's PanoramaLab, and it takes another approach to harnessing Internet data in the form of a spatial narrative (Lintermann *et al.*, 2008a). In the current version of the project the user browses the free online encyclopedia *Wikipedia* inside the panoramic screen. The cylindrical surface of the 360-degree screen becomes a large-scale browser surrounding the user, who can thus experience a panorama of his or her movements in the virtual information space. A filter mechanism ensures that only open content is displayed in the installation.

The project lets users experience Internet-based information retrieval in a new way. As the developer Bernd Lintermann describes in a video clip:

> Whereas our computer monitor only provides a restricted frame, a small window through which we experience the multilayered information landscape of the Net only partially and in a rather linear mode, the installation turns browsing the Web into a spatial experience: search queries and results are not displayed as text-based lists of links, but as a dynamic collage of sounds and images. (Lintermann *et al.*, 2008b)

CloudBrowsing exemplifies the use of visual searching, in which users traverse data primarily through visual association and not through the pages and hyperlinks of *Wikipedia*; it privileges the visual over the textual. *CloudBrowsing* immerses the user in metadata-related arrays of images around particular semantic trajectories in an endless set of permutations.

ECLOUD WW1 (2012) by Sarah Kenderdine and Jeffrey Shaw was designed for a custom designed 9-metre wide by 3.5-metre high interactive 3D projection environment and developed by the Applied Laboratory for Interactive Visualization and Embodiment (ALIVE), City University of Hong Kong, in partnership with Europeana's *1914–1918*, a crowdsourced web-based archive (Kenderdine and McKenzie, 2013).[4] The installation activates over 70,000 images of war memorabilia ascribed to 2500 individual stories collected from across Europe. The installation instantaneously aggregates the digital imagery and associative metadata of this dataset through a large-scale interactive viewing experience. The platform, as an example of embodied museography, provides a powerful experiential tool for participants to engage in an everchanging coalescence of war ephemera and the social memories attached to these objects. It also offers curators and exhibition designers innovative methodologies for the display and interpretation of metadata through the use of cultural analytics to devise user-generated database narratives.

In situ and in-the-round, *mARChive* (2014) is the new interface to Museum Victoria's collections, resulting from an Australian Research Council Linkage grant with iCinema Research Centre University of New South Wales and the museum (Morris, 2014). The project aims to investigate visual searching and emergent narratives by integrating an immense archive of museum collection data into a 360-degree 3D space, allowing for interactive access to a data cloud of 100,000 records with images. Apart from the advances in information visualization it offers, *mARChive* addresses one of the most fundamental challenges of access facing museums: only a fraction of their collections are on display. At Museum Victoria, for example, it is only 0.8%. The challenge of displaying and making sense of 100,000+ objects simultaneously from 17 different thematic areas from diverse collections including indigenous material, natural sciences data, and social history and technology presents both theoretical and practical challenges (Kenderdine and Hart, 2014).

mARChive is staged in the Advanced Visualisation and Interaction Environment (AVIE), one the nine immersive platforms that are basis for novel visualizations by the author.[5] AVIE, developed by iCinema, is the world's first omnidirectional (360-degree) 3D panoramic screen (360 degrees horizontal × 50 degrees vertical), 10 meters in diameter by 4.5 meters high. *mARChive* takes on these core challenges of information visualization inside AVIE, responding to the need for embodied interaction, knowledge-based interfaces, collaboration, cognition, and perception (as identified in Pike *et al.*, 2009). This display system is representative of the powerful qualities that distinguish *mARChive* from the panoramas of the nineteenth century: omnistereo imagery, spatial audio, real-time image generation, and interactivity (McGinity, 2014). The history of digital panoramic immersion and its affordances for embodiment are well described in a review of panoramic history and key works in new media art (McGinity *et al.*, 2007).

Panoramic Immersion

> In virtual reality, the panoramic view is joined by sensorimotor exploration of an image space that gives the impression of a "living" environment. (Grau, 2003:7)

As noted, the panorama has been at the core of the visualization paradigms described in this chapter as a conjunction of virtual reality technologies. Extrapolating from the 360-degree immersive panorama has been a basis for developing these new ways of representation, embodiment, inhabitation, navigation and narration. The mass public screen entertainment of the panorama is the subject of a number of extensive analytical histories,[6] and this led Stephen Oettermann to claim the panorama as "the first true mass medium ... " (Oettermann, 1997:7).

In current media practices, the re-emergence of the panoramic scheme as "the new image vogue" (Parente and Velho, 2008:79) is based on the desire to design virtual spaces and places that can be inhabited by the viewer — maximizing a sense of immersion and ultimately "presence." In digital heritage this is expressed as displays of either past environments made from archaeological and historical data (digital recreations), or remote real-world locations (panoramic enclosures for archaeological site visualization and documentation purposes, for example). The panorama reveals itself as a navigable space, persistent throughout media history, which is charged with sociocultural implications (Kenderdine, 2007c). Considering the re-emergence of the panoramic scheme in contemporary virtual reality reinforces the primary notion under discussion in this chapter – that is, the affordances of IIVE in relation to the embodied experience.

In a discussion of contemporary panoramic form, it is important to introduce works by media artists and engineers that also exploit panoramic imaginary. The large-scale installation artists Michael Naimark (USA), Luc Courchesne (Canada), Masaki Fujihata (Japan), and Jeffrey Shaw (Australia) have all been working within the oeuvre of extended narratives and augmented devices for immersive panoramic images since the mid-1980s, and their works are useful examples in the context of this chapter. Seminal works that invoke the panorama include, for example: *Moving Movie* (1977), *Displacement* (1984), and *Be Now Here* (1995) by Michael Naimark; *Morel's Panorama* (2003) by Masaki Fujihata; *Place – A User's Manual* (1995), *Place 'Ruhr* (2000), and the immersive platforms *EVE* (1993–2004) and *Panoramic Navigator* (1997) by Jeffrey Shaw; *Landscape One* (1997) and *Panoscope* (2001) by Luc Courchesne.

These works are of interest because they all re-enact cinematographic devices by the use of video sequences. They also combine immersive architecture with the panoramas and thereby conjoin the interactive language of the new digital interfaces with the movement of the cinema image. These artworks have laid foundations for many future possibilities of immersive and interactive cinema.

Michael Naimark, for example, traveled to heritage sites around the world to record his panoramic views for *Be Now Here* (1994). Using a 35 mm 3D stereographic camera mounted on a motor-driven tripod, he was able to capture 360-degree motion scenes at locations such as Angkor in Cambodia, Dubrovnik in Croatia, Timbuktu in Mali, and Jerusalem in Israel. His immersive display consisted of 3D video projected onto a 360-degree screen, combined with a spatial soundscape and an anthropological approach to both virtual travel and site documentation (Grau, 2003:240–2). *Be Now Here* is for a small number of viewers who stand on a platform that rotates 360 degrees every two minutes to give the illusion of panning across the images. The viewers are required to walk to keep their position respective to the fixed projection — an effective form of kinesthetic connection. The Be Now Here project website describes how this effect is "similar to the feeling when the train next to yours pulls out of the station."[7]

Jeffrey Shaw developed the idea of augmented and environmental cinema, anticipated by the painted panorama, as early as 1967 with his use of spherical projection in *Corpocinema*, which challenged the defined limits of the flat screen. This approach was further developed in 1974 with the *Diadrama*, which comprised three adjacent screens and three pairs of synchronized slide projectors, constituting a field of view of 270 degrees. Shaw's subsequent experimentations have been more or less immersive, engaging the visitor's whole body and giving priority to the gaze. Either through a projected visualization window or integrated in a system of vision, the spectator is always invited to accomplish a specific activity and to actualize the scene through a specially designed interface.[8]

Jeffrey Shaw's work, as the theorist and designer Lev Manovich describes, "evokes the navigation methods of panorama, cinema, video and virtual reality. He 'layers' them side by side" (Manovich, 2001:282). Here Manovich refers to installations such as *Place* (1995) and *Place Ruhr* (2000) that surround the visitor (who stands on a rotating platform) within a 360-degree panoramic screen. The idea of navigating panoramic constellations in *Place Ruhr* (2000) is echoed in the cultural heritage work *PLACE-Hampi* (2006). Shaw's works reframe the traditional panorama within the modalities of virtual reality. The interface allows the visitor to navigate between the various locations — each of which is depicted in panoramic cylinders that have been distributed throughout the landscape map. Once inside the individual panoramic cylinders, the user confronts a scene augmented by incidental animated effects. These works contribute to the "representation and documentation of social and economic histories of the places depicted" (Grau, 2003:240–2).

The use of the panorama in virtual, immersive environments provides a lexicon for navigable space that is "not only a topology, geometry and logic of static space" but is also transformed by "new ways in which space can function in computer culture" (Manovich, 2001:280). The notion of navigating virtual spaces is key to the success of hybrid cinematic forms such as those described in this chapter.

Embodiment in Cultural Heritage Visualization

A series of museum-based works have been created by the author since 2000, interpreting significant cultural precincts using a variety of IIVE, including the UNESCO World Heritage sites of Olympia, Greece; Angkor, Cambodia; the monuments at Vijayanagara (Hampi) and the Fort of the Hooded Cobra in Nagaur, Rajasthan, India; Dunhuang, China; and numerous sites throughout Turkey. These works are: *Virtual Olympia* (2000), *Sacred Angkor* (2004), *PLACE-Hampi* (2006), *Eye of Nagaur* (2008), *Hampi LIVE* (2009), *PLACE-Turkey* (2010), and the *Pure Land* projects (2012) which are described here.[9]

Embodiment theory is used in this chapter to examine two world-touring installations that integrate a single archaeological dataset into two distinct interfaces, with unique outcomes. These installations arise out of the digitization work (laser scanning and ultra-high-resolution photography) undertaken at the Mogao Grottoes by the Dunhuang Academy. *Pure Land: Inside the Mogao Grottoes at Dunhuang* (2012, virtual reality)[10] and *Pure Land Augmented Reality Edition* (2012, augmented virtuality)[11] have been seen by over 300,000 people in five countries and are the subject of extensive critical acclaim (e.g., Kennicott, 2012) and commentary (Kenderdine, 2013b). This chapter extends that earlier work by examining these two installations explicitly from the perspective of embodied experience, using a framework of analysis by the philosopher Mark Johnson (2007). Johnson's thesis provides a meta-level analysis for understanding the entanglement of embodied experience as *biological, ecological, phenomenological, social*, and *cultural* (Johnson, 2007: 275–8). In these two installations, immersive interactive visualization architectures combine in distinctly different ways, to provide a context for multisensory mediation of a World Heritage site.

The modalities of embodiment in the *Pure Land* projects can be described as forms of prosthetic vision, acoustic immersion, kinesthetic activation, telepresence, augmentation, inhabitation, revealing, flying, dwelling, traveling, and walking. In these installations the sensory world of participant visitors is tuned for encounter, and emergent meaning becomes possible. Such sensory experiences are being placed at the forefront of cultural analysis — overturning linguistic and textual analysis, supporting both phenomenological and experiential inquiry. Museum specialist Linda Young, in her review of *Handbook of Material Culture* (Tilley *et al.*, 2006) says:

> ... [the somatic] confronts textuality and visuality as our culture's dominant modes of
> understanding material culture, and suggests that the embodied subject and its multiple,

concomitant ways of sensing, feeling, knowing, performing and experiencing, offer dynamic routes to different perceptions of the human relation to the material ... Corporeality and sensuality open up to the concept of sense-scapes – an enticing notion. (Young, 2007)

Embodiment Theories

Embodiment theories attempt to understand the mind as a set of physical processes derived from the brain and body of a human, that ultimately serve his or her action in the physical world. Embodiment is multisensory and results from effects of visual, auditory, tactile, olfactory, and gustatory cues. Embodiment is entanglement through, and with, context and environment. Embodiment is immersive, resulting in emergent response to being in the world. And while these statements may seem obvious to us "embodied beings," as philosopher Mark Johnson describes: "Coming to grips with your embodiment is one of the most profound philosophical tasks you will ever face" (Johnson, 2007:1).

A discussion on theories of embodiment includes several broad fields of inquiry and analysis. The first area concerns the *phenomenological*, in which individuals are aware of their bodies in their thoughts and actions in relation to the world around them. The writings of phenomenologist Maurice Merleau-Ponty in *The Phenomenology of Perception* (1962) and American pragmatist John Dewey in *Art as Experience* (1934) are highly influential for subsequent theoretical development in embodiment and embodied cognition.

The wellspring of scholarship dealing with *cognitive* aspects of embodiment includes understanding the neural processes of message transmission and learning, which enables individuals to think and act. In second-generation cognitive science, empirical studies of embodied cognition are active in psychology and the neurosciences, including enactivism (as first proposed by Varela *et al.*, 1991). Enactivism provides alternatives to cognitivism, computationalism, and Cartesian dualism. For perceptual sensation to constitute experience – that is, for it to have genuine representational content – the perceiver must possess and make use of his or her sensorimotor knowledge.[12] An enactivist approach to learning, for example, understands human experience and knowledge formation as dynamically unfolding interactions with the environment (Stewart *et al.*, 2010; Noë, 2012; Hutto and Myin, 2013). The creation of experiential, progressive, and dynamic processes for students moves beyond traditional forms of procedural learning. Such approaches are multidisciplinary in nature and aligned with advanced studies in neuroscience, philosophy, robotics, artificial intelligence, as well as human–computer interaction and embodied cognition (Minsky, 1986; Bateson, 1987; Clark, 2010).

The embrace of embodiment theory also continues to drive a proliferation of research in aesthetics, linguistics and anthropology, and in specializations of philosophy including pragmatism, phenomenology, and ecology (Johnson, 2007:264; Shusterman, 2012). In recent times, we see embodiment theories reverberating in every humanities endeavor, for example: architecture (e.g., Pallasmaa, 2011, 2012), cinema (e.g., Sobchack, 2004; Bruno, 2002), post-processural archaeology (e.g., Pearson and Shanks, 2001; Tilley, 2004, 2008; Olsen *et al.*, 2012), anthropology (e.g., Howes, 2006; Mascia-Lees, 2011), cultural geography (e.g., Tuan 2001; Casey, 1998), performance (see Salter, 2012; Giannachi *et al.*, 2012), art history (see Parry, 2011; Crowther, 2009;

Pinney, 2004[13]), new media art (e.g., Duguet *et al.*, 1997; Shaw and Weibel, 2003; Grau, 2003), and digital cultural heritage (Kenderdine, 2007a, 2007b, 2007c; Flynn, 2013; Forte and Bonini, 2008), to name only a few.

The Machine–Body Ensemble

We are in the midst of a transformation, from a world of screens and devices to a world of immersive experiences. (Krzanich, 2014)

The *Pure Land* projects build upon a history of various modes of "virtual reality" for large-screen displays, which emphasize the sensorial and immersive through panoramic immersion, stereoscopy, and augmentation (see Kenderdine and Hart, 2003, for an analysis of stereoscopy, the body and immersion, and Kenderdine, 2007a, for an extensive discussion of the panorama and new media).

Pure Land: Inside the Mogao Grottoes (*Pure Land*), shown in Figure 2.1, is staged in the AVIE. Inside this 10-meter-diameter, 4-meter-high theater, up to 30 visitors are able to freely perambulate a true-to-life-scale virtual Cave 220 from Dunhuang. A handheld interface provides interaction with the digitally rendered cave — allowing the user to reveal key elements in the mural paintings on its walls. Exploiting the high-resolution photography and laser scanning data recorded by the Dunhuang Academy, *Pure Land* reframes and reconstitutes the extraordinary wealth of paintings found in the caves at Dunhuang. Inside its panoramic enclosure, visitors engage in a surrogate experience of being inside this cave temple and seeing its magnificent Buddhist wall paintings. As well as offering a powerful space of embodied representation, *Pure Land* exploits various digital image-processing techniques such as 2D, 3D animation, and 3D cinematography to further develop its experiential and interpretative capabilities.

Figure 2.1 *Pure Land: Inside the Mogao Grottoes.* Image © Applied Laboratory for Interactive Visualization and Embodiment, CityU, Hong Kong.

Figure 2.2 *Pure Land: Augmented Reality Edition.* Image © Applied Laboratory for Interactive Visualization and Embodiment, CityU, Hong Kong.

Pure Land: Augmented Reality Edition (*Pure Land AR*), shown in Figure 2.2, uses mobile media technology to create a complementary augmented-reality rendition of the same data from Cave 220. This could be better described as an augmented "virtuality" (Milgram *et al.*, 1994) Walking around inside the exhibition space holding a tablet screen in their hands, users are able to view the architecture of the cave and to explore its sculptures and wall paintings as they appear on mobile "windows" – a kinesthetic revealing of the painted architectonic space of the virtual cave at one-to-one scale. Other viewers simultaneously follow these users as they interactively reveal the cave. In this installation the walls of the exhibition room (which share the same scale as the real cave) are covered with one-to-one scale prints of Cave 220's "wireframe" polygonal mesh – which provides users with visual cues as to what to explore. In doing so, the tablet screen shifts from being considered as an object in and of itself, to functioning as a mobile framing device for the staging of a "virtual" rendering of the real cave that relies on an intricate spatial tracking system.

Embodiment in The *Pure Land*

The body carries time into the experience of place and landscape. Any moment of lived experience is thus orientated by and towards the past, a fusion of the two. Past and present fold upon each other. The past influences the present and the present re-articulates that past. (Tilley, 2004:12)

In *The Meaning of the Body*, philosopher Mark Johnson outlines an "embodiment theory" based on how the body and mind operate together in one organic process. Following John Dewey's somatic naturalism, Johnson argues that all our abstract conceptualization and reasoning, all our thought and language – all our symbolic expression and interaction – are tied intimately to our embodiment and to the pervasive aesthetic characteristics of all experience. Building on work done with George Lakoff (1999), Johnson demonstrates that human beings are metaphorical creatures and metaphor is essential for abstract conceptualization and reasoning, and that, through the nature of embodied experience, truth is not absolute. Johnson challenges us to "stop thinking of the human body as a thing" (2007:275), and argues that meaning and mind are embodied at a number of levels, simultaneously: as a *biological organism* (the body in the world as flesh); an *ecological body* (environmental context of the body in the world); a *phenomenological body* (our body as we live and experience it, the tactile-kinesthetic body); a *social body* (subjective relations); and a *cultural body* (i.e., cultural artifacts, institutions, practices that constitute "culture"). Each aspect of an embodied self cannot be removed from the others, with the implication that a study of embodiment needs to be multidisciplinary and must be subject to multiple methods of analysis.

Following Mark Johnson, it is possible to conceive a fivefold framework for the embodied nature of the *Pure Land* projects.

1. **The biological organism** (the body in the world as flesh) has different constraints in relation to the technologies employed. Every user-agent comes to the *Pure Land* projects with inherent physical capacities.

    Archaeologist Christopher Tilley demonstrates the manner in which the past can be understood and interpreted via a sensual human scale as opposed to an abstract, analytical gaze. In this context it is useful to quote his discussion of the interpretation of rock art:

    > Iconographic approaches are usually primarily cognitive in nature. … It is the mind that responds in a disembodied way. … Kinaesthetic approaches, by contrast, stress the role of the carnal human body. The general claim is that the manner in which we perceive, and therefore relate to visual imagery, is fundamentally related to the kinds of bodies we have. The body both limits and constrains and enables us to perceive and react to imagery in specific embodied ways. (Tilley, 2008:18)

    The physical nature of the *Pure Land AR* interface, for example, requires dexterous manipulation to reveal the cave: strong arms to lift the tablet aloft, strong neck to gaze at the ceiling, and strong knees and legs to crouch in front of the elaborate paintings down at ankle level (where an animation of an inscription that dates the construction of the cave is embedded, waiting to be discovered).

    Twisting and turning of the interface demands an embodied engagement by the user-agent, which is the becoming of the *phenomenological* body.

2. **The phenomenological body** (our body as we live and experience it; the tactile-kinesthetic body) provides a different way of thinking about the past in the present. The interactive features of *Pure Land* allow the virtual cave to be transformed from a mimetic representation to a navigable space, rich with layered

interpretation and fully illuminated – impossible if one were there in person. The magnifying glass, for example, acts like a prosthetic device – enabling the viewers to examine the paintings at ten times the scale. Don Ihde, post-phenomenologist and philosopher of science and technology, promotes a material hermeneutics that "gives things voices where there had been silence, and brings to sight that which was invisible" (Ihde, 2005), which is exactly the way in which the cave is brought to life. The "things" of Idhe's visual hermeneutics are viewed through the instrumental magnification of prosthetics, such as telescopes and microscopes, thus allowing perception to go where it has not gone before.

The interactive nature of *Pure Land* and *Pure Land AR* produces emergent narrative. As Jeffrey Shaw describes it, this has a particular phenomenological consequence:

> By creating virtual extensions to the image space that the viewer must explore in order to discover its narrative subjects, the navigable artwork allows the visitor to assume the role of both cameraperson and editor. (Shaw, 2003:23)

Pure Land AR is not a passive televisual environment, but an interactive performance, exactly mapping the real space of Cave 220 with the digital model. The conjunction of the actual wireframe image on the exhibition walls, and the life-like cave rendering seen on those walls via the tablet window, operates at the borderline of the indexically real and the phantasmally virtual – between re-embodiment and dis-embodiment.

Pure Land AR thus weaves a set of subtle paradoxes into its web of virtualization and actualization, and these paradoxes feed the kinesthetic excitement that is clearly evident in all visitors' astonished enjoyment of this installation. It thus aligns with the technologies of telepresence that virtually transport the viewer between the present location and another place – in this case, from the exhibition space to Dunhuang.

We see how the *phenomenological* body extends to become the *ecological* body.

3. **The ecological body** (or environmental contexts) of *Pure Land* and *Pure Land AR* are distinct, resulting in different affects in the way the work is embodied and meaning is created. They are both installations existing in standalone architectures with minimal interpretative support (except for brochures). *Pure Land* is an omnidirectional data space, rendering the virtual cave inside a spatial soundscape, and *Pure Land AR* takes place in a fully lit space. In both cases the virtual cave is rendered at 1 : 1 scale. The additional contextual settings include art biennales (Shanghai 2012), museums (Washington 2012), university exhibition venues (various through 2012 and 2103), book fairs (Hong Kong 2012), short-term exhibitions (Marseille 2013), and technology expos (Hong Kong 2013). Each venue brings different cultural audiences, prior knowledge and expectations. It should also be noted that Cave 220 is permanently closed to the public, so the digital cave is the only access for the majority of people.

The full omnidirectional potential of panoramic enclosure is fully realized in *Pure Land*, where the user is surrounded by the stereographic image space. Omnidirectional attention dispels the ego-centered view, since there is always something going on inside the same space but outside the user-agent's direct field of view. One can invoke the notions of allocentric and egocentric cognition and spatial perspectives, where the allocentric are those pertaining to a perceived, fixed external framework (a reality that exists all-around and is distinct from one-self) and the egocentric which contains your relationship with a given object or frame. A cognitive map of an omnidirectional, immersive space allows for allo- and ego-centric interpretations simultaneously (Blesser and Salter, 2006:39–40).[14] Simultaneously, all spectators are able to turn and gaze at any point in the room, irrespective of the agent-user interactions in the application (which trigger augmentations such as the magnifying glass, 2D, and 3D animations).

The mural paintings on the walls of the cave itself could be described as part of this context, and depict early Tang renderings of Buddhist sutras. The north wall portrays the Bhaisajyaguru's Eastern Paradise Sutra. The east wall illustrates the Vimalakirti Sutra, and the south wall the Western Pure Land Sutra. *Pure Land* concentrates its visualization on the Eastern Pure Land paradise of the Medicine Buddha from the north wall, which is dominated by the seven forms or emana-tions that Bhaisajyaguru can assume as a healer. The Buddha-forms stand in a row on lotus platforms with a pool below and 24 musicians and four dancers alongside (Figure 2.3). The narrative of the painting relates to the 12 great vows of the Buddha and the provision of food, drink, clothing, medicine, and spiritual aids.

We see how the *ecological* body extends to include prior knowledge by visitors who may be able to decode these images, thus becoming the *cultural body*.

Figure 2.3   *Pure Land: Inside the Mogao Grottoes.* Image © Applied Laboratory for Interactive Visualization and Embodiment, CityU, Hong Kong.

4. **The cultural body** (i.e., cultural artifacts, institutions, practices that constitute cultural life). Every installation happens in a different cultural context: Buddhist practitioners, academics, and lay people each bring their own cultural body. Some recognize the spatial and iconographic significance of the murals, while others experience something that is less familiar. As with many locations of spiritual significance (e.g., places of worship, burial sites), the spatial and iconographic arrangement is crucial to the meaning of the narrative as well as to correctly reading iconography (Kenderdine, 2013a). The correctness of the environmental context allows a devotee the transcendent experience he or she may seek in this environment, while for scholars the accuracy of color reconstructions, animations, and 3D modeling are of profound importance. It is interesting to note that the *Pure Land* projects give scholars better access to the site than if they were there in person. The ability to travel upwards to roof level (that is, to fly upwards), and to magnify the murals, provides enhanced opportunities for study.

   The *cultural* body is sensitizing and hermeneutic and spirals into the *phenomenological* body.

5. **The social body** (subjective relations). *Pure Land* demonstrates the dynamics of a single-user, multi-spectator interface that is important to the notion of museums as places of socialization. In *Pure Land*, the majority are spectators as part of a three-way relationship (user–system, user–spectators, and spectators' view of the emerging interactions). In *Pure Land AR*, the two mobile tablets allow two users and, typically, groups of 3–10 people to follow the tablets around. This method has proven to be very successful in reinforcing the social qualities of the interpretative experience. A group of people will always surround the user, and will follow, direct, gesture, prompt, and photograph the user's view of the world. This dynamic is integral to the interpretation, and to the performance of the work. The view that everyone should have his or her own tablet interface would deny the dynamic of this interchange and only advantage more isolated journeys of discovery (Kenderdine *et al.*, 2009).

   Between the user and the system, the concept of embodiment is of primary concern. Embodiment is a "participatory" status and a foundation for exploring interaction in context (Dourish, 2001). In terms of the trichotomy of the system–user–spectators, embodiment implies a reciprocal relationship with the context – encompassing users, interactive systems, spectators, co-users, physical surroundings, and the meanings ascribed to these entities (Dalsgaard and Koefoed-Hansen, 2008:5; cf. Dourish, 2001).

   Researchers of computer–human interaction address the issue of how a spectator should experience a user's interaction with the computer (Reeves *et al.*, 2005:748). Borrowing from performance theory, the user is the inter-actor with the system, and the interaction between the user and the system is the performance. As Dalsgaard and Koefoed-Hansen express it:

   > It is the ways in which the user perceives and experiences the act of interacting with the system under the potential scrutiny of spectators that greatly influences the interaction as a whole … it is precisely this awareness of the (potentiality of a) spectator that transforms the user into a performer. (Dalsgaard and Koefoed-Hansen, 2008:6)

The key to this relationship is the awareness of others, which provides the context for individual activity. The user not only acts in relation to the system but also is propelled by the knowledge that his or her perception of the system is a performance for others. Dalsgaard and Koefoed-Hansen (2008:31) call this "performing perception."

In the social, the body is interleaved with the *ecological*, *phenomenological*, and *cultural* body.

Evaluating the Embodied Experience

The evolution of visitor research in museums since the 1900s reflects an array of diverse evaluation typologies, pedagogies, collections, and curatorial trends. The museums' emphasis on the quality of their collections and scholarly frameworks has evolved to include visitors framed by these qualities. The next generations of embodied experiences described in this chapter, however, require new tools for analysis and evaluation. The subjective, affective, and embodied causalities of visitors' experiences are difficult to record — requiring visual, interactive, and engaging communication (Martinec and van Leeuwen, 2009). As this chapter has discussed, cognition is embodied when it is dependent upon features of the physical body — that is, when aspects of the person's body beyond the brain play a significant causal or physically constitutive role in processing. However, attempts to derive emotional state by gauging bodily responses (heartbeats and/or facial recognition) have proved unreliable (e.g., Kaliouby and Robinson, 2005). The gap in the task of evaluation has become the focus for a new research tool (Kocsis and Kenderdine, 2015). *I Sho U* is designed around interaction, introspection and narrative engagement and is used to determine visitor feelings and response.[15] It is based on the assumptions designers make in developing behavioral and emotional affordances. Through the design, interaction, and visualization scheme of the questions asked in *I Sho U*, visitors participate in instantaneous, collective, and participatory methods focused on their emotional, embodied, and cognitive states.

I Sho U can be compiled by museum evaluators online and deployed over the Internet, and downloaded to tablets. These tablets are distributed to visitors by docents at the museum. The average time for data gathering per person is five minutes, enabling hundreds of surveys per hour (a vast increase compared to traditional survey methods such as exit surveys or observation). *I Sho U* aggregates user responses online in real time, with cumulative and comparative interpretation. The tool undertakes audio mining and image analytics from the users' inputs.

The app encourages visitor agency through technological interface and creative visualization, and utilizes design-led integrative thinking, action, and creative data collection that are led by the visitor. Using this method positions the visitor as integral to the evolution of the design and construction of IIVEs and future museum exhibitions. *I Sho U* encapsulates the fundamental role of visitor evaluation and evolving social research to impact and improve the design, delivery, and dissemination of the museum — actual and virtual. The development of these tools is essential to begin to describe the embodied experience, from the perspective of the user.

Conclusion

The history of experimental interfaces for cultural heritage materials dates back to the 1990s in a series of works by influential media artists. In 2015, the powerful nature of these experiences is now recognized by industry and will no doubt become the basis for further developments in screen(less) technologies and immersive environments. Understanding the fundamental nature of embodied experience will put humanities scholars, and museum curators and designers, at the forefront of articulating and defining meaning in an increasingly ubiquitous screen culture. Within this context the purpose of this chapter has been to take a close reading of two immersive experiences to draw out the parameters of the embodied experience. The meaning that users and visitors to the *Pure Land* projects create as a result of their experience is contingent on the interplay of these five embodiments. By breaking down the *Pure Land* experience, it becomes clear how one *body* affects the others, and how no single aspect alone can be claimed to be the experience itself. If we can articulate these interrelationships clearly, then the kinds of social and physical environments we create will have a profound influence on our minds and our capacity for thought and reason. With proliferating datasets, the need for novel and humanistic solutions to visualization challenges must not be underestimated.

NOTES

1 Presence research is an established body of inquiry for virtual environments, e.g., the International Society for Presence Research (ISPR), available online at http://www.temple.edu/ispr (accessed June 30, 2009); Presence and Interaction in Mixed-Reality Environments (Presence II), available online at http://cordis.europa.eu/ist/fet/pr.htm (accessed June 30, 2009).

2 Myo: https://www.thalmic.com/en/myo/; Google Glass: http://www.google.com/glass/start/; Oculus Rift: http://www.oculusvr.com/ (accessed November 20, 2014).

3 See HIPerSpace at Calit2 http://vis.ucsd.edu/mediawiki/index.php/Research_Projects:_HIPerSpace; StarCAVE at UC San Diego; Allosphere at UC Santa Barbara http://www.allosphere.ucsb.edu/; AVIE, iCinema UNSW at http://www.icinema.unsw.edu.au/technologies/avie; Cave2, U Illinois at http://www.evl.uic.edu/cave2; Applied Laboratory for Interactive Visualization and Embodiment, CityU Hong Kong, at http://alive.scm.cityu.edu.hk/visualization-systems/.

4 ECLOUD WW1, available online http://alive.scm.cityu.edu.hk/projects/alive/ecloud-2012 (accessed November 20, 2014).

5 AVIE, iCinema UNSW: http://www.icinema.unsw.edu.au/technologies/avie.

6 See Oettermann (1997), Comment (2000), Altick (1978), Avery (1995). Huhtamo (2004) makes an extensive review addressing a perceived lack of historical information published before his survey on the so-called "moving panoramas" and extends this analysis in Huhtamo (2013).

7 *Be Now Here*, Michael Naimark, available online at http://www.naimark.net/projects/benowhere.html (accessed June 30, 2009).

8 For an archive of many of the works by Jeffrey Shaw see www.jeffrey-shaw.net (accessed November 20, 2014).

9 Many of these projects have been archived on the ALiVE website. See ALiVE & Related Projects http://alive.scm.cityu.edu.hk/ (accessed November 20, 2014).

10 *Pure Land: Inside the Mogao Grottoes at Dunhuang* http://alive.scm.cityu.edu.hk/projects/alive/pure-land-inside-the-mogao-grottoes-at-dunhuang-2012/ (accessed November 20, 2014).

11 *Pure Land Augmented Reality Edition.* http://alive.scm.cityu.edu.hk/projects/alive/pure-land-ii-2012/ (accessed November 20, 2014).

12 See Noë (2004). Also see the European Commission, Network of Excellence on Enactive Interfaces, available online at http://www.interdisciplines.org/enaction (accessed June 30,

2009) and the Enactive Networks, available online at http://www.enactivenetwork.org (accessed June 30, 2009).

13   Corpothetics: a term coined by anthropologist and visual theorist Christopher Pinney (2004), meaning "corporeal embodied aesthetics" – that is, the processes of image-making that consciously invoke a bodily response in the viewer. In India, darshan is considered an example of *corpothetics*.

14   As sound theorists Blesser and Salter point out, different cultures may associate different aspects

of their culture as either "ego" or "allo." The cognitive maps will vary across cultural groups; in one culture, language may be spatialized as egocentric (that is, things are described in relation to the viewer, which is good for encoding relative locations), or in the case of the Mayans, the allocentric framework means they have better sense of absolute locations and therefore navigation in wide open spaces (2006: 39–40).

15   *I Sho U* at Visitor Experience Studies, available online at http://ishou.com.au/ (accessed September 10, 2015).

REFERENCES AND FURTHER READING

Altick, R. 1978. *The Shows of London*. Cambridge, MA: Harvard University Press.

Avery, K. 1995. The panorama and its manifestation in American landscape painting, 1795–1870. Unpublished dissertation, Columbia University, New York.

Bateson, G. 1987. Men are grass: metaphor and the world of mental process. In *A Way of Knowing*, ed. W. Thompson. Hudson, NY: Lindisfarne Press.

Blesser, B., and Salter, L.R. 2006. Spaces Speak, Are You Listening? Experiencing Aural Architecture. Cambridge, MA: MIT Press.

Bonini, E. 2008. Building virtual cultural heritage environments: the embodied mind at the core of the learning processes. *International Journal of Digital Culture and Electronic Tourism* 2 (2), 113–25.

Bruno, G. 2002. Atlas of Emotion: Journeys in Art, Architecture, and Film. New York, London: Verso.

Casey, E. 1998. *The Fate of Place: A Philosophical History*. Berkeley, CA: University of California Press.

Clark, A. 2010. Supersizing the Mind: Embodiment, Action, and Cognitive Extension (Philosophy of Mind). New York: Oxford University Press.

Comment, B. 2000. *The Painted Panorama*, New York: Harry N. Abrams Inc.

Crary, J. 2001. Suspension of Perception: Attention, Spectacle, and Modern Culture. Cambridge, MA: MIT Press.

Crowther, P. 2009. *Phenomenology of the Visual Arts (Even the Frame)*. Stanford, CA: Stanford University Press.

Dalsgaard, P., and Koefoed-Hansen, L. 2008. Performing perception: staging aesthetics of interaction. *Transactions on Computer–Human Interaction (TOCHI)*, 15 (3). New York: ACM.

Dawson, P. Levy, R., and Lyons, N. 2011. "Breaking the fourth wall": 3D virtual worlds as tools for knowledge repatriation in archaeology. *Journal of Social Archaeology* 11 (3), 387–402.

DeFanti, T.A., Dawe, G., Sandin, D.J., *et al.* 2009. The StarCAVE, a third-generation CAVE and virtual reality, OptIPortal. *Future Generation Computer Systems* 25 (2), 169–78.

Dewey, J. 1934. *Art As Experience*. New York: Putnam.

Dourish, P. 2001. Seeking a foundation for context-aware computing. *Human–computer Interaction* 16 (2), 229–41.

Drucker, J. 2013. Performative materiality and theoretical approaches to interface. *DHQ: Digital Humanities Quarterly* 7 (1).

Duguet, A.M., Klotz, H., and Weibel, P. 1997. *Jeffrey Shaw, a Users Manual: From Expanded Cinema to Virtual Reality*. Karlsruhe: ZKM.

Flynn, B. 2013. v-Embodiment for cultural heritage. *Digital Heritage International Congress*, Marseille. IEEE, 347–54.

Forte, M., and Bonini, E. 2008. Embodiment and enaction: a theoretical overview for cybercommunities. *Virtual Systems and Multimedia Conference 2008*, Cyprus. IEEE.

Giannachi, G., Kay, N., and Shanks, M., eds. 2012. *Archaeologies of Presence*. London: Routledge.

Grau, O. 2003. *Virtual Art: From Illusion to Immersion*. Cambridge, MA: MIT Press.

Griffiths, A. 2008. Shivers Down your Spine: Cinema, Museums, and the Immersive View. New York: Columbia University Press.

Hooper-Greenhill, E. 2006. Studying visitors. In *A Companion to Museum Studies*, ed. S. Macdonald. Oxford: Blackwell, 363–76.

Howes, D. 2006. Scent, sound and synaesthesia: Intersensoriality and material culture theory.

In *Handbook of Material Culture*, ed. C. Tilley, W. Keane, S. Kuechler, M. Rowlands, and P. Spyer. London: Sage, 161–72.

Huhtamo, E. 2004. Peristrephic pleasures: the origins of the moving panorama. In *Allegories of Communication: Intermedial Concerns of Cinema to the Digital*, ed. J. Fullerton and J. Olsson. Rome: John Libbey, 215–48.

Huhtamo, E. 2013. Illusions in Motion: Media Archaeology of the Moving Panorama and Related Spectacles. Cambridge, MA: MIT Press.

Hutto, D.D., and Myin, E. 2013. *Radicalizing Enactivism: Basic Minds without Content*. Cambridge, MA: MIT Press.

Ihde, D. 2005. Material hermeneutics. In *Symmetrical Archaeology*. Stanford: Theoretical Archaeology Group. http://humanitieslab.stanford.edu/Symmetry/746 (accessed August 3, 2009).

Johnson, M. 2007. The Meaning of the Body: Aesthetics of Human Understanding. Chicago: University of Chicago Press.

Johnson, M., and Lakoff, G. 1980/2003. *Metaphors We Live By*. Chicago: University of Chicago Press.

Kaliouby, R., and Robinson, P. 2005. Real-time inference of complex mental states from facial expressions and head gestures. In *Real-Time Vision for Human–Computer Interaction*, ed. B. Kisačanin, V. Pavlović, and T.S. Huang. New York: Springer, 181–200.

Kasik, D.J., Ebert, D., Lebanon, G., Park, H., and Pottenger, W.M. 2009. Data transformations and representations for computation and visualization. *Information Visualization* 8(4), 275–85.

Keim, D.A., Mansmann, F., Schneidewind, J., and Ziegler, H. 2006. Challenges in visual data analysis, *Proceedings in Information Visualisation IV 2006*. IEEE: London, 9–16.

Kenderdine, S. 2007a. Somatic solidarity, magical realism and animating popular gods: Place-Hampi "where intensities are felt". *Proceedings of the 11th European Information Visualisation Conference*. IEEE Comp Society, 402–8.

Kenderdine, S. 2007b. The irreducible ensemble: Place-Hampi. In *Proceedings of Virtual Systems and Multimedia 13th International Conference*, ed. S. Kenderdine, T. Wyeld, and M. Docherty. Berlin: Springer, 58–67.

Kenderdine, S. 2007c. Speaking in Rama: panoramic vision in cultural heritage visualization. In *Digital Cultural Heritage: A Critical Discourse*, ed. F. Cameron and S. Kenderdine. Cambridge, MA: MIT Press, 301–32.

Kenderdine, S. 2013a. Place-Hampi: Inhabiting the Panoramic Imaginary of Vijayanagara. Heidelberg: Kehrer Verlag.

Kenderdine, S. 2013b. Pure Land: inhabiting the Mogao Caves at Dunhuang. *Curator: The Museum Journal* 56 (2), 199–218.

Kenderdine, S., and Hart, T. 2003. This is not a peep show! The Virtual Room at the Melbourne Museum. In *Proceedings of International Committee on Hypermedia and Interactivity*, Paris. Pittsburgh: Museum Archives and Informatics. http://www.archimuse.com/publishing/ichim03/003C.pdf (accessed June 30, 2009).

Kenderdine, S., and Hart, T. 2011. Cultural data sculpting: omni-spatial visualization for large scale heterogeneous datasets. In *Proceedings of Museums and the Web 2011*, ed. J. Trant and D. Bearman. Toronto: Archives and Museum Informatics.

Kenderdine, S. and Hart, T. 2014. mARChive: sculpting Museum Victoria's Collections. *MW2014: Museums and the Web 2014*. http://mw2014.museumsandtheweb.com/paper/marchive-sculpting-museum-victorias-collections (accessed June 20, 2015).

Kenderdine, S., and McKenzie, H. 2013. A war torn memory palace: animating narratives of remembrance. *Digital Heritage International Congress*, Marseille. IEEE, 315–22.

Kenderdine, S., Shaw, J., and Kocsis, A. 2009. Dramaturgies of PLACE: Evaluation, embodiment and performance in PLACE-Hampi. *DIMEA/ACE Conference* (5th Advances in Computer Entertainment Technology Conference and 3rd Digital Interactive Media Entertainment and Arts Conference), Athens, Volume 422, 249–56. ACM.

Kenderdine, S., Forte, M., and Camporesi, C. 2011. The rhizome of the Western Han. In *Revive the Past: Computer Applications and Quantitative Methods in Archaeology (CAA)*, Proceedings of the 39th International Conference, Beijing. Amsterdam: Pallas Publications, 141–58.

Kenderdine, S., Shaw J., and Gremmler T. 2012. Cultural data sculpting: Omnidirectional visualization for cultural datasets. In *Knowledge Visualization Currents: From Text to Art to Culture*, ed. F.T. Marchese and E. Banissi. London: Springer, 199–221.

Kennicott, P. 2012. Pure Land tour: for visitors virtually exploring Buddhist cave, it's pure fun. *Washington Post*, November 29.

Kocsis, A., and Kenderdine, S. 2015. *I Sho U*: an innovative method for museum visitor evaluation. In *Digital Heritage and Culture: Strategy and Implementation*, ed. H. Din and S. Wu. Singapore: World Scientific Publishing Co.

Krzanich, B. 2014 Keynote address. *CES 2014*.

Lakoff, G., and Johnson M. 1999. *Philosophy in the Flesh: The Embodied Mind and its Challenge to Western Thought.* New York: Basic Books.

Lee, H., Ferguson, P., O'Hare, N., Gurrin, C., and Smeaton, A.F. 2010. Integrating interactivity into visualising sentiment analysis of blogs. *IVITA '10: Proceedings of the First International Workshop on Intelligent Visual Interfaces for Text Analysis,* 17–20.

Lintermann, B., Belschner, T., Jenabi, M., and König, W.A. 2008a. Crowdbrowsing. KZM - YOU_ser 2.0: celebration of the consumer. http://www02. zkm.de/you/index.php?option=com_ content&view=article&id=59 (accessed November 30, 2010).

Lintermann, B., Belschner, T., Jenabi, M., and König, W.A. 2008b. *CrowdBrowsing.* Video clip. Karlsruhe: ZKM / Center for Art and Media Karlsruhe. http://container.zkm.de/cloudbrowsing/ Video.html (accessed November 30, 2010).

Macdonald, S. 2007. Interconnecting: museum visiting and exhibition design. *CoDesign International Journal of CoCreation in Design and the Arts* 3 (1), 149–62.

Manovich, L. 2001. *The Language of New Media.* Cambridge, MA: MIT Press.

Manovich, L. 2012. Media visualization: visual techniques for exploring large media collections. In *Media Studies* Futures, ed. K. Gates. Oxford: Blackwell.

Martinec, R., and Van Leeuwen, T. 2009. *The Language of New Media Design: Theory and Practice.* New York: Routledge.

Mascia-Lees, F.E. 2011. *A Companion to the Anthropology of the Body and Embodiment.* Blackwell Companions to Anthropology. Hoboken, NJ: John Wiley & Sons, Inc.

McGinity, M. 2014. Presence, immersion and the panorama. PhD thesis, University of New South Wales.

McGinity, M., Shaw, J., Kuchelmeister, V., Hardjono, A., and Del Favero, D. 2007. AVIE: a versatile multi-user stereo 360° interactive VR theatre. *Proceedings of the 2007 Workshop on Emerging Displays Technologies: Images and Beyond: The Future of Displays and Interaction,* San Diego, August 2007, Volume 252, New York: ACM.

Merleau Ponty, M. 1945. *Phénoménologie de la perception.* Paris: Gallimard. Published in 1962 as *Phenomenology of Perception,* trans. F. Williams. London: Routledge & Kegan Paul.

Milgram, P., Takemura, H., Utsumi, A., and Kishino, F. 1994. Augmented reality: a class of displays on the reality–virtuality continuum.

Proceedings of Telemanipulator and Telepresence Technologies 2351, 282–92.

Minsky, M. 1986. *Society of Mind.* New York: Simon & Schuster.

Morris, L. 2014. Digital cinema will allow visitors to explore museum archives. *Sydney Morning Herald,* September 18. http://www.smh.com.au/ entertainment/art-and-design/digital-cinema-will-allow-visitors-to-explore-museum-archives-20140918-10ebkh.html#ixzz3GdTsPD4x (accessed September 30, 2014).

Noë, A. 2004. *Action in Perception.* Cambridge, MA: MIT Press.

Noë, A. 2012. *Varieties of Presence.* Cambridge, MA: Harvard University Press.

Oettermann, S. 1997. *Panorama: History of a Mass Medium.* New York: Zone Books.

Olsen, B., Shanks, M., Webmoor, T., and Witmore, C. 2012. *Archaeology: The Discipline of Things.* Berkeley: University of California Press.

Pallasmaa, J. 2011. The Embodied Image: Imagination and Imagery in Architecture. Hoboken, NJ: John Wiley & Sons, Inc.

Pallasmaa, J. 2012. *The Eyes of the Skin: Architecture and the Senses.* Hoboken, NJ: John Wiley & Sons, Inc.

Parente, A., and Velho, L. 2008. A cybernetic observatory based on panoramic vision. *Technoetic Arts: A Journal of Speculative Research* 6(1), 79–98.

Parry, J.D., ed. 2011. *Art and Phenomenology.* London: Routledge.

Pearson, M., and Shanks, M. 2001. *Theatre/ Archaeology.* London: Routledge.

Pike, W.A., Stasko, J.T., Chang, R., and O'Connell, T.A. 2009. The science of interaction. *Information Visualization* 8 (4), 263–74.

Pinney, C. 2004. Photos of the Gods: The Printed Image and Political Struggle in India. London: Reaktion Books.

Preziosi, D. 2007. Brain of the Earth's body. In *Museum Studies: A Critical Anthology,* ed. B.M. Carbonell. Oxford: Blackwell.

Reeves, S., Benford, S., O'Malley, C., and Fraser, M. 2005. Designing the spectator experience. In *Proceedings of the Conference of Human Factors in Computer Systems* (CHI05). New York: ACM, 741–50.

Salter, C. 2012. Entangled: Technology and the Transformation of Performance. Cambridge, MA: MIT Press.

Shaw, J. 2000. Place Ruhr. http://www. medienkunstnetz.de/works/place-ruhr/flash/3/ (accessed June 20, 2015).

Shaw, J. 2003. Introduction. In *Future Cinema: The Cinematic Imaginary after Film,* ed. J. Shaw and P. Weibel. Cambridge, MA: MIT Press, 19–27.

Shaw, J., and Weibel, P., eds. 2003. *The Cinematic Imaginary after Film*. Cambridge, MA: MIT Press.

Shusterman, R. 2012. *Thinking Through the Body: Essays in Somaesthetics*. Cambridge: Cambridge University Press.

Smith, N., Knabb, K., DeFanti, C., *et al.* 2013. ArtifactVis2: Managing real-time archaeological data in immersive 3D environments. *Digital Heritage International Congress*, Marseille.

Sobchack, V. 2004. *Carnal Thoughts: Embodiment and Moving Image Culture*. Berkeley, CA: University of California Press.

Sommerer, C., and Mignonneau, L. 2002. *The Living Web*. http://www.virtualart.at/database/general/work/the-living-web.html (accessed November 30, 2010).

Sommerer, C., Mignonneau, L., and Lopez-Gulliver, R. 2002. Interfacing the Web: Multimodal and Immersive Interaction with the Internet. In *VSMM2002 Proceedings: The Eighth International Conference on Virtual Systems and Multimedia*, Gyeongju, Korea, 753–64.

Speer, R., Havasi, C., Treadway, N., and Lieberman, H. 2010. Visualizing common sense connections with Luminoso. *IVITA '10: Proceedings of the First International Workshop on Intelligent Visual Interfaces for Text Analysis*, 9–12.

Stafford, B.M. 2011. A Field Guide to a New Metafield: Bridging the Humanities Neurosciences Divide. Chicago: University of Chicago Press.

Stewart, J., Gapenne, O., and Di Paolo, E., eds. 2010. *Enaction: Towards a New Paradigm for Cognitive Science*. Cambridge, MA: MIT Press.

Tilley, C. 2004. The Materiality of Stone: Explorations in Landscape Phenomenology. Oxford: Berg.

Tilley, C. 2008. Body and Image: Explorations in Landscape Phenomenology. Walnut Creek, CA: Left Coast Press.

Tuan, Y.-F. 2001. *Space and Place: The Perspective of Experience*, reprint. Minnesota: University of Minnesota Press.

Varela, F.J., Thompson, E., and Rosch, E. 1991. *The Embodied Mind: Cognitive Science and Human Experience*. Cambridge, MA: MIT Press.

Wenger, E. 1998. *Communities of Practice: Learning, Meaning and Identity*. Cambridge: Cambridge University Press.

Young, L. 2007. Review of *Handbook of Material Culture*, ed. C. Tilley, W. Keane, S. Kuechler, M. Rowlands, and P. Spyer, 2006. *reCollections: Journal of the National Museum of Australia* 2 (2). http://recollections.nma.gov.au/issues/vol_2_no2/book_reviews/handbook_of_material_culture (accessed June 30, 2009).

3

The Internet of Things

Finn Arne Jørgensen

At some point in the near future, information will effortlessly flow between ourselves, the rest of the world, and the technologies we surround ourselves with. Sensors, networks, and computational capabilities will have been woven into the fabric of everyday life. Technology will do our bidding without us even having to ask, reading our intentions and divining our wishes as if through magic. Such are the countless visions of the Internet of Things that can be found in the advertisements and reports of many contemporary technology companies. One compelling example is Corning Incorporated's prize-winning "A Day Made of Glass" short film (2011), in which the glass that Corning produces serves as a slick and seductive interface between people and the Internet of Things. In the video, we follow a family through an entire day, witnessing how glass surfaces displaying customized information function like a natural, almost irresistible, way for them to interact with the Internet of Things.

Since its coining around the turn of the millennium, the concept of "the Internet of Things" has gained traction as a way of both describing and prescribing the frictionless and technologically connected world we can see in "A Day Made of Glass." This chapter will discuss the Internet of Things in two ways: First, as a term describing *the interconnectedness of technological artifacts* through sensors and communication networks, and second, as *a set of design fictions* about how these artifacts are changing the world. These two interpretations are interwoven – since the technological underpinnings cannot be separated from the visions of future applications, we need to understand both the technical and the cultural aspects of the Internet of Things.

The Internet of Things can be seen as a cluster of ideas about the future of technology that pulls in many different directions. We can find both complementary and divergent portrayals of art, interventions, and hacking on the one hand – and corporate

A New Companion to Digital Humanities, First Edition. Edited by Susan Schreibman, Ray Siemens, and John Unsworth.
© 2016 John Wiley & Sons, Ltd. Published 2016 by John Wiley & Sons, Ltd.

control, innovation, and monetization on the other. A common theme is that the Internet of Things allows anything and anyone to connect in any possible way, suggesting that as a technological infrastructure, the Internet of Things is open, neutral, and frictionless. This chapter challenges such a view of technology. Building on concepts from science and technology studies (STS), I discuss the making of standards, technologies, and discourses around the Internet of Things, particularly focusing on agency, power, and human relations, asking how potential areas of application have been imagined, visualized, and embedded in technological designs and standards, including the digital humanities.

What is the Internet of Things?

When Kevin Ashton coined the term *Internet of Things* in 1999, he envisioned a world where all things were tagged with a unique identifier that could be queried over the Internet (Ashton, 2009). Ashton – cofounder and executive director of MIT's Auto-ID Center – built upon an older set of visions about ubiquitous computing (often shortened to ubicomp) in formulating his idea. Ubiquitous computing "describes a set of processes where information technology has been thoroughly integrated into everyday objects and activities," to such an extent that this layer of information technology becomes almost invisible, even taken for granted, by the users (Dodson, 2008:7). In Ashton's implementation of the ubiquitous computing future, things automatically gather and exchange information about the world around them using radio-frequency identification (RFID), sensors, tagging, and communication networks, bridging the world of physical things with the Internet.

This is, however, only one of many possible interpretations of the Internet of Things, and there is no clear and unanimous definition of the term. We can think of it as an umbrella term covering a series of emerging practices and standards. The idea of "smartness" is central – of smart things that don't just collect information, but also act independently on that information (EpoSS, 2008). Connecting devices, including those that were previously not connected, to one another is also a key idea. Bruce Sterling (2005) calls the things of the Internet of Things "spimes," objects that can be tracked through space and time throughout their lifetime. Cory Doctorow (2005) eloquently describes a spime as a "location-aware, environment-aware, self-logging, self-documenting, uniquely identified object that flings off data about itself and its environment in great quantities." Spimes interact with the lives of people in complicated and often controversial ways, creating what Sterling (2004) calls "spime wranglers," the "class of people willing to hassle with Spimes." While this chapter is less concerned with the technical architecture of the Internet of Things than with the implications of a society permeated by the Internet of Things, we need to understand some of the basic elements of how it is all supposed to work. One way of gaining this understanding is to look at envisioned use areas.

Many visions of future applications take daily life situations as their starting point, extrapolating from them a set of technical capabilities or characteristics. One frequently encountered example – we can even call it a trope of the Internet of Things – that dates as far back as the late 1990s is the smart fridge that will monitor its contents, write shopping lists, and even suggest meals based on current food supplies. Such visions are behind the relatively recent entry of electronics companies like LG and Samsung into the slowly-moving domestic appliance market. These refrigerators have been commercially unsuccessful, partly because they are very expensive and partly because consumers simply do not see a need for this functionality, yet developers and engineers seem reluctant to let go of the idea. We will return to the engaged engineers and disinterested users of the Internet of Things in a bit.

Energy use monitoring has become a more successful implementation of Internet of Things approaches. Real-time monitoring and visualization of energy use is becoming increasingly common in households and commercial buildings alike, and the next step in the logic of the Internet of Things is to predict and automate. The Nest Learning Thermostat is one example that has been relatively successful (to the point where Google acquired Nest for $3.2 billion in 2014), building on the premise that consumers want programmable thermostats, but can't be bothered to do the actual programming. The networked, sleek, and attractive Nest thermostat learns the preferences of its users over time. After the initial learning period, it can both differentiate between day and night and recognize the difference between weekday and weekend patterns. An embedded motion sensor allows for lower temperatures where there's no one around. In other words, the Nest thermostat monitors the inhabitants of the house and their habits in order to dynamically adjust the temperature for maximum comfort and minimum energy consumption, without requiring active user involvement beyond the initial learning period. Accompanying smartphone apps enable manual control and detailed logs as well. The Nest is connected to the Internet through Wi-Fi, enabling sharing of information between multiple Nest devices in the same household, but also provides a way for Nest (and now Google) to use the collected data to improve their product. Google's move into the household automation market signals a continued interest in Internet of Things products and solutions that stay close to home. Smart power grids are also appearing, whole energy infrastructures capable of gathering and acting on information about consumer behavior and fluctuating energy supplies in order to improve the efficiency and reliability of power distribution (Verbong *et al.*, 2013). From an energy efficiency and sustainable development point of view, such automated interaction with the everyday lives of people definitely holds considerable potential.

Another set of emerging technologies centers on the interaction of the body and the Internet of Things. The so-called "Quantified Self Movement" aims to measure all aspects of our individual everyday lives, including food intake, steps walked, sleep patterns, and even mood, with the intention of optimizing and hacking habits and lifestyles (Swan, 2012). A plethora of consumer products in this category have appeared on the market in the last few years, particularly activity monitors such as the Fitbit, Jawbone UP, Nike+ Fuelband, Pebble, and the Samsung Gear Fit. Also other forms of wearable computing promise to blur the boundary between body and technology, in particular Google Glass and the Apple Watch. Yet, the ubiquitous smartphone is perhaps the best example of an already existing Internet of Things device we have – we always have one with us, it is propped full of sensors and connectivity options, and often functions as a hub for other devices.

Location-awareness is a central feature of the Internet of Things. Miniaturized global positioning system (GPS) sensors combined with digital maps and Wi-Fi triangulation have made geolocation popular among consumers. We can already find smart parking spaces that have embedded sensors that let users (or rather, a commercial middleman) know when it's available. Geofences, where actions are triggered when the users move into a particular space, also belong in this category. The Philips Hue light bulb can turn on when your smartphone enters the room, and can use more sophisticated triggers that consider the time of the day, and other factors. These interactions between people and technology are scriptable, where the user ideally will be presented with some kind of interface to these scripts, prompting a *Wired* magazine journalist to label it "The Programmable World." Here, the journalist waxed poetic when thinking about how, as soon as we get enough Things on the Internet of Things, it becomes "a coherent system, a vast ensemble that can be choreographed, a body that can dance" (Wasik, 2013).

It is hard to discuss the Internet of Things without considering the security and privacy concerns that inevitably come with the voracious data collection and exchange of spimes, especially considering the global controversy over National Security Agency (NSA) surveillance that started, post-Snowden, in 2013. Security obviously becomes a concern when all the devices of the Internet of Things are gateways to personal information, potentially allowing malicious code to enter the technologies that surround us. When an Internet security firm analyzed a spam email campaign, they found evidence of more than 100,000 hacked Internet of Things appliances, including refrigerators, sending out this mail (Proofpoint, 2014); a smart fridge can not only store spam, but also email it. When we consider that more dangerous things than refrigerators are also connected to the Internet, such as the nuclear installations that the Stuxnet computer virus targeted, there's no doubt that there's also an "Internet of Things to Worry About" out there (Mittal, 2011).

The actual development of the Internet of Things as concrete technologies and standards is to a large degree driven by business interests. During the last decade, a number of commercial forecasts and research reports have subscribed to this projected trajectory by mapping out the many envisioned applications of a fully realized Internet of Things (European Commission, 2009; Sundmaeker *et al.*, 2010; Chui *et al.*, 2010). The 2001 Forrester Report on "The X Internet" concluded that the Internet was boring, dumb, and isolated – "so remote from the real world that the media calls it by a different name – cyberspace" (Forrester Research, 2001). By looking at current trends, the report speculated that smart devices would extend the Internet from its current configuration into the physical world. The Internet of Things seems to be taken for granted as a vision of the future, but one that will "probably require dramatic changes in systems, architectures and communications ... middleware, applications support, MAC, data processing, semantic computing and search capabilities, and even low-power technologies" (Yan *et al.*, 2008: vii). In this interpretation, fully realizing the Internet of Things becomes merely a matter of technological implementation. Yet, the question of implementation and its consequences cannot be separated from its social, cultural, and political components, and thus something that the digital humanities should play close attention to.

The Internet of Things as Design Fiction

In contemporary usage, the Internet of Things has become a generic term that stands for a whole set of visions of the future, often referencing or inspired by science fiction films such as *Minority Report*. These films draw a picture of a believable future, inhabited by people using technological artifacts that have not yet been invented, but that make sense in a way that we can recognize. This projection of current technological possibilities into a vision of future society is an inseparable part of the Internet of Things. Most news reports of the Internet of Things are written in the future tense: this and this will happen, they argue, in the not too distant future (as evidenced by *Wikipedia*'s (undated) editorial caveat for its Internet of Things entry: "This article possibly contains unsourced predictions, speculative material, or accounts of events that might not occur"). The devices we see now are only the beginning, and the future they promise is just around the corner. But it has been just around the corner for a long time.

This shifting of perspectives between the past, present, and future is common when discussing the Internet of Things. "We now inhabit the future imagined by [ubicomp's] pioneers," observe Genevieve Bell and Paul Dourish (2007) in an article exploring the state of ubiquitous computing. They define this field as unusual within the computer sciences in that it is not defined by technological problems, but rather by a vision of future possibilities. The Internet of Things can be seen as the latest iteration of this ubiquitous computing vision, a new take on an old future. We find similar observations in another foundational article by Mark Weiser (1991) on "the computer for the twenty-first century," which both articulated a research agenda and set a rhetorical tone for a particular technological future. Such visions both predict the future and guide the development of future technologies, and this is by no means unique to the Internet of Things. Yet, Bell and Dourish (2007) criticize this view of technological development by arguing that placing ubiquitous computing in the proximate future renders contemporary practice irrelevant. This is where we get a gap or a mismatch between present technological capabilities and social implementation of the same technologies. The promoters of ubiquitous computing considered the implementation of their technological vision someone else's problem.

To properly understand the Internet of Things, we need to look at its storytellers, the ones selling the idea of the connected future. Technologies are always paired with stories of their use, as historian of technology David Nye (2003, 2006) demonstrates throughout his work. Design fiction can briefly be described as stories of the use of future technologies. Bruce Sterling was perhaps the first to use the term, though others have done much to develop it as an analytical concept, such as Julian Bleecker (2009), who calls design fiction an entanglement of "design, science, fact and fiction." Design fictions create a discursive space in which new futures might emerge, a "deliberate use of diegetic prototypes to suspend disbelief about change." The key concept here is "diegetic," implying that the technologies within the design fiction "exist as 'real' objects … that function properly and which people actually use." (Kirby, 2010:43). For instance, music playing from a radio in the movie is one such example of diegetic objects, while the movie soundtrack – with music that you as a viewer can hear but not the people on the screen – does not qualify as diegetic (Tannenbaum, undated). It needs to be a fully realized part of the fictional world.

A key insight of design fiction is that design does something with the world. It is part of what serves to insert a product into an existing network of potential users, enabling them to do particular things in particular ways, but also influencing their way of thinking about the world. As Sterling (undated) argues, "the point of a design fiction is to seize public attention, to affect the future thinking of the viewers, and to provoke the viral spread of the message." We can return to the smart fridge trying to gain entry into the kitchens of the world, presenting a twofold argument to its potential users that their lives would be better if they upgraded their fridge, and that it in any case is more or less inevitable that fridges will become smart and networked in the future.

Similar narrative trajectories appear in the history of the smart house, one of the most imagined sites for the implementation of the Internet of Things, from the pre-Internet push-button housewives of the 1960s to the houses of the imagined near future that already know when a button needs to be pushed (Heckman, 2008). These smart houses are infused with the networked sensors of the Internet of Things, but very few have seen any significant market adoption. Instead, they were prototype houses, laboratories, and testing grounds for particularly new information technology. Gender and technology scholars have pointed out that smart homes are also heavily gendered (Cowan, 1985; Wajcman, 2000). They are often designed by men, for women, around functionality that the designer thought sounded useful rather than based on actual use patterns and needs. As a result, the designs often center on information and communication technologies rather than targeting the actual labor that takes place in the home (Berg, 1999). The future changes rapidly, however, as demonstrated by the Norwegian Folk Museum's decision to acquire and exhibit Telenor's smart house from 2001 when the company shut down what they considered a dated vision of the future (Maihaugen, undated). Today, such visions of the smart house are still around, but the smartness has to a large degree shifted over to smart gadgets such as the Nest thermostat, the Hue light bulb, and the one smartphone to rule them all. The visionary smart houses were prototypes that are now being translated into concrete consumer products, within the reach of ordinary consumers who are not necessarily looking to replace their whole house. Functioning as spimes, these gadgets are gateways to a future Internet of Things, slowly extending its reach by connecting people and devices throughout the world.

The Internet of Things, as many other design fictions, is often accompanied by technological boosterism as well as considerable enthusiasm from its creators, but generally doesn't attempt to pry into the more problematic implications of a connected world. We should ask, however, exactly which problem such connectedness aims to solve, and for whom. Many of the more visionary explorations of the Internet of Things aim at addressing social challenges, particularly surrounding health and environmental issues (e.g., Smith, 2012). Commendable as such ambitions might be, they also demonstrate that the Internet of Things easily can fall prey to what Evgeny Morozov (2013) calls solutionism. Just because something is technologically possible doesn't mean it's a good idea, as Morozov enjoys pointing out. Nor are potentially disruptive and revolutionary new technologies necessarily transformative for all users. We see this clearly in the Achilles heel of smart kitchens, for instance. The actual labor that takes place in the kitchen is a heavily gendered issue that domestic design fictions generally ignore (Cowan, 1985; Berg, 1999).

New technologies come paired with stories of their future applications. The emerging clusters of objects, standards, and digital applications that we label "the Internet of Things" cannot be separated from its many design fictions, but these also reveal the complex sociotechnical worlds they are part of. In other words, the Things of the Internet of Things are never just things; they are assemblages of issues and controversies, entangling and connecting values, interests, and actors, never in isolation from the rest of society. An object does not have to be smart and networked in order to do this, but the Internet of Things does serve to draw our attention to both the agency of objects and our delegation of tasks to the material world.

Digital Humanities in a Programmable World

The Internet of Things is a massive conglomerate of billions of networked objects, wrapped up in visionary projections of a networked and transformed world. The scale and scope of the idea is breathtaking, yet the devil is in the details. I suggested in the introduction that the Internet of Things has two different interpretations: first as interconnected technological artifacts, second as a set of design fictions about how these artifacts are changing the world. Both of these interpretations are projected into the future, and we can by no means take it for granted what shape this future will take, and what *our place as agents* will be. This, I believe, has considerable implications for the place of the Internet of Things within the big tent of the digital humanities.

In making technological artifacts networked and traceable in space and time, the Internet of Things opens up for digital humanities projects that reach out of our computers and into the physical world. In the programmable world of the Internet of Things, the digital gets absolutely physical, and thus blurs the boundaries between what counts as a computer and what does not. We see this exemplified in projects that combine art and critical making such as Garnet Hertz's "FLY (http://139.142.46.159)" (2001), a fly with an implanted webserver. The networked fly, potentially a flying spime except that it was connected to the Internet through an Ethernet cable and thus was unable to fly, prompts us to question the nonhuman viewpoint of spimes. What do they see? How do they process what they see? How do spimes interact with the world? If we are to take the design fictions of the Internet of Things seriously, digital humanists should include not just computers, but also networked toasters, light bulbs, smart fridges, digital jewelry, cars, and yes, even flies, within the scope of their scholarship. These are all simultaneously spimes connected to the Internet of Things as well as cultural, social, and political objects that intersect with our lives.

The digital humanities needs to engage with both technology development and the cultural narratives of design fictions. If the Internet of Things consists of things talking to each other, shouldn't we be able to take part in this conversation in one way or another? One task of the digital humanities should be finding ways of inserting people into the conversation. This calls for openness, for hacking, for making and imagining. The spime-wrangler that Bruce Sterling writes into existence is a good model for digital humanities scholars to emulate. For the digital humanities, it is equally important to imagine and develop new and unexpected ways for things to fit together, but also to push things to their breaking point and examine the pieces that remain. It all comes down to the fact that all technology is social (Fischer, 2014). The Internet of Things is not merely a collection of technical protocols, but a full Society of Things.

The Internet of Things consists of smart devices that talk to each other, ideally both mirroring and shaping human behaviors and values. There is a complex process of mutual shaping going on in this relationship, what STS scholars call co-production (Jasanoff, 2004). The Internet of Things prompts us to consider the relationship between people and data. The purpose of many of the elements envisioned in the Internet of Things is to automate the routine actions of everyday life. This can free up time and attention for people to engage in more meaningful activities. But what if those actions are part of who we are? The routine actions and small decisions of everyday life are, in fact, meaning-making actions (Shove *et al.*, 2007). By delegating these to technology and predictive algorithms, are we weaving technology into the fabric of our lives or unraveling this fabric? In the Internet of Things, we not only delegate the gathering and processing of vast amounts of information to computers, but also the right to act on that information.

Such delegations to technology are not in any way new, as demonstrated by Bruno Latour in his classic essay on "the sociology of a door-closer" (Johnson, 1988). In fact, Latour's vocabulary seems to be made for untangling the complex interactions between humans and nonhumans that surround the Internet of Things. Following Latour's insistence that if we want to know what a nonhuman does, "simply imagine what other humans or other nonhumans would have to do were this character not present" (Johnson, 1988:299), it would be easy to conclude that delegation is simply replacing one or more human actions with a technology that can do the same thing in a more efficient manner. Yet, in this process of offloading tasks to the Internet of Things, new possibilities come into being, some as synergetic effects and others as unintended consequences.

Let us return to the smart refrigerator to unpack the layers of delegations, valuations, and social relations inherent in its algorithms. Say that you are one of the rare people who have a smart fridge in your kitchen, and that you leave it up to the kitchen to suggest new recipes and write shopping lists, even order groceries online directly from the store. We can assume that the algorithms directing its predictive choices might allow for some kind of user feedback and preferences, as in "no, I do not want this for dinner today," "pick ecological ingredients wherever possible," or "pick the cheapest ingredients," but what is the fridge to do when it hears from the smart bathroom scales that its owner's weight keeps increasing? Will governments require or encourage smart fridges to consider public health advice? In short, whose preferences and values have been delegated to the smart fridge, and which valuations do users reserve for themselves? When a computer anticipates your needs, the interface disappears, even the computer (Weiser, 1991). The Internet of Things is a fundamentally different way of interacting with computers, but one that requires even more awareness of the delegation of morality that takes place. Actions and ethics are profoundly interrelated, so when we delegate actions and agency to technology (which we have done for a long time) we are also delegating ethics. The question of training computers to make ethical judgments is currently facing Google's self-driving cars – if a car is in a situation where it needs to make an evasive maneuver that would likely kill one person in order to save two other people, what should it do? Whenever you automate something like this, you not only embed particular interpretations, values, and power relations in a design, but also filter away other ways of doing or valuing things. The processes through which these filters act upon the world are not always transparent and open for evaluation, something that becomes very clear in the rapidly growing commercial arena that the Internet of Things is.

Deeper consideration of "A Day Made of Glass," smart fridges, and other design fictions for the Internet of Things – in particular the stories that are not being told – can provide much insight about the place of digital technologies in contemporary society. They present us with a powerful vision of the future of a programmable world, and as such, something that humanities scholars should engage with, whether or not you choose to call yourself a digital humanist. The obviously affluent family of "A Day Made of Glass" is never overwhelmed by the information they are presented with, which has been filtered by some form of algorithm that is able to judge which information is necessary at any given time. They interact with very few people outside the screen. In fact, the urban world they inhabit seems rather empty and sterile. A screen shows us a mediated traffic congestion that is avoided when the car's GPS system guides the driver down empty side streets instead. What we are presented with is a world inhabited by things rather than people. Steven J. Jackson (2014) questions the world that much contemporary information technology seems to inhabit. "Is it the imaginary nineteenth-century world of progress and advance, novelty and invention, open frontiers of development?" he asks, pointing to a vision of the world that is similar to this frictionless future of the Internet of Things. Or is it "the twenty-first-century world of risk and uncertainty, growth and decay, and fragmentation, dissolution, and breakdown?" (Jackson, 2014:221). While it should not necessarily be the main task of the humanities to point out the depressing state of the world, it would be a useful reminder that the Internet of Things needs to find its place in a broken and messy world, full of tensions, conflicts, constraints, values, power relations, all of which are unevenly distributed.

The frictionless and smooth world we are presented with in "A Day Made of Glass" may be a seductive vision of the Internet of Things. Wrangling with spimes allows us to untangle the layers of delegations and valuations inherent in the Internet of Things in a way that sweeping visions cannot. Like all infrastructural technologies, the Internet of Things requires maintenance, modification, mediation, and domestication to become technologies that we can live with. Jackson argues that we should take breakdown, dissolution, and change as our starting point rather than innovation, development, and design. The world is constantly falling apart, but it is also constantly being repaired, reinvented, reconfigured, and reassembled. Building on Janet Abbate's work on the history of the early Internet (2000), Jackson argues that the Internet grew by breaking, "bumping up against the limits of existing protocols and practices and working around them, leaving behind almost by accident some of the properties that we now enumerate as key and distinctive virtues of the Internet" (Jackson, 2014:228).

Such breaking points open up for digital humanities investigations into the Internet of Things. Mark Sample's "Station 51000" Twitterbot (2013) is one example of how one can engage with such breaking points. He presents us with a floating spime lost at sea, infused with a certain humanity through Markov-chained content from Melville's *Moby-Dick*. Station 51000 is a data buoy that collects environmental data (wind direction, speed, and gust; atmospheric pressure; air and water temperature) for the National Oceanic and Atmospheric Administration (undated). Originally moored outside Hawaii, it went adrift in early 2013 but still continues transmitting data. However, since these buoys are supposed to be fixed in one place, it has no GPS sensor and there is no way of knowing exactly where it is. Sample's ingenious mashup lets the buoy become a sort of storyteller, sounding as lost and unmoored as the data it generates. On May 14, 2014, for instance, the lost buoy tweeted: "Note the air pressure at 30.09 inches and falling. Who in the lawless seas. It's a Hyperborean winter scene" (Station 51000, 2014). This is the Internet of Things, adrift, collecting and transmitting broken data to whoever wants to listen. In "Station 51000," Sample wrangles with a floating spime, engaging in what Ian Bogost calls carpentry – "constructing artifacts as a philosophical practice," a form of philosophical inquiry through making rather than writing (Bogost, 2012:92). As Sample (2014) has argued, one role for the humanities is to think difficult thoughts, facing and preserving ambiguities rather than striving to eliminate them. The Internet of Things is full of ambiguities and conflicting perspectives that cannot be easily resolved. The more data the Internet of Things generates, the more important the humanistic context of that data becomes. Spimes and their design fictions hold great potential – if critically and carefully deployed – for a wide range of applications in the digital humanities. Scholars like Mark Sample and Garnet Hertz have already begun actively seeking out the breaking points of connected, smart technologies. This hacking and wrangling of the Internet of Things can happen both on the technological and the narrative level, through building and breaking, introducing friction, and exploring broken data, all while questioning its meaning and significance.

The Internet of Things is just around the corner. It has been so for a while and will most likely continue to be so. In striving for the new, however, we should not be unprepared for the shock of the old. We never start from nothing. Infrastructures like the Internet of Things must function in the world as it is, layered with history, filled with elements that don't fit. The underlying standards and use patterns of the Internet of Things will likely reflect the same boundaries and power relationships as the rest of the world. We need to reflect upon the past visions of the future. When something becomes ubiquitous and pervasive, it also becomes invisible and taken for granted. One way to open this taken-for-grantedness up for analysis is to start by looking at times and places when things were otherwise, before it became ubiquitous. Not only do spimes enable awareness of ongoing practices and processes in the world; they also provide an entry point for engaging with these processes. It is up to digital humanists to meet the challenge of wrangling with these spimes in meaningful ways.

REFERENCES AND FURTHER READING

Abbate, J. 2000. *Inventing the Internet*. Cambridge, MA: MIT Press.

Ashton, K. 2009. That "Internet of Things" thing. *RFID Journal*, http://www.rfidjournal.com/articles/view?4986 (accessed May 23, 2014).

Bell, G., and Dourish, P (2007). Yesterday's tomorrows: notes on ubiquitous computing's dominant vision. *Personal Ubiquitous Computing* 11 (2), 133–43.

Berg, A.J. 1999. A gendered socio-technical construction: the smart house. In *The Social*

Shaping of Technology, ed. D. MacKenzie and J. Wajcman. Buckingham: Open University Press, 301–13.

Bleecker, J. 2009. Design fiction: a short essay on design, science, fact, and fiction. Near Future Laboratory. http://nearfuturelaboratory. com/2009/03/17/design-fiction-a-short-essay-on-design-science-fact-and-fiction (accessed May 23, 2014).

Bogost, I. 2012. *Alien Phenomenology, or What It's Like to Be a Thing*. Minneapolis: University of Minnesota Press.

Chui, M., Löffler, M., and Roberts, R. 2010. The Internet of Things. *McKinsey Quarterly* March 2010. McKinsey & Company.

Corning Incorporated. 2011. A day made of glass: Corning's vision for the future. http://www. corning.com/adaymadeofglass (accessed May 23, 2014).

Cowan, R.S. 1985. *More Work for Mother: The Ironies of Household Technology from the Open Hearth to the Microwave*. New York: Basic Books.

Doctorow, C. 2005. Bruce Sterling's design future manifesto: viva spime! *Boing Boing*. http:// boingboing.net/2005/10/26/bruce-sterlings-desi.html (accessed May 23, 2014).

Dodson, S. 2008. Foreword: A tale of two cities. In *The Internet of Things: A critique of ambient technology and the all-seeing network of RFID*, ed. R. Kranenbourg. Network Notebooks 02. Amsterdam: Institute of Network Cultures.

EpoSS. 2008. *Internet of Things in 2020: A Roadmap for the Future*. Brussels: European Commission.

European Commission. 2009. *Internet of Things*. *Strategic Research Roadmap*. Brussels: European Commission, Information Society and Media DG.

Fischer, C. 2014. All tech is social. *Boston Review*, August 4. http://www.bostonreview.net/blog/ claude-fischer-all-tech-is-social (accessed October 13, 2014).

Forrester Research, Inc. 2001. The X Internet. *The Forrester Report*, May 2001. Cambridge, MA: Forrester Research Inc.

Heckman, D. 2008. *A Small World: Smart Houses and the Dream of the Perfect Day*. Durham, NC: Duke University Press.

Hertz, G. 2001. FLY (http://139.142.46.159). Mendel Art Gallery, Saskatoon, Canada.

Jackson. S.J. 2014. Rethinking repair. In *Media Technologies: Essays on Communication, Materiality and Society*, ed. T. Gillespie, P. Boczkowski, and K. Foot. Cambridge, MA: MIT Press.

Jasanoff, S. 2004. The idiom of co-production. In *States of Knowledge: The Co-Production of Science and the Social Order*, ed. S. Jasanoff. London: Routledge.

Johnson, J. [B. Latour] 1988. Mixing humans and non-humans together: the sociology of a door-closer. *Social Problems* 35 (3), 298–310.

Kirby, D. 2010. The future is now: diegetic prototypes and the role of popular films in generating real-world technological development. *Social Studies of Science* 40, 41–70.

Maihaugen (undated). Fremtidshuset. http://www. maihaugen.no/no/maihaugen/Velg-ditt-Maih augen/Aktiviteter-for-ungdom/Fremtidshuset (accessed May 23, 2014).

Mittal, P. 2011. How digital detectives deciphered Stuxnet, the most menacing malware in history. http://www.wired.com/2011/07/how-digital-detectives-deciphered-stuxnet (accessed May 23, 2014).

Morozov, E. 2013. To Save Everything, Click Here: The Folly of Technological Solutionism. New York: PublicAffairs.

National Oceanic and Atmospheric Administration (undated). Station 51000 (LLNR 28007.5) – Northern Hawaii One – 245NM NE of Honolulu HI, http://www.ndbc.noaa.gov/station_page.php? station=51000 (accessed May 23, 2014).

Nye, D. 2003. America as Second Creation: Technology and Narratives of New Beginnings. Cambridge, MA: MIT Press.

Nye, D. 2006. Technology Matters: Questions To Live With. Cambridge, MA: MIT Press.

Proofpoint. 2014. Proofpoint uncovers Internet of Things (IoT) cyberattack. Press release, http:// www.proofpoint.com/about-us/press-releases/ 01162014.php (accessed May 23, 2014).

Sample, M. 2013. Station 51000, Twitter account. https://twitter.com/_lostbuoy_ (accessed May 23, 2014).

Sample, M. 2014. Difficult thinking about the digital humanities. http://www.samplereality. com/2014/05/12/difficult-thinking-about-the-digital-humanities (accessed May 23, 2014).

Shove, E., Watson, M., Hand, M., and Ingram, J. 2007. *The Design of Everyday Life*. Oxford: Berg.

Smith, I.G., ed. 2012. *The Internet of Things 2012: New Horizons*. Internet of Things European Research Cluster.

Station 51000. 2014. Note the air pressure at 30.09 inches and falling. Who in the lawless seas. It's a Hyperborean winter scene. Twitter, https://twitter. com/_LostBuoy_/statuses/466678617649729536 (accessed May 23, 2014).

Sterling, B. (undated). Futurism: design fiction for media philosophers. European Graduate School. http://www.egs.edu/faculty/bruce-sterling/ lectures (accessed May 23, 2014).

Sterling, B. 2004. When blobjects rule the earth. http://www.viridiandesign.org/notes/401-450/00422_the_spime.html (accessed May 23, 2014).

Sterling, B. 2005. *Shaping Things*. Cambridge, MA: MIT Press.

Sundmaeker, H., Guillemin. P., Friess, P., and Woelfflé, S., eds. 2010. *Vision and Challenges for Realising the Internet of Things*. Brussels: European Commission, Information Society and Media DG.

Swan, M. 2012. Sensor mania! The Internet of Things, wearable computing, objective metrics, and the quantified self 2.0. *Journal of Sensors and Actuator Networks* 1, 217–53.

Tannenbaum, J.G. (undated). What is design fiction? Message posted to http://www.quora.com/What-is-design-fiction (accessed May 23, 2014).

Verbong, G.P.J., Beernsterboer, S., and Sengers, F. 2013. Smart grids or smart users? Involving users in developing a low carbon electricity economy. *Energy Policy* 52 (1), 117–25.

Wajcman, J. 2000. Reflections on gender and technology studies: in what state is the art? *Social Studies of Science* 30 (3), 447–64.

Wasik, B. 2013. In the programmable world, all our objects will act as one. *Wired*, http://www.wired.com/2013/05/internet-of-things-2 (accessed May 23, 2014).

Weiser, M. 1991. The computer for the twenty-first century. *Scientific American*, September, 94–104.

Wikipedia (undated). The Internet of Things. https://en.wikipedia.org/wiki/Internet_of_Things (accessed May 23, 2014).

Yan, L., Zhang, Y., Yang, L.T., and Ning, H. 2008. *The Internet of Things: From RFID to the Next-Generation Pervasive Networkd Systems*. Boca Raton, FL: Auerbach Publications.

4

Collaboration and Infrastructure

Jennifer Edmond

Changes in a system can be either gradual and organic or sudden and disruptive in nature. Over time, digital humanities, as it is now known, has emerged as a product of both. On the surface, it would appear that the field has been largely shaped by disruptive forces. From the IBM processors that caught Father Busa's imagination, to the watershed of affordability reached by geographic information system (GIS) technologies in the 1990s, to the emergent applications of virtual world modeling, augmented reality, and the Internet of Things, the technologies that drive the digital humanities generally enter the field from outside.

But not all of the forces shaping digital humanities emerge externally. Other shifts within this area of research stem from long traditions that predate the humanities' turn toward the digital: the importance of scholarly communities, the relationship scholars have to their sources and tools, and the institutions in which these sources and tools are maintained. The emergence of collaborative practices and bespoke infrastructural models are therefore two examples of forces shaping digital humanities that have not been introduced from without, but have arisen from within, growing incrementally over time and space, taking into account and adapting around what already exists (see Edwards *et al.*, 2007). Such developments, representing as they do both change and continuity, present a challenge to disciplinary norms. This is even more the case at those points where an emergent process has threatened to supplant or alter the epistemological or methodological foundations of an established field. These norms of knowledge creation not only represent the perception of an ideal mode by which to build understanding, but often act as well as proxies for other socially important processes, for example, to measure achievement or belonging.

A New Companion to Digital Humanities, First Edition. Edited by Susan Schreibman, Ray Siemens, and John Unsworth.

The adaptation and application of new technologies or norms in the culture of humanistic scholarship therefore continues to inspire both enthusiasm and resistance. There is a long tradition of scholarly suspicion with regard to "supplements" – additions intended to assist an existing process but threatening to supplant it. Such an ambivalence surrounded many of the technological and social aids to knowledge creation that arose over the centuries, from the printing press to the typewriter to the mobile phone. Indeed this suspicion is recorded about as far back as written records themselves, appearing already in the passages in Plato's *Phaedrus*, where the invention of writing is characterized as a "pharmakon:" possibly an aid to "memory and wit," but quite possibly also a hindrance to it (Plato). Clearly, the technological side of digital humanities' development has this status – both exciting and worrying – but this can equally be said of the more organic changes that are shaping the field from within. These developments, and the polarized reactions they often bring, have implications not only for the growth of digital humanities, but for the scholarly ecosystem as a whole.

Collaboration and the Digital Humanities

In the digital humanities, the need for collaboration has the status of an essential component in the founding myth. Father Busa's challenge to the IBM scientists to live up to their motto of needing only time to do the impossible (Busa, 2009:3) represents in many ways a vision of the digital humanities ideal: cutting-edge technological development and deep analog scholarly knowledge challenging each others' paradigms, facilitating each others' work, and validating each others' results. Although digital humanities projects may by necessity be strongly collaborative, the traditional humanities environment from which they often arise and within which they operate is not generally organized, in its operational modes or training systems, to foster collaboration. The roots of the paradigm of the "singleton scholar" are very deep, and it is easy for a collaborative approach to research to become viewed not just as a supplement, but as a threat, to the traditions of scholarship. It is not that humanities researchers do not work together, for they do, in academic departments, in learned societies, and at conferences and professional meetings large and small – this is what Unsworth (2003:6) refers to as a "cooperative" rather than "collaborative" model of interaction. But, as this refinement of terminology implies, there are clear limitations to the extent to which many humanistic scholars are comfortable with co-production of knowledge, a cultural norm which is a source of mystification in many other disciplinary traditions (Real, 2012).

Even within the digital humanities, for example, publication norms still lean strongly toward single, rather than multiple, authorship, obscuring in the peer-reviewed journals of the field the central role of collaboration in how results were achieved (Nyhan and Duke-Williams, 2014). The shifts in collaborative practice can be better seen, therefore, not so much in how the work of digital humanities is disseminated, but in how its conceptualization and theorization have changed over the course of digital humanities' maturation as a field. These trends illustrate the tension, and growing synthesis, between an emergent view of the research projects as characterized by teamwork and project management requirements and the traditional values of the work as curiosity-driven and meeting the aims of scholarship.

Many scholars focusing on systemic and social issues in academic research culture have noted and investigated this tension over the past 10 years and more, in particular as the methods and approaches associated with digital humanities have become (in spite of running somewhat against the traditional grain) ever more commonplace. Some of the earliest applied work on collaboration in digital humanities (and interdisciplinary research generally) emerged from management science, with some very useful results. Some of the issues identified early on include: relationship-level versus task-level successes and failures (Kraut, 1987); potential conflicts between researcher quality goals and organizational efficiency goals (Fennell and Sandefur, 1983); the lack of a common vocabulary to describe work processes and insights between specialists from different backgrounds (Fennell and Sandefur, 1983; see also Bracken and Oughton, 2006); cultural differences (Amabile *et al.*, 2001; see also Siemens and Burr, 2013); the importance of leadership (Amabile *et al.*, 2001; see also Siemens, 2009); and the cost of insufficient attention in projects being paid to processes, management structure or role clarity (Amabile *et al.*, 2001). This tradition continues, producing work based in issues arising in digital humanities projects, but relevant across a number of work contexts, such as problems related to team members' physical proximity (or lack thereof) (Siemens and Burr, 2013).

Over time, a more specific body of work has also emerged, as the issue at hand in a digital humanities project is not just one of two or more people contributing to a common goal or output. One of the most common definitions in the literature defines collaboration as the "coming together of *diverse* interests and people to achieve a common purpose via interactions, information sharing and coordination of activities" (Jassawalla and Sashittal, 1998:51, my emphasis). Were the collaborations at the core of the digital humanities only between those from similar backgrounds, with similar epistemological expectations and similar research processes and communications norms, then the topic would surely be less fraught. But the range of interests encompassed by digital humanities is broad, covering resource development, specific research questions and methods, evaluation, policy, standards, teaching, and software development, among others (Terras, 2001). Digital humanities as a field is essentially interdisciplinary and often intersectoral, and in these characteristics lie the roots of many of the specific day-to-day challenges to collaboration in projects in this field. This variety of perspectives that digital humanities collaboration brings together requires the interweaving of very different intellectual positions and working cultures, such as a humanist trained primarily in a discipline like history or literature, a computer scientist or software developer, and a branch of information management or library science.

The key differentiator of the most successful digital humanities collaborations, therefore, is not just that they monitor and manage all of the task- and relationship-level difficulties that may befall such an undertaking, but also that they ensure from the outset that the project objectives propose interesting research questions or otherwise substantive contributions for each discipline or specialty involved, and that team members maintain a clear sense of their own roles and respect for those of their fellow team members. In short, digital humanities teams, like all high-performing teams, require trust and harmonization between individual and group goals (Siemens, 2009). These are two essential elements that can be particularly challenging to foster across disciplinary divides and between the competing demands of structured, effective project management and the nomadic nature of curiosity-driven research. If either of these essential elements is missing, insidious questions of status (not of individuals, but of whole fields of knowledge) can emerge to poison the all-important relationships between collaborators (Fennell and Sandefur, 1983; Siemens *et al.*, 2011). In the worst cases, teamwork based on an ethos of knowledge sharing can degenerate into the negotiation of uncomfortable tacit hierarchies, where some contributors (regardless of their expertise or seniority) feel like service providers working in the shadow of otherwise autonomous project leaders. Even within what should be one of the most common binaries for interdisciplinary collaboration on digital humanities projects, that is between digital humanities researchers and digital librarians, a large gulf in attitudes, preparedness, expectations, enjoyment, and overarching goals continues to exist. The related differences of perspective, if unacknowledged and unmanaged, can be hugely destructive to the framework of trust that underpins a team's morale and contributes to its effectiveness. As one digital librarian stated it: "we're very service oriented, but we don't want that to be confused with servitude" (Siemens *et al.*, 2011:342; see also Short and Nyman, 2009; Speck and Links, 2013).

The failure of a collaborative venture usually begins with a failure either to imagine likely outcomes or to encourage open dialog on the part of the project team and its leader. You cannot ensure such creativity through a project plan, but you can sometimes ensure the presence of a particular kind of figure, one that arises throughout the years of scholarship on collaborative work in the digital humanities. These individuals, described as "intermediaries" (Edmond, 2005), "translators" (Siemens *et al.*, 2011:345), or "hybrid people" (Liu *et al.*, 2007; Lutz *et al.* 2008; cited in Siemens *et al.*, 2011:345), talk across disciplinary cultures and encourage open-mindedness. And though these individuals cannot create the esteem and trust required to ensure that interdisciplinary collaborations remain enriching and productive, they can ensure that flashpoints are recognized and managed, and they can capitalize upon opportunities to develop a common language, bringing convergence to terms which might have lay and specialist meanings ("data," "standard"), and guiding the emergence of shared metaphors that can inspire across the specialties (Bracken and Oughton, 2006). It should be said, however, that the skill set required for this role remains relatively rare, and will likely do so for some time. Positive forces like the "alt-ac" movement (Nowviskie, 2010) in the United States have made significant progress in preparing the ground for such a cohort to emerge, but in general, the rewards structures and engrained hierarchies of the institutions within which this work is generally situated must give way somewhat more to a celebration of this class of generalists before such people can be systematically and fairly trained and rewarded.

There is also a further facet of collaboration in the digital humanities that reaches beyond the project and the development team. In his essay on models of collaboration, John Unsworth (2003) posits that alongside the intradisciplinary and interdisciplinary collaborative modes fostered by the digital humanities, there is a third mode of collaboration enabled by the interaction of cultural or creative data with technology, namely that with the reader. If scholarly communications in the digital age are to overcome a publication culture based on printed texts delivered in electronic format, then the reader will also engage differently with the arguments and evidence contained within, with sources and with the overt (as in thematic) or hidden (as in by database structure) organization of knowledge. This is what Davidson refers to as "Humanities 2.0": "distinguished from monumental, first-generation, data-based projects not just by its interactivity but also by openness about participation grounded in a different set of theoretical premises, which decenter knowledge and authority" (Davidson, 2008:711–12).

Infrastructure

Regardless of the nature or complexities of this move from an individual to a collaborative paradigm for humanistic research, one thing that is assured by these changes is an increase in the scale of the average research undertaking. This shift places a different set of imperatives upon the research environment. Greater scale, interdisciplinary approaches, and an overall faster cycle of communications in the macro environment define new requirements for the infrastructure required to support research.

Infrastructure, including the many more nuanced or community-specific terms used to refer to it, such as research infrastructure, knowledge infrastructure, or cyberinfrastructure, can mean very different things to different people. For example, it is clear that a functional high-speed broadband link is a necessary tool for research in the modern age. But this is a necessary tool for work generally, not just for research. Some cite preprint or institutional repositories as an example of infrastructure (Lynch, 2003; Pritchard, 2008), but while these resources contribute a great deal to institutional data and knowledge management, they do not necessarily make a direct impact on the active delivery of new research. Tools sometimes emerge and are adopted as elements of a potential infrastructure, but this does not work well in isolation, nor in profusion (which, paradoxically, intimidates rather than inspires users) (Wheeles, 2010). Knowledge sharing is also proposed as a primary goal of many candidate infrastructures (Wheeles, 2010), though how one creates a durable environment for this remains unclear. At a higher level, the term *infrastructure* has been defined for digital humanities as including "collections of digital content and the software to interpret them" (Arms and Larsen, 2007), "intellectual categories … material artifacts … organizations … business models and social practices" (Crane *et al.*, 2009), or "the institutional fabric … plus the tools of scholarship that make information accessible" (Brown and Greengrass, 2010:1).

Many initiatives with a claim to inclusion under the heading of infrastructure – from digital libraries or national repositories to tool suites, standards, data stores, and knowledge marketplaces – have now emerged and developed to relative maturity. These developments seek generally to extrapolate paradigms drawn from one of the essential knowledge bases within the digital humanities (information management, humanistic domain, software-based) at a grander scale. When a paradigm drawn from one of the parts is applied to the whole, however, often the result, which should be integration, is instead greater fragmentation than existed previously. Examples of this sort of development abound, unfortunately, in software tools without a clear application, in research projects developed according to outdated technical standards, or in digital libraries with neither the cohesion nor the metadata to address real user needs.

As with shifts in what is meant by collaboration within the scholarly community, the shift in how to provide the basic platform for knowledge creation in the humanities is not propagated as a ripple emanating outward from a definable point, but as a shift in something internal and essential to the long history of the disciplines that converge in the digital humanities. Whether or not one agrees with the characterization of cyberinfrastructure as having experienced a "long now" (Edwards *et al.*, 2007:3), it has been clear for some time that the original knowledge infrastructures, the libraries, archives, and museums, are being supplemented and pushed toward change. The current fragmented definition and conceptualization of infrastructure is another result of the organic changes that form a part of the shift that has brought digital humanities into existence, with a traditional and valued paradigm facing competition based on a new conceptualization of and by users. This may seem a modern phenomenon, but in fact its roots are historically very deep. Certainly by the nineteenth century, one could see the rise of historians such as Leopold von Ranke, with his writing of history "as it actually was," beginning to challenge the values of librarians such as Anthony Panizzi, who is remembered as much for his landmark set of 91 rules for cataloging as for denying Thomas Carlyle access to uncataloged materials in the British Museum library. These two figures epitomize the tension between the source viewed as an object to be federated and manipulated in the name of creating the historical record and one to be curated and preserved in the name of securing the historical record.

The moment when this slow divergence in perspectives finally came to a distinct and open declaration (at least in terms of digital research infrastructure for the humanities) can be pinpointed to 2006, with the release of two reports, one European, one American, announcing the arrival of the era of cyberinfrastructure. These two publications were the report by the American Council of Learned Societies, *Our Cultural Commonwealth* (2006), and the *European Roadmap for Research Infrastructures* published by the European Strategy Forum on Research Infrastructures (2006). Both of these documents pointed in a direction away from viewing digital libraries, archives, and museums as coterminous with research infrastructure for humanities, and towards a new model based on a different conceptualistion of user requirements in the digital age.

Since that moment, there has been a rush to develop operational responses to this dual call for action in the development of digital, virtual, or cyberinfrastructures for research and discovery in the cultural space. The Bamboo project (launched 2008) ended in 2014, albeit not without leaving behind the Digital Research Tools Directory (DiRT), while Nineteenth Century Scholarship Online (NINES) has both gradually transformed itself to meet its communities' needs and fostered the launch of related projects such as Eighteenth Connect and the Medieval Scholarly Electronic Alliance (MESA). In Europe, the Digital Research Infrastructure for the Arts and Humanities (DARIAH) moved from a preparatory phase to build in 2011 and has in 2014 been established as a separate legal entity under the European Research Infrastructure Consortium (ERIC) instrument of the European Commission. It too has spawned an ecosystem of related projects, defined more in terms of specific thematic communities of practice than eras, in the European Holocaust Research Infrastructure (EHRI), the Collaborative European Digital Archival Research Infrastructure (CENDARI), and the equivalent project for archaeological data, ARIADNE. Concurrent with the rise of bespoke research infrastructures whose content often lacks the provenance that would tie it back to a specific library or archive, there has also been momentum on the part of digital libraries and archives to create more researcher-friendly modes of usage, such as through the HATHI Trust Research Centre (HTRC) and the proposed development of a bespoke Europeana research platform (Dunning, 2014).

This list is by no means exhaustive, even within the limited space of large platform developments with a stated or implicit claim to being infrastructures. Myriad other candidates are listed and discussed elsewhere (e.g,. Anderson, 2013; Speck and Links, 2013). In spite of their common claim to status as digital research infrastructures for the humanities, however, even this small list represents quite a diverse range of approaches and visions. This is common in the definition of what an infrastructure is – so much so that Star and Ruhleder claim we need to recognize the relational nature of the concept of infrastructure, and ask not "what" it is but instead " … when" (1996:38). A more useful approach to defining infrastructure, therefore, is to capture not what it is, but what it does; or, to be more exact, how it does what it does. Real infrastructure, when it is working properly, disappears from view: we don't marvel at the road that delivers us to our destination or at the electrical current available from the sockets in our walls.

This is a characteristic that has been referred to as getting "below the level of the work" (Edwards *et al.*, 2007), facilitating tasks without determining how they should be carried out. It is only at this level that a support for research can become both omnipresent in scholarly work and simultaneously transparent. It is the lack of this kind of support that Gregory Crane comments on when he says, "The infrastructure of 2008 forces researchers in classics and in the humanities to develop autonomous, largely isolated, resources" (Crane *et al.*, 2009). A vision of infrastructure that responds to Crane's frustration defines its essence as existing "in the linkages and connections that will enable individuals and communities to create their own narratives around multimodal content and interfaces regardless of where that content might sit" (Anderson, 2013:18). Edwards and Anderson both see what Crane finds lacking – an integration across resources enabling flexible connections (between tools, resources, standards, and communities) to be made, revised, discarded, and remade. In short, infrastructure should never force the undesirable, but silently and seamlessly support the productive.

But getting "below the level of the work" is not as easy as it sounds, because to aim too far below that level carries as much risk as being just above it. Within infrastructural developments, a balance must always be struck between designing for the greatest possible impact, thereby risking development of an overly generic tool or environment, and designing at too high a level of functionality or specificity, well above the level of most potential users' "work." Even within the digital humanities, researchers trained in traditional humanistic methods can struggle to describe their habits of work and essential requirements sufficiently for them to be translated effectively into technology. This challenge is not unique to digital humanities. Lucy Suchman's research (1995) has demonstrated how difficult it is to speak about work in any context without unintentionally stripping away the all-important layers of contingency and interrelation between types of working knowledge. Recognition of this difficulty has contributed to the adoption of agile programming and participatory design in digital humanities, a solution based in collaboration, which has had some success. But it also remains true that, while in some cases it is the limits of our imagination that hold back the advance of digital humanities infrastructure, in other cases it is the technological intractability (Borgman, 2007) of many things that are not overly difficult for human brains, like telling jokes (Taylor and Raskin, 2013) or playing the game go (Drake and Uurtamo, 2007).

In the absence of any unified vision for a transformative digital humanities infrastructure, we continue to rely on the original knowledge infrastructures – the libraries, the archives, and the thematic collections. This model for infrastructure (that is, infrastructure as providing access to sources) is a core element of many infrastructural projects, but even the definition of a source is being challenged in the new environment. Some of this pressure is from emergent content sources, such as crowdsourced material or scholar-produced resource collections. But other questions around sources stem directly from the conceptualization of a library's or archive's function as a long-term guarantor of the physical safety of cultural material. If our goal is that "information should last forever," however, we face a dilemma. The maintenance of digital resources falls between traditional roles and areas of expertise, and therefore responsibility for it remains ambiguous. Of course many individuals will carefully maintain their projects, even through difficult transitions within or between institutions, but others may need to move on for professional or personal reasons to other projects, or indeed they may retire, leave the profession, or die. In other cases, institutional repositories or libraries (such as University of North Carolina, discussed in Kretzschmar and Potter, 2010, and the University of Nottingham, discussed in the UoN Data Repository Report, 2013), nationally funded centers (like the Data Archiving and Networked Services (DANS) in the Netherlands, the UK Networked Data Centres, or the Digital Repository of Ireland) or supernational infrastructures (like Digital Research Infrastructure for Arts and Humanities, DARIAH) may take on some projects, or some parts of them. But to guarantee that both data and interface will be available in anything approximating perpetuity is an exceptionally difficult and expensive promise to make, and it is therefore no surprise that the long-term fate of so many digital humanities projects remains uncertain.

In addition, while the open-endedness of digital scholarship is often held up as an advantage over print publication because it allows its authors to incorporate new findings and documents as they are discovered, this very open-endedness of the digital can also be interpreted as one of its greatest weaknesses. Digital projects resist completion (Kretzschmar, 2009), and even a project into which no new information is being added will require far more maintenance to remain usable over 20 years than any book. Meanwhile, the needy nature of digital objects and projects stands in direct opposition to the dominant funding model for their creation, which is based on limited-term funding to create, but not maintain, the research output.

There is a clear imperative, therefore, to make the long-term sustainability of digital resources one of the goals of infrastructural support for the digital humanities; however, different organizations have pursued this goal in very different ways. Many have picked up on the social aspects of the digital humanities, as in the NINES approach to providing peer review of online resources, or DARIAH's organization according to "virtual competency centres." Others have tried to harness technological advancements to add value without necessarily seeking to replicate the important work that digital repositories, archives, and libraries are already doing. Recognizing the power, but also the intellectual and resource limitations, inherent in the cataloging of individual collections and/or items, these projects seek instead to harness the possibilities of linked data to add value to aggregated or federated sources without making the same level of up-front investment in the content as would be required to create metadata records at time of ingest for every item in the system. Such projects as the Collaborative European Digital Archival Infrastructure (CENDARI) and the Australian Humanities Networked Infrastructure (HuNI) focus in this way on the inquiry and discovery phases of the humanities research process, looking not just to make research more efficient, but to revive the serendipitous aspects of research in physical collections, something that digital data management techniques have largely engineered out of the research process (Edmond, 2013; Burrows, 2013). Although they may still be in their developmental stages, projects like these point the way toward a new generation of digital humanities infrastructures, productively fusing the digital library with its technical and social cousins.

Challenges Ahead: Enduring Tensions in the Scholarly Research Ecosystem

How we work together and how we create a fit-for-purpose support structure for research: these key issues stand not only in the middle of the discussion about what digital humanities is and should do, but are also relevant to all scholarship in the twenty-first century. At one remove, they encourage reflection on how we understand authorship and authority in the current age; how we imagine and embed new ways to communicate our findings; how we shape and control our methodological approaches; and how we maintain a consistent dialog at a time when technological capability threatens to outstrip the adaptive capacity of potential users (Fitzpatrick, 2007). At a second remove, however, from questions of collaborative practice and infrastructural development, is a further set of yet broader issues core to the future of scholarship, such as the ethical and moral dimensions of defending traditional norms in the face of obvious shifts in circumstance, or indeed of abandoning them for the sake of greater resources and for the benefit of alignment with a set of values that may or may not serve scholarship.

It was with great understatement that the authors of one paper wrote, "Unfortunately, the academic community has a track record of resistance to new forms of scholarly communication" (Arms and Larsen, 2007). Both the past (with all of its significant and powerful habits) and the future (with all of its uncertainty) seem to hold back the long-anticipated paradigm shift from which digital humanities will emerge as an accepted norm. Claire Warwick notes that this slow uptake has been recognized since the 1990s (cited in Burrows, 2013), and attributes it essentially to resources not having been designed to get "below the level of the work." But a shift toward collaborative work methods and the new forms of research communication fostered by infrastructural developments also require a shift in the ethos of sharing – early, late, and throughout the research process. In spite of the potential, open access sharing is still perceived as offering "no real benefit other than to be seen as acting as a good citizen" (Anderson, 2013:10) and some scholars hesitate to informally communicate about their key discoveries through electronic channels such as blogs, preferring to withhold their contributions until they are formally published (Rutner and Schonfeld, 2012:32). There are conflicts emerging in this resistance, however. Researchers report unwillingness to expose their search and browse patterns to an automated system (Borgman, 2007; Brown and Greengrass, 2010), but complain of "bad searches," tacitly revealing an expectation that their research environments have the adaptive capacity of commercial systems, a capacity that is dependent on exactly such invisible data sharing. Whether or not this model is actually appropriate for systems underpinning research is, of course, another question entirely, but how sharing is viewed and managed within the scholarly community will most certainly have an impact on what can be done, and what won't be done, in the future.

Another such macro-level issue is that of whether large-scale interdisciplinarity and infrastructural development displace the locus of power in a manner that is not in harmony with the scholarly values that underpin digital humanities. "Although the primary aim of all these infrastructure programs is to support research, the rhetoric in which they are framed by the funders tends to focus on the economic and political gains to be obtained" (Anderson, 2013:7). Digital humanities can be politically attractive, aligning, as it does with the often irresistible assumption that technology produces economic benefit. Digital humanities has also been a strong promoter of humanistic research to new audiences, giving many projects more effective conduits to non-specialist users. We cannot expect, however, that all digital humanities work, or indeed all humanities work, will have these kinds of outcomes, or that planning for such an outcome always justifies the resources it will require.

Willard McCarty states, "I have no argument against infrastructure; rather my argument is for its secondary status ... The problem with advancing infrastructure as our focus is that in doing so we surrender the discipline to servitude" (McCarty, 2012:13). If McCarty's fears are justified, then the threat of the digital supplement, at least in this context, may be on the verge of realization. The achievement of scale has given digital humanities researchers the opportunity to reach large audiences beyond their research peers and invest at an unprecedented level in the essential substrate of their research. Through collaboration and infrastructure, digital humanities is increasing its impact, and its visibility. Unchecked or built upon without caution, however, these trends could create not a basis for more open and respectful cooperation among research professionals, but a new class of serfs working in service not to research, but to infrastructure for its own sake. Indeed, professionalization, in particular for those researchers working within teams or supporting infrastructures, is a further issue not determined by either collaboration or infrastructure, but ultimately perhaps ameliorated or exacerbated by them. The real challenge behind digital work in the humanities is therefore not only to grow and reach out, or to define and build the bespoke supports and networks so many have theorized and imagined; the most essential goal of the creation of infrastructures to support large-scale, collaborative work is, and should remain, the opportunity to broaden and deepen areas of knowledge, and to connect them more efficiently and effectively into the wider ecosystem. If this focus can be maintained, then scholarship as a whole, and not only digital humanities, will benefit.

REFERENCES AND FURTHER READING

Amabile, T.M., Patterson, C., Mueller, J., *et al.* 2001. Academic–practitioner collaboration in management research: a case of cross-profession collaboration. *Academy of Management Journal* 44 (2), 418–31.

American Council of Learned Societies (ACLS) Commission on Cyberinfrastructure for the Humanities and Social Sciences. 2006. *Our Cultural Commonwealth.* http://www.acls.org/cyberinfrastructure/ourculturalcommonwealth.pdf (accessed October 2014).

Anderson, S. 2013. What are research infrastructures. *International Journal of Humanities and Arts Computing* 7 (1–2), 4–23.

ARIADNE. http://www.ariadne-infrastructure.eu (accessed October 2014).

Arms, W., and Larsen, R. 2007. Building the infrastructure for cyberscholarship. Report of a workshop held in Phoenix, Arizona, National Science Foundation.

Borgman, C.L. 2007. *Scholarship in the Digital Age: Information, Infrastructure, and the Internet.* Cambridge, MA: MIT Press.

Bracken, L.J., and Oughton, E.A. 2006. "What do you mean?" The importance of language in developing interdisciplinary research. *Transactions of the Institute of British Geographers* NS 31, 371–82.

Brown, S., and Greengrass, M. 2010. Research portals in the arts and Humanities. *Literary and Linguistic Computing*, Vol. 25, No. 1, 1–21.

Burgess, H.J. 2011. New media in the academy: labor and the production of knowledge in scholarly multimedia. *DHQ: Digital Humanities Quarterly* 5 (3).

Burrows, T. 2013. A data-centred "virtual laboratory" for the humanities: designing the Australian Humanities Networked Infrastructure (HuNI) service. *Literary and Linguistic Computing* 28 (4), 576–81.

Busa, R. 2009. From punched cards to treebanks: 60 years of computational linguistics. http://convegni.unicatt.it/meetings_Busa_abstract_TLT8.pdf (accessed October 2014).

CENDARI. http://cendari.eu (accessed October 2014).

Crane, G., Bamman, D., Cerrato, L., *et al.* 2006. Beyond digital incunabula: modeling the next generation of digital libraries? European Conference on Digital Libraries. http://www.eecs.tufts.edu/~dsculley/papers/incunabula.pdf (accessed October 2014).

Crane, G., Seales, B., and Terras, M. 2009. Cyberinfrastructure for Classical philology. *DHQ: Digital Humanities Quarterly* 3 (1).

DARIAH. http://dariah.eu (accessed October 2014).

Davidson, C.N. 2008. Humanities 2.0: promise, perils, predictions. *PMLA* 123 (3), 707–17.

Digital Research Tools (DiRT). http://dirtdirectory.org (accessed October 2014).

Drake, P., and Uurtamo, S. 2007. Heuristics in Monte Carlo Go. Proceedings of the 2007 International Conference on Artificial Intelligence, 171–5.

Dunning, A. 2014. Drafting priorities for Europeana research. Europeana. http://pro.europeana.eu/blogposts/drafting-priorities-for-europeana-research (accessed October 2014).

Edmond, J. 2005. The role of the professional intermediary in expanding the humanities computing base. *Literary and Linguistic Computing* 20 (3), 367–80.

Edmond, J. 2013. CENDARI's grand challenges: building, contextualising and sustaining a new knowledge infrastructure. *International Journal of Humanities and Arts Computing* 7 (1–2), 58–69.

Edwards, P.N., Jackson, S.J., Bowker, G.C., and Knobel, C.P. 2007. Understanding infrastructure: dynamics, tensions and design. http://hdl.handle.net/2027.42/49353 (accessed November 2012).

EHRI. http://www.ehri-project.eu (accessed October 2014).

Eighteenth Connect. http://www.18thconnect.org (accessed October 2014).

European Strategy Forum on Research Infrastructures. 2006. *European Roadmap for Research Infrastructures.* http://ec.europa.eu/research/infrastructures/pdf/esfri/esfri_roadmap/roadmap_2006/esfri_roadmap_2006_en.pdf (accessed October 2014).

Fennell, M.L., and Sandefur, G.D. 1983. Structural clarity of interdisciplinary teams: a research note. *Journal of Applied Behavioral Science*, 19 (2), 93–202.

Fitzpatrick, K. 2007. CommentPress: New (social) structures for new (networked) texts. *Journal of Electronic Publishing* 10 (3).

Hathi Trust Research Centre (HTRC). http://www.hathitrust.org/htrc (accessed October 2014).

Jassawalla, A.R., and Sashittal, H.C. 1998. An examination of collaboration in high-technology new product development processes. *Journal of Product Innovation Management* 15, 237–54.

Kraut, R. 1987. Relationships and tasks in scientific research collaborations. *Human Computer Interaction* 3 (1), 229–45.

Kretzschmar, W.A. 2009. Large-scale humanities computing projects: snakes eating tails, or every end is a new beginning? *DHQ: Digital Humanities Quarterly* 3 (1).

Kretzschmar, W.A. Jr., and Potter, W.G. 2010. Library collaboration with large digital humanities projects. *Literary and Linguistic Computing* 25 (4), 439–45.

Lynch, C.A. 2003. Institutional repositories: essential infrastructure for the digital age. *ARL Bimonthly Report* 226, 1–7.

McCarty, W. 2012. The residue of uniqueness. *Historical Social Research* 37 (3), 24–45.

NINES. http://www.nines.org (accessed October 2014).

Nowviskie, B. 2010. #alt-ac: alternate academic careers for humanities scholars. http://nowviskie. org/2010/alt-ac (accessed October 2014).

Nyhan, J., and Duke-Williams, O. 2014. Joint and multi-authored publication patterns in the digital humanities. *Literary and Linguistic Computing* 29 (3), 387–99.

MESA. http://www.mesa-medieval.org (accessed October 2014).

Plato. *Phaedrus*. Trans. B. Jowett. http://classics.mit. edu/Plato/phaedrus.html (accessed November 2013).

Pritchard, D. 2008. Working papers, open access, and cyber-infrastructure in classical studies. *Literary and Linguistic Computing* 23 (2), 149–62.

Real, L.A. 2012. Collaboration in the sciences and the humanities: a comparative phenomenology. *Arts and Humanities in Higher Education* 11, 250–61.

Rutner, J., and Schonfeld, R.C. 2012. *Supporting the Changing Research Practices of Historians*. Final Report from ITHAKA S+R. http://www. sr.ithaka.org/research-publications/supporting-changing-research-practices-historians (accessed October 2014).

Short, H., and Nyhan, J. 2009. "Collaboration must be fundamental or it's not going to work": an oral history. *DHQ: Digital Humanities Quarterly* 3 (2).

Siemens, L. 2009. "It's a team if you use 'reply all'": An exploration of research teams in digital humanities environments. *Literary and Linguistic Computing* 24 (2), 225–33.

Siemens, L., and Burr, E. 2013. A trip around the world: accommodating geographical, linguistic and cultural diversity in academic research teams. *Literary and Linguistic Computing* 28 (2), 331–43.

Siemens, L., Cunningham, R., Duff, W., and Warwick, C. 2011. A tale of two cities: implications of the similarities and differences in collaborative approaches within the digital libraries and digital humanities communities *Literary and Linguistic Computing* 26 (3), 335–48.

Speck, R., and Links, P. 2013. The missing voice: archivists and infrastructures for humanities research. *International Journal of Humanities and Arts Computing* 7 (1–2), 128–46.

Star, S.L., and Ruhleder, K. 1996. Steps toward an ecology of infrastructure: design and access for large information spaces. *Information Systems Research* 7 (1), 111–34.

Suchman, L. 1995. Making work visible. *Communications of the ACM* 38 (9), 56–64.

Taylor, J.M., and Raskin, V. 2013. Natural language cognition of humour by humans and computers: a computational semantic approach. *12th IEEE Conference on Cognitive Informatics & Cognitive Computing (ICCI*CC)*, July 16–18, 2013, 68–75.

Terras, M. 2001. Another suitcase, another student hall – where are we going to? what ACH/ALLC 2001 can tell us about the current direction of humanities computing. *Literary and Linguistic Computing* 16 (4), 485–91.

University of Nottingham. 2013. UoN Institutional Data Repository. http://www.nottingham.ac.uk/ research/research-data-management/data-sharing-and-archiving/depositing-and-archiving. aspx (accessed November 2013).

Unsworth, J. 1999. The library as laboratory. Paper presented at the Annual Meeting of the American Library Association (New Orleans, Louisiana). http://people.brandeis.edu/~unsworth/ala99. htm (accessed October 2014).

Unsworth, J. 2000. Scholarly primitives: what methods do humanities researchers have in common, and how might our tools reflect this? Paper presented at *Humanities Computing: Formal Methods and Experimental Practice*, King's College, London. http://people.brandeis.edu/~unsworth/ Kings.5-00/primitives.html (accessed October 2014).

Unsworth, J. 2003. The Humanist: "Dances with Wolves" or "Bowls Alone"? Paper presented at the Association of Research Libraries conference (Washington DC). http://www.arl.org/about/ tour-this-website/1207#.VEY6cildUdU (accessed October 2014).

Unsworth, J. 2009. The making of "Our Cultural Commonwealth." *DHQ: Digital Humanities Quarterly* 3 (4).

Wheeles, D. 2010. Testing NINES. *Literary and Linguistic Computing* 25 (4), 393–403.

Part II
Creation

5

Becoming Interdisciplinary

Willard McCarty

What makes bad poets worse is that they read only poets (just as bad philosophers read only philosophers), whereas they would benefit much more from a book of botany or geology. We are enriched by frequenting disciplines foreign to our own. (Emile M. Cioran, 1973)[1]

Being Curious

Temptation to explore the knowable and the ease with which exploring may begin have increased many-fold in recent years due to the Web. As a result, being curious may seem remarkable only in its absence, and only its censure abnormal. Conviction of its utter normality is bolstered by Aristotle's testimony that the desire to find things out is basic to humans,[2] and by Edmund Burke's that it is "The first and simplest emotion which we discover in the human mind" (1757:1). Primatologists and ethologists since Darwin have observed curiosity among "the higher animals … similar passions, affections, and emotions, even the more complex ones."[3] At least behaviorally, if not cognitively, blurring into the hunger of life for life, it would seem reasonable to suppose that curiosity in some sense does not stop with Darwin's "higher animals" but is synonymous with being or even becoming alive. Konrad Lorenz has written in *The Foundations of Ethology*, on "exploratory behavior or curiosity," that

A free play of innumerable factors, a play neither directed at any goal nor predetermined by any cosmic teleology, a play in which nothing is determined except the rules of the game has, on the molecular level, led to the origin of life. It has caused evolution and

A New Companion to Digital Humanities, First Edition. Edited by Susan Schreibman, Ray Siemens, and John Unsworth.

moved phylogenetic development in the direction from lower to higher organisms. ... It would seem that this free play is the prerequisite for all truly creative processes, for those of human culture just as for those of evolution. (1981/1978:334)

But what individuals and societies actually do with this inherent, biologically rooted if not cosmic tendency to free play is another matter. G.E.R. Lloyd has, for example, detailed the struggle in ancient Greece and China between the freedom to look anywhere, ask anything, and the beholdenness which ensures continuity across time. At the end of *The Ambitions of Curiosity* he concludes that against the constraints they faced these "were often just that, just ambitions. But what ambitions: for in one context after another, they held out the hope of understanding what had never been understood before" (2002:147).

I begin with conflict of the fundamental urge to *know* (in the full sense Heinlein rescued in *grok*)[4] against an equally fundamental resistance so that both remain firmly in sight as I take up curiosity's interdisciplinary manifestations. Given our time and place, this urge to know may only appear in the ghostly form of a mundane duty or means of advancement, and resistance to it be mistaken as an irrelevant historical artifact. The strong inducements from funding agencies and universities to lay claim to interdisciplinary research may wrongly suggest that professionalized curiosity is merely part of an academic job description, that it is only a matter of acquiring "domain knowledge." Hence we may also conclude that the old moral injunctions, weighted with the authority of Augustine and Aquinas among others,[5] against a "blameable ... disposition to inquire too minutely into anything" and "inquisitiveness in reference to trifles or matters which do not concern one" – senses the *Oxford English Dictionary* marks obsolete – have no modern form. But Lloyd's careful exploration of the ancient struggle and Lorraine Daston's well-informed reminder that "Curiosity has never been allowed free rein" (2005:36) recommend that while keeping in mind the "free play ... neither directed at any goal nor predetermined by any ... teleology" we ask not whether but how resistance manifests itself to us and how to equip ourselves for the struggle of the freedom to inquire against beholdenness to disciplines.

In this chapter I will first briefly consider the historical push to interdisciplinary research and the growth of interest in curiosity in order to justify explicit attention to exploration of disciplines other than one's own. I will then bring the difficulties into focus, and discuss the aims of interdisciplinary research and some practical strategies.

A warning: my approach fits somewhat uncomfortably into the burgeoning literature on the subject, which in the last decade or so has orbited the abstraction called "interdisciplinarity" and devoted considerable energy to its inter-, multi-, trans-, and other relations.[6] I take the view that in dicing and re-dicing the *what*, this literature has not paid enough attention to the *how* (whatever good may have been done for the sociology of knowledge). In consequence it has been less than helpful to the adventurous but inexperienced scholar and to the discussion of changing research practices as a whole. Much of this literature begins with the abstraction and as a result gets stuck in taxonomic debate that from my perspective is a *Glasperlenspiel*.

Recent History of Interest

The term "interdisciplinary" (or "interdiscipline" used adjectivally) goes back to the young social sciences in the early twentieth century. Despite the enormous impetus to and development of interdisciplinary research in the sciences during World War 2, the word was still new enough in 1976 that the founding editor of *Interdisciplinary Science Reviews* felt the need to note that it "is a relatively new term, although its concept reaches back to the beginnings of modern science" (Michaelis, 1976; 2001:310). In 1979 the Association for Integrative Studies was founded.[7] In the following year Clifford Geertz observed for the social sciences that "the lines grouping scholars together into intellectual communities, or (what is the same thing) sorting them out into different ones, are these days running at some highly eccentric angles" (1980:169). Writing in 1988, in a valuable history of the word, Roberta Frank noted that it had "started out with a reasonably bounded set of senses [but] subjected to indecent abuse in the 50s and 60s ... acquired a precocious middle-aged spread" (1988:139). That spread has expanded just as interdisciplinary has become a thing to be taxonomized. In 1990 William H. Newell's edited collection *Interdisciplinarity: Essays from the Literature* demonstrated a thoughtful and widespread interest. Now "interdisciplinarity" has the attention of a 580-page *Oxford Handbook* (Frodeman *et al.*, 2010) and many other signs of a vigorous industry.[8]

Mainstream attention to curiosity has likewise grown dramatically in recent years. When at the beginning of the 1980s Michel Foucault spoke of his "dream of a new age of curiosity" (1996/1980:305), and Lorraine Daston and Katharine Park published their first study of marvels, prodigies, and curiosities, academic interest in the topic was rare, they noted.[9] By 1998, when their book *Wonders and the Order of Nature 1150–1750* was published, "Wonder and wonders [had] risen to prominence on a wave of suspicion and self-doubt concerning the standards and sensibilities that had long excluded them (and much else) from respectable intellectual endeavors" (1998:10).[10] Since then several other signs of interest have appeared, for example Brian Dillon's *Cabinet* (2000–), a magazine intended "to encourage a new culture of curiosity" (http://cabinetmagazine.org); Barbara M. Benedict's *Curiosity: A Cultural History of Early Modern Inquiry* (2001); Neil Kenny's *The Uses of Curiosity in Early Modern France and Germany* (2004) – "timely now that once again curiosity is being nudged into the cultural limelight," Daston commented in her review (2005); and Dillon's 2013–14 traveling exhibition *Curiosity: Art and the Pleasures of Knowing*, accompanied by a catalog with essays by him and Marina Warner.[11] "The world at large, in all its glory or stupidity, is wide open for investigation," senior curator Robert Malbert declared enthusiastically in his Foreword to the catalog (Dillon and Warner, 2013:9).

The moment, it seems, is upon us.

Curiosity's Machine and the Individual

Unsurprisingly, curiosity's digital machine has been intimately involved. In a sense this chapter is an educated guess as to the outcome for the humanities.

But we do not have to guess entirely in the dark. Without yielding authority to the physical and biological sciences, we can get some insight from observing changes in them, where there can be little doubt that, as John von Neumann foresaw, computing is bringing about "nothing less than the second half of the scientific revolution" (Glimm 1990:185). According to many voices at the Blankensee Colloquium of 2007,[12] for example, the pressure to conceive scientific "theories and models … as computable from the outset" has become increasingly difficult to resist. Consensus seems to be that in many areas of research, models and theories "will become decreasingly successful" if not "conceived from their conception as computable."[13] What these sciences do and what they do not do in consequence, or even what becomes inconceivable within them as a result, and so what it means to be a science, would seem in question.

In the humanities, attempts at corresponding algorithmic power for analysis have had limited success at best. The effects of curiosity's machine have come principally through slowly growing digital collections of primary sources and secondary literature. In consequence the great majority of scholars have had less than 20 years to experiment with these effects.[14] During this time they have been lumbered by the weak and operationally misleading analogy implicit in the notion of a "digital library," which has tended to obscure the great differences of action. At one time not so long ago the name of the game for digital collections was "information retrieval," a phrase splicing epistemic data to old library structures and habits. Experts defined the ideal to be the impossible combination of perfect precision (the relevance of retrieved items) and recall (the percentage of relevant items found). But classical information retrieval in fact works quite poorly, especially for the humanities – the disconnect between the meaning we seek and its encoding in character-strings is simply too great. More sophisticated mechanisms do much better by following what our and others' actions show we want rather than what we say we want in Boolean language. They do not so much filter out the irrelevant as more effectively locate possibilities likely to tempt us. The irony is that the failure of these mechanisms (especially the Boolean ones) to aid specialist inquiry offers a far greater though traumatic benefit to scholarship, bringing together, say, articles belonging to English literature with others in theoretical biology, medieval history, anthropology, and cognitive science. Who could not be curious? I wish I could say, no one.

This I call the default condition of research in the twenty-first century. It is what happens when you, I, our colleagues, and students use JSTOR, for example, though again we may choose to deny the temptations. Some recoil from what they see as info-glut. But from the perspective of research, which by nature cannot arrive at a final *result*, for which the brick-in-the-wall metaphor of knowledge is all wrong,[15] what we get isn't necessarily debilitating chaos but potentially a fructifying though traumatic cornucopia. And so my immediate question is how we are to deal with plenty in the form it now takes.

In other words, the problem that concerns me here is the imminent consequence of so much genuinely meaningful diversity. We are all aware of the threat to focused research posed by centrifugal proliferation of intriguing possibilities. We all know well the frustrations of being lured into time-wasting bouts of online prowling that yield cascades of material as impractical to explore as they are compelling – and unusable unless explored. This, I know, is not strictly new. It is also the peril that has always lurked in any research library. But for obvious reasons it is so much easier to be way-laid, so much easier to succumb. One is so much more likely to encounter material that formerly would have been found on another floor or kept in another, perhaps distant building. So what do you do?

The initial problem is an old one. A well-known historical example of an attempt to deal with it is Vannevar Bush's rearguard response at the end of World War 2 to the "growing mountain of research" which, he said, the investigator "cannot find time to grasp, much less to remember" (Bush, 1945:101; see also Nyce and Kahn, 1991). In celebrating Bush's imagined Memex, however, we tend to overlook the fact that he designed it to aid specialization "increasingly necessary for progress," not to unbind the book, break down disciplinary fences, and all those other things his Memex is said to have inspired. We overlook his view in "As we may think" that "the effort to bridge between disciplines [is] correspondingly *superficial*" (1945:101; my emphasis). Bush's geometrical metaphor (*superficies*, having length or breadth without thickness), though undoubtedly intended as merely a common adjective, makes the point elaborated in another context by Richard Rorty (2004/2002): that the implicit model of knowledge at work here privileges singular truth at depth, reached by the increasingly narrower focus of disciplinary specialization, and correspondingly trivializes plenitude on the surface, and so the bridging of disciplines. Hence the epistemic question that the Web makes so difficult to avoid: is this plenitude *only*, *necessarily* trivial or trivializing? Must its interdisciplinary pursuit be conceived as mentally enervating? Is depth of knowledge necessarily and always good – or, as we say revealingly, *profound*?

The obvious answer, no, leaves us with a problem of practical epistemology: how then do we do research? Rorty argues from Gadamer that we are faced with an entirely different way of conceiving the pursuit for truth, not going deep to find the one answer but going wide to collect many witnesses, many views, then filtering, sorting, and reclassifying according to the question at hand (2004/2002).

The Aim and the Difficulties

As curious inquirers empowered by curiosity's machine and encouraged to do interdisciplinary work, what is our goal?

I have entitled this chapter "Becoming interdisciplinary" with care, not only to focus attention on individual practice but also to answer the charge leveled against all such work by Stanley Fish in his formidable interdiction, "Being interdisciplinary is so very hard to do" (1989). The title is deliberately ironic: he argues that it is *impossible* to be interdisciplinary, warning his reader off in a relentless, closely reasoned argument.

His target is more serious than the many specious claims to interdisciplinary work and the handwaving that attends them. Fish's concern is with the goal of *achieving* a neutral, *perfectly* interdisciplinary standpoint, and so with the claim to a kind of absolute truth transcending all disciplines – a panoptic god's-eye view from which they might all be observed doing their limited things (The claim to the panoptic view lurks, for example, in the casual rhetoric about "breaking down" the boundaries that disciplines construct and police, to make from a partitioned landscape a great open field of knowledge. Indeed the very idea of the panopticon is illuminating: see Foucault, 1991/1975; Bentham, 1995; Lyon, 2006.) I think we must agree with Fish thus far, that such a goal is delusional – this side of godhead no such perfect neutrality is possible, and that belief in it is dangerous in its programmatic absolutism. I refer you to his article for the details. But what I would like you to note here in particular is his further, and I think quite wrongheaded, assertion that *attempting* a broader view is therefore not only doomed but also morally wrong.[16] Such a fundamentalist position would by analogy have us argue that one should abandon *any* attempt to be good because achieving perfect goodness is, as we all know, impossible. Just as we, knowing that being perfectly good is unachievable, do not run amok but try our best, should we not strive to extend ourselves beyond what we have been conditioned to know in the ways we have been conditioned to know it? Isn't that what education is for?

Those other than Fish who have considered the problem seriously – I name only Gillian Beer (1996:115–45; 2006), Greg Dening (1996:39–41), Thomas Kuhn (1977:5–6), Marilyn Strathern (2004), Peter Galison (2010), and Myra Strober (2010) – attest that making the attempt is severely challenging. We learn from them all, and from many others who have written on the topic,[17] but my focus here is narrower. Strober's sociological concern is with colleagues in university departments and how they might most productively combine their research interests. Her interdisciplinarity is the collaborative kind. Strathern's anthropological and Galison's historical concerns are with interchanges of knowledge and knowledge-objects between established groups across what Galison has called "the trading zone." Mine here, like Beer's, Dening's, and Kuhn's, is with the individual rather than with groups, with cognitive rather than professional strategies. On the basis of my own experience in making the attempt (but necessarily always falling short), I want to sketch out what is involved. Whether alone in the study or together with others in a research team, the individual faces the same challenge in attempting to take on a foreign disciplinary culture. So, I would argue, the broad relevance of the individual's dilemma to scholarship, whether alone or in teams.

In *Open Fields: Science in Cultural Encounter* (1996) Beer reflects a lifetime of experience. "Interdisciplinary work crosses over between fields," she writes: "it transgresses. It thus brings into question the methods and materials of differing intellectual practices and may uncover problems disguised by the scope of established disciplines" (1996:115). Elsewhere she enumerates the hazards:

> how to distinguish what's central from what's peripheral in this other zone; how to tap into the hinterland of controversy that lies behind the works on the shelf; how to avoid becoming merely disciples because not in control of a sufficient range of knowledge. ... The converse of this is true as well: the problems preoccupying those working in another discipline may sometimes (initially, arrogantly) seem quite simple – because we are not familiar with the build up of arguments across time that has reached this moment of dilemma.
>
> And then, crucially, there is the matter of competence. ... Others have spent years acquiring the skills that the interdisciplinarian needs. Is this a raiding party? Is there time to question and to learn? How much must be taken on trust? Are we accessing others' materials but still applying the mode of analysis learnt in our native discipline, or are we seeking new methods of analysis too? Either of these approaches may in fact yield fruit. And it is essential that we do not abandon the long learnt skills that go with our own disciplinary formation: they will be fundamental in any contribution we can make to new knowledge (Beer, 2006)

And then there is the profound intellectual trauma that attends the understanding of what is involved. Kuhn (philosopher, historian, and physicist) wrote from his belief in disciplinary incomensurability of "a personal wrench, the abandonment of one discipline for another with which it is not quite compatible" (1977:5). Here Karin Knorr Cetina's term "epistemic culture" is suggestive (1991). It connotes the integrity of disciplines as social institutions, their internal coherence, the respect for them we find in those who have explored most successfully beyond the limits of their own – and the culture shock that movement among them entails.

For my purposes here I take disciplines, then, as autonomous epistemic cultures from which explorations begin and to which they usually return, bringing change with them. Each of them, including the one you start from, is characterized by a "normal discourse," as Rorty has called it. However permeable or open, each thus orbits "an agreed-upon set of conventions about what counts as a relevant contribution, what counts as answering a question, what counts as having a good argument for that answer or a good criticism of it" (1979:320). These conventions are seldom if ever written down; agreement is mostly or entirely tacit, embodied in works of scholarship taken by consensus to be exemplary – for a time. Rorty notes that his idea of "normal discourse" is a generalization of Kuhn's "normal science," and that, as in Kuhnian science, disciplinary normality is from time to time upset and refigured by revolutionary changes in a field. For the interdisciplinarian these are events to learn from.

Disciplinary normality is policed – sometimes not too strong a term for the passionate attacks on new ideas.[18] More serious is the silent way in which, as Dening notes, disciplines function as "ways of making a blinkered view of the world seem mythically true" (1996:40), hence other views wrong, insignificant, or even undetectable. For this reason, in proportion to differences in its conventions, research in a discipline to which one is alien is difficult to see as good research, or even to see as research at all (Imagine from an old-fashioned philologist's likely perspective what publications in computer science or in cultural studies would look like, and vice versa.) The outsider presenting to insiders is apt to be greeted by incomprehension, misapprehension, indifference, hostility – or, what is worst of all, he or she may not be heard as saying much of anything, as if a tiny insect had flown into the room and was making a barely audible, slightly annoying buzz.

In its etymology, "barbarian" encodes the sociointellectual problem that becoming interdisciplinary aims to overcome.

The Meta-Discipline of Interdisciplinary Explorations

I have argued that the interdisciplinarian cannot get away from his or her discipline of origin, at least not completely, and I have implied that the more disciplines he or she investigates the more diversely encultured he or she will become. And I have hinted in my reference to epistemic cultures that interdisciplinary exploration itself cannot be innocent of disciplinary guidance, that there must be a meta-discipline at play, i.e., social anthropology.[19] Let me now bring that meta-discipline into the open.[20]

If disciplines are epistemic cultures in the anthropological sense, then we have not just silos or islands of knowledge but islands populated by communities of knowers, their languages, habits, histories, and artifacts. I referred earlier to Galison's trading zone, which applies chiefly to contact between disciplines motivated, as traders are, by their own agendas. Thus, in the transfer of objects from one to the other, Galison describes "a partial peeling away, an (incomplete) *dis*encumbrance of meaning" (1997:436). The interdisciplinarian may only be wanting a like depth of contact, but here I am assuming the objective to be more than that – to be acquisition of what Clifford Geertz calls, with care, "the native's point of view" (1983). In one place he describes the "characteristic intellectual movement ... [as] a continuous dialectical tacking between the most local of local detail and the most global of global structure in such a way as to bring them into simultaneous view" (1983:69); in another as "a Jamesian hum of buzz and implication ... [a] double image, clarity from a distance, jumble up close" that "critiqued, developed, filled out, moralized upon, and brought to bear on more exact experiences ... turned into my most general conception of what it was that was driving things" (1995:13). For the ethnographic historian Greg Dening, whose Oceanic natives and European strangers vanished long ago, all such explorations are performances "on the beaches of the mind" (2002). *The Death of William Gooch: A History's Anthropology* (Dening, 1995) is a magnificent, inspiring example.

By singling out two of the scholars to whom I am most indebted I may seem to be in imminent danger of falling into one of the traps Beer warns us against: becoming a mere disciple "because not in control of a sufficient range of knowledge" – which is, I must admit, a fair warning. But I offer Geertz and Dening not as icons for your mantelpiece but to illustrate the beginnings of a way of finding structure and methodological guidance. The fluid combination of distance and intimacy in interdisciplinary exploration is otherwise very difficult to navigate. One could do *much* worse than those two, though many others have thought extensively about ethnographic practice and may provide better help in different circumstances. But whether there is a more effective meta-discipline I very much doubt.

The range of possibilities in interdisciplinary research is from theft to assimilation. At the former extreme is Beer's "raiding party," which we can see frequently occurring in the poaching of equations, methods, and other expressions of process from one discipline for use in another.[21] Such is also characteristic of creative artists, who take and adapt with equally little regard for the source. It can be seen in the long-term behavior of disciplines or whole groups of them, for example, the "refiguration of social thought" brought about by a shift of influence from the natural sciences to the humanities (Geertz, 1980). The effects can be disastrous (cf. Franck, 2002). Now, with consensus on the importance of material culture and its "thing knowledge" (Baird, 2004; Daston, 2004; see also Galison, 1997; Gorman, 2010), we cannot doubt that poaching has its not always foreseeable consequences.

At the other extreme is the one-way migration, to establish a new discipline (e.g., molecular biology, digital humanities) or to resettle in an old one as an ex-pat.

Between these two is what seems to me the ideal – a combination, not compromise, of centrifugal freedom and centripetal beholdenness. This is expressed, for example, by Northrop Frye in *On Education*: "every field of knowledge," he writes, "is the centre of all knowledge ... [I]t doesn't matter so much what you learn when you learn it in a structure that can expand into other structures" (1988:10). Such would seem what Ian

Hacking describes in his role as "complacent disciplinarian" (2004): "not interdisciplinary in the sense of trying to break down disciplinary boundaries, but rather a philosopher who tries to be disciplined enough to pick up what is going on in other disciplines" (Hacking, undated). Sociologist Jerry A. Jacobs' critical study, *In Defense of Disciplines: Interdisciplinarity and Specialization in the Research University* (2014), argues that quite contrary to the talk of "silo mentality" knowledge passes quite readily from one discipline to another.[22]

The How

Interdisciplinary research is like the ordinary curiosity-motivated kind in that it is exploratory and unpredictable within the domain to be explored. But (to paraphrase Beer) because the interdisciplinarian brings into question the methods and materials of a differing intellectual practice, possibly uncovering problems disguised by the scope of the discipline under investigation, the security of that discipline's embrace is unavailable. Again the interplay of freedom and beholdenness: while the constraints of the foreign discipline must be recognized and respected, the interdisciplinarian struggles to be as much free of them as of those belonging to his or her discipline of origin. In a sense Alan Rauch is right, that the help we need is to "find our way in a world that is always already interdisciplinary" (Austin *et al.*, 1996:274) — so long as we understand this to mean both that no one gets it quite right and that no completely right take on it is to be had.

Basic skills that are required begin with the old one of following trails in books and articles through their footnotes and bibliographies, watching for repetition of references to the same source that signals its regard within its discipline's normal discourse. Reviews are an obvious way to measure the reactions of a discipline to new work. Edited collections (despite the ill-deserved contempt in which they are held by "research excellence" exercises) can be invaluable, especially if they set out, as they often do, to give a synopsis of research in the discipline. So also special issues and dedicated sections of journals devoted to themes important to particular disciplines. Deliberately crafted presentations to outsiders can likewise be valuable, for example contributions to the Oxford University Press' *Very Short Introductions* series; overviews commissioned by professional societies for their websites; and explicit gestures from individuals, such as Peter Berger's well-known *Invitation to Sociology: A Humanistic Perspective* (1963) and his later reversal in "Sociology: a disinvitation?" (1992). Public lecture series frequently give senior scholars the opportunity to take just such an overview as the interdisciplinarian would wish for: for example, the BBC Reith Lectures and the American Council of Learned Societies Howard Homer Haskins Prize Lectures.[23] Colleagues and friends can sometimes be helpful, but often a native informant will be influenced too much by a particular school of thought within a discipline to be useful.

Native informants are also likely to be so caught up with the current state of the discipline that they not only lack the overview you need but also miss what I like to call the trajectory of the discipline, its long-term direction or sense of purpose, which they may lack the perspective to see. Looking back to origins may help. In *The Muse*

Unchained: An Intimate Account of the Revolution in English Studies at Cambridge (1958), E.M.W. Tillyard argues that, "When a new freedom comes into being, the kind of thing it leads to depends largely on the characters of the people who first enjoy it. ... Thus it follows that any fitting account ... must deal largely with persons and their characters. ... It must have as its main topic certain people: by what accidents they became involved ... what ideas they had, and how they translated them into action" (11–12). As I've argued elsewhere for digital humanities (McCarty, 2013:46), we know from various sources that social phenomena are marked, often indelibly, by the historically specific contexts of their origins. They are, as we say, *imprinted* (Stinchcombe, 1965; Lounsbury and Ventresca, 2002). So there is strong argument in favor of the writings of founders. A good example of a recent case is cultural studies, for which the works of Raymond Williams and Richard Hoggart are particularly important: for example, for Williams, his luminous essay "Culture is ordinary" (2001/1958). Such originating works may lead to others commenting precisely on what made them foundational, thus Terry Eagleton on Williams in "Resources for a journey of hope" (1989) and Lindsey Hanley on Hoggart in her introductory essay to the recent edition of *The Uses of Literacy: Aspects of Working Class Life* (2009).

Just as colleagues and friends may be helpful, so also popular cultural materials, such as, again, for cultural studies, the BBC television drama *The Chatterley Affair*, on the obscenity trial at the Royal Courts of Justice in 1960 against D.H. Lawrence's *Lady Chatterley's Lover*. In that trial Hoggart (played accurately by David Tennant) gave crucial testimony that led, as you may know, to the funding which made possible the inaugural center for cultural studies at Birmingham, by the grateful publisher of the novel, Penguin Books. In following such leads, one strays far from the confines of rigorous scholarship, but so do scholars in their ordinary lives. To paraphrase sociologist Maurice Halbwachs (1992:22) and anthropologist Mary Douglas (1986/1987:45), while interdisciplinary understanding of a problem can draw strength from a base in a socially organized body of people, it is individuals who understand and so must be understood. The group is not mind writ large; rather the mind of the individual is the group writ small and made intellectually coherent.

Digital Humanities

I have so far avoided discussing two things: the particular situation of digital humanities among the disciplines, and cookbook procedures for interdisciplinary research.

The latter I will not do. A comparison of any introductory handbook on ethnographic method to the writings of such as Geertz and Dening will demonstrate how much is lost and how much distorted by reducing a powerful role to a set of rules or textbook account. As Geertz's famous description of the Balinese cockfight makes clear, his and his wife's "sudden and unusually complete acceptance into a society extremely difficult for outsiders to penetrate" did not come from a "generalizable recipe for achieving that mysterious necessity of anthropological field work, rapport" but from their own equally sudden and complete acceptance of village life in a telling moment (1972:4). It's unlikely that interdisciplinary fieldwork will ever be quite as memorable as that cockfight, but the principle is the same and stands persuasively against any attempt to describe how to perform the role this chapter has sketched its way around.

The former, to consider interdisciplinary research from our starting point in digital humanities, is unavoidable in the context of the *New Companion* and important also because this discipline's nature is unique. I can see three ways in which it is, with corresponding points to be made about becoming interdisciplinary.

First, digital humanities is new. Although it has been practiced for over six decades, self-awareness only came to the discipline in the last decade, with the publication of the first *Companion* in 2004 and my own *Humanities Computing* in 2005. Because it is new, the discipline needs help from its peers. Just as physics at its beginning took from the arts and crafts, mechanics and mathematics, and made something different from them, so also digital humanities must take as need be and transform what it takes. All outward explorations from any discipline into others render it vulnerable to being diverted by tacit thing knowledge, as I said earlier, but digital humanities is particularly at risk because it lacks a strong sense of itself. I also noted that its necessary openness to relationships is another source of vulnerability. To become interdisciplinary means to become radically reciprocal.

Second, digital humanities has (to paraphrase the medieval *centrum ubique, circumferentia nusquam*) a centre all over the disciplinary map and a circumference that is at best uncertain. Here is not the place to argue how far the Big Tent extends, nor what activities, if any, or in what sense, belong under it and nowhere else (Pannapacker, 2011). But it is clear that interdisciplinary research is simply how it operates. That fact makes becoming interdisciplinary neither easy nor simple, however. It is not easy, for reasons I have taken pains in this chapter to explore. Digital humanities does not get a pass. It is not simple, because the techno-scientific instrument on which the practice is based means that the digital interdisciplinarian brings the whole inheritance of the Two Cultures to the table. But like it or not, the techno-sciences are part of the conversation.

Third, in consequence of that inheritance, digital humanities offers a middle ground or conjectural space within which, data being simply data, the objects of study dear to the humanities may be treated temporarily *as if* they were objects of nature, like rocks or stars, then the results of that treatment juxtaposed to how we see them and questions asked. I have argued the case at length elsewhere (McCarty, 2007). But the core of it is this: that via the conjectural space digital humanities inherits without surrender of authority to the sciences far more than the debate C.P. Snow started in 1959. It inherits many centuries of now relevant work that has been foreign to the humanities since Galileo.

Coda

My aim here has been to suggest that not just the need to tackle great problems but also curiosity's latest historical moment are with us, that becoming interdisciplinary both rides the urge to know and struggles to hang on against the possibility of being thrown by it. I have put great emphasis on faithfulness to a discipline's self-understanding as countermeasure to solipsism, but at the same time the well-attested history of fruitful poaching cannot be denied.

Is becom*ing* interdisciplinary – always that participle, Dening insisted – a good thing? Anyone struggling to finish a major piece of writing against the commanding temptations on all sides is allowed to wonder. But the cornucopia opened to us by curiosity's digital machine is not a force of nature like the tide. It is a direct consequence of human action, bringing back a dark, riddling answer to an implicit question: what if curiosity were operationalized? We have no clear answer yet but feel the force of the question.

NOTES

1 "Ce qui rend les mauvais poètes plus mauvais encore, c'est qu'ils ne lisent que des poètes (comme les mauvais philosophes ne lisent que des philosophes), alors qu'ils tireraient un plus grand profit d'un livre de botanique ou de géologie. On ne s'enrichit qu'en fréquentant des disciplines étrangères à la sienne."

2 Metaphysics 980a21.

3 *The Descent of Man* (1871:47), where he dismisses the opinions of "many authors who have insisted that man is separated through his mental faculties by an impassable barrier from all the lower animals". Other keen observers of the natural world attest to what Konrad Lorenz calls the autonomous exploratory behavior of "the most highly organized animals ... [which] can, in subjective phenomenology, be described as curiosity" (1981/1978:292; see also 333–5), e.g., fellow Nobel laureate Nikolaas Tinbergen's *Curious Naturalists* (1969/1958).

4 "to understand so thoroughly that the observer becomes a part of the observed – to merge, blend, intermarry, lose identity in group experience" (Heinlein 1961:287). See all of *OED* s.v. *know*.

5 See *Conf.* 10.35; but note also 1.14; *Summa* Q167; cf. Foucault 1996/1980:305.

6 Not everyone who uses the abstract noun engages in the ontological exercise; my point is that the abstraction raises the question, what is *it*?

7 Now the Association for Interdisciplinary Studies; see http://www.units.muohio.edu/aisorg/ (accessed January 27, 2014).

8 Locating and sorting those signs I leave as an exercise in interdisciplinary research for the reader. But note esp. Fuller (2013).

9 Daston and Park, 1998:9–10. Social history demonstrates that extra-academic curiosity about matters formerly kept hidden or dismissed erupted in popular culture from the mid 1960s; the Swedish films *I am Curious (Yellow)* and *I am Curious (Blue)*, released in 1967 and 1968 respectively, are representative.

10 Academic attention to curiosity blurs into the anthropology and social history of magic, shamanism, witchcraft, demonology, satanism, the paranormal and so on, which show a much less well defined trajectory.

11 For the exhibition see http://www.south-bankcentre.co.uk/find/hayward-gallery-and-visual-arts/hayward-touring/future/curiosity-art-and-the-pleasures-of-knowing (accessed January 8, 2014).

12 For the Blankensee-Colloquia (another good example of recent interest in interdisciplinary research) see http://www.wiko-berlin.de/en/institute/projects-cooperations/blankensee-colloquia/; for the 2007 event, http://userpage.fu-berlin.de/~gab/info/blankensee-colloquium2007.html.

13 Gramelsberger 2011:12 (proceedings of the 2007 Colloquium), paraphrasing Thomas Lippert; see also Humphreys, 2004.

14 See, for example, the first two papers discussing "information retrieval" in the ACM Digital Library, Perry *et al.*, 1954, and Ridenour, 1955.

15 The case does not have to be made for the humanities; for the sciences see Rheinberger, 2010.

16 Liu (2008) is the only other argument along these lines that I know.

17 Apart from Frodeman *et al.*, 2010, see esp. Fuller, 2013, and the many publications of Julie Thompson Klein, csid.unt.edu/about/people/klein (accessed February 11, 2014), e.g., Klein, 1990.

18 For one of the more spectacular examples see the reaction of historians to the importation of computing (in the form of "quantification") from economic history, e.g., Davis *et al.*, 1960:540; Bridenbaugh, 1962; Fischer, 1970:104; Plumb, 1973:64ff; Barzun, 1974:14,158; Stone, 1987.

19 According to David Apter, Clifford Geertz "once entertained the notion of doing an anthropological study of the disciplines as savage tribes" (2007:112). Alas, he did not act on it.

20 Ethnography is standard practice in computer science (see e.g., Crabtree *et al.*, 2012; Nardi, 2010).

21 For the sciences in general see Hacking (2002) on styles of scientific reasoning. Examples of pattern-finding tests in statistics are numerous and telling; see Hacking (1990). See also McCarty (2005:68–9) on the remarkably migratory Michaelis–Menten equation. Digital humanities is based on the migratory power of methods across disciplines.

22 I discovered Jacobs (2014) too late to take proper account of it. A quick scan of it suggests that its sociological argument, while not central to my purpose, strengthens my case on behalf of disciplines as starting points for intellectual growth. His critical attack on the rhetoric of disciplines as isolating silos of knowledge and barriers to its movement looks telling.

23 For the Reith Lectures see http://www.bbc.co.uk/radio4/features/the-reith-lectures/about; for the Haskins Lectures, http://www.acls.org/pubs/haskins.

REFERENCES AND FURTHER READING

Apter, D.E. 2007. On Clifford Geertz. *Daedalus* 136(3), 111–13.

Austin, T.R., Rauch, A., Blau, H., *et al.* 1996. Defining Interdisciplinarity. *PMLA* 111 (2), 271–82.

Baird, D. 2004. *Thing Knowledge: A Philosophy of Scientific Instruments*. Berkeley: University of California Press.

Barzun, J. 1974. Clio and the Doctors: Psycho-History, Quanto-History and History. Chicago: University of Chicago Press.

Beer, G. 1996. *Open Fields: Science in Cultural Encounter*. Oxford: Oxford University Press.

Beer, G. 2006. The challenges of interdisciplinarity. Speech for the Annual Research Dinner, Durham University, 26 April 2006. www.dur.ac.uk/ias/news/annual_research_dinner (accessed February 11, 2014).

Benedict, B.M. 2001. *Curiosity: A Cultural History of Early Modern Inquiry*. Chicago: University of Chicago Press.

Bentham, J. 1995. *The Panopticon Writings*. Edited by M. Božovič. London: Verso.

Berger, P. 1963. *Invitation to Sociology: A Humanistic Perspective*. Garden City, NY: Doubleday.

Berger, P. 1992. Sociology: a disinvitation? *Society* 30 (1), 12–18.

Bridenbaugh, C. 1963. The great mutation. *The American Historical Review* 68 (2), 315–31.

Burke, E. 1757. *A Philosophical Enquiry into the Origin of our Ideas of the Sublime and Beautiful*. London: R. and J. Dodsley.

Bush, V. 1945. As we may think. *The Atlantic Monthly* 176 (1), 101–8.

Cioran, E.M. 1973. *De l'inconvénient d'être né*. Paris: Gallimard.

Crabtree, A., Rouncefield, M., and Tolmie, P. 2012. *Doing Design Ethnography*. Heidelberg: Springer Verlag.

Darwin, C. 1871. *The Descent of Man and Selection in Relation to Sex*. New York: D. Appleton and Company.

Daston, L., ed. 2004. Things that Talk: Object Lessons from Art and Science. New York: Zone Books.

Daston, L. 2005. All curls and pearls. Review of *The Uses of Curiosity in Early Modern France and Germany*, by Neil Kenny. *London Review of Books* 27 (12) (23 June), 37–8.

Daston, L., and Park, K. 1998. *Wonders and the Order of Nature 1150–1750*. New York: Zone Books.

Davis, L.E., Hughes, J.R.T., and Reiter, S. 1960. Aspects of quantitative research in economic history. *Journal of Economic History* 20 (4), 539–47.

Dening, G. 1995. *The Death of William Gooch: A History's Anthropology*. Honolulu: University of Hawai'i Press.

Dening, G. 1996. A poetic for histories. In *Performances*. Chicago: University of Chicago Press, 39–63.

Dening, G. 2002. Performing on the beaches of the mind. *History and Theory* 41, 1–24.

Dillon, B., and Warner, M. 2013. *Curiosity: Art and the Pleasures of Knowing*. London: Hayward Publishing.

Douglas, M. 1987/1986. *How Institutions Think*. London: Routledge & Kegan Paul.

Eagleton, T. 1998/1989. Resources for a journey of hope: Raymond Williams. In *The Eagleton Reader*, ed. S. Regan. Oxford: Blackwell, 311–20.

Fischer, D.H. 1970. Historians' Fallacies: Toward a Logic of Historical Thought. New York: Harper & Row.

Fish, S. 1989. Being interdisciplinary is so very hard to do. *Profession 89*. New York: Modern Language Association, 15–22.

Foucault, M. 1991/1975. *Discipline and Punish: The Birth of the Prison*. Trans. Alan Sheridan. New York: Vintage Books.

Foucault, M. 1996/1980. The masked philosopher. In *Foucault Live: Collected Interviews, 1961–1984*, ed. S. Lotringer. Trans. L. Hochroth and J. Johnston. New York: Semiotext(e).

Franck, R. 2002. General introduction. In *The Explanatory Power of Models*, ed. Robert Franck. Dordrecht: Kluwer, 1–8.

Frank, R. 1988. "Interdisciplinary": the first half century. *Issues in Integrative Studies* 6, 139–51.

Frodeman, R., Klein, J.T., and Mitcham, C., eds. 2010. *The Oxford Handbook of Interdisciplinarity*. Oxford: Oxford University Press.

Frye, N. 1988. *On Education*. Markham, ON: Fitzhenry & Whiteside.

Fuller, S. 2013. Deviant interdisciplinarity as philosophical practice: prolegomena to deep intellectual history. *Synthese* 190 (11), 1899–916.

Galison, P. 1997. *Image and Logic: A Material Culture of Microphysics*. Chicago: University of Chicago Press .

Galison, P. 2010. Trading with the enemy. In Gorman 2010, 25–42.

Geertz, C. 1972. Deep play: notes on the Balinese cockfight. *Daedalus* 101 (1), 1–37.

Geertz, C. 1980. Blurred genres: the refiguration of social thought. *The American Scholar* 49 (2), 165–79.

Geertz, C. 1983. "From the native's point of view": on the nature of anthropological understanding. In *Local Knowledge: Further Essays in Interpretative Anthropology*, 3rd edition. New York: Basic Books.

Geertz, C. 1995. *After the Fact: Two Countries, Four Decades, One Anthropologist*. Cambridge, MA: Harvard University Press.

Glimm, J. 1990. Scientific computing: von Neumann's vision, today's realities, and the promise of the future. In *The Legacy of John von Neumann*, ed. J. Glimm, J. Impagliazzo, and I. Singer. Proceedings of Symposia in Pure Mathematics, vol. 50. Providence, RI: American Mathematical Society, 185–96.

Gorman, M.E., ed. 2010. *Trading Zones and Interactional Expertise: Creating New Kinds of Collaboration*. Cambridge, MA: MIT Press.

Gramelsberger, G., ed. 2011. *From Science to Computational Sciences: Studies in the History of Computing and its Influence on Today's Sciences*. Zürich: Diaphanes.

Hacking, I. 1990. *The Taming of Chance*. Cambridge: Cambridge University Press.

Hacking, I. 2002. "Style" for historians and philosophers. In *Historical Ontology*. Cambridge, MA: Harvard University Press, 178–99.

Hacking, I. 2004. The complacent disciplinarian. Interdisciplines: Rethinking Interdisciplinarity, 5 January. http://apps.lis.illinois.edu/wiki/download/attachments/2656520/Hacking.complacent.pdf (accessed February 11, 2014).

Hacking, I. (undated). Ian Hacking: education. http://www.ianhacking.com/education.html (accessed February 11, 2014).

Halbwachs, M. 1992. *On Collective Memory*. Edited and translated by Lewis A. Coser. Chicago: University of Chicago Press.

Hanley, L. 2009. Introduction. In *The Uses of Literacy: Aspects of Working Class Life*, by Richard Hoggart. London: Penguin, ix–xxiv.

Heinlein, R.A. 1961. *Stranger in a Strange Land*. New York: Ace Books.

Humphreys, P. 2004. *Extending Ourselves: Computational Science, Empiricism, and Scientific Method*. Oxford: Oxford University Press.

Jacobs, J.A. 2014. *In Defense of Disciplines: Interdisciplinarity and Specialization in the Research University*. Chicago: University of Chicago Press.

Kenny, N. 2004. *The Uses of Curiosity in Early Modern France and Germany*. Oxford: Oxford University Press.

Klein, J.T. 1990. *Interdisciplinarity: History, Theory, & Practice*. Detroit: Wayne State University Press.

Knorr Cetina, K. 1991. Epistemic cultures: forms of reason in science. *History of Political Economy* 23 (1), 105–22.

Kuhn, T. 1977. The relations between the history and philosophy of science. In *The Essential Tension: Selected Studies in Scientific Tradition and Change*. Chicago: University of Chicago Press, 3–20.

Liu, A. 2008. The interdisciplinary war machine. *Local Transcendence: Essays on Postmodern Historicism and Database*. Chicago: University of Chicago Press, 169–85.

Lloyd, G.E.R. 2002. The Ambitions of Curiosity: Understanding the World in Ancient Greece and China. Cambridge: Cambridge University Press.

Lorenz, K. 1981/1978. *The Foundations of Ethology*. Trans. K.Z. Lorenz and R.W. Kickert. New York: Springer Verlag.

Lounsbury, M. and Ventresca, M.J. 2002. Social structure and organizations revisited. *Research in the Sociology of Organizations* 19, 3–36.

Lyon, D., ed. 2006. *Theorizing Surveillance: The Panopticon and Beyond.* Cullompton: Willan Publishing.

McCarty, W. 2005. *Humanities Computing.* Basingstoke: Palgrave.

McCarty, W. 2007. Being reborn: the humanities, computing and styles of scientific reasoning. *New Technology in Medieval and Renaissance Studies* 1, 1–23.

McCarty, W. 2013/2006. Tree, turf, centre, archipelago – or wild acre? Metaphors and stories for humanities computing. In *Defining Digital Humanities: A Reader,* ed. M. Terras, J. Nyhan, and E. Vanhoutte. London: Ashgate.

McCarty, W. 2013. The future of digital humanities is a matter of words. In *A Companion to New Media Dynamics,* ed. J. Hartley, J. Burgess, and A. Bruns. Chichester: John Wiley & Sons Ltd.

Michaelis, A.R. 1976. Editorial. Future affirmative. *Interdisciplinary Science Reviews* 1 (1), iii-xi. DOI: 10.1179/isr.1976.1.1.iii. http://www.maneyonline.com/doi/abs/10.1179/isr.1976.1.1.iii (accessed June 20, 2015).

Michaelis, A.R. 2001. *The Scientific Temper: An Anthology of Stories and Matters of Science.* Heidelberg: Universitätsverlag C. Winter.

Nardi, B.A. 2010. *My Life as a Night Elf Priest.* Ann Arbor: University of Michigan Press.

Newell, W.H., ed. 1990. *Interdisciplinarity: Essays from the Literature.* New York: College Entrance Examination Board.

Nyce, J.M., and Kahn, P. 1991. *From Memex to Hypertext: Vannevar Bush and the Mind's Machine.* Boston: Academic Press.

Pannapacker, W. 2011. "Big Tent digital humanities": a view from the edge, Part I. *The Chronicle of Higher Education,* 31 July. http://chronicle.com/article/Big-Tent-Digital-Humanities/128434 (accessed March 5, 2014).

Perry, J.W., Berry, M.M., Luehrs, F.U., and Kent, A. 1954. Automation of information retrieval.

AIEE-IRE '54 (Eastern): Proceedings of the December 8–10, 1954, Eastern Joint Computer Conference: Design and Application of Small Digital Computers. New York: Association for Computing Machinery.

Plumb, J.H. 1973. Is history sick? manipulating the past. *Encounter* 40, 63–7.

Rheinberger, H.-J. 2010. *On Historicizing Epistemology: An Essay.* Trans. D. Fernbach. Stanford: Stanford University Press.

Ridenour, L.N. 1955. Storage and retrieval of information. AIEE-IRE '55 (Eastern): Papers and Dscussions Presented at the November 7–9, 1955, Eastern Joint Computer Conference: Computers in Business and Industrial Systems. New York: Association for Computing Machinery.

Rorty, R. 1979. *Philosophy and the Mirror of Nature.* Princeton: Princeton University Press.

Rorty, R. 2004/2002. Being that can be understood is language. In *Gadamer's Repercussions: Reconsidering Philosophical Hermeneutics,* ed. B. Krajewski. Berkeley, CA: University of California Press, 21–9.

Stinchcombe, A.L. 1965. Social structure and organizations. In *Handbook of Organizations,* ed J.G. March. Chicago: Rand McNally, 142–93.

Stone, L. 1987. Resisting the New. Review of *The New History and the Old,* by Gertrude Himmelfarb. *New York Review of Books* 34 (20).

Strathern, M. 2004. Commons and Borderlands: Working Papers on Interdisciplinarity, Accountability and the Flow of Knowledge. Oxford: Kingston.

Strober, M. 2010. Interdisciplinary Conversations: Challenging Habits of Thought. Stanford: Stanford University Press.

Tillyard, E.M.W. 1958. The Muse Unchained: An Intimate Account of the Revolution in English Studies at Cambridge. London: Bowes and Bowes.

Tinbergen, N. 1969/1958. *Curious Naturalists.* Garden City, NY: Doubleday.

Williams, R. 2001/1958. Culture is ordinary. In *The Raymond Williams Reader,* ed. John Higgins. Oxford: Blackwell, 10–24.

6

New Media and Modeling: Games and the Digital Humanities

Steven E. Jones

Video games are among the most widely experienced and influential forms of new media today. And games have been central to the history of computing itself, from chess-playing mechanical automata, to Turing's thought experiments (imagined explicitly in terms of a "game"), to the earliest actual computer games – *Tennis for Two* (1958), *Spacewar!* (1962), and *Adventure* (1977) – to more recent developments in expert systems, such as IBM's Watson, which plays chess, and *Jeopardy*, to serving as the source for many of the conventions operating in non-game simulations and virtual worlds (such as avatars and point of view). Because games are algorithmic systems that test the player's freedom within programmed formal constraints, and because they combine computing with modes of cultural expression associated with the humanities – storytelling, design, aesthetics, social communication – they would seem to be of obvious interest to the digital humanities. But, perhaps because they possess a stigma as mass entertainments, and despite the deep interest in games shown by many digital humanities practitioners, for several decades they were mostly excluded from digital humanities research, which focused on linguistic and textual analysis, and, later, on the markup of texts for editing and archiving. To put this in historical perspective: in the 1960s, as early researchers in humanities computing were working on stylometrics, attribution studies, and computational linguistics, researchers and graduate students at MIT were playing *Spacewar!* after hours on a DEC PDP-1 computer, exploiting the representational and modeling affordances of the system in a creative way, anticipating the later explosion of games as a popular medium (Brand, 1972).

The text-based linguistic work of pioneering scholar Father Roberto Busa, SJ, is often said to have inaugurated that earlier era in humanities computing. But over 40 years after he began the *Index Thomisticus*, in a foreword to the first edition of the

A New Companion to Digital Humanities, First Edition. Edited by Susan Schreibman, Ray Siemens, and John Unsworth.

Companion to Digital Humanities, Father Busa called for "the automation of *every* possible analysis of human expression" (Busa, 2004; my italics). By then, changing practices and changing platforms, along with the rise of media studies in universities, had already led to an increased focus within digital humanities on born-digital forms of media, including video games. In an oral history published in 2013, Ray Siemens recollects his own early programming of games, and his desire as an undergraduate to bring together the study of games and literature, a desire frustrated at a time when computers were viewed as tools for working on humanities content, not themselves as platforms for new kinds of content or as the object of critical attention (Nyhan, 2012). As Siemens goes on to observe in the interview, in recent years, games and gaming culture have become "a part what we now consider DH to be, or in an area that DH services and is served by." Looking back, we can see that, even during the period when they were relegated to after-hours cycles, as it were, games and gamelike environments have served as sources of inspiration and increasingly as objects of attention for the digital humanities, from early MUDs and MOOs in the 1980s and 1990s, to the "game of interpretation," *IVANHOE* (2000), to digital forensics and preservation, which have included games as boundary-testing examples of born-digital objects (McDonough *et al.*, 2010), to the pedagogical and theoretical deployment of games in humanities contexts, and the interdisciplinary analysis and critique of game systems in platform studies. More generally, video games are quintessentially modeling systems, and modeling and simulation, as Willard McCarty (2004) has argued, is a key affordance of computing in general for digital humanities research. In recent years, with the advent of mobile, geospatial, physical, and ubiquitous computing, games have provided especially valuable models of the culture's shifting relationship to networked technology itself in today's mixed-reality environment.

In the 1980s and 1990s, the first digital peer-reviewed journal in the humanities, *Post Modern Culture*, was established and edited by John Unsworth. It is worth remembering that the journal was closely associated at the time with its own dedicated gamelike space online, the PMC-MOO. MOO stands for MUD, Object Oriented, and a MUD is a Multi User Dungeon, a form of text-based virtual world first developed in the 1970s and then connected to the emerging public Internet in the 1980s. MUDs and MOOs have deep roots in games such as *Adventure* and *Zork* (as Nick Montfort wryly points out, "the 'D' in 'MUD' stands for *Zork*": Montfort 2003:223), which had in turn descended in part from *Dungeons and Dragons*. These roots are exposed inside the MUD as conventions and formal elements in the virtual spaces: avatars, programmer Wizards, puzzles to solve, creatively or wittily described dungeons or rooms, NPC (non-player character)-like programmable bots, and other programmed objects (including weapons and tools) with which the player can interact, by manipulating them and collecting them in inventory, for example. One difference from the earlier games from which they descended is that MUDs allowed multiple users to play at the same time in a shared space. PMC-MOO and other academically connected MOOs served primarily as synchronous online meeting spaces, but a sense of ludic excess, a gamelike sense of play, often accompanied and extended the chat sessions beyond utilitarian necessity. Even online academic conferences might involve settings, avatars, and objects inspired by games, such as user-created and programmed Eliza-style bots, tools, and rooms, and a certain amount of dungeon-crawling-style navigation.

Unsworth's 1996 account of the social and political implications of the MOO explains that participants belong to three classes, players, programmers, and Wizards, and refers to the MOO as a programmable space comparable to other "forms of gaming and/or virtual reality environments," observing in conclusion that such environments highlight increasing tensions between work and play in the digital age. Game DNA, as it were, is embedded in MOO code, and this had subtle influences on the work (and play) that took place in these spaces, which were important to the formation of various overlapping communities of humanities computing and media studies that eventually became known as the digital humanities.

A number of MOOs were in operation in the 1990s among early practitioners of humanities computing, including one that Carl Stahmer, Neil Fraistat, (later) Ron Broglio, and I created at the Romantic Circles Website in 1997, the *Villa Diodati MOO* (named after Byron's residence on Lake Geneva, where Mary Shelley famously conceived of *Frankenstein*). Text-based precursors to graphical virtual worlds such as *Second Life*, MOOs were widely used for educational applications, where they retained gamelike elements. In 1998–1999 we built inside the larger *Villa Diodati MOO* a game called *MOOzymandias*, which was also meant as an experimental collaborative "edition" of Shelley's famous sonnet about textually inscribed objects, the ruins of a colossal statue discovered by a traveler in the desert. In designing the space, we explicitly imagined the editor as playing the role of game master, defining challenges for players and guiding player interactions with the text, and we imagined the linked spaces inspired by the poem as a puzzle-adventure game for pedagogical and interpretative ends. We received a grant from the National Endowment for the Humanities (1999–2002) to develop *MOOzymandias*, along with other texts and other spaces in the MOO, as an online learning resource for high school and college literature students.

As I write, the *Villa Diodati MOO* is still running on Romantic Circles servers, although unbeknownst to most of our users, accessible in a text-only form via any Telnet connection. The chambers of the *MOOzymandias* game remain accessible, for the most part, beginning with the conventional second-person text: "You find yourself in the gigantic antechamber of an Egyptian tomb. You look around for a way in. ... You see a book here." Typing the right commands will allow you to open the book, take objects and interact with them, traverse the tunnels and chambers, solve puzzles related to the text and context of Shelley's poem. The rooms and tunnels, puzzles, bots, and other objects were created by the game's master-editors or by players (including students), which is to say, they were written in both MOO programming code and natural language descriptions, prompts and narratives, "scripts" in a double sense. Despite the hybrid Web-MOO's use of some images and HTML objects, the space was still essentially text-based, not far removed in that way from its mainframe ancestors, *Adventure* and *Zork*. The MOO was already a kind of historical or legacy platform by the time we created *MOOzymandias*. Early MMORPGs (massively multiplayer online role-playing games) and virtual worlds were essentially graphical MUDs. The coming of *EverQuest* and *World of Warcraft* and the 3D virtual world, *Second Life,* made the MOO's text-based virtual reality environment seem primitive, even obsolete to most users in the era of ever-increasing immersive online experiences. In retrospect, however, MOOs offer historical evidence of the role played by games and game-like environments – their conventions and structural premises, as well as a general ethos of collaborative experiment and play – in the field of humanities computing in the 1990s and early 2000s.

One advantage of MUD and MOO platforms was their accessibility. The MOO programming language was relatively easy to learn and the command-line interface was used for both programming the environment and experiencing it. The metaphorically vertical architecture of the platform was "flattened" as a result, the distance between lower-level operating system and higher-level game scripts and interface features felt closer than with later games for consoles or computers. The Unix-derived text input for MOOs engaged the player in an activity that was one step away from coding. Even students using the space were exposed to a command-line interface by necessity, and usually found it easy to learn a little code in order to manipulate the environment and the objects in it. Through an inherited game convention of "leveling up" they could, if the permissions settings allowed, gain programmer status and collaborate in making the environment itself. At the very least, the structure of the MOO encouraged players to more intuitively understand the structure of any game taking place in the environ-ment (even when they were not helping to create it). For example, MUDs and MOOs revealed in a vivid way the interconnection between fictive and structural elements in any game, the imagined world on the one hand and the procedures for interaction with that world on the other hand. MUDs and MOOs are closely related genealogically to game-like interactive fictions, such as the works published in the 1980s by Infocom, as Nick Montfort has explained. And any interactive fiction consists of two basic features: a world model (which can be mapped), and a parser (a script that processes the player's input in a meaningful way) (Montfort, 2003:viii–ix). Although Montfort is careful to distinguish interactive fiction from video games per se, both forms are clearly parts of the same media family and share cultural conventions, structures, assump-tions, and gameplay mechanics, with many of today's role-playing games (RPGs), action games, and puzzle adventures. I would argue that the basic duality Montfort identifies – world model and interactive parser, or, to put it more generally, world model and data about the world – is crucial for understanding video games of all kinds. The world model can take the form of a grid painted on a board, a series of scrolling platforms, or a cinematic 3D virtual reality, and the data can be cards, tokens, numbers generated by rolling dice or some other counter, or statistics, items in inventory, character history, and level. To play a game is to engage the game world through the lens of dynamic data, most explicitly represented in the heads-up display (HUD) overlay typical in video games, in which game and player statistics, inventory, navigation, and other data are displayed in a visual interface, literally overlaid on the graphical images of the game world. It's true in some sense that, as one influential theory has it, games are played inside a "magic circle," in which we suspend ordinary life and agree to the conditions, rules, and conventions of the game (Huizinga, 1950). But the layered consciousness that characterizes gameplay is a reminder that we actu-ally play on the perimeter of the magic circle, rather than within its boundary, a perimeter perhaps better imagined in any case materially, as a chalk circle, say, like the kind we draw on the spot to designate a space for playing a game of marbles, or as the mutually agreed and staked-out territory of a game of make-believe war, or, for that matter, the shared digital maps, represented in the HUD, defining a campaign level of a video game. Such agreed-upon "circles," or gameplay enclosures, are not magic. They are social phenomena, always therefore part of the real world, never entirely apart from it. And the game actually takes place, via the agency of players, back and forth across the socially constructed perimeter, with players experiencing the game in a state of layered self-consciousness.

That kind of layered, engaged play at the circumference of a socially delineated gamespace begins to look at lot like hermeneutic engagement in general, once we understand interpretation as a playful, ludic activity. In an experimental search for ways of representing (and promoting) such ludic interpretation, Jerome McGann, Johanna Drucker, Bethany Nowviskie, and Stephen Ramsay, with others, collaborated starting in 2001 on a project to develop and test a game of interpretation. As McGann said at the time, the best models for self-conscious collaborative interpretation "descend to us through our culture in games and role-playing environments" (McGann, 2001:164). The result was IVANHOE, a role-playing game of interpretation. Like MUDs and MOOs, IVANHOE was essentially text-based. It was in fact first played as a text-only game, in email exchanges (Walter Scott's romance-adventure novel, *Ivanhoe*, was the first literary work around which the game was played, giving the project its name.) Although a number of interface designs were prototyped, with varying features, the game developed in blogs and, later, employed a pie-chart style visualization interface showing moves made by players within a discourse field (the big circle) spun out of a shared text. Gameplay involved writing and rewriting the text (with its intertexts and paratexts) in revisionary acts of rewriting as "deformance," with every player's competitive or cooperative move tracked and visualized by the dynamically updated graphical tool. The graph visualized ongoing contributions to the discourse field, and colored "marbles" represented players and their positions in relation to that field. Players adopted a role, represented as a mask or avatar, whether based on a character chosen from within the central shared text, or the author, or some real or imagined character from within the pre-text or reception history of the text. The relation of character to discourse field is what the game was meant to test, through competitive and cooperative gameplay, in the form of acts of rewriting.

IVANHOE emerged from the Applied Research in Patacriticism (ARP) group at the University of Virginia, whose key theoretical inspiration was the twentieth-century avant-garde discourse of Alfred Jarry. An emphasis on deformative, aleatory, algorithmic, and ludic practices shaped its development. As Geoffrey Rockwell (another very early play-tester and developer of IVANHOE) has said, gaming "is research in the human-ities in that it is a return to play as one of our subjects and methods, play with the defining technology of this age, the computer as a toy at hand" (Rockwell, 2003:97). In this way, IVANHOE anticipated a number of characteristics of then-emergent digital humanities practices, including the reconceptualization and analysis of texts, aided by algorithmic processes and represented in visualizations and graphs, in order to expose otherwise hidden patterns and raise new questions. Another early developer and play-tester of IVANHOE, Stephen Ramsay, has in recent years argued for an algorithmic criticism, for "computationally enacted textual transformations," which he sees as merely a "self-consciously extreme" version "of those hermeneutical procedures found in all interpretive acts" (Ramsay, 2011:13,16). Even Father Busa's mainframe-assisted concordance building, Ramsay points out, was "algorithmic in the strictest sense" (19), a kind of computationally assisted dissolution and reconstitution of the text, as a massive, lemmatized list of its words, for the purpose of revealing otherwise imperceptible patterns, hidden dimensions. In this way, Ramsay links *IVANHOE* to more recent digital humanities transformations of very large corpora of texts via quantitative analysis and data visualizations, and to the earliest forms of humanities computing. *IVANHOE* reveals the potentially deformative, experimental, or ludic dimensions of even the most traditional text-based practices in the field. More pragmatically, in terms of method, the development of the *IVANHOE* game at the University of Virginia anticipated (and directly inspired) the emphasis within later digital humanities on hands-on prototyping and building things, and on collaborative or competitive play, as modes of investigation.

In the new century, video games have played another important role for digital humanities: as use-cases of the preservation and curation of born-digital media objects. The methods of digital forensics and media archaeology have overlapped with work in digital humanities, as seen most prominently in Matthew Kirschenbaum's work, and these methods have frequently been applied to the study of video games. Kirschenbaum's award-winning *Mechanisms* (2008), for example, focuses in literally microscopic detail on the 1980 game *Mystery House*, using a disk image and a hex editor program to perform a close reading, at the level of the binary data, of the game's complex material textuality. And the book applies its media-forensics approach to the game-like multimedia work by William Gibson, *Agrippa*. The artist's book containing a digital poem was part of a larger staged happening in 1992, the reach of which included the Internet. The result looks in retrospect like nothing so much as a trans-platform alternate reality game (ARG). Both of these cases raise questions about preservation of and access to digital media once their original platforms, including machines and operating systems and interface software, become functionally obsolete, and about the importance of understanding multiple materialities in the scholarly study of games and other new media.

Kirschenbaum was one of the researchers on the *Preserving Virtual Worlds* project (2010), initially a two-year multi-institutional research collaboration, which investigated the cultural-heritage problem of how to preserve and archive computer games and works of interactive fiction, which it recognizes as complex objects, "layers of logical abstractions mediated by the conventions of digital computing" (McDonough *et al.*, 2010). Part of an initiative of the Library of Congress, the project included social spaces like *Second Life*, but seven of its initial eight case studies were video games, ranging historically from *Spacewar!* (1962), to *Mystery House* (1980), to *Warcraft III* (2002), mainframe, console, and online games. The project focused on social and institutional as well as technological difficulties faced by libraries and archives when it came to handling this kind of new-media object.

> Unlike a book in a library, computer games have very poorly defined boundaries that make it difficult to determine exactly what the object of preservation should be. Is it the source code for the program? The binary executable version of the program? Is it the executable program along with the operating system under which the program runs? Should the hardware on which the operating system runs be included? Ultimately, a computer game cannot be played without a complex and interconnected set of programs and hardware. (McDonough *et al.*, 2010:13)

In dealing with basic questions of metadata ontologies, for example, and practical questions of how to make games playable into even the near future in the face of the obsolescence of their original systems, the project confronted the complexities of games as systems, as multilayered programmed expressive works, dependent on particular material hardware and software platforms, including network environments.

Preserving Virtual Worlds had a good deal in common with the approach known as platform studies, as articulated in the book series published by MIT Press and edited by Nick Montfort and Ian Bogost. As an approach, platform studies investigates underlying computing systems of all kinds, the "foundations of digital media," and how software and hardware shape creative and expressive work done on those systems – "artistic, literary, gaming, and other creative development" (foreword to Jones and Thiruvathukal, 2012:viii). It pays attention to all the layers in a platform's metaphorical "stack," including, at the lower levels, the machine and its code, then, moving up, the operating system, application software, and interface, all interacting to produce the effects of a given game or other work of cultural expression. This attention to platform is I think fundamental to today's digital humanities in general, whether applied to the study of new media or demonstrated in a general self-consciousness about the platforms through which scholarship – in the form of text, data, or code – is created and shared. My own contribution to the platform studies series, with my co-author George K. Thiruvathukal, was explicitly conceived of as a digital humanities project, *Codename Revolution*, a study of the Nintendo Wii video game console. When it was introduced in 2006, the Wii helped to usher in the era of casual gaming by tapping into the mass market of first-time gamers or non-gamers. It did this by design, by shifting attention away from the rendering of realistic, 3D virtual game worlds and to the physical and social space of the player's living room. The Wii was designed as a constellation of a sometimes klugy set of motion-control peripherals, all connected through accelerometers and other sensors and channels of communication to create a personal area network for embodied gameplay, turning the living room into game space. And that's where Wii gameplay takes place, not in some imaginary world on the other side of the screen (This is true to some degree of all gaming, but the Wii was designed from the start to foreground and enhance the mixed physical and digital space of gameplay.) When Microsoft's Kinect appeared in 2010, it was marketed as gadget-free. But it actually works by taking the sensors and gadgets out of the user's hands (or out from under her feet) and placing them up by the screen, looking back out at the room. In practice, Kinect play is very much like Wii play: both focus on the player's body in physical space. A range of hacks and homebrew applications for Kinect followed upon the release of a version for PC, and for the most part these focused not on virtual reality, but on connecting digital data and the physical world in various ways, including for example 3D scanning and 3D printing.

The Wii is a vivid example of the social nature of all platforms, the ways in which its components were designed and experienced in shared cultural contexts, so that it is impossible, finally, to separate software and hardware configurations from the social and cultural facts that influenced them and help to determine their effects. My co-author is a computer science professor, and our collaboration involved combining his perspective with mine as a literary and textual scholar. We wrote the book starting from two premises: (1) that games and game systems are a fruitful focus of interdisciplinary attention; and (2) that attention to the materialities of platforms is a key feature of digital humanities today. Games provide valuable use-cases for digital humanities because they have a well-established history for making meaning within the limits of specific computing platforms. And digital humanities can provide a useful theoretical perspective on that history, and on the cultural significance of particular games and game systems: the materialities of computing and the cultural significance of creative works. Viewed in this way, a platform-studies approach to games is by definition a digital humanities approach.

In recent years, a variety of digital humanities projects and research centers have taken a range of approaches to the study of video games. Just to name a few examples: an NEH-funded Gaming Institute was held at the University of South Carolina in 2010; a collaborative team led by Kari Kraus and Derek Hansen received funding from the National Science Foundation (NSF) in 2013 to study ARGs and transmedia storytelling; Geoffrey Rockwell and a team at the University of Alberta has collaborated with Ritumeikan University in Kyoto, Japan, to form a global game studies group, holding an international symposium on Japanese gaming in Alberta, in August 2012. In summer 2014, a course on "Games for Digital Humanities" – which provided a hands-on look at the medium of games as an object of research – was scheduled for the influential Digital Humanities Summer Institute at the University of Victoria, amidst other courses on topics such as text encoding, digitization, and geographic information systems (GIS). Among the centers and research groups around the world that have focused on the study of games, I could cite for example the Greater Than Games lab at Duke University, led by N. Katherine Hayles (whose own research has included interpretation of games); or HASTAC, the Humanities, Arts, Science, and Technology Alliance and Collaboratory, led by Cathy Davidson. In 2013, two THATCamps (The Humanities And Technology Camps) were held with a focus on games, at the University of Maryland and at Case Western Reserve University. Many scholars, based in different disciplines, have researched video games within recognizable digital humanities frameworks, although only some of these were explicitly declared as such, including (just to name a few prominent examples), Mark Sample, Zach Whalen, Patrick Jagoda, Rita Raley, Kari Kraus, Edmond Chang, Patrick LeMieux, Stephanie Boluk, Tim Lenoir, and Victoria Szabo. Indeed, game studies and new media work not explicitly identified as digital humanities have offered many contributions to the emerging field. I have already cited Nick Montfort and Ian Bogost, for example, neither of whom would call himself a digital humanities scholar, but both of whose work has been extremely influential in digital humanities, contributing via publications, conferences, and workshops, and on social media.

Besides being a significant cultural medium deserving of scholarly attention, video games are particularly valuable to the digital humanities because they are essentially modeling or simulation systems, not only models *of* (an imaginary undersea dystopia, or a crime-ridden American city very much like Los Angeles) but models *for*[1] – for experimenting with different ways of interoperating with algorithmically generated narrative possibilities, for example, or for cooperating with (or competing against) many other players in order to make a meaningfully expressive architecture, or to manage resources toward the completion of a goal – or, for that matter, any number of other social and material possibilities and situations that can be imagined. The point is that as a "pervasive medium, one as interwoven with culture as writing and images," as Ian Bogost has argued, video games have "valid uses across the spectrum, from art to tools and everything in between" (Bogost, 2011:7) – but this is in part because video games represent a vernacular tradition of experimentation with dynamic modeling or simulation. As Willard McCarty has argued, the capacity for modeling is key to the digital humanities: "properly understood, modeling points the way to a computing that is of as well as in the humanities: a continual process of coming to know by manipulating representations" (McCarty 2004). As McCarty reveals, games represent an already developed tradition of computer simulation.

> In the humanities we have known for some years that computer-based simulations, in the form of pedagogical games, can play a role in teaching. An old but very good example is The Would-Be Gentleman, a re-creation of economic and social life in seventeenth-century France in which the student-player must realize and put aside his or her modern preconceptions in order to win. ... In other words he or she must become a seventeenth-century Frenchman mentally and emotionally. From more recent and far more technically advanced VR applications, such as Richard Beacham's and Hugh Denard's reconstruction of the theater of Pompey in Rome ..., one can predict a scholarly future for simulation in many areas of humanistic research. (McCarty, 2004)

This goes beyond so-called sim games, a genre where the main point of gameplay is to simulate a city, or a roller-coaster theme park, or a quotidian suburban household. It is the way games work on a deeper structural level: they abstract and represent dynamic systems in ways the player can interact with them and experience various outcomes and effects. Gameplay itself, viewed this way, is an iterative experimental process, a series of moves adding up to a process of learning over time, in other words, through acts of recursive modeling. Across a variety of genres and platforms, games are models within which to practice modeling: a given game is a model of an existing or imagined world, and every act of gameplay models possible pathways and outcomes within the game.

Consider one of the most popular games of the past decade, _Minecraft_ (2009). Initially created by independent developer Markus Persson (known as "Notch"), it has been widely played across various platforms and has won awards and critical attention and sold many millions of copies. A sandbox construction game, it allows users to build freely using cubes that they "mine" in the game world. Everything you build in _Minecraft_ is made from 3D pixel (or voxel)-looking primitives, $16 \times 16 \times 16$-bit 3D blocks (defined in the game world as 1 meter square). You dig them up as raw materials of various kinds and then stack or connect them to make stylized buildings, vehicles, objects, and structures of all kinds. It is like playing with Lego blocks, and part of the challenge is to make something that looks organic or realistically rounded out of the digital Legos. Aesthetically, the results look decidedly retro-styled, pixelated in a 16-bit way, which adds to the appeal. Eschewing realistic graphics for stylized forms allows for a resource-efficient massive game world, much like MOOs in their day. You can travel very far in the virtual world of _Minecraft_. It is not technically an infinite terrain, but it feels infinite to most players, since the game procedurally generates on the fly the part of the world you travel to, rendering it in successive chunks of $16 \times 16 \times 128$-pixel blocks as you get to them. Often, you can see this happening as the world forms out in front of you, in the same way that a "slippy map" (such as in *Google Maps*) loads digital tiles as you scroll or swipe. In its purely sandbox or Creative mode, *Minecraft* allows you just to build and explore. In Survival mode, however, you become vulnerable to monsters that spawn at night, so you have to build adequate shelter quickly in order to protect yourself and stay alive. In both modes, players have built elaborate virtual objects, including many models of existing objects in the physical world or in pre-existing fictional worlds, from the Taj Mahal or Eiffel Tower to the Starship *Enterprise*, to working virtual hydraulic, mechanical, and electronic devices (one category of block, Redstone, provides and conducts electricity). There have even been working, playable replicas of classic video games created inside *Minecraft*. Some mods of the game have been applied to city planning, used to model possible future layouts of existing urban neighborhoods in the physical world (Goldberg and Larsson, 2013/2011:184–6). But the game is not just about modeling objects, cities, buildings, or even machines or dynamic systems. It self-consciously models – is about – modeling, the relationship between the digital and the physical. For example, you can export 3D models from software programs such as Google SketchUp into the game, and, conversely, you can build models in the game that can be extruded as physical objects using a 3D printer. *Minecraft* is a flexible system for modeling that self-consciously calls attention to its digital primitives and, thematically as well as procedurally, foregrounds the transit between physical and digital objects of various kinds, in the process figuring the multidirectional relationship between the physical world and the digital network.

That network is no longer adequately figured as virtual reality or "cyberspace," as it was in the popular imagination for roughly two decades. When author William Gibson coined the term *cyberspace* in 1982, he was inspired by watching arcade video-game players as they leaned into their machines, staring at the screens, working the controls and bumping the cabinets. Gibson – not himself a gamer – assumed that the players must have been longing for total immersion in the virtual world on the other side of the screen, and from that assumption he extrapolated a digital world apart from the physical world, a transcendent world of pure data (Jones, 2014:18–20). As a metaphor, cyberspace was always gamespace in another guise, gamespace displaced. In the past decade, the metaphor of cyberspace has given way to a new prevailing concept of our relation to the network. As Gibson himself has said, cyberspace is *everting*, turning inside out and spilling out into the physical world. It is in this environment that the digital humanities has taken hold in the public imagination during the past decade, I think because the new digital humanities is also premised on a view of the networked world as mixed reality, a space of interplay between digital and physical materialities, the network immanent in the world (Jones, 2014).

Games have always modeled mixed reality, the relationship of the digital and physical dimensions, even in classic 2D side-scrolling platformers. A number of recent independent games pay tribute to this convention and focus on navigating mixed reality in their central gameplay mechanics. Take Polytron's *Fez* (2012), for example. It's a game about the need to see from different perspectives the dimensional possibilities hidden in plain sight, possibilities you can't see or take advantage of until you (literally) turn the problem around, using the left and right triggers of the Xbox controller to rotate the whole game world 90 degrees in one direction or the other, shifting from 2D to 3D – or back to 2D. As the opening of the game says, you rotate the game world in order to change your perspective – in more than one sense. You play as Gomez, a small all-white cartoon character in a colorful pixelated universe of giant tower-worlds floating in the sky that are reminiscent of the tiled landscapes of *Super Mario Bros.* or the birds-eye maps of early adventure RPGs like the *Zelda* or *Final Fantasy* series, but turned on their side, as it were. Doors take you to interior rooms or other levels, cubes hover overhead until you grab them by jumping up to hit them. Negative-space niches, ledges, overhangs, look as if they were created by removing or rearranging the basic cubes with which the game world was created. *Fez* often looks almost as blocky as *Minecraft* (and, yes, there are recreations of *Fez* inside *Minecraft*), and as in that game, the blocks are metaphors for pixels or bits (there are eight "cube-bits" to find in the first level), again, figurative primitives signifying "the digital." The opening cutscene is glitchy, revealing in sputtering glimpses the digital realm behind the visible game world, then shifting to a "reboot" of the game, complete with conventional game logos. Developer Phil Fish has said that the game world of *Fez* is a "computer world ... and every now and then the universe becomes unstable and has to defragment itself and reboot." Though he describes the game world as existing inside a computer, of course gameplay takes place at the boundary of the imaginary computer game world and the player's physical world. Every time you flip dimensions, you call attention to that perspective on the boundary, and the self-conscious glitchy moments remind the user at the controls that the larger gamespace of *Fez* is a actually hybrid digital and physical space.

You navigate in the usual platformer way, by running, jumping, and climbing, looking for shiny golden cubes and the invisible "anticubes" that are their counterparts. Especially for a first-time player or uninitiated watcher, the most noticeable thing about the game – the visual feature that most stands out – is the repeated shifting in perspective triggered by the player as he or she searches for a platform to jump to or a way around an obstacle. And the rotation is striking precisely because it causes an alternation between 3D and 2D views. Click, and everything is flat like a classic side-scrolling platformer. Click again, and the same structure has depth and the two square platforms you just jumped between are revealed in another dimension to be many feet or meters apart, one floating behind another in space. In that new third dimension, the same objects are transformed, either expanded or reduced, along with what they afford or constrain in your gameplay. What we think of as the optical illusion – that the two square ends of platforms viewed straight on appear to be alongside one another when aligned along the horizontal y-axis, even though they are "actually" cubes and are very far apart along the z-axis (once you can visualize depth) – turns out to be a navigable reality within the game, a kind of viable parallel universe of only two dimensions. Toggling with the controller triggers has a leveling effect, relativizing the 2D and 3D worlds, revealing them as interpenetrating dimensional realities, alternatives always available, despite the evidence of your senses, accessible with a simple but world-altering shift in perspective. Even your square heads-up inventory frame, which shows the number of cube shards and keys you have collected, can be rotated using the triggers to reveal that it's actually itself a cube, with space to store other items, such as a treasure map, for example.

Fez is a puzzle platformer game, and most of its puzzles not directly about jumping involve decoding of one sort or another, from using in-game QR codes (you actually aim your smartphone at the screen to scan them in order to obtain a secret button combination) to a cryptic alphabet you first glimpse on tablet-like slabs in the opening cutscenes. The characters of the fictional alphabet are clearly reminiscent of the Tetrimino shapes from the ur-puzzle game, *Tetris*, which are in fact sculpted into surfaces throughout *Fez*. As with the 8-bit or 16-bit graphics, the tribute to *Tetris* is part of the game's retro aesthetic, but it also calls attention to the importance in games, and in the digital world as a whole, of puzzles, acts of encryption and decryption, encoding and decoding. When combined with the game's central mechanic, rotating the game world, the puzzles reinforce the sense that *Fez* is about the need to decrypt the world in order to reveal its digital foundations. *Fez* can be understood as a playable meditation on the cryptic but ultimately meaningful relationship between different dimensions of the world, and the need to navigate between those dimensions. The pixelated style, all the blocks, tiles, or bits in increments of 8, 16, 32, and 64 – as well as its epiphanic glitches revealing the hidden digital infrastructure – suggest that you must navigate among physical and digital dimensions, already intricately combined in a mixed-reality environment. *Fez* models a number of things, but in a high-level thematic and metaphorical way, it models the exigencies of the human– computer relationship in a mixed-reality environment.

A best-selling children's game franchise, Activision's *Skylanders* (2011), may provide the most vivid model of mixed reality among recent games. Its *Pokémon*-like collectible toys, plastic cartoony figurines, "come to life" inside the game when you place them on the Portal of Power, a small round glowing platform that the product website calls "a gateway between our world and the amazing world of Skylands." The Portal glows, the action figure glows, and the character appears in the game animated and fully playable. If you swap out the toy on the portal for another, the new one appears in the game, and you can place two on the portal to activate Co-op mode. The figurines are a product of the spread of 3D printing and maker culture, and the resultant ability of a small shop to design objects in software that are then turned into physical objects. They can be painted and even have round radio-frequency identification (RFID) tags inserted in their base to make them working to-scale prototypes (The later *Giants* and *Swap Force* games use NFC [near field connection] chips, so the connection is made even before the figurine touches the Portal of Power.) The figurines are meant to be imagined as in suspended animation, their vitality stored as "memories," data on their embedded chips, to be awakened in the digital game world. Every time someone puts a little plastic statue on the glowing portal and it appears, animated, inside the game, the process recapitulates in reverse the way that very figure's prototype, at least, was produced: from drawings on paper and in a computer to a physical object hot off the 3D printer. The developers say that the Wii inspired *Skylanders*, and, like the Wii, the game is imagined as a distributed system out in physical space – a constellation of small tags, processors, and sensors – a system that models the eversion of the network as a whole. *Skylanders* is even more far-flung than the Wii, truly cross-platform in significant ways, situating the game out in the world, in a social space where toys and cards are handled and traded, as well as in the digital space defined by the game's hardware and software. The gameplay is the opposite of cyberspatial, in other words, the opposite of being trapped in a world behind the screen. It's a game of the eversion, of mixed reality. *Skylanders* suggests a world in which the normal relationship to the network and its data takes the form of repeated *transduction* back and forth across a porous boundary between the physical and the digital, in mixed-reality spaces, a world of connected data-linked things, layers of things both physical and digital. Playing with them means digitizing them, interacting with them in both physical and digital environments, collecting and curating the data with which the things become tagged and annotated, sharing and collectively curating the experience of them with other users across a variety of platforms.

There are obvious connections between this kind of game technology and today's digital humanities – starting with a shared inspiration from maker culture and its emphasis on building things using open-source software and hardware. But in a more general way, by citing all of these specific examples I mean to suggest some of what the digital humanities might learn from video games when it comes to modeling systems, not just at the pragmatic level of experimental simulations but at the higher level of social and cultural dynamics. Video games are a vital medium, one which offers a rich arena for creative experimentation with the larger cultural issues – and the emerging digital-and-physical platforms – at the heart of the digital humanities today. Whatever else they simulate, video games necessarily simulate the relation between human and computer. If, as Willard McCarty (2004) has said, "modeling points the way to a computing that is of as well as in the humanities: a continual process of coming to know by manipulating representations," that may be one reason video games have played such a central role in the history of humanities computing and the digital humanities. Games provide playable models of human–computer interactions in our era of the everted network, our mixed reality. If the digital humanities is about taking a humanities perspective on computing as much as it is about bringing computing to bear on humanities research, then video games amount to possibility spaces for further experimentation.

NOTE

1   These terms – "model of" vs. "model for" – are discussed in McCarty, 2004. Conventionally, a simulation is a dynamic model unfolding over time, but the words "model" and "simulation" are often used interchangeably, and in my discussion I deliberately combine more general senses of "modeling," as understood in the arts and various humanities disciplines, with more precise computer-science senses of the term.

REFERENCES AND FURTHER READING

Bogost, I. 2011. *How to Do Things With Video Games*. Minneapolis: University of Minnesota Press.

Brand, S. 1972. Spacewar: fanatic life and symbolic death among the computer bums. *Rolling Stone* December 7. http://www.wheels.org/spacewar/stone/rolling_stone.html (accessed June 20, 2015).

Busa, R. 2004. Foreword: Perspectives on the digital humanities. In *A Companion to Digital Humanities*, ed. S. Schreibman, R. Siemens, and J. Unsworth. Oxford: Blackwell. http://www.digitalhumanities.org/companion (accessed June 20, 2015).

Goldberg, D, and Larsson, L. 2013/2011. *Minecraft: The Unlikely Tale of Markus "Notch" Persson and the Game that Changed Everything*. Trans. J. Hawkins. New York: Seven Stories Press.

Huizinga, J. 1950. *Homo Ludens: A Study of the Play Element in Culture*. Boston: Beacon Press.

Jones, S.E. 2014. *The Emergence of the Digital Humanities*. New York; Routledge.

Jones, S.E. and Thiruvathukal, G.K. 2012. *Codename Revolution: The Nintendo Wii Platform*. Cambridge, MA: MIT Press.

Kirschenbaum, M.G. 2008. *Mechanisms: New Media and the Forensic Imagination*. Cambridge, MA: MIT Press.

McCarty, W. 2004. Modeling: a study in words and meanings. In *A Companion to Digital Humanities*, ed. S. Schreibman, R. Siemens, and J. Unsworth. Oxford: Blackwell, 2004: http://www.digitalhumanities.org/companion (accessed June 20, 2015).

McDonough, J.P., Olendorf, R., Kirschenbaum, M., *et al.* 2010. *Preserving Virtual Worlds Final Report*. http://hdl.handle.net/2142/17097 (accessed June 20, 2015).

McGann, J. 2001. *Radiant Textuality: Literature After the World Wide Web*. New York: Palgrave.

Montfort, N. 2003. Twisty Little Passages: An Approach to Interactive Fiction. Cambridge, MA: MIT Press.

Nyhan, J., ed. 2012. Video-gaming, *Paradise Lost* and TCP/IP: an Oral History Conversation between Ray Siemens and Anne Welsh. *DHQ: Digital Humanities Quarterly* 6 (3). http://www.digitalhumanities.org/dhq/vol/6/3/000131/000131.html (accessed June 20, 2015).

Ramsay, S. 2011. *Reading Machines: Toward an Algorithmic Criticism*. Urbana: University of Illinois Press.

Rockwell, G. 2003. Serious play at hand: is gaming serious research in the humanities? *Text Technology* 12 (2), 89–99.

Unsworth, J. 1996. Living inside the (operating) system: community in virtual reality. In *Computer Networking and Scholarship in the Twenty-first-Century University*, ed. T.M. Harrison and T. Stephen. New York: SUNY Press. http://hdl.handle.net/2142/195.

7

Exploratory Programming in Digital Humanities Pedagogy and Research

Nick Montfort

How Humanists Benefit from Learning to Program

The book *Digital_Humanities* lists a variety of technical skills, rooted in text encoding and in information technology project management, that are important to the digital humanities (Burdick *et al.*, 2012). Although determining the appropriateness of scripting languages is listed, being able to program is not mentioned. Similarly, *Debates in the Digital Humanities* (Gold, 2012), a collection that features a section on "Teaching the digital humanities," has nothing to say about whether programming should be taught. Typically when DH pedagogy is discussed, the real topic is how to use pre-constructed DH systems to deliver education. Humanities students can surely be offered the same opportunity that Seymour Papert, using Logo (1980), and Alan Kay, using Smalltalk (Kay and Goldberg, 2003), successfully offered to young children. Humanities students, too, can be allowed to learn programming.

The case for programming education would not be as strong if programming were merely instrumental and involved nothing more than completing an already-established plan. In advocating that humanists and artists should program, I consider a type of programming practice that I call exploratory programming, one which involves using computation as a way of inquiring about and constructively thinking about important issues.

In what follows, I outline programming's cognitive, cultural, and social value with reference to what some important thinkers and researchers have determined. This outline, and this argument, is mainly intended for those who determine curriculum, who teach courses that could include programming, and who advise humanities students on which electives are appropriate.

A New Companion to Digital Humanities, First Edition. Edited by Susan Schreibman, Ray Siemens, and John Unsworth.
© 2016 John Wiley & Sons, Ltd. Published 2016 by John Wiley & Sons, Ltd.

Those who decide to become new programmers often find the motivation to do so in their encounters with computers and with others who are using programming to think about interesting problems. They often have concrete and personal reasons for engaging with computing, and do not need to consult the sort of argument that I present here. The discussion here might, however, help humanities and arts students better articulate their interest in programming to fellow students and to faculty members.

One humanist who has advocated for programming education recently – both in print and by teaching students to engage with programs in humanities classes – is Matthew Kirschenbaum. He argues:

> Computers should not be black boxes but rather understood as engines for creating powerful and persuasive models of the world around us. The world around us (and inside us) is something we in the humanities have been interested in for a very long time. I believe that, increasingly, an appreciation of how complex ideas can be imagined and expressed as a set of formal procedures – rules, models, algorithms – in the virtual space of a computer will be an essential element of a humanities education. (Kirschenbaum, 2009)

Kirschenbaum is one of several humanists who have already been teaching programming to undergraduate and graduate students in different contexts. I have taught programming to media studies students at the Massachusetts Institute of Technology (MIT) and the New School and have undergraduate MIT students doing computational writing projects in "The Word Made Digital" and "Interactive Narrative" (my course web pages are linked from http://nickm.com/classes). Daniel C. Howe developed and taught the course "Programming for Digital Art and Literature" (http://www.rednoise. org/pdal) at Brown and Rhode Island School of Design (RISD). At Georgia Tech, Ian Bogost has taught courses that include a "Special Topics in Game Design and Analysis" section (syllabus at http://www.bogost.com/teaching/atari_hacks_remakes_ and_demake.shtml) devoted to programming the Atari VCS. Allison Parrish teaches Python programming in "Reading and Writing Electronic Text" (current course page at http://rwet.decontextualize.com), regularly offered in New York University (NYU)'s Interactive Telecommunications program. Others who have taught programming to humanists include Michael Mateas and Stephen Ramsay. There are also many courses for artists and humanists in Processing, which was created by Ben Fry and Casey Reas to help designers learn programming and is ideal for developing interactive sketches.

In the following sections, I will offer arguments that programming:

- allows us to think in new ways,
- offers us a better understanding of culture and media systems, and
- can help us improve society.

After this, I'll return to the ways that programming can be enjoyable, explaining what special qualities of programming may make it a particularly pleasing way to occupy our time and to contribute new creative work to the world. And, finally, I will further characterize the specific practice I call exploratory programming, which is distinct from developing software to specification.

Cognitively: Programming Helps us Think

One useful perspective on how computing can improve the way we think has been provided by educational researchers, who chose to

> distinguish between two kinds of cognitive effects: Effects *with* technology obtained during intellectual partnership with it, and effects *of* it in terms of the transferable cognitive residue that this partnership leaves behind in the form of better mastery of skills and strategies. (Salomon *et al.*, 1991:2)

The first of these effects is obvious in many domains. The person using a spreadsheet to try out different budgets and scenarios is better prepared to innovate in business than the person who lacks such a system and must calculate by hand. A civil engineer modeling an unusually-designed bridge with a computer is better able to ensure that it is safe than is one who must rely on earlier methods. A radiologist using a modern, computational magnetic resonance imaging (MRI) system is able to deliver a diagnosis in cases where x-rays would not be adequate.

This positive effect of computation is what computer pioneer Douglas Engelbart called "augmenting human intellect" (Engelbart, 2003).Although there are very many domains in which thinking *with* computers has proven effective, some are nevertheless resistant to the idea that thinking with computers can be helpful in the humanities and arts. However, computing can be used to model artistic and humanistic processes, just as it can be used to model business and economic processes, bridges from an engineering perspective, the human body from a medical perspective, and so on. Thus, programming has the potential to improve our humanistic and artistic thinking as well. Improving the reader's ability to think *with* the computer in this way is a primary interest of mine.

There is also hope that thinking computationally can enhance the way we think more generally, even when we are not using computers. Indeed, there is evidence that adding computational thinking to the mix of our experiences and methods can improve our general thinking. Perhaps an obsessive focus on programming could be detrimental. But those who have a background in the arts and humanities and who choose to learn programming are diversifying their ways of thinking, adding to the methods and perspectives that they already have. Programming can help them consider the questions they care about in new ways.

The research that has been done about whether programming improves cognition has focused on younger learners who are still developing cognitively, not students in higher education. Nevertheless, to provide some insight into the effects *of* computer programming, I offer some results from the literature on whether learning to program can help people of that age group improve their cognition.

Modeling Humanistic and Artistic Processes is Thinking

Edward Bellamy (1888), in *Looking Backward: 2000–1887*, projected a character more than a hundred years into the future to explain his utopian vision of society. Similarly, Douglas Engelbart wrote about how computation could augment human intellect in a more or less science fictional mode. Writing in the voice of a hypothetical augmented human, Engelbart explained more than 50 years ago why people using computers as tools (even if they were using the advanced technology that he envisioned) should understand computer programming:

> There are, of course, the explicit computer processes which we use, and which our philosophy requires the augmented man to be able to design and build for himself. A number of people, outside our research group here, maintain stoutly that a practical augmentation system should not require the human to have to do any computer programming – they feel that this is too specialized a capability to burden people with. Well, what that means in our eyes, if translated to a home workshop, would be like saying that you can't require the operating human to know how to adjust his tools, or set up jigs, or change drill sizes, and the like. You can see there that these skills are easy to learn in the context of what the human has to learn anyway about using the tools, and that they provide for much greater flexibility in finding convenient ways to use the tools to help shape materials. (Engelbart, 2003:93–4)

Engelbart presents one way of understanding the computer metaphorically, as a workshop that allows people to build things. Not being able to program is akin to not being able to change a drill bit. A person *can* use a workshop in such circumstances, but is limited in what he or she can build. Another way of understanding the computer is as a laboratory. If people can use the equipment that is there, but are unable to change the experimental setup, they are limited in what experiments they can do. Seeing the computer in these ways, as a means of thinking constructively or experimentally, helps to explain why people who are artists and critical thinkers would want to be able to adjust computation in a variety of ways. Such adjustment was done in Engelbart's time, and still is done, by computer programming.

Perhaps the most problematic aspect of the statement by the hypothetical augmented human is the mention of how people often "learn anyway" about aspects of programming. Environments for programming (typically, BASIC) became easily available to the everyday home computer user in the late 1970s and 1980s, but as powerful, complex integrated development environments (IDEs) and compiled languages have been developed, programming has in some cases become more difficult to access once again, and people do not encounter it casually in the ways they used to. This means that some unnecessary complexity has been hidden, but some flexibility has also been removed. Still, those who delve into HTML, learn to use regular expressions to search documents, and start to develop short shell scripts do end up gaining some familiarity with their computational tools and can build on that to begin to learn skills relevant to programming.

Engelbart's work focused on improving complex processes and on facilitating teamwork, and he was also very engaged with building models of salient aspects of the world. While Engelbart was not focused on humanistic and artistic work, constructing computational models is useful in the arts and humanities as much as in economics, biology, architecture, and other fields. One way to frame this sort of model building in the humanities and arts is as "operationalization," and this was the term used at the Media Systems workshop in 2012 (Montfort, 2013; Wardrip-Fruin, 2013). Presenters there discussed numerous systems that modeled humanistic and artistic theories, giving a glimpse of the many computational systems that have provided new insights.

I gave examples there of one small-scale and one large-scale system that implements particular concepts from narratology. A different sort of demo (and a much more visually appealing one) was given by Ken Perlin. He showed his procedural animation system, one which also operationalizes ideas, in this case, artistic ones about how different animation techniques can be used to produce expressive behavior. Others who did related work and were in attendance included Michael Mateas, whose *Façade* (a joint project with Andrew Stern) implements Aristotelian dramatic concepts; Ian Bogost, who builds models that engage with concepts of procedural rhetoric; computational creativity researcher Mary Lou Maher, who showed work across different domains of creativity; Michael Young, developer of narrative systems based on ideas from narrative theory; and Ian Horswill, who has modeled virtual characters using various psychological theories, including Reinforcement Sensitivity Theory. These cases, as the report of the workshop noted, showed that "operationalization almost always involves novel scholarship both in computational systems and in the area being modeled." Unfortunately, "few individuals are prepared to do both types of research, while interdisciplinary teams are difficult to assemble and support" (Wardrip-Fruin and Mateas, 2014:48–9). If exploratory programming were undertaken more often by humanists and artists, these explorers and programmers would be able to do this work of operationalization more easily, both individually and in collaborating teams.

Systems of these sorts, whatever domain they are in, inherently embody arguments about the theories they draw upon. For instance, at the most abstract level, they seek to show what parts of a theory can be formalized and what that formal representation should be. Such systems, by virtue of how they are constructed, also argue that certain aspects of a theory are independent and others are linked. These models can be used for reflection by scholars and researchers, for poetic purposes (to make new, creative works) or for study. However, a computer implementation by itself, even without a human-subjects experiment, is a way of engaging with a theory and attempting to understand and apply it in a new way.

Programming could Improve our Thinking Generally

Considerable educational research was undertaken in the 1970s and 1980s to assess the value of computers in grade-school education; some of this focused on computer programming specifically. The results varied, but in 1991 a meta-analysis of 65 of them, which involved coding the results from each and placing them all on a common scale, was published. It considered quantitative studies available in university libraries that took place in classrooms (at any grade level) and assessed the relationship between computer programming and cognitive skills (Liao and Bright, 1991:253–4).

> The results of this meta-analysis indicate that computer programming has slightly positive effects on student cognitive outcomes; 89% of positive study-weighted [effect size] values and 72% of positive ESs overall confirm the effectiveness of computer-programming instruction. ... Students are able to acquire some cognitive skills such as reasoning skills, logical thinking and planning skills, and general solving skills through computer programming activities. (Liao and Bright, 1991:257–62)

The researchers noted that the effect was moderate, and that their analysis did not assess whether computer programming was better to teach than were other alternatives. Also, the study was assessing grade-school education research rather than programming education in colleges and universities. Still, the conclusion was that, at least for young learners, there were observable cognitive benefits to learning programming.

This meta-analysis also determined that the benefits of learning to program could go beyond a specific programming language. However, it suggested that the selection of an appropriate language was important, since programming education with Logo had the greatest effect size (Liao and Bright, 1991:262). Logo was not used exclusively for exploratory programming in the 1970s and 1980s, but I suspect that its use was significantly correlated with an exploratory programming approach, which was part of Seymour Papert's original vision for the langauge. So, I read these results as consistent with (although not clearly demonstrating) the value of exploratory programming in particular.

True, these are K–12 studies, and the instruction provided was almost certainly simply in programming itself or was related to math. The effect, too, was not a strong one, but it was not clear that other types of instruction would have offered more benefit. The significant gains from programming education – as determined in this analysis of 65 studies – are quite relevant to the arts and humanites, however. While older students are developmentally different, if opportunities remain to improve students' "reasoning skills, logical thinking and planning skills, and general solving skills," doesn't that, by itself, speak in favor of teaching programming as a method of inquiry in the humanities and arts? Do any of the other humanistic methods that we teach to these advanced students offer documented, general cognitive benefits, observed at any grade level?

Culturally: Programming gives Insight into Systems of Communication and Art

The argument here is twofold. First, as critics, theorists, scholars, and reviewers, those who have some understanding of programming will gain a better perspective on cultural systems that use computation – as many cultural systems increasingly do. Second, after learning to program people are better at developing cultural systems as experiments about, interventions into, augmentations of, or alternatives to the ones that already exist.

Programmming Allows Better Analysis of Cultural Systems

Douglas Rushkoff writes: "For the person who understands code, the whole world reveals itself as a series of decisions made by planners and designers for how the rest of us should live" (2010:140). By understanding how media and communications systems are programmed, we gain insight into the intentions of designers and the influence of material history, protocols, regulations, and platforms. In many cases, a full understanding of, for instance, a Web application will involve understanding not only the decisions made by the developer of that application, but also the decisions that have been made in creating and upgrading underlying technologies such as HTML, CSS, and programming languages (JavaScript, PHP, Java, Flash).

Consider a few questions related to culture and computing: Why do many games for the venerable Nintendo Entertainment System share certain qualities, while different qualities are seen in even earlier Atari VCS games? How do the options offered for defining video-game characters, virtual-world avatars, and social network profiles relate to our own concepts of identity? How does word-processing software, with its formats, typographical options, and spell- and grammar-checking, relate to recent literary production? How have tools such as Photoshop participated in and influenced our visual culture? How did a small BASIC program exist in cultural and computational contexts and have meaning to computer users of the 1980s? Because the cultural systems relevant to these questions are software machines built out of code and hardware machines made to be programmed, knowledge of programming is crucial to understanding them.

Scholars in the humanities have already used their knowledge of programming and their understanding of computation to better understand the history of digital media. Extensive discussion of this sort has been provided in book-length studies. These include studies of early video games by Nathan Altice (2015) and Nick Montfort and Ian Bogost (2009); of identity in digital media by D. Fox Harrell (2013); of word processing by Matthew G. Kirschenbaum (2014); of Photoshop and visual culture by Lev Manovich (2013); and of a one-line Commodore 64 BASIC program by Montfort *et al.* (2013). In several of these cases, the methods of inquiry these scholars used included developing software and learning from the process of programming. In all of these cases, these scholars brought their understanding of computing – developed in part by doing at least some amount of programming and exploration – to bear on these questions. While these particular studies have been done, many open questions remain regarding how these and other programmed systems participate in our culture.

Programming Enables the Development of Cultural Systems

To ground this aspect of programming in practical concerns, consider that, by learning to program, people enlarge their ability to develop new cultural systems and to collaborate on their development. Michael Mateas, writing of his experience developing a course in programming (one aspect of procedural literacy) for artists and humanists, explains how an awareness of computation allows work on new sorts of projects:

> Procedurally illiterate new media practitioners are confined to producing those inter-active systems that happen to be easy to produce within existing authoring tools. ... collaborative teams of artists, designers and programmers ... are often doomed to failure because of the inability to communicate across the cultural divide between the artists and programmers. Only practitioners who combine procedural literacy with a conceptual and historical grounding in art and design can bridge this gap and enable true collaboration. (Mateas, 2008)

Mateas is not simply claiming that artists and humanists should learn computing jargon so as to be able to bark commands at programmers. He is discussing communication at a more profound and productive level, the sort that allows for the exploration and expression of new ideas.

To close the "two cultures" gap that Mateas identifies in new media and the digital humanities, it would of course be ideal for those who are technically expert to learn something about the humanities as well. While the methods and goals of humanistic research may not be obvious to all programmers, it is quite difficult to find programmers (at least, ones in the United States) who have never taken a course in the humanities at all, who have never studied a novel or taken a history course. It is still easy, however, to find artists and humanists who have no experience with programming.

Socially: Computation can Help to Build a Better World

Programming not only can contribute to social and utopian thought; I believe it is uniquely suited to building productive utopias. I consider a utopia to be a society (usually represented or simulated in some way, although there are utopian communities that are actual societies) that is radically different from our own and yet is also engaged with our own society. A utopia might be an attempt to provoke people, or it might be offered as a serious model that could be emulated. In any case, a utopia is not an escapist vision, nor it is it an alternative place with no relation to our society, the sort of place that has been called an atopia.

Utopias don't have to be perfect to be useful to social and political thought. In terms of provoking people to think about important issues in new ways, utopias can be presented that are worse than our current society. These are called dystopias; because they present arguments about how our society might improve, I consider them to be in the broad category of utopias as well.

Programming can be used to develop utopias via computer games and simulations. The original *Sim City*, for instance, can be read as a model city that promotes mass transit and nuclear power. (Modified versions of it can present other simulated societies, using computation to make different arguments.) Or, programming can enable new social spaces and developments, such as pseudonymous online support groups that are open to people around the world.

Both types of potential are indicated by Douglas Rushkoff: "We are creating a blueprint together – a design for our collective future. The possibilities for social, economic, practical, artistic, and even spiritual progress are tremendous" (Rushkoff, 2010:14). To take this idea seriously, rather than cynically dismissing it: if we are to be designers of our collective future, what does that sort of design entail, and what skills should we have to participate in this collaborative activity?

Rushkoff offers his answer, that we should fully develop our ability to write online, using computers:

> Computers and networks finally offer us the ability to write. And we do write with them on our websites, blogs, and social networks. But the underlying capability of the computer era is actually programming – which almost none of us knows how to do.

We simply use the programs that have been made for us, and enter our text in the appropriate box on the screen. We teach kids how to use software to write, but not how to write software. This means they have access to the capabilities given to them by others, but not the power to determine the value-creating capabilities of these technologies for themselves. (Rushkoff, 2010:19)

Given this perspective, it seems hard to justify that developing social media wiles specific to whatever the current proprietary systems are – the ability to skillfully use Friendster, Facebook, or Twitter, for example – really constitutes the core skill for the collective designers of our future. It sounds like arguing that we will be able to develop a progressive new society because we know how to navigate our local IKEA. If we envision ourselves as empowered to determine a better future together, we will need to know much more than navigation, more than how to shop, consume, select, and inhabit existing corporate frameworks. We will need to know how to participate in creating systems, whether the goal is incremental development or a radical provocation. In Engelbart's terms, we will need the full use of our "home workshop," to have all of the tools available to us and adjustable.

Programming ability has been used to develop new cultural systems, of course. One example is a system launched in 2009 by a for-profit company. This system, Dreamwidth, aimed to correct problems with LiveJournal, which runs on free software code, by forking that code to create a new system. The company improved the way the site could be accessed on screen readers, provided a different privacy model for journal viewing, and published the first widely discussed diversity statement. This cultural system was developed with a focus on writers, artists, and others who were contributing creatively. The community of developers that works on the Dreamwidth code (and, because this is free software, also has full access to this code for any purpose) is remarkable. By the first year after launch, half of the developers were people who had never programmed in Perl or contributed to a free software project before, and about 75% were women (Smith and Paolucci, 2010). To put this in perspective, as of that year, estimates of the percentage of women participating in free software projects overall ranged from 1.5% to 5% (Vernon, 2010).

The Dreamwidth response involved not just a verbal critique of the problems with LiveJournal (where the Dreamwidth co-founders worked); it also involved more than just producing a proposal or mock-up of what might be better. The response was a project to build a new system with the participation of programmers, including many new programmers. The result was a site that hosts a diverse community and an inclusive group of developers.

With that specific example in mind, consider one more statement from Rushkoff about the importance of participating in and humanizing computing:

[T]he more humans become involved in their design, the more humanely inspired these tools will end up behaving. We are developing technologies and networks that have the potential to reshape our economy, our ecology, and our society more profoundly and intentionally than ever before in our collective history. (Rushkoff, 2010:149)

Programming is Creative and Fun

At the risk of trivializing what I understand as a cognitively empowering practice, one that is capable of providing us better cultural understanding that can help us build a better society, it would be remiss of me not to mention that programming is an activity that gives the programmer poetic pleasure, the pleasure of making and of discovery through making. I discussed earlier how programming is not *only* a hobby to fill the time; this particular aspect of programming that I am discussing now is indeed connected to some types of productive hobbies as well as to artistic practices. It's worth noting, though, that there are special creative pleasures of programming.

It is enjoyable to write computer programs and to use them to create and discover. This is the pleasure of adding something to the world, of fashioning something from abstract ideas and material code that runs on particular hardware. It involves realizing ideas, making them into functional software machines, in negotiation with computational systems. The strong forumlation of this impulse to make and implement in the digital humanities specifically is the declaration that the only true digital humanists are those who build systems ("hack") rather than theorize ("yack") (Ramsay, 2011). To note that programming is creative and fun, however, does not require excluding other types of involvement in a field, nor does it mean that it is not also fun to critically or theoretically yack. It simply involves admitting the pleasure and benefits of hacking, of exploring with programmming.

Writing a program offers enjoyment that is not entirely unlike other types of making in the arts and humanities: the way sound and sense grow and intertwine on the lattice of a poem; the amazing configuration of voices, bodies, light, and space in a play; the thrill of new connection and realization that can arise from a well-constructed philosophical argument. This, by itself, isn't meant to justify the inclusion of programming in a humanities or arts curriculum, but it is meant to suggest that the activity of programming can be consistent with more traditional activities: writing, developing arguments, creating works of art, and so on.

Exploratory Programming

The idea of exploratory programming is not supposed to provide the "one true way" to approach computing in all circumstances; it's not a suggestion that programmers never develop a system from an existing specification and ship or launch it. It's meant, instead, to be one valuable mode in which to think, to encounter computation, and to bring the abilities of the computer to address one's important questions, artistic, cultural, or otherwise.

A problem with programming as it is typically encountered is that many people who gain some ability to program – particularly those whose formal training ends with an introductory class or two, or those who learn in the context of implementing one very specific project in predetermined ways – never learn to explore at all. There are substantial challenges involved in learning how to program and in learning how computing works. If one is interested in mastering basic data structures and gaining the type of understanding that a computer science student needs, it can be difficult to also discover how to use programming as a means of inquiry.

What constitutes a good introduction to computer science is not always ideal for artists and humanists. Linked lists and binary trees are essential concepts for those learning the science of computation, but a great deal of exploration through programming can be done without understanding these concepts. Those working in artistic and humanistic areas can learn a great deal by seeing, initially, how computing allows for abstraction and generalized calculations. They can gain comfort with programming, learn to program effectively, see how to use programming as a means of inquiry – all without becoming full-blown computer scientists. For those who don't plan on getting a degree in computer science, it can sometimes be difficult to understand the bigger picture, hard to discern how to usefully compute on data and how to gain comfort with programming while also dealing with the more advanced topics that are covered in introductory programming courses. It can be hard to see the forest for the binary trees, as students focus on understanding the detailed mechanisms of computation but often neglect the cultural situation of computing.

Beyond that, many of those who haven't yet learned to program can have the impression that programming is simply a power tool for completing an edifice or a vehicle used to get from one point to another. While the computer can have impressive results when used in instrumental ways, it can be used for even more impressive purposes when understood as a sketchpad, sandbox, prototyping kit, telescope, and microscope. As a system for exploration and inquiry, the computer is unmatched. Exploratory programming is about using computation in this way.

In my book *Exploratory Programming for the Arts and Humanities* (Montfort, forthcoming), I aim to provide a course for individual or classroom learners who wish to do exploratory programming and better understand cultural systems. This book is meant to particularly relate to the digital humanities, to the cultural aspects of programming, and to different ways of analyzing and generating media. There are plenty of other ways to begin to program, however, and good resources for doing so. I encourage humanists and artists to get started in whatever ways seem appealing. There are already excellent books that introduce programming in Processing (Shiffman, 2009) and Ruby (Pine, 2005). New programmers can use these and other resources to understand the essentials of computing and begin putting together interesting projects in many ways. Effective ways to get started do not require a particular programming language or a formal class, but they do benefit from an exploratory approach to programming – along with the awareness that programming can help us think socially and as individuals, humanistically and as artists.

References and Further Reading

Altice, N. 2015. *I AM ERROR: The Nintendo Family Computer / Entertainment System Platform*. Cambridge, MA: MIT Press.

Bellamy, E. 1888. *Looking Backward, 2000–1887*. Boston, MA: Ticknor and Company.

Burdick, A, Drucker J., Lunenfeld, P., Presner, T., and Schnapp, J. 2012. *Digital_Humanities*. Cambridge, MA: MIT Press.

Engelbart, D. 2003. From augmenting human intellect: a conceptual framework. In *The New*

Media Reader, ed. N. Wardrip-Fruin and N. Montfort. Cambridge, MA: MIT Press, 93–108.

Gold, M.K., ed. 2012. *Debates in the Digital Humanities.* Minneapolis: University of Minnesota Press.

Harrell, D.F. 2013. *Phantasmal Media: An Approach to Imagination, Computation, and Expression.* Cambridge, MA: MIT Press.

Kay, A., and Goldberg, A. 2003. Personal dynamic media. In *The New Media Reader*, ed. N. Wardrip-Fruin and N. Montfort. Cambridge, MA: MIT Press, 391–404.

Kirschenbaum, M. 2009. Hello worlds: why humanities students should learn to program. *Chronicle Review*, January 23, 2009. http://chronicle.com/article/Hello-Worlds/5476 (accessed June 20, 2015).

Kirschenbaum, M.G. 2014. *Track Changes: A Literary History of Word Processing.* Cambridge, MA: Harvard University Press.

Liao, Y.C., and Bright, G.W. 1991. Effects of computer programming on cognitive outcomes: a meta-analysis. *Journal of Educational Computing Research* 7 (3), 251–68.

Manovich, L. 2013. *Software Takes Command.* New York: Bloomsbury.

Mateas, M. 2008. Procedural literacy: educating the new media practitioner. In *Beyond Fun: Serious Games and Media*, ed. D. Davidson. Pittsburgh: ETC Press, 67–83.

Montfort, N. 2013. Talks from Media Systems. http://nickm.com/post/2013/09/talks-from-media-systems (accessed June 20, 2015).

Montfort, N. (forthcoming). *Exploratory Programming for the Arts and Humanities.* Cambridge, MA: MIT Press.

Montfort, N., and Bogost, I. 2009. *Racing the Beam: The Atari Video Computer System.* Cambridge, MA: MIT Press.

Montfort, N., Baudoin, P., Bell, J., *et al.* 2013. *10 PRINT CHR$(205.5+RND(1)); : GOTO 10.* Cambridge, MA: MIT Press.

Papert, S. 1980. *Mindstorms: Children, Computers, and Powerful Ideas.* New York: Basic Books.

Pine, C. 2005. *Learn to Program.* Dallas, TX: Pragmatic Bookshelf.

Ramsay, S. 2011. Who's in and who's out. Paper presented at the History and Future of Digital Humanities panel, Modern Language Association Convention, Los Angeles, January 6–9, 2011. http://stephenramsay.us/text/2011/01/08/whos-in-and-whos-out (accessed June 20, 2015).

Rushkoff, D. 2010. *Program or Be Programmed: Ten Commands for a Digital Age.* New York: OR Books.

Salomon, G. Perkins, D.N., and Globerson, T. 1991. Partners in Cognition: Extending Human Intelligence with Intelligent Technologies. *Educational Researcher* 20 (3), 2–9.

Shiffman, D. 2009. *Learning Processing: A Beginner's Guide to Programming Images, Animation, and Interaction.* Burlington, MA: Morgan Kaufmann, 2009.

Smith, M., and Paolucci, D. 2010. Build your own contributors, one part at a time. Presentation slides. January 20, 2010. http://www.slideshare.net/dreamwidth/build-your-own-contributors-one-part-at-a-time (accessed June 20, 2015).

Vernon, A. 2010. Dreadfully few women are open source developers. *Network World* March 5. http://www.networkworld.com/community/node/58218 (accessed June 20, 2015).

Wardrip-Fruin, N. 2013. Nick Montfort on "The art of operationalization" (Media Systems). Expressive Intelligence Studio. https://eis-blog.soe.ucsc.edu/2013/09/montfort-art-of-operationalization (accessed June 20, 2015).

Wardrip-Fruin, N., and Mateas, M. 2014. *Envisioning the Future of Computational Media: The Final Report of the Media Systems Project.* Santa Cruz: University of California Center for Games and Playable Media. https://games.soe.ucsc.edu/envisioning-future-computational-media-final-report-media-systems-project (accessed June 20, 2015).

8
Making Virtual Worlds

Christopher Johanson

"Experience endless surprises and unexpected delights in a world imagined and created by people like you." So says the advert for *Second Life*, what one scholar has called "the quintessential virtual world" (Jones, 2014:104). Yet these worlds were not built by people like you. Development was guided by tacit assumptions that multi-user, persistent, world-generating systems should aim to approximate the basic affordances of physical reality. The needs of the academic community played no part. A sandbox was created, but the toys within enable only specific kinds of technologically determined experiences.

Through rapid technological advances, humanists can do more than construct virtual worlds confined within parameters developed by others. They can now create the interface and define its affordances. Tools of narrative, annotation, citation, refutation, and markup can be foregrounded. The humanities virtual world is an interrogative laboratory, interactive collaboratorium, immersive dissemination medium, and/or multivocal reading and authorship tool. For some questions, humanities-based virtual worlds offer the best tools for the job, but only if the humanist is also the maker.

Definitions

A virtual world persists, it interacts in real time, it is shared, it has rules – the so-called physics of the world – and, most important, it embodies (Bartle, 2004:3–4). A virtual world may or may not recreate, simulate, and allow for, support, or mandate play. One can find love in a virtual world, build with digital Legos, join a club of virtual penguins, achieve equine form and earn points for a well-groomed mane, suck the blood from

A New Companion to Digital Humanities, First Edition. Edited by Susan Schreibman, Ray Siemens, and John Unsworth.
© 2016 John Wiley & Sons, Ltd. Published 2016 by John Wiley & Sons, Ltd.

one's virtual spouse in a lavishly textured, particle effects-laden Victorian land, or float in a bubble above a fantastical steampunk city. And you can do all this now, today, through a range of technological interfaces, screens, mobile devices, head-mounted displays and operating systems. You will almost always have to download software, and, invariably, sign up for an account. And, with the exception of worlds like *Club Penguin*, *Howrse* – "breed horses or ponies, and discover the responsibilities of managing an equestrian center!" – and *NeoPet*, you often must be over 18 to play.

Definitions of virtual worlds are inextricably and inevitably connected to that of virtual reality. Like a linguistic false friend, the terms are mistakenly exchanged by even those who know better. Here is what they share: a sense of being somewhere else for a time, that is, *presence*. They also share their virtuality, but *virtual* is itself a fraught term. In vernacular English, virtual is often opposed to the real, and *residents* of virtual worlds will often refer to their *real* life outside the virtual world. Such usage ignores the paradox of the very real life lived in the idealized space of the virtual. The more accurate and more technical definition contrasts *concrete* or *actual* reality with its *virtual* counterpart. One simultaneously inhabits the actual, while exploring the virtual (Shields, 2003). There is a vast gulf between creating idealized *realities* and idealized *worlds*, however. Virtual reality aims to simulate an individual user's *actual* reality by supplying interfaces that hijack and immerse one or more of the senses (Craig *et al.*, 2009:1–32). A virtual world, in contrast, is the setting, comprising computationally generated rules and 3D content. Interfaces open windows into the virtual world, but they do not define the experience. While you can turn off virtual reality, as a user you most likely won't be able to turn off a virtual world. It persists on a networked server, always waiting for someone to visit via screen, mouse and keyboard, handheld device, or even virtual reality interface plugged directly into your brain.

Interventions in History

Before there were computer-based virtual worlds, there were video games. One can build a virtual world using game technologies, and one can build a game in a virtual world, but the Venn diagram of these activities yields a very small overlap. There is no intrinsic reason to be exclusionary, but certain boundaries need to be set to work with and profit from virtual worlds. The video game and the virtual world are sometimes separated by miles of code. Rather than rehearse a general history of the virtual world, *this* history of virtual worlds will focus specifically on meaningful influence and critical interventions that directly affect the humanist maker of worlds. They are, in order, the first-person shooter, real 3D, MMORPGs, the embodied avatar, the open world, and the commodification of game development platforms.

A first-person maze set the blueprint for virtual world development. Created in the early 1970s at the NASA Ames Research Center, *Maze War* pitted two players against each other in a networked race through a primitive 3D maze (Pinchbeck, 2013). You were represented as an eyeball, moving through a world of vector display graphics, like the sort created with lasers at concerts today. Commodity hardware was not yet ready to support more sophisticated interaction in a 3D world, but the maze would remain the fundamental organizing principle for first-person gaming.

The maze was fully weaponized in 1992 with the release of *Wolfenstein 3D*, one of the first in a new gaming category, the first-person shooter (FPS) (Bissell, 2010:131). Id Software created a gaming engine to support seamless motion through a quasi-3D world, termed 2.5D, with a significant twist: the player was armed, literally. You could see your hands and the things they carried. The scene was set: a human form was inhabited by the player, to be used as a proxy to explore a digital world. As John Carmack, the lead programmer behind *Wolfenstein 3D* notes, "[Y]ou're going in there, you're interacting with a simulation at some level, but it's not necessarily a simulation of reality … [T]he thing that hooked people, that got them in there, was that it was really the first time in gaming you had the ability to project yourself into this world" (Pinchbeck, 2013:19). The avatar was born, or at least the preliminary idea of the avatar. Once you got into an FPS, you could of course shoot, by equipping those bare hands with a pistol, a flamethrower, or a chain gun.

Id Software changed everything again, when it created the *Quake* engine, in 1996. The *Wolfenstein* engine, and the *Doom* engine, which followed it in 1993, were still fundamentally maze-based games. Their worlds were designed as 2D mazes, with attributes given to rooms and walls, and were reproduced for the user by using a ray-casting technique. It was as if the world you inhabited was the ground floor of an apartment building. If you wanted to go to the next floor, the computer would throw away the current floor as you climbed the stairs. The *Quake* engine, however, supported a fully formed 3D environment, and leveraged the power of OpenGL, the open source graphics library that had already received widespread adoption in research labs. OpenGL supported fully realized 3D Cartesian worlds integrated into computer graphics cards built specifically to support 3D matrix calculations. If you could carry a 3D printer back to 1996 and extract the *Quake* environment from its digital confines, you could print a 1 : 1 replica of the computer-generated world.

It was not until 1997 that the second major transformation occurred: the rise of the massively multiplayer online role-playing game (MMORPG). Though not the first, *Ultima Online* was the game-changer. Its graphics were 2.5D, but it established first principles that would ramify through future virtual world development. Its new world was persistent. One could quit the game today, restart tomorrow, and see the changes made by yourself and others. Its inhabitants, both human and computer-controlled, could interact with each other. And a substantial portion of gameplay mechanics involved augmenting one's personal character through the acquisition of skills and weapons.

Two years later, the MMORPG collided with the FPS. Released in 1999, *EverQuest* simultaneously deepened the connection between virtual worlds and RPGs while borrowing heavily from FPS gameplay mechanics. Rooted in analog role-playing games first designed in the 1970s, where one could choose classes of characters with certain attributes, the *EverQuest* experience centered wholly on the care and feeding of a partly customizable avatar. One chose a class, such as Ranger, Wizard, or Thief, and then one customized hair and eye color and race (e.g., human, dwarf, half-elf, but not ethnicity). As in *Ultima Online* before it, through experience, acquisition of treasure, luck, and skill in the game world, one could dress and equip the avatar with more interesting and powerful stuff. And unlike most MMORPGs of the time, *EverQuest* allowed you to move through this networked, persistent world like a character in

Quake. You were no longer even limited to a first-person view with ghost hands floating in front. Now you could zoom out to view your character from above or behind, and thus the avatar grew up.

In 2003 Linden Lab's *Second Life* transformed the digital discourse. Following the spirit of games that offered capacities for multiple users embedded in three-dimensional space, *Second Life* was a self-contained three-dimensional sandbox for world builders. No longer did one log in to walk through a static context, in a world built by others; now one logged into a place that was built by fellow users – at least, that was how the marketing went. Prior to *Second Life*, to build an online, multiplayer experience required advanced technical expertise, training in CAD/CAM modeling software and a robust computational infrastructure. *Second Life* eliminated all such requirements.

Like the MMORPGs, and now almost codified as part of the virtual world experience, *Second Life* focused first on the avatar. To register for an account, you assumed a persona by choosing a first name, selecting a surname from a prepopulated list, and then select-ing a customizable avatar representation. Avatar customization was the most easily accessible, most robust, and first interactive encounter by a new *resident*. Beyond avatar tweaking, users could also interact with each other in new ways. Chat was imple-mented via text and later via microphone. Sitting, standing, hanging out, and dancing were also built-in avatar actions. The sorts of mundane activities that one can do in real life. No longer was running and killing privileged. Hanging out was the innovation: the ability to interact in 3D with others within a shared world, without the express task of competing with or against, attacking, or killing them.

Unlike MMORPGs, *Second Life* also let the user customize the world itself. Using a rudimentary interface, the user's avatar could construct elements in-world. The primitives, called *prims*, were boxes and spheres and cones, with optional images applied to them. Process and making were privileged above product (Malaby, 2009). You could watch a fellow user's avatar build in real time. And a currency was established: by spending a certain amount of US dollars one received Linden dollars, which could be used to purchase virtual real estate, or hire virtual contractors. Sophisticated builders and modders quickly emerged, who were eager to trick out avatar form and behavior or construct in-world architecture, for a fee. The latter is where something fascinating happened at a rapid rate: a new user of *Second Life* could enter the environment, access an embodied virtual labor pool, and contract out work to be done in-world.

While the hype surrounding *Second Life* waxed first and then slowly waned (Shirky, 2006; Lacy, 2012; Van Geel, 2013), FPS game worlds had been undergoing yet another transition: from closed to open. The fundamental element of the original FPS was the wall. Mazes were constructed, and the 3D geometry was generated from a 2D maze. Views were bounded. Walls eventually disappeared, but remained as invisible barriers, or carefully constructed Potemkin villages. The player moved from zone to zone, interacting, most often by shooting, with non-player characters (NPCs) within a bounded space. The player might try to leave the prescribed space, but the narrative would have to allow it first. Doors might be in view, but would not open until the next narrative element had been achieved. Even when the games moved outdoors, the walls remained. Apparently boundless scenes were presented to the player, but if you walked to a nearby lake, for example, an invisible barrier stopped you from entering.

Though the world was 3D and could enable unlimited motion in all directions, in practice the linear story arc and the limitations of graphics technology created invisible barriers. One could see the beyond in the game, but one couldn't actually get there.

The gradual opening of 3D worlds began with *Ultima Online*, but was elevated and expanded through city-based games, such as *Grand Theft Auto*, and fantasy games like the *Elder Scrolls*. Algorithms supporting real-time shading, fluid dynamics, and particle effects made for beautiful imagery. Even though there was a game to be played and an end goal, smelling the flowers, or, at least, looking at them, was inherently part of the pleasure. The freedom to move anywhere within a world led to endless possibilities from a narrative perspective. One could stall out on one side of the world, while all the action, and all the narrative was, or should be, happening on the other side. So guidance came from the *quest* (Wardrip-Fruin, 2009:47–80). As the player wanders about the world, interacts with the NPCs, discovers buildings, islands, caves, and mountain sanctuaries, quests can be assigned. The player can choose to follow a specific quest to engage with a specific story. While one is engaged in a quest in an open world, save for moments of critical action, interaction with an NPC, unlocking a door, reading a hidden book, or finding a monument, one is mostly walking through the environment with purpose. Just as one might drive to the Disney Concert Hall in Los Angeles, but on the way, spontaneously, decide to stop to refuel the car or decide to rob a bank, before ultimately going to the show, so questing in an open world allows for similar player choice. Save that, for most quests, even the timing is secondary. The quest waits patiently to be pursued. If you miss the concert tonight, just come back again tomorrow. These are layered stories, almost, but not quite rhizomatic. The way one moves, the paths one takes, contributes to the narrative at both macro and micro levels.

From a phenomenological perspective, the gamer, or simply the reader, is sculpting a highly individualized memory of story and narrative. The paths one walks, the order in which one quests, the battles one fights, and the way those battles are won are unique experiences. The fundamental choice of avatar, the critical element that continues to define one's gameplay experience, guides the direction of the story. One remembers the paths taken and can recreate them again. It is rarely the case, however, that the events of one's day convey a cohesive story. Rather, they are the raw material, but the cohesive tissue that connects the game's end goal to your personal wanderings comes from somewhere else.

The cut-scene is the open world's narrative crutch (Wardrip-Fruin, 2009:71–80). Rather than let the player wander and create by interacting with the scenery, the NPCs, and other embedded narrative elements, the cut-scene spoon-feeds a script to the player. When they first appeared in the 1980s video game, *Pac-Man*, cut-scenes were scripted, silly, animated interludes between *waka waka* pellet chomping. In time, cut-scene storytelling soon included text subtitles, like the narrative text in a silent movie, live-action video, and pre-rendered animation. Short-form offered the same storytelling affordances as their long-form cousins, but in the process created a significant rupture in interactivity and experiential gameplay. Nonetheless, these scripted interludes, in their various forms, advanced the narrative, serving as milestones between sequences of 3D gameplay. In such modes, the "end" of the game and the story rarely involved direct, embodied action by the player, such as the defeat of the last villain or the completion of the final puzzle. Instead, it was a scripted scene – often in radically different aesthetic mode than the gameplay – that explained for you what it was you had just done and why you had done it.

Technological advances continued to determine narrative possibilities by preserving the fundamental unit of gameplay, the embodied experience. Once rendering engines could deliver real-time lighting and shading at a level similar to pre-rendered animations, the cut-scene could blend more seamlessly into the narrative. Now the same avatar controlled by the user could be hijacked for a moment of scripted storytelling. You were always *present*. Early iterations limited some actions of the avatar, allowing for only minimal head motion, to control the first-person/third-person view. Later, avatars triggered moments of gameplay by entering rooms or walking near critical objects. The surrounding characters would begin to tell stories, which the player could choose to listen to. The character is still free to wander about, walk away from the storyteller, or even attack the narrator. Likewise, the narrator, or participating narrators, could use simple math to look directly at the player, to point to areas of key interest, or to beckon onward. In the actual world, Odyssey Works' *An Audience of One* provides a useful analogy for this type of storytelling moment (Colin, 2012). A theater-goer buys a ticket, with time and location specified. The actor(s) arrive, and the play begins when the troupe addresses you, takes your hand and walks you through the play, the city, and the narrative, just like a virtual-world cut-scene.

Fast Making

Parallel with the development of open-world 3D games came the single most important advance for the digital humanist: the commodification and proceduralization of the environments for making these open worlds, including landscape, flora, and fauna.

The fundamental building block of the real-time 3D digital world remains the mesh, which is a cohesion of polygons, itself comprising a collection of vertices, which are in turn intrinsically a data structure consisting of an ordered list of three-dimensional coordinates that define its surfaces, e.g., the front face of a cube with an origin of 0,0,0 might look like this:

−1.0, −1.0, 1.0,
1.0, −1.0, 1.0,
1.0, 1.0, 1.0,
−1.0, 1.0, 1.0.

The computer connects the dots between each point to create a surface, and continues to connect the dots to create more surfaces, building forms that, upon closer inspection, look like facets on a diamond. Connecting these dots can be as complicated as typing the coordinates by hand to draw each brick of a digital house, to tracing these points out in virtual 3D space with mouse and keyboard, or as simple as clicking a "house" button, inputting the desired house, e.g., Tudor or Craftsman, and letting the computer follow a set of rules to create the structure in order to plant the house in a landscape.

As tools have developed, making a virtual world involves assembling pieces, rather than constructing polygons. If representing actual reality is a concern, the maker can be hyper-precise, and ultra-accurate. By using laser scanning technology, or using an array of photographs taken from a consumer-grade camera, one can automatically build a 3D model, with millimeter-level precision. Or, conversely, by using CAD/CAM software, one can build a detailed world of abstracted forms, hypothetical futures based on architectural blueprints, or reconstructed past environments. The maker can, if desired, rely on generative software to create and sculpt landscape in extraordinarily rapid fashion. Geographic information system (GIS)-based data and digital elevation models (DEMs) from landscape surveys can be transformed into terrain. You can also play floral God. If you want trees, you select or create a type, or a collection of types, and spray-paint them onto a landscape. You can also use a system of pre-built or user-modified rules to control the motion of the trees, that is, to simulate the wind. And you do so using the same middleware technology employed by the most successful gaming companies. All this software is more accessible and more powerful than it has ever been.

You can even customize yourself. In early iterations of *Second Life*, customization features were limited to approximations, and to appearance alone. One might select eye color, hair color, clothing to create an avatar that was both not very realistic and looked not very much like you. Adding customized animations, extracted from motion capture systems, took time, and were themselves limited in duration. Combining the avatar, which is also a simple mesh, and animations that control how the avatar moves, walks, runs, jumps, sits, reads, rides a bike, etc. was an exceedingly complicated process. First the avatar needed to be *rigged*, that is, a skeletal system needed to be added, then joints specified, often done through proprietary systems by specialists. Now, however, middleware companies have produced complete avatar generation systems that can rig any 3D mesh, and use motion capture or simple videos for animating motion. And other middleware companies exist to let you scan your own physical body, to generate a digital version of you, replete with facial expressions acquired through your computer's onboard camera.

Each of these elements on its own does not constitute world building. Only by weaving these pieces together and injecting interactivity, gameplay, storytelling, and the like does one begin to *make* a virtual world. The critical question for makers is simple: *where* do you want to make the world, from within or without? Do you wish to adapt an existing virtual world's technologies or create your own? For many applications, existing virtual-world-based technologies are seemingly the most ideal place to stage a virtual world, but the advent of low-cost game development engines has radically altered the landscape of making. A video game is not, strictly speaking, a virtual world, especially from the point of view of the virtual-world denizens of today. The reason many of the residents inhabit a virtual world is primarily social, to create, in fact, a second life. These large-scale worlds offer a base for the non-programmer to interact and construct. They don't offer the same possibilities for the programmer, or graphic designer, or the student of human–computer interaction. They aren't necessarily as interoperable and are constrained by limitations of scripting languages and interface, but for the study of embodied social interaction, nothing can compare.

Unlike large-scale virtual-world systems, the game development engine exists to do precisely its titular claim, to build games, not virtual worlds. Recall, however, the critical interventions thus far: the avatar-based game, and the multiplayer open world. One can use gaming technology to build the functional equivalent of virtual worlds. As gameplay in an open-world environment has approached the level of avatar-based interactivity offered in virtual worlds, so the game development environment becomes an increasingly more enticing mode of making. While large-scale virtual world environments have focused on building infrastructure for in-world construction and avatar-based transactions, game development environments are designed to promote goal-seeking and storytelling, and tuned to capitalize on the latest advances in graphical representation.

These critical interventions, culminating in the development of consumer-grade world-building software, enable extraordinarily powerful modes of virtual-world-based experience and storytelling. There are many paths to making a virtual world, but questions need to be addressed at the outset. What will the world look like? Who is your intended audience? How would you like that audience to experience your world? Above all, the existential question matters most: why should your world exist?

Documentation

> Imagine human beings as if they were in a cave-like dwelling underground, with a broad opening to the daylight across the whole width of the cave. They have been there since childhood, chained not just by their legs but by their necks, so that they can't move and can only look ahead of them – the neck-chain makes it impossible for them to turn their heads round. Light reaches them from a fire that burns way above and behind them; and in between the fire and the prisoners, high above, there is a path across the cave, beside which you need to imagine a little wall, built like those screens puppeteers have in front of their audience so that they can show their puppets above them. ... Next, along this little wall, imagine people carrying a whole collection of manufactured objects that stick up above it, including human statues and representations of other kinds of creatures fashioned out of wood and stone and all sorts of other things; as you'd expect, some of the carriers are speaking, others are silent. ... [F]rom every point of view ... what people in that situation would think of as the truth would be nothing but the shadows of the manufactured objects behind them. (Plato, 2012:514a–515c)

Oft-cited as the first conceptualization of a virtual world, Plato's allegory of the cave is an attempt to articulate how one might experience the Forms, a kind of idealized notion of ideas, in which, for example, the chair that you and I sit in can only be called a chair because there exists in the heavenly ideascape an ideal form of chair to which all others relate. To see the Forms would be as if we had previously experienced pale two-dimensional shadows of what was actually a three-dimensional, Kodachrome world. The analogy will seem familiar to readers of Abbott's *Flatland* (1885), in which the concept of a four-dimensional spatial universe is introduced through similar fictional narrative. In *Flatland* we are asked to imagine first what a denizen of a Cartesian 2D, plane-based world might see, should a sphere pass through it: a growing and shrinking, two-dimensional circle. So it goes for those of us in 3D space. The passing four-dimensional object would appear in 3D for us, but its fourth dimension would be inconceivable. Therefore, the argument goes, a virtual world is a pale reflection of reality. It is not.

The virtual world is an abstraction comprising bits and bytes, derived from, in every single instance, data. These data, though sometimes arbitrarily conceived, nonetheless are available for recovery and analysis in ways that cannot occur in the actual world. It is exceedingly difficult to trace the lineage of the smallest unit of organic form in the real world. One might be able to target and measure a particular molecule in a particular human's hand, but at some point, as you try to find the smallest component of that molecule, you will arrive at the immeasurable. You might be able to say precisely where, in this world, according to an imposed geographic coordinate system, you will find the corner of a stone in a lane in rural Arkansas, but it is only because you impose this system of measurement on the stone. Whereas in the virtual world built with modern, real-time graphics libraries, all locations are known at all times because you, or the computer, at your behest, put them there. The coordinate system already and necessarily exists. Furthermore, you can demonstrate, if you take the time, the lineage of an individual pixel or an individual polygon, and show why it is the precise color at one moment in time. Or, at one degree of abstraction, you can also say precisely how a virtual stone in virtual Arkansas came to be located at x,y,z, and how this stone came into existence. You can, if you made the world, and if you propose to call this world a work of scholarship. This is an extraordinarily powerful feature.

Plato's allegory reminds us what is at stake for those who wish to make virtual worlds. The maker designed and built the puppets, generated the fire, determined how it flickers, gave it directionality, controlled the lighting in the cave and the shapes of the shadows on the wall. A maker of virtual worlds built the cave, and the interface to it, and perhaps the form of the prisoners as well. The maker is the author, or the *makers* are the *authors*. Those chained to the stone floor? They are the readers, the game players, or the virtual-world denizens. And this is a good thing for scholarship, so long as the readers are aware of their state and can shed the neck chain and look back at the fire.

Since the active reader is still, for the moment, chained to the desk or at least to the device, the makers have a powerful documentary toolset. It does not matter at all what the prisoners believe a triangle might look like in 3D space, all that matters is that the shadow the first prisoner sees is the *same* shadow as that seen by the second prisoner. It is the shadow created by the author. The virtual world can enforce documentary principles in a way that a text-based fictional world cannot. To wit, fiction author Neil Gaiman celebrates the storytelling possibilities of his project *A Calendar of Tales*, where he crowdsourced illustrations to add to his text-based narrative: "I really love the different ways people have been illustrating the stories and the way they've been illustrating the characters. Everyone imagines them differently, and nobody's wrong. What you have is a hundred thousand different versions of right." (Gaiman, 2013). Once the author has a bit of fire, some puppets, and a few chains, those hundred thousand versions are reduced to one.

The virtual world, from a spatiotemporal perspective, is a solipsistic, multidimensional documentary tool. It documents activity in-world with exactitude and precision. Historians and researchers concerned with the study of antiquity have been early adopters and persistent users of virtual-world technology to document and experience historical spaces and places. Their use cases offer valuable guidance for would-be makers. Reconstructing, resurrecting, representing, or simply diagramming spaces and places of the past all demand detailed adherence to documentable documentary principles (Bentkowska-Kafel *et al.*, 2012). Often, however, the maker of virtual worlds is doing so outside of the virtual-world apparatus. After all, the virtual world is not a reflection of the actual world, it is a world unto its own. Documenting real-world spaces will most often occur using world-building software. Documents processed, data transformed, and meshes produced will be imported into a virtual world, and placed precisely using a shared coordinate system. It is, however, a simple step to transform the x,y,z system within a virtual world to a geographic system that reads data from the actual world. Thus, the virtual world can capitalize on actual-world correspondences. And once these physical spaces are realized in-world, connected to a coordinate system that spans the virtual and the actual, everything is documentable. The actions and interactions of the virtual-world denizens can be the objects of study. The actions of the avatars can be recorded and played back, their conversations studied and situated into the documentary record. Once in this space, every action can be, and often is, recorded. Every motion. Every word typed, or spoken, every note taken, and every object created.

Annotation

Unlike in the actual world, four-dimensional annotation is a feature of the virtual world genre. In the actual world, a tour guide can, for example, become a kind of real-time annotation machine, by walking, climbing, pointing, and talking. Physical signposts provide further annotation. A human could conceivably develop a non-digital system of annotation, a kind of 3D Post-it note system to tag buildings, trees, leaves, other people, etc., but a virtual human is a mouse-click away from such a system. It is traditionally very difficult to talk about, in detail, specific elements of architecture, and of spaces in general, in context, with photograph and text alone. The virtual world offers continuous context *and* the ability to mark that context up, to point to it with virtual Post-it notes. To document paths walked and items of interest highlighted in order to replay them. For a humanities virtual world, each of these annotations ought to be accessible and citable, individually or collectively.

Annotation need not be a solo experience. Synchronous and asynchronous collaborative experiences are both hallmarks of virtual words. Why walk through the world alone when one might move through the world as a group of researchers, or a group of students, marking up spaces, discussing them, and leaving a trail for others to follow? These multivocal annotations can also be performed collaboratively, in real time, or asynchronously, with one layer building upon another. Through this process the source material used to construct the virtual world can be revealed, or criticized. One might remark on the inappropriate use of a plan, or an unsuccessful attempt to build 3D geometry from evidence. A superficial analog is the textual footnote and the experience of collaborative document editing. In the virtual world, however, an avatar can point to specific parts of the world. Fellow avatars can likewise examine the identified area, point to it with a virtual pointer, discuss, debate, and affix a 3D comment as a record for others to read and critique.

These comments transform the virtual world from experimental lab to published scholarship. Once a comment, or by analogy a footnote, or perhaps simply an analogical page, chapter, and sentence demarcation, is fixed in-world, it need only link outward to enter into a scholarly conversation. So long as some combination of 3D state, viewing location, direction of gaze, and, if necessary, text/audio description, are collectively encompassed under a DOI, the virtual experience can be accessed and cited by others. The *entire* in-world virtual experience can be accessed, examined, observed, and, in a potentially unending stream of comment, cited by text-based scholarship, or embedded in map-based investigations, or cited and accessed in the same virtual world, or in other virtual worlds centered on the same geographic area.

Interpretation

Everything represented in the virtual world constitutes an interpretation. What is visible and what isn't both function as data points in the interpretative enterprise. It is easy to forget this critical point when engaged in the details of world construction. This is *your* world, and, as world-maker, you must accept that the world you have created will always be built entirely in the image of its creators, or at least informed by their theoretical leanings. The key to critical making in the humanities is understanding and communicating the chain of custody that led to the world you have made. Once that chain of custody is controlled, you can then articulate who or what has made the interpretative intervention to display knowledge within your virtual world.

To build a virtual landscape, for example, you can begin with a set of survey points, each one defined in x,y,z space. These points might number in the tens or the hundreds, if gathered in the real world via traditional survey methodology, or in the thousands or millions if generated through some computational technique. The next step is to interpret the data, either by drawing contour lines or by directing a computer to draw them for you – from this point on, the data have entered the realm of multilevel interpretation. The contours are transformed into a grayscale raster file where the shade of gray represents elevation. This raster file is the basis for generating a 3D mesh terrain. The data points have been interpreted, the contour lines serve as interpretations as well; next, the representation of the ground. If there is a real-world referent, is it covered with grass? What kind? Can you document it? How long must it be? Do you understand how the grass was cut and what its appearance ought to be? Should there be crabgrass? Clover? Is the grass symbolic? Or does every blade matter? Or are you copying this grass, this texture, this image, this original intellectual work, from someone else? These are all questions one asks when working with words, but are exactly the sort that are forgotten when working with imagery, no matter what its dimensions are. Answering each of these questions requires interpretation of the underlying data (Johanson, 2009).

A virtual world contains a multitude of data, of imagery, of text, of three-dimensional form, and it will rarely be the case that the world created is static. It can be made to change and to facilitate comparison. The virtual world might present alternative realities of the past, the present, or the future, and these realities might be juxtaposed with each other. You might, for example, compare different proposed building projects for a university, or you might examine different possible reconstructions of a historic landscape or a historic cityscape. As you explore the world with your avatar or your band of avatars you might then interpret the city as you see it.

For the virtual world, the model *is* the territory. While there may exist external referents, and these should be clearly documented and annotated, the model is also, in the end, the subject of interrogation and interpretation. The virtual world provides mechanisms to explore complex visualizations, to do so in embodied form, to do so as a solitary scholar, or as a group. At one extreme, the experience can be subjected to phenomenological analysis; at the other, sight-lines and view-sheds can be explored, analyzed, and contextualized. Questions such as, "Was it possible for the audience in the Roman Forum listening to Cicero's third Catilinarian to have seen the statue of Jupiter recently erected on the Capitoline?" can be assessed in virtual context. As more data are revealed, so more questions can be asked. What do such visual interrelationships mean? If an accurate aural model is implemented, one might then ask, what might have been the extent of audible range for the audience of such a speech?

Or interactions of another kind might be the subject of inquiry. Avatar interaction inside a tightly controlled artificial world is, save for the limitations of screen-based interfaces, a powerful tool for the scientific study of virtual human interaction. All variables can be controlled, in order to facilitate the study of the physical response to addiction triggers (where the virtual world stands in for what was once a videotaped system), for example (Bordnick *et al.*, 2011). Or, in the same control environment, the virtual world can serve as an experimental platform for natural language processing and machine-based interpretation (Bretaudière *et al.*, 2011). An anthropology of virtual worlds has arisen. One can also study the interaction between human and artificial intelligence in a world where embodied actors are visually indistinguishable from computer-controlled NPCs (Boellstorff, 2008, 2012). There are also studies of interaction and biases related to race and gender, within historical or present-day environments (Kafai *et al.*, 2010). As pedagogical exercises or research endeavors, the virtual world, when its known parameters are tightly controlled, serves up limitless interpretative possibilities, save that, of course, they all must be interpretations of the virtual, rather than the actual. As a laboratory, the virtual world shines, but it is worth proceeding carefully should one choose to publish the lab. Though not untested, these scholarly waters are treacherous.

Argumentation

[A]ny writer who is not interested in what we are now calling "video games" is a bystander to one of the most important conceptual shifts between story and storyteller in a hundred years. (Bissell, 2011)

To argue is the stuff of scholarship. One can hold exhibits, offer presentations, record and play back events within virtual worlds, but to participate in scholarly conversation, to argue, assert, test, and refute in public, through the use of this new medium is yet a novelty. Is a video game an argument? Is it a work of art? A game? A cartoon? Yes. Intrinsically, all have the capacity to tell stories, and can be interpreted as story, especially if the burden is placed on the reader to provide interpretation. As noted above, the interpretative leaps made at even the documentation and annotation stages constitute arguments of a kind. Nonetheless, it can hurt no one to aim for clarity. Rarely is it the case for scholarship to communicate a clear and concise argument by asking the reader to infer the main points. Even the most visual argument could be clearer with some captioning.

The bulk of virtual-world- and game-based academic endeavors are best taken as published laboratories rather than the functional equivalent of the academic article. The reasons are manifold. First, whether a story or narrative can even be told effectively within traditional games is still a question that causes significant disagreement (Wardrip-Fruin and Harrigan, 2004). Absent explanatory text that establishes the nature of the argument and the ways that evidence will be brandished, it is difficult to contend that a virtual-world exploration of, for example, the ancient agora is a scholarly argument, if it doesn't marshal some of the trappings of traditional scholarly argumentation (Balmer, 2014). It is certainly avant-garde, and an obvious case can and should be made for its scholarly merit, but its ability to participate in an ongoing conversation or spark a new one requires clarification.

What might a virtual-world-based argument look like? Not all arguments are visual and kinetic, but some are particularly well-suited to embodied, interactive explication. If the argument revolves around spaces, especially those that are unbuilt, have fallen into ruin, or require hypothetical adornment, additions, or subtractions, the virtual world works. If an argument depends upon a walk, or a run, or a drive, or a carriage ride in order to see and experience a narrative, the virtual world works. If the argument needs to show virtual humans and needs to put the reader into a first-person interrogation of a simulated event, or of a live performance, the virtual world works. If the argument involves allusivity in Silver Latin poetry, the virtual world may not. Nonetheless, if the virtual world fits the problem, it offers a clear path to a superior kind of space-based argumentation.

Virtual worlds come with ludic baggage that must be acknowledged and harnessed. They exhibit some of the trappings of the gaming world, and they reinforce some of the stereotypes, right or wrong, of virtual reality. Game technology implies fun, at some level. Argumentation, as much as it can, takes place in a gamified mode. There are levels to conquer, puzzles to solve, quests to complete, experience points to acquire, and dragons to slay. While not obviously useful for academic conversation, such features are, or could be if deployed properly, essential for both scholarly discourse and pedagogical experiment. Build a virtual world on gaming technology without acknowledging "fun" at your peril.

The mechanics of the in-world argument matter, but equally important is the design and the interface (Bogost, 2007:233–60). To make a scholarly virtual world in an extant virtual-world sandbox cedes control of the argument. There are norms of interaction for avatar-based experiences, but those norms should not determine content or interpretation. The skin of the data and the skin of the interface both contribute to the argument. If every pixel should have provenience, then for an argument it should also convey meaning. The *Second Life* logo and the boatloads of extraneous menu items all influence the reading experience. The simple hurdle of avatar creation as a first step privileges an activity that is not necessarily the primary goal of the virtual-world-based argument. If an argument is the goal, the commodification of game-development environments provides all the tools to sculpt game mechanics, interface, and design precisely as you like.

Build the argument on a deep map (Bodenhamer *et al.*, 2015). Not all virtual worlds will have a real-world referent, but those that do can build three-dimensionally on the extant properties of the deepest of maps. Layers of information ranging from census data to photographic archives and ancient places have been mapped to real-world coordinates, and many are already being published as Linked Open Data. If the virtual world uses a geographic coordinate system as its Cartesian core, the geo web is available for integration, citation, and consumption within this world.

The same geographic coordinate system, coupled with time-based markup, enables geo-temporal argumentation. The on-site tour can now come to life and remain interoperable. The author of a virtual world that juxtaposes in-world experience with out-of-world annotation can create the functional equivalent of a virtual tour, or an analog of an archaeological park's signage. Walk near point A, which is defined by geographic coordinates, themselves defined by an externally accessible markup file, and a text or NPCs tell you a story. Walk near point B, and a citable cut-scene makes the counterpoint. Or scroll through the marked-up text in a separate interface and watch the virtual world transport you, the avatar-based reader, from point A to point B as you read from paragraph to paragraph.

Virtual worlds provide the scholarly opportunity to transform complex data that are inherently visual into a shared laboratory for argumentation and refutation. The author now points the reader to the specific areas in space and time under discussion. If the author has diligently documented, annotated, and interpreted, the visual portion of the argument (along with the textual) is transformed into a quantifiable subject of technical and qualitative critique. The world imagined by the author is the world seen by the reader. If all elements, including the landscape, the grass, the trees, the buildings, the graphical artifacts (e.g., the jagged, aliased lines sometimes created by graphics hardware), the shadows, the light, the tone, the dirt, the interface, the style of avatar, its clothing, its hairstyle and skin color, and its method of locomotion, in short if everything is documented clearly by the author and annotated to show provenience, the author's interpretation and documentation process can be replicated through the reader's virtual experience, critiqued, cited in other works, challenged, and even refuted.

Refutation is the guiding principle for making an argumentation machine that harness multimedia forms and three-dimensional experience. How can the reader refute the argument? Unlike a game, in which participants control elements of the story, but, in the end, are unable to permanently affect the underlying content, a virtual world, built with gaming technology, invites the reader to follow the argument of the author, and then examine the evidence in detail. The reader can link to components of the argument to comment, to be sure, but even more powerful, he or she can create annotations in-world, or create alternative interpretations and alternative narratives. These layered arguments form the foundation for the kind of tool that can and will advance significantly the way that space- and place-based arguments are effected.

Conclusions

Future possibilities are almost realities. Gangs of readers might swarm a virtual world to critique it *en masse*, as a multivocal review. Conferences can be held in-world, or in and out of world. The geographic core enables the overlay of real-world information, *and* the overlay of the virtual world *onto* the actual world. When one walks through twenty-first-century Rome, one might, with the right type of interface, simultaneously walk through the virtual world version of the fifteenth-century city. Avatars might interact with readers who are simultaneously walking the actual world and the virtual, reporting live to each other what they see, on the ground of a modern archaeological site or on the virtual version. *Ad infinitum.*

Like so many new technologies, their future is enticing, but their present, in the case of virtual worlds, is already provocative. Humanists are creating virtual-world projects and serious games at a rapid rate. The technological barriers to entry have never been lower. As in all areas of scholarship, planning, time, and resources must be managed, and the work is always hard, but end goals have never been more attainable. The most critical element, however, is the simplest and most straightforward. Commercial enterprises built and supported by the largest and greatest players in the digital landscape have not, yet, been built by people like you. To make a virtual world for scholarship in the humanities requires precisely those tools that currently exist in the humanist's scholarly toolbox. They need only be reapplied to a new landscape that includes broader fields of inquiry. It is all too easy to set them aside at the moment when they are most necessary. Make no excuses for the technological shortcomings of software built by others. Instead, make these virtual worlds yourself, in your image, with the clarity of structured argumentation incumbent on a practicing humanist.

REFERENCES

Abbott, E. 1885. *Flatland: A Romance of Many Dimensions, by A Square.* Boston, MA: Roberts Brothers.

Balmer, J. 2014. Review: Digital Hadrian's Villa Project. *Journal of the Society of Architectural Historians* 73 (3), 444–5. doi:10.1525/jsah.2014.73.3.444.

Bartle, R.A. 2004. *Designing Virtual Worlds.* Indianapolis: New Riders.

Bentkowska-Kafel, A., Denard, H., and Baker, D., eds. 2012. *Paradata and Transparency in Virtual Heritage.* Farnham: Ashgate.

Bissell, T. 2010. *Extra Lives: Why Video Games Matter.* New York: Pantheon Books.

Bissell, T. 2011. Press X for beer bottle: on L.A. Noire. *Grantland* June 10. http://grantland.com/features/la-noire/.

Bodenhamer, D.J., Corrigan, J., and Harris, T.M., eds. 2015. *Deep Maps and Spatial Narratives.* Bloomington: Indiana University Press.

Boellstorff, T. 2008. Coming of Age in Second Life: An Anthropologist Explores the Virtually Human. Princeton: Princeton University Press.

Boellstorff, T. 2012. *Ethnography and Virtual Worlds: A Handbook of Method.* Princeton: Princeton University Press.

Bogost, I. 2007. Persuasive Games: The Expressive Power of Videogames. Cambridge, MA: MIT Press.

Bordnick, P.S., Carter, B.L., and Traylor, A.C. 2011. What virtual reality research in addictions can tell us about the future of obesity assessment and treatment. *Journal of Diabetes Science and Technology* 5 (2): 265–71.

Bretaudière, T., Cruz-Lara, S., and Rojas Barahona, L. 2011. Associating automatic natural language processing to serious games and virtual worlds. *Journal for Virtual Worlds Research* 4 (3). https://journals.tdl.org/jvwr/index.php/jvwr/article/view/6124 (accessed June 20, 2015).

Burdick, A, Drucker J., Lunenfeld, P., Presner, T., and Schnapp, J. 2012. *Digital_Humanities*. Cambridge, MA: MIT Press.

Colin, C. 2012. Odyssey Works makes art for and about one person. *New York Times* October 4, sec. Arts / Art & Design. http://www.nytimes.com/2012/10/07/arts/design/odyssey-works-makes-art-for-and-about-one-person.html (accessed June 20, 2015).

Craig, A.B., Sherman, W.R., and Will, J.D. 2009. *Developing Virtual Reality Applications: Foundations of Effective Design*. Burlington, MA: Morgan Kaufmann.

Cudworth, A.L. 2014. Virtual World Design Creating Immersive Virtual Environments. Boca Raton, FL: CRC Press.

Frischer, B., and Dakouri-Hild, A., eds. 2008. *Beyond Illustration: 2d and 3d Digital Technologies as Tools for Discovery in Archaeology*. BAR International Series 1805. Oxford: Archaeopress.

Gaiman, N. 2013. *BlackBerry 10 & Neil Gaiman Episode IV A Calendar of Tales*. 2013. http://www.youtube.com/watch?v=mxMXHPD1dew&feature=youtube_gdata_player (accessed June 20, 2015).

Hinrichs, R.J., and Wankel, C. 2011. *Transforming Virtual World Learning*. Bingley: Emerald. http://www.emeraldinsight.com/2044-9968/4 (accessed June 20, 2015).

Johanson, C. 2009. Visualizing history: modeling in the eternal city. *Visual Resources: An International Journal of Documentation* 25 (4), 403. doi:10.1080/01973760903331924.

Jones, S.E. 2014. *The Emergence of the Digital Humanities*. New York: Routledge.

Kafai, Y.B., Cook, M.S., and Fields, D.A. 2010. "Blacks deserve bodies too!": Design and discussion about diversity and race in a tween virtual world. *Games and Culture* 5 (1), 43–63. doi:10.1177/1555412009351261.

Lacy, S. 2012. Philip Rosedale: the media is wrong, SecondLife didn't fail. *PandoDaily* July 6. http://pando.com/2012/07/06/philip-rosedale-the-media-is-wrong-secondlife-didnt-fail (accessed June 20, 2015).

Malaby, T.M. 2009. *Making Virtual Worlds Linden Lab and Second Life*. Ithaca, NY: Cornell University Press. http://site.ebrary.com/id/10457566 (accessed June 20, 2015).

Pinchbeck, D. 2013. *DOOM: SCARYDARKFAST*. Ann Arbor: University of Michigan Press. http://quod.lib.umich.edu/cgi/t/text/idx/l/lvg/11878639.0001.001/1:3/−doom-scarydarkfast?g=dculture;rgn=div1;view=fulltext;xc=1 (accessed June 20, 2015).

Plato. 2012. *Republic*. Trans. C.J. Rowe. London; New York: Penguin.

Schell, J. 2008. *The Art of Game Design: A Book of Lenses*. Amsterdam; Boston: Elsevier/Morgan Kaufmann.

Shields, R. 2003. The Virtual. *Key Ideas*. London; New York: Routledge.

Shirky, C. 2006. A story too good to check. *Gawker* December 12. http://gawker.com/221252/a-story-too-good-to-check (accessed June 20, 2015).

Van Geel, I. 2013. MMOData.net: Version 4.1 thoughts and comments. *MMOData.net*. December 28. http://mmodata.blogspot.com/2013/12/version-41-thoughts-and-comments.html (accessed June 20, 2015).

Wardrip-Fruin, N. 2009. Expressive Processing : Digital Fictions, Computer Games, and Software Studies. Cambridge, MA: MIT Press.

Wardrip-Fruin, N., and Harrigan, P., eds. 2004. *First Person: New Media as Story, Performance, and Game*. Cambridge, MA: MIT Press.

FURTHER READING

Theoretical reading can help the cause, but before surveying the literature, one ought to first immerse in practice. There is no single point of entry into the art of making virtual worlds better than, for better or for worse, direct immersion in Linden Lab's *Second Life*. The story of *Second Life*'s rapid rise and subsequent slow decline is told best by analyses of its user data, first questioned by Shirky (2006), but conveniently graphed by Van Geel (http://users.telenet.be/mmodata/Charts/PCUShard.png), and put into context by Lacy (2012). Those who are already residents of the Linden community but armed with programming skills might then turn to OpenSimulator (http://opensimulator. org) or Unity3D to craft world and interface combined.

To engage with discussions of any *virtual* thing, start with Shields (2003). Though not strictly speaking about virtual worlds, Craig *et al.* (2009) offer a practical definition of virtual reality and give an excellent introduction to issues surrounding real-time immersive application development. For extensive and illuminating dissection of gamification, see Schell (2008). Though slightly dated and idiosyncratic, Bartle (2004) provides a nearly comprehensive introduction to the design of virtual worlds. Burdick *et al.* (2012:68–9) present a concise outline of how one might organize a virtual-world-based academic study, Cudworth (2014) gives a user-friendly guide to working with and designing virtual worlds, and Hinrichs and Wankel (2011) collect real-world experiences of educators doing the same.

For a wealth of discussion covering virtual worlds in entertainment, cultural heritage, game design, and virtual reality, a general survey of the following journals is most productive: *International Journal of Computer Games Technology*, *Virtual Reality*, *Games and Culture*, *Journal of Gaming and Virtual Worlds*, and the *International Journal of Gaming and Computer-Mediated Simulations*.

For an anthropological analysis of virtual world communities, see Boellstorff (2008). For a different approach to the study of "making virtual worlds," see Malaby (2009), who analyzes the community that designed and built the *Second Life* virtual world and its codebase. Though there are now many studies of avatars in virtual worlds, Kafai *et al.* (2010) present a compelling holistic study of one of the most important issues surrounding avatar design: inclusion and exclusion.

Lastly, when building world environments that are meant to be used as scholarship, even non-historians and non-archaeologists would do well to consult the London Charter (www. londoncharter.org), which outlines "principles for the use of computer-based visualisation by researchers, educators and cultural heritage organisations."

9
Electronic Literature as Digital Humanities

Scott Rettberg

Electronic literature is an umbrella term used to describe various forms of literary practice that take advantage of the computational, multimedia, and networked properties of the contemporary computer in the production of born-digital experiences and works of a narrative or poetic nature that are specific to this context. Some of the forms and genres of electronic literature include hypertext fiction, kinetic multimedia poetry, interactive fiction, generative poetry and fiction, interactive drama and cinema, database narratives, locative narratives, network "styles" based on new writing practices specific to networked communication technologies, and text-based new-media art installations. The creative production of this type of work can itself be understood as a digital humanities practice: not an application of digital tools to a traditional form of humanities research, but rather experiments in the creation of new forms native to the digital environment.

In both the broader digital humanities and in electronic literature there is a recognition that there are at least three levels of scholarly practice, of roughly equivalent value:

1. theory and analysis;
2. toolmaking and platform development; and
3. applied research.

While many other humanities fields can be defined by generic, temporal, and regional qualities, the boundaries of emergent fields of the digital humanities tend to be more fluid and contingent. Both "electronic literature" and "digital humanities" are loosely defined not by their attachment to a historic period or genre but by a general exploratory engagement with the contemporary technological apparatus. Electronic literature is a

A New Companion to Digital Humanities, First Edition. Edited by Susan Schreibman, Ray Siemens, and John Unsworth.
© 2016 John Wiley & Sons, Ltd. Published 2016 by John Wiley & Sons, Ltd.

field that explores the effects and affordances of computational devices and the network on literary practice, while the digital humanities is a broader area primarily focused on research derived from digital methods within established areas of study in literature, history, and other humanistic disciplines. Because they are defined primarily by approach rather than content, both electronic literature and the digital humanities are defined by cultural affiliations within research communities as much as they are by a particular object of study.

New academic disciplines often emerge from within existing ones. Electronic literature has an obvious relationship to literary studies, but it does not necessarily function as a subfield of literature. Some academics working in e-lit teach in English departments, but there is significant crossover with a range of other disciplines, including fine arts, design, computer science, film, and communications. One of the defining characteristics of the field of electronic literature has been that the critics, theorists, and practitioners tend to converge in the same environments, presenting and exhibiting creative work and scholarship at the same conferences. Both the Electronic Literature Organization (ELO) conferences and the E-Poetry Festivals bring artists and critics together, and theoretical and creative trends tend to co-evolve.

Electronic literature has emerged as a distinctive digital humanities field in its own right, with conferences, festivals, journals, and a growing body of dissertations, monographs, and edited collections addressing the subject. Electronic literature functions as a field of digital humanities research on a number of different levels, each with their own defining characteristics. These include:

1. creative digital media practice in electronic literature;
2. the development of specific platforms for creative practices in digital media;
3. theoretical work and analysis works of electronic literature to build new understandings of contemporary textuality and "digital vernaculars";
4. the establishment of networked scholarly practices, digital publications, research infrastructures, and social networks particular to the digital media research environment; and
5. meta-analysis and visualization research based on electronic literature metadata.

Creative Writing in Digital Media as Digital Humanities Research

The relationships between humanities research and creative practice in humanities disciplines are typically somewhat strained. While for example in the United States, many language and literature programs offer courses in creative writing and include creative writers on faculty, there is often a pronounced cultural divide between the creative writing program and the literature program "proper" – a sort of begrudging understanding that while it is good to have poets and novelist about, their research outputs should not be spoken of in the same breath as the work of their scholarly cousins. In academic departments that host both literature and creative writing programs, separate systems of evaluation and metrics of achievements apply. The professional networks of creative writing and literature are similarly segregated, creative writing programs doing much of their hiring and congregating at the

Association of Writers & Writing Programs (AWP) and literature programs doing the same at the Modern Language Association (MLA). Creative practice and scholarship are more complexly intertwined in electronic literature. This is in part because creative projects are presented in the same contexts as critical writing in the field, but also because of the nature of creative outputs in the field of electronic literature.

Electronic literature projects are forms of creative expression, but they are also often experiments in the scientific sense, sometimes in multiple disciplines simultaneously. A novelist working in hypertext is not only writing a fiction, but also experimenting with alternative models of textual navigation and user interaction. The author of a short story producing a narrative generator is not only writing a story but collaborating with a machine environment and coding a potential narrative system. A poet working in a CAVE environment is both writing a poem and exploring the aesthetics of embodied interaction in a 3D environment. A filmmaker producing a generative database film is both producing a film and exploring the effects of aleatory combinatorics on visual narrative. It has become difficult to speak of genre in electronic literature, in part because it seems as if nearly every new piece is producing its own new genre.

One way of thinking about electronic literature practice is that it functions as a research and development wing for new literary forms that engage with technology on an aesthetic level. New works function as individual artistic expressions but also as documented experiments in applied technology and formal innovation. Writers working in new media are both creating discrete literary experiences and testing the chemistry of a particular creative admixture of writing and technological apparatus. While during the 1980s and 1990s these experiments took place mainly within the confines of applications made for the personal computer screen, and then increasingly the global network, the scope and diversity of digital poetic environments has expanded in recent years as ubiquitous computing has taken hold.

The development team that produced the first version of Storyspace, the hypertext authoring system in which many of the hypertext fictions published by Eastgate Systems in the 1990s were produced, is one example of how creative work and digital humanities practices have gone hand in hand in electronic literature. As Michael Joyce was authoring *afternoon, a story* (1990), the most-often-cited hypertext fiction, he was also working with Jay David Bolter and John Smith in developing the authoring system of Storyspace. The creative work was both a standalone literary artifact and a testing framework for a platform which was then used both by other authors and as a pedagogical environment. After publishing *afternoon*, Joyce used Storyspace in the classroom for several years before publishing *Of Two Minds: Hypertext Pedagogy and Poetics* (1995) which among other topics explored the usefulness of hypertext authoring in writing classroom situations including developmental writing. The same process that resulted in the hypertext fiction also resulted in the development of a software platform, its applied use in the classroom, and a pedagogical study.

The first major wave of critical engagement with electronic literature was focused primarily on hypertext fiction and poetry, although interactive fiction – the text-parser-based form based on the genre of text-adventure games popular during the early days of home computing – also enjoyed an active developer and readership community. Hypertext had its heyday during the 1990s, first in works distributed individually on floppy discs and CD-ROM, and then on the Web. During the late

1990s and early 2000s, various forms of interactive and non-interactive multimedia poetry were most prominent. The rise of the platform of Flash is particularly notable within work produced during this period. Projects such as the early-2000s online journal *Poems That Go* (Ankerson and Sapnar*et al.*, 2000) pushed high-end visual design, interaction design, and multimedia capabilities of this platform in kinetic poetry. In the post-millennial years a great diversification has taken place as writers work within a variety of platforms and multimedia modalities. Presentation venues have also greatly diversified. While some means of dissemination are similar to those of print culture, such as online journals and digital anthologies, electronic literature is also now frequently presented in art gallery and museum contexts, as well as within live performance environments. If the range of artistic experimentation in e-lit has branched off in many different directions, the general trend in the field of electronic literature has been away from traditional models of poetry and fiction and towards a deeper engagement with digital poetics – that is, with exploring the specific constraints and affordances of the contemporary computational environment. Forms of literary engagement such as "codework" – literary expressions that address and present the poetics of code both on the machine level and in human language – are a more explicit manifestation of a field that is more generally focused on the creative affordances for language, storytelling, and poetics presented by a network-mediated, ubiquitous computing culture.

E-lit projects often cross over into experimental research in other disciplines, including computer science and human–computer interface research. Michael Mateas and Andrew Stern's *Façade* (2005) for example is an interactive narrative in which the interactor negotiates a one-act drama in the form of a visit to the apartment of a couple of old friends who are in the midst of a critical marital argument which could spell the end of their relationship. The user/player/reader of this work responds to the characters in the drama, providing typed responses to Grace and Trip, the marital combatants at the center of the work. Although *Façade* was clearly an interactive narrative artwork, it also resulted in a number of computer science research publications on natural language processing and expressive artificial intelligence. Projects such as Nick Montfort's *ppg256* series (2008) also function to explore computer science problems as well as formal poetics, in this case by exploring both the "elegance" standards of programming (producing maximal computational effect from minimal lines of code), and constraint-driven poetics. The works are Perl Poetry Generators in 256 characters, very compact computer programs that each result in the production of some of form of intelligible or semi-intelligible generated poetry.

Montfort and Stephanie Strickland's *Sea and Spar Between* (2010), and Mark Sample's follow-on project *House of Leaves of Grass* (2013) result in e-lit projects that can also serve as a type of deconstructive comparative analysis tool useful in the contemplation of two remixed source texts. In Montfort and Strickland's work, phrases and lines from the poetry of Emily Dickinson are recombined with phrases and lines from Melville's *Moby-Dick* using a quantitatively determined corpus and recombined according to certain human aesthetic-determined qualitative methods applied algorithmically. The poem is presented as an enormous canvas of potential poetry. The authors describe the work on the project site as "a poetry generator which defines a space of language populated by a number of stanzas comparable to the number of fish in the sea, around

225 trillion." By adjoining Dickinson and Melville's language in this way and presenting us with an interface to browse all the potential combinations of strings from the arrays, the piece in turn serves as an analytic tool inviting reflection on the qualities and patterns used by the authors of the source text. Sample's *House of Leaves of Grass* takes advantage of the platform developed by Montfort and Strickland to develop a new work and a new exploration, in this case of Mark Danielewski's *House of Leaves* and Whitman's *Leaves of Grass*, to explore the effects of juxtaposition on samples selected from the two works according to either frequency of appearance or thematic significance and then algorithmically remixed into couplets based on seven templates. In developing his selected corpus, Sample explicitly used digital humanities tools *N-Gram Tools*, *Voyant Tools*, and the *Stanford Named Entity Recognizer*. Both projects show how the same tools used to perform quantitative textual analysis for other digital humanities projects can be integrated into an artistic practice that results in artworks that can themselves serve as a kind of comparative textual analysis tool.

A number of e-lit projects have also served as experiments in the poetics and narrative effects of resituating the reading experiments within physically embodied interactive environments. If works of electronic literature first resituated reading from the page to the screen, more recent waves of exploration have pushed beyond the screen. The Brown University CAVE project *Screen* for example developed a narrative experience within an immersive 3D environment (Wardrip-Fruin *et al.*, 2003). A narrative reflection on human memory, forgetting, and loss, the piece literally immerses the reader in language that peels off the walls and swirled about the embodied visual space. Language was in this case not merely representational but an objective correlative materialized in embodied physical space.

Bruno Nadeau and Jason Lewis's *Still Standing* (2005) similarly explores the connections between the user's embodied interaction and the act of reading. As the user approaches the work, letters jostle about on the bottom of the screen in an unreadable pile. As machine vision captures the shadow of the user/reader's body, the letters react as if kicked about by the user. The poem remains unreadable as long as the user is moving or playing with the space of the text. Only when the user stands still do the words finally settle into shape, and the poem takes the shape of the reader's body. The poem itself reads "five chapters of addiction for my personal commotion bring my brain to a stop the inception of sedation is need for the waves to break and the spin to reduce letters to litteral the motionless moment hides my sight to seduce." While, as an interactive installation, the work on one level encourages the user to move about and play with it, it finally encourages stillness and reflection in reaction to technological immersion and information overload.

Locative narratives such as Jeremy Hight, Jeff Knowlton, and Naomi Spellman's *34 North 118 West* (2002) are part of a strand of the field that is taking digital narrative and poetics out of the paradigm of reader-at-screen and into the physical world, using mobile devices to add layers of narrative and other forms of literary expression to environments the reader moves through. Collective writing projects such as the database narrative *The Last Performance* (2007) by Judd Morrissey and Mark Jeffery *et al.* are expanding the range and effects of techniques such as machine reading and visualization, as well as the integration of live time-based performance as an element of the presentation of the work.

There are certain costs associated with this form of creative practice – among them that cycles of technological development and obsolescence are such that many works produced using "cutting-edge" technologies or experimental methods are fragile from a preservation standpoint. Many works of e-lit have already been lost to changes in the underlying codebase of existing platforms with updates that render obsolete works produced in earlier versions of software, to the complete loss of platforms, to the exigencies of storage media, and like problems. Works that are published on the Web, for example, are not replicated in the same way as printed artifacts. If the original website is hacked or neglected, the entire work can be destroyed. Other strains on the practice of digital writing include the fact that outside of academe, there are few paths to economic success from the production of e-lit. Although there is now some market for apps developed for tablets and mobile devices, few authors have actually made a living solely through the production of works of e-lit.

In part because of the tentative and experimental nature of the enterprise, many authors of e-lit document and "write up" their projects in forms that have something in common with the lab reports produced in scientific contexts. While acid-free paper and libraries do much of the work of preservation of print fiction and poetry, the development of a robust culture of documentation is essential to the growth and sustainability of electronic literature. If we consider the project of the field of electronic literature as a totality, one of its aims must be to produce such a record. Given that a high percentage of works produced during this experimental period will not survive, documentation is necessary in order that other writers, audiences, and scholars may learn from precedent works which may or may not be accessible in the near future. Paratexts and critical commentary provide a basis for the continued development of the field. Efforts such as the Electronic Literature Organization's publication of the pamphlets *Acid Free Bits: Recommendations for Long-Lasting Electronic Literature* (Montfort and Wardrip-Fruin, 2004) and *Born-Again Bits: A Framework for Migrating Electronic Literature* (Liu *et al.*, 2005) also help to mitigate the problems of preserving electronic literature by putting forth best practices for both authors and archivists.

Beyond Creative Production: Platforms, Scholarship, and Research Infrastructure in Electronic Literature

While creative practice is central to the existence of the field of electronic literature, it is also a bustling hub of critical activity and research infrastructure development.

As in the digital humanities more broadly, credit is due to the toolmakers who develop platforms for their own work and for others to build upon, often on an open-source model. While it is not the case that electronic literature is produced exclusively in "e-lit platforms" – virtually any platform ranging from HTML to Twitter to the Unity 3D engine can be bent to experimental literary purposes – there are some prominent examples of digital developers releasing applications or libraries for others to build on. This is a core practice of the interactive fiction community, for example, where platforms such as INFORM, TADS, and Twine provide complete development and publishing environments for an active creative community. Daniel Howe's RiTa provides a free and open-source toolkit for experiments in natural language and generative literature. Even individual works of electronic literature can serve as platforms as authors hack and adapt others' source code. The series of adaptations which have taken place of Nick Montfort's poetry generator *Taroko Gorge* (2009) provide a prominent example of this.

Critical analysis of electronic literature provides models of understanding changes in contemporary culture and textuality, and of developing new social models of humanities research. The critical field of electronic literature is active and eclectic in its range of investigation. While much early theoretical writing about hypertext, such as George Landow's *Hypertext: The Convergence of Contemporary Critical Theory and Technology* (1992), emphasized its relation to poststructuralist theory as a central focus, more recent criticism has found a full range of approaches to the subject.

N. Katherine Hayles's work in electronic literature offers one model of a humanities researcher who analyzes and uses works of electronic literature in her critical work as "tutor texts" to investigate, illustrate, or expand the context of a theoretical paradigm she has developed across her work, specifically the framework of the posthuman. In works such as *Electronic Literature: New Horizons for the Literary* (2008) Hayles developed a method of media-specific analysis, and used careful readings of works of electronic literature such as Shelley Jackson's *Patchwork Girl* (1995), Talan Memmott's *Lexia to Perplexia* (2000), and Stephanie Strickland's *slippingglimpse* (2006) to extend theoretical explorations of materiality, embodiment, the machine as an active cognizer, and the complex symbiotic relationships developing between human and machine intelligence and networked forms of cognition.

Chris Funkhouser's studies *Prehistoric Digital Poetry: An Archeology of Forms 1959–1995* (2007) and *New Directions in Digital Poetry* (2012) provide examples of a more historiographic approach to understanding the history of digital poetry, first as an outgrowth of and reaction to twentieth-century experimental poetic traditions such as visual poetry and sound poetry and then as a series of evolving traditions in their own right. Funkhouser's approach is both longitudinal and direct. He traces patterns, but his work is based on what are essentially short close readings of individual digital poems. This can be more complex than it sounds, as some of the poems he reads are generative and vary on each reading.

Jessica Pressman, Mark Marino, and Jeremy Douglass's work *Reading Project* (2015), a case study using William Poundstone's *Project for the Tachistoscope {Bottomless Pit}*, provides an example of an exciting trend towards collaborative practice in new media scholarship. The logic of their project was that there would be many ways to slice a critical reading of Poundstone's work. In order to bring several digital humanities reading methods into conversation, the three authors each applied a different methodology. Jessica Pressman read onscreen aesthetics, Mark Marino analyzed the programming code, and Jeremy Douglass used cultural analytics to show how data-visualizations stimulate literary interpretations. A distinctive aspect of this approach is that the three critics were not only providing three readings of the same work, but considering how those readings could inform one another. In a field that involves many background disciplines and critical approaches, this type of collaborative reading holds great promise for future studies of individual works.

The field of electronic literature itself can provide a rich and rewarding object of study. One of the central concerns of the 2010–2013 HERA-funded ELMCIP project (*Developing a Network-Based Creative Community: Electronic Literature as a Model of*

Creativity and Innovation in Practice) was developing an understanding of how techno-logically mediated network-based creative communities function differently from prior networks of literary practice and dissemination. Some of the fruits of those investiga-tions are available in two "electronic literature communities" issues of the journal *Dichtung Digital* which together provide as complete an analysis of different creative communities in electronic literature drawn together by regional histories, shared interest in particular platforms or genres, institutional initiatives, and so forth as has been developed to date (Rettberg and Tomaszek, 2012). Many of these essays have been collected in a volume *Electronic Literature Communities* (Rettberg *et al.*, 2015).

Because the field of electronic literature has dealt with comparatively strange literary objects, and has developed largely independently of any parent discipline, it initially lacked scholarly networks and research infrastructure suited to the particular-ities of the field. The Electronic Literature Organization, founded as a literary non-profit organization in 1999, was established largely in attempt to address that lacuna, and over the past 16 years has been successful at establishing a robust research network based on electronic literature. The organization's conferences interweave creative production – presentations, performances, and exhibitions of new works – with papers and panel discussions. The opportunities these conferences provide for in-person contact between critics, theorists, developers, writers, and artists working in electronic literature have been essential to its development as a transdisciplinary field.

If the human network is essential, so too are the research infrastructure projects of the ELO and other affiliated projects and organizations. The ELO's *Electronic Literature Collection, Volume One* (Hayles *et al.*, 2006) provided a new publishing model situated between prior models of commercial and completely independent publishing on the Web. In gathering together a collection of 60 diverse works of electronic literature, and publishing them both on physical media in a case suitable for library distribution and on the Web, the *Collection* addressed issues related both to the difficulty of locating works in transient media and, to some extent, to those of preservation. All of the works were further published under a Creative Commons license, in order to encourage their free distribution and circulation. A second volume of the *Collection* was published in 2011 (Borrás *et al.*, 2011), and in 2012 the ELMCIP project published the *ELMCIP Anthology of European Electronic Literature* (Engberg *et al.*, 2012). While none of these projects is intended to establish a fixed canon of electronic literature, each provides durable selections of works of e-lit selected by editorial collectives on the basis of submissions via an open call and peer-review process and goes some way towards estab-lishing a stable set of references for teaching and learning about e-lit.

Digital collections and anthologies have been vital to the growth of the field over the past decade, but perhaps even more essential for its long-term survival is the existence of databases, directories, and archives, each of which address the challenges of documenting and preserving digital literature in a different way. The ELO's *Electronic Literature Directory* (ELD) was first established in the early 2000s and re-launched with a new information architecture in 2009. Focused on concise critical descriptions of works of e-lit, the ELD harnesses the collective effort of scholars around the world in creating a kind of encyclopedia of electronic literature that will be essential to the collective memory of the field. NT2 is a major ongoing research project based in Quebec and focused on providing a similar resource for the francophone world. While it shares some aspects in common with the ELD, the NT2's *Réserche Repertoire*, established in 2005, is more distinctively focused on the use of semantically structured metadata to categorize works within a media- and genre-driven taxonomy. The *Repertoire* also includes "enhanced fiches" of particular works that include extra rich-media documentation, such as video captures of users interacting with the work. The distinctive aspect of the ELMCIP *Electronic Literature Knowledge Base*, established in 2010, is that it provides an information architecture for documenting works of electronic literature in a critical ecology that also includes extensive documentation of critical writing, authors, publishers, organizations, events, databases, and teaching resources. The primary goal of the ELMCIP *Knowledge Base* is to document and make available for analysis the relations between the different objects and actors that define the field, by documenting cross-references between the different objects that automatically update the other records they connect with. For example, every time a work of critical writing is entered, the contributor is asked to also include references to the creative works it addresses. Over time this establishes a history of the critical reception of a given work. Likewise, whenever a conference or festival is documented, references are included to the works and critical articles presented there, enabling a kind of temporal mapping of the field. Once these relations are mapped, new types of distant reading and visualization-based research become possible. Using data harvested from the ELMCIP *Knowledge Base*, members of the Bergen Electronic Literature Research Group are beginning to explore the use of these digital methods to map patterns in the field, for instance by doing citation analyses to consider questions such as if we can identify a canon in the field on the basis of how works have been cited over time. By gathering large collections of abstracts and full-text resources in the database, other types of data mining will also soon be possible.

Perhaps the most exciting large-scale digital humanities development in the field of electronic literature is the establishment and collaborative work of the Consortium for Electronic Literature. This entity was formed to bring the international actors in the field, particularly the organizations and projects developing research databases and archives, into closer contact with one another, not only to support better communication in the field but also to establish machine-level interaction between participating databases and archives. As a first step, the consortium has established a set of core bibliographic fields for describing works of electronic literature. Upcoming projects will include a shared search engine, which will allow for users to search within all of the participating databases from the interface of any of them. A name authority is also planned to help tie authors and entities to a fixed identifier. Together, these efforts should help to increase international research communities' awareness of work being done in other cultural contexts, to reduce the duplication of effort, and to ensure the preservation of the information developed by all of the participating projects.

References and Further Reading

Ankerson, I., and Sapnar, M. 2000. *Poems That Go*. http://poemsthatgo.com (accessed March 11, 2014).

Borrás, L., Memmott, T., Raley, R., and Stefans, B.K., eds. 2011. *The Electronic Literature Collection, Volume Two*. Cambridge: The Electronic

Literature Organization. http://collection.
eliterature.org/2 (accessed March 11, 2014).

CELL: Consortium for Electronic Literature. http://
eliterature.org/cell (accessed March 11, 2014).

Electronic Literature Organization. *The Electronic
Literature Directory*. http://directory.eliterature.
org (accessed March 11, 2014).

ELMCIP. *The ELMCIP Electronic Literature
Knowledge Base*. http://elmcip.net/knowledge
base (accessed March 11, 2014).

Engberg, M., Memmott, T., and Prater, D. 2012.
*ELMCIP Anthology of European Electronic
Literature*. Bergen: ELMCIP. http://anthology.
elmcip.net (accessed March 11, 2014).

Funkhouser, C. 2007. *Prehistoric Digital Poetry:
An Archeology of Forms 1959–1995*. Tuscaloosa:
University of Alabama Press.

Funkhouser, C. 2012. *New Directions in Digital
Poetry*. London: Continuum.

Hayles, N.K. 2007. *Electronic Literature: New
Horizons for the Literary*. South Bend, IN:
University of Notre Dame Press.

Hayles, N.K, Montfort, N., Rettberg, S., and
Strickland, S., eds. 2006. *The Electronic Literature
Collection, Volume One*. College Park, MD: The
Electronic Literature Organization. http://collection.
eliterature.org/1 (accessed March 11, 2014).

Hight, J., Knowlton, J., and Spellman, N. 2002. *34
North 118 West*. Documentation. http://34n118w.
net/34N (accessed March 11, 2014).

Jackson, S. 1995. *Patchwork Girl*. Watertown, MA:
Eastgate Systems.

Joyce, M. 1990. *afternoon, a story*. Watertown, MA:
Eastgate Systems.

Joyce, M. 1995. *Of Two Minds: Hypertext Pedagogy and
Poetics*. Ann Arbor: University of Michigan Press.

Landow, G. 1992. *Hypertext: The Convergence of
Contemporary Critical Theory and Technology*.
Baltimore: Johns Hopkins University Press.

Liu, A., Durand, D., Montfort, N., *et al.* 2005.
*Born-Again Bits: A Framework for Migrating
Electronic Literature*. http://eliterature.org/pad/
bab.html (accessed April 8, 2014).

Mateas, M. and Stern, A. 2005. Procedural Arts.
Façade. http://www.interactivestory.net (accessed
March 11, 2014).

Memmott, T. 2000. *Lexia to Perplexia*. http://
collection.eliterature.org/1/works/
memmott__lexia_to_perplexia.html (accessed
March 11, 2014).

Montfort, N. 2008. *ppg256 (Perl Poetry Generator in
256 Characters)*. http://nickm.com/poems/
ppg256.html (accessed March 11, 2014).

Montfort, N. and Strickland, S. 2010. *Sea and Spar
Between*. Dear Navigator, Winter 2010. http://
blogs.saic.edu/dearnavigator/winter2010/nick-
montfort-stephanie-strickland-sea-and-spar-
between (accessed March 11, 2014).

Montfort, N., and Wardrip-Fruin, N. 2004. *Acid
Free Bits: Recommendations for Long-Lasting
Electronic Literature*. http://eliterature.org/pad/
afb.html (accessed April 8, 2014).

Montfort, N. *et al.* 2009. *Taroko Gorge* (and descendants). http://nickm.com/poems/taroko_gorge.
html (accessed March 11, 2014).

Morrissey, J., Jeffery, M., *et al.* 2007. *The Last
Performance {dot org}*. http://thelastperformance.
org/title.php (accessed March 11, 2014).

Nadeau, B. and Lewis, J. 2005. *Still Standing*.
Documentation video. In *The Electronic Literature
Collection, Volume Two*. http://collection.eliterature.
org/2/works/nadeau_stillstanding.html
(accessed March 11, 2014).

NT2. *NT2 Réserche Repertoire*. http://nt2.uqam.ca/
fr/search/site/?f%5B0%5D=type%3Arepertoire
&retain-filters=1 (accessed March 11, 2014).

Pressman, J., Marino, M., and Douglass, J. 2015.
*Reading Project: A Collaborative Analysis of
William Poundstone's Project for Tachistoscope
{Bottomless Pit}*. Iowa City: University of Iowa
Press.

Rettberg, S. and Tomaszek, P. 2012. *Dichtung Digital*
41, 42. Special issues on electronic literature
communities. http://dichtung-digital.de/editorial/
2012_41.htm (accessed March 11, 2014).

Rettberg, S., Tomaszek, P., and Baldwin, S., eds.
2015. *Electronic Literature Communities*.
Morgantown, WV: Computing Literature Books.

Sample, M. 2013. *House of Leaves of Grass*.
http://fugitivetexts.net/houseleavesgrass (accessed
March 11, 2014).

Strickland, S. 2006. *slippingglimpse*. http://
www.slippingglimpse.org (accessed March 11,
2014).

Wardrip-Fruin, N., Carroll, J., Coover, R., *et al.*
2003. *Screen (2002)*. Documentation video. In
The Electronic Literature Collection, Volume Two.
http://collection.eliterature.org/2/works/
wardrip-fruin_screen.html (accessed March 11,
2014).

10
Social Scholarly Editing

Kenneth M. Price

Creating scholarly editions has always been to some degree social, though we are more aware of how collaborative we are in a digital environment than we were in a print-based world. When working in print, editors typically spent little time on issues of design, layout, distribution, and long-term preservation, but all of these issues (and more) are typical concerns for editors of digital texts. If editors in a digital age face increased burdens, we also enjoy greater possibilities, including larger and more engaged audiences for our work and new ways for that work to be reused. This chapter considers both the promise and the perils of social editing. Although the word *social* in "social editing" can be construed in various ways, I concern myself primarily with an emerging usage in which "social" implies user-generated content. The very idea of user-contributed content has been greeted with enthusiasm in some quarters and with skepticism and anxiety in others. We can learn from the crowdsourcing efforts under-taken thus far and can glimpse some of the new possibilities on the horizon. To what extent might users of electronic editions help projects address the extensive and costly work that stands in the way of the realization of a digital scholarly edition? (I avoid saying completion of a digital scholarly edition, because many of them, embedded within electronic archives or digital thematic research collections, are conceived in such ambitious and open-ended ways as to defy completion.) How can we best nego-tiate the roles of scholarly specialists and interested users, and, in particular, how can we establish quality control without discouraging user involvement?

Our era is witnessing an explosion of amateur contributions to knowledge in many arenas, most visibly through *Wikipedia*. The roles of the amateur and the professional academic can sometimes be effectively integrated, but there are often different assump-tions and goals held by each. The professional and amateur roles now being negotiated

A New Companion to Digital Humanities, First Edition. Edited by Susan Schreibman, Ray Siemens, and John Unsworth.

are comparable to those that in the eighteenth century sometimes brought together and sometimes divided antiquarians and historians, the former interested in relics of the past and discrete facts, the latter interested in narratives of the past and their implications for the present and future. By making this comparison, I acknowledge a key difference: it is professionals who have the training, institutional backing, and other advantages that enable them to formulate large research questions. Generally speaking, amateurs contribute to projects devised by professionals rather than the other way around. To say this is not to make invidious distinctions but merely to recognize a pattern in how large-scale projects have emerged thus far and likely will into the future.

As we strive to harness the talents of both specialists and lay people, we can find inspiration by observing how much amateurs have added to scientific knowledge, especially in the field of astronomy. The creators of *Galaxy Zoo*, convinced that thousands of human observers are better at the recognition of patterns than powerful computer systems, have undertaken a collaborative astronomy project involving several universities and tens of thousands of volunteers. The goal of the project is to have 20 separate users classify every galaxy from the *Sloan Digital Sky Survey* (an ambitious survey that created three-dimensional maps of more than 930,000 galaxies) because multiple classifications will enable the creation of "an accurate and reliable database, that will meet the high standards of the scientific community" (Galaxy Zoo team, 2007). In this case, the sheer massiveness of user involvement promises to yield highly reliable results. The project leaders hold that the aggregate analysis of 20 lay people is no more subject to error than the informed analysis of one or two experts. The allure of the project for volunteers is explained by Chris Lintott, one of its leaders and an advocate for public outreach: "You get to see parts of space that have never been seen before. These images were taken by a robotic telescope and processed automatically, so the odds are that when you log on, that first galaxy you see will be one that no human has seen before." Since 2007 amateur astronomers numbering in the hundreds of thousands – and from more than 100 countries – have examined and documented remote corners of the universe (Adams, 2012).

Other scientific projects address issues closer to those faced by literary and historical editors. The *North American Bird Phenology Program* (NABPP), for example, gathered records created by volunteer observers between 1880 and 1970, tracking the "first arrival dates, maximum abundance, and departure dates of migratory birds across North America." The goal of this program, coordinated by the US government and sponsored by the American Ornithologists' Union, was to aggregate these observations so that they could be used to shed light on almost a century of migration patterns and changes in bird populations. The program exists now as "a historic collection of six million migration card observations." The original documents were scanned and made available via the Internet by nearly 3000 volunteers. The work of this citizen science program has made this material accessible to academic and lay users; it is fully searchable and analyzable, and can be used for many purposes, including an assessment of the consequences of climate change (North American Bird Phenology Program, 2011; US Geological Survey, 2012).

The massive amounts of data confronting *Galaxy Zoo* and NABPP – in the millions of records each – have been important factors driving scholar–volunteer collaboration. One might argue that few humanities editing projects operate on a comparable scale, but some do include massive numbers of texts. In fact, one of the dramatic changes in humanities research in recent decades is the new availability of increasingly vast portions of the human record in electronic form, making texts available not so much for reading (sheer quantity makes that impossible) but for the analysis of patterns that can be detected and then explored in more detail (Ramsay, 2005:181). Mass digitization projects have created enormous troves of information, typically by relying on optical character recognition (OCR), an automated means of converting a digital scan or photographic image into machine-readable electronic text. This conversion process is almost always imperfect, and, not surprisingly, when the original print quality is poor (because of broken fonts, smudging, stains, gaps, or other damage) we get disappointing results – so-called dirty OCR text – with a high rate of error. Given the amount of dirty OCR in the large datasets humanists increasingly work with, we can only welcome any effort that leads to the progressive improvement of these texts. The situation for humanists is further complicated by the fact that OCR has had little success with converting handwritten documents into usable electronic texts; accordingly, most of the manuscript record of the past is omitted in the data-mining efforts conducted. As in the sciences, humanists require accurate and reliable data. For massive digitization projects, the question is how to achieve a very high degree of textual reliability. We remain so deeply shaped by print culture that the early release of material, of work still in progress, faces stiff resistance in some quarters. Yet given the malleability of electronic texts and thus our ability to correct errors and to accommodate new discoveries, a more suitable goal than flawlessness, particularly in large datasets, is the early release of strong rather than perfected content. Material should be accurately labeled, so that material not fully vetted is understood as such. If material is released early, it should ideally be followed by progressive and sustained improvement of the textual corpus. Such progressive improvement can be aided by user feedback and contributions of various kinds. In this type of scenario, opening our work so that everyone may participate can be highly effective.

Increasing the accuracy of electronic texts is a vital editorial goal. The drive toward greater accuracy is ongoing and manifests itself across many different types of projects. A dramatic case in point is *Trove*, the Australian newspaper digitization program. *Trove* began with a soft launch in 2007, providing no press releases and relying instead on word of mouth so that usage would increase at a gradual rate (though now Rose Holley, Digital Librarian at the National Library of Australia, manages more than 30,000 volunteers). Volunteers needed no advance training because of the relative simplicity of comparing a transcription generated by OCR with an image and then correcting the transcription as necessary. The project presents volunteers with a screen split between an image from a microfilmed original on one side and a transcription on the other. The interface is simple and largely self-explanatory, including an option to "fix this text." Clicking this link opens a text box that allows for editing and saving of a revised transcription. The corrected copy is then stored in an SQL database. If vandalism occurs at any time, the project can roll back to an earlier state of the transcription.

Intrigued by the site, I decided to try a search for "Walt Whitman" in Australian newspapers. To correct articles, I needed to first solve a "captcha" test ("Completely Automated Public Turing test to tell Computers and Humans Apart"). Even allowing for this delay, I was able to correct text within seconds. Some articles were reasonably accurate, and the few changes needed were obvious ones. For example, I encountered this short news item:

> Walt Whitman.
> London, October 27. – **WaltWfcitman**, the
> American poet, is reported to be in a
> critical state of health. He is in his 72nd
> year.

And another:

> Walt Whitman.
> LOaNDoi, Wednoeday.-**Walt Whitman**,
> the Ameriean poet, who has been seriously
> ill for some time, is now reported to be in a
> critical condition.

In both of these cases, the original newspaper had no spelling errors. The problems stemmed entirely from the translation of the image into text by the OCR software.

The print quality of early Australian newspapers is often poor, because the first printing presses were those that had been withdrawn from service in England, and a lack of suitable paper in the colony only made matters worse (Holley, 2009).

The OCR of a Tasmanian newspaper, *The Cornwall Chronicle* from 3 April 1858, clarifies why social editing is so important, why we have to pin our hopes on crowd-sourcing, given the size of *Trove* and given how impracticable it would be to clean it all by paid library staff:

> for the chlmnev eiretp aai Her Majesty (lie
> Quocn.'
> Here is another stloct i!ioi:glit ? -
> ' The thought struck me Hie other d«y
> that the Lord will have in heaven somo --(
> thoso very big sinncif that have guile furili-'i
> astray llun anybody that cwv livid, the must
> extraordinary e'ltrnv^ausviB ol vice, jibt to
> m.iko themelndy cumiilute liy eingirg eomo oi
> thoao supijtiiu notes ivttie.lt you &nd I, bevausti
> wo Imve not (jouu .... Sir aniay, will never 'ja
> »l.ln io inter. I »uii-W H-liolher nr.o Im*
> stepped into this e'n.ipi'l Ihn iiioriiing wIkjiii
> God has selected to Uke ? id of Iliosf *!(-;
> uoteB in tlw scale 1 1 ivnise'; I'crhapi tlwve is
> on9 p'lch h'e. li.! how will euch. a one
> mug, if grace – flea (jiace – ahall have mercy
> upon him.'

Within *Trove* as a whole, it is unclear what the relative proportions are of accurate to inaccurate OCR. I suspect that even with the progress made thus far this comment about the collection is an understatement: "digital outputs (image quality, OCR text) may not be good enough to enable adequate full text retrieval or to meet user expectations" (Holley, 2009).

Fortunately, as indicated, Rose Holley and the *Trove* team have erected few barriers to participation: volunteers are not even required to get a log-in. The process of correcting text can be strangely satisfying and captivating: some volunteers are so passionately committed to *Trove* that they have worked up to 50 hours per week. The project encourages these individuals by listing the names of those who have corrected the most lines of text, updating their totals as the work progresses. In "Crowdsourcing: how and why should libraries do it?" Holley (2010) provides guidance for others interested in initiating their own crowdsourcing projects. The overall success of the Australian initiative has encouraged similar newspaper projects elsewhere, including at the National Library of Finland and the National Library of Vietnam. In the United States, digitized newspaper sites that offer public text correction and transcription include the Louisville *Leader* (from the University of Louisville Library); Cambridge, Massachusetts, newspapers (from the Cambridge Public Library); Tennessee newspapers (from the University of Tennessee Library); and Virginia newspapers (from the State Library of Virginia).

Like Rose Holley, Laura Mandell is keenly interested in improving the accuracy of electronic texts generated through OCR. Mandell and 18thConnect.org, an organization she leads, have developed TypeWright, a tool designed to improve the OCR texts generated from Gale's *Eighteenth Century Collections Online (ECCO)*. She explains her reliance on Gamera, an open-source program developed by Professor Ichiro Fujinaga of McGill University:

> Because Gamera was originally created for recognizing musical characters, it is less dependent than other OCR software on recognizing characters only if they occur on the same line as others. This feature is valuable for scanning texts produced before 1820 because the characters in those texts are often not evenly aligned along a baseline, the result of the punch not being situated in the matrix with mathematical precision when the type was made. We have already been able to train Gamera to distinguish between the long s and the lowercase f, something that was previously possible only through dictionary look-up. There are, however, some things Gamera may not do as well as Gale's OCR, so we are further developing automated correction, and the centerpiece of our process is a crowd-sourced correction tool. (Mandell, 2011:302)

Through a grant from the Andrew Mellon Foundation, Mandell and her team are able to train Gamera on a particular set of fonts commonly used in the eighteenth century. The TypeWright correction tool enables crowdsourced correction and the "training" of OCR engines (what Mandell calls an optimization of human–computer interaction). The corrected texts make possible improved searching and analysis of this material. Mandell has negotiated an agreement with Gale that allows for the release of the page images and the corrected text from Gale's copyright claim. This innovative agreement is a mutually beneficial swap: Gale benefits from an improved product and better search results as they gradually replace deeply flawed texts with ones corrected at no expense; scholars benefit also from the improved product and from the growth of open-access content.

OCR is only one way that errors and inconsistencies get introduced into digital texts. The *Text Creation Project* (TCP), a vast undertaking centered at the University of Michigan, creates encoded electronic text editions of early printed books. TCP staff transcribe and mark up the text from the millions of page images in ProQuest's *Early English Books Online*, Gale Cengage's *Eighteenth Century Collections Online*, and Readex's *Evans Early American Imprints*. The TCP's tag lines – "Transcribed by hand. Owned by libraries. Made for everyone" – are effective, but the texts they have created nonetheless still need a good deal of amelioration. They employ vendors to do the transcription, and the results are often problematic.

Efforts are now under way to improve these texts. In "How to fix 60,000 errors," Martin Mueller (2013) describes AnnoLex, a project making a "systematic effort to harness the energy and imagination of undergraduates as editors and explorers of old plays in new forms." Based on electronic texts first developed by the TCP, *AnnoLex* is a collection of 630 Early Modern English plays, pageants, and other entertainments by non-Shakespearean writers – a corpus of approximately 15 million words. Recognizing that the TCP transcriptions contain many errors and omissions, Mueller has identified a group of undergraduate students to improve these texts. Unlike the example of *Trove*, the problem here is not dirty OCR but instead inadequate or inconsistent transcription and encoding. Mueller encourages the creation of "Young Scholar" editions, "where proofreading of professional quality is a *sine qua non*" (Mueller, 2013).

With smaller projects, concerns about accuracy and authority intensify, because these projects ordinarily focus on canonical writers whose verbal choices and even punctuation practices – witness the attention given to Emily Dickinson's dashes – are closely scrutinized. More focused editorial work has typically emphasized painstakingly careful treatment of the text (however text is conceived) and contextualization of it through an introduction, annotations, and other apparatus. This approach highlights the writing of an original creator or creators and relies on the expertise of the editorial team. The highest level of expertise is not required for every aspect of editorial work, however, and sound results can be achieved with user-generated content, assuming the right checking and controls are in place. In short, involving our users does not lead inevitably to a relaxation of scholarly standards.

The *Bentham Project* at University College London successfully blends user engagement and high scholarly standards in its long-term editing of *The Collected Works of Jeremy Bentham* (projected to be 70 volumes, and under way since the 1950s). The *Bentham Project* was motivated to experiment with crowdsourcing because of the truly vast amount of content it faces – 60,000 manuscript folios (approximately 30 million words) – and because of the languishing state of the print edition. Significantly, the project's work on the utilitarian philosopher maintains a commitment to creating an "authoritative" edition even while experimenting with Transcribe Bentham, an effort to crowdsource the transcription of manuscript material. Some of these manuscripts are dauntingly complex and all but illegible. Every transcription submitted by a volunteer to the *Bentham Project* is examined by paid staff and, where necessary, corrected.

The *Bentham Project* had good fortune in gaining publicity from a *New York Times* article by Patricia Cohen (2010), and the novelty of their undertaking also served them well. One early article on the *Bentham Project*, "Transcription maximized; expense minimized? Crowdsourcing and editing *The Collected Works of Jeremy Bentham*," expressed worries about the cost-effectiveness of crowdsourcing, since initially the amount of time paid staff had to spend setting up the infrastructure and protocols along with vetting the contributions seemed to amount to more than would have been spent had the staff just transcribed the materials directly themselves (Causer *et al.*, 2012:130–3). Fortunately, as the *Bentham Project* refined the system, it ultimately became cost-effective, a crucial result given the limited availability of grant funding. The project coordinators have discovered that "crowd sifting" may be a more exact term than crowdsourcing. After they established their system and located a handful of "super transcribers" – a small group of people who have done the majority of the transcriptions – the results were favorable. That is, out of many volunteers, relatively few people transcribed more than one or two documents. In fact, the "overwhelming bulk of the transcription has been done by fifteen 'Super Transcribers', who comprise the strong core of *Transcribe Bentham*, and whose work generally requires minimal editorial intervention" (Causer and Terras, 2014). The coordinators of this project foresee a time when some of the super transcribers can help with the vetting of other volunteer contributions. Appropriately, if a transcription is used, the volunteer is credited for his or her contribution to the edition. Causer and Terras (2014) analyze the remarkable improvements made after the initial period of experimentation.

Tackling material even more complicated than that of the *Transcribe Bentham* project, Ray Siemens has led efforts to transcribe the Devonshire Manuscript, a document containing the widely varying scripts of its assorted authors. Composed in the 1530s and early 1540s, the Devonshire Manuscript is a miscellaneous collection of poetry written by an assortment of men and women and now edited by many hands. Siemens' group is attempting to model the social edition in the context of social media. They have created one version described as an "authoritative version of the text, which has undergone a thorough review by an international advisory group of Early Modern and Renaissance scholars" (Crompton and Siemens, 2012). They then make this text available through *Wikibooks* for discussion and commentary. Ultimately the *Wikibooks* edition will be compared with the text established by the scholars and their advisory group. The use of the term "authoritative version" is unfortunate, because we have learned from twentieth-century efforts to create "authoritative" and "definitive" editions how elusive these goals are when new discoveries are frequently made and new approaches to editing emerge. They announce two key goals: (1) to produce the first "truly socially mediated edition of the Devonshire Manuscript for publication," and (2) to "change the role of the scholarly editor from the sole authority on the text to a facilitator who brings traditional and citizen scholars into collaboration through an ongoing editorial process" (Crompton and Siemens, 2012). However, if Siemens' team regards the text as "authoritative," it is not entirely clear why they put it on a wiki. Nor is it clear if their goal in doing so is to prompt readers to comment on passages, thus serving as a type of annotation, or to improve the accuracy of the transcription, or both. Nevertheless, their approach promises to engage their audiences with the scholarship as it is being created. With added participation, we have the potential to increase interest and loyalty and perhaps even to build a community. It is reasonable to hope that we can gain from the new perspectives, fresh insights, and the sheer knowledge brought to bear by the public – or at least that self-selected group interested enough to engage seriously with something like the Devonshire Manuscript.

Convinced of the advantages of community-wide efforts, Peter Robinson, building on his long history of distinguished digital editing, has recently gained support from the University of Saskatchewan to initiate *Textual Communities*. Robinson has been working toward this project for more than a decade, as is clear from his essay "Where we are with electronic scholarly editions, and where we want to be":

> Scholarly electronic editions up to 2003 have rarely extended beyond the model of print technology, either in terms of product (the materials included and the ways they are accessed) or process (the means by which they are made and by which they may be manipulated). However, some edition projects are beginning to explore the possibility of the electronic medium, and others may follow their lead as the basic tools for their making become more widely distributed. Yet this may only be a prelude to a much greater challenge: the making of what may be called fluid, co-operative and distributed editions. (Robinson, 2004:123).

Robinson points out that the amount of work that needs to be done is vast (there are 84 manuscripts of the *Canterbury Tales* alone). Robinson, like so many of us, needs a community of people to locate and procure images, and to transcribe, compare, and analyze documents. He envisions the social editions that will result from scholars and readers working together as the "work of many and the property of all." Robinson acknowledges that this approach will strain "currently deployed data and organizational models" and require rethinking of entrenched practices in the academy, but he rightly notes that the potential benefits are significant (Robinson, undated).

In some ways, of course, it is easiest if one's "user community" is also a group of scholars or students with shared training and assumptions. One example of an editorial community of peers is John Bryant's *Melville Electronic Library* (MEL), a project allowing interested editors and scholars to obtain a log-in and contribute to the editing of Herman Melville's texts. TextLab, a tool created for MEL, enables multiple revision sequences and accompanying narrative explanations to exist together and to be compared, with the aim of deepening understanding of Melville's creative process. Through TextLab – described as a "text and image tool for transcribing and explaining revision" – users can mark up a manuscript image, transcribe the leaf's text using a TEI-XML editor that automates coding, and comment on the nature and sequencing of Melville's revisions (Melville Electronic Library, undated). This technique lowers the barrier to social editing, since filling in boxes is less daunting than is learning the fine points of XML encoding (Interestingly, the *Transcribe Bentham* project uses a similar technique in that they use a bespoke toolbar which adds the relevant XML tags.) If fully realized in practice, Bryant's system, with its emphasis on fluidity (building on his conviction that texts are far more fluid than we customarily acknowledge, existing in different forms and morphing as they move from manuscript to print, from edition to edition, and from early incarnations to later adaptations) will lead to a proliferation of versions. For example, with *Billy Budd*, a work Melville left in manuscript at his death, we will see not only the three significantly different printed versions that appeared at intervals in the twentieth century but also the range of new readings of tangled passages put forth by various editors of MEL (not to mention later theatrical and film versions). We are at the outset of this editorial experiment, and so it is too early to say whether this project will leave readers awash in too much fluidity and multiplicity or will be a resounding success.

These social editing efforts can also be turned to pedagogical purposes. In an approach akin to Bryant's, Elizabeth Dillon and Nicole Aljoe are in the beginning stages of developing the *Early Caribbean Digital Archive*. This project addresses the lack of any "pan-Caribbean digital or analog archive of pre-20th century materials" (Dillon *et al.*, undated). The project aims to "reframe the literary history of the early Caribbean as one where something new is preserved – voices beyond the imperial history of the Caribbean." Dillon and Aljoe plan to invite users – projected to be primarily scholars and their students – to participate in the transcription of early Caribbean texts. As of now, they emphasize compiling texts rather than editing them: in various documents describing the *Early Caribbean Digital Archive* the word "editing" does not appear. They see the first order of business for this project as collecting texts and making them available. Yet editing of some sort occurs willy nilly, with greater or lesser degrees of self-consciousness, whenever a text is transmitted from one state to another. In the past, literary studies have seen editorial efforts lavished on white writers without comparable efforts devoted to writers of color (where is the good scholarly edition of Charles Chesnutt, or the complete correspondence of Paul Laurence Dunbar or W.E.B. Du Bois, for example?). For Caribbean studies, we need both greater access to texts and better-edited texts.

The initial phase of the *Early Caribbean Digital Archive* will focus on acquiring materials from the Anglophone Caribbean, but for this promising project – and for other cultural resources – we need to become multilingual as rapidly as possible. I foresee an increasing reliance on users particularly in efforts to internationalize our resources. In an age of global content production and usage, we need to move scholarly editions beyond the usual monolingual model. Given the time constraints and linguistic limitations of staff on any one project, our best hope for the multilingual development of resources is no doubt through social editing. At the *Walt Whitman Archive* we have worked in recent years to make our site increasingly multilingual and have cultivated translators across many different languages and national traditions. Eventually, we hope to digitize all book-length translations of *Leaves of Grass* published during Whitman's lifetime as well as important translations that appeared after his death. Currently, the first full-length Spanish-language translation, a two-volume German translation of selected poetry and prose by Whitman, two Russian translations that were important in shaping the reception of Whitman in Russia in the early twentieth century, and a translation of the deathbed edition of *Leaves of Grass* in Portuguese (by a Brazilian translator) are available.

Encouraging multilingual editions could be seen as a radical opening up of our work. Another very important way to open our work is through appropriate licensing. We should allow our editions to be used as widely as possible, without restriction, so that our work has the best chance to be preserved and so that it can join forces with unforeseen collaborators. Unfortunately, too often creative commons noncommercial restrictions are imposed. Thoughtful discussions of licensing by Paul Klimpel (2012), Bethany Nowviskie (2011), and others make the case that those of us who have imposed a noncommercial restriction are being short-sighted with this licensing (and for the moment the *Walt Whitman Archive* remains in that camp). The line between commercial and noncommercial is porous and ambiguous. While it may seem counterintuitive, we would probably be wise to *want* our material to be reused without restriction, even if it means that someone else profits. We should not want to stop people from creatively reusing and perhaps improving on what we have created. Open content needs to be fully and truly open, not open only after an author has granted permission.

As we look toward the future of editing, it becomes clear that the magnitude of what we will edit will require changes in method. Overwhelming quantity creates new needs: the US National Archives has collected 8 million emails from the Ronald Reagan and George H.W. Bush administrations, another 20 million from the Clinton administration, and 240 million from the George W. Bush administration. No human will live long enough to read all of them, much less edit them and annotate them with regard to relevant context and (often) accompanying handwritten notes, voice recordings, and video further filling out the historical record. If this material and that of the Obama and future administrations is to receive scholarly treatment in the future, some parts of the editorial work will need to be undertaken by users.

Occasionally, we hear people say that if they can't find something on the Internet, then it doesn't exist at all. Regrettably, our students are sometimes reluctant to enter a library or to work through manuscripts in the archives despite the fact that a staggering amount of material is *not* available online. The Council on Library and Information Resources has studied so-called "hidden collections," and has concluded that cultural institutions "collectively hold millions of items that have never been adequately described and therefore are all but unknown to, and unused by, the scholars it is our mission to serve" (Tabb, 2004:123). A 1998 Association of Research Libraries survey of special collections at 99 North American research universities discovered that 15% of printed volumes, 27% of manuscripts, and at least 35% of video and audio materials remained unprocessed or uncataloged, and thus hidden. Given recent cuts at many state archives and universities, we can be confident that the situation has grown worse in the intervening years. There is, in short, a huge volume of material that is unknown and inaccessible to scholars. One of the key tasks of editorial work, as always, has been to discover and make available material otherwise beyond our ken.

Going forward, we need to be increasingly developing interactive systems and promoting mutual exchange of ideas and information. Users are potentially more engaged when there is less mediation between them and the past. Our earliest online editions approached editing in ways similar to their print brethren – as static intellectual constructs, resources to be consulted and used. Yet changes in the online environment, so-called Web 2.0, have altered what can be done, and, crucially, user expectations about their involvement. The success of crowdsourcing with intrinsically difficult material is heartening. It is not clear how many new crowdsourcing projects the public can sustain, and participant fatigue – or at least lessened interest – may set in when crowdsourcing seems less novel. Crowdsourcing efforts seem most likely to be successful with writers or texts with a huge following.

Does every project need to engage social media, to give users a platform for contributions and commentary, to proceed with crowdsourcing? I think not. Social editing is a new approach that promises to be a big help for some projects, and offering opportunities for commenting on projects or contributing to them can bring advantages that merit consideration. Still, much depends on where a project is in its life cycle. Long-term projects start at one moment of possibility and, inevitably, find themselves in another moment later in their work. Many long-term textual editing projects – think of the Thomas Jefferson, Benjamin Franklin, and Adams Family papers – began in the days of the letterpress edition only to find themselves maturing into a world of online publishing (where they occasionally had to face threats that federal funders would only support open-access development). Even if we favor open-access work, as I do, it is easy to see how historical changes can create dilemmas for a project, say, that established a long-term contract with a publisher well before online publishing was a viable option. To some extent it seems as unfair as it is unavoidable to have the rules changed midstream on a project. For a print project that may be 10 or more volumes into a multi-volume series to have to rethink its editorial procedures, its way of procuring images, its dissemination and preservation plans is both costly and likely to result in an unseemly mix of print and electronic sources – a product neither fully realized nor satisfactory. There may be an analogy here for electronic projects, like the *Walt Whitman Archive*, that began in a Web 1.0 world only now to find themselves in a Web 2.0 world. Should these projects try to realize their original vision or try to be as nimble as possible in reacting to new opportunities? And do such projects have the time, energy, and personnel sufficient to thoroughly revamp how they engage their audiences with the content they now have in place? User-generated content and user involvement is all the rage now, but will it remain so? Perhaps this is a fundamental change that is here to stay, though Web 2.0 markers may one day look like cranks on cars or fax machines – quaint reminders of 2014, the early 1900s, and the 1990s, respectively (Gopnik, 2014).

Walt Whitman's poem "This Compost" provides means for thinking about the theory of social editing. Whitman contemplates corruption, purification, and the mysterious means by which the mass perfects things:

> O how can it be that the ground itself does not sicken?
> How can you be alive you growths of spring?
> How can you furnish health you blood of herbs, roots, orchards, grain?
> Are they not continually putting distemper'd corpses within you?
> Is not every continent work'd over and over with sour dead?
>
> Where have you disposed of their carcasses?
> Those drunkards and gluttons of so many generations?
> …
>
> Behold this compost! behold it well!
> Perhaps every mite has once form'd part of a sick person – yet behold!
> The grass of spring covers the prairies,
> The bean bursts noiselessly through the mould in the garden,
> The delicate spear of the onion pierces upward,
> The apple-buds cluster together on the apple-branches,
> The resurrection of the wheat appears with pale visage out of its graves,
> …
>
> What chemistry!
> That the winds are really not infectious,
> That this is no cheat, this transparent green-wash of the sea which is so amorous
>   after me,

That it is safe to allow it to lick my naked body all over with its tongues,
That it will not endanger me with the fevers that have deposited themselves in it,
That all is clean forever and forever,
That the cool drink from the well tastes so good,
That blackberries are so flavorous and juicy,
That the fruits of the apple-orchard and the orange-orchard, that melons,
    grapes, peaches, plums, will none of them poison me,
That when I recline on the grass I do not catch any disease,
Though probably every spear of grass rises out of what was once a catching
    disease.
Now I am terrified at the Earth, it is that calm and patient,
It grows such sweet things out of such corruptions (Whitman, 1892:285–7)

Whitman's meditations, born out of environmental crises in his own era, can be translated to the corruptions – both textual and environmental – of our own time (Farland, 2007:799). Notwithstanding Whitman's optimism, ultimate transformation and purification is far from guaranteed, and, at least at the textual level much will depend on whether the mass of people can be as powerful as the poet imagined the renewing powers of the earth to be. Perhaps if we get enough editors, or contributors, we have reason to hope we will get a better text or corpus. Establishing a more perfect text is one goal, and just getting hidden or huge texts out there is another, of social editing. "This Compost" speaks to the former idea at the level of its chemistry reflection, to the latter in its attempt to expose the editorial processes of the earth. Whitman recognized the mystery and grandeur and even fear-inducing power of forces beyond the individual as he contemplated the workings of the multitude.

REFERENCES AND FURTHER READING

Adams, T. 2012. Galaxy Zoo and the New Dawn of Citizen Science. *The Guardian | The Observer*, March 17. http://www.theguardian.com/science/2012/mar/18/galaxy-zoo-crowdsourcing-citizen-scientists (accessed February 12, 2014).

Causer, T., and Terras, M. 2014. Crowdsourcing Bentham: beyond the traditional boundaries of academic history. *International Journal of Humanities and Arts Computing* 8 (1), 46–64.

Causer, T., and Wallace, V. 2012. Building a volunteer community: results and findings from Transcribe Bentham. *DHQ: Digital Humanities Quarterly* 6 (2).

Causer, T, Tonra, J., and Wallace, V. 2012. Transcription maximized; expense minimized? Crowdsourcing and editing *The Collected Works of Jeremy Bentham*. *Literary and Linguistic Computing* 27 (2), 119–37.

Cohen, P. 2010. Scholars recruit public for project. *New York Times*, December 27. http://www.nytimes.com/2010/12/28/books/28transcribe.html?pagewanted=all&_r=0 (accessed February 17, 2014).

Crompton, C., and Siemens, R. 2012. The social edition: scholarly editing across communities. http://www.dh2012.uni-hamburg.de/conference/programme/abstracts/the-social-edition-scholarly-editing-across-communities (accessed February 2, 2014).

Devonshire Manuscript. http://en.wikibooks.org/wiki/The_Devonshire_Manuscript/A_Note_on_this_Edition (accessed February 2, 2014).

Dillon, E., Aljoe, N.N., Doyle, B., and Hopwood, E. (undated). The Early Caribbean Digital Archive. http://www.northeastern.edu/nulab/the-early-caribbean-digital-archive/ (accessed February 3, 2014).

Farland, M. 2007. Decomposing city: Walt Whitman's New York and the science of life and death. *ELH* 74 (Winter), 799–827.

Galaxy Zoo Team. 2007. *Galaxy Zoo Newsletter* #1, http://zoo1.galaxyzoo.org/Article_020807.aspx (accessed February 16, 2014).

Gopnik, A. 2014. A point of view: why I don't tweet. *BBC News Magazine*, February 7, http://www.bbc.co.uk/news/magazine-26066325 (accessed Februrary 7, 2014).

Holley, R. 2009. Many hands make light work: public collaborative OCR text correction in Australian historic newspapers. http://www.nla.gov.au/ndp/project_details/documents/ANDP_ManyHands.pdf (accessed February 1, 2014).

Holley, R. 2010. Crowdsourcing: how and why should libraries do it? *D-Lib Magazine* 16 (3/4). http://www.dlib.org/dlib/march10/holley/03holley.html (accessed January 25, 2014).

Jones, S.E. 2014. *The Emergence of the Digital Humanities*. New York: Routledge.

Klimpel, P. 2012. Consequences, risks and side-effects of the license module "non-commercial use only – NC." http://openglam.org/files/2013/01/iRights_CC-NC_Guide_English.pdf (accessed January 20, 2014).

Mandell, L. 2011. Brave new world: a look at 18thConnect. *The Age of Johnson* 21, 299–307.

Melville Electronic Library (undated). Editions. http://mel.hofstra.edu/editions.html (accessed February 17, 2014).

Mueller, M. 2013. How to fix 60,000 errors. Scalable reading blog, https://scalablereading.northwestern.edu/2013/06/22/how-to-fix-60000-errors/ (accessed February 16, 2014).

North American Bird Phenology Program. 2011. https://www.pwrc.usgs.gov/bpp/BPP_Factsheet_2011.pdf (accessed February 9, 2014).

Nowviskie, B. 2011. Why, oh why, CC-BY? http://nowviskie.org/2011/why-oh-why-cc-by/ (accessed January 15, 2014).

Ramsay, S. 2005. In praise of pattern. *Text Technology* 2, 177–90.

Robinson, P. 2004. Where we are with electronic scholarly editions, and where we want to be. *Jahrbuch für Computerphilologie* 5: 123–43. http://computerphilologie.uni-muenchen.de/ejournal.html (accessed January 5, 2014).

Robinson, P. (undated). Textual communities. http://www.textualcommunities.usask.ca/web/textual-community/wiki/-/wiki/Main/ (accessed January 5, 2014).

Siemens, R., Timney, M., Leitch, C., Koolen, C., and Garnett, A., with the ETCL, INKE, and PKP Research Groups. 2012. Toward modeling the *social* edition: an approach to understanding the electronic scholarly edition in the context of new and emerging social media. *Literary and Linguistic Computing* 27 (4), 445–61.

Tabb, W. 2004. "Wherefore are these things hid?" A report of a survey undertaken by the ARL Special Collections Taskforce. *RBM: A Journal of Rare Books Manuscripts, and Cultural Heritage.* 5: 123–6. http://rbm.acrl.org/content/5/2/123.full.pdf+html (accessed February 18, 2014).

Terras, M. 2010. Crowdsourcing manuscript material. http://melissaterras.blogspot.com/2010/03/crowdsourcing-manuscript-material.html (accessed January 17, 2014).

US Geological Survey. 2012. *Preserving science for the ages: USGS data rescue.* USGS Fact Sheet 2012–3078. http://pubs.usgs.gov/fs/2012/3078/pdf/fs2012-3078.pdf (accessed January 29, 2014).

Whitman, W. 1892. *Leaves of Grass*. Philadelphia: David McKay, 1892. Also available at http://www.whitmanarchive.org/published/LG/1891/poems/205 (accessed February 17, 2014).

11

Digital Methods in the Humanities: Understanding and Describing their Use across the Disciplines

Lorna Hughes, Panos Constantopoulos, and Costis Dallas

In the past 20 years, there has been an increased uptake of digital scholarship in the humanities, as evidenced by an increase in "digital humanities" posts, greater funding opportunities to develop digital humanities projects, and the establishment of new digital humanities centers and initiatives around the world (Svensson, 2012). In his introduction to *Debates in the Digital Humanities* (2012), Gold reprised "coverage of the Digital Humanities in popular publications such as the *New York Times*, *Nature*, the *Boston Globe*, the *Chronicle of Higher Education*, and *Inside Higher Ed*" as confirming that the digital humanities is not just "'the next big thing,' as the *Chronicle* claimed in 2009, but simply 'the Thing,' as the same publication noted in 2011 (Pannapacker)."

Digital humanities conferences, journals, and books have proliferated, and additional funding has been allocated to digital humanities initiatives. In the United Kingdom, "Digital Transformations" has been identified as a key funding theme by the Arts and Humanities Research Council (AHRC). Participants are invited to "cross refer" standard research grant applications with this theme, embedding digital humanities approaches more firmly into "traditional" humanities research. Elsewhere, we have seen the establishment of the National Endowment for the Humanities (NEH) Office of Digital Humanities (http://www.neh.gov/divisions/odh) and national initiatives including Huma-Num in France (http://www.huma-num.fr) and DigHumLab in Denmark (http://www.dighumlab.com). The Andrew W. Mellon Foundation estimated in 2004 that "taken together, grants with a technological emphasis in the library and scholarly communication, research in information technology, and other programs, represent just over 20% of total Foundation grant making today" (Bowen, 2005).

This activity has been extensively documented elsewhere (such as in updates in the *Chronicle of Higher Education* on the topic of "digital humanities"), but it is instructive

A New Companion to Digital Humanities, First Edition. Edited by Susan Schreibman, Ray Siemens, and John Unsworth.
© 2016 John Wiley & Sons, Ltd. Published 2016 by John Wiley & Sons, Ltd.

to consider some of the main drivers for these developments. The first is the expansion of freely accessible digital collections created by museums, libraries, archives, and universities, thanks to large-scale investment in the creation of digital content over the past 20 years (JISC, 2007). These initiatives have increasingly made available the primary source materials for the study of literature, history, linguistics, classics, musicology, performance studies, and related disciplines. Primary resources are the foundation of scholarship, and ease of access to their digital surrogates has led to a ubiquity around the adoption of digital humanities approaches (Ell and Hughes, 2013). The second is the development of web-based digital tools and approaches, making it easier to create, analyze, and share digital research. Specifically, Web 2.0 technologies, and the transition from static web pages to the creation of an online environment that supports greater interactivity with digital content, as well as the managing and recording of this interaction, have changed the way that the World Wide Web is used, especially through social media, into a participatory culture (Dafis *et al.*, 2014). This has led to the widest dissemination of research that integrates primary sources and digital approaches. Leading on from this, the third factor is the increasing recognition of the value of interdisciplinary scholarship, where humanities, scientific, and engineering disciplines can collaborate and add value to each other's research. In the USA, this has been seen in initiatives like the NEH *Digging into Data* challenge, which has funded a great deal of research that is highly collaborative. In the UK, the Arts and Humanities e-Science initiative ran from 2005 to 2008 to investigate collaborative approaches to addressing new research challenges (archived documentation can be found at http://www.ahessc.ac.uk).

This proliferation of digital content, its dissemination, and greater interdisciplinary collaboration has led to the flourishing of "digital humanities," but it has also led to calls for a better articulation and definition of what constitutes "digital humanities." Definitions of digital humanities are as prolific as the field itself (Kirschenbaum, 2010:60), but frequently cited as an initial conceptual framework are the "scholarly primitives." This was used in the context of the digital humanities by Unsworth (2000) to denote the basic functions that have been common to scholarship across the disciplines: discovering, annotating, comparing, referring, sampling, illustrating, and representing.

Unsworth's conceptualization echoes earlier research on scholarly information behavior which sought to identify the information processes and needs underlying the work of scholars as they seek, manage, and use primary sources and secondary information resources (Stone, 1982; Ellis, 1993; Bates *et al.*, 1995; Palmer and Neumann, 2002). This is brought to bear on the definition of requirements and affordances of information services and infrastructures in the digital environment (University of Minnesota Libraries, 2006; Palmer *et al.*, 2009; Benardou *et al.*, 2013). In fact, understanding the humanities research process as a special case of a business process has been recognized as a crucial condition to ensure that planned digital infrastructures serve the needs of scholars (Bearman, 1996; American Council of Learned Societies, 1998). As it has been argued, the rise of digital scholarship calls for "a broader examination of the methodology and practice of the humanities, and of the function of information resources and scholarly communication," and for the identification of "scholarly tasks corresponding with specific 'modes' of research [to be] matched with a tool-set of systems and interface capabilities (e.g., annotation and attribution, comparison and presentation, synthesis)" (Dallas, 1999). The emergence of digital infrastructures such as DARIAH, CLARIN, and EHRI in the context of the European Commission's e-Infrastructures program led to several studies drawing from an examination of scholarly research processes to develop insights on the capabilities of these infrastructures (Benardou *et al.*, 2010; Speck and Links, 2013; Blanke and Hedges, 2013).

Reconceptualizing Unsworth's "scholarly primitives," the common elements of humanistic inquiry, as *methods* that constitute the basis of analog and digital scholarship is a useful place to start to build a systematic account of digital humanities in action. Thinking of the "digital methods" used in digital humanities as the "scholarly primitives" done in a digital way is a useful way to reflect on the practice of digital humanities as a means of deploying the technical "state of the art" to humanistic inquiry. Simply put, doing digital humanities involves the creation of an academic workspace where scholarly methods assume the form of computer-based techniques that can be used to create, analyze, and disseminate research and pedagogy.

A definition of digital methods in the humanities was proposed in 2007 by the arts-humanities.net project, based at King's College, London:

"Methods" refer to the computational methods used by artists and humanists. Computational methods are defined as the following:

1. The term "method" broadly denotes all the techniques and tools that are used to gain new knowledge in the various academic fields that constitute the arts and humanities.
2. A method is a computational one if it is either based on ICT (i.e., database technology), or critically dependent on it (i.e., statistical analysis).
3. Methods are used in the creation, analysis and dissemination of digital resources.

Looking at this definition, the dependencies in the use of digital methods are clear. The use of these methods is part of a scholarly ecosystem where they are applied to digital content, and they inform the use of computational tools for analysis. For example, a scholar may use a high-resolution digital image of a medieval manuscript (content) as the source on which they use a shared annotation technique (method) using a digital editing platform like KILN (tool).[1] This leads to a conceptualization of the process of digital humanities having *content*, *tools* and *methods* as its core elements. Digital *content* is the raw primary source material of research; digital *tools* enable the interpretation and analysis of this raw material; and expertise in scholarly *methods* – both tried and tested, and emerging – gives the researcher a framework for accomplishing results in the digital workspace.

Digital methods – including text analysis and mining, image analysis, moving image capture and analysis, and quantitative and qualitative data analysis – can be found at a key point of intersection between disciplines, collections, and researchers. Data-rich disciplines (e.g., archaeology, library and information science, and musicology) have refined new ICT methods, and within the data-driven sciences research methods have emerged around data and information processes. The use of advanced

ICT methods can produce significant benefits in arts and humanities scholarship. They can enhance existing research methods (for example, by harnessing the processing power of high-performance computing to allow large datasets to be searched quickly and efficiently, or in complex or novel ways); and they enable new research methods (for example, hyperspectral imaging of manuscripts). Sometimes, the use of digital methods comes about through collaboration with other disciplines, and the adoption of their methods to humanities source materials. For example, a UK Arts and Humanities e-Science program project, *REACH* (Researching e-Science Analysis of Census Holdings, http://www.ucl.ac.uk/dh/reach), based at University College London, applied record linkage research methods developed by physicists working on the *AstroGrid* project to carry out pattern-matching of data in historical census datasets (Hughes, 2011). These examples also demonstrate how the use of digital research methods in the humanities binds practitioners to research infrastructures in "ways that are deeper and more explicit than we are generally accustomed to in scholarship and depend on networks of people" (Kirschenbaum, 2010).

The use of digital content, tools, and methods is transforming humanities research through greater access to materials and new modes of collaboration and communication. These approaches facilitate the type of research that changes the paradigms of understanding and creates new knowledge in two ways:

- Firstly, by facilitating and enhancing existing research, by making research processes easier via the use of computational tools and methods.
- And secondly, by enabling research that would be impossible to undertake without digital resources and methods, and asking new research questions that are driven by insights only achievable through the use of new tools and methods (Hughes, 2011).

Gregory Crane, Humbolt Professor at the University of Leipzig, has referred to this work as *e-Wissenschaft*, reflecting that the best examples of digital humanities are a new intellectual practice with elements that distinguish qualitatively the practices of intellectual life in this emergent digital environment from print-based practices (Crane, 2009).

The best way to truly understand the role of methods in digital humanities, therefore, is to examine and observe digital humanities in practice, to understand the many ways that digital content, tools, and methods are crucial to arts and humanities research, expanding and transforming scholarship in all aspects of data capture, investigation, analysis, modeling, presentation, and the communication of the results of this work to the widest possible audience using traditional and non-traditional publishing approaches. This enables greater engagement with research, and use and reuse of research data, than was previously possible.

Digital Methods Identified: The AHRC ICT *Methods Network*

From 2005 to 2008 in the UK, the AHRC funded a research support initiative called the ICT *Methods Network* (http://www.methodsnetwork.ac.uk). This was the first interdisciplinary program of its kind, with the groundbreaking remit of understanding the impact of digital content, tools, and methods on humanities and arts scholarship. The

Network was based at King's College, London, but worked in partnership with researchers and institutions around the UK to establish a network of over 50 activities that showcased digital humanities in practice, in order to build awareness of transformative and innovative ICT-based research across the disciplines. Through its activities and publications, the Network gathered evidence of the value and broader impact of digital collections, and the ICT methods, tools, and collaborations that underpin their use in the scholarly research cycle. Through this, the impact of digital scholarship could be seen in several ways:

- generating new research questions and findings
- doing traditional research in significant new ways
- extending the evidence base for research
- institutional and disciplinary impact
- fostering the impact of the digital humanities on developments in ICT in other fields (e.g., the impact of the Text Encoding Initiative on the development of XML)
- extending the social and economic impact of the arts and humanities (by expanding the communities of users).

Initial Classification and Expression of Digital Methods

One of the most significant outputs of the AHRC ICT *Methods Network* was an initiative to document the use of digital content, tools, and methods and articulate them formally. The use of digital methods requires an understanding of the method in question, its suitability in the context in which it is to be applied, and exemplars of its application. Accordingly, there was a need to express the interaction between content, analytical and interpretive tools and technologies, methodological approaches, and the communities of practice that have emerged around their use. The Network built on two existing pieces of work that had been developed to articulate digital research methods in the arts and humanities, contributing to the awareness of the need for better documentation and descriptions of digital methods and the scholarly ecosystems that underpin them.

"Methodological Commons"

The first was an expression of the "Methodological Commons" as an intellectual and disciplinary map (or "ecology") of digital arts and humanities in the context of modeling humanities research processes. The map was developed by Harold Short with Willard McCarty at the Centre for Computing in the Humanities (CCH) at King's College, and was initially presented at an Association for Literary and Linguistic Computing (ALLC) meeting in 2002 (also published in McCarty, 2005). The map went through various refinements and it continues to evolve, although as a matter of presentation rather than the underlying concept.[2] The thinking behind the "Methodological Commons" also informed the development of the AHRC ICT Methods Network, co-directed by Short (Greengrass and Hughes, 2008).

In Short and McCarty's model, the "Methodological Commons" has the following core elements:

- technical methods from discipline areas outside the arts and humanities, e.g., engineering and computer science, e.g., for mining, visualization, and modeling of digital content
- new modes of collaboration across disciplines and communities, particularly in partnership with scientific, engineering, and cultural heritage science disciplines
- combinations of data types, technical methods, and multiple technologies are frequently needed, for example, combinations of text, database, image, time- based data (video or sound), and geographic information systems (GIS)
- formal methods for analysis and design of source data and modeling of possible technical approaches
- methods for working with large-scale data sources, as well as aggregating materials from multiple collections or sources.

The AHDS Taxonomy of Computational Methods

In a separate initiative in 2003, Sheila Anderson and Reto Speck of the UK's Arts and Humanities Data Service (AHDS) began development of the *Taxonomy of Computational Methods in the Arts and Humanities* (or *ICT Methods Taxonomy*) as part of the Projects and Methods Database project (Speck, 2005).[3] This taxonomy classified digital methods used in the creation, management, and sustainability (the "digital curation" life cycle) of digital resources in the arts and humanities, and developed a controlled vocabulary. The taxonomy classified methods by behavioral similarity at two levels:

- *Content types* describe the type of digital resource created, for example: text; image, audiovisual data, dataset, or structured data; 3D object; or spatial dataset.
- *Function types* describe the broad functions commonly undertaken in digital resource creation processes. These include: *capture*, i.e., the conversion of analog information into (raw) digital data (via "digitization"); *structuring and enhancement*, i.e., the organization and integration of the data captured from one or various sources into a uniform conceptual framework, via, for example, normalization, standardization, or enhancement of data, or markup; *analysis*, i.e., the extraction of information/knowledge/meaning from the resource; and *publication and presentation*, i.e., the digital presentation or communication of the resource. These functions are not mutually exclusive but can overlap in significant ways. Therefore, for the purposes of the taxonomy, certain computational methods can be classified under more than one function type heading (e.g., the method "Record linkages" is classified as both as a structuring/enhancing method and as an analytical one).

In 2007, the AHRC ICT *Methods Network* built on this existing taxonomy to include the methods used for the *use and analysis* of digital content and its wider *dissemination*, including *interaction* with digital content. The expanded taxonomy was then used to classify the digital methods used by approximately 400 research projects funded by the AHRC that had a digital output, in the context of providing a detailed description of these projects to serve as exemplars of digital humanities as practiced in the UK at that time. This was published online in the arts-humanities.net resource.

The taxonomy was also adopted by the Digital Humanities Observatory (DHO) in Ireland (which adopted it as the basis of their DRAPIER project, http://dho.ie/drapier), and by the Oxford University Digital Humanities Programme, which has refined it further and uses it currently as a means of describing digital humanities projects that are based at Oxford (http://digital.humanities.ox.ac.uk/Methods/ICT-methodology.aspx). The current structure of the taxonomy, as maintained by the Oxford University Digital Humanities Programme, is simple. It has the following high-level categories:

- communication and collaboration
- data analysis
- data capture
- data publishing and dissemination
- data structuring and enhancement
- practice-led research
- strategy and project management.

Within each of these are sublevels, where more detail is provided. For example, the "data analysis" level, which is defined as the "extraction of information, knowledge or meaning from a digital resource, using techniques such as searching and querying or feature measurement," contains the following sublevels:

- audiovisual analysis
- searching and linking
- statistical analysis
- text analysis
- other analysis
- visualization.

To drill down further, the subcategories of method within "text analysis" are: collating, collocating, content analysis, indexing, parsing, stemmatics, and text mining.

For each method, the user can link directly to examples of projects that use them. Because of this essential link with projects, the taxonomy provides a framework for understanding how digital methods sit within and enable existing research practice in the arts and humanities, and how they might be replicated by others in the field. Presenting digital methods in this project-based way also makes clear how methods work with content and tools, and overcomes the distinction between defining methods by content type or function, as arts-humanities.net enabled the user to search methods in both ways. The framework of existing activity also shows work that is yet to be done, and can be used to inform decisions about applying tools or methods in other relevant contexts. However, because the context of projects was so essential to understanding the underlying descriptions of digital methods, it became clear as the funded period of arts-humanities.net came to an end (in 2011) that such "registries" only have value if the data that underpins them is constantly updated, an activity that requires dedicated, funded attention.

The methods taxonomy as a concept has been adopted by DARIAH-DE, the German arm of the European Research Infrastructure initiative, *DARIAH* (Digital Research Infrastructure for the Arts and Humanities, http://www.dariah.eu) and the US-based Bamboo Digital Research Tools wiki (*BambooDiRT*) project (http://dirt.projectbamboo. org). The resulting Taxonomy of Digital Research Activities in the Humanities (TaDiRAH, http://tadirah.dariah.eu) refined the AHDS/Oxford taxonomy further, seeking community input to enrich the data, adopting a collective intelligence approach rather than dedicated, funded data gathering. The current high-level categories in the taxonomy can be seen below.

Research activities

1 **Capture**
conversion
data recognition
discovering
gathering
imaging
recording
transcription

2 **Creation**
designing
programming
web development
writing

3 **Enrichment**
annotating
cleanup
editing

4 **Analysis**
content analysis
network analysis
relational analysis
spatial analysis
structural analysis
stylistic analysis
visualization

5 **Interpretation**
contextualizing
modeling
theorizing

6 **Storage**
archiving
identifying
organizing
preservation

7 **Dissemination**
collaboration
commenting
communicating
crowdsourcing
publishing
sharing

Scoping Digital Methods in Practice: The Network for Digital Methods in the Arts and Humanities (NeDiMAH)

The best way to understand the use of digital methods in the humanities is by example. However, this means understanding their role not only in a specific project, but also in regular scholarly practice, which can provide practical demonstrations of how digital content, tools, and methods are transforming scholarship. This can expand the above attempts to classify and define digital methods, and extend the existing taxonomy to include the broadest range of methods used across the disciplines. As described above, there has been a large-scale investment in digital content and international initiatives to support the curation, management, and preservation of this content. There have also been investigations in ways that researchers' use of digital content has become integrated into their research practice (for example, Houghton *et al.*, 2003). Nevertheless, remarkably little work has been done in scoping widest scholarly practice in the digital humanities. There has been very little investment in researching what scholars actually do with digital content in terms of advanced research, and how the "methodological commons" and the new ways of working it enables are transforming research. Apart from the UK's AHRC ICT *Methods Network* and the DHO in Ireland, few initiatives have had this as their remit.

In 2011, the European Science Foundation (ESF) addressed this gap by funding NeDiMAH, a Research Network Program on Digital Methods in the Arts and Humanities (http://www.nedimah.eu). NeDiMAH was funded through support from 16 ESF member organizations[4] and the Network's program was operational from 2011 to May 2015. The core objective of NeDiMAH was to examine the practice of, and evidence for, digital research in the arts and humanities across Europe. Through a series of network events, it built collaborations and networking between the community of European scholars active in this area, as well as other stakeholder groups from scientific disciplines, technical areas, libraries, archives and museums, and those engaged in the creation and curation of scholarly and cultural heritage digital collections. The key area of distinction between NeDiMAH and the AHRC ICT Methods Network is that the taxonomy of classification of digital methods developed by the Methods Network was very much based on projects, whereas NeDiMAH sought to scope practice that has become embedded into research work across the scholarly life cycle. Building on this information, NeDiMAH activities and research have contributed to the classification and expression of digital arts and humanities via three key outputs:

- a map visualizing the use of digital research across Europe;
- an ontology of digital research methods; and
- a collaborative, interactive online forum for the European community of practitioners active in this area.

Through a structured set of activities, NeDiMAH built a collaborative forum for arts and humanities researchers that enables them to describe, develop, and share research methods that allow them to create, and make best use of, digital methods, tools, and content.

It also sought to address the need to understand the underlying infrastructures – human and technical – that enable this work. NeDiMAH's work was therefore based on collaboration with the EC-funded DARIAH and CLARIN (*Common Languages Resources and Technology Infrastructure*, http://www.clarin.eu) e-research infrastructure projects, as well as other national and pan-national initiatives (including, for example, the *European Holocaust Research Infrastructure* [EHRI, http://www.ehri-project.eu], the *COnnecting REpositories* [CORE] project, and the *Collaborative European Digital Archive Infrastructure* [CENDARI]). NeDiMAH also investigated the impact of digital research methods on scholarly publishing, especially the evaluation of digital scholarship and its outputs. NeDiMAH showcased the ways in which arts and humanities researchers have engaged with practitioners from other disciplines, and how arts and humanities tools and methods support collaboration within this environment. This fostered a human, collaborative infrastructure, and a practical exemplar of the "methodological commons" that underpins digital arts and humanities scholarship.

The structure of NeDiMAH supported methodological investigation across the disciplines. Activities were organized by six thematic working groups, each focusing on a specific area of research where disparate methods, tools, and content were used by interdisciplinary communities of practice, linking disparate methods and approaches researched by small groups of specialists or individuals. The charge to each working group was to consider specific methodological areas from three areas of scientific focus:

- investigating the use of related methods and gathering information about specific European projects that use them;
- analysis of current practice, with a view to developing meaningful case studies, as well as understanding which methods and technologies are accepted as "best practice" and to identify where gaps exist; and
- modeling ways in which the method can be applied across the disciplines in scholarly practice.

Some findings of each working group are outlined below, with an overview of the specific methodological areas addressed based on the research carried out by each group.

1 *Space and Time*

As high-level, cross-cutting concepts, space and time provide important reference points that transcend disciplinary boundaries in the digital humanities. ICT approaches to representing and analyzing these dimensions include GIS, statistical distribution metrics, dynamic web mapping, geo-referencing, network analysis, mobile computing, augmented reality, and semantic annotation of places, periods, and events. Geospatial technologies are increasingly widespread in the arts and humanities, often in partnership with cultural heritage and memory organizations. ICT methods for dealing with time have an equally high potential of opening up new avenues of research. This working group explored the concepts of "place" (spatial concepts), "period" (temporal concepts), and "event" (concepts intersecting space and time) as both coordinate-based and conceptual entities. The working group also identified current and emerging methods for the representation and analysis of the data, and identification of the current state of multidisciplinary approaches to time and space modeling in the humanities. The working group identified a baseline of digital methods as a means to evaluate and address the use of those that emerge and to assess their implementation for practical work in the area of cultural heritage as well as for further research (NeDiMAH Space and Time working group, 2011). The main disciplinary areas that contribute methods in this area are geography, history, and archaeology, as well as linguistics, performance, social sciences, and literature.

The key methods used for analyzing and visualizing space and time require spatial and temporal data, and temporal GIS (for example, http://www.hgis-germany.de), or spatial databases such as PostGIS tools (Obe and Hsu, 2010). These also require the creation, maintenance, and application of other data, including thesauri, gazetteers, and other conceptual schemes,[5] and atlases (e.g., the *Digital Atlas of Roman and Medieval Civilization* [DARMC], http://darmc.harvard.edu/icb/icb.do), to describe specific entities such as places, periods, and events; and spatial and temporal ontologies that describe the relationships between them.[6] While spatial and temporal representation and analysis methods have been primarily implemented by geographers and historians, archaeological methods also have the widest applicability, including geo-electric and geomagnetic prospecting, and ground radar (e.g., *ArcLand: Archaeo Landscapes Europe* [www.arcland.eu]). Also of increasing importance are semantic methods of extracting chronology from narrative sources, and methods of reducing uncertainty about place from descriptions in archival sources (Eide, 2013). Because of this inclusion of a conceptual approach to place, period, and event, methods for mapping and representing uncertainty are also of great importance in this area (Kauppinen *et al.*, 2010).

2   *Information Visualization*

Visualization refers to techniques used to summarize, present, and enact rich materials visually, and it is becoming increasingly important as an integrated part of the research processes in the humanities. Visualization is taken to include different types of interaction (e.g., sensor technology), technologies (including high-resolution and multiple displays), as well as materials such as geographical datasets, images, 3D representations, graphs, tables, networks, and archival materials. Technology and research methodology can together improve research in the humanities. However, these technologies need to be used critically, particularly in areas rich in ambiguity and complexity.

Visual components in digital environments are used for both description and analysis. They bring together research methods from disciplines including archaeology, literature, classics, information science, architecture, and history. The field includes methods for selecting data, data capture, modeling and representation, searching and querying data, and visual representation. These include 3D modeling and 3D visualization, to create three-dimensional reconstructions of cultural heritage objects or material culture, and motion capture. As visualization can relate to exact representations (for example, architectural models, or archaeological models created through 3D laser scanning, e.g., the *Archaeology in Saxony* project [http://www.archaeologie. sachsen.de/951.htm]), reconstructions based on incomplete or fragmented information (such as reconstructions of historic buildings from descriptions or old maps), and visualizations of literary or artistic worlds, the field must address elements of game theory, and the development of editions and layers of digital narratives. See, for example, the *IVANHOE* game (www.ivanhoegame.org), for an integration of literary narrative and game theory to create a visualized environment. Again, methods for representing uncertainty are essential (Latour, undated), whether spatial or temporal, as covered in projects like *Mapping the Jewish Communities of the Byzantine Empire* (http://www.byzantinejewry.net) or in documenting the decision-making process in developing a historic visualization with ambiguous data.[7] This is an area where inter- (and trans-) disciplinarity can also bring in challenges: new tools can be like "Trojan horses," bringing with them epistemological assumptions from their home disciplines (Drucker, 2011).

3   *Linked Data and Ontological Methods*

The use of ontologies, or conceptual models, provides the semantic definitions and clarifications to transform disparate, localized information into a coherent resource, be it within a project or an institution or on a global level. In this way, the use of common or compliant ontologies enables information exchange and integration between heterogeneous sources of information by, for example, Linked Open Data, expressed in compliance with the Resource Description Framework (RDF) standard. A specific theme addressed by the NeDiMAH working group on this topic was ontology-based annotation in text studies, including methods for the representation and analysis of text. This is a new way of approaching text as a computer-based model that can be manipulated for analysis, or compared to related material.

Approaches include the use of the open annotation data model, a method of encoding annotations using RDF, adopted by both the scientific and humanities disciplines. Examples of initiatives using these methods are the *Australian Electronic Scholarly Editing* (AustESE) Framework (http://www.itee.uq.edu.au/eresearch/projects/austese), and the *CaNeDiMAHn Writing Research Collaboratory* (CWRC) (http://www.cwrc.ca), which uses multiple, formal external annotations. These approaches lend themselves well to large-scale collections of digital data that are suitable for data modeling, and in a form from which formal data can be inferred.

4 Building and Developing Collections of Digital Data for Research

The use of ICT methods requires good practice in all stages of the digital life cycle to ensure effective use and reuse of data for research. Building digital collections of data for research involves consideration of the subsequent use and reuse of these collections for scholarship, using a variety of digital methods and tools. The ultimate use of digital materials by researchers is a consideration that impacts on decisions made at every stage of this life cycle: selection, digitization, description, structuring, curation, preservation, and, most importantly, sustainability and access (in terms of authorization and interoperability) over the long term. The way that digital resources end up being used may be unanticipated at the outset; or they may have value for different communities and disciplines than originally intended. Conversely, some digital resources are less "valuable" to scholarship because their creator did not factor methodologies of use into the development of the resources.

Methods that are currently considered in creating digital resources include encoding, that is digitally encoding or enriching digital objects with metadata and markup, including categorization of words or information about the object described. This is typically done using XML, or TEI, or an RDF/linked open data encoding scheme, and the results can be seen in projects like the *Haskala Republic of Letters* (www.jnul.huji. ac.il/eng/smw.html) or the *Controversia et Confessio Projekt* (www.controversia-et-confessio. adwmainz.de). Similarly, corpora building methods have been refined by initiatives in linguistics, theology, or historical studies, to create large-scale text collections including the *British National Corpus* (www.natcorp.ox.ac.uk), the *Digitale Bibliotek* or *TextGrid* (http://www.textgrid.de), and *Monsaterium* (www.monasterium.net).

5 Using Large-scale Text Collections for Research

Digital tools and methods, such as information retrieval and extraction methods (including topic modeling, text and data mining, and statistical analysis), can reveal new knowledge from large amounts of textual data, extracting hidden patterns by analyzing the results and summarizing them in a useful format. The examination of practice in this area by NeDiMAH was informed by the work of corpus linguistics and related disciplines to develop a greater understanding of how large-scale text collections can be used for research.

6   Creating Digital Editions

Digital tools and methods are essential to the transformation of the production and dissemination of scholarly and documentary editing, and can enable interoperability and accessibility of digital data. Digital editions are now establishing themselves as the norm in many areas of philological endeavor, with a number of current methods used in this area, including encoding, annotation, transcription, and collaborative text editing. Examples include the *Women Writers* project (www.wwp.northeastern.edu) or the *Jean Paul Portal* (www.jean-paul-portal.uni-wuerzburg.de). A key focus of this NeDiMAH working group was to document practice with a view to encouraging the wider adoption of those methods, through training and awareness of the IT competencies required in this area.

The NeDiMAH and DARIAH Research Methods Ontology Project

One of the main deliverables of NeDiMAH has been the development of a research methods ontology along with a shared vocabulary for the digital humanities. NeDiMAH has convened an international, interdisciplinary working group for this purpose,[8] which has scoped existing work done on digital humanities taxonomies described above, including the AHDS digital research methods taxonomy, the Oxford methods taxonomy, the TaDiRAH methods taxonomy, as well as the information organization schemes applied in the DHO, and arts-humanities.net. It has explored the collaborations required to bring this initiative together, building on synergies with the DARIAH-EU Virtual Competency Centre on Research and Education (VCC2), as well as outlining what has been learned about digital methods from research carried out by the six NeDiMAH working groups. The design and implementation of the NeDiMAH Methods Ontology (NeMO) was carried out by researchers from the Digital Curation Unit–IMIS, Athena Research Centre, Greece.

Why an Ontology?

As already mentioned, *content*, *tools*, and *methods* have been identified as core elements of the conceptualization of digital humanities advanced in this study.

Understanding and charting the ecosystem of digital humanities evolves along a major axis, which is the challenge of analyzing and modeling humanities research processes, and includes explicitly specifying the dependencies between content, tools, and methods. This has consistently been the context of inquiry, though often implicit, ever since the early work on scholarly primitives, to later developments on methodological commons, method taxonomies, and NeDiMAH with its multifaceted approach. During the preparatory phase of DARIAH, the need for an explicit model of the research process, capturing the interplay of all the important elements of the eco-system, was identified, and a Scholarly Research Activity Model (SRAM) grounded on empirical evidence was proposed, subsequently validated, and extended in the EHRI project by a research team based in the Athens-based Digital Curation Unit (Benardou *et al.*, 2010, 2013). Finally, NeDiMAH undertook the development of a comprehensive formal model, incorporating existing relevant taxonomies and synthesizing previous relevant research.

A model of the research process should enable the development of, firstly, a common understanding and vocabulary within the digital humanities community; secondly, an environment of interoperable resources and services for discovering, understanding, contributing, and linking content, tools, and methods; and, thirdly, the information base to tackle the fundamental question of "How does the way people work, alone or together, change due to the use of information technology?" To this end, an adequate model of scholarly research process must comprise a set of precisely defined general concepts representing the main elements of the humanities research ecosystem, their intrinsic structure, and the kinds of relations pertaining among them. Such a model is an *ontology*. Taxonomies, on the other hand, are purely hierarchical structures intended to capture a systematic organization of the various kinds of entities in the domain in question (e.g., actors, tools, methods) as specializations or subdivisions of the general concepts, and they are routinely included in an ontology. The distinctive trait of an ontology, in comparison to a taxonomy, is the explicit representation of relations among concepts. These give rise to representations of research processes in the form of semantic networks better suited for associative, exploratory investigations and inferences.

The Scholarly Research Activity Model

One of the outcomes of the earlier work on analyzing and modeling scholarly activity in the DARIAH and EHRI projects by the Digital Curation Unit, IMIS-Athena Research Centre, was the Scholarly Research Activity Model (SRAM) (Benardou *et al.*, 2010, 2013) intended to support the elicitation of requirements, and the design and development of information repositories and services in digital humanities infrastructures. This was inspired on one hand by business process modeling and on the other by activity theory, an approach which views an activity as a "purposeful interaction of a subject with the world," employing appropriate "mediating tools", and fulfilling some objective or motive that in turn is intended to meet a specific need. An activity system is then seen as a hierarchy of activities, composed of conscious actions designed to meet hierarchically structured goals (Engeström, 1987, 2000; Kaptelinin and Nardi, 2007). SRAM was developed on the basis of the CIDOC Conceptual Reference Model (CIDOC CRM, accepted as ISO 21127) ontology for cultural documentation by specializing the relevant CRM general concepts and adding compatible new ones so as to capture research activities in the spirit of activity theory, and to address patterns of use of resources and dependencies among activities as suggested by Malone *et al.* (2003).

SRAM captures information on actors, activities, methods, procedures, resources, formats, tools and services, and goals, including the relations among them (Figure 11.1).

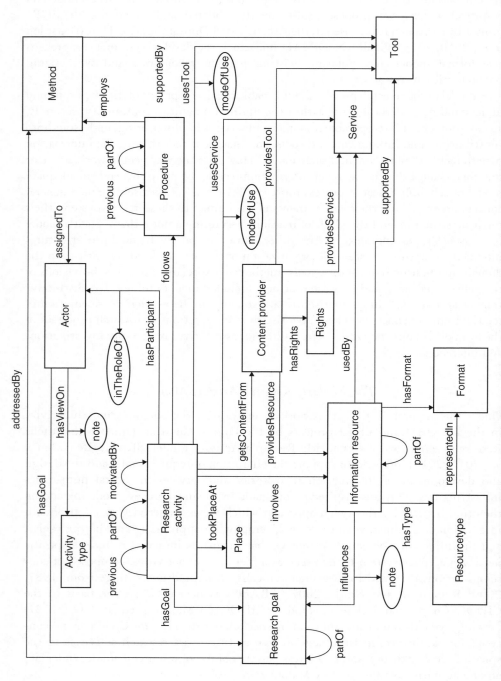

Figure 11.1 The Scholarly Research Activity Model.

The model distinguishes between descriptive and prescriptive views on activities through the concepts of *activity* and *procedure* respectively, while the concept of *method* represents specific ways of working in performing steps of activities or procedures. The concept of *goal* provides the context and drives the steps of research activity and the use of particular resources, methods, and tools. SRAM entities effectively capture the main viewpoints of investigation of the nature of research activity and the use of information resources in its course, while the relations between those entities provide the semantic threads of investigation (Benardou *et al.*, 2013).

NeMO: The NeDiMAH Methods Ontology

The outcome of the research project presented in this chapter is an ontology delivered in both document and machine-readable forms, and a Web service comprising a database containing the ontology definition and the appropriate functionality to support access to and evolution of the ontology. The NeDiMAH Methods Ontology (NeMO) includes types of objects and/or concepts, and their properties and relations, representing the domain of arts and humanities scholarly practice in the digital age. The scope of entities in the ontology encompasses scholarly disciplines and fields, methodologies, techniques, procedures, research data and resources, epistemic objects, research actors, as well as environments, tools, services, and infrastructures. SRAM provided a useful starting point for developing the ontology, since it already complied with an established ontology (CIDOC CRM) of the cultural domain and addressed prevalent concerns in research practice understanding as formalized in CHAT and business process modeling. This approach extends the content, tools and methods triplet to a richer set of basic concepts that enable an integrated description and analysis of research practices from three basic viewpoints: agency, resource, and process (Figure 11.2).

Looking at the analysis of the research practice as a set of interrelated questions, the agency viewpoint addresses *who*, *what*, and *why*, while the process and resource

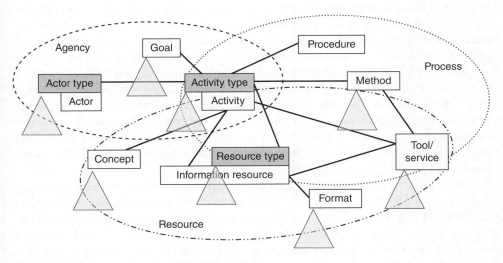

Figure 11.2   The ecosystem of scholarly activity.

viewpoints address respectively the task and object aspects of *what* and *how*. Accordingly, the agency viewpoint comprises notions of activity, actor, and goal; the process viewpoint comprises notions of activity, procedure, method, and tool/service; and the resource viewpoint comprises notions of activity, concept, information resource, format, and tool/service. The common ground of all three viewpoints is, not surprisingly, the central notion of activity. Activity can have structure, defined in terms of both composition from sub-activities and sequence relations; it has time and place of occurrence; and it is related to the actors involved in various roles, to resources and tools used as well as outcomes produced (concepts and resources), to methods employed and possibly established procedures, and to the goals pursued. The notion of goal captures the successive refinement from high-level objectives down to narrower goals to concrete questions, thus enabling, together with the notion of topic, the representation of the research context. This provides an explicit support for reasoning about research practices.

Two major classes of analysis are supported by the NeMO ontology: recording and analyzing empirical evidence collected through field research (e.g., in the form of examples), and recording knowledge and supporting inference at the categorical level. To this end the notions of actor, activity, and resource are complemented by corresponding notions of type. These type notions enable developing and subsuming taxonomic classification schemes under the basic notions of the ontology. Thematic taxonomies, such as the aforementioned ones, can be reviewed for adaptation and integration into this overall scheme, thus contributing to an evolving knowledge base about research practices in the humanities. In this framework, accounts of empirically attested scholarly practice, such as the use of a particular research method by a specific digital humanities research project to process a dataset or body of scholarly evidence into an interpretive model, syllogism, or publication, can be represented as instances of relevant entities and properties of the ontology.

The domain addressed by the ontology encompasses both digital humanities work in the stricter sense, and digitally enabled work by humanities researchers in general. In terms of disciplinary scope, it seeks to include a broad spectrum of humanities disciplines, including those occupied with the study of textual and visual resources, material and intangible cultural heritage, and quantitative and qualitative modes of analysis. It also seeks to cover in equal measure methods of information seeking, use and modification of digital resources used in scholarly practice, and research methods in the proper sense of the word, as they are used by humanities scholars in all phases of the scholarly research life cycle, from the initiation of a research field, idea, or conjecture, to publication and review by the scholarly community. In addition, it is not limited strictly to academic research, but also seeks to model practices of humanities scholars related to academic teaching, and to those supporting the public understanding of scholarly knowledge.

In document form, the ontology includes definitions of entities and properties, and examples of occurrence and use. In machine-readable form, the ontology is defined in RDF/S (RDF Schema), in order to support its use in a wide range of applications accessing registries and knowledge bases that contain information about methods and their context of use. Furthermore, the taxonomic parts of the ontology comply with SKOS (Simple Knowledge Organization System). The compliance with standards indicated above caters for syntactic as well as semantic interoperability between future registries and applications employing NeMO knowledge bases and other CIDOC CRM – and SKOS – compliant information systems in the arts and humanities and in libraries, museums, and archives. Architecturally, the ontology comprises three layers: the lower level captures fine-grained aspects of research practices and is expected to evolve rather dynamically; the middle layer addresses specific but quite broad concepts and is expected to be relatively stable; and the upper layer contains the most general notions and acts as a frame of reference. Finally, the ontology is available through a Web service which offers the ontology definition, examples, use cases, mappings from other taxonomies to the NeMO type system, and the appropriate functionality to support access and evolution.

The NeMO ontology will contribute to the formalization and codification of the expression of work in the digital arts and humanities. It will give greater academic credibility to the digital humanities and support peer-reviewed scholarship in this area, while maximizing the value of national and international e-research infrastructure initiatives by developing a methodological layer that allows arts and humanities researchers to develop, refine, and share research methods that allow them to create and make best use of digital methods and collections. The ontology will help elicit and prioritize the functional requirements for planned digital infrastructures in the arts and humanities on the basis of actual evidence, on what humanities scholars do and need. And most of all, it will contribute to the development of a commonly agreed nomenclature on digital methods in the nascent field of digital humanities: something that typically happens with the maturing and consolidation of a discipline or research domain.

Conclusion

A report commissioned by OCLC mentioned digital humanities scholars who "often consider wrestling with digital methods to be an integral part of their intellectual inquiry" (Schaffner and Erway, 2014:8). One of the reasons for this "wrestling" is perhaps the lack of available, accessible registries that adequately map current methods and show their integration into the digital humanities methodological commons, and their relationships with content and tools, and dependencies across the disciplines. There have been several efforts to overcome this by building taxonomies of digital methods, and the initiative to build on these and develop an ontology of methods is therefore timely. Understanding how methods are used in the digital humanities clarifies the practice and extent of digital humanities, illustrating how it is influenced by, and influences, methodological innovation and development across the academic disciplines, including those outside the humanities. It will make clear to those investing in digital humanities – whether funding agencies or those responsible for institutional investment – what the value and reach of the digital humanities is. It will also help digital humanities to migrate from being a separate entity with obscure language and rituals to becoming part of the accepted suite of research practices available to scholars, and just part of doing not digital research, but good research.

NOTES

1   KILN is a framework for building and deploying complex XML-based websites, and is primarily used for electronic editions, including
the AHRC-funded project *The Cult of Saints in
Wales: Medieval Welsh-language sources and their
transmission* (www.welshsaints.ac.uk). KILN was
developed at the Department for Digital Humanities, King's College, London: https://kclpure.
kcl.ac.uk/portal/en/publications/kiln%284
6591d52-afc1-452e-9223-977f6d118efe%29/
export.html.

2   It was previously maintained on the ALLC
website, but has since been incorporated into
the European Association of Digital Humanities
(EADH) website: http://www.eadh.org.

3   Its aim was to establish a register containing
detailed information on current and recent arts
and humanities research projects using ICT,
and on the computational methods employed
by such projects. It became part of the broader
ICT Guides project (http://www.ictguides.
ac.uk) and was subsequently incorporated into
arts-humanities.net.

4   The contributing member organizations
are: Bulgaria, Bulgarian Academy of Science
(BAS); Republic of Croatia, Croatian Science
Foundation; Denmark, Danish Council of
Independent Research (FKK); Finland, The
Academy of Finland – Research Council for
Culture and Society; France, Centre National
de Recherche Scientifique (CNRS); Germany,
German Research Foundation (DFG);

Hungary, Hungarian Academy of Sciences
(MTA) and the Hungarian Scientific Research
Fund (OTKA); Ireland, Irish Research Council
for the Humanities (IRCHSS); Luxembourg,
Luxembourg National Research Fund (FNR);
Netherlands, Netherlands Organisation for
Scientific Research (NWO); Norway, Research
Council of Norway (NCR); Portugal,
Foundation for Science and Technology (FCT);
Romania, National Research Council (CNCS):
Sweden, Swedish Research Council (VR);
Switzerland, Swiss National Science
Foundation (SNSF); United Kingdom, Arts
and Humanities Research Council (AHRC).

5   This is an area where crowdsourcing methods
for gathering data have been successful,
including *Cymru1900Wales* (http://www.cym
ru1900wales.org).

6   These currently mostly address geometric and
topological relations. A resource indexing
these ontologies is available at http://labs.mon
deca.com/dataset/lov/details/vocabularySpace_
Space-Time.html.

7   A community-adopted method for representing uncertainty in cultural heritage visualizations is paradata, described at http://www.
londoncharter.org/glossary.html.

8   Members of the working group include, Lorna
Hughes, Christian-Emil Ore, Costis Dallas,
Matt Munson, Torsten Reimer, Erik Champion,
Leif Isaksen, Orla Murphy, Panos Constanto-
poulos, and Christof Schöch.

REFERENCES AND FURTHER READING

American Council of Learned Societies. 1998.
*Computing and the Humanities: Summary of a
Roundtable Meeting.* Occasional Paper No. 41.
Chicago: ACLS.

Bates, M.J., Wilde, D.N., and Siegfried, S. 1995.
Research practices of humanities scholars in an
online environment: the Getty online searching
project report no. 3. *Library and Information
Science Research* 17 (1), 5–40.

Bearman, D. 1996. Overview and discussion points.
In *Research Agenda for Networked Cultural Heritage.*
Santa Monica, CA: Getty AHIP, 7–22.

Benardou, A., Constantopoulos, P., Dallas, C.,
and Gavrilis, D. 2010. Understanding the
information requirements of arts and humanities

scholarship: implications for digital curation.
International Journal of Digital Curation 5,
18–33.

Benardou, A., Constantopoulos, P., and Dallas, C.
2013. An approach to analyzing working practices of research communities in the humanities.
*International Journal of Humanities and Arts
Computing* 7, 105–27.

Blanke, T., and Hedges, M. 2013. Scholarly primitives: building institutional infrastructure for
humanities e-science. *Future Generation Computer
Systems* 29 (2), 654–61. doi:10.1016/j.future.
2011.06.006.

Bowen, W.G. 2005. *Mellon Foundation 2004
Annual Report: President's Report.* http://www.

mellon.org/about/annual-reports/2004-presidents-report (accessed November 9, 2014).

Crane, G. 2009. Cyberinfrastructure for classical philology. *DHQ: Digital Humanities Quarterly* 3 (1). http://www.digitalhumanities.org/dhq/vol/003/1/000023.html#N10167 (accessed November 9, 2014).

Dafis, L.L., Hughes, L.M., and James, R. 2014. "What's Welsh for crowdsourcing?" Citizen science and community engagement at the National Library of Wales. In *Crowdsourcing our Cultural Heritage*, ed, M. Ridge. London: Ashgate, 139–60.

Dallas, C. 1999. Humanistic research, information resources and electronic communication. In *Electronic Communication and Research in Europe*, ed. J. Meadows and H.-D. Boecker. Luxembourg: European Commission, 209–39. http://hdl.handle.net/123456789/792 (accessed June 20, 2015).

Drucker, J. 2011. Humanities approaches to graphical display. *DHQ: Digital Humanities Quarterly* 5 (1). http://www.digitalhumanities.org/dhq/vol/5/1/000091/000091.html (accessed November 9, 2014).

Eide, O. 2013. Text to map: rooms of possibilities. Paper presented at *Computer Applications and Quantitative Methods in Archaeology*, Perth, Australia, March 25–28. http://www.oeide.no/research/caa2013/TextsAsMapsAbstract.pdf (accessed November 9, 2014).

Ell, P., and Hughes, L.M. 2013. E-Infrastructure in the Humanities. International *Journal of Humanities and Arts Computing* 7, 24–40. DOI: 10.3366/ijhac.2013.0079 (accessed November 9, 2014).

Ellis, D. 1993. Modeling the information-seeking patterns of academic researchers: a grounded theory approach. *Library Quarterly* 63 (4), 469–86.

Engeström, Y. 1987. Learning by expanding: an activity theoretical approach to developmental research. http://lchc.ucsd.edu/mca/Paper/Engestrom/Learning-by-Expanding.pdf (accessed November 9, 2014).

Engeström, Y. 2000. Activity theory as a framework for analyzing and redesigning work. *Ergonomics* 43 (7), 960–74.

Gold, M.K., ed. 2012. *Debates in the Digital Humanities*. Minneapolis: University of Minnesota Press.

Greengrass, M., and Hughes, L.M. 2008. *The Virtual Representation of the Past*. London: Ashgate.

Houghton, J.W., Steele, C., and Henty, M. 2003. *Changing Research Practices in the Digital Information and Communication Environment*. Canberra, Australia: Department of Education, Science and Training. http://www.cfses.com/documents/Changing_Research_Practices.pdf (accessed November 9, 2014).

Hughes, L.M. 2011. Using ICT methods and tools in arts and humanities research. In *Digital Collections: Use, Value and Impact*, ed. L.M. Hughes. London: Facet, 123–34.

JISC. 2007. Evaluation of the JISC Digitization Programme, Phase One. http://www.jisc.ac.uk/whatwedo/programmes/digitisation/reports/evalphase1.aspx (accessed November 9, 2014).

Kaptelinin, V., and Nardi, B.A. 2007. *Acting with Technology: Activity Theory and Interaction Design*. Cambridge, MA: MIT Press.

Kauppinen, T., Mantegari, G., Paakkarinen, P., *et al.* 2010. Determining relevance of imprecise temporal intervals for cultural heritage information retrieval. *International Journal of Human–Computer Studies*, 68 (9), 549–60. DOI: 10.1016/j.ijhcs.2010.03.002 (accessed November 9, 2014).

Kirschenbaum, M.G. 2010. What is digital humanities and what's it doing in English departments? *ADE Bulletin* 150, 55–61. http://www.ade.org/bulletin (accessed November 9, 2014).

Latour, B. (undated). Mapping Controversies on Science for Politics (MACOSPOL). http://mappingcontroversies.net/Home/PlatformOverview (accessed November 9, 2014).

Malone, T.W., Crowston, K.G., and Herman, G.A. 2003. *Organizing Business Knowledge: The MIT Process Handbook*. Cambridge, MA: MIT Press.

McCarty, W. 2005. *Humanities Computing*. Basingstoke: Palgrave Macmillan.

NeDiMAH Space and Time working group. 2011. European Science Foundation Event Report: Place, Period, Event-based Approaches to Space and Time. http://www.nedimah.eu/reports/place-period-event-entity-based-approaches-space-and-time (accessed November 9, 2014).

Obe, R.O., and Hsu, L.S. 2010. *PostGIS in Action*. Shelter Island, NY: Manning Publications

Palmer, C.L., and Neumann, L.J. 2002. The information work of interdisciplinary humanities scholars: Exploration and translation. *Library Quarterly* 72 (1), 85–117.

Palmer, C.L., Teffeau, L.C., and Pirmann, C.M. 2009. *Scholarly Information Practices in the Online Environment*. Dublin, OH: OCLC. http://0-www.

oclc.org.millennium.mohave.edu/programs/
publications/reports/2009-02.pdf (accessed June
20, 2015).

Schaffner, J., and Erway, R. 2014. Does every
research library need a digital humanities
center? Dublin, OH: OCLC Research. http://
www.oclc.org/content/dam/research/publica
tions/library/2014/oclcresearch-digital-humanities-
center-2014.pdf (accessed November 9, 2014).

Speck, R. 2005. The AHDS Taxonomy of
Computational Methods. http://www.ahds.
ac.uk/about/projects/documents/pmdb_tax
onomy_v1_3_1.pdf (accessed November 9,
2014).

Speck, R., and Links, P. 2013. The missing voice:
archivists and infrastructures for humanities
research. *International Journal of Humanities and
Arts Computing* 7 (1–2), 128–46. doi:10.3366/
ijhac.2013.0085.

Stone, S. 1982. Humanities scholars: information
needs and uses. *Journal of Documentation* 38 (4),
292–313.

Svensson, P. 2012. Beyond the big tent. In *Debates
in the Digital Humanities*, ed. M.K. Gold.
Minneapolis: University of Minnesota Press,
36–49.

University of Minnesota Libraries. 2006. *A Multi-
Dimensional Framework for Academic Support:
Final Report*. Minneapolis: University of
Minnesota Libraries. http://purl.umn.edu/5540.

Unsworth, J. 2000. Scholarly primitives: what
methods do humanities researchers have in
common and how might our tools reflect this?
Paper presented at *Humanities Computing:
Formal Methods and Experimental Practice*, King's
College, London, May 13. http://people.bran
deis.edu/~unsworth/Kings.5-00/primitives.
html (accessed November 9, 2014).

12

Tailoring Access to Content

Séamus Lawless, Owen Conlan, and Cormac Hampson

Introduction and Motivation

Supporting users in searching and exploring large volumes of content presents significant challenges, particularly when different users have different and evolving needs. Content itself can be in a variety of different forms, text, image, and video. Moreover, several additional models and content forms may be extracted from an original content collection. In the case of historic manuscript collections, for example, there can exist a wide range of content forms and extracted models, including high-quality scans, manual transcriptions, manually written metadata, automatically generated normalizations, automatically extracted entity models (people, places, events), and social-network graphs of the persons mentioned. An example of such a collection is the *1641 Depositions*, a corpus of over 8000 handwritten manuscripts detailing the 1641 Rebellion in Ireland (http://1641.tcd.ie). The recent growth in digitization projects has resulted in the proliferation of digital archives and heterogeneous content collections.[1] For example, the Early English Books Online (EEBO) project presents a large collection of digitized material online (http://eebo.chadwyck.com). EEBO collects together more than 125,000 titles, but many of these titles are only offered as digital images of the individual pages. For these titles the words are not searchable, as the text has not been extracted from them. This extraction is often a costly and time-consuming process, as modern optical character recognition (OCR) techniques that scan images of text to extract words work best on modern fonts.

This chapter will present a variety of techniques and technologies that may be used to support tailored access to content in its wide variety of forms. This includes an introduction to the continuum of personalization, which strives to tailor how this wide range

A New Companion to Digital Humanities, First Edition. Edited by Susan Schreibman, Ray Siemens, and John Unsworth.
© 2016 John Wiley & Sons, Ltd. Published 2016 by John Wiley & Sons, Ltd.

of content is presented to meet the needs of individual users. It will also examine the applicability of different personalization techniques for different user groups and highlight how users may be offered increasing levels of control over this personalization.

The interdisciplinary field of digital humanities offers compelling opportunities for the application of personalization. It sits at the intersection of information and communications technology (ICT), knowledge management (which seeks to support the discovery and management of content in a structured manner), and a wide range of humanities disciplines. These disciplines have research practices which tend to be very labor-intensive, solitary, and characterized by research material which is often disconnected and non-digitized. This has presented a particular obstacle to novice researchers and to appreciation by the general public, as access to content is often a significant barrier. Digitization represents an important step forward, but the requirement remains for specialist environments which can offer a rich, personalized, and stimulating engagement with the digitized material to empower users with different backgrounds and experiences to interact with such collections.

Personalization and adaptive contextualization technologies such as adaptive hypermedia, adaptive web, intelligent systems, and recommendation systems have been successful in many application areas such as education, tourism, and general information sites. Personalization attempts to ensure that content and services are tailored to individual users' personal preferences, goals, and context while at the same time making the reuse of such media easier. Brusilovsky, one of the early innovators in the area of adaptive hypermedia (Brusilovsky, 2007), described some fundamental considerations for adaptive systems (Brusilovsky, 1996). De Bra was also instrumental in the creation of the early adaptive hypermedia systems with the development of *AHA!* (De Bra and Calvi, 1997). Recent research in adaptive hypermedia has sought to weave together content and interactive services to deliver personalized experiences (Conlan *et al.*, 2013). Such adaptive technologies reconcile each user's interests, prior experience, or location to provide personalized navigations of relevant digital resources (adaptive personalization) or suggest personalized recommendations concerning digital resources of interest based on similar users' behavior and feedback (social recommendation). These types of systems build an inferred model of users' interests by examining their interactions with the system. For example, if a user browses and bookmarks many documents about a particular person it may be inferred (possibly with a low confidence) that the user is currently interested in that person. If someone creates an annotation over a discrete piece of a document that contains a mention of that person the confidence may be increased. Such implicit modeling may be augmented with explicit modeling, i.e., taking direct guidance from the user, to adjust confidence levels and to add/remove items from the user's model. This evolving model of the user is used to adjust how the systems present information or make recommendations, with the systems attempting to prioritise content that will be of value to the user.

The rise of "i," "me," and "my" prefixes for various web portals (e.g., iGoogle, which transitioned to be the main Google search interface) and web services is intended to give the impression of some form of personal adaptation of content and service to an individual user's needs, preferences, or history to enhance the individuals experience. Typically however, such services tend to focus on (a) identification and ranking of relevant content (web pages) or services (Teevan *et al.*, 2005; Agichtein *et al.*, 2006;

Dou *et al.*, 2007); (b) simplistic "personalization" of the content presentation by inclusion of the user's name and historical information/recently used resources; or (c) simple augmentation of screen layout (Ankolekar *et al.*, 2008). However, typical adaptive personalization technologies have three general weaknesses:

- They fail to take into account the broader community of which the user is a member, thus neglecting a valuable source of insight into user intention.
- They also fail to personalize in response to a sufficiently broad diversity of criteria, e.g., user intent (based on context of use) or level of user interaction control.
- They are unaware of the structure and internal dynamics of the material to which they offer access. Such "domain awareness" is an important input to the selection and sequencing of material presented by an adaptive system to the user.

These are all areas in which research in the field of digital humanities can offer insight and guidance. Recent large-scale digitization initiatives have made many important cultural heritage collections available online. This makes them accessible to the global research community and interested public for the first time. However, the full value of these heritage treasures is not being realized. After digitization, these collections are typically monolithic and difficult to navigate, and they can contain text which is of variable quality in terms of language, spelling, punctuation, and consistency of terminology and naming. As a result, they often fail to attract and sustain broad user engagement and so have only limited communities of interest. If such collections were augmented with personalized access they might become more accessible, thus unlocking their huge potential.

This chapter addresses the challenges associated with effectively empowering communities of researchers with personalized mechanisms which support their exploration, interrogation, and interpretation of complex digital cultural artifacts. A number of use-cases are presented to exemplify how these challenges may be addressed. Achieving balance between open exploration and personalized recommendation presents the most significant challenge, as offering just automated adaptivity is not enough. The danger of heavy-handed personalization is that users are presented with a highly prescriptive portal through which they interact with content, and that the portal filters content in a restrictive or biased fashion. This does not typically fit with the hypothesis building and research processes found in many humanities disciplines. Ensuring that the user is in control of the personalization process is essential to the success of explorative environments. Such user-centered control may be enhanced through: correlating usage patterns with self-expressed user goals; predefined research strategies; and the provision of appropriate tools for users to explore and navigate large cultural heritage information spaces. For example, personalization systems should empower their users to examine and control what the system has modeled about their interests, thus offering as much control as possible to generate the most appropriate and engaging experience for the user.

Next-generation adaptive systems aim to make digital humanities artifacts more appealing and more usable to a broader public, as well as supporting the activities of professional researchers. This will lead to larger and more active communities of interest focused on the artifacts. Such communities are key not only to sustaining interest in our heritage but also to promoting deeper understanding of, and contribution to, digital humanities artifacts. Such communities can form the basis for sustained and richly rewarding engagement with digital humanities artifacts.

Innovative personalization can be achieved by taking into account a range of variables, such as individual user intent and diversity of use, awareness of the activities and interests of the community to which the user belongs, and in-depth analysis of the structure and features of digital humanities artifacts and collections. The following sections of this chapter discuss the key aspects that are needed to effectively tailor access to content. First, the importance of understanding each individual user, including that person's short- and long-term interests, is discussed. This is balanced with the need to give users control over how an adaptive environment models them and adapts to their needs. The following section then describes how personalization may be achieved by adapting elements of an environment. This section includes a discussion of how personalization may be introduced without limiting how a user may explore artifacts. The chapter then concludes with a discussion of some of the opportunities that this form of tailored access to content offers for the future.

Users and Content

Overview: It is not possible for a computing system to really know and understand a person! Therefore, personalization systems need a model of both the individual and the content of interest, in order to make algorithmic decisions on how to best support that individual.

A wide variety of personalization techniques may be deployed to promote individualized access to content. For example, personalization techniques which offer high-level overviews of the themes within a collection may be more suited to the general public, whereas researchers who are intimately familiar with a content collection and the context in which it may be interpreted can gain more value from on-the-side guidance and connections to related resources. When developing an environment that aims to give access to content, it is essential that potential end users and key user communities be identified from the outset. If an environment is being designed to give tailored access to content via adaptive technology, then a range of user communities need to be addressed, potentially ranging from members of the general public – perhaps encountering the specific content collections for the first time – to experienced professional researchers. This presents a difficult challenge, as each individual user may wish to engage with this content in a variety of different ways. However, this is the challenge personalization techniques are designed to address.

Users vary in terms of their prior knowledge, experience with a collection, and the goals they wish to achieve. In this sense there exists a continuum of experience to which users belong. While it could be conveniently assumed that a member of the general public has less experience than a professional researcher, this is not strictly the case. For example, professional researchers may have specific artifacts or themes in a collection that focus their interest, whereas a general user may be bringing a lot of informal knowledge about the collection. There is another dimension of experience, beyond knowledge of the content, which should be considered. Users will also have varying experience of how to make effective use of the tools offered in an environment to meet their needs. This stems both from general technical literacy/confidence and from specific experience using such tools. This aspect of experience can have a significant bearing on how the user approaches individual tasks.

In order to successfully model the user, it is important to have deeper information about the content and artifacts that user is working with. This information, such as the entities mentioned within a text, can be used to augment the user's model. For example, if the user navigates to several documents about the same person, an interest in that person may be implicitly assumed. There are a number of challenges with this approach: the first lies in successfully identifying the entities that are relevant to an artifact; the next comes from trying to determine a user's degree of interest in an artifact; and the third lies in ensuring the user has appropriate control over the user model, to scrutinize and control what has been modeled.

Content Modeling

Overview: It is difficult or often impossible for computer systems to "understand" content. An abstracted model of the content, often referred to as metadata, is required to allow personalized systems to work with content.

Modeling the key characteristics in a piece of content is a necessary step if content is to be recommended to users and used to help determine their evolving interests. This modeling may take different forms, but typically it involves trying to identify the characteristics which may be pertinent to the users exploring the content. At a basic level, this may include simple entities such as people, places, and events. Even at this basic level issues may arise in ensuring the entities are accurately identified within the artifact. For example, anaphora resolution may require interpretation, either by a human annotator or from a piece of software to appropriately identify an entity. Specifically named entities in a piece of content tend to be easier to model and make explicit in the metadata describing the artifact.

The goal of modeling content, whether performed manually or with a (semi-) automated process, is to create a metadata representation of the document. This acts as a surrogate representation of the document and highlights the key entities related to the document. Ideally, these entities should be objectively verifiable and easily verified. If feasible, the entities should also be tied to different pieces of the artifact. For example, if a person is mentioned in a piece of text it is valuable to identify where, via character offsets, that mention occurs. This abstracted view of an artifact will enable the user modeling features to correlate user activity around an artifact with entities that the user may potentially be interested in.

User Modeling

Overview: Users vary in their experience, preferences, and abilities. For personalization systems to tailor experiences for each individual user, an abstracted model of that user is required.

Central to the adaptive services provided within any adaptive environment is the user model (Kobsa, 93). A model of each user is built silently as a user interacts with the system. All actions a user performs are recorded in order to build up detailed information on each user. The user model is a key input in any adaptive strategy employed by an adaptive environment.

For example, there are a number of different user actions that result in user model updates. These include viewing, bookmarking, and annotating content; performing a search; interacting with visualizations; and clicking recommendations. Each action results in different weightings being applied to the relevant entities that are stored within the user model. The entities are identified by examining the specific piece of content that the user is interacting with. For instance, viewing a page that contains specific mention of an individual, results in a small increase to the weighting of that person within the user model. Other less passive actions receive greater increments. For example, viewing a visualization of a particular document increases the weighting of relevant entities by a higher margin, while bookmarking a page increases the weighting even further, as does creating a note or annotating specific entities within a document. The weightings associated with these actions can be easily adjusted up or down, and new actions added that also impact entity weightings within the user model. This flexibility is key in tailoring the user model correctly. An example of a user model that is constructed in this manner can be found in the *CULTURA* research environment (Bailey *et al.*, 2012).

It is important that a model of a user has some form of decay function that factors in how recently the user has shown interest in certain entities. For example, a user may show a lot of interest in a certain city in the early stages of exploring a collection, but may move on to more refined expression of interest in a locale as the exploration progresses. The weightings applied to the original entity should decay with time, or more precisely with interactions. It is also possible to maintain a variety of different models for a user that represent shorter- and longer-term interests. One approach is for an environment to maintain two models, one complete model that captures and decays all user actions and another that only captures a finite number of interactions. In this way different recommenders may be built to account for short-term versus long-term interest. Regardless of the modeling approach employed, it is important to give the user as much control as possible over the model, to allow it to be adjusted to meet each user's needs.

Transparency, Reflection, and User Control

Overview: Sometimes computers get it wrong! Offering users an insight into what the personalization system has modeled about them and the ability to tweak and control that model is important to ensure the system behaves as they wish.

Often users are curious as to why specific recommendations are being made to them, but they generally have no way of seeing the model of interest representing them in the background. This may be tackled in two ways.

Firstly, when recommendations are made to a user, an explanation should be provided as to why they are being presented. For instance, in *CULTURA* recommendations are accompanied by explanatory text indicating that links are relevant to an entity (person, place, event, etc.) that the user has encountered in their explorations. In Figure 12.1 the items in each list link to resources that are related to the place entities "Lismore," "Trim," and "Meath." This box is rendered beside the deposition text and enables users to quickly locate new resources that may be relevant to their

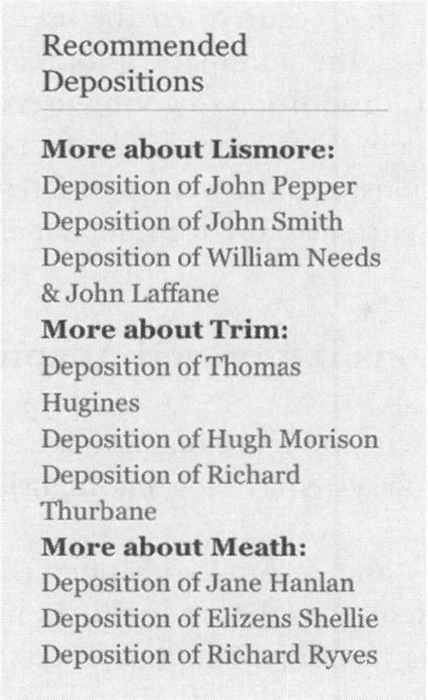

Recommended Depositions
More about Lismore:
Deposition of John Pepper
Deposition of John Smith
Deposition of William Needs & John Laffane
More about Trim:
Deposition of Thomas Hugines
Deposition of Hugh Morison
Deposition of Richard Thurbane
More about Meath:
Deposition of Jane Hanlan
Deposition of Elizens Shellie
Deposition of Richard Ryves

Figure 12.1 Personalized recommendations based on user interests.

Increase Weight
Decrease Weight
KilmcCaloge Victim captivity words
Apostate Deponent Mentioned Denounced
Lieutenant assault Wife Lady Debtor Captain
Joiner apostacy military_action Succour killing
arson

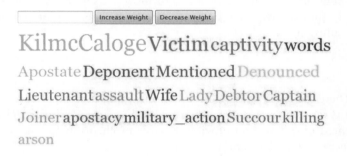

Figure 12.2 User model rendered as a tag cloud.

exploration and interests. The box indicates why these resources are being recommended to them. In this way, it is clear why the recommendations are there, even if the user does not necessarily agree on their relevance (Hampson *et al.*, 2014).

This potential disagreement resonates with a second feature that an adaptive environment should offer: a mechanism to display the entities that are having most influence on a user's model. One mechanism for manifesting such information is to use a tag cloud. This is used to promote reflection and to allow the user to understand and manipulate the model. Importantly, the tag cloud is not static, and a user can adjust the relative influence of various entities through the interface offered (Figure 12.2). For example, if there are a number of terms that the system thinks are of interest to the user in the current context, but which the user disagrees with, then it is easy to select the terms and either delete them entirely or reduce their individual sizes in the tag cloud. In addition, the user can add new terms manually, or increase the size of entities within the model. Any change in an entity's size has a direct impact on the recommendation calculations that occur when the user resumes browsing a content collection. This process makes the automatic processing that is occurring in the background more transparent, in addition to giving users significant control over how their user models represent them. Different clouds can be rendered for different types of entities (people, organizations, etc.) as well as different clouds detailing the user's overall model of interest and current short-term model of interest.

Personalization and Adaptivity

Overview: The user and content models alone are not enough to generate a tailored experience. The personalization systems need some algorithms and logic to decide how best to support the user.

Personalization techniques and technologies offer the promise of tailoring each user's access to content in response to that individual's information need, knowledge, preferences, and so on. These techniques support a continuum of engagement with content, ranging from highly prescriptive offerings based upon a model of each user's behavior to less constrained, user-centric curation of content collections, for a spectrum of user categories. A four-phase model of personalization has been proposed to support this continuum of engagement and to allow users to move seamlessly between a constrained, guided navigation and more freeform, open exploration of a content collection (Hampson *et al.*, 2014).

Four-Phase Model of Personalization

Overview: There are many approaches to personalizing user experiences, but few are tailored for the forms of exploration performed by humanities scholars. The four-phase model presented in this section provides flexible mechanisms for enabling personalized experiences over a wide variety of content.

One reason why novice users struggle to engage with large cultural collections is a lack of guidance when they initially encounter the set of resources. The four-phase personalization approach has been designed to counteract this by providing a structured introductory pathway into a collection, without restricting users from exploring the material as their interest is piqued. The four phases defined by the approach are *guide*, *explore*, *suggest*, and *reflect*.

Users with little experience of the content typically start their investigations within the *guide* phase. Here a "narrative" is employed, which enables resources within a collection to be sequenced on a specific theme (e.g., the evolution of a form of illumination in fifteenth-century Padua; Agosti *et al.*, 2013). Furthermore, how these resources are rendered to the user (text, visualization, etc.) can also be specified within the narrative metadata, which is encoded as XML. This process is especially useful for providing users with a path through specific content, though it does not limit their ability to use these sequenced narratives as a springboard for their own investigations. Within the four-phase personalization approach, this involves stepping from the *guide* phase to the *explore* phase (number 1 in Figure 12.3). Narrative pathways are discussed in more detail in the next section.

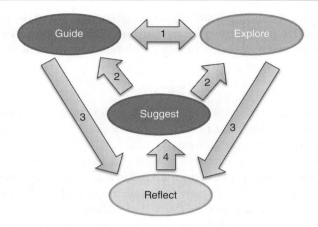

Figure 12.3   The four-phase approach to personalization.

In the *explore* phase, tools are offered to support the exploration and browsing of the underlying content collections. These tools can include data-enriched maps, entity-oriented search, social-network analysis and visualization, amongst many others. At any stage users can return to where they left their path in the *guide* phase, and users with little prior knowledge of the resources often flick between the *explore* and *guide* phases several times. In contrast, professional researchers with a deep understanding of the collection typically spend the majority of their time within the *explore* phase, and may never involve themselves with the more structured *guide* phase.

Importantly, by monitoring the user model as a user explores the content, the narrative path presented in the *guide* phase can be adapted by the system. This is achieved by selecting documents for the user's path that most closely match that user's interests or information needs. This can result in the path being enriched with further resources, exploration points, and concepts.

Whether within the *guide* or *explore* phase, a user will be given personalized suggestions for content, or tools which offer exploration points. These suggestions are based upon the system's interpretation of the user's actions and interests, as manifest in the user model. This process occurs in the *suggest* phase (which works in parallel with the *guide* and *explore* phases), with on-the-side, noninvasive recommendations presented to users (number 2 in Figure 12.3). These recommendations are influenced by both long- and short-term interests of the user as indicated by the user's actions – search terms submitted, entities viewed, annotations created, and so on.

At any stage within the *guide* or *explore* phases, users may enter the *reflect* phase. This involves viewing their user model and seeing what interests the environment has associated with them (number 3 in Figure 12.3). The *reflect* phase is not static, and users can edit their user model. They can add or delete terms, or manually increase or reduce the size of existing terms (thus changing their degree of influence). Importantly, any changes made during the *reflect* phase directly impacts upon the *suggest* phase and the recommendations that eventually filter down into the *guide* and *explore* phases (number 4 in Figure 12.3).

By espousing the four-phase personalization approach, digital humanities environments can dynamically adapt to users, support the various ways in which they wish to engage with a content collection, and render useful suggestions to them at appropriate times. Moreover, this process provides mechanisms that are appropriate for a range of users with different levels of ability or different interests in the underlying resources.

Narrative

Overview: Inexperienced users can often find it daunting when confronted with a large collection of artifacts. Narratives provide flexible guided pathways across artifacts to gently introduce the user to the content available.

In personalized systems, a narrative represents a navigation structure based upon relationships between concepts in a domain (Conlan *et al.*, 2013). This navigation structure is designed to meet an objective, such as providing a guided introduction to a topic in a content collection. At design time this strategy is authored to represent the variety of potential conceptual pathways that can be used to generate a user experience. During execution, these potential pathways are reconciled with the user model to select the most appropriate or relevant for that individual. Each step on this pathway can be a piece of content, or a service such as a network visualization or entity-oriented search.

When using an environment designed using the four-phase approach to personalization, users with little experience of a content collection will typically start their investigations within the *guide* phase via a narrative module. This "narrative" module, which in the example in Figure 12.4 is rendered to users as a lesson block within the

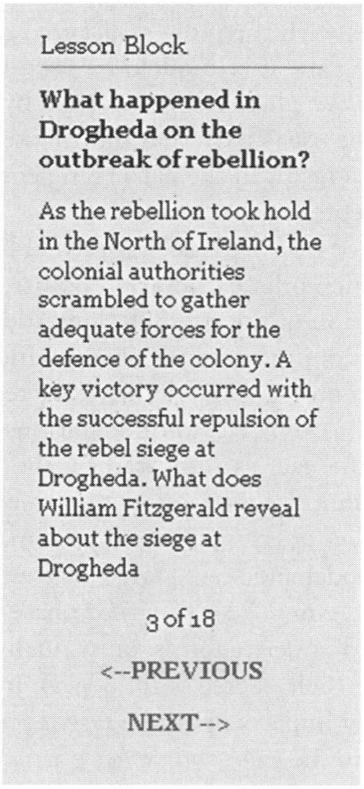

Lesson Block
_____

What happened in Drogheda on the outbreak of rebellion?

As the rebellion took hold in the North of Ireland, the colonial authorities scrambled to gather adequate forces for the defence of the colony. A key victory occurred with the successful repulsion of the rebel siege at Drogheda. What does William Fitzgerald reveal about the siege at Drogheda

3 of 18

<--PREVIOUS

NEXT-->

Figure 12.4   A guided lesson plan.

user interface, enables resources within the collection to be sequenced on a specific theme, such as a chain of derivation of illustrations in an illuminated manuscript collection, or the reliability of witness statements in a collection of depositions.

These lessons are developed by domain experts, and they contain paths of various lengths (with optional and compulsory parts), so that users with different levels of interest can be accommodated. Furthermore, how these resources are rendered to the user (text, visualization, etc.) can also be specified within the narrative.

As described above, being on a guided path does not limit the more adventurous user from exploring the collection in a more freeform manner by using the services offered as part of the explore phase. In fact, many narratives explicitly encourage users to do so, by including services in the narrative which can be a springboard for the user's own investigations.

Personalized environments can monitor a user's progress through a narrative, and if the user shows sufficient interest in particular concepts, the narrative can be dynamically augmented through the addition of further relevant resources. Importantly, users can also explicitly adjust narratives as they make progress (by choosing to see more resources on a specific concept), which gives them ultimate control of their experience.

Personalized Search

Overview: Searching online is a very familiar process for most users. However, for a given query, offering the same set of results to every user does not account for their individual differences. Personalized search uses the user model to tailor the results for each user.

Unprecedented amounts of digital humanities content is now available online, in digital libraries, repositories, and archives. This information is available in many formats, and offers wonderful opportunities for knowledge discovery, but also presents many complex challenges for the discovery, combination, and exploration of appropriate information from disparate sources.

Personalizing the process of searching for information online has been demonstrated to be a very effective method of supporting users in the navigation of these increasingly large volumes of content. Personalized search attempts to deliver customized results to meet specific user interests, preferences, information needs, and contexts (Micarelli *et al.*, 2007; Zhou *et al.*, 2012). This is achieved by using information about a user to adapt the content selected and presented to that user's needs, preferences, knowledge, and interests, and to automatically resolve potential ambiguity in searches. As described above, providing users with some control over these user models and how the personalization process influences the search is key to ensuring satisfaction and promoting adoption (Ahn *et al.*, 2008).

When using a search interface to explore and investigate a cultural heritage collection, users' information needs are continuously evolving as they acquire knowledge and gain context. As a result, an individual's perception of the relevance of a piece of content will also continuously change. Relevance, which was traditionally viewed as a static state in search systems, must now be considered more fluid and adaptive.

Recommendation

Overview: One potential problem with exploring collections online is that a user who does not search for a particular piece of content may never become aware of it. Recommendation enables personalization systems to highlight content that is relevant to the user's activities and interests.

Recommendation is an approach to information filtering which attempts to identify content that is likely to be of interest to an individual user. Recommendation is usually achieved by analyzing the content of a collection and matching items from that collection to a user model (Ricci *et al.*, 2011). We have already discussed how such user models are constructed based upon a user's previous actions. Another approach to recommendation is known as collaborative filtering (Resnick *et al.*, 1994), where the system attempts to predict what content a user will find relevant based upon that user's similarity to other users.

An example of how collaborative filtering can be used is the recommenders developed by the *CULTURA* project (http://www.cultura-strep.eu). In this approach, two distinct sets of recommendations are offered to users as they explore a cultural heritage collection. These recommendations are delivered by two tools, a "Hybrid Recommender" and a "Global Recommender." These tools implement the *suggest* phase of the four phase personalization approach.

The Hybrid Recommender generates a list of recommended content based upon an individual's user model and the content that the user is currently viewing. Specifically this involves looking at the entities extracted from each resource and blending them with respect to the weighted entities of interest stored within the user model. The Hybrid Recommender can also access the weighting between entities that have been a recent focus of interest to the user, as opposed to those terms that consistently appear to be of relevance to the user. After this analysis and blending of results takes place, links to relevant content are generated and rendered within a side block in the environment. This provides the user with a useful, noninvasive mechanism for further browsing of the cultural archive.

While the Hybrid Recommender takes into account the current content that the user is viewing and balances the entities contained within that content with those entities in the user model, the Global Recommender gives recommendations based solely on the individual's user model. This recommender is designed to provide initial starting points for exploration rather than providing links to complementary resources while in the middle of an exploration.

Conclusion

This chapter has introduced some of the challenges encountered in offering tailored access to content. It has discussed how analyzing both the user's actions and the artifacts in a collection can yield a number of possibilities for generating a personalized experience. However, caution must be exercised in realizing these possibilities. Users should be supported in their explorations, and any personalization offered should be peripheral. The users interacting with collections of content have a variety of backgrounds and different levels of experience. When tailoring access to these collections, all of these users should be effectively supported in the tasks they are trying to accomplish.

Any personalized solution offered should leave the user very much in control. The four-phase model for personalization allows seamless movement between guidance, exploration, suggestion, and reflection, thus empowering users to maximize their engagement with a content collection. Of key importance in this model is the reflection phase, which enables the user to scrutinize and adjust the user model, upon which personalization is based. Engaging in reflection not only allows this control, but can also help users to identify relevant topics and entities they 'were not explicitly aware of. The guidance phase enables novice users to receive directed support in navigating across key artifacts in a collection. This guidance is offered through narrative, a curated path and commentary linking a number of artifacts together. Again, this guidance is offered alongside the artifacts, so that users can engage in exploration whenever they choose. The key point when offering personalized experiences is that users should be empowered to follow their interests and explore the content as they wish, with the personalized recommendations, narratives, and search offering appropriate support along the way.

NOTE

1   Further examples of such collections are: The Old Bailey Online (http://www.oldbaileyonline.org); Google Library Archives (http://www.google.com/googlebooks/partners.html); Eighteenth Century Collections Online (http://find.galegroup.com/ecco/start.do?prodId=ECCO&userGroupName=tcd); BHL-Europe (http://www.bhl-europe.eu).

REFERENCES AND FURTHER READING

Agichtein, E., Brill, E., and Dumais, S. 2006. Improving web search ranking by incorporating user behaviour information. Proceedings of the 29th Annual International ACM SIGIR Conference on Research and Development in Information Retrieval, Seattle, Washington, USA, 2006, 19–26.

Agosti, M., Manfioletti, M., Orio, N., Ponchia, C. 2013. Enhancing end user access to cultural heritage systems: tailored narratives and human-centered computing. In *New Trends in Image Analysis and Processing: ICIAP 2013 International Workshops, Naples, Italy, September 2013*, ed. A. Petrosino, L. Maddalena, and P. Pala. Berlin: Springer, 278–87.

Ahn, J., Brusilovsky, P., He, D., Grady, J., and Li, Q. 2008. Personalized web exploration with task models. *Proceedings of the 17th International Conference on World Wide Web, WWW 2008, Beijing, China, April 21–25, 2008*. New York: ACM, 1–10.

Ankolekar, A., Krötzsch, M., Tran, T., and Vrandečić, D. 2008. The two cultures: mashing up Web 2.0 and the Semantic Web. *Journal of Web Semantics* 6 (1).

Bailey, E., Lawless, S., O'Connor, A., *et al*. 2012. CULTURA: supporting enhanced exploration of cultural archives through personalisation. *Proceedings of the 2nd International Conference on Humanities, Society and Culture, ICHSC 2012, Hong Kong, China, October 27–28, 2012*.

Brusilovsky, P. 1996. Methods and techniques of adaptive hypermedia. *User Modeling and User-Adapted Interaction* 6 (2–3), 87–129.

Brusilovsky, P. 2007. Adaptive navigation support. In *The Adaptive Web*, ed. P. Brusilovsky, A. Kobsa, and W. Neidl. Lecture Notes in Computer Science, 4321. Berlin: Springer, 263–90.

Conlan, O., Staikopoulos, A., Hampson, C., Lawless, C., and O'Keeffe, I. 2013. The narrative approach to personalization. *New Review of Hypermedia and Multimedia* 19 (2), 132–57.

De Bra, P., and Calvi, L. 1997. Creating adaptive hyperdocuments for and on the Web. *Proceedings of the AACE WebNet'97 Conference, Toronto*, 149–54.

Dou, X., Song, R., and Wen, J. 2007. A large-scale evaluation and analysis of personalized search strategies. *Proceedings of 16th International Conference on World Wide Web (WWW16), Banff, Alberta, Canada.*

Hampson, C., Lawless, S., Bailey, B., *et al.* 2014. Metadata-enhanced exploration of digital cultural collections. *International Journal of Metadata, Semantics and Ontologies* 9 (2), 155–67.

Kobsa, A. 1993. User modeling: recent work, prospects and hazards. In *Adaptive User Interfaces: Principles and Practice*, ed. M. Schneider-Hufschmidt, T. Kühme, and U. Malinowski. Amsterdam: North-Holland.

Micarelli, A., Gasparetti, F., Sciarrone, F., and Gauch, S. 2007. Personalized search on the world wide. In *The Adaptive Web*, ed. P. Brusilovsky, A. Kobsa, and W. Neidl. Lecture Notes in Computer Science, 4321. Berlin: Springer, 195–230.

Resnick, P., Iacovou, N., Suchak, M., Bergstrom, P., and Riedl, J. 1994 GroupLens: an open architecture for collaborative filtering of netnews. *Proceedings of the ACM Conference on Computer-Supported Cooperative Work, Chapel Hill, NC,* 175–86.

Ricci, F., Rokach, L., and Shapira, B. 2011. Introduction to Recommender Systems Handbook. In *Recommender Systems Handbook*, ed. F. Ricci, L. Rokach, B. Shapira, and P.B. Kantor. New York: Springer, 1–35.

Teevan, J., Dumais, S.T., and Horvitz, E. 2005. Personalizing search via automated analysis of interests and activities. *28th International ACMIR Conference on Research and Development in Information Retrieval, Salvador, Brazil, 2005.*

Zhou, D., Lawless, S., and Wade, V. 2012. Improving search via personalized query expansion using social media. *Journal of Information Retrieval* 15, 218–42.

13
Ancient Evenings: Retrocomputing in the Digital Humanities

Matthew G. Kirschenbaum

A hobbyist wires a mothballed Macintosh Plus (it has no on-board Ethernet or Wi-Fi) to a Raspberry Pi so he can use it to surf today's Web (Keacher, 2013). An archivist for a small New York City-based arts organization reconstructs a legendary bulletin board system known as "The Thing" using everything from backup data on 5¼-inch floppy disks to 35 mm slides depicting the original BBS in operation (Kopstein, 2013). A Romanticist who edited the work of the poet Percy Bysshe Shelley in the 1980s turns to forensic computing to recover his files from legacy media so that the manuscript transcriptions they contain can serve as copy-texts for a new TEI-encoded edition online (Olsen, 2013). A scholar and curator of electronic literature ships a consignment of 30-year-old machines to the annual meeting of the Modern Language Association, where she stages an exhibit to allow attendees to encounter – and *read* – early works of digital fiction and poetry on their native platforms (Pathfinders, 2013). All of these are examples of "retrocomputing," a set of hands-on practices devoted to preserving, engaging, and extending the historical legacy of outdated and outmoded computer systems for purposes of documentation and recovery, education, experimentation, critical and artistic expression, and sheer satisfaction.

Retrocomputing is a colloquial term with no fixed, canonical definition. It overlaps with the activities of professional digital preservationists, but is also unmistakably a hobbyist endeavor, improvisational and freewheeling while cultural heritage institutions tend towards standards, best practices, and curatorial conservatism. Yuri Takhteyev and Quinn DuPont (2013) describe retrocomputing as "a set of diverse practices involving contemporary engagements with old computer systems," while Patricia Galloway (2011) finds retrocomputing characterized by "amateurism" (in the sense that its practitioners are rarely compensated), the focused application of "technological

A New Companion to Digital Humanities, First Edition. Edited by Susan Schreibman, Ray Siemens, and John Unsworth.
© 2016 John Wiley & Sons, Ltd. Published 2016 by John Wiley & Sons, Ltd.

skill," and a "persistent interest" born of a "sincere identity" with the aims of the retrocomputing community; she also notes the analogy to other forms of "technological tinkering," such as ham radio. While the archetype for retrocomputing may be the engineering retiree who donates time and expertise to a computer history museum to restore vintage equipment, generational criteria are inadequate. Much of the activity in the retrogaming community is by teenagers, for example, and other segments of retrocomputing, such as the demoscene (Tassäjarvi, 2004), attract adherents who weren't even born when the original systems debuted. Galloway calls attention to the role of so-called "tacit knowledge" in such enterprises, where the participants typically come by their expertise experientially, from hands-on learning and over-the-shoulder interactions. Physical space is thus vital for retrocomputing, not only as a site for collective work and knowledge sharing, but also for creating opportunities for public access and exhibition. Regional clubs and collectives are commonplace, though of course the community has important online forums and outlets as well. Retrocomputing shares important affinities with maker and DIY culture, steampunk, hardware modding activities such as overclocking, design fiction, device art, and even (I would argue) fan culture forms such as fan fiction and cosplay, as well as historical re-enactment. There are also clear commonalities with emerging theoretical approaches in digital and new media studies, including media archaeology, platform studies, software studies, and critical code studies. My goal in this chapter is to examine retrocomputing from the standpoint of the digital humanities specifically, and to ask what its practices, attitudes, and perspectives can offer to the conduct and identity of digital humanities at the present moment.

Digital humanities typically prides itself on the cutting edge. Those of us who run centers or labs, or who administer courses and curricula, go to great lengths to keep hardware and software current. We attend workshops, institutes, and conferences to be up to speed. We read blogs and feeds, follow Twitter, and have conversations with colleagues, all in an effort to stay informed. Research often tends to gravitate toward what's new, with the advent of new tools and techniques, new platforms and devices serving as a catalyst to critical and creative thinking: "I wonder what this corpus would show me if I tried topic modeling?" "How can I deliver this scholarly function-ality on this new touchscreen?" Given all of this impetus toward the new, it would seem counterintuitive to knowingly embrace technologies that are decades out of date and which physically lack the means (literally, at the level of hardware and protocol) to interact with the thriving digital world surrounding them. And while some readers may bear some affection toward their old machines and even keep them on hand, they typically ascribe such tendencies to personal nostalgia and do not view them as an integral part of their practice as scholars and researchers in digital humanities itself.

Yet it would be a mistake to allow retrocomputing's significance to digital humanities to rest solely upon its contrarian impulses, the opposition between old and new. Several writers have worked to dissolve that particular binary in critical ways; Takhteyev and DuPont (2013), for example, note the importance of a "remix" ethos in the practice of retrocomputing, where legacy components often find themselves fully integrated with new technologies, fabricated or jury-rigged to extend or replace their functionalities. Indeed, they see retrocomputing's primary significance not in its conservationist ten-dencies, but in its ability to act as a "transformative" practice, "producing assemblages of physical and digital fragments originating from different time periods and 'remixed' in novel ways" (Takhteyev and DuPont, 2013:358) (The Internet-enabled Mac Plus described above, which relies on a combination of legacy hardware and contemporary components, as well as vintage software – but still from a later era than the original hardware – is an example of just such an assemblage.) Similarly, they note a balance between rigorous authenticity and more playful or whimsical engagements, illustrating the point with a Commodore 64 painted a wholly unhistorical (but striking) shade of blue in order to recapture the sense of joyousness that originally accompanied using the machine (Takhteyev and DuPont, 2013:362). Such examples, as well as the sheer strangeness of the industrial design, form factors, and ergonomics of old systems, can remind us of the importance of the affective dimension of computer systems, that they are objects and artifacts in the world, not just instrumental portals to supposedly "virtual" places.

Jonathan Sterne (2007), meanwhile, has argued compellingly that computers are "new" primarily with respect to other computers, and not to external forms of media or technology. "Today, computers and other digital hardware displace their own counterparts more than anything else," he states (Sterne, 2007:19). Sterne also notes the radically compressed progression from the "new" to the merely "useful" to the obsolete that governs our temporal experience of computing: his point is that perceptions of old and new are almost always functions of marketing strategies and societal pressures, and not the inherent properties of the technology itself, which performs just the same as it always did (My father did his online banking with an Apple II and a 1200-baud modem well into the early 1990s; the rest of the family scoffed, but it worked – so were the rest of us really just channeling the pressures of the marketplace?) Sterne then reminds us that everyday computing is often characterized by the juxtaposition of old and new, with last year's computer still lurking in the corner of the office or on a shelf in the closet, and a snarl of cables, connectors, and adapters inevitably bundled in some desk drawer. No one who is confronted by these mute material remainders (and reminders), literally the *products* of planned obsolescence, can subscribe to a view of technological novelty that is wholly progressive and positivistic. Retrocomputing may thus offer a vantage point from which to locate other kinds of markers and delimiters in our chronologies of computing, individual and idiosyncratic rather than those imposed exclusively by external marketing cycles. Such stances are epitomized by a novelist like George R.R. Martin, who still prefers the keyboard-driven word processor WordStar to any GUI alternative. If our tools really *do* shape our ideas and our thinking (as Nietzsche famously claimed with regard to his typewriter), then digital humanities bears a responsibility to critically examine the material legacy of its own technologies and instruments: this includes their implications in consumer commodity culture, their ranges of emotion and affect, and their status as historical and material – which is to say irreducibly humanistic – artifacts.

The remainder of this short chapter will consider what this might mean from the standpoint of two potential areas of digital humanities activity: data preservation and recovery, which opens opportunities for collaboration with libraries and archives that are increasingly acquiring born-digital content (see the earlier example of the Shelley scholar's embrace of forensic computing); and the historical study of digital cultural forms, including creative explorations, which also overlap with the burgeoning interest in critical making (like the electronic literature exhibition described above). I conclude with suggestions for individuals and centers interested in building their own retrocomputing collections.

Preservation and Recovery

If digital humanities is to concern itself with the full sweep of our collective past then it must, like a Klein bottle, also come to terms with the born-digital objects and artifacts that characterize cultural production in all areas of human endeavor in the decades since the advent of general-purpose computers. We take it as paradigmatic, after all, that digital humanities concerns itself with digital representations of the analog cultural record, as well as analytical operations – of many and diverse kinds – upon those surrogate digital representations. Alan Liu (2013) recognizes these same two sets of operations as the predominant ones in his essay on "The meaning of the digital humanities," concluding: "On the one hand, leading text encoding and digital archiving projects find it necessary to create their own analytic, processing, and visualization tools to present materials. And, on the other hand, text analysis, visualization, and other processing projects often have to go to great lengths to select, clean, and prepare pre-existent digital materials as a usable corpus" (Liu, 2013:411–12). Retrocomputing offers digital humanities tools and methods that are comparable to both "digitization" and "analysis" when it comes to the cultural artifacts of the computer age. Put another way, retrocomputing affords a set of applied practices for embedding the digital in a cultural and historical framework, the necessity of its specialized devices, procedures, and software confirming the now fundamental historicity of these once "new" objects.

The first and most basic of these practices involve recovering data from legacy media. This is where barriers to access are literally the most palpable. Because digital data is both invisible to the naked eye (at least under normal conditions) and encoded using arbitrary sign systems, the media must typically be rendered operational, at least to some degree, to attempt recovery. The whole tangle of ports, cables, and device drivers that govern interactions between an operating system and its peripherals must therefore be recreated, circumvented, imitated, or otherwise accounted for. Sometimes these transfers can be effected simply by using a chain of more or less contemporary components, for example a slightly older computer that still accommodates a particular media device; Doug Reside has termed these serendipitous hardware configurations "Rosetta computers," and gives the example of the Macintosh "Wall Street" Powerbook G3, which came with a so-called Superdisk (capable of reading 3½-inch disks recorded at various data densities), an Ethernet port, and a CD-ROM drive. The CD-ROM allows for installation of an alternative operating system such as Linux, the Superdrive means the computer can accommodate a variety of legacy media, and the Ethernet port provides the means for exporting the data (third-party cards even permitted the addition of USB devices via the machine's native PCMCIA slots). The Forensic Recovery of Evidence Device, or FRED, manufactured by Digital Intelligence, is essentially a purpose-built Rosetta computer that has connectors for a variety of magnetic and optical media, including all of the most common hard-drive interfaces.

But the retrocomputing community has also produced its own special-purpose tools for accessing even older forms of legacy media. The most common of these are floppy-disk controller cards, which allow a 5¼-inch disk drive to be connected to a contemporary operating system via a USB bridge. These cards tend to come and go, since they are hobbyist endeavors manufactured in small batches, sometimes even on-demand. The best-known is perhaps the KryoFlux, so called because it captures not individual "bits" per se but rather the sequences of magnetic fluxes that make up data in its physically recorded form. Importantly, this means that the card can often bypass corrupted tracks and sectors, vestigial copy-protection schemes, and other formatting idiosyncrasies since it is not seeking to interpret the data but merely obtain a recording of the signal duplicated from the magnetic fluxes on the surface of the media.

The purpose of all of the tools described above is the capture of what's known as an "image" of the original media. This is not of course a photographic image (though those too are sometimes obtained for preservation purposes) but rather a so-called "stream" consisting of every individual bit, whether in its raw signal state or interpreted as a binary value. Such bitstreams (or disk images), when obtained under sound forensic conditions, can function as legal surrogates for the original media, their digital evidence admissible in a court of law. Checksums ensure that not a single bit has been altered, inadvertently or otherwise, in the transfer process (While this might seem excessive from the standpoint of cultural heritage, consider the implications of a scholar staking an argument – and perhaps her tenure and career – on archival evidence obtained from born-digital media.) The disk image can then be analyzed, searched for keywords and strings or other forms of data and metadata, and even "carved" to look for unallocated and incomplete file fragments. A disk image is the best way of preserving the "original order" of a set of born-digital materials, since it will be inured from having its date- and time-stamps reset as part of its interactions with the new host operating system. From a scholarly standpoint, a disk image should therefore be regarded as a facsimile, an extremely high-fidelity surrogate of (in fact mathematically indistinguishable from) the "original." Because of our interest in these matters at the Maryland Institute for Technology in the Humanities (MITH), we have served as institutional collaborators on the BitCurator project, in which, together with researchers at UNC Chapel Hill, we are working to develop an open source digital forensics processing environment with exactly these capabilities (Figure 13.1).

There is thus an opportunity space for digital humanities here: while some libraries and archives now have these capabilities in-house as part of their mandate to process born-digital collections materials, many still do not. Moreover, those institutions are typically concerned with processing very large collections in aggregate, and often lack the time and resources as well as the appropriate workflows and procedures to take on boutique assignments. At MITH, we've been able to intervene in several important digital recovery projects – in effect, "digitizing" a born-digital object by migrating it from obsolescent media to a contemporary platform, where it can become an object for preservation and further analysis, reuse, or remixing. Doug Reside was able to use the aforementioned Rosetta computer to recover an unaltered disk image of William Gibson's famous and supposedly self-destructing or self-encrypting poem "Agrippa" from one of the original source disks; with the disk image in hand, the poem could be "played" in a Macintosh System 7 emulator to experience it in its original on-screen

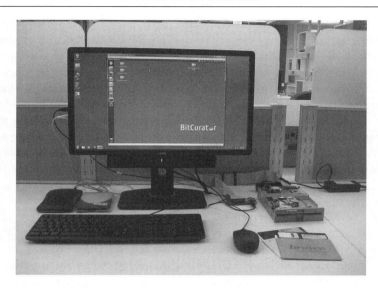

Figure 13.1   Digital forensics workstation at MITH running the BitCurator environment with various media drives, a write-blocker, and a Kryoflux controller card also visible. Source: photo by author.

presentation. Among the discoveries that emerged were that the poem contained crude sound effects included among its scripted behaviors. Similarly, I used a floppy controller card of the sort described above to recover Paul Zelevansky's animated digital game-text *SWALLOWS*, originally written in Forth-79 for the Apple II. With a 140 kB image file from the original 5¼-inch diskette, Zelevansky released a 2.0 remix of the work, which had not been seen since the mid-1980s. Other critics, such as Lori Emerson, have used the data thus recovered to do important new critical work on Zelevansky, helping to restore his place in the canon of electronic literature. A final example concerns IBM's Magnetic Tape Selectric Typewriter, or MT/ST, which was the first product ever marketed as a "word processor" (debuting in 1964, it weighed some 200 lb [90 kg] and carried a $10,000 price tag). We have one on site at MITH owing to my current work on the literary history of word processing, and are in the process of restoring it; specialists at a DC-area archival institution have tape cartridges originally prepared with an MT/ST, and are waiting on our restoration efforts to attempt their own data recovery.

That last example is representative of a kind of partnership that may enjoy further uptake. Because not every cultural heritage institution needs to retain the capacity to handle all esoteric media and device formats, a network of exchanges might take shape wherein the various institutional stakeholders would maintain mutually supporting repositories of vintage equipment. The OCLC is in fact experimenting with just such an initiative in an effort it has dubbed Software and Workstations for Antiquated Technology, or SWAT. They note that

> A SWAT site might have a wide array of computing platforms, including the software and drives to read many types of media. Alternatively, a SWAT site could specialize in one particular challenge, such as punched cards, early word-processing disks, or Apple II

media. Services could be offered to other archives (and, conceivably, to businesses, law enforcement, and individuals), perhaps on a cost-recovery basis ... (Erway, 2012:5)

Digital humanities centers are potentially excellent candidates for SWAT sites in that they typically enjoy greater institutional flexibility than, say, a library special collections unit. Regardless, the tools and expertise to recover data from outmoded media formats ought to be within the capacity of digital humanities centers as well as individual practitioners, just as we take it for granted that access to scanners, digital photography stations, and other forms of media transfer and digitization – and the competencies to make use of them – are indispensable components of digital humanities work.

Digital Culture

In 1952 Christopher Strachey, nephew of Bloomsbury stalwart Giles Lytton Strachey, programmed the Manchester Mark I computer to generate love letters according to a set of simple rules for creating sentences out of word lists. This is arguably the beginning of digital computing used for purposes of creative and artistic expression, though of course other dates and milestones are possible. Regardless, computers have been an essential element of creativity in the visual and literary arts, as well as music, film, and of course their own native medium, throughout the second half of the twentieth century, and especially since the advent of personal computing in the late 1970s. Just as scholars in a field such as the history of the book routinely pay very close attention to the material particulars of their subject matter – how a particular book is typeset, bound, or illustrated, but also more macro concerns as well, such as print runs and marketing – so too have scholars of digital culture now begun asking analogous kinds of questions regarding programming languages, software interfaces, hardware affordances, and network architectures. It matters, as Noah Wardrip-Fruin (2011) has discovered about Strachey's program (through archival research with its source code at the Bodleian), that its word lists *do* in fact contain the word "love" and its variants, thus refuting a reading by Alan Turing's biographer (Turing and Strachey were acquainted) that this was a computer program that "dared not speak its own name." Similarly, depending on the kinds of questions one is asking, it may matter whether a novelist was running WordStar on an Osborne 1 with a 3 × 5-inch screen, or whether he was using Pages on a pair of 21-inch plasma displays configured to operate in tandem. How many lines are visible on the screen at once? Did that constraint affect the writer's approach to the revision process? In recent years much of digital cultural studies and new media theory has undergone a "material" turn, and a plethora of new approaches have emerged, bearing names like media archaeology, platform studies, software studies, and critical code studies. Though not at all interchangeable – media archaeology in particular comes out of some very different contexts, primarily continental European – what is relevant for our purposes is that retrocomputing furnishes the specific technical resources that such scholarship demands, whether it's access to a functioning Osborne 1 or more specialized tools such as hex editors, emulators, decompilers, and disassemblers.

Digital humanities centers with the resources and a setting for retrocomputing are thus positioned to forge substantive collaborations with scholars working in areas of contemporary media and culture, including game studies, digital art, and electronic literature. Indeed, this is a particularly effective way to move digital humanities out of its traditional focus on public domain material, which too often results in twentieth- (let alone twenty-first-)century subjects being neglected. Moreover, digital humanities centers and programs are sometimes better positioned to appreciate the value of early computer games and software, which in other circles might be dismissed as mere pop culture ephemera. There are thus opportunities to build substantial holdings in those areas. At MITH we are the stewards of two large collections of hardware, software, data files, and manuscript materials from a pair of authors who have been associated with literary hypertext since its earliest years, Deena Larsen and Bill Bly (Figure 13.2). The Larsen and Bly Collections resemble typical literary manuscript collections in a number of respects; as I have described in greater detail elsewhere, they consist of both analog and digital content spanning multiple genres and forms in either state, ranging from correspondence and journals to drafts, proofs, proofs of concept, and the ultimately uncategorizable (Kirschenbaum, 2013). We initially acquired the Larsen Collection to serve as a research testbed for projects we were then undertaking in the digital preservation space, but even at the time we understood our long-term obligations as the caretakers and stewards of the material. Crucially, and with both Larsen and Bly's blessing, we have adopted an access model that resembles that of the University of Virginia's Rare Book School, where collections materials are routinely handled, shared, stressed, and even dismantled for pedagogical purposes. For us, one of Larsen's Macintosh computers is not only an object of preservation in its own right but also an operable platform that we don't hesitate to employ to access legacy media or furnish a

Figure 13.2 Part of MITH's retrocomputing collections, including materials from the Deena Larsen and Bill Bly Collections. Source: photo by author.

user with an authentic period experience. Recently we have developed a joint stewardship model with library special collections at Maryland, which ensures that these items will receive the same level of protection and long-term care as other special collections material; just as importantly, they will now be discoverable through the special collections interface via finding aids prepared in accordance with normal manuscript processing procedures. The preceding examples demonstrate the way in which retrocomputing resources open the door to collaborations with diverse campus entities, as well as partners in the surrounding community and beyond.

The *Pathfinders* project is another case in point (http://dtc-wsuv.org/wp/pathfinders). Directed by Dene Grigar and Stuart Moulthrop, and funded by the National Endowment for the Humanities (NEH) Office of Digital Humanities, *Pathfinders* addresses itself to the question of how one documents digital literary history in the context of the climate of accelerated technological change described by Sterne, where the kind of machines that were used to author and disseminate a particular work of electronic literature are all long obsolesced and scrapped. Emulators – which are essentially computer programs that are programmed to duplicate the operations of other computer programs, or even complete hardware and chip sets – are a partial solution, of course, but they are not infallible and can often fail to capture what archivists would term the "significant properties" of an original digital work (Not all emulators support sound, for example.) Drawing on Grigar's own extensive collection of vintage computers, *Pathfinders* has adopted a case-study approach, which consists of working with five important early authors of electronic literature (including Bly) to document the kinds of literary and interactive experiences their work produced. *Pathfinders* conducts oral history interviews with those authors and, crucially, records what the project terms "traversals," which are video sessions of both the authors themselves and other readers navigating the literary work on a restored exemplar of the original system for which it was designed (These in fact are both approaches that have previously been employed in the game preservation community, where there is a much larger constituency of persons interested in safeguarding their creative legacy.) Part digital preservation, part literary and textual studies, and part computer history, *Pathfinders* is a bracing example of the retrocomputing ethos harnessed for focused academic inquiry.

No act of preservation, of course, can fully restore every absent context for a given experience, whether digitally mediated or otherwise. The balance between the "lure of authentic experience" as Henry Lowood (2013) has recently termed it, and the kinds of concessions that have to be made because of limited curatorial resources and competing demands – for example, a museum exhibit that runs original hardware but directs the output to large-screen displays for easy viewing – is ever-present; and while locating and sustaining that balance is the source of much curatorial anxiety, it is also a fascinating area for scholarly and theoretical investigation, one that brings the importance of recent approaches like media archaeology and software or platform studies to the fore. For example, Lowood notes, "Another problem with the Authentic Experience is that often it is just not that useful to the researcher; it may not be the most useful way to understand historical software in execution." He offers the example of an emulator which, while perhaps requiring concessions with regard to authenticity as described above, also compensates by "offering real-time information about system states and code execution." This is a direct counterpoint to the positions of a media archaeologist such as Wolfgang Ernst (2011), who routinely asserts the primacy of technological agency in his writings and maintains a lab of restored computers and media devices. "'Historic' media objects are radically present when they still function, even if their outside world has vanished," he declares (Ernst, 2011:242), an insistence which dovetails with the plain joy of watching an antiquated machine flicker and return to life. Retrocomputing and digital preservation are thus the kinds of undertakings where competing theories must be put in to practice, with choices and trade-offs in the face of limited resources and material roadblocks. One could say the same, of course, about most any form of digital humanities.

Going Retro

While retrocomputing activities can readily be performed by individuals, since the resources required tend to be relatively inexpensive, the focus on collaborative work, the need to store and maintain material artifacts, and opportunities for public display and access make it particularly conducive to activities in centers and labs. As discussed above, MITH at Maryland shares joint stewardship of two literary manuscript collections that include extensive retrocomputing assets; in addition, MITH has also accumulated a substantial collection of computers, software, and other early computer memorabilia not affiliated with either the Larsen or Bly materials, including the MT/ST unit also described above, as well as a wide array of legacy drives, cables, connectors, and other peripherals to support various forms of digital recovery. Probably the single most extensive collection of vintage computers in North America in an overtly humanistic setting is the Media Archaeology Lab directed by Lori Emerson at the University of Colorado Boulder (http://mediaarchaeologylab.com), which maintains dozens of vintage machines, all in working order, including such rarities as a functioning Apple I replica and an Altair. Likewise, Nick Montfort founded the Trope Tank at MIT as a space where students can experiment with a variety of vintage platforms including an original *Asteroids* arcade machine (http://trope-tank.mit.edu). (While that last might seem indulgent, think about what it has to teach the student of human–computer interaction and computer games: the difference between vector and raster graphics; the affordances of push-button controllers; the ergonomics of standing upright at the console; and the aesthetic impact of the boldly painted cabinet.) Dene Grigar of the *Pathfinders* project maintains the Electronic Literature Lab, also with similar resources and capabilities (http://dtc-wsuv.org/wp/ell).

Importantly, all of these spaces are not just about preserving the past, but are also creating new work in various media – precisely the kinds of remixes described by Takhteyev and DuPont. The Media Archaeology Lab, for example, sponsors residencies from visiting artists who make use of their collections. A recent participant, Matt Soar, writes this about his project:

> My focus ... will be to use various "raw" materials (16 and 35 mm film leaders) to make work using artifacts from the MAL collection. The goal will be to create "happy accidents": composite images, projections, and time-based media that highlight and celebrate the ephemeral, paratextual aspects – the "metadata" – of film. (Media Archaeology Lab, 2013)

The MAL also sponsors lectures, class visits, and open houses, where members of the public can try out the vintage hardware, play games, and so forth. The Trope Tank, meanwhile, was instrumental to a book Montfort co-wrote with nine other authors. *10 PRINT CHR$(205.5+RND(1));:GOTO 10* (2013) is a rigorous technical and theoretical study of the cultural, technological, and imaginative significance of that single line of eponymous code, which draws a continuously and randomly computed maze-like pattern on the screen of a Commodore 64. Montfort routinely demonstrates the program on an actual C64, noting that it relies on the user's access to special character codes printed directly on the original keyboard, which, while replicable with an emulator, are not visually present as a feature of the host system. The intensive scrutiny of the *10 Print* program has also led Montfort and his collaborators to write new programs (in the original BASIC as well as contemporary languages) inspired by it. Besides remixes at the level of code and the conceptual elements of computing, retrocomputing also entails hands-on engagements with boards, circuits, and other physical components, resulting in such dramatic creations such as Jeri Ellsworth's fusing of a Commodore 64 to the neck of bass guitar, so that signals from its pick-ups are processed through the C64's original sound card (she frequently performs with the instrument while on roller skates) (Louisgoddard, 2012).

For both individuals and centers or institutes, perhaps the best way to begin developing a collection for retrocomputing is with a "honeypot." Take an old computer, preferably still working, and display it prominently in a heavily trafficked space. Visitors and passers-by will take note, and offer up that Osborne they still have in the attic or that Kaypro in their closet. As Sterne reminds us, many people tend to hang on to their old computers and peripherals, and the opportunity to donate them to a space where they might enjoy active use from an interested and engaged community will prove irresistible. Indeed, in short time you will find that you will want to develop a collections policy so that you are not just acquiring hardware and software aimlessly. Considerations include: Do you want to collect broadly or in a specific time period? Machines of any particular type or make? Is it important that they be in working order, or do you have the resources to repair them? Who will be the users for this equipment? Will any of it be unique or valuable in its own right? Do you want to preserve and restore the machines, or do you want them to be taken apart and reassembled? What about peripherals like printers? What about storage media, and can you ensure privacy for any data that might remain accessible on them? And so on. *eBay* and *Craig's List* are both excellent places to find potential collections material as well as spare parts and components, although some institutions will also confront bureaucratic obstacles when purchasing from these sources (a nontrivial consideration, in fact). Equally opportune are the surplus storefronts that many campuses maintain. Along with the actual hardware, it is worth configuring one or more contemporary machines as a retrocomputing hub, outfitted with software resources like emulators, and specialized equipment such as the Retrode2, which allows users to play Nintendo SNES cartridges with the original controllers through an emulator on a contemporary computer, while also allowing users to extract their ROM files (Donahue, 2012). (As the preceding suggests, retrocomputing can sometimes become a legally grey area, and individual institutions will have to research what issues may obtain and find their individual comfort level.) Finally, one should not overlook the fact that a great deal of digital culture and computer history exists in *print*, in the form of manuals, books, magazines, and newsletters, as well as the packaging and promotional material that accompanied early software products. This too is an essential element for collections building, and the manuals and documentation can often be had for pennies on the dollar. A sizable reference library can be built up very quickly.

For data recovery activities, while one can spend a lot of money on specialized digital forensics resources, as Porter Olsen (2013) has demonstrated the necessities can also be covered very inexpensively. Elements to consider including sources for the necessary drives and controller cards, a write-blocker for ensuring data integrity, and software with forensics capabilities. Legacy floppy drives for both 3½- and 5¼-inch disks are easily and inexpensively found on the second-hand markets. The former can come with a USB connection, so compatibility with current platforms is a non-issue; the latter will require a specialized controller card of the kind described above, and these are somewhat more expensive (though not prohibitively so). A write-blocker is a physical hardware device that ensures data is not inadvertently passed to the legacy media from a host computer in the process of obtaining a disk image; it is an essential component for professional forensics work, and also a good idea for archival and cultural heritage applications. Software options include several high-end packages with yearly licensing fees, as well as a number of open-source utilities, the best known of which is called *The Sleuthkit*. The aforementioned BitCurator project gathers and packages a number of the open-source digital forensics utilities and allows a user to access them from both a custom Linux installation and a virtual machine.

Retrocomputing is thus very affordable. It is not the province solely of long-established centers at elite institutions. On the contrary, it is most frequently supported through gift economies and barter, collaboration, swaps, collectives, meet-ups, and second-hand markets. Retrocomputing is a reminder that computers afford diverse forms of interaction, including those *not* always characterized by ease, efficiency, immediacy, or accessibility. It is thus a theoretically replete valance for digital humanities activity, and perhaps even more important in that regard than the preceding has suggested. For if old versus new is ultimately a difficult binary to sustain, a more productive one, at least in the present moment, is arguably to be found in the contrast between big and small. Much digital humanities is now characterized by engagements with so-called "big" data; this in itself is a relatively recent phenomenon, driven by the widespread availability of vast research corpora from repositories such as the HathiTrust, as well as the desktop tools with which to analyze them. Distant reading, macroanalytics, cultural analytics, culturomics, big humanities, the humanities "at scale," and "the massive" are all influential tropes and terms, as other contributions to this volume will confirm. Against this backdrop, retrocomputing perhaps opens a space for the unapologetically small, the uncompromisingly local and particular: this machine, *that* pin, *that* screw (the one you scraped your knuckle getting loose), *that* board (the one you burned yourself soldering). Digital humanities, however one elects to define it, has to be big enough for the tiny things too.

Acknowledgments

I am grateful to Ted Underwood for a clarifying Twitter exchange that helped me in my thinking about retrocomputing and its relation to "big" data.

REFERENCES AND FURTHER READING

Donahue, R. 2012. Preserving virtual SNES games. Maryland Institute for Technology in the Humanities, October 25. http://mith.umd.edu/preserving-virtual-snes-games (accessed June 20, 2015).

Emerson, L. 2014. *Reading/Writing/Interfaces: From the Digital to the Bookbound*. Minneapolis: University of Minnesota Press.

Ernst, W. 2011. Media archaeography: method and machine versus history and narrative of media. In *Media Archaeology: Approaches, Applications, and Implications*, ed. E. Huhtamo and J. Parikka. Berkeley and Los Angeles: University of California Press, 239–55.

Ernst, W. 2013. *Digital Memory and the Archive*. Minneapolis: University of Minnesota Press.

Erway, R. 2012. *Swatting the Long Tail of Digital Media: a Call for Collaboration*. Dublin, OH: OCLC Research. http://www.oclc.org/research/publications/library/2012/2012-08.pdf (accessed June 20, 2015).

Galloway, P. 2011. Retrocomputing, archival research, and digital heritage preservation: a computer museum and ischool collaboration. *Library Trends* 59 (4), 623–36.

Goto80. 2013. *Computer Rooms*. Bräkne-Hoby, Sweden: Click Festival.

Keacher, J. 2013. How I introduced a 27-year-old computer to the Web. http://www.dailydot.com/opinion/mac-plus-introduce-modern-web (accessed June 20, 2015).

Kirschenbaum, M.G. 2008. *Mechanisms: New Media and the Forensic Imagination*. Cambridge, MA: MIT Press.

Kirschenbaum, M.G. 2013. The .txtual condition: digital humanities, born-digital archives, and the future literary. *DHQ: Digital Humanities Quarterly* 7 (1). http://www.digitalhumanities.org/dhq/vol/7/1/000151/000151.html (accessed June 20, 2015).

Kirschenbaum, M.G. 2014. Software, it's a thing. https://medium.com/@mkirschenbaum/software-its-a-thing-a550448d0ed3 (accessed June 20, 205).

Kopstein, J. 2013. "The Thing" redialed: how a BBS changed the art world and came back from the dead. The *Verge*, March 15. http://www.theverge.com/2013/3/15/4104494/the-thing-reloaded-bringing-bbs-networks-back-from-the-dead (accessed June 20, 2015).

Lee, C.A., Woods, K., Kirschenbaum, M., and Chassanoff, A. 2013. *From Bitstreams to Heritage: Putting Digital Forensics into Practice*. Chapel Hill, NC: The BitCurator Project. http://www.bitcurator.net/docs/bitstreams-to-heritage.pdf (accessed June 20, 2015).

Liu, A. 2013. The meaning of the digital humanities. *PMLA* 128, 409–23.

Louisgoddard. 2012. Commodore 64 transformed into hybrid bass keytar. *The Verge*, July 9. http://www.theverge.com/2012/7/9/3146354/commodore-64-bass-guitar (accessed June 20, 2015).

Lowood, H. 2013. The lures of software preservation. In *Preserving.exe: Toward a National Strategy for Preserving Software*. Washington DC: Library of Congress. http://blogs.loc.gov/digitalpreservation/2013/10/preserving-exe-report-toward-a-national-strategy-for-preserving-software (accessed June 20, 2015).

Manovich, L. 2013. *Software Takes Command*. New York: Bloomsbury.

Media Archaeology Lab. 2013. Matt Soar. http://mediaarchaeologylab.com/matt-soar (accessed June 20, 2015).

Montfort, N. and Bogost, I. 2009. *Racing the Beam: The Atari Video Computer System*. Cambridge, MA: MIT Press. A demonstration of the platform studies approach.

Montfort, N., Baudoin, P., Bell, J., et al. 2013. *10 PRINT CHR$(205.5+RND(1)); : GOTO 10*. Cambridge, MA: MIT Press.

Olsen, P. 2013. Building a digital curation workstation with BitCurator (update) *BitCurator*, August 2. http://www.bitcurator.net/building-a-digital-curation-workstation-with-bitcurator-update (accessed June 20, 2015).

Parikka, J. 2013. *What is Media Archaeology?* Cambridge: Polity. A short and accessible introduction to the topic.

Pathfinders. 2013. Curatorial plan for the Pathfinders exhibit at the MLA 2014. http://dtc-wsuv.org/wp/pathfinders/2013/12/16/curatorial-plan-for-the-pathfinders-exhibit-at-the-mla-2014 (accessed June 20, 2015).

Reside, D. 2010. Rosetta computers. In *Digital Forensics and Born-Digital Content in Cultural Heritage Collections*, ed. M. Kirschenbaum, R. Ovenden, and G. Redwine. Washington DC: CLIR, 20.

Sterne, J. 2007, Out with the trash: on the future of new media. In *Residual Media.*, ed. C.R. Acland. Minneapolis: University of Minnesota Press, 16–31.

Takhteyev, Y., and DuPont, Q. 2013. Retrocomputing as preservation and remix. *Library Hi Tech* 31 (2), 355–70.

Tassäjarvi, L., ed. 2004. *Demoscene: The Art of Real-Time*. Even Lake Studios.

Wardrip-Fruin, N. 2011. Digital media archaeology: interpreting computational processes. In *Media Archaeology: Approaches, Applications, and Implications*, ed E. Huhtamo and J. Parikka. Berkeley and Los Angeles: University of California Press, 302–22.

Part III
Analysis

14

Mapping the Geospatial Turn

Todd Presner and David Shepard

The subfield of mapping, geo-temporal visualization, and locative storytelling within the digital humanities has exploded in recent years. Reasons for this development include the recent ubiquity of web- and GPS-enabled devices, the simplification of the technical software required to make maps, and the wide availability of historical imagery and geographic datasets. Attempts to characterize this field have used a number of convergent terms to describe the "spatial turn" in the digital humanities, the rise of "spatial humanities" as a field of research and a methodology, and the emergence of "geohumanities" as place-based investigation at the creative intersection between geography and humanities (Guildi, undated; Bodenhamer *et al.*, 2010; Dear *et al.*, 2011). It would be reductive to claim that quantitative methods stemming from geographic information systems (GIS) are simply brought to bear on qualitative, historical, and interpretative methods from the humanities; rather, "geohumanities" has precipitated a scholarly reconceptualization of the significance of place in relationship to narrative, practices of representation, and digital technologies. "Space" and "time" are not empty containers or given categories; instead, they are situated constructions and conceptual problems that call for a multiplicity of approaches to mapping. They, therefore, demand a historical awareness of differential and culturally specific ways of conceptualizing "space" and "time."

On its most basic level, a map is a kind of visualization that uses levels of abstraction, scale, coordinate systems, perspective, symbology, and other forms of representation to convey a set of relations. The map may or may not have some kind of referent to an "external reality" (however one defines that), but maps are always

A New Companion to Digital Humanities, First Edition. Edited by Susan Schreibman, Ray Siemens, and John Unsworth.
© 2016 John Wiley & Sons, Ltd. Published 2016 by John Wiley & Sons, Ltd.

relational, from the moment that something is inscribed relative to something else. Within the history of cartography, critical cartography studies, and, more recently, radical cartography, maps have been shown to be "systems of propositions," to use Denis Wood's term, in that they always make arguments and claims (and, in so doing, also exclude, silence, and erase other arguments and claims) (Wood, 2010:34). The history of cartography betrays the many ways that maps are implicated in ideologies of discovery, ownership, and control in fashioning the power and reach of the nation-state, fostering the colonial will to know, and encoding power dynamics as naturalized expressions of a world supposedly "out there." Much work has been done in the humanities, geography, and critical cartography studies to "denaturalize" the map and expose the structuring assumptions, epistemologies, and worldviews that govern its propositional form.[1]

Mapping in the digital humanities ranges from historical mapping of "time-layers" to memory maps, linguistic and cultural mapping, conceptual mapping, community-based mapping, and forms of counter-mapping that attempt to de-ontologize cartography and imagine new worlds. In the 1950s, the members of the experimental Situationist group developed an approach to experiencing urban spaces that they termed "psychogeography" in order to create a new critical awareness of urban environments. Similarly speculative, cognitive maps are used to model experience in many domains of human life where qualitative properties are given dimension and formal value in visual form. Additionally, with locative media, the physical landscape and built environment are curated and annotated to produce augmented experiences. Data landscapes can be curated in the physical space of the city, allowing a user with a Global Positioning System (GPS)-enabled mobile device, for example, to listen to geo-coordinated soundscapes while walking down a sidewalk, follow in the footsteps of the dead, or hear stories told by generations of immigrants about a neighborhood. Such locative investigations bring together the analytical tools of GIS, the structuring and querying capacities of geo-temporal databases, and delivery interfaces on GPS-enabled mobile devices.

While critiques of GIS and GPS technologies rightly point out their investment in and deployment by military and corporate infrastructures (Parks, 2005), these same technologies have also been repurposed in profound ways that destabilize physical borders and facilitate critical forms of counter-mapping, subversion, and hacktivism. For example, Ricardo Dominguez, founder of the *Electronic Disturbance Theater*, developed the "transborder immigrant tool," a recycled phone equipped with a GPS receiver, GIS maps, and a digital compass to guide immigrants to water caches and safety in the desert between Mexico and southern California. As Elizabeth Losh explains Dominguez's project, "the global migrant underclass unable to afford so-called smart phones would no longer be 'outside of this emerging grid of hyper-geo-mapping-power' ('Transborder Immigrant Tool'), and the harsh reality of the border landscape could be digitally augmented to promote a different form of politics" (Losh, 2012:169). In other words, as Laura Kurgan has argued in her own work on both using and subverting digital technologies of location, it is possible to reclaim, repurpose, and politicize these mapping technologies by prying apart "their opacities, their assumptions, and intended aims" through critical and activist modes of creativity (Kurgan, 2013:14).

A Brief History of GPS and GIS

The history of remote sensing satellites stretches back to the 1960s with the launching of the first military spy satellites and the research to build the Global Positioning System (GPS). Completed in 1993, the 24 satellites and five ground stations provide signals that allow receivers to accurately calculate and potentially target any point on the planet according to latitude, longitude, altitude, and time. GIS – variously called geographic information systems or sciences – refers to the computational tools and software for analyzing geographic data and producing maps based on such data. GIS resulted from a network of competing and intersecting interests, ranging from corporate and military interests to governmental and civil libertarian ones. It was only because of this corporate–governmental interchange that the tools and the political challenges of open spatial data that we now know came into being. Today, web-based mapping applications such as *Google Earth*, *OpenStreetMap*, and *WorldMap* have brought the analytic tools of GIS to the general public, and are changing the way people create, visualize, interpret, and access geographic information.

The first location-based technologies were developed in the 1960s by a variety of government interests focused on land management. One of the first large GIS programs was CGIS, the *Canada Geographic Information System*, developed for the Canada Land Inventory, which began in 1962 (Tomlinson, 2012). But the development of large-scale GIS systems did not begin until the end of the 1970s, with the creation of MOSS (*Map Overlay and Statistical System*) by the US Fish and Wildlife Services. MOSS was developed by the Federation of Rocky Mountain States, a nonprofit organization, and was the first broadly deployed, vector-based, interactive GIS (Reed, 2004). Likewise, the Army Corps of Engineers developed GRASS (*Geographic Resources Analysis Support System*) in 1982. MOSS and GRASS were the first large-scale deployed systems used by a variety of customers in different offices. GRASS was eventually made available to the international academic community and had about 6000 users by the early 1990s. The presence of two widely used systems (plus others) with different strengths led users to want to exchange data between the two. The GRASS Interagency Steering Committee (GIASC) and the GRASS users' group merged to form the Open GRASS Foundation (OGF). OGF brought together private companies, government agencies, and academic users to drive the development of shared standards for interoperable software. OGF eventually became the Open Geospatial Consortium, the organization we know today (McKee, 2013). The standards it created were to ensure compatibility between applications rather than to generate open data for public consumption.

Arguably the first computerized humanistic mapping project followed shortly after the development of GIS technology. In the early 1970s, linguists Mario Alinei, Wolfgang Viereck, and Antonius Weijnen led a research project to map language use patterns in Europe, the *Atlas Linguarum Europae* ("Linguistic Atlas of Europe"). The ALE sent fieldworkers to 3000 locations from Portugal to Russia to survey locals on the words they used for particular concepts, with the goal of describing language usage independent of national boundaries or categories of language like "Italian" or "Spanish," which gloss over regional dialects and other languages spoken in those nations. The results were mapped using a computerized plotter (Weijnen and Alinei, 1975) and published as a series of print maps beginning in 1983 (Alinei, 2008). The project has been updated and is ongoing. Aside from the ALE, however, mapping technology was not widely deployed in the humanities in the 1970s and 1980s because of the cost and esoteric nature of GIS; the ALE could make use of these cutting-edge technologies because it was an international effort spread across multiple universities that received funding from UNESCO.

In the 1990s, as the Open Geospatial Consortium was growing, the field of "web mapping" emerged alongside the development of web browsers. This transition from desktop to web GIS was profound in a number of ways ranging from the technical to the social. While there were certainly many technical challenges to overcome to make web mapping available to the general public, the biggest transformation came in the mentality and public work of mapmakers themselves. Desktop-based GIS systems were primarily used to produce print maps, while web-based maps were intended for a (potentially) global audience. Static maps were replaced by dynamic, real-time, interactive animated maps, and at times, even immersive 3D environments. Data were fungible and could be manipulated by users who could interactively modify *what* they saw on a map, via options such as spatial queries, filters, toggles, time sliders, panning, and zooming. The development of web mapping began in earnest in 1994, when Xerox PARC presented a rudimentary map server at the first World Wide Web conference (Putz, 1994). Web mapping took another significant step when MapQuest released its first web map in 1996. ESRI released its first professional web GIS products, *Map Objects*, *ArcGIS*, and *ArcIMS*, in 1998, 1999, and 2000, respectively. *ArcGIS* (as we know it today) was first released as version 8.0 in 1999, and combined two other products, *ArcView* and *Arc/Info*. While these early tools were primitive by modern standards, and pale in comparison to what *Google Maps* could do in 2005, they opened the door for public interest in Web-based maps that could be merged with other kinds of data.

With the sudden visibility of geographic data, spatial data standards became a political matter, not just a matter of compatibility. In 2000, OGC released its first mapping standard, *Web Map Service*, and another in 2003, *Web Feature Service*. When Google purchased Keyhole, Inc. and with it the program that became *Google Earth*, they submitted Keyhole's in-house *Keyhole Markup Language (KML)* to the OGC for formal standardization (Open Geospatial Consortium, 2008). At the same time, the geo-developer community began creating alternatives to government and corporate-provided software and data. *OpenLayers*, an open-source alternative to *Google Maps*, was released in 2006. *OpenStreetMap*, a volunteer-driven mapping initiative, began the same year, out of frustration with the British government's refusal to release an open version of its Ordnance Survey maps (OpenStreetMap, undated). Today, *GeoServer* (http://geoserver.org) is the open-source software server certified by the OGC to share interoperable, standards-compliant spatial data, maps, and geo-visualizations globally. Other platforms, such as the ESRI community site, *GeoCommons* (http://geocommons. com), have also come online in recent years to openly share geo-data.

This transition to web mapping thus shifted the dynamics of *who* was able to create maps. No longer were governments, militaries, corporations, and professional geographers, urban planners, and cartographers the only or the only authoritative mapmakers. The expansion to the Web, coupled with the availability of satellite imagery, data providers, and map APIs from *Google* to *OpenLayers*, took away the time-consuming aspect of having to acquire basemaps and learn abstruse software. It empowered an entire generation of mappers who were now able to create web maps with just a little bit of programming knowledge. To this day, the push for open spatial data exchange continues to come from many directions.

Despite the changes in technologies, it seems fitting that 30 years later, some of the original GIS programs are still viable open-source projects that interoperate with new web mapping technologies. GRASS (http://grass.osgeo.org) runs under Windows, Mac OS, and Linux today, and still has a robust user community. What were once government tools have found new life as open-source projects, in the same way that we repurpose corporate web mapping software and data collected from spy satellites to empower community organizations and nonprofits to tell their own stories and create their own maps. The standardization that began as a compatibility concern has led to the ability to tell other narratives and make counter-maps.

The Spatial Turn in the Digital Humanities

When Google released its *Maps application programming interface (API)* in the summer of 2005 (followed by its *Earth API* shortly thereafter), a small revolution occurred. Anyone with basic programming skills could now integrate Google's world map and the accompanying satellite imagery into individual websites, create and mark up maps using this imagery, and even develop new software using Google Maps. Quite suddenly, the esoteric world of GIS was opened up to the masses of neo-geographers on the web, and map mashups flourished almost overnight. Geographic and temporal markup became indispensable metadata fields for a vast array of Web content, prompting Michael Jones, Google's chief technologist, to emend his company's mission: "to *geographically* organize the world's information and make it universally accessible and useful" (Jones, 2007).

While Google hardly invented (let alone organized) the geospatial web, it is remarkable that the number of digital mapping projects has exploded since mapping technologies, geo-data, and satellite imagery have been put in the hands of the masses. Far from going unrecognized, as Martyn Jessop argued in a provocative article published in 2007, the geo-revolution has been taken up by the digital humanities in countless ways, despite – or perhaps because of – the very fundamental problems that he identified to explain the supposedly slow uptake of geographic analysis and visualization in the humanities: the fuzzy nature of humanities data; the fact that most humanists work with textual, visual, and sonic sources that do not lend themselves to geometric or mathematical abstractions; and the persistent disciplinary silos which have prevented serious collaborations between humanists and geographers, urban planners, architects, archaeologists, anthropologists, and others working with spatial data.

Over the past decade, the geospatial turn in the digital humanities has been catalyzed by a number of convergent institutional, technological, and intellectual changes. These include the efforts of major libraries and museums, such as (among others) the Newberry, the Huntington Library, the University of Southern California, the University of Virginia, and the New York Public Library, as well as private initiatives such as the *David Rumsey Map Collection*, to geo-code historical atlases and maps, newspapers, and photograph collections. At the same time, a number of historical GIS platforms, such as *Social Explorer*, have come online. *Social Explorer* (www.socialexplorer.com) provides demographic information, from median income to religious affiliation, for the United States since 1790 at various geographic levels, from state and county to census tract, block group, zip code, and census place.[2] An analogous project is *A Vision of Britain through Time* (www.visionofbritain.org.uk), which allows users to download census reports throughout the nineteenth and twentieth centuries, a wide range of historical maps, statistical geo-data, and even geo-encoded travel writing.

One of the largest and most impactful early infrastructure and community-building initiatives was the *Electronic Cultural Atlas Initiative* (ECAI), an international effort that originated at UC Berkeley in 2001. ECAI created a federation of scholars working on humanities GIS and became a clearinghouse for cultural-historical geo-data, especially digital gazetteer development (structured dictionaries of geographic places). ECAI mapping projects were quite diverse, mapping languages in the Pacific, the cultural impact of the Silk Road, and the history of Sydney, Australia, among other things. It also provided software for displaying geographic data over time, such as "timemap," although the programs have since been replaced by more up-to-date tools. Nevertheless, these efforts played a significant role in the maturation of historical GIS, the development of metadata standards, and linked geo-data, giving rise to comprehensive gazetteers such as Ruth Mostern and Elijah Meeks' *Digital Gazetteer of the Song Dynasty* (http://songgis.ucmerced.edu).

Similar projects and efforts were also under way in other historical disciplines. Begun in 1993 and completed in 2007, Edward Ayers' *The Valley of the Shadow* project (http://valley.lib.virginia.edu) is a place-based investigation of two communities during the American Civil War, one Northern and one Southern. While not, strictly speaking, a mapping project, the archive features a trove of letters, diaries, soldier records, newspaper articles, census records, and other documents that allow queries based on county, time period, and document type. Rather than presenting a global view with pretensions to objectivity, *The Valley of the Shadow* acts as a rudimentary form of what we have come to call a "thick map," a map that exposes a variety of sources that can be bought together to tell any number of smaller stories. Other projects, such as *Atlantic Europe in the Metal Ages* at King's College London (www.aemap.ac.uk), have used GIS to test specific hypotheses, in this case whether and how Celtic evolved from Indo-European in Atlantic Europe during the Bronze Age, using a body of historical, linguistic, and archaeological data.

The surge of large-scale text digitization and markup projects begun in the 1990s paved the way to develop geo-encoding standards through the Text Encoding Initiative (TEI) and Geography Markup Language (GML). While place data can be indicated at many levels (from point data and address to city or country), the most granular markup gives location in terms of latitude and longitude based on a standard coordinate system, usually World Geodetic System 84 (WGS:84). While humanities data may sometimes fit within such a frame of reference, other times these data do not, especially when we consider uncertainty or variability in the historical record, imaginative or speculative geographies, non-Western ways of conceptualizing space and place, or subjective experiences of space that simply do not map onto standard coordinate systems or projections. At the same time, standard coordinate systems and projections allow data to be shared across platforms, something that potentially enables more users and communities to tell their own stories by making their own maps. Led by David Germano, the *Tibetan and Himalayan Digital Library* (www.thlib.org) offers a publishing platform, networked information system, and multilingual library for accessing and analyzing a wide range of spatially encoded information, including texts, images, videos, historic maps, and GIS data layers, related to the Tibetan plateau and the southern Himalayas. It also facilitates participatory scholarship in local communities by empowering "citizen scholars" to document and tell their own stories while adhering to standards and facilitating the interoperability of data.

In archaeology and classics, mapping has exploited the third and fourth dimensions through digital reconstruction projects. The *Digital Roman Forum* (http://dlib.etc.ucla.edu/projects/Forum), led by Bernard Frischer and Diane Favro between 1997 and 2003 as part of UCLA's Cultural Virtual Reality Laboratory, built digital models of the Roman Forum based on archaeological and textual evidence of how it looked in antiquity. The models featured time-stamps and geographical data in three dimensions, which, several years later, could be exported into and viewed in other geographically aware environments, such as Google Earth. Other multidimensional modeling projects have followed, including *Digital Karnak* (http://dlib.etc.ucla.edu/projects/Karnak), a model of the enormous temple complex at Karnak that enables viewers to follow the architectural, religious and political development through a time slider and thematic maps. More recently, the *Venice Time Machine* (http://partenariats.epfl.ch/page-92987-en.html), which originated at the École Polytechnique Federal de Lausanne (EPFL) and Ca' Foscari University in Venice, is an attempt to digitize and interpret the city government's extensive historical archives. Among the current projects making use of the archive are several mapping initiatives, including a three-dimensional virtual-reality model of the city throughout its long history, and a map of shipping routes and trade networks in different periods.

Far from simply "recreating" historical environments and making historical data available to the wider public, however, the digital humanities has also developed a rich critical vocabulary to understand the rhetoric of mapping and geo-visualization. Unlike conventional approaches to mapping, which tend to be positivistic and mimetic, the digital humanities has imagined critical practices of geo-temporal narration, forms of counter-mapping, and notions of "deep mapping" or "thick mapping," which privilege experiential navigation, time-based approaches, participatory mapping, and alternative rhetorics of visualization (Bodenhamer, 2010, 2014; see also Presner *et al.*, 2014). Maps and models are never static representations or accurate reflections of a past reality; instead, they function as arguments or propositions that betray a state of knowledge. Each of these projects is a snapshot of a state of knowledge, a propositional argument in the form of dynamic geo-visualizations.

Humanities Mapping

Prior to the burst of interest in GIS and geo-visualization technologies in the humanities, the significance of the geographic and the spatial dimensions of cultural production had not gone unrecognized by humanities scholars. After all, some of the most significant theorizations of the cultural production of space have been made by humanists, such as Fredric Jameson's concept of "cognitive mapping" linked to Los Angeles, Michel de Certeau's notion of "everyday life" in New York, and David Harvey's studies of the modernity of capitalism in Paris and London. Further, building on the writing of Edward Said, much work has been done in transnational and postcolonial studies to examine the "spatial strata" of cultural production and power. One need only think of studies such as Paul Gilroy's "black Atlantic," Arjun Appadurai's "global ethnoscapes," Homi Bhabha's "location of culture," James Clifford's anthropological study of "routes," and Stephen Greenblatt's call for "mobility studies" to focus on questions of diaspora, exile, and displacement in literary and language studies, and the call for renewed attention to psycho-geographies, imaginary landscapes, and practices of *détournement* rooted in situationist ideas of urban engagement and cognitive dissonance.

In literary studies, Franco Moretti's *Atlas of the European Novel* (1998) and *Graphs, Maps, Trees* (2005) explore the "geography of literature" as both the journeys characters take as a kind of literary mapping, and the mapping of literary texts themselves to shed light on market forces, urban topographies, and the growth of the nation-state. More recently, Robert Tally has developed an approach called "geocriticism," derived from Bernard Westphal's *Geocriticism: Real and Fictional Spaces* (2011), which explores the role of space and place in fiction through literary cartographies (e.g., Tally, 2009). And with a robust collaboration of methods across literary studies and GIS, mapping has started to investigate new aspects of literary history. Ryan Cordell's "Reprinting, circulation, and the network author in antebellum newspapers" (2015) is a study of the growth of American authors' readership through mapping the journals that reprinted them. He juxtaposes these publication maps with demographic data and the history of the American railways system, in essence performing Greenblatt's call for "mobility studies."

The study of history has also taken a spatial turn, precisely as GIS has taken a historical turn.[3] These blended approaches situate and investigate historical questions on spatial platforms, without uncritically embracing or cavalierly dismissing GIS. Richard Marciano and David Theo Goldberg's T-RACES project (http://salt.umd.edu/T-RACES), for example, brings together the history of redlining maps produced by the Home Owners' Loan Corporation in the 1930s with archival documents linked to census tract, in order to reveal the complex ways in which exclusionary spaces were created throughout the United States to preserve racial homogeneity. In T-RACES, a massive archive of American racial history has been geo- and temporally marked up in a discovery and historical visualization platform built on the *Google Maps* engine. Another project, *Mapping the Republic of Letters*, developed at Stanford University (http://republicofletters.stanford.edu), visualizes the correspondence networks through which European and American intellectuals debated politics, philosophy, and government theory during the eighteenth century. For instance, the Italian thinker Francesco Algarotti exchanged letters with

Americans like Benjamin Franklin and Samuel Engs, and Voltaire wrote to Czarina Catherine II of Russia. The project demonstrates the international scope of these correspondence networks, something that is difficult to appreciate when considering any one of these thinkers' work in isolation.

For historians such as Richard White, the director of Stanford's Spatial History project, mapping, modeling, and visualization are methods of research to test hypotheses, discover patterns, and investigate historical processes and relationships. He argues that spatial analysis and visualization are

> not about producing illustrations or maps to communicate things that you have discovered by other means. **It is a means of doing research**; it generates questions that might otherwise go unasked, it reveals historical relations that might otherwise go unnoticed, and it undermines, or substantiates, stories upon which we build our own versions of the past. (White, 2010)

Other historians, including Philip Ethington, have begun to conceptualize and design new cartographic approaches to history that foreground place and place-making as ways to visualize and narrate cities in deep time. Ethington (2007:466) argues that "knowledge of the past ... is literally cartographic: a mapping of the places of history indexed to the coordinates of spacetime." Maps work, he argues, primarily by juxtaposition and simultaneity, bringing discrete data together to delve into the layered histories impacted in a given place. Together with verbal text, which is syntactically linear and narratological, history – as told through "ghost maps" – can be thought of as topoi to envision the many pasts of Los Angeles (Ethington, 2011; Ethington and Toyosawa, 2014). Experienced as a complexly layered visual and cartographic history, Ethington's history of Los Angeles, *Ghost Metropolis*, demonstrates how history literally "takes" and "makes" place, transforming the urban, cultural, and social environment as various "regional regimes" leave their impression on the landscape of the global city of Los Angeles.

In concert with these developments, new institutional configurations such as "urban humanities" have developed, which ally architecture, design, urban planning, computational analysis, GIS, and the humanities to investigate the complexity of cities – as embodied, lived in, built, imagined, and represented spaces. Like the digital humanities, these configurations lead to different kinds of research questions, in terms of scale, method, content, and output. How might we begin to map the cultural, social, and architectural history of megacities, where some 10% of the earth's population now resides? How can we respond to the grand challenge of designing and building a more democratic city? To respond to such questions, a plurality of perspectives and expertise as well as partnerships beyond the walls of the university with nongovernment organizations (NGOs), city councils and regional governments, developers, museums, and countless cultural and social constituencies are, of course, needed. These kinds of collaborations are starting to be established in many places, especially at "spatial research centers" such as Harvard's Center for Geographic Analysis, Stanford's *Spatial History Project* (part of its Center for Spatial and Textual Analysis), Columbia's Spatial Information Design Lab, UCLA's Experiential Technologies Center, and multi-institutional collaborations such as the Virtual Center for Spatial Humanities (http://thepoliscenter.iupui.edu/index.php/spatial-humanities/project-1).

As more and more humanistic and technological projects have converged and matured, sophisticated general-purpose tools have been developed for radically inter-disciplinary humanities mapping. *WorldMap* (http://worldmap.harvard.edu), an open-source platform from Harvard for exploring, visualizing, and publishing geographic information, allows users to assemble thematic collections of GIS data in many formats to publish on the Web. Built on *Google Earth*, *HyperCities* (http://hypercities.com) is a "thick mapping" tool for crafting geo-temporal narratives out of historical maps, GIS data, and other geo-encoded materials. ESRI recently released a narrative mapping tool, *Story Maps* (http://storymaps.esri.com), while the University of Virginia released *Neatline* (http://neatline.org), an interactive tool for telling stories using maps, time-lines, and exhibition resources through *Omeka*. These projects, among others, strive to make what was once esoteric – creating maps with various kinds of spatial data – accessible to the general public, while embracing a critical notion of mapping as propositional, situated knowledge.

There are still many challenges ahead, not least the creation of a qualitative GIS that deepens humanistic interpretative methods by enabling multi-perspectival mapping, ambiguity and uncertainty, and differential approaches that de-colonize maps, map-making, coordinate systems, and standardized projections. The specter of positivism and objectivism still looms large in this field. As more theoretical rigor and experi-mental methods emerge, we are likely to see new forms of "thick mapping" that build toward a multiplicity of modalities for participatory storytelling, counter-mapping, and site-specific meaning making. Far from the Apollonian eye looking down from a transcendental view, "thick mapping" betrays the contingency of looking, the ground-edness of any perspective, and the embodied relationality inherent to any locative investigation.

To imagine such alternatives, perhaps one of the most promising new direc-tions for the field is immersive mapping through avatar-based, virtual-world gaming environments (e.g., the Humanities Virtual Worlds Consortium, http://virtualworlds.etc.ucla.edu). As an experiential and experimental modality for con-structing, exploring, and interacting with three-dimensional models situated within a time-based GIS framework, researchers pose questions and test hypotheses within dynamic environments embodied by human avatars. This interaction enables the investigation of embodied, on-the-ground perspectives in and on built spaces and landscapes, especially to study time-based events (like orations, parades, or funerary processions through the Roman Forum). While the advances described above have resulted in innovative projects, the field continues to change rapidly as new technologies and new archives become available. Much work still remains to be done in marking up and curating the physical environment in ways that aug-ment knowledge, deepen community, and preserve the complexity of cultural memories through mapping.

Acknowledgments

The authors thank our UCLA colleague Yoh Kawano for his contributions to this chapter, particularly his help with the history of GIS.

NOTES

1   In addition to Wood, see Harley and Woodward (1987–1995), Harvey (2001), Harley (2002), Pickles (2004).
2   In the USA, the US Census Bureau provides TIGER (Topologically Integrated Geographic Encoding and Referencing) datasets for the most recent census (2010) as well as theme maps, gazetteer files, and other geographic data, primarily since 1990 (although some data stretch back to 1790) in the form of shapefiles: http://www.census.gov/geo. In other countries such as Ireland, the Irish census publishes indices of place names, which allows enhanced gazetteers to be produced.
3   For temporal or historical GIS, see Johnson (2004) and Knowles (2008).

REFERENCES AND FURTHER READING

Alinei, M.L. 2008. Forty years of ALE: memories and reflexions of the first general editor of its maps and commentaries. *Revue Roumanie de Linguistique* 52, 5–46.

Appadurai, A. 2003. *Modernity at Large: Cultural Dimensions of Globalization*. Minneapolis: University of Minnesota Press.

Bhabha, H. 1994. *The Location of Culture*. New York: Routledge.

Bodenhamer, D.J. 2010. The potential of spatial humanities. In *The Spatial Humanities: GIS and the Future of Humanities Scholarship*. Bloomington: Indiana University Press, 14–30.

Bodenhamer, D.J., ed. 2014. *Deep Maps and Spatial Narratives*. Bloomington: Indiana University Press.

Bodenhamer, D.J., Corrigan, J., and Harris, T.M., eds. 2010. *The Spatial Humanities: GIS and the Future of Humanities Scholarship*. Bloomington: Indiana University Press.

Clifford, J. 1997. *Routes: Travel and Translation in the Late Twentieth Century*. Cambridge, MA: Harvard University Press.

Cordell, R. 2015. Reprinting, circulation, and the network author in antebellum newspapers. *American Literary History* 27 (3).

Dear, M., Ketchum, J., Luria, S., and Richardson, D., eds. 2011. *GeoHumanities: Art, History, Text at the Edge of Place*. London: Routledge.

Ethington, P. 2007. Placing the past: "groundwork" for a spatial theory of history. *Rethinking History* 11 (4), 465–93.

Ethington, P.J. 2011. Sociovisual perspective: vision and the forms of the human past. In *A Field Guide to a New Meta-Field: Bridging the Humanities–Neurosciences Divide*, ed. B. Stafford. Chicago: University of Chicago Press.

Ethington, P.J., and Toyosawa, N. 2014. Inscribing the past: depth as narrative in historical spacetime. In *Deep Maps and Spatial Narratives*, ed. D.J. Bodenhamer. Bloomington: Indiana University Press.

Gilroy, P. 1995. *The Black Atlantic: Modernity and Double Consciousness*. Cambridge, MA: Harvard University Press.

Greenblatt, S., ed. 2009. *Cultural Mobility: A Manifesto*. Cambridge: Cambridge University Press.

Guldi, J. (undated) Spatial humanities: a project of the institute for enabling geospatial scholarship: http://spatial.scholarslab.org/spatial-turn/what-is-the-spatial-turn (accessed June 20, 2015).

Harley, J.B. 2002. *The New Nature of Maps: Essays in the History of Cartography*. Baltimore: Johns Hopkins University Press.

Harley, J.B., and Woodward, D., eds. 1987–1995. *The History of Cartography*, 6 volumes. Chicago: University of Chicago Press.

Harvey, D. 2001. *Spaces of Capital: Towards a Critical Geography*. New York: Routledge.

Jessop, M. 2007. The inhibition of geographical information in digital humanities scholarship. *Literary and Linguistic Computing* 22 (1), 1–12.

Johnson, I. 2004. Putting time on the map: using TimeMap for map animation and Web delivery. *GeoInformatics* 7 (5), 26–9.

Jones, M. 2007. The future of Local Search – Google's strategic vision. Presentation at Where 2.0 (May 29, 2007).

Knowles, A.K., ed. 2008. *Placing History: How Maps, Spatial Data, and GIS are Changing Historical Scholarship*. Redlands, CA: ESRI Press.

Kurgan, L. 2013. *Close Up at a Distance: Mapping, Technology and Politics*. New York: Zone Books.

Losh, E. 2012. Hacktivism and the humanities: programming protest in the era of the digital university. In *Debates in the Digital Humanities*, ed. M.K. Gold. Minneapolis: University of Minnesota Press, 161–86.

McKee, L. 2013. OGC History (detailed). http://www.opengeospatial.org/ogc/historylong (accessed June 20, 2015).

Moretti, F. 1998. *Atlas of the European Novel: 1800–1900*. London: Verso.

Moretti, F. 2005. *Graphs, Maps, Trees: Abstract Models for a Literary History*. London: Verso.

Open Geospatial Consortium. 2008. OGC® OWS-5 KML Engineering Report. http://www.opengeospatial.org/standards/kml (accessed June 20, 2015).

Parks, L. 2005. *Cultures in Orbit: Satellites and the Televisual*. Durham, NC: Duke University Press.

Pickles, J. 2004. *A History of Spaces: Cartographic Reason, Mapping, and the Geo-Coded World*. New York: Routledge.

Presner, T., Shepard, D., and Kawano, Y. 2014. *HyperCities: Thick Mapping in the Digital Humanities*. Cambridge, MA: Harvard University Press.

Putz, S. 1994. Interactive information services using World-Wide Web hypertext. http://web.archive.org/web/20110628195239/http://www2.parc.com/istl/projects/www94/iisuwwwh.html (accessed June 20, 2015).

Reed, C. 2004. MOSS: a historical perspective. http://www.scribd.com/doc/4606038/2004-Article-by-Carl-Reed-MOSS-A-Historical-perspective (accessed June 20, 2015).

Tally, R. 2009. *Melville, Mapping and Globalization: Literary Cartography in the American Baroque Writer*. London: Continuum.

Tomlinson, R. 2012. Origins of the Canada Geographic Information System. *ArcNews*. http://www.esri.com/news/arcnews/fall12articles/origins-of-the-canada-geographic-information-system.html (accessed June 20, 2015).

OpenStreetMap (undated). History of OpenStreetMap. http://wiki.openstreetmap.org/wiki/History_of_OpenStreetMap (accessed June 20, 2015).

Weijnen, A.A., and Alinei, M.L. 1975. *Introduction. Atlas Linguarum Europae*. Assen: Van Gorcum, 1975.

Westphal, B. 2011. *Geocriticism: Real and Fictional Spaces*. Trans. R. Tally. New York: Palgrave Macmillan.

White, R. 2010. What is spatial history? http://web.stanford.edu/group/spatialhistory/cgi-bin/site/pub.php?id=29 (accessed June 20, 2015).

Wood, D. 2010. *Rethinking the Power of Maps*. New York: Guilford Press.

15

Music Information Retrieval

John Ashley Burgoyne, Ichiro Fujinaga, and J. Stephen Downie

Music information retrieval (MIR) is "a multidisciplinary research endeavor that strives to develop innovative content-based searching schemes, novel interfaces, and evolving networked delivery mechanisms in an effort to make the world's vast store of music accessible to all" (Downie, 2004). The methods of MIR research are almost invariably computational, but the particular techniques used vary as widely as music itself and the different roles it can play in one's life. MIR is behind the technologies that make personalized recommendations for new music one might wish to purchase, software that estimates the key and tempo of tracks to help DJs mix smoothly, scanners that can convert printed music into digitally editable scores, and many other digital interfaces to musical information. As more and more consumers interact with music digitally, the importance of MIR will only continue to grow.

MIR research is applied research and strongly task-oriented. Because of its computational underpinnings, one can classify these tasks most naturally by examining the type of input data they entail and the type of data desired for output. The input data for MIR are always digital music data, which primarily take one of four forms: *images* of printed or handwritten music; so-called *symbolic formats,* such as the Musical Instrument Digital Interface (MIDI) standard, that seek to represent musical scores in a machine-interpretable form; *digital audio*; and *metadata*, either of traditional categories associated with library catalogs or of newer forms such as blogs, social-media posts, reviews, or other online texts about music. The space of possible outputs is much larger, but there are three fundamental categories: *information retrieval* tasks, which primarily seek to return a piece of music to a user based on some kind of query (e.g., recommending new music based on past music purchases); *classification or estimation* tasks, which seek to assign a single label or value to the input data (e.g., identifying the composer or

A New Companion to Digital Humanities, First Edition. Edited by Susan Schreibman, Ray Siemens, and John Unsworth.

estimating the tempo); and *sequence-labeling* tasks, which rather than assigning a single label to the input data, seek to label the input data in multiple locations as it unfolds in time (e.g., providing a sequence of chord labels that correspond to an audio file).

Although there are large overlaps and co-attendance at important conferences, the core concerns of MIR are distinct from those of musicology, including computational musicology and music theory; music cognition; and sound engineering, including sound synthesis and compositional techniques. Musicological questions in general are more open-ended and descriptive than MIR questions – for example, a description of the stylistic characteristics of music by Josquin (musicology) vs. an automated system for predicting whether a piece of music is by Josquin or one of his contemporaries (MIR). Computational research in music cognition tends to focus on models of the human mind, whereas MIR prefers the best-performing models regardless of their cognitive plausibility (compare Fujinaga's study of timbre [1998], which takes an MIR approach, with McAdams's [1999], which seeks a cognitive interpretation). MIR research on audio shares with sound engineering an emphasis on signal processing research in sound synthesis, but MIR tasks tend to focus on labeling or retrieval rather than creation. Nonetheless, there is growing interest in filling the gaps between MIR and these fields, as one can see from the list of keynote speakers at conferences of the International Society for Music Information Retrieval (ISMIR): Nicholas Cook and Dmitri Tymoczko from music theory (2005; 2008); David Huron, Carol Krumhansl, and Emmanuel Bigand from music cognition (2006 & 2011; 2010; 2012); and François Pachet from sound engineering and computational creativity (2013).

This chapter begins with a sketch of the history of MIR, including the development of the ISMIR conference and the annual Music Information Retrieval Evaluation eXchange (MIREX), wherein the newest techniques in MIR are shared and compared. A more detailed summary of the most important branches of MIR research follows, organized by the four primary types of data that MIR researchers use: images, so-called *symbolic* digital formats, audio, and metadata about music. The chapter concludes with a discussion of some of the open questions in MIR and likely directions for development over the next five to ten years.

A Brief History of MIR

In some ways, MIR with symbolic data has the longest history, a history that extends back much further than the moniker *music information retrieval* itself. As modern statistical methods developed in the late nineteenth and early twentieth century, some scholars were already applying them to music. Without computers available to support their research, these early MIR scholars tabulated musical features by hand, directly from musical scores, and sought to specify stylistic characteristics based on these features. One of the earliest such studies, for example, demonstrated that larger melodic intervals occur less frequently in folk music than smaller melodic intervals (Myers, 1907). Some early ethnomusicological work used such tabulations of musical features to distinguish or describe the styles of non-Western musical cultures, such as Tunisian music (Hornbostel, 1906) or Native American music (Watt, 1924).

As computers became more widely available to researchers in the 1960s and 1970s, interest grew in computerized analysis of music. The terms *computational musicology* and *music information retrieval* were born: both first used in the titles of academic papers in the mid-1960s (Kassler, 1966; Logemann, 1967). Many early research efforts were concentrated solely on optimal representations for symbolic encoding of music for the computer (Lincoln, 1972). Other scholarly concerns in this era were primarily stylistic and would be considered computational musicology today: horizontal and vertical intervals in the masses of Josquin (Mendel, 1969), for example, or so-called *stemmatic analysis* of the relationships among extant sources for Josquin's *Missa Beata Virgine* (Hall, 1975). Pioneering work on analysis of musical audio data also began in these decades, including detailed analysis on musical instrument timbre (Slawson, 1968; Risset & Mathews, 1969; Grey, 1975); research in pitch tracking, which started in the speech domain and was later applied to music (Moorer, 1975; Askenfelt, 1976; Piszczalski & Galler, 1977); and prescient work by Chafe *et al.* (1985), which discussed extracting pitches, keys, meter, and tempo.

Excepting a few bright spots, such as the launch of *Computing in Musicology*, a periodical compiling active research in computational musicology, and early work on extraction of rhythm from audio (Schloss, 1985; Desain & Honing, 1989), there was a relative lull in computational research on music during the 1980s. (Music cognition, on the other hand, flourished, including the founding of *Music Perception*, still one of its leading journals today.) One of the possible reasons computational musicology did not grow as quickly as expected during this time, especially as compared to computer-aided text analysis, was a lack of large datasets. Without optical music recognition technology to convert scanned images of printed music to a machine-readable encoding, all musical data had to be entered manually, which was (and still is) cumbersome, expensive, and error-prone (Pugin *et al.*, 2007a).

In the 1990s, two things occurred that helped MIR to grow again. One was the increasing amount of music that was becoming easily available as digital audio, which solved the problem of encoding. The other was the surge in the computing power of desktop computers allowing researchers to analyze music easily. The earliest papers uniquely on MIR, introducing the ever-popular query-by-humming research, appeared in the first half of the decade (Kageyama *et al.*, 1993; Ghias *et al.*, 1995), followed by papers on searching through databases via audio content (Wold & Blum, 1996; McNab *et al.*, 1996). In August 1999, an "Exploratory Workshop in Music Information Retrieval" was held within the ACM SIGIR (Association for Computing Machinery, Special Interest Group on Information Retrieval) conference in Berkeley, California. That September, another "Music Information Retrieval" workshop was held in London as part of the Digital Resources for the Humanities annual conference at King's College.

These workshops inspired the first ever International Symposium for Music Information Retrieval, held in Plymouth, Massachusetts, in October 2000. This workshop grew into an annual conference, known as the International Society of Music Information Retrieval (ISMIR) Conference since the incorporation of the Society in 2008. To date, the ISMIR proceedings comprise nearly 1500 papers spanning the full range of MIR concerns, and the conference has become the pre-eminent venue for disseminating new research in the field. ISMIR is particularly important because there is no single academic journal that spans the breadth of MIR research.

MIREX

As ISMIR became more established, and in particular as certain core tasks became more defined, MIR researchers sought to ascertain the relative strengths and deficiencies of their algorithms under rigorous sets of test conditions. The Music Information Retrieval Evaluation eXchange (MIREX) was developed to meet that need, and, like ISMIR itself, MIREX has contributed greatly to the growing success and impact of MIR research (Downie, 2008; Downie *et al.*, 2010; Cunningham *et al.*, 2012).

MIREX held its first suite of evaluations in 2005 (Downie *et al.*, 2005). It operates on an annual cycle wherein like-minded researchers gather together to tackle a specific MIR sub-problem such as pitch detection or score alignment. Once a group has come together they create a MIREX "task" under which the participants will run their evaluations. They then need to construct the three principal components that make up each MIREX task: (1) a common set of data to be analyzed; (2) a common set of queries or procedures to be run against the data; and (3) a common set of metrics and evaluations to be used to evaluate the outputs of each algorithm. The application of one algorithm against one dataset that provides one set of results is called a "run" in MIREX parlance. Runs are usually completed in the late summer of each year, in time for the submitters to reflect upon their results in anticipation of their presenting posters at the special MIREX session held at each ISMIR conference. After the MIREX session at ISMIR, the cycle begins anew.

The MIREX model borrows shamelessly from the older Text Retrieval Conference (TREC) evaluation campaign. Unlike TREC, however, MIREX follows a nonconsumptive research paradigm wherein algorithms are brought to the data (stored at the University of Illinois) rather than having the datasets distributed to the MIR researchers. The nonconsumptive model helps MIREX to avoid costly and complicated intellectual property arrangements that plague those doing research on digital music materials. This nonconsumptive model is also now being deployed to allow for algorithmic access to the vast collection of copyright-restricted textual materials found in the HathiTrust corpus (Kowalczyk *et al.*, 2013).

In parallel with MIR research in general, MIREX has grown significantly over the years. MIREX 2005 used 10 datasets to generate 86 runs across nine tasks using algorithms submitted by 82 participants. MIREX 2013 deployed a record 37 datasets spanning 24 tasks. MIREX 2013 saw the evaluation of more than 300 runs of algorithms submitted by over 100 individual researchers. Since 2005, MIREX has evaluated more than 2000 runs. Beyond simple growth, MIREX has played a role in moving MIR research forward. For example, in 2007, the top average precision score in the Audio Cover Song Identification (ACS) task was 52%. By MIREX 2009, the best average precision score had reached 75%.

The MIR Pipeline

MIR tasks, for MIREX or otherwise, tend to follow a fairly standard pipeline, illustrated in Figure 15.1: feature extraction to convert the input data into a useful intermediate representation, followed by inference to convert the features to the desired output. If the input data are particularly complex (e.g., full-quality audio files or high-resolution color images), the pipeline may sometimes include some kind of pre-processing to simplify the data prior to feature extraction, for example, converting stereo audio to mono or binarizing a color image to strictly black and white. MIR researchers may focus on any or all of these steps in the pipelines of tasks that interest them.

Machine learning, the use of data to tune the parameters of an algorithm automatically, is important throughout the MIR pipeline, and one important question for MIR

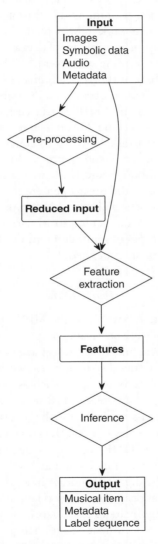

Figure 15.1 The pipeline for a typical MIR task. After an optional pre-processing step, features are extracted from musical input that are used to infer the best output: usually a musical item itself (information retrieval), an unknown piece of metadata such as the artist name (classification or estimation), or a sequence of labels, such as a chord transcription. Researchers interested in a given task may focus their energy on any of the three diamonds in the pipeline.

researchers at each step of the pipeline is the appropriate balance to strike between machine learning and expert human knowledge. In general, the balance for feature extraction has been tipped in favor of expert knowledge and the balance for inference has been tipped in favor of machine learning. Researchers in automatic chord estimation from audio, for example, know in advance that a useful feature to extract might be how much sound energy is in each pitch class (C, C sharp, D, etc.), but when inferring actual chord labels from these so-called chroma vector features, they may prefer to let a machine decide precisely where the thresholds should be between particular chords. Cutting across this general trend is the fact that machine learning is only feasible when there are large amounts of data available. Thus, the earliest work in MIR tended to favor expert knowledge at all levels of the pipeline, whereas given the amount of data available today, there is a growing trend in MIR to prefer machine learning whenever possible (Humphrey *et al.*, 2013).

Whether learned by a machine or tuned by a human expert, each step of the pipeline also must work within the natural constraints and possibilities of the input data. As a result, there are a number of canonical MIR tasks that have taken shape and are likely to remain stable for some time to come. Given a large collection of images of musical scores, for example, the natural task is to try to convert those images into faithful symbolic representations of the same score, a process known as optical music recognition (OMR). Extracting a symbolic score is likewise a natural task for audio data as well, although it remains one of the great open engineering challenges in the field; MIR with audio data tends to focus on intermediate representations such as key detection, chord estimation, beat tracking, or tempo estimation. Table 15.1 lists the classical MIR tasks, organized by the types of input and output. The remainder of this section discusses each block of the table in more detail.

Image Data

There is relatively little variation possible in the MIR pipelines that stem from image input, in part because the space of conceivable outputs is so restricted. It is difficult to imagine a practical use case where images of musical scores would be the query rather than the response to an information retrieval system. Even classification or estimation tasks are conceivable only in niche applications at best, such as identifying the scribe who was responsible for a particular page of a manuscript (Bruder *et al.*, 2003). The canonical MIR output for an image of a musical score is a symbolic representation of that same score, a process known as optical music recognition (OMR), by analogy to optical character recognition (OCR) in the text domain. OMR is of particular interest as an accompaniment to large music digitization projects at libraries and archival institutions, as it can create a machine-readable catalog of the digitized content in a symbolic format that lends itself easily to search and to computational musicology (Hankinson *et al.*, 2012).

The OMR pipeline typically includes a substantial amount of pre-processing prior to feature extraction, including document image analysis to identify page regions containing music rather than text or decoration, binarizing the image to black-and-white, removing staff lines, and identifying connected components of black pixels (Rebelo *et al.*, 2012). Feature extraction and inference vary widely, depending on the source material. Much work is devoted to common music notation (as well as several commercial products), but other research groups focus explicitly on early printed

Table 15.1 Classical MIR tasks, by input and output type.

	Information retrieval	Classification & estimation	Sequence labeling
Images	—	Scribe/printer identification	Optical music recognition (OMR)
Symbolic data	Query-by-tapping Melodic/harmonic similarity measures Theme finding (audio or score)	Performer identification Composer identification Genre classification Mood classification	Expressive timing Voice separation Automated harmonic analysis Pitch spelling
Audio	Cover-song identification Query-by-humming Similarity measures/recommendation Fingerprinting Playlist generation	Performer identification Composer identification Genre classification Emotion/mood classification Tag estimation Key finding Tempo estimation Meter estimation	Multiple f0 estimation and tracking Melody extraction Score following Chord estimation Onset detection Beat/bar tracking Structural segmentation Source separation
Metadata	Music recommendation Database search and federation Playlist generation	Tag completion/clustering Artist clustering	—

music and music manuscripts, for which there is unlikely ever to be sufficient commercial interest to produce a viable project. Common output formats include MusicXML, the Music Encoding Initiative (MEI), and the formats of commercial music notation systems such as Finale or Sibelius.

Recent developments are encouraging more OMR to take place online. Audiveris has launched an online OMR service for common music notation, and the SIMSSA project is striving toward a similar service for earlier musics (Hankinson *et al.*, 2012).

Symbolic Data

In contrast to image data, symbolic data lends itself naturally to a broader range of possible outputs. A large portion of computational as well as traditional musicological research is score-based, and many MIR tools for symbolic data can be seen as potential support tools for musicological researchers.

One of the canonical uses for symbolic data is as a query for information retrieval: identifying a piece of music based on a few notes of one of its most memorable themes. Long before the advent of computers, dictionaries of musical themes such as Barlow and Morgenstern's (1948) included indices based on melodic patterns. Themefinder is one of the earliest and perhaps still the best-known large-scale computerized search engine for musical themes (Sapp *et al.*, 2004), and interfaces for melody-based searching are becoming an almost standard component of online musical databases, for example, the Peachnote corpus and the Global Chant Database. MIREX also features tasks for related tasks like query-by-tapping, whereby users seek to retrieve a melody from a database by way of its rhythm, and attempts to mimic human judgment of melodic similarity, which can improve the quality of search results when users' queries are imperfect.

Classification and estimation tasks are also common for symbolic data. This category of output tends to correspond with the links to computational musicology. Style analysis, as mentioned earlier, has long been a concern of computational musicology, and the converse problem is identifying the composer of an unknown piece of music. MIREX has also included tasks for identifying the genre of pieces within symbolic corpora (McKay & Fujinaga, 2005), and recently added a task for discovering repeated themes and sections (Collins *et al.*, 2013).

Labeled sequential outputs for symbolic data come in two kinds, one oriented toward musical performance and the other toward musical analysis. The musical performance stream comprises a large body of research in finding ways for computers to play back symbolic scores less mechanically, in particular, *expressive timing* (Kirke & Miranda, 2013). The other stream focuses on musicological tools, such as automated harmonic analysis (Temperley, 2001) or *pitch spelling* to handle ambiguities of enharmonic equivalents in formats like MIDI that do not record the distinction naturally (Chew, 2014).

Audio

Audio has dominated MIR research for the past two decades. In part, this is because there is no one "natural" output or pipeline for audio; almost anything is possible. Digital audio is ubiquitous, and despite the legal challenges of working with copyrighted material, it is relatively easy for most research groups to acquire digital audio in great quantity.

Like image data, audio data tends to be too large and complex to use directly for feature extraction. Some kind of pre-processing is typical, including techniques such as collapsing stereo or multichannel recordings to mono, reducing the sampling rate, and breaking the audio down into short overlapping *frames* from which features can be extracted independently. The result is a collection of parallel sequences of different feature values, which are then used for inference.

The canonical audio information retrieval task is *query-by-humming*, whereby users hum a tune into a microphone and ask a computer to identify the piece of music that they are attempting to perform. Although perhaps less popular than it used to be, query-by-humming has been part of MIR research since the mid-1990s and has had some successful commercial implementations, including the SoundHound music service (Dannenberg *et al.*, 2007). Query-by-humming is a specific case of *audio fingerprinting*, which seeks to mark audio fragments of any kind in such a way that they can work effectively for retrieving music from a database, with applications ranging from identifying music playing in one's surroundings to ensuring copyright compliance (Chandrasekhar *et al.*, 2011). There are also many applications for fuzzier fingerprinting, identifying audio that is merely similar to a query rather than exactly the same. Predicting audio similarity has challenges both cognitive and computational, but it also has many applications, including music recommendation systems, playlist generation systems, and cover-song identification (Flexer *et al.*, 2012).

Audio lends itself to similar classification and estimation tasks to the symbolic domain, and a battery of MIREX tasks on artist, composer, genre, and mood classification has been standard for a number of years now. In addition to these tasks, there are a number of musicological support tasks that are relevant for audio because they seek to recreate some of the most useful pieces of information that are apparent from a musical score but not from an audio file: key finding, tempo estimation (especially useful for DJs), and meter estimation. As social media surrounding music becomes more important, tag prediction has become an especially interesting classification task: trying to guess how users would label a piece of music themselves given a free choice of descriptors to use, such as the tags used for the Last.fm music service (Turnbull *et al.*, 2008; Bertin-Mahieux *et al.*, 2011a).

Sequence labeling tasks are in many ways the holy grail of MIR tasks for audio data. The greatest challenge would be to render a direct transcription from audio to a symbolic score, but there are no systems (to date) that can accomplish this task completely successfully (Benetos *et al.*, 2013). In many cases, however, a complete transcription is unnecessary, and somewhat simpler tasks are sufficient. In a performance environment, for example, *score following*, whereby a machine follows a symbolic score in time with a live performance, is often sufficient for synchronizing performance events, and several such systems have been deployed successfully (Cont, 2011). For other applications, only a specific aspect of the score is necessary, such as the melody (Salamon, 2013) or a chord transcription (McVicar *et al.*, 2014). Performance for these types of tasks is increasing rapidly and may eventually blur the distinction between working with symbolic versus audio data.

Metadata

Image, symbolic, and audio data all pertain directly to the music itself, so-called *content-based music information retrieval*. It is also possible to work with metadata about music, such as titles, artists, lyrics, or music blogs and journalism, either exclusively or in tandem with content-based features. Sequence labeling is not possible from metadata alone, but several important information retrieval and classification tasks are. One of the most effective uses of metadata has been for music recommendation (Celma, 2010), but these types of "cultural features" or "community metadata" have also proven helpful for genre classification (Whitman, 2005; McKay *et al.*, 2010) and artist clustering (Schedl *et al.*, 2011) among other tasks.

The Future of MIR

Relatively few of the classical MIR problems are truly solved, and we expect that considerable research energy will be devoted to improving the state of the art in the core tasks for some time to come. We also see four more general areas where MIR might develop and strengthen its connections to related fields like computational musicology and music cognition over the next few years. These key areas are (1) higher-level output possibilities, such as chords rather than fundamental frequencies; (2) social media and crowdsourcing as data sources; (3) big data; and (4) multivalent user interfaces.

High-level Output

MIR was borne of computational musicology, but as digital audio became more widely available in the 1990s, interest veered away from the symbolic data that had traditionally been of concern to musicologists and focused instead on audio. That bias continues to haunt the field today: approximately 95% of MIREX tasks involve audio signal processing, with only a handful uniquely dealing with symbolic data. Concomitant with this bias, MIR has also traditionally emphasized "low-level" tasks, those that are necessary to process audio but are not especially interesting musicologically in themselves, over "high-level" tasks that would be of greater musicological and cultural interest. The MIREX Audio Onset Detection, Multiple Fundamental Frequency Estimation, and Audio Beat Tracking tasks, for example, would be low-level, in contrast to higher-level tasks such as Audio Chord Estimation, Discovery of Repeated Themes and Sections, and Structural Segmentation.

These tendencies have hindered collaboration between musicologists and MIR researchers (Cook, 2005). Not only are the many low-level MIR tasks uninteresting musicologically, musicology has also insisted on a higher level of accuracy for the high-level tasks than early algorithms were able to provide (although see Pugin *et al.*, 2007b, for an example of how it can be possible to bootstrap an otherwise weak MIR tool quite profitably in some contexts). Nonetheless, a strong interest in refilling the gap between computational musicology and MIR remains (Volk & Honingh, 2012), and as the performance of high-level audio tasks improves, we could be re-entering a golden age of computational musicology, in partnership with MIR.

The release of several new tools and datasets may also revive interest in MIR with symbolic data. The *music21* toolkit, an attempt to address some perceived shortcomings of the *Humdrum* toolkit, is seeing wider adoption (Cuthbert & Ariza, 2010). The McGill *Billboard* project has released over 1000 expert chord transcriptions of American popular music as well as tools for parsing these data (Burgoyne *et al.*, 2011; De Haas & Burgoyne, 2012). The *Electronic Locator of Vertical Interval Successions* (ELVIS) project has collected and released a large dataset of symbolic scores of early music, along with new tools for analyzing contrapuntal relationships with *music21*. Far from supplanting traditional musicology, these projects are opening rich veins of investigation that would have been unimaginable even 15 years ago.

Social Media and Crowdsourcing

By way of its interest in metadata, MIR has embraced social media from the beginning, and given the constant need for more data and ubiquity of digital music, MIR was an early adopter of crowdsourcing for gathering data from the general public. We expect that these trends will continue and even accelerate in the near future. Research attention has recently turned toward mining microblogs such as Twitter (Schedl *et al.*, 2011; Weerkamp *et al.*, 2013), and the use of games as a tool to encourage crowdsourcing continues (Aljanaki *et al.*, 2013). Crowdsourcing and social media also offer particular advantages for improving collaborations with musicology and music cognition, because they reflect how music is consumed "in the wild" and how people describe music in their own words (cf. studies of language and musical diaries in music cognition: Bernays & Traube, 2011; Van Zijl & Sloboda, 2011).

Big Data

Perhaps surprisingly, given the strong influence of machine learning in MIR, few data-sets used in MIR to date are truly "big." One notable exception is the Million Song Dataset, which expressly sought to challenge MIR to work on a commercial scale and has also been used to investigate musicological questions about the evolution of pop music (Bertin-Mahieux *et al.*, 2011b). The *Structural Analysis of Large Amounts of Music* (SALAMI) project sought to bootstrap human annotations with supercomputers to build a dataset on a similar scale (Smith *et al.*, 2011). The *Peachnote* corpus has made an unprecedented number of scores available for symbolic analysis (Viro, 2011). Much social media data can also fall into the big-data category. Big data has implications both for MIR itself – more data makes it possible to rely more on machine learning for feature extraction (Humphrey *et al.*, 2013) – and the types of questions it can answer.

Much like Moretti's (2005) case for big-data methods in literature, machines can consume more music than one person could do in a lifetime, and recent studies have started to trace changes in style that would have been impossible to examine as thoroughly using traditional methods (Serrà *et al.*, 2012; Burgoyne *et al.*, 2013; Zivic *et al.*, 2013). These recent studies also show the interpretative challenges of big-data research in MIR, especially in communicating such results across disciplines and using statistical techniques appropriately and responsibly (Huron, 2013). We expect the number of methodological and communicative techniques for big data in MIR to evolve rapidly over the next few years.

Multivalent User Interfaces

For the most part, researchers have studied each of the classical MIR tasks independently of other tasks. That is changing, though, in response to a growing concern within the MIR community over MIR's relative inattention to users and the user experience. Although the complaint is not new (Wiering, 2007), it has been increasing in urgency recently (Lee & Cunningham, 2013). One response has been to develop multivalent user interfaces that integrate multiple MIR technologies into a single interface. The SALAMI project, for example, combined multiple approaches to music similarity and structural analysis to devise a unique interface for browsing the output of many popular segmentation algorithms over a large database of 350,000 songs (more than two years of continuous audio) (Bainbridge *et al.*, 2012). The SIMSSA project is attempting a similar feat for a broad range of OMR technologies, and is seeking to integrate crowdsourcing to improve data quality and provide new training material for machine learning (Hankinson *et al.*, 2012). The Songle project integrates crowdsourcing with a wide range of different audio MIR tasks: meter estimation, beat tracking, meter extraction, chord estimation, melody

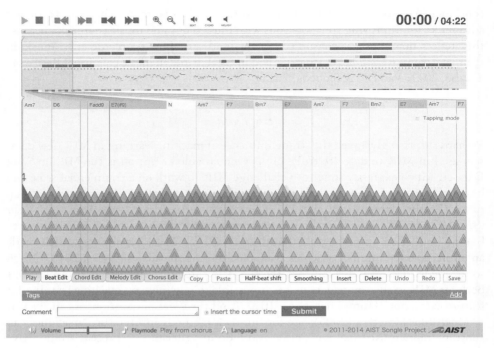

Figure 15.2 A screenshot from Songle, a web service from Japan's National Institute of Advanced Industrial Science and Technology (AIST). Songle conducts a number of typical MIR sequence-labeling tasks automatically – beat detection, chord estimation, melody extraction, and structural segmentation – and provides an attractive interface for users to view and edit the results (Goto *et al.*, 2011). Source: http://songle.jp.

extraction, and segmentation (Goto *et al.*, 2011; Figure 15.2). All of these projects emphasize actual use by real persons, a trend that we expect to continue; MIREX itself is undergoing discussions at the time of writing to integrate user-interface evaluation as a permanent part of its battery.

Conclusion

As soon as computers became a part of the academic infrastructure, researchers became interested in using them to study music. Over a period of some decades, the computers have gotten better at answering research questions, and meeting demonstrated needs. The past two decades have seen a particularly strong growth in the field of music information retrieval (MIR). MIR researchers work on musical data in all its forms – images, symbolic data, audio, and metadata – and they answer many classes of questions, from classic information retrieval to simple estimation or classification, to complex sequence labeling. Most digital music services now integrate some kind of MIR technology, and the ubiquity and importance of digital music throughout contemporary culture suggests that the field will only continue to grow.

REFERENCES AND FURTHER READING

Aljanaki, A., Bountouridis, D., Burgoyne, J.A., *et al.* 2013. Designing games with a purpose for music research: two case studies. In *Proceedings of the Games and Learning Alliance Conference*. Paris, France.

Askenfelt, A. 1976. Automatic notation of played music (status report). *Quarterly Progress and Status Report STL-QPSR* 17 (1), 1–11.

Bainbridge, D., Downie, J.S., and Ehmann, A.F. 2012. Structured audio content analysis and metadata in a digital library. In *Proceedings of the 12th ACM/IEEE-CS Joint Conference on Digital Libraries*, 431–2.

Barlow, H., and Morgenstern, S. 1948. *A Dictionary of Musical Themes*. New York: Crown.

Benetos, E., Dixon, S., Giannoulis, D., Kirchoff, H., and Klapuri, A. 2013. Automatic music transcription: Challenges and future directions. *Journal of Intelligent Information Systems* 41 (3), 407–34.

Bernays, M., and Traube, C. 2011. Verbal expression of piano timbre: multidimensional semantic space of adjectival descriptors. In *Proceedings of the International Symposium on Performance Science*. Toronto, ON.

Bertin-Mahieux, T., Eck, D., and Mandel, M. 2011a. Automatic tagging of audio: the state-of-the-art. In *Machine Audition: Principles, Algorithms, and Systems*. Hershey, NY: Information Science Reference, 334–52.

Bertin-Mahieux, T., Ellis, D.P.W., Whitman, B., and Lamere, P. 2011b. The millon-song dataset. In *Proceedings of the 12th International Conference on Music Information Retrieval, Miami*, 591–6.

Bruder, I., Finger, A., Heuer, A., and Ignatova, T. 2003. Towards a digital document archive for historical handwritten music scores. In *Digital Libraries: Technology and Management of Indiginous Knowledge for Global Access*, ed. T.M.T. Sembok, H.B. Zaman, H. Chen, S.R. Urs, and S.-H. Myaeng. Berlin: Springer, 411–14.

Burgoyne, J.A., Wild, J., and Fujinaga, I. 2011. An Expert Ground-Truth Set for Audio Chord Recognition and Music Analysis. In *Proceedings of the 12th International Conference on Music Information Retrieval, Miami*, 633–8.

Burgoyne, J.A., Wild, J., and Fujinaga, I. 2013. Compositional data analysis of harmonic structure in popular music. In *Mathematics and Computation in Music: Fourth International Conference*, ed. J. Wild, J. Yust, and J.A. Burgoyne. Berlin: Springer, 52–63.

Celma, Ò. 2010. Music Recommendation and Discovery: The Long Tail, Long Fail, and Long Play in the Digital Music Space. Berlin: Springer.

Chafe, C., Jaffe, D., Kashima, K., Mont-Reynaud, B., and Smith, J.B.L. 1985. Techniques for note identification in polyphonic music. In *Proceedings of the International Computer Music Conference*, 399–405.

Chandrasekhar, V., Sharifi, M., and Ross, D.A. 2011. Survey and evaluation of audio finger-printing schemes for mobile query-by-example applications. In *Proceedings of the 12th International Society for Music Information Retrieval Conference, Miami*, 801–6.

Chew, E. 2014. Mathematical and Computational Modeling of Tonality. Berlin: Springer.

Collins, T., Arzt, A., Flossmann, S., and Wedmer, G. 2013. SIARCT-CFP: improving precision and the discovery of inexact musical patterns in point-set representations. In *Proceedings of the 14th International Conference on Music Information Retrieval, Curitiba, Brazil*, 549–53.

Cont, A. 2011. On the creative use of score following and its impact on research. In *Proceedings of the 8th Sound and Music Computing Conference, Padova, Italy*.

Cook, N. 2005. Towards the compleat musicologist? [Invited talk, Sixth Annual Conference on Music Information Retrieval, London, England].

Cunningham, S.J., Bainbridge, D., and Downie, J.S. 2012. The impact of MIREX on scholarly research (2005–2010. In *Proceedings of the 13th International Society for Music Information Retrieval Conference, Porto, Portugal*, 259–64.

Cuthbert, M.S., and Ariza, C. 2010. music21: a toolkit for computer-aided musicology and symbolic music data. In *Proceedings of the 11th International Society for Music Information Retrieval Conference, Utrecht, the Netherlands*, 637–42. Retrieved from http://web.mit.edu/music21

Dannenberg, R.B., Birmingham, W.P., Pardo, B., *et al.* 2007. A comparative evaluation of search techniques for query-by-humming using the MUSART testbed. *Journal of the American Society for Information Science and Technology* 58 (5), 687–701.

Desain, P., and Honing, H. 1989. The quantization of musical time: a connectionist approach. *Computer Music Journal* 13 (3), 56–66.

Downie, J. S. 2004. The scientific evaluation of music information retrieval systems: Foundations and future. *Computer Music Journal* 28 (2), 12–23.

Downie, J. S. 2008. The Music Information Retrieval Evaluation Exchange (2005–2007): a window into music information retrieval research. *Acoustical Science and Technology* 29 (4), 247–55.

Downie, J.S., West, K., Ehmann, A., and Vincent, E. 2005. The 2005 Music Information Retrieval Evaluation eXchange (MIREX 2005): Preliminary overview. In *Proceedings of the 6th International Conference on Music Information Retrieval, London, UK*, 320–3.

Downie, J.S., Ehmann, A.F., Bay, M., and Jones, M.C. 2010. The Music Information Retrieval Evaluation eXchange: some observations and insights. In *Advances in Music Information Retrieval*, ed. Z.W. Rás and A.A. Wieczorkowska. Berlin: Springer, 93–115.

Flexer, A., Schnitzer, D., and Schlüter, J. 2012. A MIREX meta-analysis of hubness in audio music similarity. In *Proceedings of the 13th International Conference on Music Information Retrieval, Porto, Portugal*.

Fujinaga, I. 1998. Machine recognition of timbre using steady-state tone of acoustic musical instruments. In *Proceedings of the International Computer Music Conference*, 207–10.

Ghias, A., Logan, J., Chamberlin, D., and Smitch, B.C. 1995. Query by humming: musical information retrieval in an audio database. In *Proceedings of ACM Multimedia*. San Francisco, CA.

Goto, M., Yoshii, K., Fujihara, H., Mauch, M., and Nakano, T. 2011. Songle: a web service for active music listening improved by user contribution. In *Proceedings of the 12th International Society for Music Information Retrieval Conference, Miami*, 311–16.

Grey, J.M. 1975. An exploration of musical timbre. PhD dissertation, Stanford University.

Haas, W.B. de, and Burgoyne, J.A. 2012. Parsing the Billboard chord transcriptions. Technical report UU-CS-2012-18. Utrecht University, the Netherlands.

Hall, T. 1975. Some computer aids for the preparation of critical editions of Renaissance music. *Tijdschrift van de Vereniging voor Nederlandse Muziekgeschiedenis*, 25, 38–53.

Hankinson, A., Burgoyne, J.A., Vigliensoni, G., and Fujinaga, I. 2012. Creating a large-scale searchable digital collection from printed music materials. In *Proceedings of the 21st ACM Conference on the World Wide Web*, 903–8.

Herrera-Boyer, P. and Gouyon, F., eds. 2013. MIRrors: music information research reflects on its future. *Journal of Intelligent Information Systems* 41 (3) [special issue].

Hornbostel, E.M. von. 1906. Phonographierte tunesische Melodien. *Sammelbände der Internationalen Musikgesellschaft* 8 (1), 1–43.

Humphrey, E.J., Bello, J.P., and LeCun, Y. 2013. Feature learning and deep architectures: New directions for music informatics. *Journal of Intelligent Information Systems* 41 (3), 461–81.

Huron, D. 2013. On the virtuous and the vexatious in the Age of Big Data. *Music Perception* 31 (1), 4–9.

International Society for Music Information Retrieval. http://www.ismir.net (accessed June 20, 2015).

ISMIR Cloud Browser. http://dc.ofai.at/browser (accessed June 20, 2015).

Kageyama, T., Mochizuki, K., and Takashima, Y. 1993. Melody retrieval with humming. In *Proceedings of the International Computer Music Conference*, 349–51.

Kassler, M. 1966. Toward musical information retrieval. *Perspectives of New Music* 4 (2), 59–67.

Kirke, A., and Miranda, E. 2013. An overview of computer systems for expressive music performance. In *Guide to Computing for Expressive Music Performance*, ed. A. Kirke and E. Miranda. Berlin: Springer, 1–47.

Klapuri, A. and Davy, M., eds. 2006. *Signal Processing Methods for Music Transcription*. New York: Springer.

Kowalczyk, S.T., Sun, Y., Peng, Z., *et al.* 2013. Big data at scale for digital humanities: an architecture for the HathiTrust Research Center. In *Big Data Management, Technologies, and Applications*, ed. H. Wen-Chen and N. Kaabouch. Hershey, PA: IGI Global, 207–94.

Lee, J.H., and Cunningham, S.J. 2013. Toward an understanding of the history and impact of user studies in music information retrieval. *Journal of Intelligent Information Systems* 41 (3), 499–521.

Li, T., Ogihara, M., and Tzanetakis, T., eds. 2012. *Music Data Mining*. Boca Raton, FL: CRC Press.

Lincoln, H.B. 1972. Uses of the computer in music composition and research. In *Advances in Computers*, ed. M. Rubinoff. New York: Academic Press, 73–114.

Logemann, G. 1967. The canon in the Musical Offering of J.S. Bach: an example of computational musicology. In *Elektronische Datenverarbeitung in der Muiskwissenschaft*, ed. H. Heckmann. Regensburg: Gustave Bosse, 63–87.

McAdams, S. 1999. Perspectives on the contribution of timbre to musical structure. *Computer Music Journal* 23 (3), 85–102.

McKay, C., Burgoyne, J.A., Hockman, J., Smith, J.B.L., Vigliensoni, G., and Fujinaga, I. 2010.

Evaluating the genre classification performance of lyrical features relative to audio, symbolic and cultural features. In *Proceedings of the 11th International Society for Music Information Retrieval Conference, Utrecht, the Netherlands*, 213–18.

McKay, C., and Fujinaga, I. 2005. The Bodhidharma system and the results of the MIREX 2005 Symbolic Genre Classification contest. In *Proceedings of the 6th International Conference on Music Information Retrieval, London*, ed. J.D. Reiss and G.A. Wiggins.

McNab, R., Smith, S., Witten, I., Henderson, C., and Cunningham, S.J. 1996. Towards the digital music library: tune retrieval from acoustic input. In *Proceedings of the ACM Conference on Digital Libraries*, 11–18.

McVicar, M., Santos-Rodríguez, R., Ni, Y., and De Bie, T. 2014. Automatic chord estimation from audio: a review of the state of the art. *IEEE Transactions on Audio, Speech, and Language Processing* 22 (2), 556–75.

Mendel, A. 1969. Some preliminary attempts at computer-assisted style analysis in music. *Computers and the Humanities* 4 (1), 41–52.

MIREX Wiki. http://music-ir.org/mirex.

Moorer, J.A. 1975. On the segmentation and analysis of continuous musical sound by digital computer. PhD dissertation, Stanford University.

Moretti, F. 2005. Graphs, Maps, Trees: Abstract Models for a Literary History. London: Verso.

Myers, C.S. 1907. The ethnological study of music. In *Anthropological Essays Presented to Edward Burnett Tylor*, ed. W.H.R. Rivers, R.R. Marett, and N.W. Thomas. Oxford: Clarendon Press, 235–53.

Piszczalski, M., and Galler, B.A. 1977. Automatic music transcription. *Computer Music Journal* 1 (4), 24–31.

Pugin, L., Burgoyne, J.A., and Fujinaga, I. 2007a. Reducing costs for digitising early music with dynamic adaptation. In *Proceedings of the European Conference on Digital Libraries, Budapest, Hungary*, 417–74.

Pugin, L., Burgoyne, J.A., Eck, D., and Fujinaga, I. 2007b. Book-adaptive and book-dependent models to accelerate digitization of early music [paper, poster and lecture presentation at the Neural Information Processing Systems Conference Workshop on Music, Brain and Cognition]. Whistler, BC.

Rás, Z.W. and Wieczorkowska, A.A., eds. 2010. *Advances in Music Information Retrieval*. Studies in Computational Intelligence, 274. Berlin: Springer.

Rebelo, A., Fujinaga, I., Paszkiewicz, F., *et al.* 2012. Optical music recognition: state-of-the-art and open issues. *International Journal of Multimedia Information Retrieval* 1 (3), 173–90.

Risset, J.-C., and Mathews, M.V. 1969. Analysis of musical-instrument tones. *1969* 22 (2), 23–30.

Salamon, J. 2013. Melody extraction from polyphonic music signals. PhD dissertation, Universitad Pompeu Fabra, Barcelona, Spain.

Sapp, C.S., Liu, Y.-W., and Selfridge-Field, E. 2004. Search-effectiveness measures for symbolic music queries in very large databases. In *Proceedings of the 5th International Conference on Music Information Retrieval*.

Schedl, M., Knees, P., and Böck, S. 2011. Investigating the similarity space of music artists on the micro-blogosphere. In *Proceedings of the 12th International Society for Music Information Retrieval Conference, Miami*, 323–8.

Schloss, W.A. 1985. On the automatic transcription of percussive instruments. Ph. D dissertation, Stanford University.

Serrà, J., Corral, Á., Boguñá, M., Martín, and Arcos, J.L. 2012. Measuring the evolution of contemporary Western popular music. *Nature Scientific Reports* 2 (521).

Slawson, A.W. 1968. Vowel quality and musical timbre function of spectrum envelope and fundamental frequency. *Journal of the Acoustical Society of America* 43 (1), 87–101.

Smith, J.B.L., Burgoyne, J.A., Fujinaga, I., De Roure, D., and Downie, J.S. 2011. Design and creation of a large-scale database of structural annotations. In *Proceedings of the 12th International Society for Music Information Retrieval Conference, Miami*, 555–60.

Temperley, D. 2001. *The Cognition of Basic Musical Structures*. Cambridge, MA: MIT Press.

Turnbull, D., Barrington, L., Torres, D., and Lanckriet, G. 2008. Semantic annotation and retrieval of music and sound effects. *IEEE Transactions on Audio, Speech, and Language Processing* 16(2), 467–76.

Viro, V. 2011. Peachnote: music score search and analysis platform. In Proceedings of the 12th International Conference on Music Information Retrieval, Miami, 359–62.

Volk, A., and Honingh, A., eds. 2012. Mathematical and computational approaches to music theory, analysis, composition and performance. *Journal of Mathematics and Music* 6 (2) [special issue].

Watt, H.J. 1924. Functions of the size of interval in the songs of Schubert and of the Chippewa and Teton Sioux Indians. *British Journal of Psychology* 14 (4), 370–86.

Weerkamp, W., Tsagkias, M., and Rijke, M. de. 2013. Inside the world's playlist. In Proceedings of the 22nd ACM International Conference on Information and Knowledge Management, San Francisco, 2501–4.

Whitman, B. 2005. Learning the meaning of music. PhD dissertation, Massachusetts Institute of Technology.

Wiering, F. 2007. Can humans benefit from music information retrieval? In *Adaptive Multimedia Retrieval: User, Context, and Feedback*, ed. S. Machand-Maillet, E. Bruno, A. Nürnberger, and M. Detyniecki. Berlin: Springer, 82–94.

Wiering, F. 2012. Balancing computational means and humanities ends in computational musicology.

Talk in the Humanities Lectures series at Utrecht University. http://www.staff.science. uu.nl/~wieri103/presentations/DHlecture WieringDecember2012.pdf (accessed June 20, 2015).

Wold, E., and Blum, T. 1996. Content based classification, search and retrieval of audio. *IEEE Multimedia* 3 (3), 27–36.

Zijl, A.G.W. van, and Sloboda, J. 2011. Performers' experienced emotions in the construction of expressive musical performance: an exploratory investigation. *Psychology of Music* 39 (2), 196–219.

Zivic, P.H.R., Shifres, F., and Cecchi, G.A. 2013. Perceptual basis of evolving Western musical styles. *Proceedings of the National Academy of Sciences* 110 (24), 10034–8.

16
Data Modeling

Julia Flanders and Fotis Jannidis

Nowadays computers can do many things: they anticipate how share prices will develop, they describe how rockets fly, they allow us to dig into thousands of books from many libraries to find common topics, or present us with maps and events from times long gone. For all these tasks computers need models: models of the share prices and the factors involved in their development, models of how a physical object like a rocket will behave in the atmosphere, models of books, and models of regions and events. The models provide formalized perspectives on their subjects, expressed in a way that makes it possible to gather specific information about the subject. In short, the formalized model determines which aspects of the subject will be computable and in what form.

Though it is obvious how central modeling is to computing, there is no disciplinary field concerned with modeling in the digital realm. What we do have is a group of different fields engaged in discussing digital modeling: for example, in computer science "data modeling" refers to the design of databases (Simsion, 2007) and "object modeling" often refers to the design of entities in the context of software development: for example, with the help of the Unified Modeling Language (UML). Mathematical modeling covers areas like discrete dynamical systems or growth models (Mooney and Swift, 1999) and also statistical models (Freedman, 2009), and these have been applied not only to physics and biology but also to economy and sociology (Miller and Page, 2007). And data modeling, especially the digital modeling of text, has a long history of intense debate in the digital humanities, concerning issues such as how to model textual materiality, how to represent the semantics of data models, and whether models should be driven by function or by higher-level descriptive goals. Thus far, these discussions have only been partially informed by research on modeling in other fields: there is as yet no unifying theory. As the domain of digital humanities matures,

A New Companion to Digital Humanities, First Edition. Edited by Susan Schreibman, Ray Siemens, and John Unsworth.
© 2016 John Wiley & Sons, Ltd. Published 2016 by John Wiley & Sons, Ltd.

however, modeling has become an increasingly visible topic, and some common strands of research are starting to emerge.

There are different forms of modeling, and they are usually divided into two groups: process modeling and data modeling. The first describes processes like the development of share prices or the growth of nations, while the second describes objects: either real-world objects and their digital surrogates, or objects created in digital form. In the discussion that follows we will be concentrating on data modeling in the digital humanities, because the research in the digital humanities has focused on finding the best ways to express the specific properties of cultural artifacts and thus has influenced data modeling practices in general, while there is no comparable research on process models.

Data Modeling: An Integrated View

Data modeling is fundamental to many different activities in digital humanities: for example, creating databases to capture important aspects of cultural objects, creating digital editions by using a TEI-conformant schema to mark up text, creating software for research purposes to work on specific datasets. The results of data modeling can be found in manuals, schemas, database designs, software designs, stylesheets, and many other places. So what exactly is data modeling? The question of how to define data modeling in this context is of central concern, not only as a matter of terminological clarity, but also in order to situate data modeling in the appropriate context.

In computer science, data modeling is "a collection of conceptual tools for describing data, data relationships, data semantics, and consistency constraints" (Silberschatz *et al.*, 1996:7). So the data model is not identical with the data, but rather a description of it that includes the semantics of the data and from which one can derive more formal aspects like the structural properties of the data or consistency constraints that apply to it. So data modeling can be understood as process of abstraction, starting with real (or digital) objects and ending with very abstract descriptions in a very formal notation.

In data models one can distinguish three levels, which are also often seen as three steps in a modeling process:

1. *Conceptual data modeling*: identification and description of the entities and their relationship in the "universe of discourse" (the established term for that part of the world a modeler is modeling) and notation of the findings, for example in an entity-relationship diagram.
2. *Logical data modeling*: defining the tables of a database according to the underlying relational model.
3. *Physical data modeling*: optimization of the database for performance. There seems to be a consensus that this third level is at (or even beyond) the periphery of data modeling proper.

It is important to note here that despite the strong relationship specifically with database design, this modeling process is understood in quite an abstract and generalizable sense. Ideally both the conceptual and the logical model should be designed without any reference to a specific implementation, so that the implementation can be optimized or even entirely replaced with a different one at a later point in time.

Furthermore, even if the distinction between the logical and the conceptual level is a result of specific database modeling techniques, it captures an important general aspect of data modeling. While the conceptual model has its origins in structures of meaning, the emphasis of the logical model is on providing a structure for the data that allows the user to use a set of algorithms to answer questions of interest in relation to the data. This computability is usually achieved by using a mathematical model: the relational model in case of databases, or tree structures in the case of XML. In these cases the logical model is a powerful formal abstraction, but it achieves this power at the cost of omitting semantic information. The conceptual model, on the other hand, retains the semantic information and offers an integral and embedded view of the data while at the same time it organizes the information in such a way that the logical model either can be derived automatically or is at least very easy to derive.

This distinction between the conceptual model and the logical model has a strategic value in designing and managing data, but the question is whether and how it can be extended beyond the domain of database design, where it arose. Does the distinction have an equivalent in other data modeling systems? In XML, for example, the underlying mathematical model is the tree, and hence an XML schema occupies the role of the logical model. But when we try to find an equivalent to the conceptual model, the situation is more complex and until now no conceptual model for XML has been successful. Maler and El Andaloussi (1995), for example, proposed a tree diagram which has some of the functionality of an entity-relationship diagram, and there have also been attempts to extend existing technologies such as the Unified Modeling Language (UML).

One approach that has seen wide use within the digital humanities is the Text Encoding Initiative (TEI). The TEI guidelines describe an XML language in which the schema is first modeled using a system called ODD (One Document Does it all). The ODD format is a document that contains XML schema fragments and their documentation; it also contains mechanisms for expressing specific choices and constraints, such as the application of local controlled vocabularies or the omission of specific elements. Because the ODD creates an explicit linkage between the semantic domain of documentation and the logical/structural domain of the schema (which is generated directly from the ODD file), it offers a kind of conceptual modeling. In addition, because the TEI language is designed (in principle at least) without reference to a specific logical model, the ODD could in theory be used to generate other kinds of constraint systems using logical models other than XML.

Chen and Liao (2010), reviewing proposals for conceptual modeling of XML, observe a fundamental conflict in modeling XML data at a conceptual level:

> On the one hand, the conceptual modeling requires a high level abstraction, which means the details for data organization should not be exposed. On the other hand, if we want to capture XML-specific in conceptual model, we have to reveal some features on data organization. (Chen and Liao, 2010, transcribed as written)

As the authors note, conceptual modeling holds value not only for the expression of semantics and real-world concepts, but also because it reflects the intuitions of end users – in the case of digital humanities, the scholars who are really responsible for modeling the data. The same logic holds true for other data modeling systems such as

RDF (resource description framework): the distinction between the conceptual and logical data model seems useful even in cases where, as in XML, no obvious mechanism for representing the conceptual model yet exists in common usage.

In a more or less formalized way, data models describe structures of data, and hence we can draw a difference between the data itself and its information structure. From computer science we can borrow the distinction between three aspects of modeled data:

- a *modeled instance*: for example, the structure of a text expressed through XML markup, or an address book organized as a table
- a *data model*: for example, the schema to which the textual markup conforms (e.g., an XML language such as TEI), or the structure of a database table
- a *meta model*: for example, the XML metalanguage or the relational model

At least in the XML world, the relationship between the modeled instance and the data model can vary considerably: the modeled instance very often instantiates only one of many quite different possible relationships of the elements specified in the data model. That is, the instance belongs to the class described by the data model, while the class may contain many instances which can differ considerably from one another. Conversely, if we look at a collection of instances and consider how to model it, our model may express what those instances have in common at a greater or lesser level of generality. For instance, a collection of four-line, six-line, and ten-line poems might yield a very specific data model that permitted only those precise forms, or a more general one that permitted poems to have any number of lines (or any even number, or any number up to 10, etc.)

If we map these different aspects of the data model onto the levels we identified above we can represent the results as a matrix:

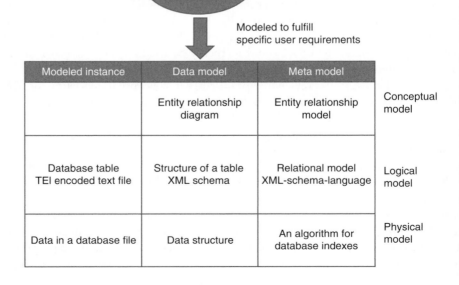

Modeled instance	Data model	Meta model	
	Entity relationship diagram	Entity relationship model	Conceptual model
Database table TEI encoded text file	Structure of a table XML schema	Relational model XML-schema-language	Logical model
Data in a database file	Data structure	An algorithm for database indexes	Physical model

This matrix offers a way of understanding how the different activities of data modeling are instantiated in different kinds of artifacts, and how these artifacts operate within the overall information ecology. However, to get a full picture of how modeling operates in a humanities context there are two more dimensions to consider.

The first of these has to do with the motivations behind the model. It is a common feature of literature on data modeling that in order to create and evaluate a model one has to have a clear understanding of the user requirements for the data model. On the one hand, data models support what we might term "curatorial" activities by users and user communities including archivists, libraries, and historical societies. These activities often involve the remediation of print materials for preservation purposes, or the creation of digital archives that are intended to offer a primary research function similar to their physical counterparts. We might characterize these user groups as *curation-driven modelers* in the sense that their modeling efforts are oriented towards creating reusable resources that capture the most common, uncontroversial, "neutral" features of the text that can be taken as serving a very wide potential audience of users, and that lend themselves to large-scale digitization at low cost. One good example of this modeling approach is the TEI in Libraries family of schemas, which provide a tiered system of incrementally more complex TEI schemas that permit libraries to digitize large text collections for general search and retrieval, with gradual enrichment of the markup over time. A radical example is TEI Tite, which was designed as a data capture schema for libraries working with digitization vendors to do the most basic kind of data capture at very low cost.

On the other hand, data models also exist whose function is to express specific research ideas for individual scholars and projects, whom we might characterize as *research-driven modelers*. For example, researchers building a corpus to be used in training a machine-learning algorithm might model the corpus in ways that serve that goal to the exclusion of most others. While curation-driven modelers also make assumptions about what features of the digital objects are of interest for most users and in most use cases, research-driven modelers typically concentrate on producing data that will be more specifically directed towards their own research needs. These two groups also tend to differ in the way they adopt standards: curation-driven modelers find standards essential as a way of constraining the diversity of data within manageable bounds, and as a way of providing common tool sets and interfaces that scale across large data collections, while research-driven modelers may find that their research requires modeling that is not yet supported by existing standards.

The second dimension – closely related to the first – concerns the context within which the model will be used. On the one hand there are models that are explicitly designed to work optimally within the context of specific application, and which take advantage of the application's features. For instance, before the standardization of HTML in the early days of the Web, web pages were often modeled for use within a specific web browser whose features required specific coding. The strengths and limitations of this approach are clear: the modeled data is much less portable, but in its intended environment it works better than a more generalizable model might, and the cost of developing a workable model for a limited application context is often considerably less. The converse approach is to design models that attempt to be application-independent, with the trade-off that such models may work less optimally in any given context than a model designed for that context alone, and may be more expensive to develop.

These considerations operate practically and strategically to frame the activities of data modeling. We now turn to the question of how data modeling operates within a humanities context, and whether it requires a specialized theoretical approach.

Data Modeling for the Humanities

Although the tools for data modeling in the humanities come to us largely unchanged from the sciences, their use in a humanities context is strongly inflected by the world of discourse in the humanities. In computer science most practitioners regard data modeling as a description of a real and objective world (which includes the possibility of measuring the correctness of data models), while only a minority views it as a design process. In digital humanities there seems to be a general understanding that a data model is, like all models, an interpretation of an object, either in real life or in the digital realm. Similarly, most assume that data modeling is primarily a constructive and creative process and that the *functions* of the digital surrogate determine what aspects have to be modeled. The constructed nature of models becomes clearer as we move from features about which there is strong consensus (such as the identifiability of individual persons) towards features whose boundaries and relations are inflected through disciplinary or interpretative perspectives (such as the meaning of a textual strike-out or the structural function of a piece of a ruined building). As we have noted earlier, there may be motives that draw researchers towards consensus or away from it, but even in cases of strong consensus practitioners in the humanities tend to understand that consensus as a societal function rather than as evidence of an objective reality. As a result, modeling systems operating within the humanities are often designed to be somewhat adaptable, permitting modification of terminology or structural assumptions in order to accommodate divergent perspectives. The popularity of "bottom-up" or "user tagging" approaches in recent years reflects this desire for modeling to inductively reflect a diversity of perspectives rather than operating from a pre-established position of authority. The design of XML languages (notably the TEI and DocBook) to be customizable by users is a more complex instance of such an accommodation. Even when the practical disadvantages of these approaches discourage their use – since fluidity diminishes the effectiveness of the model in supporting efficient workflows for data creation – humanists commonly acknowledge that their models are social constructs.

At the same time, we have a sense that while models may not represent an objective reality, this does not imply that all models are equally good. It is possible to construct data models that fail to match any of our shared ideas about how the universe is organized, and it is also possible to construct models that represent that universe in a flawed, inelegant, or inefficient way. It may thus be useful to assess data models in terms of their persuasiveness, intellectual elegance, or strategic value even if we do not find it useful to speak of their truth-value. A classification system for literary works might legitimately omit genre as a category, as a way of arguing that genre is analytically irrelevant to modern literary criticism, or might propose any number of genre-based classifications with varying degrees of persuasiveness, elegance, and strategic value. On the other hand a classification system that categorized all literary works as either "lyric" or "non-fiction" would fail on all three metrics. To take another example, the modeling of tables in XML varies widely from language to language, but most models agree in treating the row as the primary unit of organization (with columns represented in a secondary manner through the number and width of cells in the row). Clearly a table "in reality" consists of both rows and columns, either of which could in principle be treated as primary, but there is strategic value and intellectual economy in modeling it in the common manner. We can find analogous examples in humanities scholarship: for instance, the modeling of textual variants in a scholarly edition, which might entail a classification of variants according to some scheme (for instance, distinguishing substantives from accidentals, or distinguishing orthographic variants from lexical variants). These classifications represent a local consensus within a specific community of practice, reflecting both strategic value and intellectual elegance. The representation of paragraphing within prose documents can also be understood as such a consensus – admittedly one that is more widely shared, but still by no means universal.

Once we have established this initial set of conditions for modeling in the humanities, we can turn our attention to some further complexities arising from the ways that humanities data models are used in scholarship. Many of the artifacts modeled in digital humanities have characteristic features distinguishing them from natural objects: they are created with a purpose by identifiable agents and they have a history which is part of their identity. Museum and cultural heritage institutions have developed ontologies – notably the CIDOC Conceptual Reference Model (CRM) – in which concepts like provenance and purpose are explicitly represented. Furthermore, our models need in many cases to represent not only the history of the artifact itself, but also the history of the ways in which it has been described and contextualized. Finding aids, catalogues raisonnés, archaeological descriptions, and other records are discursive constructs with their own complex traditions, blind spots, and modes of discourse. There is thus already a layering of rich description which is to be formalized, and in which information about the entities involved may be coded in ways that are embedded in tradition and may be challenging to unpack. Our models of the data these descriptions provide must also enable us to see and work with those layers of mediation. In the development of standards such as the Encoded Archival Description (EAD), the issue of how, and how much, to represent the documentary conventions of such resources so as to permit the underlying data to be used effectively has been a significant development challenge.

In the digital humanities, strong attention is paid to the mediatedness of digital research objects, and to the mechanisms of that mediation. At a practical level, representational systems like the TEI Guidelines include explicit mechanisms within the digital object itself for documenting the details of transcriptional and editorial methods, areas of uncertainty, textual interventions, and other processes that help constitute the digital object and its signifying practices. Researchers in digital humanities likewise view the intellectual work on this layer as important work in its own right: the annual Digital Humanities Conference includes myriad research papers in which the examination, comparison, and evaluation of such mechanisms is of central concern, and over time appropriate practices have emerged and have been instantiated in standards and documentation. However, in most cases these have not yet been formalized at the level of our data models, and it is not immediately clear how this might be possible. For instance, one of the crucial informational layers in humanities data modeling is the representation of uncertainty. In a very informal way, humanities researchers accept that all representations of research materials – texts, objects, spaces, and so forth – carry some degree of uncertainty by virtue of being human creations. Longstanding practices in fields such as diplomatic transcription or epigraphy can capture uncertainty using formal notation, and these practices in turn have informed the development of systems such as TEI which include provision for uncertainty as an explicit feature of the markup. However, this feature is implemented unevenly: uncertainty about details of the transcription is modeled in one way, while uncertainty about the chosen markup is modeled in another, and there are some aspects of uncertainty that cannot yet be modeled effectively in TEI. We might say therefore that uncertainty is not built formally into the *data model* of the TEI even though it is representationally present and its importance is strongly acknowledged. A similar situation obtains with other information layers such as attribution of responsibility, assignment of dates to specific modeling interventions, identifying sources for specific layers of information, or indeed identifying those layers as distinct informational units.

One final source of problems in digital humanities is felt more by those who try to formalize their knowledge about one work than by those who are interested in modeling many works at the same time. In the last 200 years humanists have emphasized the uniqueness of works of art and have described and analyzed their unique ways of meaning making in detail. And it has been part of their social function to reduce the flood of cultural traditions to a canon that represents the aesthetic and ethical values of a society. This function determines a habitus (says the French sociologist Pierre Bourdieu) which valorizes the individual before the general. Obviously there is a conflict of values here: the computer-science perspective makes us look for a good general description applicable to all entities, while the humanities perspective makes us look for those features which make this entity special: models conceal when they reveal (McCarty, 2005:52). As digital humanists we feel the pull in both directions, and simple solutions would only sacrifice one side to the other. Some of the most fertile and urgent areas of digital humanities research involve the question of how to develop data modeling approaches that accommodate both the self-reflexivity required by humanities research and the actionability and computational clarity required by the digital domain.

References and Further Reading

Buzzetti, D. 2002. Digital representation and the text model. *New Literary History* 33, 61–88.

Chen, H., and Liao, H. 2010. A survey to conceptual modeling for XML. In *2010 3rd IEEE International Conference on Computer Science and Information Technology (ICCSIT)*, IEEE, Chengdu, China.

Coombs, J.H., Renear, A.H., and DeRose, S.J. 1987. Markup systems and the future of scholarly text processing. *Communications of the ACM* 30 (11), 933–47.

Freedman, D.A. 2009. *Statistical Models: Theory and Practice*, revised edition. Cambridge: Cambridge University Press.

Maler, E., and El Andaloussi J. 1995. *Developing SGML DTDs: From Text to Model to Markup.* Upper Saddle River, NJ: Prentice Hall.

McCarty, W. 2005. Modelling. In *Humanities Computing.* Basingstoke: Palgrave Macmillan, 20–72.

Miller, J.H., and Page, S.E. 2007. Complex Adaptive Systems. An Introduction to Computational Models of Social Life. Princeton: Princeton University Press.

Modern Language Association (undated). Guidelines for evaluating work in digital humanities and digital media. http://www.mla.org/guidelines_evaluation_digital (accessed June 20, 2015).

Mooney, D., and Swift, R. 1999. *A Course in Mathematical Modeling.* Mathematical Association of America.

Silberschatz, A., Korth, H.F., and Sudarshan, S., eds. 1996. *Database System Concepts,* 3rd edition. New York: McGraw-Hill.

Simsion, G. 2007. *Data Modeling: Theory and Practice.* Bradley Beach, NJ: Technics Publications.

Sperberg-McQueen, C.M., and Huitfeldt, C. 2011. Ten problems in the interpretation of XML documents. In *Modeling, Learning, and Processing of Text-Technological Data Structures,* ed. A. Mehler, K.-U. Kühnberger, H. Lobin, *et al.* Berlin: Springer, 157–74.

17

Graphical Approaches to the Digital Humanities

Johanna Drucker

The digital humanities have adopted conventions of information visualization and user interface that come from disciplines whose epistemological premises are fundamentally at odds with humanistic methods. The implications of this permeate every aspect of digital work. The challenge of addressing graphical approaches in/to/from/for the humanities requires that we engage in a critical description of visualization and interface from a humanistic-critical perspective, that we analyze the epistemological assumptions built into their development, that we think through the issues in adapting these for the humanities, and that we envision alternatives.

Visualization and Interface

Visualization tools have been integrated into digital humanities projects with great rapidity, but this process has not been accompanied by an equal increase in attention to the intellectual implications of the use of graphical arguments built on tools borrowed from other disciplines. Meanwhile, the dependence of digital humanities on the basic operations of the graphical (and now tactile) user interface, rendered almost invisible by its familiarity, passes without substantive critical comment. Thirty years after WISYWYG, and more than twenty years after the browser-enabled display of networked materials, it's about time to reflect on the relations between graphical approaches to the humanities and the humanistic aspects of interpretation and knowledge production for which they are being used. Understanding the rhetorical force of graphical formats is a critical task to which humanities scholars are aptly suited by their training in close reading, though the language of visual modes of meaning production is still a foreign tongue for many. From analysis springs invention,

A New Companion to Digital Humanities, First Edition. Edited by Susan Schreibman, Ray Siemens, and John Unsworth.

and the push for innovation of graphical expressions suited to the needs and methods of humanists should get a boost from exposing the operations and limitations of current conventions.

Both major areas of graphical expression – information visualization and interface display – are premised on assumptions about data, knowledge design, content models, and file formats that need explicit attention if they are going to be understood from humanistic perspectives and reworked for humanities projects.

Start with a basic typology of visualization types and their appropriate uses: bar charts (comparison of value), pie charts and tree maps (percentage of values), scatter plots (discrete values), continuous graphs (change over time), network diagrams (relations and connections), directed graphs (influence or force), tree diagrams (relations of hierarchy), bubble diagrams (relative scale and value, though they tend towards distortion more than other formats). Galleries of good and bad, best and worst, hideous and prize-winning graphics abound online, and they are useful for teaching and research.[1] Many standard platforms or packages, from basic Excel charts to ManyEyes (www-958. ibm.com/software/analytics/manyeyes) or Tableau (www.tableau.com), make use of these same formats. They are the stock in trade of creating what Edward Tufte (2001), the high-profile designer, called the "visual display of quantitative information." The history of information graphics tracks the development of these formats from an impulse towards "political arithmetik" that arose in the eighteenth century as a part of bureaucratic administration of economies, demographics, and resources.[2] Some are older, of course, such as the spreadsheet grid whose content modeling capacities were already embraced by Babylonians for accounting purposes as well as the study of geometry (Drucker, 2014). And some are newer – such as the rectangular area "tree maps" whose surfaces would be difficult to calculate without the automated methods that are one of the strengths of digital processing.

The design of accurate and appropriate representations of quantitative information is an art, not a mere push-the-button mechanical task. Graphical organization, dimensions, scale, the labeling and ordering of lines, bars, symbols, textures, and so on all create artifacts whose visual form is what is present to a reader/viewer. The adage that an information visualization allows complex datasets to be perceived in an efficient manner, rendering patterns legible across sets of numbers whose relation is almost impossible to discern in spreadsheet form, should always be accompanied by a warning to be wary of reading the artifactual features of the graphic as if they are an unmediated presentation of underlying information. A simple change in the scale of the x or y axis exaggerates or minimizes the significance of any difference across values. Those interested in creating effective graphics can look to the classic works of practitioners (Calvin Schmid is an excellent example) for fundamental principles (Schmid, 1983). Get the basics right, and the rest will follow. But all visualizations are artifacts in their own right, and knowing how to read them *as graphical expressions* is crucial. The means by which a graphic produces meaning is an integral part of the meaning it produces. While excellent guides to production of graphics exist (albeit out of sight of the mainstream of digital platforms, whose automatic parameters and packaged solutions come without intellectual instructions), few, if any, guides articulate the meaning production mechanisms of graphical formats. Much work can and will be done in this area ahead. Here are a few suggestive thoughts towards that engagement.

The basic formats of information visualization retain the imprint of their disciplinary origins. Graphics come with arguments in their form, before they are linked to specific information sets. The columnar form of the spreadsheet, for instance, which, as noted above, goes back into Mesopotamian times, structures the assignation of values in columns and rows that can be read against each other. The power of this invention is mind-boggling, really, as the generative potential of the grid arrangement allows for combinatoric selection of values across its entire contents – you can read the areas of intersection for each column and row from a single graphic presentation. The format has been used for sorting and managing information for millennia. The discrete boxes and boundaries and the grouping of "data" in a field or column with a single designation allow for powerful epistemological moves. The articulation of the row/column format is complex, even if the presentation is simple, and the structure allows for generative reading of values in varying combinations. The use of a grid in this structure emphasizes the spaces/fields for content, while a continuous graph makes use of a grid for the points at intersections of lines/values.

Grid forms do not express a hierarchy in their graphical system. Tree diagrams (not to be confused with tree-maps, which are area-based charts), by contrast, declare a parent–child relation linked by derivation and continuity. Nodes in a tree always have some connection to each other, and thus the articulation of the graphic form determines meaning as an aspect of these relations. Tree diagrams track their history to ancient images of the Tree of Life, but achieve widespread use in genealogical tables from the Tree of Jesse to the tracking of bloodlines across generations in humans, pedigree animals, and other systems where direct connections are being mapped (Watson, 1934; Cook, 1974; Klapisch-Zuber, 2007). In an interesting twist, the Sephirotic Tree of Jewish mysticism, though it maps a hierarchy with a divine being at its top, is often abstracted, combined with the traditional squares of opposition to create a logical structure whose meaning production relies on multiple crossings from node to node. Squares of opposition are formal graphic structures invented in classical antiquity to represent propositions in Aristotelian logic. While they enjoyed particular prominence in European medieval philosophy, squares of opposition were part of George Boole's formal studies in the nineteenth century as well as being adopted for structuralist and semiotic analyses (Boole, 1854; Parsons, 2012). The apparent simplicity of their form belies the complexity of argument and issues to which they can be put, and, like grids, they are generative in their provocation of multiple readings and interpretations.

Bar charts came relatively late into the family of graphics, invented for accounting and statistical purposes, and thus pressed into service in the eighteeenth century, with only rare exceptions beforehand. They depend on underlying statistical information that has been divided into discrete values before being mapped onto a bivariate graph. The techniques belong to the natural and social sciences, to the externalized standards of empirical metrics, to the presumption of repeatable results and observer-independent phenomena. Bar charts express discrete quantitative values as visual features (one value per bar), but the size, scale, and height of a bar becomes a significant aspect of its impact. By contrast, scatter plots display discrete values as points on an x,y grid, as single points in a set. Bar charts imply that a value is achieved by aggregation, a collection that has reached a certain level (like water in a rain column), while scatter plots merely mark a value produced against a metric. Though all metrics are constructs, of course, the scatter-plot point expresses an intrinsic value (like temperature, date, or weight) rather than an accumulated one (17 inches of snow). These distinctions are the essence of graphical literacy, and should be used in determining the fitness of any particular visualization to a particular task.

Bubble charts and area graphs are inventions of nineteenth- and twentieth-century information designers, though their precedents in using plane geometry, cartographic and architectural foundations of plans and maps of property, also have ancient origins. The difference between using geometry to represent and divide territory on a representation and the creation of graphics that use area as an effect of changing variables to generate a display requires an intellectual leap. The amount of calculation necessary to refigure the area of the circles in a bubble diagram or the subdivisions of area in a tree-map is nontrivial in analog calculations but formulaic in digitally automated ones. Distortions abound in any representation of value that relies on circles, since the tendency to vary the radius results in a dramatic increase in area that does not correspond to the actual proportion of change. Florence Nightingale is credited with inventing the coxcomb diagram to communicate the dramatic level of fatalities from post-battle infection and disease. She made deliberate use of their distorting properties to be persuasive. Tree maps are more accurate, less distorting, and allow nesting and hierarchy to be displayed in the same system as proportion or percentage of value. The hard-edged rectangular format is highly legible, within reason, and can be remarkably efficient as a presentation of enormous amounts of complex information.

Network diagrams, directed graphs, and other depictions of relationships have become extremely popular forms of visualization in the humanities. They seem to work well to show communication systems, social relations, power and influence, or markets, as well as other kinds of relation-based phenomena. The edges and nodes that constitute the language of networks are reductive, and though they can be loaded with attributes that provide extra information and description to the depiction, they are basically static expressions of complex systems. The level of complexity necessary to model dynamic systems introduces another order of challenge into the analysis of information and its transformation into visualization. The family resemblance of one network diagram to another seems so much stronger than its individual character that it should give pause. Though usefully compact for communicating information, network diagrams often create their graphical display using algorithms that optimize legibility within the limits of screen real estate, organizing their nodes and neighborhoods for efficiency rather than for semantic or meaning-driven origins within the original materials. When we turn our attention, as we will in a moment, to the fundamental issue of data creation and extraction that lies under any visualization, these issues become even more clear.

The use of geographic information systems (GIS) and conventional maps for humanities projects opens a whole Pandora's box of issues – from historical anachronism to the assumptions that space is a static, *a priori* given, rather than a culturally contested and socially constructed phenomenon. The use of *Google Maps*, in particular, produces a set of images based on unquestioned assumptions about the ideology of cartographic rendering that no serious geographer would tolerate. Humanists tumble wholesale into the mapping exercise with rampant enthusiasm for sticking virtual pins in virtual

maps, using terms like "geo-rectification" as if they were mere mechanical conveniences rather than acts of interpretative distortion (often enacting hegemonic values).
Space and time, the two great philosophical concepts, are suddenly treated as givens in
the digital humanities, as if the full weight of millennia of reflection on their
philosophical complexity – the distinctions, for instance, between time as a container
and temporality as a relational system, with its parallel in space/spatiality – were of no
use whatsoever in the new enterprise. The challenges are central to digital humanities
as a field, but will require more effort than is currently being put to their conceptual
formulation if humanistic approaches are to find their way into visualizations of
these profoundly significant and substantive issues. For now, this brief mention will
have to suffice, standing in for elaborate discussions ongoing elsewhere (Thrift, 2007;
Drucker, 2009).

   The basic rules of information graphic design suggest adopting a graphic format
appropriate to the argument and the "data" (more on the scare quotes in a moment)
using only as many graphic variables/elements as there are dimensions in the
information (color, size, shape, tonal value, texture, orientation, position), and making
the graphic as legible as possible, with as little distortion as can be managed. These
are admirable principles, but they are grounded in an assumption of transparency in
which the visualization is meant to "show" the form of the pre-existing dataset. One
problem is that datasets, while they have structure and form, are not graphical, so the
graphic expression is always a translation and remediation. In many cases, the resulting graphic has so much extra information that it gets read for its artifactual qualities
rather than its informational ones. From a functionalist point of view, the directive to
digital humanists is to learn the basic language of graphics and use it in accord with
the professional guidelines developed by statisticians. From a critical point of view,
however, the message is more skeptical and suggests a radical rethinking of the epistemological assumptions that the statisticians have bequeathed us. The fault is not
with the source, since it is the borrowing for humanistic projects that is problematic,
not the statistical graphics themselves. They work just fine for statistical matters
(Börner, 2010).

   This tiny glimpse into the graphical rhetoric structured in visualization conventions is meant to make the point that the use of any of these formats engages processes
of meaning production that are built into its structures and derived from disciplinary
origins whose epistemological viewpoint is embodied in the form. The same can be
said at the micro-level, where the distinction between formats has implications for the
ways information is encoded. Graphic image formats are either pixel-based or scalable
vector graphics. This distinction divides the digital world into "pictures" – that is,
images that can describe anything through patterns of color values in a tapestry on
screen – and "shapes" – images with properties that constrain them. Many techniques
are used for rendering images, but the rendering effects conform to data structures
that are either descriptive or scalable. The challenge for the humanities is to consider
ways the attributes in a scalable graphic can be given values that enact humanistic
properties. One concrete way to think about this is to consider the "edges" or lines of
connection (relations) in the network diagrams discussed above. "Nodes" (points or
entities) can carry attributes that vary in a complex way, and modeling a relationship
so that factors affect each other, as in an adaptive system, makes more sense than

merely giving them weight or a value or quality that remains static. To create visualization programs that accommodate these considerations would be a move towards asserting the methodological foundations of humanities and their role in a computational environment.

In addition to the ongoing use of information visualizations, humanists are involved, as are all users of screen-based technologies, in the mediated experience of the user interface. The graphicality of interface has become almost invisible in the digital environment. Even though its conventions are recent, they are so familiar we take for granted the navigation bars, search boxes, drop-down and sidebar menus. Even when our movement through them is performed by pinching or swiping, the information structures are graphic. The basic tensions in interface between offering cues for behavior and presenting an information structure are part of digital humanities projects just as much as they are present in commercial, news, or entertainment sites. The difference of domains is not marked by functional features, but by the absence of ads, a consistency throughout the site, subtle but distinctive branding, and other elements of graphic design. Similarly, the difference between a scholarly book and a storybook does not reside in its structure — both are bound pages with an open fore-edge and book block within covers — but in the details of type, font, layout, paratext, scholarly apparatus, and content. The conventions for ordering and organizing information in digital humanities projects are less established than the codes of interface. In other words, the use of navigation features, breadcrumbs, and so forth may be more or less standard, but the content model of a project on a major historical event will vary radically from one on the letters of an important political figure or the study of a collection of publications. Communicating the contents of a digital project is a knowledge design problem — since the multifaceted aspect of database structures offers different views into the materials. The decisions about presentation of a project's contents constitute an argument de facto, though they may or may not be considered in using the more or less default features of an interface with its "search," "home," and "contents" tabs. An interface usually has to balance between showing a model of the intellectual content or creating cues for user behaviors (Garrett, 2002). The question of making the organization of knowledge accessible and legible is a difficult one to address through design without overwhelming a user or constraining their engagement through a too-limited menu of access points. These are problems in any interface design, and in the humanities, where the shape of content is itself content, the question carries a certain extra weight.

Our understanding of the design issues in a digital environment can benefit from retrospective consideration of the ways analog artifacts provide a semantically inflected armature for meaning production. Or, put another way, we ought to pay more attention to the ways form is meaning, or presentation encodes the instructions that already determine how meaning is produced through such basic features as juxtaposition, hierarchy, sequence, proximity, continuity, rupture, position, scale, orientation, and so on. These basic graphical principles construct meaning. We read the top header on a page differently from a line within a text block, a title differently from a footnote, and so on. Each is positioned within the semantic field according to hierarchies that structure meaning as part of the performance of the image/text files/content that are presented in that armature.

The current conventions of graphical interface design are not the natural expression of any order in the social or natural world. They are conveniences that make optimal use of screen space. Techniques for introducing humanistic perspectives would begin with parallax views or any point-of-view system that inscribes a non-singularity within the information field and display. Difference, the recognition of the incommensurable distinction between one reading and another, one interpretative act and every other, can be rendered in subtle graphical ways, marking the trace of a subject's presence within the field of display. Point-of-view systems are central to the history of visual representation. They exist in all images, whether marked or not, whether they are conspicuously present, as in one-point perspective renderings, or rendered neutral and omniscient, as in axono-metric and isomorphic projections. A point-of-view system places any and all represen-tations into a subject position, away from value-neutral and observer-independent claims to simply be what *is*. This shift, from presentation to representation, from an image that presents itself as *what is* to one that marks its *constructed-ness*, is the crucial shift from a non-humanist to a humanist perspective. This is the move that registers the presence of an individual or collective subject within the system of knowledge production.

In the early days of hypertexts and before the conventions of the Web, interface conventions were not fixed. The archives of the Electronic Literature Organization (http://eliterature.org) are an excellent resource for looking at the imaginative engage-ment with design of experience and navigation. What was being communicated and how in the structure of those early designs, and how might some of their experiments rejuvenate our imagination? The very fact that the designs force an awareness of the act of reading, of making one's way, and of being in the digital work seems useful as a way to de-naturalize the experience. Transparency has its place, of course, and not every work should be a meta-work, one that trips us at every turn, forces extremes of self-consciousness about the user experience. Such novelties grow tedious. But for interface design to come of age within a humanistic framework, to embody the subjective, interpretative, and user-dependent, historically situated conditions of knowledge will require some design work that has not yet been done. Likewise, for information visu-alizations to carry the inflected, affective, and multidimensional variety and subtlety of humanistic documents into a display for purposes of analysis, re-representation, mediation, or study requires an extension of the current techniques. Affective metrics are crucial, as are co-dependent variables, so that the scene that emerges does not stand in static relation to an always-fictive *a priori* given, but embodies the made-ness of interpretation as a practice. We'll return to this below.

Analysis of Assumptions

As stated at the outset, information visualization techniques borrowed from statistical social sciences, natural sciences, and the business of bureaucratic management work poorly for the humanities. The bad fit begins at the very moment of parameterization (using a metric to generate quantitative information). This is when the demonstration that data is *capta*, constructed and not given, is most evident and most critical, since the initial decisions about *what* will be counted and *how* shape every subsequent feature of the visualization process.

Content modeling (giving shape to the data through a database or other structure), builds layers of interpretative framing on top of the original decisions. Consider, for instance, the example of census data and the counting of members of different ethnic or racial groups, then consider the use of such quantified "data" in contrast to other parameters, such as education, longevity, income levels. The first set of decisions about how to determine ethnicity is highly problematic, but once it is used to generate information, the information separates itself from that initial process. The "data" appear to be self-evident, rather than being, as they are, the effect of a construct. In the humanities, the process of data creation often depends on an act of remediating knowledge and/or experience from analog form to digital form (transcription of texts, re-recording of film or vinyl sound to digital file formats). The continuous spectrum of analog phenomena is chunked into the discrete form of digital units. Once these exist, they are highly tractable to all manner of analytical processing, but the information is at a remove from the original.

Born-digital humanities materials present themselves with an analog face. Texts, images, music, video, documents of all kinds may be made with a digital camera, keyboard, or program, but they are experienced in the same way as analog humanities texts. All digital formats are fungible, and the form of input or source does not have to determine the output. Sound signals can be output as light, text files as music, and so on, and any file can be subject to some kind of quantitative analysis that allows some variable to be charted against another (e.g., length of track and range of notes) in a graphic form.

Visualizations are all based on this sequence: parameterization (assigning a metric), quantification (counting or measuring what has been parameterized), and translating this captured, constructed information into a graphic. Visualizations are interpretative translations, but they pass themselves off as *images of data*. It is not too strong a statement, therefore, to say that *almost all information visualizations are reifications of mis-information*, and this is particularly true in the humanities, where the initial parameterization is often a radical intervention into and reductive extraction from an original artifact, corpus of documents, or other phenomena. Stated another way, visualizations are all *representations* (substitutes and surrogates) that pass themselves off as *presentations* (the information itself), as if the "form follows data" dictum of Tufte (2001) were accurate, and as if the artifact on the screen were an actual image of the data. The misinformation which is at the heart of data creation becomes amplified, and each act of display creates an artifact. This often presents viewers with a situation where they are reading the features of the artifact and taking incidental elements as expressions of a dataset. The dataset is already an extraction from a corpus, text, or aesthetic work, and a remediation. The image is another level of translation, further removed from the original act of creating *capta*.

Humanities documents and aesthetic artifacts are not "data" and they don't contain "data." They have to be remediated to become "data" – quantified and discrete information units, and in the process several issues come into play. For one thing, the plane of discourse and plane of reference are conflated. Data mining can be performed on any digital file, but only on the discourse – the literal information encoded in the ASCII coding or the stream of bits or other features of the file. The file does not have to be in a database or higher order of organization to be subjected to processing. Once the data-mining operation is run, it produces a "derivative" that then passes as "information" to be visualized. Not only is this information removed from and different from the source, but it is fraught with other problems that build on each other. Take a simple-seeming example of performing data mining on a text. A search algorithm can find every instance of a word, even create a keyword-in-context analysis, but the search is being performed on what we call, in semiotic terms, the plane of discourse. On the plane of discourse, the information of the digital file is simply code. But what can we capture of the plane of reference? The distinction of discourse/reference is the same as the difference between the telling and the told. We cannot capture the told because it is a performance, made anew in every instance, but also, it has no material instantiation in the substrate, only in the reader/viewer's experience. And yet, the told, not the telling, is where meaning is produced by a reading or viewing of any text, image, artifact, sound or music file. The content of scientific texts, legal texts, or business documents is similarly constructed, though the aim of most of these is to create as close a connection between discourse and reference as possible to avoid ambiguities (as in contracts or treaties).

My point is that every instance of the word "amoeba" might be more closely related to every other across a body of scientific texts than every instance of the word "feeling" across even a single aesthetic text. And much of the data mining that leads to visualization ignores this fact, so that the process of word counting, or string searching, is based on a flawed method that conflates literal discourse and symbolic/interpreted reference. In an art-historical context, this would be the equivalent of counting instances of the color red across a collection of images without discriminating between symbolic and representational functions. The reds are not the same, and can not be counted the same way, put into the same category, or re-represented as data for visualization in a graph or chart, without monstrous distortion.

The next set of critical issues in using visualizations from outside the humanities involves the distinctions between quanta and qualia. Data are discrete, not continuous; they are explicit, not ambiguous; they are modular and bounded, not vaguely defined; they are sorted into categories that do not support contradiction; they are put into relations according to hierarchies, structures, or other ordering principles that have a very limited and highly defining set of qualities. In other words, "data" are antithetical to humanistic artifacts, they are fundamentally different in nature from the artifacts from which they are derived. Creating a humanities dataset, or culling quantitative or statistical information from humanities documents or corpora is problematic on many levels. Humanistic data are rarely discrete. A word is not reducible to its letters, for instance, and 20 instances of "the same" word are likely 20 different linguistic formulations in which the word is being given value and meaning through use. Some words have an enormous resonance, and inflect an entire paragraph, while others might serve a helper function, or a relatively passive role. None of this can be recorded by a string search, and again, counting words for data mining produces qualified results that need to be treated according. Not all instances of the same word mean the same thing (homonyms and puns are the most striking instances). Neither are words always explicit, and much of the impact of language use is in its subtlety, its implications, suggestions, nuances, and these are created by proximity to other words – a delicate situation is not delicate in the same way as a delicate piece of lace. Likewise, humanities data are rarely bounded – When does an event begin? End? What are its contributing factors and forces? What do we do to measure effects that exist without actual causes?

Phenomena in the world of humanistic experience and also in the varied and complex discourse fields of aesthetic documents do not lend themselves to representation within bounded, carefully delimited parameters. The metrics used to weight or characterize humanities phenomena are more complex than single value systems can represent, so a network diagram that shows "relations" among various nodes in a cultural system, among documents, authors, concepts, and so on, that is grounded in a single metric value for the edge-node relations, is painfully reductive. Relationships, whether among human beings or humanistic concepts, are dynamic, fluid, flexible, and changeable. They are always in flux, not static or fixed. Humanistic phenomena are co-dependent with their conditions of production: Is a news event an effect or a cause, a representation or a driver, force or a reflection of the system of social conditions in which it participates?

Obviously these are questions that cannot be answered; they are posed to expose the limits of representational systems built on *a priori* or outset conditions of decision making on which subsequent analyses are made. By the time we are looking at a network diagram, a bar chart showing frequency of word use, or a scatter plot mapping dates of historical events, we are in deep complicity with the process whereby the artifact of visualization is mistaken for the phenomena it has (mis)represented.

As we have seen, the process of information visualization involves a series of distinct and dependent phases: extraction of data as information through parameterization and quantification, their remediation in forms and format that express the statistical, quantitative features of a dataset according to conventions. These have been adopted (almost exclusively) from fields that not only have nothing to do with the humanities, but that are often theoretically and methodologically antithetical to its core values and beliefs. The range of information visualizations that allows data to be created, displayed, and analyzed is comprised of charts, graphs, and diagrams whose pedigrees link them to statistical, managerial, and bureaucratic domains. The simple act of swapping contents from the humanities for those of the business or government offices is not sufficient to change the epistemological imprint. And therein lies the crux of the problem with using these techniques in the humanities. The difficulty is not just that the suit of clothing is ill-fitted, but that the body of evidence and argument on which it needs to hang is constructed in fundamentally different ways in the humanities than in fields whose relation to statistical processing is less problematic.

The basic graphical environment for visualizations seems counter to the principles by which interpretation works. The graphic conventions of information visualizations are almost all Euclidean. They are all structured on regular divisions of space and standard units of measure. When the value of a word, image, note, or other unit of meaning production varies by context, by inflection, by conditions of reception, its value needs to be represented in a graphical system that reflects these nuances and complexities. The content models that create structured data, in database or other formats, require that knowledge representations get sorted into named, identified boxes or fields. The imprint of that nomenclature over-determines the value of the information entered into the field, and thus the data structure becomes as powerful a part of the argument to be represented as the information it contains. A similar observation extends to the ways graphical interface scaffoldings create semantic value through their structuring principles.

The structuring principles for designing experience on the screen through the creation of a human–computer interface is driven largely by engineering sensibilities that prioritize efficiency, user satisfaction, and short-cycle results and rewards that are grounded in a model of the user as consumer, not producer or scholar. A "user" is not the same as a "subject" or "interpreter." The premises of a consumerist model of the user experience are different from those that would inform an interpretist one. And yet, the graphical formats of screen display that have become familiar conventions for reading, processing, understanding, and meaning production within networked environments come as much from commerce and entertainment as from literary or scholarly precedents. We now navigate, search, orient, and understand the materials we encounter in a networked environment according to a set of codes whose graphic conventions are only occasionally an object of critical study.

Towards Alternatives

Rethinking graphical display in humanistic terms would involve designing point-of-view systems, partial knowledge representation, scale shifts, ambiguity, uncertainty, and observer dependence into our visualizations and interface. These could be custom-built boutique projects, but it would be better to develop conventions designed to engage and expose principles of cultural conditions, hegemonies, and power structures.

To address this we have to address first principles: how to create methods for generating capta that have some of the characteristics of humanities documents and expressions. These have to embody ambiguity, complexity, fluidity, dynamic change, co-dependence, and other features of humanistic phenomena. If we take seriously even the most basic premises about meaning production from twentieth-century philosophy of language, that meaning is dependent on use, then modeling conditions of use is a prerequisite for mapping word frequency and usage over a corpus.

Beyond the basic modeling of phenomena, and the creation of mathematical and conceptual designs that are more appropriate to their specific character and quality, we face the challenge of creating conventions of visualization that are legible, rhetorically useful, and effective in communicating arguments about influence, development, slippage, and other interpretative dimensions.

Most conventions of interface act as concealments: they are devices for hiding what has been structured in the back-end of the site. No matter how simple (a mere HTML outline and hierarchy) – or complex (a vast and elaborate content management system customized to the last degree of granularity) – the back-end structures what the front-end displays. The display covers the design process, decision making, and all the many aspects of the content model in order to provide a means of access through the user experience. This is not pernicious, but it does have implications, and the ideology of document design, the rhetoric of the database, and the hegemonic force of information structures all play their part in the ongoing instrumentalization of knowledge regimes. We know this, and recognize it in architecture, text production, spectacle, and performance – and the critical study of new-media artifacts intersects here with digital humanities in useful ways. The point is to figure out how the workings of concealment act, what are their techniques, modes, and capacities, and what techniques for allowing interpretation to engage with the design of knowledge in database and digital formats might look like. That would be the beginning of a humanistic interface.

As for visualizations, they are the reification of misinformation, representations passing themselves off as presentations. All data is *capta*, made, constructed, and produced, never given. What counts is what can be counted, what can be parameterized. So the first act of creating data, especially out of humanistic documents, in which ambiguity, complexity, and contradiction abound, is an act of interpretative reduction, even violence. Then, remediating these "data" into a graphical form imposes a second round of interpretative activity, another translation. An original question, how many of "x" are there in this text, becomes a statement in the bar chart graphic showing exactly how many "x's" were in these texts. But what are these presumed equivalences really based on? Are the various "x's" really the same? Data translations are fictions, distortions, misrepresentations, and then they become reified as visualizations, statements that pass as self-evident. The graphic shows just how many "x's" were in a body of texts and everyone forgets how they got there. Reading the image for its rhetorical force requires yet another set of critical exercises, for the scale of the graph, its own interior metrics, its regularized and static metrics. The use of visualizations from outside the humanities, from fields whose foundations are based on empirical observation, suggests that the presentation of interpretative analysis can be performed with the same tools as those of business management or census taking. What an impoverished point of view. One might as well write poetry with a table of weights and measures, or perform a sonata using a mechanical watch. The tools are too crude for the task. The challenges to the humanities are clear: construct systems of graphic designs to show humanistic values and methods within the visualizations and interfaces of our work.

NOTES

1   For best and worst visualizations, see: Visualising data, http://www.visualisingdata.com/index.php/2013/02/best-of-the-visualisation-web-january-2013/; EagerEyes, Visualization and Visual Communication, Robert Kosara, http://eagereyes.org/blog/2008/ny-times-the-best-and-worst-of-data-visualization; and many others.

2   The term is generally traced to the seventeenth-century economist, William Petty, whose book *Political Arithmetic* was posthumously published in 1690: http://en.wikipedia.org/wiki/William_Petty. See also the work of William Playfair, *An Inquiry into the Decline and Fall of Powerful and Wealthy Nations* (London: Greenland and Norris, 1807).

REFERENCES AND FURTHER READING

Boole, G. 1854. *An Investigation of The Laws of Thought*. London: Macmillan.

Börner, K. 2010. *The Atlas of Science: Visualizing What We Know*. Cambridge, MA: MIT Press.

Cook, R. 1974. *The Tree of Life*. New York: Avon Books.

Drucker, J. 2009. *SpecLab*. Chicago: University of Chicago Press.

Drucker, J. 2014. *Graphesis*. Cambridge, MA: Harvard University Press.

Garrett, J.J. 2002. *The Elements of the User Experience*. Upper Saddle River, NJ: Peachpit Press.

Klapisch-Zuber, C. 2007. The tree. In *Finding Europe: Discourses on Margins, Communities, Images ca. 13th – ca. 18th Centuries*, ed. A. Molho, D.R. Curto, and N. Koniordos. New York: Berghahn Books, 293–314.

Parsons, T. 2012. The traditional square of opposition. *Stanford Encyclopedia of Philosophy*. http://plato.stanford.edu/entries/square (accessed June 20, 2015).

Schmid, C. 1983. *Statistical Graphics: Design Principles and Practices*. Hoboken, NJ: Wiley.

Serna, S.P., Scopigno, R., Doerr, M., et al. 2011. 3D-centered media linking and semantic enrichment through integrated searching, browsing, viewing and annotating. *VAST'11: Proceedings of the 12th International Conference on Virtual Reality, Archaeology and Cultural Heritage*. Aire-la-Ville: Eurographics Association, 89–96.

Thrift, N. 2007. *Non-Representational Theory: Space | Politics | Affect*. New York: Routledge.

Tufte, E. 2001. *The Visual Display of Quantitative Information*. Cheshire, CT: Graphics Press.

Watson, A. 1934. *The Early Iconography of the Tree of Jesse*. Oxford: Oxford University Press.

18

Zen and the Art of Linked Data: New Strategies for a Semantic Web of Humanist Knowledge

Dominic Oldman, Martin Doerr, and Stefan Gradmann

Meaning cannot be counted, even as it can be counted upon, so meaning has become marginalized in an informational culture, even though this implies that a judgment – that is, an assignment of meaning – has been laid upon it. Meaning lives in the same modern jail which houses the soul, the self, the ego, that entire range of things which assert their existence continually but unreasonably. (Pesce, 1999)

This chapter discusses the Semantic Web and its most commonly associated cogwheel, Linked Data. Linked Data is a method of publishing and enabling the connection of data, while the Semantic Web is more broadly about the meaning of this information and therefore the significance and context of the connections. They are often thought of as being synonymous, but the use of Linked Data in practice reveals clear differences in the extent to which the Semantic Web is realized both in terms of expressing sufficient meaning (not just to support scholarly activity but also interesting engagement) and implementing specific strategies (Berners-Lee *et al.*, 2001).

These differences, particularly reflected in the approaches and outputs of different communities and disciplines operating within the humanities, bring to the fore the current issues of using Semantic technologies when working with humanities corpora and their digital representations. They also reflect more deep-seated tensions in the digital humanities that, particularly in the Open Data world, impede the formation of coherent and progressive strategies, and arguably damage its interdisciplinary objectives. We make the case for consistent forms of knowledge representation across all humanist scholarly activities correctly reflecting humanist discourse and epistemology. We also discuss the significant role that structured data, much of which has been

A New Companion to Digital Humanities, First Edition. Edited by Susan Schreibman, Ray Siemens, and John Unsworth.
© 2016 John Wiley & Sons, Ltd. Published 2016 by John Wiley & Sons, Ltd.

contributed by humanists employed within memory institutions and recorded in institutional information systems for the last 30 years, can potentially have in the open environment of the Semantic Web. These sources have been largely overlooked as a significant source for analytical humanities research[1] (Prescott, 2012), but could provide valuable and unique meaning, context and perspective, at both micro and macro levels of research.

If the digital humanities are the "intersection between humanities scholarship and computational technologies" (Pierazzo, 2011), then Linked Data and the Semantic Web could be seen as representing polarized viewpoints from these two disciplinary cultures. As they race forward towards this imagined intersection they may either combine in a fascinating development of digital infrastructure, computer reasoning, interpretation, and digital collaboration, or instead participate in a dismal collision, leaving only a mechanical meaningless shell in its wake. Linked Data "is not enough for scientists" and therefore is not enough for humanists, and "publishing data out of context would fail to respect research methodology nor would it respect the flow of rights and reputation of the researcher" (Bechhofer *et al.*, 2013). This should apply throughout the research life cycle.

The World Wide Web sets humanists up with an almost cruel challenge. It hosts huge amounts of information about the world and its history which is increasingly difficult for the traditionalist to ignore. On the surface it provides an accessible and friendly environment for most non-technical users to browse and explore, and exerts an unquestioning acceptance about its place in the world. But as soon as we attempt to assert academic integrity onto it we find exactly the same pre-Web issues (Unsworth, 2002),[2] except they are magnified and more complicated. The options are to abandon scientific approaches and convince ourselves that the advantages of quantity and the initial accessibility of the Web of Data outweigh the concerns of loss of control, provenance, transparency, reproducibility, and all the other elements of good research (and believe that perhaps technology will sort it out later), or accept that to build a Web that truly supports the development of humanities knowledge means not accepting technology as it is served up to us, but asserting ourselves and our disciplines onto it and its development.

Linked Open Data and the Semantic Web?

> The Web is more a social creation than a technical one. I designed it for a social effect – to help people work together – and not as a technical toy. (Berners-Lee and Fischetti, 2008)

The Semantic Web, it is argued, is the Web of meaningful data that can be processed by computers and employs "Linked Data" as the mechanism for publishing structured data to the World Wide Web where that data can be linked and integrated. It uses the same HTTP protocol (Hypertext Transfer Protocol) and a similar way of identifying data (Uniform Resource Identifiers [URI] or "web resources"), as that employed by web pages (W3C Technical Architecture Group, 2001).[3] However, in contrast to an HTML (HyperText Markup Language) Web page, the Web of Data uses a simple meta-model called RDF (Resource Description Framework) consisting of only three elements: a subject, a predicate, and an object, commonly known as a "triple."[4] An example of such a triple statement would be:

Subject: "http://www.digbib.org/Franz_Kafka_1883/ Das_Schloss"

Predicate: "http://www.cidoc-crm.org/rdfs/cidoc-crm#P14_ carried_out_by"

Object: "http://viaf.org/viaf/56611857"

(the last element could also be the literal value "Franz Kafka"), or again rendered graphically:

Such triples can be combined into large, sophisticated graph structures which can be organized using a "grammar" written in the RDF Schema (RDFS)[5] language, which includes constructors for declaring sub and super classes and properties. It also incorporates the concept of inheritance, enabling simple, deterministic logical operations on such aggregations of RDF triples ("reasoning").

The Semantic Web has strong alignment with knowledge representation (a way of representing the real world designed for interpretation by computers), but information can be published as Linked Data that provides very little scope for meaningful interpretation. The clarion call from Tim Berners-Lee for open data publication has been promoted with a priority on "raw data now," with few additional public qualifications (Berners-Lee, 2009). Since the use of RDF does not mandate that data has an unfettered open license, Linked Open Data has a particular significance. If computers, rather than humans, are following and exploring links, then licensing restrictions create barriers and complexity limiting the ability to exploit the full benefits of Linked Data and Semantics – one of the main challenges cited by John Unsworth (2006) in establishing digital infrastructures. Therefore the Web of Data goes hand in hand with campaigns to change the nature of data publication to an open model that supports the advancement of more progressive knowledge objectives and outweighs the current restrictive business models entrenched in the existing Web of Pages (Renn, 2006).

The use of RDF solves substantial data integration issues by addressing the problem of schema mismatch (information modeled in different structures) and providing a platform for potentially resolving differences and equivalences in semantics. These problems of mismatch are present in other types of data model, most notably those used in relational databases and in Extensible Markup Language (XML), a format well known to many humanists as the model used for the Text Encoding Initiative (TEI).[6] The most common system of data management, relational databases, use related (or joined) tables of fields (usually highly normalized) together with a set of constraints. The associated management systems (relational database management system, RDMS) employ standards for data query and retrieval,[7] but differences between vendors, together with different data models (different fields and structures) used for similar information mean that in practice they are unsuitable for large-scale Open World data integration. In particular, it is not possible to effectively embed the semantics of data into the underlying models.

Despite strong examples of the use of relational databases in the digital humanities, particularly in the area of prosopography,[8] lack of syntactic and semantic interoperability has inevitably limited the ability of structured data projects to reach beyond relatively narrow scopes, and has arguably contributed to a fragmentation of information and an accumulation of siloed (even if "linked") data repositories. The use of XML has provided some answers to the problem of data sharing (and is still dominant in this role) through a common and open syntax with a flexible and extensible structure. However, XML also does not address the issue of semantic interoperability and does not effectively encode meaning and relationships even within agreed schemas. Its main advantages of flexibility and extensibility create sustainability problems in that any small changes can easily break systems dependent on data integration, requiring potentially expensive ongoing maintenance and creating a constant and unacceptable risk of instability.

RDF also has its problems, but it differs in that the model is consistent across all implementations (the three main elements of the model – subject, predicate, and object – are fixed) and therefore syntactically it cannot break regardless of the information that is encoded within. Of particular significance to humanists is that semantics can be embedded (rather than described separately) within exactly the same structure. This provides far greater potential for integrating vast repositories of data using the standard Web protocol, and provides the foundation for additional technology layers with increasingly sophisticated levels of expressivity. It also provides the type of flexibility that researchers require to quickly incorporate new information and data structures that are necessary as their research progresses, and creates the opportunity for consistent forms of knowledge representation for all research activities.

The RDFS defines triples with special meaning that provide the basic building blocks for implementing hierarchical ontologies. Ontologies, in the computer science sense, are used to represent knowledge and employ poly-hierarchical structures of classes and properties reflecting different levels of specificity (or levels of knowledge) from which inferences can be made. Of particular importance for information integration is the distinct capability of RDF to formulate specialization/generalization relationships between properties or "data fields." The Web Ontology Language (OWL),[9] which really refers to a number of different implementations of knowledge representation logic, provides additional support for varying degrees of automated computer reasoning, alongside other systems,[10] to define computable relationships between concepts of different provenance.

The Semantic Web provides both short-term and long-term challenges for humanists in promoting a more meaning-orientated approach to data representation. In order to handle the tools of knowledge representation, humanists, Linked Data software developers, and infrastructure owners must develop an understanding about what kind of meaning humanists need that can be represented in these tools, and what it requires to express this meaning in terms of skills, distribution of labor, and infrastructure, for humanists and developers alike.[11] Because of a lack of deeper understanding and effective communication between these partners, and the tendency to regard technology as the solution for self-evident applications that users "discover" and that will evolve by use on their own (Aberer *et al.*, 2004), Linked Data is often seen as the finishing line without any real sense of its benefit and ultimate usefulness – it is just something that we are urged to do (Schraefel, 2007). While basic Linked Data publication may well be useful for some kinds of data, it is usually counterproductive for many types of humanities sources unless adapted to reflect specific methods and practices, and integrated into the epistemological processes they genuinely belong to.

The advanced methods of the RDF/OWL framework to express meaning and to relate and exchange it globally can only become effective if humanists engage with them and learn how to express their concepts, methods, and processes in detail, and in formalized ways. Knowledge engineering becomes a major concern in its own right. The shortcomings of the prevalent idea, that collections of intuitive lists of predicates (such as the so-called application profiles[12]) and terminology form a sufficient interface between technology and the humanists' discourse and episte-mology, are reflected by the relative stagnation of developing "metadata vocabularies" and the poor results of applying reasoning methods to them, despite the continuing promises (Brown and Simpson, 2013). Humanists on their own will not be able to harness the expressive power latent in the tools without an interdisciplinary collabo-ration with technologists and managers in which all parties have a common under-standing of the possibilities of Semantic technologies and the structure and complexity of the humanists' discourse.

Meaning and the Semantic Web

The challenge of the Semantic Web, therefore, is to provide a language that expresses both data and rules for reasoning about the data and that allows rules from any existing knowledge-representation system to be exported onto the Web. (Berners-Lee *et al.*, 2001)

Many computer scientists are familiar with Shannon's "mathematical theory of com-munication," which describes how information sources are encoded, transported, decoded and received in a form that is as complete and intact as possible (Shannon, 1948). Shannon assumed that the sender and receiver of a message are in perfect agreement on the meaning of the signals used. He did not consider larger numbers of users communicating via varying symbols. While the purpose of communication is to convey some meaning, the theory simply deals with the engineering problem to which the "semantic aspects of communication are irrelevant" (Shannon, 1948:349). Therefore what Shannon's theory never attempted to address was, how is meaning derived from information? This has been described as the "information paradox," in that "how can a system process information without regard to its meaning and simultaneously gen-erate meaning in the experience of its users?" (Denning and Bell, 2012). The explana-tion provided by Denning and Bell added the concept that information consists of both signs and referents, and it is the association between the two that allows recipi-ents of new information to derive new knowledge.

While this explanation fills the gap left by Shannon, it allows us to think more clearly about the importance of this association. If the signs and referents are ambiguous, ill-defined, and disconnected from original sources, then the value of the association in deriving knowledge is diminished. While some types of simple information carry more generally understandable signs and referents with less ambiguity, this is not true of all information, and the potential for meaning to be lost, particularly in large-scale data publication, is great. This is especially true of information consisting mostly of naming "universals" that focus on the nature and type of things – "essence." In Bertrand Russell's words, information that concentrates solely on these universals, is "incomplete and insubstantial; they seem to demand a context before anything can be done with them" (Russell, 2011:64). Just as importantly, the meaning of one piece of information is not necessarily carried in one fragment. Its meaning is informed by other information (context) around it. Therefore, not only is the context of a single statement important to understand the association, but also the context provided by intentionally (and, with data integration, unintentionally) associated information.

If information (encoded knowledge) cannot provide adequate clarity (and is divorced from other contextualizing information), then this clearly becomes a problem for any further analysis because a digital representation must first and foremost provide a faithful, understandable, and explainable representation of a source as a basis for further valid scholarly investigation. It becomes difficult to produce any useful or meaningful information, however skilled the researcher and regardless of the scholarly tools wielded, if the data has weak correspondence with its original meaning. While the location of motorway roadworks or the times of trains from King's Cross Station may require less contextual framing, information in the humanities, particularly historical information, relies heavily on meaningful context from sources with different perspectives. The lack of context in digital environments is not only problematic for scholarly methodology but also impacts on any meaningful engagement of subsequent audiences. However, much of the historical information published in quantity in the Linked Data format provides very little context and therefore includes large amounts of ambiguity and misrepresentation. This can be explained, in part, by the lack of engagement or involvement of domain experts themselves in the digital representation of their data, and their lack of knowledge about the possibilities of Semantic technologies, ultimately resulting in the dominance of the technologist at the so-called intersection of digital humanities.

Computer science also seems to underestimate the challenges of representing the dependency of data on complex contexts in humanities, and does not readily assist humanists with adequate or appropriate solutions.[13] Equally, humanists are often not aware of the complexity of their own disciplinary developments and the means to structure it (as, for instance, demonstrated by Roux and Blasco, 2004) in the Linked Data world. Consequently they do not require and encourage computer scientists to take up the issue. The more insubstantial and meaningless the information published, the more humanities scholars rightfully reject it as a legitimate scholarly resource, and the less likely it is that institutions will seriously invest in Linked Data, because of a lack of benefits it provides.

The systematic and mechanical publication of data has limited practical benefits, but in the long run it is detrimental to the promotion of the disciplinary objectives of digital humanities. In the context of the "two cultures" debate, Matthew Arnold[14] (in the nineteenth century) warned of an impending anarchy created by a "blind faith in machinery" (Arnold, 1869:sec.934), a position that has parallels with a current blind faith in Linked Data and its "anarchic," unsustainable, and un-strategic deployment. While the digital research community express concerns, these tend to concentrate on more high-level aspects such as the mechanics and functional aspects of cyberinfra-structures, particularly the role of scholarly functions or "primitives" (see below). Despite great expertise in knowledge representation in other areas of digital human-ities scholarship,[15] it is often lacking in larger Open World environments, affecting the quality and meaning of information represented.

While Linked Data has become an increasingly popular way to publish data, OWL, the mechanism that supports knowledge representation on the Web, has yet to make significant inroads, with only the simplest of features being generally implemented (Glimm *et al.*, 2012). While RDF provides the basis for syntactic harmonization, it is RDFS and OWL engineering (for example) that provide the key to semantic harmoni-zation and computer interpretation, and it is this aspect of the Semantic Web that humanists might have been expected to have expressed a particular interest and con-cern in. This can only happen if the meaning of the predicates, terms, and vocabularies employed are more systematically developed as humanist theories in their own right, with methodologies empirically oriented towards the inference rules of the humanist discourse, such as discussed in Gardin (1990), rather than regarding human interpre-tation as a "black box" (Gangemi *et al.*, 2005).[16]

Modeling and the Semantic Web

> There is this constant opposition between data and text. In order to process text we have to treat it as if it were data, as if text were composed of nice measurable things like characters that can be constituted into other things like words, phrases and syn-tagmatic objects of various kinds, and equally when we process data we try to pretend that we're doing it in a way that's not textual ... that data is self-evidently not subject to interpretation. ... and I am not convinced of that. (Bernard, 2011)

Modeling was argued, in the original *Companion* (McCarty, 2004), to be a fundamental activity of humanities computing and a method shared with other established disci-plines. In association with knowledge representation, it has been developed in a number of different areas of humanities research. Modeling, distinguished from a model, is the ability to simulate the effects of introducing different variables and inputs. The use of acknowledged scholarly methods demonstrates academic integ-rity, which is important for a new field trying to establish itself. But equally impor-tant is the need to show how activities like modeling, but also other scholarly activities, continue to be applied, generating a history of development, expansion, and growing sophistication. McCarty pointed out the advantages of using com-puters for modeling humanities corpora in contrast to more manual approaches. Computers provide "tractability" and "absolute consistency" in an environment in which models can be manipulated with astonishing speed, but which also satisfies the computer's and modeling's necessity for precision. This makes the creation, management, and control of larger digital datasets, representing a wider range of knowledge, problematic (McCarty, 2004:259) – and this creates a challenge for Linked Open Data environments.

McCarty identified the importance of "a structured correspondence between the model and the artifact, so that by playing with one we can infer facts about the other" (McCarty, 2004:259). In the analysis of literature this might involve the manipulation of words and word patterns and comparing the effect of these changes between an original representation of the text and subsequent manipulated versions. To produce these different outcomes (inferences) these vocabulary manipulations should operate consistently across all versions of the model within the same overall context and within the same framework of representation. In retrospect, McCarty's ultimate dissatisfaction, primarily through the modeling of Ovid's *Metamorphoses* (McCarty, 2014; see also McCarty, 1996), included the perceived inability to model context (at a micro level) objectively: "The resultant model produced interesting results but reached an impasse when I realised that its structure was not so much incomplete as arbitrary" (McCarty, 2007) (we come back to this). The development of distant reading provides a means of identifying context more systematically but from a macro or "bird's eye" position. This is where the production of Linked Data from structured information systems can provide valuable and broader historical context at all levels.

For humanities structured data (much of which comes from the information systems of cultural or memory institutions) the issue of context is different. In most organizational systems it is generally implicit, and therefore we overlook it and mistake the data for just a list of nouns.[17] However, using the knowledge of domain experts, context can be identified and represented precisely and purposefully. Making explicit this context allows analysis at both a micro and a macro level (and many levels in between), creating a highly effective knowledge system, particularly when integrated with other data. This is an extremely important aspect of the structured data that is constantly being produced by humanists like curators, librarians, and archivists. For this type of information the relationship of correspondence is different. The use of inference and analogy is not with the artifact as source material, like the text in McCarty's example, but rather it has a more direct association with *the scholar* who produces information (which is only partially recorded in an information system) that may be categorized as expressions of knowledge that are either "known facts" (often originating from those with proximity to the artifact), or expressions that are "possibly being." When these differences are distinguished and understood, the data starts to become very useful.

Semantic Web technologies provide the architecture for working with large amounts of data containing different types of fact from heterogeneous sources even within the anarchic conditions of the Web of Data, making forms of "big data" analysis possible, but still with difficulties. Modeling to find patterns in a single work of literature, like Ovid's *Metamorphoses* (McCarty, 1996) is one thing; modeling patterns *of history* (as opposed to modeling to find particular patterns within distinct historical data in which similarities and differences may be located using computer reasoning and inference) is likely to attract far more skepticism, since no system can hope to include all relevant data and context or compare with the fact that "the computer in our heads has, or can have, historical experience built into it" (Hobsbawm, 1998:38).

The question of modeling history (with its implied ability to predict future events) from large repositories of information brings to the fore a strong implicit assumption prevalent in digital humanities, that research systems should primarily contain and manipulate representations of the subject matter of humanities studies just as, for example, mechanics in physics might create a model of how rigid objects might move around. This narrow interpretation of scope immediately provokes doubt about such an endeavor in the humanities, where regularities in the subject matter are subtle, fuzzy, or rare, and the factors of influence (disciplines, mission, history, local perspectives, and so on) are countless. Even in natural sciences and in so-called "e-science," working with models of the observed or assumed reality of ultimate interest is a quite minor part of the services information systems provide. It is possible that only the discipline of meteorological forecasting broadly focuses on continually evaluating coherent models of "reality," and history works on vastly larger timescales (*longue durée*!).

The major role information systems (that now feed Linked Data repositories) can and should play is the support of the epistemological processes, i.e., what knowledge exists, where it comes from, where it has been used, where it can be used, and where it should be used – a conclusion also reached by McCarty, who described "analytic modeling,"[18] – "to raise the epistemological question of how we know what we somehow know" (McCarty, 2007:7).[19] The information system must not be seen as a surrogate of reality bound to some sort of view or filter (the use of the term "digital surrogate" is symptomatic of this confusion). Rather, it must be seen as a platform for the "externalization of argument" (Serres, 2011) to trace how different pieces of knowledge relate and how consistent they are with a past or with categorical theories possible within the limits of all known facts.

Information modeling, rather than attempting to deal with or model unlimited facts, instead pertains to the way we observe, how and under which conditions we would accept sources and adopt belief contained in them, what sorts of sources and knowledge we would use in arguments, and which sort of reasoning paradigm we apply. The final result of any academic study in the humanities or sciences constitutes only the tip of the iceberg of fact-seeking, fact-collecting and fact-evaluating activities, along with the respective documentation.

All this epistemological flow of information needs to be managed in structured data. Done adequately, it should become a representation of a combination of human behavior acting on information – the epistemology – tightly integrated with models of the reality – the ontology – that describes reality up to the level relevant to our ability to argue about them. For instance, the difference between a water glass and a wine glass may be sufficiently modeled by relating "glass" to "function," with context of "use" and "intended use," in order to relate scholarly knowledge to it. Such a model, in which the correspondence with the scholar can more easily associate relevant contextual information within a computer-compatible format, appears to be a more relevant and a far simpler way to integrate knowledge than knowing the two contextualized terms and their specializations in all languages.

In the semantics of the structural elements, the relationships which can be expressed explicitly within Linked Data become critical to the application, much more than the world describes. Even the smallest piece of information, placed in context, may provide the missing link needed to unlock a chain of relationships in data sourced from diverse locations. The discovery of potentially related facts through the use of a particular pattern of context allows us to debate similarities and differences which we can reuse to further infer and assert various arguments and apply other evidence.

This type of Linked Data can operate on a micro level, allowing the isolation of particular information (with its perspective and context intact), or the grouping of information to provide a macro, more distant perspective. In other words, within certain types of contextual model (such as the CIDOC Conceptual Reference Model) the micro level is never lost or distorted, it simply becomes part of a density of data that can not only supply quantitative information but also "zoom" to individual instances that provide local context. Researchers can switch between facts and arguments at different levels of knowledge abstraction.

The same principles and mindset established in more discrete digital research activities should be applied to large repositories of Linked Data, and we should not be distracted by quantity. This requires the removal of a "'two cultures'" history that implies that memory institution database systems have less value than, for example, crafted TEI-type representations (Prescott, 2012).[20] Linked Data resources become richer the more they integrate (Crofts, 2004:ii) and can provide independent or complementary contexts. They should not be seen as being in opposition or competing.

In the Linked Data world we therefore have four major issues:

1. We need to differentiate between "known" facts and "possible" facts.
2. We require a model of nested (as opposed to flat) relationships, to provide the possibility of integrating data that properly represents the scholar's knowledge.
3. We need to provide information with a description of reality to the level that allows us to participate in meaningful discourse at any level.
4. We must always be able to trace the provenance of knowledge back to the source micro-level (with its original context and perspective intact).

This was impossible in the past, and is a new "innovative" ability digital humanities can provide. By representing the implicit relationships embedded in institutional datasets, an opportunity exists to establish a knowledge base that is both rich and broad enough to fuel more sophisticated digital humanities methods supported by numerous and varied historical perspectives. Collaboration with memory institutions on this single issue of digital data curation could dramatically improve the quality of humanities research, with wide-ranging benefits for society.

Digital Humanities and the Semantic Web

> You find things by the wayside or you buy a brochure written by a local historian, which is in a tiny museum somewhere, which you would never find in London. And in that you find some odd details which lead you somewhere else, and so it's a form of unsystematic searching, which of course for an academic is far from orthodoxy, because we're meant to do things systematically. (Max Sebald: Cuomo, 2011)

Anecdotal evidence suggests that those working in more established areas of the digital humanities can be skeptical of Linked Data as a disruptive threat to established methods. The current problem of "meaning" and Linked Data inevitably leads to unbalanced comparisons on quality, as if Linked Data technology itself was responsible for poor-quality data publication or the thoroughness of an institution's data recording processes.[21] This chapter has identified some of the reasons for poor-quality outputs, but in any event these comparisons of technology are not particularly useful. Knowledge representation, independent of implementation technology, is the more important foundational step for working with computers and information. All technology formats, whether XML, relational databases, or even RDF, have advantages and disadvantages. However, the purpose of the Semantic Web is to provide support for and integrate all knowledge representation systems from different domains and communities. It "allows rules from any existing knowledge-representation system to be exported onto the Web" (Berners-Lee *et al.*, 2001). It is far more productive to talk about common issues of knowledge representation and understand how these systems can be improved and information better integrated. Linked Data and the Semantic Web do not invalidate existing methods of knowledge representation, and support the concept that historical studies rely on many different contexts, both digital and non-digital. This is important in gaining the confidence of a wider range of humanities scholars.

The CIDOC Conceptual Reference Model (CRM),[22] an ontology designed originally for the cultural heritage domain, but with far more scope, provides a useful case study. The CRM came about through a realization that cultural heritage institutions represented such a wide variety of different knowledge that attempting to model or integrate this within established meta-models (relational databases, or XML, for example) would be unsustainable and semantically limiting. The creation of a "bottom-up" knowledge representation method based on a continuously harmonized hierarchy of entities and relationships solved these problems and allowed the vast variety of knowledge to be sustainably managed and integrated (Doerr and Crofts, 1998).[23] The different levels of generalization and specialization created a less complex, more compact and sustainable model, but with far richer semantics enhanced using an "event"-based approach that empirically emerged from the analysis of data structures and expert practices.

As the TEI project has developed, using an XML model, it has also experienced a problem in managing an increasing level of variability and specialization, creating both management and data-integration issues. It also suffers from a lack of support for contextual semantics. Despite differences in objectives, there are similarities between the experience of humanists working with and representing structured data, and those involved in representing and analyzing text and literature. However, it would be extremely beneficial to the digital humanities as a whole if knowledge from these two communities could be better integrated.

The issues of representation for humanists working with digital text and debates about context are summarized in a number of recent conference papers. The lack of tools for semantic markup, and early initiatives and proposals for introducing RDF based solutions, were discussed at the 2010 Digital Humanities Conference (Sperberg-McQueen *et al.*, 2010). At the 2014 TEI Conference a paper pointed out that "XML is a poor language for semantic data modeling" and proposed an extension to the TEI project to include a TEI "'ontology"' and the use of RDF and Semantic Web reasoning (OWL) tools (Ciotti and Tomasi, 2014). At the 2012 Digital Humanities Conference, bearing in mind McCarty's frustration with attempting to provide a systematic approach to markup of context at the close (micro) level, scholars challenged a suggestion that distant reading makes close reading redundant and stated that the "reality is that quantitative methods are most effective when used alongside the close textual reading that allows us to contextualize the current glut of information" (Gooding *et al.*, 2012). The paper argued that quality needs the continued use of micro or close reading analysis. This last point reflects a clear tension created by the lack of correspondence in digital text techniques between macro and micro approaches, something addressed in the structured data world using ontologies like CIDOC CRM. For modernists (and critics of postmodernism such as Jameson, 1991) there is still an uneasiness when we gloss over the details of history and dehumanize our memories of events that should be remembered and discussed in a more human context.

In terms of convergence, there have been ongoing attempts to bring TEI into the Semantic Web world. This has included a proposed alignment of the CIDOC CRM ontology and TEI with the objective of promoting integration between literary and textual projects, and larger repositories of cultural heritage structured data (Eide and Ore, 2007). While TEI's context is "dependent on and anchored to the objects (texts) being modeled," and CIDOC CRM relies "on a specified model of the world" (Ciula and Eide, 2014), the addition of event-based features in TEI P5[24] (names, dates, people, and places), "designed to cover a wide variety of real-world descriptions," makes it possible both to integrate the TEI P5 tag set with the real world of CIDOC CRM (Ore and Eide, 2009) and to use contextual markup by asserting CIDOC CRM entities and relationships into text directly.

The British Museum, a major knowledge and memory institution, digitally publishes its collection using CIDOC CRM knowledge representation as the basis for supporting research environments and developing better engagement possibilities.[25] At the Digital Classicist Summer Seminar in 2014 it presented a method of tagging text (in this case the Ancient Egyptian *Book of the Dead* spells and their currently unpublished translations by Egyptologist and software designer Dr. Malcolm Mosher) using CIDOC CRM (and the CRM extension FRBRoo,[26] used for bibliographic data) and RDFa,[27] which provides the ability to insert RDF Linked Data into HTML, SHTML, and XML). This allows the *Book of the Dead* text to become part of a much wider body of contextual structured information from cultural heritage sources (perhaps from Ancient Egyptian collections but also related information from other cultures and periods), blurring the border between structured databases and textual representation, creating a model that traverses the two (Norton and Oldman, 2014). While this may not address all the objectives of a TEI implementation, it nevertheless demonstrates a powerful tool for bringing text and structured historical data together.

Slowly but surely there is a move away from technology solutions that perform badly both in terms of syntax and semantics, and a renewed debate about context and its relationship with quality research. Crucially, these approaches have the potential to lead currently separated digital humanities communities towards a more integrated mode of operation and encourage the creation of integrated systems of reusable information that retain the different and valuable perspectives of the expert groups that created them – regardless of specialism. It also opens up the possibility of uniting and strengthening the digital humanities discipline in terms of establishing a consistent representation of argument and belief that could be used across all types of humanities corpora, supporting contextual identification at both macro and micro levels, including "unsystematic" subjective propositions (not arbitrary ones) working alongside more objective but "distant" methods. In reality, unsystematic micro methods fit the big-data paradigm just as well as more systematic macro methods, as Max Sebald, carrying on from the quote above, describes:

> If you look at a dog following the advice of his nose, he traverses a patch of land in a completely unplottable manner. And he invariably finds what he's looking for. I think that, as I've always had dogs. I've learned from them how to do this. And so you then have a small amount of material and you accumulate things, and it grows; one thing takes you to another, and you make something out of these haphazardly assembled materials. (Cuomo, 2011)

Infrastructure and the Semantic Web

> Libraries, galleries, archives, museums are the very stuff of research, its heart and soul, not infrastructures. (Prescott, 2013)

Building a digital knowledge infrastructure (also known as a cyberinfrastructure) that works for the digital humanities is a complex undertaking. The report *Revolutionizing Science and Engineering Through Cyberinfrastructure* (Atkins *et al.*, 2003) was an 84-page attempt to provide a comprehensive rationale for, and description of, a digital research environment that could work for any discipline. The recommended structure consists of an architectural layer with underlying components for computation, storage, and networking; a middle layer of enabling hardware, algorithmic tools, software, and operational support; and finally a service layer with applications, services, data, knowledge, and practices. The risk for such a blueprint is its own lack of correspondence with the dynamics and reality of any particular knowledge domain.

Such an environment cannot ensure successful research, because "research infrastructure is not research just as roads are not economic activity" (Rockwell, 2010). Just as Linked Data provides syntactic integration without necessarily conveying any meaning, the general-purpose cyberinfrastructure is conceived for, but uneducated by, any specific scholarly domain requirements (including the issues of data meaning and context), with the risk that technology can "distort" the methods of research (Rockwell, 2010) and that digital research can become technology-led, an issue that has arisen again and again (Oldman *et al.*, 2014).

Since the Atkins report, different flavors of cyberinfrastructure have appeared with different specialisms. Some projects (e.g., Europeana; www.europeana.eu) have focused on content, becoming known as "data aggregators" and encouraging the community to create services that build on the resources they manage (although their noncollaborative methods of harvesting data have meant compromises in quality). Others have concerned themselves with providing a framework of good methodological processes under which individual projects might operate and encourage synergies, taking a "bottom-up" approach; others have focused on specific tools and services. Almost none have focused on quality or context issues and their long-term relationship with data providers. However, current projects, for example DARIAH (*Digital Research Infrastructure for the Arts and Humanities*; www.dariah.eu) and DM2E (*Digitised Manuscripts to Europeana*; http://dm2e.eu), have focused in part on how scholarly activities might themselves be integrated. Although the functionality of tools can be informed by defining and analyzing scholarly primitives, what are their inputs and outputs and how are they practically and meaningfully connected?

The DARIAH project, in assessing data management used in individual projects, confirmed that semantics "were for the most part left implicit in these relational databases, and were complicated further by the variety of conventions used in representing data." The Semantic Web and Linked Data were thought to have "great potential … as they allow researchers to formalise resources and the links between them more flexibly, and to create, explore and query these linked resources." Further still, "ontologies can thus act as the semantic mediator between heterogeneous datasets, enabling researchers to explore, understand and extend these datasets more productively and so improve the contributions that the data can make to their research" (Blanke and Hedges, 2013:8). Similarly for DM2E, Semantic technologies play a crucial role in bringing together (providing the semantic glue) to ensure that components and processes work together effectively with a consensus as to the basic ontology of scholarly work, formalized using Linked Data (RDF) environments. Despite this, however, the focus is still currently on "functions," "operations," and "mechanics."

The next focus of attention must, if belatedly, be the sources of information that feed these scholarly activities and, as research creates new information, the outputs that these research functions produce. Traditionally, digital humanities projects have mostly crafted their own datasets limited by the resources available to any individual project. While the research questions they addressed have been useful and informative, projects lack the ability to call upon larger repositories, despite the significant amounts of accumulated data created by the large investments in digitization on the part of memory institutions over the last 30 years. This has again led to criticisms that research projects concentrate disproportionately on the technology rather than on the content they analyze and the scope of questions they address, raising the question of whether "ever-more sophisticated online resources freed up scholars to explore new ideas, or made them slaves to the digital machine" (Reisz, 2011).

The other criticism is that digital humanities initiatives have not engaged with the wider community (Zorich, 2008). This lack of connection is understandable, since institutions and aggregators have failed to document, represent, and integrate data in ways compatible with basic research standards (Terras and Ross, 2011:92). Regardless, there seems to be a distinct reluctance to work more closely with memory institutions on an equal intellectual basis to improve quality and practices in scholarly data publication (Poole, 2013: para.23). This in turn prompts comments such as "I dislike intensely the term research infrastructure. It suggests that libraries, archives, etc., [are] somehow subsidiary to research" (Prescott, 2013).

The infrastructure problem for the humanities cannot be resolved independently of addressing the sources of knowledge. The objective of Linked Data and Semantic technologies is to encourage digital collaboration, and "help people work together" (Berners-Lee and Fischetti, 2008). It matters not how "state of the art" a cyberinfrastructure can be made, or how well scholarly methods are defined and incorporated, if the information that these components operate on lacks sufficient meaning and context. This is as true of Open World modeling as it was for McCarty's Closed World modeling – they involve the same scholarly activities and should use the same level of detail and quality.

In the humanities domain there are two significant challenges. The first is how to maximize the potential of existing sources of information, since many organizations that provide data have, by adopting digital information systems, been using Closed World models (again, semantics are "implicit," not explicit) that were never intended to fuel the type of cyberinfrastructure that we continually attempt to build. Converting this data into something that can be used by researchers requires more than a flat mechanical extraction, but rather the engagement of the community, particularly curators, archivists, and librarians, at source to provide meaningful contextualization of data before it is exported. The second is to support the transition of these source systems into ones that are specifically designed to meet the needs of a wider Open World audience, and this implies improved digital curation (Doerr and Low, 2010).

In response to these problems, ontologies have emerged that allow memory organizations to provide a research quality representation of their "closed" data models which are compatible with the Linked Data standard and fully utilize Semantic technologies.[28] Ultimately, source organizations must be involved in encoding the meaning of their own information, using their accumulated knowledge to deliver information relevant to research and a range of other uses. The investment of large amounts of money in one-size-fits-all harvesting mechanisms, and then converting this to Linked Data, removes much of its original value and provides no correspondence to original knowledge. This seems to go against the very spirit and nature of why Linked Data and Semantic technologies were created, in which enfranchisement is a key goal.

Scholarly Primitives and the Semantic Web

> Let's assume that I download onto my computer *La critique de la raison pure*, and that I start to study it, writing my comments between the lines; either I possess a very philological turn of mind and I can recognize my comments, or else, three years later, I could no longer say what is mine and what is Kant's. We would be like the copyists in the Middle Ages who automatically made corrections to the text that they copied because it felt natural to do so – in which case, any philological concern is likely to go down the drain. (Eco and Origgi, 2003:227)

In the discussion about infrastructure we found an increasing interest in revisiting and developing Unsworth's original list of scholarly functions and activities, commonly known as the "scholarly primitives": discovering, annotating, comparing, referring, sampling, illustrating, representing (Unsworth, 2000). This original illustrative list has since been expanded by various contributions (e.g., McCarty, 2003; Palmer *et al.*, 2009; TaDiRAH, 2014). Increasingly different initiatives have attempted to use the primitives as a vehicle for defining and promoting frameworks that create the "conditions" for improved data sharing and collaboration. These frameworks are intended to provide more focus and even to inform reference models to support the processes and workflows of research projects, tools, and also infrastructures.

However, while the core scholarly primitives are useful in classifying and defining activities that researchers recognize, they provide a relatively high-level standpoint and lack overall purpose in terms of insightful research outputs. Despite attempts at defining consensual definitions of the primitives, projects nevertheless create scholarly tools with a wide variation of methodological interpretation. For example, the scholarly primitive of "annotation" has been the focus of many projects over the years and a large number of annotation tools have been produced, recent ones with Linked Data outputs. In practice the exact nature of annotation as a function will always be viewed, interpreted, and manifested differently in different projects. Creating an annotation tool that works for every researcher and project would seem an unlikely outcome. In this respect the development of research activity taxonomies starts to feel similar to the development of the many other structured data terminologies. Just as application profiles are unable to define a common set of fields that can be agreed by the community, so the primitives are unable to define a fixed set of properties which belong to them, and risk becoming a diversion to supporting epistemological processes.

However, most of the core primitives are indirectly or directly related to making assertions and the generation of new facts to be encoded as new information[29] that are part of an *implicit* argument and belief value system.[30] Researchers represent, discover, compare, sample, and so on so that they can assert new statements about the materials under analysis. While the scholarly primitives are useful to identify common modes of activity, their discussion, in isolation from the representation of research outputs and conclusions, has limited the dialog about knowledge representation at the other end of the research workflow. Without attending to the representation of the results of scholarly activity we end up in a similar position to that discussed in relation to source data and its representation on the Semantic Web, but for the outputs of research. The symptoms are the same in that the community continues to define a wider and broader scope of activities that muddy the knowledge representation waters and emphasize the variability of subject matter. The unbalanced interest in the scholarly primitives might also support this chapter's contention that we are currently unable to implement a meaningful representation of scholarly work on the Semantic Web. While we understand that Semantic technologies may provide answers to these issues, the skills and knowledge necessary to move from activity definition to knowledge representation, and make the implicit explicit, are still in their early stages.

Above, we emphasized the need for correspondence between the sources of data and the analysis and layers of new information that are created as a result of research activities. The conclusion was that the propositions that we create as part of research, if they are to be analyzed in combination with, and maintain a correspondence to, source or canonical data, must be represented using the same ontological approach (with appropriate methods of differentiation).

The ontology CRMinf (an extension of the CIDOC CRM: the specification is available from www.ics.forth.gr) is one of the first knowledge representation systems to fully implement this approach. CRMinf extends the knowledge representation principles of the CIDOC CRM and incorporates concepts from a number of argument and belief value systems (Doerr *et al.*, 2011).[31] It provides the means to assert new facts using the same Linked Data patterns (graphs) implemented in the initial representation of data, but additionally supports the explicit representation of important contextual information regarding attribution and the scientific concepts of observation, inference, and belief adoption to new scholarly assertions. Additionally, it provides the means to bring different information sources with different representation systems into a common scholarly discourse even if source data itself cannot be practically integrated. A database record, a spreadsheet, a section of text, or indeed any other type of information object can be used as a premise to conclude new beliefs and create a connected and robust discourse of argument.

Argumentation, rather than just being an attachment or add-on to scholarly discourse, becomes fully integrated into the model. Extending the same principles of knowledge representation to a researcher's assertions means that computer reasoning can be used across all facts with transparency and full academic provenance. Since argumentation theory is interdisciplinary, it provides the necessary focus and appropriate scope to bring other research activities, or primitives, together.

Conclusions

In some form, the semantic web is our future, and it will require formal representations of the human record. Those representations – ontologies, schemas, knowledge representations, call them what you will – should be produced by people trained in the humanities. (Unsworth, 2002)

Linked Data is the technical method of linking structured data, and provides an invaluable tool for bolting together, not pages of information, but structured information. Knowledge representation and Semantic technologies provide the means of elevating Linked Data to meaningful statements by communicating the intended meaning necessary for understanding these statements and their connections, in terms of not just description, but also context and provenance. This provides a basis for delivering information capable of informing a robust epistemological approach ultimately resulting in argument and belief, for which the results of other scholarly activities, including modeling and annotation, can become part of an integrated and more collaborative endeavor.

However, many internal information systems that store relevant humanities data use technologies that do not make meaning explicit, and this makes it difficult for technologists, without help from domain experts, to understand how it should be correctly represented. While a large amount of expertise and knowledge has been developed in other areas of digital humanities, some new skills are necessary to allow humanists to operate in and influence the complexities of Open World Semantics. Until this happens, the "intersection" of the digital humanities in this growing and important area will be unbalanced and waste valuable resources. This is an uncomfortable situation for humanists who regularly campaign for higher-quality information, and at the same time feel out of their depth when confronting the Linked Data community. This has a profound effect on the ability of the Web to become a Web of Knowledge and a place to conduct serious humanities research.

Knowledge representation (an activity independent of technology), and the Semantic Web (an environment that insists on cross-disciplinary collaboration) provide the fundamental elements of a common cyberinfrastructure in which humanists can pursue individual and specialist research but in which the divisions between different research areas can be bridged. The correct application of appropriate ontologies to the highly variable outputs of humanities sources can still be integrated without a loss of local meaning and perspectives and used as context across a far broader range of research questions. The use of ontologies such as the CIDOC CRM creates a platform for precise micro and macro analysis, which can be used as supporting context for other sources of information in many different research areas. For example, digital literary history research can be enhanced by the additional context gained through structured data from memory institutions, and vice versa.

This more integrated view of research means treating cultural organizations, archives, libraries, museums, and other relevant information system sources as a part of the Academy, and part of an overall research infrastructure that promotes data quality in both inputs and outputs, as a primary concern. Experts in these institutions are part of the humanist community, not junior partners, interested practitioners, or neutral service providers (Prescott, 2012). Knowledge representation of information should, if possible, be consistent from its production to its aggregation and integration, and throughout its analysis and the assertion of argument. The representation of argument and belief should be a fundamental focus of research environments, formalized so that it can be harmonized with, differentiated from, and ultimately influence authoritative sources (and become authoritative). This provides a new dimension to analytical data modeling activities (like semantic reasoning), which can be applied across heterogeneous datasets and, in the same process, include enriching propositions made by researchers from different disciplines and organizations.

The academic community has a responsibility to ensure that the results of their work feed back into the information systems of memory institutions, and that generations of humanities scholars are able to build on the work of others, producing a stable rather than fragmented digital legacy (McGann, 2010; Prescott, 2012). There is an ongoing responsibility to improve the development of data to include, from the start, the information about significance and relevance that is currently absent from Closed World information systems (Russell *et al.*, 2009). All stakeholders should be concerned with developing improved systems of digital curation, not just the memory institutions themselves.

While we need to apply the same duty of care to structured data sources as we do in the case of other humanities sources, we need to be careful about diverting attention to objectives that are not currently within our reach and are peripheral to the solid disciplinary development of the digital humanities. This means not expending scarce resources on "dangerous exercises in futurology which think out the unthinkable as an alternative to thinking out the thinkable" (Hobsbawm, 1998:72). Humanists still need to acquire the skills that allow a more expert and authoritative contribution to the discussion of digital and web infrastructures which are currently, and unhelpfully, dominated by computer scientists and technologists.[32] In this respect the words of John Unsworth quoted at the head of this conclusion, written well over a decade ago, remain true.

Acknowledgments

We thank Ellen Van Keer (Library of Antiquity, Royal Museums of Art and History) for her kind assistance.

NOTES

1 Rather than simply a reference.

2 Issues of integrity in digital projects are discussed under the term "Charlatanism" (cf. Tito Orlandi) (Unsworth, 2002).

3 Note that the term URI encompasses web resources that include URLs or web page addresses.

4 Although most systems employ another optional field, to identify a set of triples (named graphs), making a quad.

5 An RDF-based schema that provides the basic classes and properties for defining ontologies (http://www.w3.org/TR/rdf-schema).

6 See the website of the initiative at http://www.tei-c.org/index.xml.

7 The query language for relational systems is SQL (Structured Query language), informed by ISO/IEC 9075:2011.

8 For example, the *Prosopography of Anglo Saxon England* (PASE): http://www.pase.ac.uk.

9 http://www.w3.org/2001/sw/wiki/OWL.

10 For example, SPIN (http://spinrdf.org).

11 These processes are currently being defined in the CIDOC CRM Special Interest group initiative, Synergy, which provides a reference model for collaborative data provisioning. See www.cidoc-crm.org/docs.

12 Defining, amongst other things, a set of data or metadata elements that apply to a particular application but which have little application in the humanities, where these profiles cannot be defined without misrepresentation.

13 An example may be the still hesitant technical support of reification mechanisms or Named Graphs in the Semantic Web, which can be seen as a mandatory element to represent data-related argumentation in a coherent way (Doerr *et al.*, 2011). For instance, the Open Annotation Model avoided the use of Named Graphs because of concerns about their maturity, resulting in relatively complex workarounds in contrast to those presented in Serna *et al.* (2011).

14 A poet and educationalist – he debated with Thomas Huxley on the balance of culture and science in society.

15 TEI, for example, is a form of knowledge representation.

16 As opposed to "glass box," where "we can treat the internal structure of those data *as if* it is the internal structure of an expertise." The reason why ontologies like CIDOC CRM (see below) are "bottom-up" in design.

17 For example, "The 'nouns' are the pieces of data or information the user wants" (Winesmith and Carey, 2014).

18 Rather than attempting to model history.

19 McCarty lists five trajectories with the more practical at the top. "1. A world-wide, semi-coordinated effort to create large online scholarly resources; 2. Out of this activity, the slow development of new genres in something like a digital Library; 3. Analytic modelling, to raise the epistemological question of how we know what we somehow know; 4. Synthetic modelling, to reconstruct lost artefacts from fragmentary evidence, blurring gradually into a 5. Modelling for possible worlds".

20 For an example, see http://sites.tufts.edu/liam/2014/04/23/trends.

21 See LiAM (2014): an example of comparing TEI sources with Linked data from structured sources.

22 www.cidoc-crm.org – "provides definitions and a formal structure for describing the implicit and explicit concepts and relationships used in cultural heritage documentation."

23 Also see the CIDOC CRM Primer at http://www.cidoc-crm.org/docs/CRMPrimer.pdf.

24 http://www.tei-c.org/Guidelines/P5.

25 A Linked Data interface at http://collection.britishmuseum.org, and ResearchSpace at http://www.researchspace.org.

26 An object-orientated ontology version of the model, Functional Requirements for Bibliographic Records.

27 See http://www.w3.org/TR/xhtml-rdfa-primer.

28 Most notably the CIDOC CRM (Conceptual Reference Model), although this, while having the ability to be implemented using Linked Data, is technology-agnostic.

29 Tools like the DM2E Pundit annotation system (http://dm2e.eu/digital-humanities) show a movement towards a full argument and belief value system.

30 An analogy to the implicit relationships in structured data information systems.

31 Includes argumentation examples from the following papers: Toulmin (2003), Kunz & Rittel (1970), Pinto *et al.* (2004).

32 For example, see the W3C Linked Open data and Semantic Web mailing lists.

REFERENCES AND FURTHER READING

Aberer, K., Cudré-Mauroux, P., Ouksel, A.M., *et al.* 2004. Emergent semantics principles and issues. In *Database Systems for Advanced Applications*, ed. Y. Lee, J. Li, K.-Y. Whang, and D. Lee. Belin: Springer, 25–38. http://link.springer.com/chapter/10.1007/978-3-540-24571-1_2 (accessed October 12, 2014).

Antoniou, G., and Van Harmelen, F. 2004. *A Semantic Web Primer*. Cambridge, MA: MIT Press. http://www.dcc.fc.up.pt/~zp/aulas/1415/pde/geral/bibliografia/MIT.Press.A.Semantic.Web.Primer.eBook-TLFeBOOK.pdf (accessed October 31, 2014).

Arnold, M. 1869. *Culture and Anarchy*. London: Smith, Elder & Co.

Atkins, D., Droegemeier, K.K., Feldman, S.I., *et al.* 2003. Revolutionizing Science and Engineering Through Cyberinfrastructure: Report of the National Science Foundation Blue-Ribbon Advisory Panel on Cyberinfrastructure. National Science Foundation. https://arizona.openrepository.com/arizona/handle/10150/106224 (accessed September 17, 2014).

Bechhofer, S., Buchan, I., De Roure, D., *et al.* 2013. Why linked data is not enough for scientists. *Future Generation Computer Systems* 29 (2), 599–611.

Bernard, L. 2011. *Data vs. Text: Forty Years of Confrontation. Hidden Histories Symposium (UCL)*. Hidden Histories. University College London. http://hiddenhistories.omeka.net/items/show/8 (accessed August 5, 2013).

Berners-Lee, T. 2009. The next web. http://www.ted.com/talks/tim_berners_lee_on_the_next_web (accessed September 17, 2014).

Berners-Lee, T., and Fischetti, M. 2008. Weaving the Web: The Original Design and Ultimate Destiny of the World Wide Web by Its Inventor. San Francisco: Harper.

Berners-Lee, T., Hendler, J., and Lassila, O. 2001. The semantic web. *Scientific American* 284 (5), 28–37.

Blanke, T., and Hedges, M. 2013. Scholarly primitives: Building institutional infrastructure for humanities e-Science. *Future Generation Computer Systems* 29 (2), 654–61.

Brown, S., and Simpson, J. 2013. The curious identity of Michael Field and its implications for humanities research with the semantic web. In *Big Data, 2013 IEEE International Conference on*. IEEE, 77–85. http://ieeexplore.ieee.org/xpls/abs_all.jsp?arnumber=6691674 (accessed October 10, 2014).

Ciotti, F., and Tomasi, F. 2014. Formal ontologies, Linked Data and TEI. In *Decoding the Encoded*. Evanston, IL: Text Encoding Initiative. http://tei.northwestern.edu/files/2014/10/Ciotti-Tomasi-22p2xtf.pdf (accessed October 29, 2014).

Ciula, A., and Eide, Ø. 2014. Reflections on cultural heritage and digital humanities: modelling in practice and theory. In *Proceedings of the First International Conference on Digital Access to Textual Cultural Heritage*. New York: ACM, 35–41. http://doi.acm.org/10.1145/2595188.2595207 (accessed October 29, 2014).

Crofts, N. 2004. Museum informatics: the challenge of integration. University of Geneva. http://archive-ouverte.unige.ch/unige:417 (accessed July 23, 2014).

Cuomo, J. 2011. A conversation with W.G. Sebald (interview). In *The Emergence of Memory: Conversations with W.G. Sebald*, ed. L.S. Schwartz. New York: Seven Stories Press, 93–118.

Denning, P.J., and Bell, T. 2012. The information paradox. *American Scientist* 100, 470–7.

Doerr, M., and Crofts, N. 1998. *Electronic Esperanto: the role of the oo CIDOC Reference Model*. Citeseer. http://citeseerx.ist.psu.edu/viewdoc/download?doi=10.1.1.47.9674&rep=rep1&type=pdf (accessed August 26, 2013).

Doerr, M., and Low, J. T. 2010. A postcard is not a building why we need museum information curators. In *ICOM General Conference, Shanghai, China*. https://www.ics.forth.gr/_publications/

CIDOC_2010_low_martin.pdf (accessed November 1, 2014).

Doerr, M., Kritsotaki, A., and Boutsika, K. 2011. Factual argumentation: a core model for assertions making. *Journal on Computing and Cultural Heritage*, 3(3), p.1–34.

Eco, U., and Origgi, G. 2003. Auteurs et autorité: un entretien avec Umberto Eco. *Texte-e: Le texte à l'heure de l'Internet*, 215–30.

Eide, Ø., and Ore, C.-E. 2007. From TEI to a CIDOC-CRM Conforming Model: Towards a Better Integration Between Text Collections and Other Sources of Cultural Historical Documentation. In *Get Swept Up In It*. Digital Humanities 2007, University of Illinois, Urbana–Champaign. http://www.edd.uio.no/artiklar/tekstkoding/poster_156_eide.html (accessed October 28, 2014).

Gangemi, A., Catenacci, C., Ciaramita, M., and Lehmann, J. 2005. A theoretical framework for ontology evaluation and validation. *SWAP*. Citeseer. http://www.loa.istc.cnr.it/old/Papers/swap_final_v2.pdf (accessed October 28, 2014).

Gardin, J.-C. 1990. The structure of archaeological theories. In *Mathematics and Information Science in Archaeology: A Flexible Framework*, ed. A. Voorrips (ed.). Studies in Modern Archaeology 3. Bonn: Holos, 7–25.

Glimm, B. Hogan, A., Krötzsch, M., and Polleres, A. 2012. OWL: yet to arrive on the Web of Data? arXiv preprint arXiv:1202.0984. http://arxiv.org/abs/1202.0984 (accessed September 14, 2014).

Gooding, P., Warwick, C., and Terras, M. 2012. The myth of the new: mass digitization, distant reading and the future of the book. In *Digital Humanities 2012, Hamburg*. http://www.dh2012.uni-hamburg.de/conference/programme/abstracts/the-myth-of-the-new-mass-digitization-distant-reading-and-the-future-of-the-book.1.html (accessed October 29, 2014).

Gradmann, S., and Meister, J.C. 2008. Digital document and interpretation: re-thinking "text" and scholarship in electronic settings. *Poiesis & Praxis* 5 (2), 139–53.

Heath, T., and Bizer, C. 2011. *Linked Data: Evolving the Web into a Global Data Space*. San Rafael, CA: Morgan & Claypool.

Hobsbawm, E. 1998. *On History*, new edition. London: Abacus.

Hooland, S. van, and Verborgh, R. 2014. Linked Data for Libraries, Archives and Museums: How to Clean, Link and Publish Your Metadata. London: Facet.

Jameson, F. 1991. Postmodernism, or the Cultural Logic of Late Capitalism. Durham, NC: Duke University Press.

Kunz, W., and Rittel, H.W.J. 1970. *Issues as Elements of Information Systems*. Institute of Urban and Regional Development, University of California.

LiAM. 2014. Trends and gaps in linked data for archives. LiAM: Linked Archival Metadata. http://sites.tufts.edu/liam/2014/04/23/trends (accessed October 28, 2014).

McCarty, W. 1996. Finding implicit patterns in Ovid's *Metamorphoses* with TACT. *CH Working Papers*. http://journals.sfu.ca/chwp/index.php/chwp/article/view/B.3/91 (accessed December 27, 2011).

McCarty, W. 2003. Humanities computing. *Encyclopedia of Library and Information Science 2*, 1224.

McCarty, W. 2004. Modeling: a study in words and meaning. In *A Companion to Digital Humanities*, ed. S. Schreibman, R. Siemens, and J. Unsworth. Oxford: Blackwell. http://www.digitalhumanities.org/companion (accessed December 27, 2011).

McCarty, W. 2007. Looking backward, figuring forward: modelling, its discontents and the future. In *Digital Humanities 2007*, University of Illinois Urbana–Champagne. http://www.mccarty.org.uk/essays/McCarty,%20Looking%20backward.pdf (accessed October 24, 2014).

McCarty, W. 2014. Getting there from here: remembering the future of digital humanities. Roberto Busa Award lecture 2013. *Literary and Linguistic Computing* 29 (3), 283–306.

McGann, J. 2010. Sustainability: the elephant in the room. In *The Shape of Things to Come*. A Mellon Foundation Conference at the University of Virginia. http://shapeofthings.org/papers/JMcGann.docx (accessed May 18, 2014).

Moretti, F. 2007. Graphs, Maps, Trees: Abstract Models for a Literary History. London: Verso.

Nen, E.H. 2012. Publishing and Using Cultural Heritage Linked Data on the Semantic Web. San Rafael, CA: Morgan & Claypool.

Norton, B., and Oldman, D. 2014. A new approach to digital editions of ancient manuscripts using CIDOC-CRM, FRBRoo and RDFa. In *Digital Classicist London & Institute of Classical Studies seminar 2014, UCL, London*. http://www.digitalclassicist.org/wip/wip2014-10do.html (accessed October 29, 2014).

Oldman, D. Doerr, M., de Jong, G., Norton, B., and Wikman, T. 2014. Realizing lessons of the last 20 years: a manifesto for data provisioning and aggregation services for the digital humanities (a position paper). *D-Lib Magazine* 20 (7/8). http://www.dlib.org/dlib/july14/oldman/07oldman.html (accessed July 15, 2014).

Ore, C.-E., and Eide, Ø. 2009. TEI and cultural heritage ontologies: exchange of information? *Literary and Linguistic Computing* 24 (2), 161–72.

Palmer, C.L., Teffeau, L.C., and Pirmann, C.M. 2009. Scholarly Information Practices in the Online Environment: Themes from the Literature and Implications for Library Service Development. Dublin, OH: OCLC Programs and Research. http://www.oclc.org/programs/publications/reports/2009-02.pdf (accessed October 13, 2014).

Pesce, M. 1999. SCOPE1: information vs. meaning. In *Hyperreal, Vienna*. http://hyperreal.org/~mpesce/SCOPE1.html (accessed October 5, 2014).

Pierazzo, E. 2011. Digital humanities: a definition. http://epierazzo.blogspot.co.uk/2011/01/digital-humanities-definition.html (accessed July 16, 2013).

Pinto, H.S., Staab, S., and Tempich, C. 2004. DILIGENT: towards a fine-grained methodology for DIstributed, Loosely-controlled and evolvInG Engineering of oNTologies. In *ECAI 2004: Proceedings of the 16th European Conference on Artificial Intelligence*, ed. R. López de Mántaras. Amsterdam: IOS Press, 393–7.

Poole, A. 2013. Now is the future now? The urgency of digital curation in the digital humanities. *DHQ: Digital Humanities Quarterly*, 7 (2). http://www.digitalhumanities.org/dhq/vol/7/2/000163/000163.html (accessed October 24, 2014).

Prescott, A. 2012. An electric current of the imagination. *Digital Humanities:Works in Progress*. http://blogs.cch.kcl.ac.uk/wip/2012/01/26/an-electric-current-of-the-imagination (accessed March 15, 2012).

Prescott, A. 2013. Andrew Prescott (@Ajprescott) | Twitter. https://twitter.com/Ajprescott (accessed October 17, 2014).

Reisz, M. 2011. Surfdom. *Times Higher Education*. http://www.timeshighereducation.co.uk/story.asp?storycode=418343 (accessed December 28, 2011).

Renn, J. 2006. Towards a web of culture and science. *Information Services and Use* 26 (2), 73–9.

Rockwell, G. 2010. As transparent as infrastructure: on the research of cyberinfrastructure in the humanities. *openstax cnx*. http://cnx.org/contents/fd44afbb-3167-4b83-8508-4e70885b6136@2 (accessed September 21, 2014).

Roux, V. and Blasco P. 2004. *Logicisme et format SCD: d'une épistémologie pratique à de nouvelles pratiques éditoriales Hermès*. Paris: CNRS-éditions.

Russell, B. 2011. The Problems of Philosophy. Vook.

Russell, R., Winkworth, K., and Collections Council of Australia. 2009. *Significance 2.0: A Guide to Assessing the Significance of Collections*. Rundle Mall, SA: Collections Council of Australia.

Schraefel, M.C. 2007. What is an analogue for the semantic web and why is having one important? *ACM SIGWEB Newsletter*, Winter 2007. http://eprints.soton.ac.uk/264274/1/schraefelSWAnalogueHT07pre.pdf (accessed September 17, 2014).

Serres, M. 2011. Interstices: les nouvelles technologies, que nous apportent-elles? *Interstices*. https://interstices.info/jcms/c_15918/les-nouvelles-technologies-que-nous-apportent-elles (accessed October 16, 2014).

Shannon, C.E. 1948. A mathematical theory of communication. *The Bell System Technical Journal* XXVII (3). http://www3.alcatel-lucent.com/bstj/vol27-1948/articles/bstj27-3-379.pdf (accessed September 21, 2014).

Sperberg-McQueen, C.M., Marcoux, Y., and Huitfeldt, C. 2010. Two representations of the semantics of TEI Lite. In *Cultural Expression, Old and New. Digital Humanities 2010, King's College, London*. http://dh2010.cch.kcl.ac.uk/academic-programme/abstracts/papers/html/ab-663.html (accessed October 29, 2014).

TaDiRAH. 2014. TaDiRAH: Taxonomy of Digital Research Activities in the Humanities. *Dariah*. http://tadirah.dariah.eu/vocab/index.php (accessed October 13, 2014).

Terras, M., and Ross, C. 2011. Scholarly information-seeking behaviour in the British Museum online collection. In *Museums and the Web 2011, Philadephia*. http://www.museumsandtheweb.com/mw2011/papers/scholarly_information_seeking_behaviour_in_the.html (accessed October 29, 2014).

Toulmin, S.E. 2003. *The Uses of Argument*. Cambridge: Cambridge University Press.

Unsworth, J. 2000. Scholarly primitives: what methods do humanities researchers have in common, and how might our tools reflect this? Paper presented at *Humanities Computing: Formal Methods and Experimental Practice*, King's College,

London. http://people.brandeis.edu/~unsworth/Kings.5-00/primitives.html (accessed October 2014).

Unsworth, J. 2002. What is humanities computing and what is not? http://computerphilo logie.uni-muenchen.de/jg02/unsworth.html (accessed December 27, 2011).

Unsworth, J. 2006. Our Cultural Commonwealth: the report of the American Council of learned societies commission on cyberinfrastructure for the humanities and social sciences. ACLS: New York. https://www.ideals.illinois.edu/handle/2142/189 (accessed September 22, 2014).

W3C Technical Architecture Group. 2001. *Architecture of the World Wide Web, Volume One.* http://www.w3.org/TR/webarch (accessed September 14, 2014).

Winesmith, K., and Carey, A. 2014. Why build an API for a museum collection? San Francisco Museum of Modern Art. http://www.sfmoma.org/about/research_projects/lab/why_build_an_api (accessed November 9, 2014).

Zorich, D. 2008. *A Survey of Digital Humanities Centers in the United States.* Washington, DC: Council on Library and Information Resources. http://www.clir.org/pubs/reports/pub143/contents.html (accessed November 9, 2014).

19
Text Analysis and Visualization: Making Meaning Count

Stéfan Sinclair and Geoffrey Rockwell

Un des problèmes de la sémiotique serait … de définir la spécificité des différentes organisations textuelles en la situant dans *le texte général (la culture)* dont elle font partie et qui fait partie d'elles. (Julia Kristeva)[1]

Which Words are used to describe White and Black NFL Prospects?

In May of 2014 the sports website *Deadspin* carried an article about the words used by National Football League (NFL) scouts reporting on black and white prospects (Fischer-Baum *et al.*, 2014). They found differences. White players were more likely to be called "intelligent" and blacks more likely to be called "natural." They had compiled a collection of texts – a corpus – and analyzed it with *Voyant Tools*.[2] Digital humanities methods and tools had come to sport journalism.

But *Deadspin* went a step further. Instead of discussing the difference in vocabulary they provided an "interactive" for readers to try comparisons (they use "interactive" as a noun, a ellipsis for something like an interactive widget). You type in a word to search for and the interactive returns a simple bar graph that you can drop into a comment (Figure 19.1), as hundreds of readers did. They used a simple interactive text visualization to make their point.

This chapter is about such text analysis and visualizations.[3] The analytical practices of the digital humanities are becoming ubiquitous as digital textuality continues to surround and overwhelm us. This is an introduction to thinking through the analysis and visualization of electronic texts. We start by asking again what an electronic text is in the context of analysis – a preliminary but crucial first step. Then we look at how

A New Companion to Digital Humanities, First Edition. Edited by Susan Schreibman, Ray Siemens, and John Unsworth.
© 2016 John Wiley & Sons, Ltd. Published 2016 by John Wiley & Sons, Ltd.

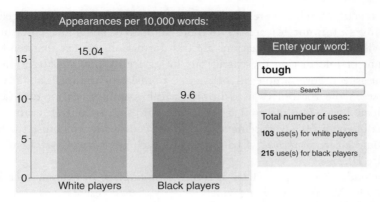

Figure 19.1   An interactive text analysis and visualization widget by *Deadspin*.

analysis takes apart the text to recompile it in ways that let you reread it for new insights. Finally we will return to how interactive visualizations bear meaning.

Ubiquitous Text

Text may be less flashy and less glamorous than other forms of communication such as sound, image, and video, but it remains the dominant way that humans communicate, discover, and process information. It is estimated that every day some 200 billion emails are sent and some 5 billion Google search queries are performed – and they are nearly all text-based.[4] The hundred hours of video uploaded to YouTube every minute would remain largely inaccessible were it not for text-based searches of the title, description, and other metadata. Even if we hesitate to join the poststructuralist theorists (like Kristeva, quoted above) in saying that *everything is text*, we can certainly agree that *text is everywhere*.

For humanities scholars and students working with texts as cultural artifacts, it is reassuring to recognize that people from every sector in our digital society are struggling with how to derive meaning from texts, from high-school students researching an essay topic to journalists combing through leaked security documents, or from companies measuring social media reaction to a product launch to historians studying diversity of immigration based on more than two centuries of trial proceedings.[5] The particular texts, methodologies, assumptions, and objectives vary widely between different applications, of course, but fundamentally we are all trying to gain insights from the vast amount of text that surrounds us.

We are unrelentingly bombarded by text in our lives and we have access to unfathomable quantities of other texts.[6] Yet for some, the problem is the opposite one: a dearth of readily accessible and reliable digital texts, whether because of legal reasons (like copyright or privacy), technical challenges (such as the difficulty of automatically recognizing characters in handwritten documents), or resource constraints that make it impractical to digitize everything (parish records scattered throughout the world, for instance). As a result, there is a significant inequality in the availability of digital texts, one that has a profound effect on the kinds of work that scholars are able to pursue.

When text *is* available there can be so much of it that we naturally seek ways of representing significant features of it more compactly and more efficiently, often through visualization. Visualizations are transformations of text that tend to *reduce* the amount of information presented, but in service of drawing attention to some significant aspect. For example, if you wanted to make an argument about the differences between the vocabulary used in mainstream commercials for toys targeted at girls compared with toys targeted at boys, you could simply compile examples from a sample set of about 60 advertisements and invite your reader to peruse the full texts. Or you could create *word cloud* visualizations for each gender, as Crystal Smith (2011) did (Figure 19.2).

Word clouds such as these have become commonplace in content such as advertising, posters, and presentations, which is to say that representations of data derived from analytic processes of digital texts have become normalized, they are not the preserve of an obscure branch of the humanities or computer science. Word clouds are especially conducive to wider audiences because they are relatively simple and intuitive – the bigger the word, the more frequently it occurs.[7] However, word clouds are usually static or very limited in their interactivity (animation for layout, hovering and clicking on terms). They provide a snapshot, but do not allow exploration and experimentation.

We have also witnessed in the past years an increase in the number of more complex text-oriented visualizations in mainstream media on the web. The *New York Times* in particular has produced several rich interactive visualizations of digital texts, including an interface for exploring American State of the Union addresses, shown in Figure 19.3.

It is worth drawing attention to several aspects of this interface:

1. The explanatory caption provides succinct context for the visualization and explicitly invites the reader to *analyze* the texts (a much more participatory activity than conventional newspaper reading).
2. The interface provides open-ended search capabilities.
3. It also provides suggested terms to explore.
4. There is a visual representation of the entire corpus – seven State of the Union addresses in what Ruecker *et al.* call a "rich prospect view" (2011) – with the distribution of term occurrences clearly shown.
5. For each occurrence of a term of interest, the surrounding text (context) can be displayed.
6. The frequency of terms can be compared, not only of the same term across multiple years, but also multiple terms.
7. There is a link to the entire 2007 State of the Union address.

With such rich and sophisticated analytic environments, do we even need to read texts anymore? Our reaction to this question reveals much about our purposes for interacting with texts. If we read text for pleasure – a compelling story, a nuanced description, a detailed account of an historical event, etc. – text analysis and visualization are unlikely to be satisfying in the same ways. If we are interested in examining linguistic or semantic features of text, analytic tools may be of help. In our (the authors') own practice as digital humanists, we have tended to combine these activities: we read

(a)

(b)

Figure 19.2 *Wordle* word cloud visualizations of vocabulary from commercials for (a) toys targeted at boys and (b) toys targeted at girls.

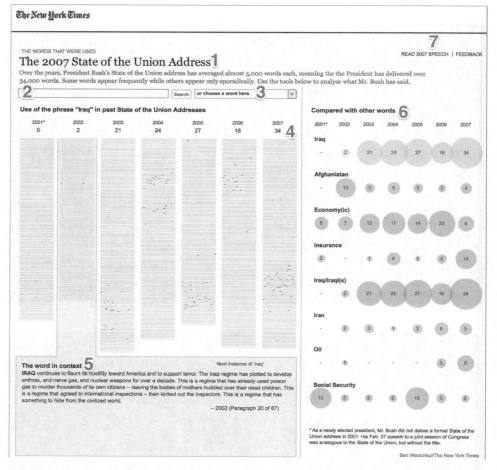

Figure 19.3   2007 State of the Union Address: an interactive text analysis and visualization interface from the *New York Times*.

texts we enjoy, we then explore and study them with analytic tools and visualization interfaces, which then brings us back to rereading the texts differently. This is what we call the *agile interpretive cycle*.

In the rest of this chapter we will explore this circling between reading, analysis, and visualization in more detail, but first we will have a closer look at what is a text.

What is a Text for Analysis?

The availability and prevalence of analytic tools and interactive visualizations can easily lead us to begin experimenting without a proper grasp of the nature and diversity of digital texts. For some purposes this naïveté is acceptable, but using tools effectively and creatively usually entails a full understanding of the materials used. Moreover, the history of digital humanities is as much about a rich tradition of reimagining text as it is about algorithmic analysis – McGann's *Radiant Textuality* (2001) provides one of the most notable examples.[8]

Bits and Bytes

Digital text is fundamentally a sequence of characters in a string, which is to say it is composed of tiny bits of discrete information that are encoded with a chosen character set in a sequence. Typically we treat textual information at the character-level of granularity, whether it is a character in the Roman alphabet (upper- or lowercase *a* to *z*, an Arabic number (0 to 9), a Chinese ideogram (such as 三 or *sān*, meaning "three"), an Emoji character (like ☺), a control character (like a tab), or any other value from a predefined character set. There are many different character sets, so the crucial thing is consistency – if a text has been encoded with a particular character set, then any future processing of the text must use a compatible character set to avoid problems. This is especially the case for plain text formats where no formatting (and no character-set information) is stored with the text, which is only a sequence of codes from the set.

Unicode is a family of character sets that has helped resolve many issues related to incompatible character sets, but it is far from used universally (Mac OS X uses the incompatible MacRoman character set by default, for instance), and of course there are also huge stores of plain text files that predate Unicode. Character encoding is not an obscure technical issue in text analysis; it remains a common challenge for text analysis and visualization. Unfortunately, there is no reliable way to determine a plain text file's character encoding short of trying different character encoding settings in a text viewer (such as a browser) or plain text editor.[9]

Some character sets are limited to one byte per character, where a byte is composed of eight bits, and one bit is a binary value of 0 or 1. Other character sets (such as Unicode, and in particular UTF-8) can use from one to four bytes to represent a character. In other words, a single Unicode UTF-8 character may actually be represented by a cohesive sequence of up to 32 digits (0s and 1s). The character is typically the smallest unit of information with digital texts, but it is an atom composed of even smaller particles (and tools can misguidedly split an atom apart when character encoding mistakes are made).

Still, the magic of digital texts is that they are composed of discrete units of information – such as the character unit – that can be infinitely reorganized and rearranged on algorithmic whims. Extract the first 100 characters of a text? Sure. Reverse the order of characters in a text? OK. Isolate each occurrence of the character sequence "love"? Done. Digital text is conducive to manipulation – it invites us to experiment with its form in applied ways that print text cannot support. This is the essence of what Ramsay calls *algorithmic criticism*, made possible by the low-level character encoding of digital texts.

Format and Markup

Whereas plain text files only contain the characters of a text, other formats can also express information about character encoding, styling, and layout (on screen or in print), metadata (such as creator and title), and a variety of other attributes *about* the text. Some file formats use a markup strategy to essentially annotate parts or the entirety of a text. Compare the different ways these markup languages indicate that the word "important" should be presented in bold:[10]

Rich Text Format (RTF)	This is {\b important}.
LaTeX	This is \textbf{important}.
HyperText Markup Language (HTML)	This is important.
Markdown	This is *important*.

It is worth noting that each of these formats can be readily edited with plain text editors, because the markup language itself uses a simple set of characters. Many other file formats are not editable in plain text editors, often because they are stored in a binary format (such as MS Word, OpenDocument, or PDF). Whether a file is editable in plain text or encoded in binary is independent of whether it is a proprietary (closed) format or an open standard. EPUB, for instance, is an open e-book standard that is distributed in binary form (as a compressed file) where much of the content is typically encoded in an HTML format. With concern for preservation and access, and deep roots in library culture, digital humanists have long favored human-readable (not binary) and open formats.

One of the crown jewels of the digital humanities community is the Text Encoding Initiative (TEI), a collective project founded in the 1980s to standardize markup for digital texts in a human-readable and open format.[11] Just as consistency and compatibility are crucial for character encoding, the same is true for other types of markup: how to encode a paragraph or a person mentioned in a text, for instance.

Although the TEI has traditionally been more focused on detailed encoding for preservation, there are definitely analytic benefits to the markup. Imagine we wanted to examine the term "lady" in Shakespeare's *Macbeth*. In a plain text file each character name is indicated before the speech, which means that a frequency count of the word "lady" might also misleadingly include "Lady Macbeth" the character name. With TEI, the character name is marked up with the <speaker> element, which makes it easier to reliably to filter out those occurrences. Conversely, we may want to only consider speeches by Lady Macbeth – again, a relatively trivial transformation of the text. Digital texts are infinitely reorganizable, and markup (such as TEI) serves to proliferate the number of logical moves that can be made, like extra grips on a climbing wall.

Despite all this, one of the first operations performed on a painstakingly marked-up text is often to strip out the markup. This is partly because many analytic operations do not benefit from the markup (indeed the markup can interfere with the proper functioning of the tool) and partly because there is still a dearth of tools that truly allow the markup to be exploited.[12]

Shapes and Sizes

Texts and text collections come in different formats, but also have different shapes and sizes, which also help determine what is possible and what is optimal.

A corpus is a *body* of texts (though a corpus can have only a single text). The kinds of text analysis operations that can or should be performed will of course be determined in part by the compatibility between what we call the *geometry* of the corpus and the design of the tools. One size does not fit all. A tool like *Poem Viewer* (Figure 19.4; ovii.oerc.ox.ac.uk/PoemVis) is intended primarily to assist in close reading of single poems, whereas the Google *Ngram Viewer* (Figure 19.5; books.google.com/ngrams) is intended to enable queries of millions of books (but no reading of text). These represent very different kinds of intellectual work, determined in part by the nature of the corpora.

Just as bits of a single digital text can be rearranged, texts within a digital corpus can be rearranged and sampled for a variety of purposes. Imagine a collection of articles from philosophy journals from the past 150 years[13] – this is a coherent corpus, but one that can spawn any number of other corpora based on a variety of logics for ordering, grouping, and filtering. For instance, we might want to have all documents ordered by year of publication and then author name, or by journal and then year and then author. Similarly, we might want to create new, aggregate texts that combine all articles by decade or by philosophical period. Or perhaps we just want to work with articles

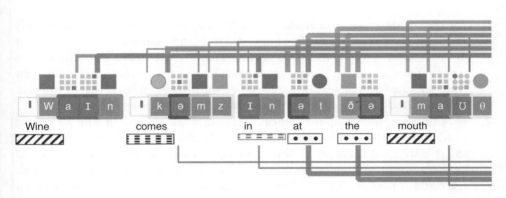

Figure 19.4 *Poem Viewer*, for close reading of linguistic features in poetry.

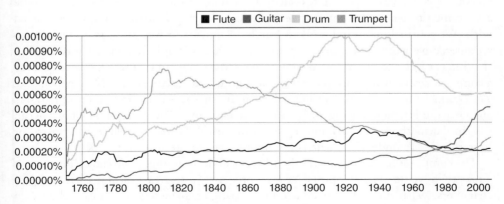

Figure 19.5 Google *Ngram Viewer*, which allows querying on millions of books.

published outside of Anglophone countries. In addition to corpus decomposition and reorganization, there are cases where a single text can generate a new corpus with many texts: all speeches from each speaker in a play in separate documents, for instance, or each item in an RSS feed becomes its own document.[14] A digital corpus is a bit like a bag of Lego where pieces can be built up in various configurations, but it is even better than that, since digital texts are trivial to clone and documents can exist in several structures a once (an infinite bag of Lego).

The presence of markup and of metadata is crucial for this kind of flexible and dynamic creation of corpora. Since the structuring and reorganization steps are often specific to the local research context (the available corpus and its format, the tools at-hand, the types of questions to ask, etc.), we have found that a bit of programming competency for parsing and processing document sets is valuable.

Analysis and Reading

In all these applications, the appeal to computers as an aid to processing texts can be largely summarized by two types of questions:

1. For texts with which I am already familiar, how can computers help me identify and study interesting things I had not noticed before, or things I had noticed but did not have reasonable means to pursue? Digital texts enable a proliferation of representations to explore linguistic and semantic characteristics and produce new representations and new associations, all of which can help to solidify intuitions we may already have had or generate entirely new perspectives.
2. How can computers help me identify and understand texts with which I am not familiar or which I cannot reasonably read? Human reading is time-consuming and selective, and retention of content is idiosyncratic. Computers can help extend human reading and understanding, especially for large collections of texts that you couldn't read in a lifetime. Computers can help identify what you might want to read.[15]

Of course, you have been doing text analysis all along. Readers on the web have become accustomed to embedded interactive analytics, like the *Deadspin* example we started with. We routinely use Find tools to search documents or web sites. It is common to see interactive word clouds in a blog that show you the high frequency words used in that blog at a glance. *Wordle* word clouds, like those shown in Figure 19.2, have become a common design feature for posters about digital humanities events. Newspapers like *The Guardian* have special data journalism units that specialize in gathering datasets and creating interactive widgets for readers to explore.[16] The question is, How we can use similar methods to study and represent historical documents, philosophy texts, or literatures?[17] To understand what we can do we need to return to strings.

The computer has a fundamentally different understanding, if we can call it that, of a text than we do. The computer "reads" (processes) a text as a meaningless string of characters. What it can do is operate on this string of characters, and it can reliably do very repetitive operations. For example, a computer can compare a short string like a word to every position in a much longer string, like a novel. That is how searching works. The computer checks every word against what you want to find. It does this menial work quickly and reliably.

The computer can do more than just find words. The computer can find more complex patterns. Let's say you want to find either "woman" or "women" – the computer can be given a pattern in the form of a regular expression, "wom[ae]n."[18] Or you can do a truncation search that searches for any words that begin with "under" – "underwater," "understand," and so on. The regular expression for this, depending on the system, might look like "under.*" – where the "." means any character and the "*" means any number (of any character). Library database systems will typically assume that you want variants of your word, especially the plural with "s" on the end. One can, in fact, do a lot of text analysis just with regular expressions that describe the patterns you want to find and return the passages that match.[19]

But what is a word? We tend to think of a word as a unit of meaning that often has an analog in the real world. The word "cat" in "the cat is on the mat over there" refers to that furry thing I'm pointing at. A computer doesn't know what a word is and certainly has no sense of what words might refer to.[20] For a computer to handle words you need to define what the orthographic (written) word is in a string, and we typically do that by identifying the characters that demarcate a word. Words are usually bounded by spaces and punctuation, and a computer can be told to split a long string (text) into shorter strings (words) by looking for the demarcation characters – though this splitting up into words, a process called tokenization, is highly challenging in some languages that do not have characters to indicate word boundaries, such as Japanese and Thai. The rules for splitting a text into word tokens can get complex, and these rules vary from language to language, but this splitting or tokenization is a basic first step to text analysis since words are important to us, particularly since so many tools operate on the lexical (word) level, rather than other units such as phrases. Tokenization, it should be noted, is not a quantitative operation – it is a phase of text analysis that has to do essentially with symbolic processing and recognition of patterns, with some similarities to how humans read.

This brings us back to analysis, which etymologically means a breaking apart into smaller units. Text analysis, like any form of analysis, is a process of decomposition, and as such is a standard way of understanding something. When we try to understand any complex phenomenon, one way to start is to break it into smaller parts – ideally into atomic parts. Bodies can be understood in terms of organs and then cells. Histories can be understood in terms of epochs and events. Texts can be understood in terms of chapters, paragraphs, sentences, and finally words (even if meaning spans across these units). Where we can formally define these parts, the computer can help us decompose the text.

What then do we do with a text in tiny little parts? Well, we can build indexes for the end of the book or concordances that show each word in a line of context. Concordancing was in fact one of the original uses for computers in the humanities, as it is what Father Busa wanted IBM support for in the late 1940s (Hockey, 2004). Concordances, especially of the Bible, are tools with a history that goes back to the thirteenth century. They allow you to quickly scan all the instances of a word such as "love" in an important text. They are better than an index, which just tells you on

```
moon (29)
I.1/577.1   four happy days bring in | Another moon: but, 0, methinks, how
I.1/577.1      0, methinks, how slow | This old moon wanes! she lingers my
I.1/577.1         away the time; | And then the moon, like to a silver bow |
I.1/577.2   faint hymns to the cold fruitless moon. | Thrice-blessed they
I.1/577.2        to pause; and, by the nest new moon-- | The sealing-day
```

Figure 19.6   Key Word In Context (KWIC) of "moon" in *A Midsummer's Night Dream* from TACTWeb.

what pages you can find the word, because the lines of text containing the word that represents the concept of interest are arranged to make it easier for one to see patterns in the appearance of the word.

Searching for words and presenting them on the screen has evolved from the print concordance into very large search engines like Google. Computers can arrange the passages of text with the word concorded in different ways, like the Key Word in Context (KWIC), where the key word (e.g., "moon") lines up so you can see what words come before and after (Figure 19.6). Until personal computers and then the Web came along and there were easy ways of publishing electronic texts directly for the computer screen, batch concording tools such as COCOA and OCP were used to create large print concordances. Text analysis, up until the first interactive tools like ARRAS, was more a matter of taking apart a text and then rearranging it so that you could print the rearrangement. It was the print concordance that was then used as a study tool.

Another use of text analysis was to identify patterns of word usage by particular authors, a field called stylistics. Not only can computers find patterns, but they can count patterns and compare counts. By counting function words, which do not convey a lot of semantic content, but which are important syntactically (and which occur in greater numbers, making them more statistically significant), one can get a sense of an author's writing style. Writing style, once formally described, can then be measured and compared (Kenny, 1982), and you can even use it as one more tool in trying to identify anonymous authors like the Unabomber (Foster, 2000).

Text analysis is not just analysis, it is also synthesis. Text analysis tools such as concordances not only break apart a text, but they put it back together in new ways. These new ways range from KWICs to visualizations that are increasingly abstract representations of the text. Text analysis synthesizes a new text, like stitching Frankenstein's monster out of parts, and it allows you to study the original in a new light. It is the textual equivalent of sampling and synthesizing new musical works, or making a collage out of images cut up from elsewhere. This synthesis can be done for artistic purposes or it can be done for interpretative purposes. The emphasis on creativity and experimentation align well with contemporary maker culture and its core tenet that *doing* (constructive creation) fosters learning and discovery. Thinking through choices of how and what to create, as well as observing and critiquing what is created, can provide generative moments of insight. Moreover, the mere ability (or affordance) to perform actions on texts can be empowering for readers and serves to further unseat the notion of rigid, canonical texts (if any such notions remain after the rise of electronic literature and hypertext).

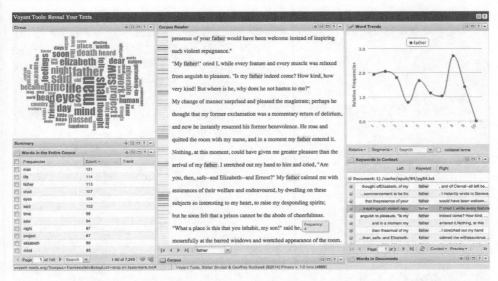

Figure 19.7 The *Voyant Tools* standard reading skin, showing Mary Shelley's *Frankenstein* for analysis.

We use the word *hermeneutica* for the interactive and interpretative analytical tools that facilitate the rearranging and manipulation of texts in order to better study and understand them. *Voyant Tools* (Figure 19.7), for example, lets you click on a word in the cloud (Cirrus) and then see the distribution of the word over the text (Word Trends). Clicking on the histogram shows the keyword in context, and clicking on an instance in the Keywords in Context panel jumps the full-text Corpus Reader to the right location. Each panel shows a different view on the text which can be used to control other views. Be careful, however, that you don't depend only on the stitch-ups. They are semi-automated rearrangements that should be questioned just like any other interpretation. Their very existence depends on a wide range of human choices, from the encoding of the digital text and the programming of the analytic tool to the parameters selected by the user and ways that results are read. Text analysis and visualization data are taken, not given, as Johanna Drucker reminds us, in her poetics of computer-mediated humanistic inquiry (2011).

Analysis and Visualization

Both print and digital text is represented visually for reading, and typography is about the graphical representation of characters in a particular medium.[21] In this simple sense, text is already a type of visualization, an instantiation of a more notional text that is not concerned with specificities like page numbers or scrolling position.[22] Emphasizing displayed text as visualization has the benefit of allowing us to take into account a full spectrum of text visualizations. Consider a text with only slight stylistic changes, such as having all adjectives display in green. Is this a text or a visualization? It is both.

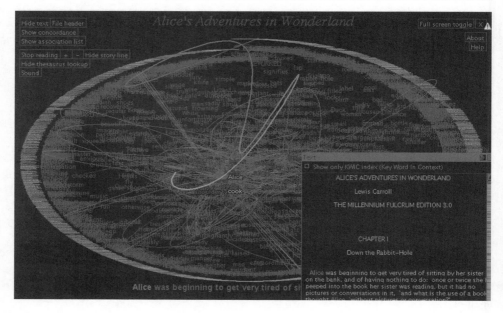

Figure 19.8   *TextArc* by Bradford Paley, showing *Alice in Wonderland* as text around the perimeter and as distributed terms within the perimeter.

We can iteratively add additional variations to the text rendering to change other stylistic attributes (italics, size, orientation, etc.) and even begin unhinging words or other lexical units from their original sequential position. A classic example of rich text visualization is Bradford Paley's *TextArc* (textarc.org), where words from a text are actually displayed twice, once in linear order arranged around the perimeter clockwise from the top (hovering over the tiny representation of a line causes a more legible version to appear), and then again by plotting each content word within the circle as if each occurrence in the perimeter pulled the terms toward it gravitationally (also called a centroid). As a result, the location of the word conveys information about its distribution in the document – "king" and "queen" occur more in the last third of *Alice in Wonderland*, for instance (Figure 19.8).

The spectrum of text visualizations thus includes a variety of stylistic and positional transformations, but also more abstract representations of textual attributes. One example of this is the *Knots* interface in *Voyant Tools*, which represents lexical repetition by introducing a kink in a line every time a selected term occurs. The more "knotted" a line, the greater the repetition (Figure 19.9).

Even though *Knots* is a more abstract and qualitative expression of repetition, it is only possible because of underlying data and algorithmic operations. The apparent dichotomy between the quantitative and qualitative can be misleading, particularly since text visualizations depend on a symbiosis between them.

Text visualizations can use a very wide spectrum of graphical features, from subtle typographical attributes in a sequential text to complex geometric forms produced from textually derived data. Reading practices are equally expansive: we read text to understand or experience something, and the same can be said about reading data visualizations.

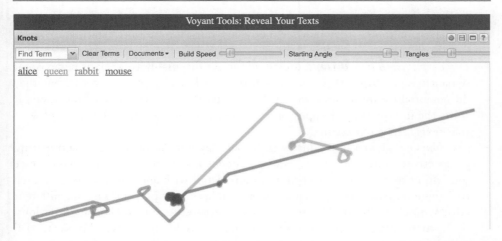

Figure 19.9 *Knots* visualization of *Alice in Wonderland* – some terms repeat often and regularly (e.g., "Alice," near the middle) while others occur very locally (e.g., "mouse," which shoots off to the right).

There is an important distinction between how to read a text visualization and how to interpret what is being visualized: understanding the mechanics of consumption compared to the understanding of what is being consumed. Once we have learned to read text in a language, we should be able to read most texts in that language, though the text may not always make sense to us. The same cannot be said for all text visualizations – we know when we are looking at text, but with some text visualizations we may be led to ask "what are we looking at?" Visualizations make use of a visual grammar, just as language requires a linguistic grammar, and we need to be able to parse what we see before attempting to analyze and understand it (see Tufte, 2001, for foundational work in studying visual information in graphs). We have developed common visual literacies for representations such as simple charts, maps, and time-lines, but other representations (like *TextArc* and *Knots*) are likely to require explanation. The effectiveness of a visualization will depend in a first instance on the ability of the reader to decipher what is being seen, either because of familiarity with the visual paradigm or through a willingness to become familiar with it. One way we often make sense of the visual features is to play with the parameters or interactive controls, which is why interactive visualizations can be easier to understand. With interactives, the play becomes a way of understanding the rearranged text, but also the tool as text.

Making Meaning Count

It would be convenient if there were a reliable set of text visualizations that were guaranteed to produce new insights, but interpretation is never that formulaic (thankfully). Sometimes the relative simplicity and sparseness of a word cloud is useful to get an overview of a text, at other times a simulated 3D representation of term clusters in a scatter-plot graph showing correspondence analysis results is an effective way of studying a corpus.[23]

We have found two principles to be important when engaging with text anlaysis and visualization tools – they may seem obvious, but they are worth stating:

- *Don't expect much from the tools*. Most tools at our disposal have weak or nonexistent semantic capabilities; they count, compare, track, and represent words, but they do not produce meaning – we do. When you don't expect much from tools, it shifts the interpretative responsibility for making sense of the rich variety of ways that texts can be represented.
- *Try things out*. Taken individually each tool may not do much, but accumulating perspectives from many tools can be beneficial. One tool may help you notice something that is worth exploring in more detail with another tool. Within each tool there may be settings that are worth tinkering or playing with for different effects (Sinclair, 2003). We use tools not to get results but to generate questions, so the more things we try, the more questions we're likely to have. Ramsay (2014) calls this the screwmeneutical imperative.

These two principles are expressed in part in the *Voyant Tools* environment that we have developed: the individual tools are designed to be simple and modular in order to favor interaction *with* and *between* the tools. The tools are intended to facilitate the augmented hermeneutic cycle by enabling navigation between reading text, analysis, and visualization at various scales ("differential reading" that slides between close and distant reading practices – see Clement, 2013).

Voyant Tools has the benefit of being readily accessible on the web and relatively user-friendly, but there are many other tools and interfaces that are worth exploring. For text analysis and visualization from a digital humanities perspective we suggest exploring resources listed on the *Text Analysis Portal for Research* (tapor.ca) and the text-mining section of DiRT (bit.ly/1sRGAuI).

The idea that text analysis and visualization are interpretative practices may seem paradoxical at first glance, since the digital is founded on matching and counting, but no amount of counting can produce meaning. On the other hand, digital tools do facilitate experimentation with the representation of digital texts, and those representations can lead us, as readers, to observe noteworthy phenomena and connections, some of which, we may argue, are meaningful. Sometimes we also get interested in the interpretation of these tools of interpretation, but that is another type of text analysis.

NOTES

1   This quotation is from Kristeva's "Texte clos" (1968). We have added emphasis to highlight Kristeva's poststructuralist move to conceptually equate text with culture (everything is text). Here is an English translation: "One of the problems for semiotics is ... to define the specificity of different textual arrangements by situating them in the general text (culture) of which they are a part and which, in turn, is part of them" (Kristeva, 1980:83).

2   *Voyant Tools* is a suite of text analysis tools we developed for the web. You can try them at http://voyant-tools.org.

3   This chapter is based on *Hermeneutica*, a forthcoming book on text analysis. See http://hermeneuti.ca.

4   The scale of the numbers is more significant here than exact values, which are notoriously difficult to determine. The estimate for emails comes from a widely cited report from the Radicati Group (2014), and Google search numbers are estimated from Google's own documentation and comCore statistics (http://bit.ly/1s3deqZ).

5   These examples are intended to be generic and representative but are inspired by specific examples such as (1) a high-school student doing text analysis on *the Game of Thrones* (bit.ly/1m6H9if); (2) an independent analyst parsing Canadian security documents leaked by Edward Snowden (bit.ly/1iyAWpC); (3) a car company like Kia tracking the response to a new model of vehicle (buswk.co/1mIsf4i); (4) a historian studying immigration using 200,000 documents from the Proceedings of the Old Bailey in London (bit.ly/1satlmL).

6   It would take well over 100 years to read just the 45,000 e-books in Project Gutenberg (gutenberg.org), assuming one could sustain the unlikely pace of one e-book a day.

7   Other aspects of word clouds may appear intuitive but are not – typically the position of words has little meaning, for instance. Word clouds have detractors who justifiably argue that they are often misused (when other visualizations would be more appropriate), insufficiently contextualized and reductive, and informationally misleading (like the color of words in some instances); see for instance Harris (2011).

8   See also Ryan Cordell's excellent "On ignoring encoding" (2014), which attempts to recalibrate the disproportionate attention paid to text analysis compared to digital editing and encoding practices.

9   Some text editors (like JEdit) and analytic tools (like *Voyant*) have built-in heuristics to try to guess character encoding, but in most instances it remains a guess, and it is best to specify the character encoding if it is known.

10 LaTeX may be the least familiar format presented here, but it is widely used as a document preparation format for scientific publications.

11 See Renear (2004) and Hockey (2000) for more information on the TEI.

12 One notable exception is TMX (textometrie.ens-lyon.fr).

13 We are beginning work on a corpus of philosophical texts from the past 150 years, provided by JSTOR.

14 RSS is Really Simple Syndication, an XML-based format that allows for multiple items (like news articles or blog posts) to be included in a single document.

15 Franco Moretti (2005) downplays reading in his description of distant reading, but we don't buy it: Moretti is still very much in the business of reading and interpretation.

16 See http://www.theguardian.com/media/datablog/2012/mar/07/open-data-journalism for an entry point into their Datastore and Datablog.

17 For an exploration of text analysis for teaching, see Sinclair and Rockwell (2012).

18 We are focusing on simple searching here, but of course it is also possible to have computers perform morphological analysis to find word variants that belong to the same family.

19 For more on regular expressions, see Stephen Ramsay's classic "Using regular expressions" (http://solaris-8.tripod.com/regexp.pdf). Ramsay also treats of patterns in *Reading Machines* (2011.)

20 Some of the challenges of natural language processing from the last half-century can be summarized by the difference in semiotic models between humans and computers: for humans, language refers to concepts that are learned through experience; for computers, language is a formal representation of lower-level binary data.

21 Braille for the visually impaired is an exception, because characters are represented for tactile rather than visual sensing.

22 The claim that there is a notional text prior to any printed or displayed instantiation will seem contentious to some, but we are especially interested in emphasizing that any form a text takes is already laden with visual specificities (font face, size, and color, page layout, etc.) that are bound to influence the experience of reading text.

23 A correspondence analysis graph for the archives of the Humanist Discussion Group listserv is a useful way to study shifts in concerns over time of the digital humanities community: see bit.ly/1ljh2BT, as well as Wang & Inaba (2009).

REFERENCES AND FURTHER READING

Clement, T. 2013. Text analysis, data mining, and visualizations in literary scholarship. In *Literary Studies in the Digital Age: A Methodological Primer*, ed. K. Price and R Siemens. New York: MLA Commons.

Cordell, R. 2014. On ignoring encoding. http://ryancordell.org/research/dh/on-ignoring-encoding (accessed June 20, 2015).

Drucker, J. 2011. Humanities approaches to graphical display. *DHQ: Digital Humanities Quarterly* 5 (1).

Fischer-Baum, R., Gordon, A., and Halsley, B. 2014. Which words are used to describe white and black NFL prospects? *Deadspin*. http://deadsp.in/1iNz1NY (accessed June 20, 2015).

Foster, D. 2000. *Author Unknown: On the Trail of Anonymous*. New York: Henry Holt and Company.

Harris, J. 2011. Word clouds considered harmful. *Nieman Journalism Lab*. http://bit.ly/QKNMdD (accessed June 20, 2015).

Hockey, S. 2000. *Electronic Texts in the Humanities*. Oxford: Oxford University Press.

Hockey, S. 2004. The history of humanities computing. In *A Companion to Digital Humanities*, ed. S. Schreibman, R. Siemens, and J. Unsworth. Oxford: Blackwell, 2004. http://www.digitalhumanities.org/companion (accessed June 20, 2015).

Jockers, M. 2013. *Macroanalysis: Digital Methods and Literary History*. Urbana: University of Illinois Press.

Kenny, A. 1982. *The Computation of Style*. Oxford: Pergamon Press.

Kristeva, J. 1968. Le texte clos. *Langages* 3 (12).

Kristeva, J. 1980. *Desire in Language: A Semiotic Approach to Literature and Art*. Trans. T. Gora, A. Jardine, and L.S. Roudiez. New York: Columbia University Press.

McGann, J. 2001. *Radiant Textuality: Literature After the World Wide Web*. New York: Palgrave.

Michel, J.-B., Shen, Y.K., Aiden, A.P., *et al.* 2011. Quantitative analysis of culture using millions of digitized books. *Science* 331 (6014), 176–82.

Moretti, F. 2005. Graphs, Maps, Trees: Abstract Models for a Literary History. London: Verso.

Radicati Group. 2014. Email statistics report, 2014–2018. http://bit.ly/1o6GmQA (accessed June 20, 2015).

Ramsay, S. 2011. *Reading Machines: Toward an Algorithmic Criticism*. Urbana: University of Illinois Press.

Ramsay, S. 2014. The hermeneutics of screwing around; or what you do with a million books. In *Pastplay: Teaching and Learning History with Technology*, ed. K. Kee. Ann Arbor: University of Michigan Press.

Renear, A. 2004. Text encoding. In *A Companion to Digital Humanities*, ed. S. Schreibman, R. Siemens, and J. Unsworth. Oxford: Blackwell. http://www.digitalhumanities.org/companion (accessed June 20, 2015).

Ruecker, S., Radzikowska, M., and Sinclair, S. 2011. Visual Interface Design for Cultural Heritage: a Guide to Rich-Prospect Browsing. Burlington, VT: Ashgate.

Sinclair, S. 2003. Computer-assisted reading: reconceiving text analysis. *Literary and Linguistic Computing* 18 (2).

Sinclair, S., and Rockwell, G. 2012. Teaching computer-assisted text analysis: approaches to learning new methodologies. In *Digital Humanities Pedagogy: Practices, Principles and Politics*, ed. B.D. Hirsch. Cambridge: OpenBook. http://www.openbookpublishers.com/htmlreader/DHP/chap10.html#ch10 (accessed June 20, 2015).

Sinclair, S., and Rockwell, G. 2014. *Voyant Tools*. http://voyant-tools.org (accessed June 20, 2015).

Sinclair, S., Ruecker, S., and Radzikowska, M. 2013. Information visualization for humanities scholars. In *Literary Studies in the Digital Age: A Methodological Primer*, ed. K. Price and R Siemens. New York: MLA Commons.

Smith, C. 2011. Word cloud: how toy ad vocabulary reinforces gender stereotypes. *The Achilles Effect*. http://bit.ly/1osjjji (accessed June 20, 2015).

Tufte, E. 2001. *The Visual Display of Quantitative Information*. Cheshire, CT: Graphics Press.

Wang, X., and Inaba, M. 2009. Analyzing structures and evolution of digital humanities based on correspondence analysis and co-word analysis. *Art Research* 9. http://bit.ly/1jLWnbX (accessed June 20, 2015).

20

Text-Mining the Humanities

Matthew L. Jockers and Ted Underwood

Why Mine?

In the humanities, more often than not, the focus of scholarly attention is on the details – often subtle and nuanced details that are revealed only through slow, thoughtful, close reading. The usual method of analysis is one largely driven by synthesis. Scholars read and make associations; they discover and reveal what is not obvious to the casual reader, and to the extent that computation is leveraged in this activity, it is usually at the level of simple keyword search: a scholar wonders about Melville's thoughts on God and then performs a search for *God* in the digital text in order to find passages that will be studied under the microscope of informed close reading. Computers are very good at this task, and for some types of questions computational keyword searching is all that is warranted. But what of other questions, questions of scale that have not been asked until quite recently?

In 1988, Rosanne Potter wrote that "until everything has been encoded, or until encoding is a trivial part of the work, the everyday critic will probably not consider computer treatments of texts" (93). She was right, and the same might be said for the tools as well. Until everything has been digitized, why bother building tools to analyze them? Potter's "everyday critic" could not imagine computer treatments of texts because the texts did not exist, and even if they had existed, the state of the tools was such that those critics would not have been likely to make huge discoveries. In fact, a number of scholars – including several who are sympathetic to the digital humanities – have in the past argued exactly this point: namely, that computer treatments of texts have had little impact on the mainstream humanities. Mark Olsen wrote in 1993 of how "computerized textual research has not had a significant influence on research in

A New Companion to Digital Humanities, First Edition. Edited by Susan Schreibman, Ray Siemens, and John Unsworth.
© 2016 John Wiley & Sons, Ltd. Published 2016 by John Wiley & Sons, Ltd.

the humanistic disciplines" (309), and Stephen Ramsay, in 2007, of how the "digital revolution, for all its wonders, has not penetrated the core activity of literary studies" (478). But already these comments feel rather antiquated, and they feel so exactly because the pace of change, even since 2007, has been so incredibly rapid. Not only do we now have massive digital archives,[1] but we also have new and sophisticated tools for studying them. And the importance of the tools should not be underestimated. Tim Lenoir has argued rhetorically, but convincingly, that quarks would not exist today were it not for the particle accelerators that were built to discover them.[2] Some of the most sophisticated and most promising new tools for text analysis and text mining have only recently come to the attention of scholars in the humanities, and embracing them, leveraging them, means that humanities scholars must learn from research in the seemingly unrelated fields of natural language processing and machine learning.

Background

Quantitative approaches have a long history in the humanities, but contemporary text mining is also a deeply interdisciplinary project with affinities to computer science, statistics, linguistics, sociology, and other social sciences. In the space available here, we can only sketch a few important lines of development.

As John Unsworth (2013) has pointed out, quantitative analysis of text has a history stretching back to the nineteenth century. Quantification was often understood as a way of getting at something called "style," either in order to understand the history of style writ large, as in L.A. Sherman's *Analytics of Literature* (1893), or in order to identify works by a particular author, as in the research of T.C. Mendenhall (1887, 1901). In the twentieth century, the project of authorship attribution came to be closely associated with the more general and varied practice of "stylometry," and it remains an important aspect of text mining today. Twentieth-century linguists approached style as a social phenomenon, particularly in a subfield called "stylistics." Stylistics, in turn, overlaps with quantitative approaches to language that don't necessarily characterize their object of inquiry as "style" – for instance, with corpus linguistics, which uses collections of samples (corpora) to describe real-world linguistic variation.[3]

The phrase *text mining* itself is modeled on *data mining*, an informal name for a subfield of computer science also known as knowledge discovery in databases (KDD). Coalescing in the late 1980s, this field emerged from the broader project of artificial intelligence, and especially from efforts to model and automate learning processes. The terms *KDD*, *data mining*, and *machine learning* are bound together in a complex topology, and it is not easy to separate intellectual history from prescriptive definition.[4] Today, *data mining* often implies unsupervised learning, whereas *machine learning* is more commonly applied to supervised learning processes (see below). But this boundary can be drawn in several different ways: sometimes *data mining* names the practice that corresponds to *machine learning*'s theory.

Textbooks on data mining often include a chapter on text mining, which is seen by computer scientists as a subfield devoted to the extraction of knowledge from unstructured text.[5] But in humanistic practice, text mining is an interdisciplinary endeavor that also borrows freely from corpus linguistics and computational linguistics, as well as social-scientific traditions like social network analysis. Perhaps most importantly, humanistic text mining seeks to frame questions that contribute meaningfully to existing traditions of humanistic inquiry. Given this complex confluence of disciplines, it is not surprising that controversies about text mining commonly involve differences of opinion about the relative weighting of different disciplinary methodologies.

Methods: Machine Learning and Text Mining

The terms *text* (or *data*) *mining* and *machine learning* are frequently conflated and sometimes confused but do represent two different practices. Generally speaking *mining* is applied to techniques focused on exploration and discovery whereas *machine learning* refers to techniques or methods that are designed for prediction. The former is generally referred to as *unsupervised* learning and the latter as *supervised* learning. At a deeper level of specificity, these kindred practices may be called machine *clustering* and machine *classification*. The simplest way of differentiating between them is to consider the role of the researcher and whether or not that researcher has advanced and specific knowledge of the structure and composition of the data.

In machine *clustering*, for example, we do not have a preconceived notion of how the data is or might be organized and do not pre-label the individual data points as belonging to one group or another; the objective is to discover hidden structure in data by machine grouping, or clustering, the data objects based on the similarity of their features. If we were clustering shapes, for example, we might have a feature called "number of sides." Given this data about the features of these shapes, an unsupervised algorithm might cluster three-sided objects into one pile and four-sided objects into another. The machine would not, however, be given information about these *classes* of shapes in advance. The machine is only given the features and attempts to group the objects into categories or classes based on analysis of the features.

In text mining, we frequently wish to group documents together according to their similarity. Similarity is often based on, or measured by, some finite set of textual features, such as the relative frequency of the most frequently occurring words. If we are interested in clustering texts according to the similarity of their style, for example, we know from years of authorship-attribution research that the most effective features for distinguishing one author's style from another's are high-frequency features such as the words "the," "of," "him," "her," and "and," as well as common marks of punctuation.[6] But, of course, machine clustering can be used for much more than authorship analysis. Say we are interested in exploring the extent to which Irish authors have a distinct literary-linguistic style.[7] For the sake of illustration, we constructed a random sample of 300 nineteenth-century novels: 100 by British authors, 100 by Irish authors, and 100 by American authors.[8] For each novel we calculated the total number of instances (the *tokens*) of each unique word and mark of punctuation (the *types*). We then divided the raw count of each feature in a given text by the total number of words in the text in order to calculate the relative frequency of each word type.

This information can be represented as a data matrix in which each row is a text (in the nomenclature of machine learning, each text is an *observation*) and each column a different word type (each word is a *feature*). In this example, the resulting matrix was 300 rows by

154,312 columns. Since we are interested in computing stylistic similarity based on the use of high-frequency features, this matrix was then reduced by keeping only those features with a mean relative frequency across the corpus of at least 0.1. This *thresholding* resulted in a new matrix of 107 features.[9] With the matrix reduced in this manner, the machine was then configured to cluster the texts using this set of 107 features and a measure of similarity called Euclidean distance.[10] The result of such clustering can be visualized as a tree dendrogram, and since the dendrogram is hierarchical, it is possible to identify groups by "cutting" the tree at specific points. Figure 20.1 shows a representation of the full tree and – through the use of shading and dotted branch lines – shows three distinct clusters. The cluster in black (Cluster Two) contains 36% of the Irish texts and exactly 0% of the British and 0% of the Americans (Table 20.1).

In a world where there were perfectly distinct stylistic differences between the three nations, splitting the dendrogram at three branches would have resulted in a perfect separation of the three nationalities: one cluster of 100 Irish-authored novels, another containing the 100 British texts, and a third of 100 Americans. Instead of perfect separation, we observe some mixing of the texts, but the absence of any British and American texts from Cluster Two is suggestive; it suggests that there is indeed something distinct about at least 36% of the Irish novels in the corpus: the aggregate *signal* – expressed through the 107 features in these 36 books – is not at all like the *signal* typical to American and/or British novels.

As noted previously, unsupervised clustering is often viewed as an exploratory method in which we seek to uncover some hidden structure in the data. A researcher

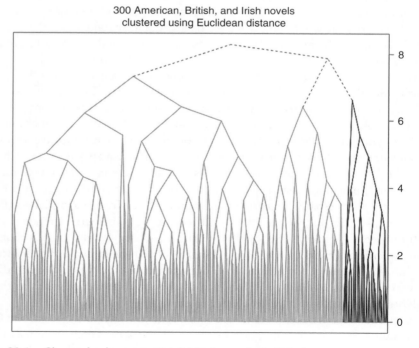

Figure 20.1   Cluster dendrogram, with Irish cluster shaded black.

Table 20.1 Three-cluster test.

	Cluster One	Cluster Two	Cluster Three
American	15	0	85
British	24	0	76
Irish	18	36	46
Total in cluster	57	36	207

observing this result might now go back to the data and examine how the features in these 36 Irish books differ from those Irish-authored books found in the other clusters. Upon deeper inspection, it may be discovered that some other factor such as religion, or class, or gender is responsible for the separation. The results of this test might also be considered good enough to warrant further testing using supervised methods of classification.

In *supervised document classification*, a researcher establishes, in advance, a set of known text classes and then writes a program to classify unseen documents based on the similarity or difference between the unseen text and the known classes of documents. The classic example of this is the authorship attribution problem. A document of unknown or uncertain authorship is processed and classified according to its statistical similarity to a known author within a closed set of candidates. As with unsupervised clustering, the greatest difficulty often comes in having to determine the features that will be compared. Say, for example, you have a closed set of two-dimensional objects: squares, triangles, and circles. *Closed* here means that these are the only types of objects that will be considered. Each of these classes is defined by some set of features. For this example, let's assume there are only three features: "shape size" (measured in area), "shape color," and "number of sides." We begin by gathering many examples from each class, and for each we extract the feature information for these three features. Assume that we have 100 different triangles, 100 different squares, and 100 different circles. For each object, we extract three data points: the area of the object, the color of the object, and the number of sides. This data are then fed into a classifier: a computer algorithm designed to identify statistical differences between the classes. In this case, the classifier is told in advance (supervised) that these shapes are representative of three distinct classes of two-dimensional objects. The machine "knows" which shapes are which and is able to use that information to organize the data. In this example, the classifier examines all of the data and identifies, or figures out, that the *number of sides* feature is incredibly useful in differentiating between the classes.[11] The classifier identifies that the *area* and *color* features seem to fluctuate randomly between classes and therefore finds no correlation between shape *size* and shape class or between shape *color* and shape class. In this way the machine is *trained* to recognize which types of object are members of which predefined classes. Once trained in this manner, the machine can be given a new object and asked to classify it according to its similarity to the known classes. If the new object happens to be an oval, this hypothetical classifier would guess that (i.e., *classify*) the oval is most likely a circle: like the circle, the oval only has one side.[12] If we gave this classifier a rectangle, it would be classified as a square: though not exactly the same as a square (i.e., with sides of equal length), the rectangle is most like the square in having four sides. Naturally, in text classification, the problems are a lot harder because the feature sets are much larger than just three features. An important point worth emphasizing here, however, is that regardless of whether the problem is simple or hard, we can perform a test of the model in order to determine how well it is performing. This is not something we can do in unsupervised clustering where we have not already established a predefined set of classes. In classification, we execute this performance test by first training a model using a randomly selected subset of the total observations and then testing the model by seeing how well it classifies the remaining held-out samples.[13]

Consider the example used above in which we clustered novels and then examined whether author nationality could be seen as an explanatory factor in how the books clustered. Using this same corpus, a classification experiment can be constructed in which a classifier is trained to identify American, British, and Irish novels based on the same 107 features used in the clustering. The process begins by having the computer randomly select a subset of the novels from each nation for training. For this example, we used 66% of the American-authored books, 66% of the British and 66% of the Irish; the remaining 34% were held out for testing the trained model. In supervised classification, unlike the unsupervised clustering done above, we (and the machine) already know the possible groups or classes (e.g., triangles, circles, and squares, or American, British, and Irish novels), and we want the computer to take a particular object that it has never seen before and classify it into one of these known groups. In order to do this, we provide the machine with information about the typical features of the squares, circles, and triangles (or the national literatures), by giving the computer lots of examples of these objects. We say, "here are some typical American books and here are some typical British and Irish books; take these objects and build a model that understands what features are most common or most typical to each class." From these examples the computer builds a model of what constitutes an American signal, a British signal, and so on. Then when the machine is given a new object, it looks at all of its features and figures out which of the known classes is most similar to the new object.

In this example classification test, we used the nearest shrunken centroid (NSC) classification algorithm, and we were able to accurately identify author nationality in the held-out data with an average accuracy of 71%.[14] Considering that chance in this experiment is 33%, the observed result of 71% is considerably better than what could be expected from a machine simply guessing at random. To really understand how the machine performed, however, it is useful to examine the confusion matrix and understand what is meant by *precision* and *recall*.

Table 20.2 shows the confusion matrix for this classification test. The confusion matrix is produced as part of the cross-validation routine that iteratively samples from the data in order to train and test a series of models. The first column in the table indicates the true class of each sample. So we begin with the row of data labeled with the class *American*. In this test, when the actual class was *American*, the machine guessed *American* 52 out of 66 times; these 52 we call the *true positives*. Five times it guessed *British* and nine times it guessed *Irish*; these we call the *false negatives*. We represent the *recall* (shown in the fifth column of the table) of this result by dividing the number of correct guesses by the combined number of correct guesses and incorrect guesses, in this

Table 20.2   Confusion matrix from classification test.

	American	British	Irish	Recall
American	52	5	9	0.79
British	0	44	22	0.67
Irish	1	20	45	0.68
Precision	0.98	0.64	0.59	

case 52/66. The resulting figure (0.79) tells us how good the classifier is at recognizing books that are written by American authors.

If we look at the second row, we notice that the machine had no problem guessing that British-authored books were not American. The model never guessed that the author of a British book was an American. About a third of the time (22 cases), however, the machine misrecognized a British book as Irish. So even though the machine assigned no British-authored books to American authors, it still only managed to correctly recognize 67% of British books. The third row shows the results for the Irish-authored books. One book was thought to be of American authorship and 20 were thought to be British. Here again, the model had little trouble differentiating Irish and American writing, and more difficulty differentiating Irish and British writing.

This difficulty will not come as a huge surprise: readers of these national literatures would expect to find greater affinity between British and Irish texts. But *recall* only tells part of the story. If recall tells us how often a given category was correctly recognized, *precision*, shown in the last row, tells us how often a given prediction was correct. Precision expresses the number of true positives (correct classifications) divided by the number of true positives *and* false positives. So, in the case of the *column* labeled *American*, we take the total number of true positives and divide by the sum of true positives and false positives. In this case, the precision is excellent: 52/(52 + 1) or 0.98. The model only guessed *American* incorrectly once. Put another way, when the machine guesses that a work is by an American author, it guesses correctly 98% of the time. Alternatively, when the machine guesses that a book is Irish-authored, it only guesses correctly 59% of the time.

In terms of overall classification accuracy, the results of this experiment, especially when viewed in the context of mere chance, were not too bad. Sometimes the overall accuracy of a classification experiment such as this will be generalized into what is called an *F-measure* or *F-score*, a measure that attempts to provide a weighted average of the precision and recall. In this example, the *F*-score is 0.72. Other times, researchers may simply describe the total number of correct classifications divided by the total number of cases: in this example, 0.71. Though we might consider these classification results fairly good, a lot about how we interpret these results depends upon the domain in which we are working and upon the stakes. If these were text samples from suspects in a murder case, we might not be satisfied with these cross-validation results. What is clear from this example, however, is that there is a fairly marked difference between American texts and those of Irish and British authorship. Given such a result, it can be productive to explore the actual features that the model found to best distinguish between the groups. Of the three groups in this test, for example, the Americans showed a greater fondness for the *comma* and for the word *the*, the Irish were next, and then the British. British authors, on the other hand, showed a substantially higher preference for the *period*, followed in turn by the Americans, and then the Irish.[15]

Adapting Algorithms to Concrete Problems

In both examples above, the learning algorithms work on a list of features produced simply by selecting the most common words (or punctuation marks) in the corpus. Other feature-selection strategies are possible. A researcher can use all the words in a corpus as features, or use measures like *information gain* to identify the features that most effectively discriminate a particular pair of classes.[16] Feature-selection strategies may depend on the problem being explored: sets of common words distinguish authors effectively, but might be less effective at distinguishing subject categories. Finally, there are many things aside from words that can be treated as features: for instance, one can use two-word phrases (bigrams).

Expanding the frame of reference to include phrases raises a larger set of issues that we can only glance at briefly here. Newcomers to text analysis are often surprised that so many algorithms rely on a "bag-of-words" model, discarding word order in order to focus simply on the frequencies of individual words.[17] Our everyday experience of text is sequential, and intuitions based on that experience would suggest that the meaning of a text depends entirely on sequence. For some purposes this is true, but for many purposes word order is surprisingly dispensable. Classifiers using a bag-of-words model often perform just as well as algorithms that consider multiword phrases (Bekkerman and Allan, 2003). On the other hand, there are certainly kinds of analysis where word order becomes central. Natural language processing toolkits, which rely on supervised models, can tag each word with a part of speech, parse sentences to iden- tify grammatical dependencies, and extract named entities (people, places, organiza- tions, and so on).[18]

Introductory textbooks on data mining list a range of algorithms that are known to work well on text. Naïve Bayes, regularized logistic regression, and support vectors are often used for supervised classification; clustering may involve *k*-means, mixed-model, or hierarchical methods. Computer scientists and statisticians are constantly refining these algorithms to improve performance, and performance may also improve when multiple models are combined in an *ensemble*. But even specialists in machine learning recommend trying relatively simple methods first, because "small gains in laboratory performance ... may be swamped by other factors when machine learning is applied to a practical data mining problem" (Witten *et al.*, 2011:377–8). The time a researcher might spend optimizing an algorithm is often better spent improving the data.

On the other hand, it is useful to understand how simple methods can be adapted to address a range of different problems. Classification algorithms do not necessarily have to characterize documents by predicting membership in a single class; in *multilabel classification*, for example, they can assign a document to multiple classes (perhaps characterizing each prediction with a different degree of confidence) (Tsoumakas and Katakis, 2007). Fuzzy and mixed-model clustering provide an unsupervised equivalent. When training data is relatively scarce, approaches like *active learning* can conserve human effort by identifying selected cases where human guidance would help the algorithm improve its performance most significantly (Han *et al.*, 2012:433–4). When a problem is imperfectly defined (often the case in the humanities), *semi-supervised learning* may be appropriate, since it allows a researcher to provide initial guidance without fully determining the range of possible classes in a model (Han *et al.*, 2012:432). Finally, there are cases where humanists may need to collaborate with computer scientists in order to develop new methods appropriate to a particular domain. *Probabilistic graphical models* support this kind of innovation with a flexible language for representing human assumptions and translating them into algorithms.[19]

Challenges

There are more potential applications of text mining in the humanities than existing research projects, because projects unfortunately confront a number of significant barriers in the start-up phase. The main obstacle is the interdisciplinary character of the enterprise itself. The parts of the data-mining process that are easy to standardize generally have been standardized: implementations of popular algorithms are readily available in toolkits like *Weka* (Hall *et al.*, 2009) and MALLET (McCallum, 2002). But tools are never a complete solution. Since every research question is different (almost by definition), each entails some problems that resist standardization. Idiosyncratic types of metadata need to be gathered, special-purpose analyses need to be performed, and results need to be translated into visualizations that address a specific question. Many of these steps are likely to require familiarity with programming and with the humanistic discipline being explored; some steps may also require knowledge of statistics. As a result, humanistic text-mining problems often call for interdisciplinary teams, or researchers with an unusual breadth of experience, or both.

It is a proverbial truth that data preparation often consumes more time than analysis. This can be true even in projects that begin with relatively structured data, since names and dates come in a variety of formats that may need to be standardized before meaningful comparison is possible. Preparation of unstructured text can be even more challenging, and researchers in the humanities confront special difficulties associated with historical change. As a reader travels back across the centuries, for instance, the rules of capitalization, word division, and spelling change. These changes could be viewed as subjects of linguistic inquiry in their own right. But a scholar who is studying the history of medicine rather than English spelling may want to ensure that "physic" and "physick" are treated as a single word. More debatably, a researcher might decide to treat occurrences of "any body" in the eighteenth century as equivalent to twenty-first-century "anybody." Normalization can be taken even further through processes of *stemming* or *lemmatization* – flattening the distinctions between possessives, plurals, and verb tenses to associate them with a single root.

Although we often speak casually about data "cleaning," decisions to standardize different aspects of text involve trade-offs that are far from straightforward. Details that count as *noise* in one context might become *signal* in another. Lemmatization, for instance, can improve the efficiency of search engines, but discards grammatical inflections that might be useful as clues about authorship or genre. For this reason, there is no single agreed-upon process of data preparation, although resources do exist, for instance, to support normalization of spelling variants when researchers want to normalize them.[20]

In an ideal world, all texts would be available in accurate copies, marked up with TEI, or some similar standard, to distinguish footnotes and running headers from body text.[21] In reality, the texts in large digital libraries are usually transcribed by optical character recognition (OCR). The OCR process produces errors (particularly on older texts), and does not provide many explicit clues to distinguish body text from paratext. Confronted with these challenges, humanists sometimes despair. Our disciplines have taught us that identifying an accurate edition is the first step in responsible research; here it seems impossible. Alternatively, we may look for a fixed accuracy cutoff that would guarantee our results are "good enough."

A more useful approach to this problem might begin with the nature of the questions being posed, and their relation to specific kinds of error. On a macroscopic scale, truly random errors are not necessarily a big obstacle for analytical methods that consider words individually. If every word in a given language had a constant 10% chance of random mistranscription, volume-level classification and methods such as topic modeling might proceed almost undisturbed. Volume-level word counts are redundant, and since the random strings produced by mistranscription will be individually rare, they are likely to fall out of the analysis. Some errors are close to being this random: coffee spots, ripped corners. But problems arise because other errors are distributed unequally across a corpus. Paper quality or worn metal type make some volumes more prone to mistranscription than others. The worst problems are those that preferentially affect specific words in specific periods – for instance, in some eighteenth-century books using the notorious "long s," "ship" will almost always be mistranscribed as "fhip" or "flip." Left uncorrected, these systematic errors could distort analysis. Fortunately, there are algorithms we can use to correct OCR even in tricky cases like the confusion between "ship" and "flip" (Tong and Evans, 1996).

Since different kinds of error have radically different effects, there is no single accuracy percentage that proves a text is good enough to support analysis. But some general principles are clear. The small category of errors that occur often and systematically, because of ambiguous typefaces or ligatures, are more problematic than the much larger category of uncommon errors. (Collectively, uncommon errors become numerous, but collectively they also approximate randomness.) It follows that partial OCR correction, addressing a limited number of predictable errors, may be adequate for many research purposes. On the other hand, different kinds of research have different degrees of sensitivity. Bag-of-words methods are more robust to random error than natural language processing, where a single misspelling can make a whole clause hard to parse. More research is needed to establish the relative robustness of different methods. Research is also under way to support automatic separation of text from paratext (Underwood et al., 2013).

So far, we've focused on challenges specific to text mining. But some of the most important challenges confronting this work are those it shares with other fields of the humanities. By allowing a researcher to survey a larger set of documents, text mining promises to give a picture of the print record that is "more representative" than an account based on a few hand-selected examples. But representative of what? Digital libraries, largely based on university libraries, do not include every book ever published. Moreover, even if we had a copy of every book, the print record itself would not reflect the demographic reality of the past, since access to print has been shaped by class, gender, and race. One could argue for a stratified corpus, rebalanced to redress these inequalities. More commonly, critics of text mining seize the other horn of the dilemma, suggesting that it would impose a misleading equality to count every title once. Perhaps popular and widely reprinted titles (or "important" titles) should carry more weight in the corpus (Rosen, 2011)?

None of these questions are new. They are versions of a debate that humanists have long pursued under the rubrics of "culture" and "canonicity" – a debate that is not likely to be resolved soon. Fortunately, it does not have to be resolved before we attempt macroscopic research. Text mining is not bound to any particular model of representation, and needn't presuppose consensus on the topic. Nothing stops us, for instance, from creating a demographically stratified corpus, or a corpus where frequently reprinted titles do count more than once. As long as researchers are clear about the criteria of selection they have used, these are all valid avenues of inquiry. We might even learn more this way than by debating abstract definitions of "representativeness." By posing the same question to corpora constructed differently, researchers can discover what difference criteria of selection make for specific questions. In some cases, selection criteria have turned out to make less difference than one might suppose – e.g., because the history of genre has broadly similar outlines in popular and less popular works (Underwood *et al.*, 2013). In short, the questions about representativeness that are often presented as obstacles to text mining would be better construed as opportunities.

One obstacle that does still loom ominously on the horizon involves the question of whether or not mining texts and producing derivative data about those texts is in fact a violation of copyright. The simple fact of the matter is that text miners need digital texts to mine, and "modern copyright law," as Loyola law professor Matthew Sag (2012) puts it, "ensures that this process of scanning and digitization is ensnared in a host of thorny issues" (2). Because of a lack of clarity around what exactly constitutes fair use, many researchers have thus far limited themselves to the study of texts produced before 1923.[22] The legal troubles began in the USA in 2005, shortly after Google announced that it was scanning and digitizing the collections of a number of private and public academic libraries in order to make their collections searchable. The Authors Guild, an advocacy group that represents member authors, sued Google, claiming that these scanning efforts were a violation of copyright.[23] After more than eight years of back and forth litigation, the case was settled on November 14, 2013 with a summary judgment in which Judge Denny Chin ruled in favor of Google. In that judgment, Chin wrote that *Google Books*:

> advances the progress of the arts and sciences, while maintaining respectful consideration for the rights of authors and other creative individuals, and without adversely impacting the rights of copyright holders. It [*Google Books*] has become an invaluable research tool that permits students, teachers, librarians, and others to more efficiently identify and

locate books. It has given scholars the ability, for the first time, to conduct full-text searches of tens of millions of books. (Authors Guild v. Google, p. 26)

Chin goes on to write specifically about the opportunities for humanities scholars interested in text mining. He cites an amicus brief that was submitted to the court on behalf of Digital Humanities and Law Scholars:

> in addition to being an important reference tool, Google Books greatly promotes a type of research referred to as "data mining" or "text mining." (Br. of Digital Humanities and Law Scholars as Amici Curiae at 1 (Doc. No. 1052)). Google Books permits humanities scholars to analyze massive amounts of data – the literary record created by a collection of tens of millions of books. Researchers can examine word frequencies, syntactic patterns, and thematic markers to consider how literary style has changed over time. (Authors Guild v. Google, p. 9–10)

Though this phase of the case was resolved with Judge Chin's ruling, at the time of writing the Authors Guild has vowed to appeal. If they make good on this promise, then the case will go before the Second Circuit and possibly then to the Supreme Court. Sag believes the possibility one of these higher courts would overrule Chin is very unlikely because, among other reasons, the Authors Guild failed to convince the judge that Google's scanning efforts have been in any way harmful to the copyright holders.

Regardless of what happens in the case between Google and the Authors Guild, humanities researchers can take some comfort in knowing that the HathiTrust Research Center has now received permission from the HathiTrust Board, with the approval of its host, the University of Michigan, and with the backing of Indiana University and the University of Illinois, to begin providing computational access to the copyrighted material held in HathiTrust's repository. This decision came after the HathiTrust won a similar lawsuit that was also brought by the Authors Guild. The ruling in that case made clear that the HathiTrust's use of books scanned as part of Google's book scanning project was fair use under US law.[24] At the time of this writing, HathiTrust has indicated that access will begin at the end of 2014 or early in 2015.

Despite these challenges, the future of text mining in the humanities is very promising. At no time in history have we ever had such access to the written record, and though that record is imperfect in many ways, it now marks a moment of great promise and great progress. And though this chapter may have overemphasized applications of text mining to literary studies (and unashamedly revealed the biases of the authors), text mining has already also been applied to a wide range of problems in other areas of the humanities. While many projects explore digital libraries, which contain mostly printed books, historians are actively working on newspapers, legal scholars on court cases, and scholars in media studies have done a great deal of text mining on social media. When scholars work with contemporary material, the boundary between "humanistic text mining" and "computational social science" can become porous. On the other hand, it is also possible for text mining to be applied to individual works, in service of interpretive projects that are quite distinct from social science. Below we offer a short list of exemplary projects.

Exemplary Projects and Examples of Text Mining in the Humanities

- Cameron Blevins. *Topic Modeling Martha Ballard's Diary* (http://historying. org/2010/04/01/topic-modeling-martha-ballards-diary). In this blog post, Blevins uses topic modeling to better understand the 27-year diary of Martha Ballard, an American midwife born in 1735.
- Dan Cohen. *With Criminal Intent* (http://criminalintent.org). This project uses computational models to explore and visualize the history of crime as it is expressed in the court records of the Old Bailey.
- David Bamman, Jacob Eisenstein, and Tyler Schnoebelen. *Gender identity and lexical variation in social media* (http://arxiv.org/abs/1210.4567). A study of the relationship between gender, linguistic style, and social networks, using a corpus of 14,000 users of Twitter.
- Jean-Baptiste Michel *et al*. *Culturomics* (http://www.culturomics.org). A project undertaken in conjunction with Google to study "culture" as it gets expressed in the Google Books Corpus.
- Matt Wilkens. *The Geographic Imagination of Civil War-Era American Fiction* (http:// mattwilkens.com/2013/12/02/new-article-in-alh). Explores representations of place in a corpus of over 1000 novels by American authors published in the USA between 1851 and 1875.
- Robert K. Nelson. *Mining the* Dispatch (http://dsl.richmond.edu/dispatch). Uses topic modeling to explore the social and political life of Civil War Richmond as it is expressed in the pages of the *Daily Dispatch* from 1860 to 1865.
- Ryan Cordell, Elizabeth Maddock Dillon, and David Smith. *Viral Texts: Mapping Networks of Reprinting in 19th-Century Newspapers and Magazines* (http://www.viraltexts. org). This project explores the reuse of text in 19th century newspaper reportage in order to analyze the culture of reprinting in the United States before the Civil War.
- Sarah Allison, Ryan Heuser, Matthew Jockers, Franco Moretti, and Michael Witmore. *Quantitative Formalism* (http://litlab.stanford.edu/LiteraryLabPamphlet1. pdf). A report on a study designed to establish whether computer-generated algorithms could "recognize" literary genres in the nineteenth-century British novel.
- SEASR (http://www.seasr.org). A multi-year, Mellon-funded project that seeks to create a text-mining platform for scholarly research. A number of text-mining projects, including several by the authors of this chapter, have been completed in collaboration with SEASR.
- The HathiTrust Research Center (http://www.hathitrust.org/htrc). A virtual research center for large-scale, high-performance, and secure computation with the materials in the HathiTrust collection (as of 2014, about 4 billion pages of text in many languages, from many periods).

NOTES

1 For example: Project Gutenberg, Google Books, HathiTrust.

2 Lenoir has made this argument on multiple occasions, primarily in lectures on pragmatic realism and social construction. He has written about this extensively in his book *Instituting Science* (1997), particularly the chapter on Haber-Bosch, in which he

discusses this idea at length. See also Hacking (1983).

3   See, for example, Biber (1998). Corpus linguistics is particularly valuable for identifying features that are over-represented in one group of sources relative to another: see Kilgarriff (2001).

4   For instance, practitioners have influentially claimed that data mining is properly understood as part of a "KDD process," but that's not necessarily how the phrase originated, or how it is used in the wild today (Fayyad *et al.*, 1996).

5   See, for example, Witten *et al.* (2011:386–9). Note further that there is no consensus on what exactly constitutes "structured" versus "unstructured" data or text. In the linguistics community there tends to be a preference for thinking of text as highly structured, whereas in computer science and related fields, text is often considered *unstructured* and the term *structured* is typically reserved for discussions of databases and tables that impose a meta-structure onto the objects contained within that structure. This was the topic of a lively debate on the Corpora-List in December 2013 under the subject heading "Quotable Statistics on Unstructured Data on the WWW" (http://mailman.uib.no/public/corpora/2013-December/019362.html).

6   For a useful study of how feature set composition impacts attribution accuracy, see Grieve (2007).

7   This is not an arbitrary example. In *Representative Irish Tales*, W.B. Yeats identified two basic categories of Irish fiction characterized by what he called "the accent of the gentry and the less polished accent of the peasantry" (Yeats, 1979). Other scholars including Thomas MacDonagh (1916), Thomas Flanagan (1959), John Cronin (1980), and most recently Charles Fanning (2000) have all commented upon the distinct and specific use of language that appears to characterize Irish narrative and, moreover, the extent to which this use of language reflects, or does not, the unique position of Irish and Anglo-Irish writers in a country where the use of English evolved in a rather dramatic fashion. Though Mark Hawthorne has written that the "Irish were not accustomed to the English language and were unaware of its subtleties and detonations" (Hawthorne, 1975), Fanning and Cronin have separately argued that the Irish became masters of the English language and employed, in Fanning's words, a mode of "linguistic subversion" (Fanning, 2000).

8   This random sample was derived from the larger collection of 3500 novels that Jockers collected for his work in *Macroanalysis*. You can download the sample data and the necessary R code for repeating this experiment at http://www.wiley.com/go/schreibman/digitalhumanities. *British* here encompasses authors of the British Isles excluding the island of Ireland.

9   Features here include both words and marks of punctuation. Column headers for marks of punctuation in the sample data begin with a "p": e.g., the column for the *comma* is headed *pcomma*.

10   Euclidean distance is a fairly standard mathematical formula for calculating the "distance" between points in a multidimensional dataset. That said, readers wishing to employ distance metrics should be aware of potential problems with such measures. The so-called *curse of dimensionality* describes a situation in which the number of dimensions becomes so large that the data become sparse and all observations seem to be very dissimilar. In this example, we have reduced the feature space to 107 dimensions, and we have 300 observations.

11   It is difficult to avoid anthropomorphic representations of what the machine is doing in these examples. Obviously the machine doesn't actually "know" or "figure out" what objects are which. The machine merely calculates based on the rules that we set as programmers and then gives the appearance of "learning" something about the data. The analogy to human learning is useful, especially for a short chapter such as this, but readers are advised not to take the analogy too far.

12   Mathematically, of course, a circle doesn't really have any sides, at least if we define *side* as something unique to polygons. Some might argue that a circle has infinite sides. In either case, in this example, the oval is most like the circle.

13   There are various techniques for this type of testing, and *k*-fold cross validation is probably the most common, with *k* most frequently set to 10. Two other typical cross-validation tests include *repeated subsampling* and *leave-one-out* methods. A full description of each of these is beyond the scope of this chapter, but all of these methods share the common goal of training a model on a randomly generated subsample of the larger corpus and then testing the model's accuracy using the held-out data not selected in the randomization process.

14 NSC has been used effectively in several authorship attribution studies, including a benchmarking study (Jockers and Witten 2010) which demonstrated its efficacy in this type of problem. See also Tibshirani *et al.* (2002).

15 In a larger and more nuanced study of author nationality, Jockers discusses how nineteenth-century British authors tended to favor words indicative of absolutes and determinacy: words such as "always, should, never, sure, not, must, do, don't, no, always, nothing, certain, therefore, because, can, cannot, knew, know, last, once, only, right" are popular indicators of British prose. The classifier found that the Irish novels were best distinguished by words that can be thought of as characteristic of imprecision and indeterminacy, words such as "near, soon, some, most, still, less, more," and "much." Taken together, the former suggest confidence, whereas the later suggest uncertainty or caution. Interested readers should consult the chapter titled "Nation" in Jockers's *Macroanalysis* (2013).

16 For an introduction to the feature-selection problem see Yang and Pederson (1997).

But note also that for some contemporary algorithms (e.g., support vector machines) feature selection becomes less critical than it was in 1997.

17 Topic modeling, which has become very popular in recent years, is an excellent example of a powerful technique that relies entirely upon a bag-of-words representation of text.

18 See, for example, http://nlp.stanford.edu/software/corenlp.shtml and/or http://nltk.org/

19 For an example of this process, see Bamman *et al.* (2013).

20 For normalization of early-modern spelling, see Baron (2013). For later texts see Underwood (2013).

21 TEI is an XML standard developed by the Text Encoding Initiative. See http://www.tei-c.org/index.xml.

22 Copyright has expired for all works published in the United States before 1923.

23 An excellent overview of the case can be found on Matthew Sag's blog (http://matthewsag.com).

24 As with the Google case, the Authors Guild is appealing this decision to the Second Circuit.

References and Further Reading

Authors Guild v. Google Inc., 770 F. Supp. 2d 666 – Dist. Court, SD New York 2011.

Bamman, D., O'Connor, B., and Smith, N.A. 2013. Learning latent personas of film characters. *Proceedings of the 51st Annual Meeting of the Association for Computational Linguistics*, 352–61.

Baron, A. 2013. *Variant Detector: (VARD2)*. http://ucrel.lancs.ac.uk/vard/about (accessed June 20, 2015).

Bekkerman, R., and Allan, J. 2003. Using Bigrams in Text Categorization. CIIR Technical Report. http://people.cs.umass.edu/~ronb/papers/bigrams.pdf (accessed June 20, 2015).

Biber, D. 1998. *Corpus Linguistics: Investigating Language Structure and Use*. Cambridge: Cambridge University Press.

Bird, S., Klein, E., and Loper, E. 2009. *Natural Language Processing with Python*. O'Reilly Media. http://nltk.org/book (accessed June 20, 2015).

Clement, T. 2008. "A thing not beginning or ending": using digital tools to distant-read Gertrude Stein's *The Making of Americans*. *Literary and Linguistic Computing* 23 (3), 361–82.

Cronin, J. 1980. *The Anglo-Irish Novel*. Totowa, NJ: Barnes & Noble.

Fanning, C. 2000. *The Irish Voice in America: 250 Years of Irish-American Fiction*, 2nd edition. Lexington: University Press of Kentucky.

Fayyad, U., Piatetsky-Shapiro, G., and Smythe, P. 1996. From data mining to knowledge discovery in databases. *AI Magazine* 17, 37–54.

Flanagan, T. 1959. *The Irish Novelists, 1800–1850*. New York: Columbia University Press.

Grieve, J. 2007. Quantitative authorship attribution: an evaluation of techniques. *Literary and Linguistic Computing* 22 (3), 251–70.

Hacking, I. 1983. *Representing and Intervening: Introductory Topics in the Philosophy of Natural Science*. Cambridge: Cambridge University Press.

Hall, M., Frank, E., Holmes, G., *et al.* 2009. The WEKA data mining software: an update. *SIGKDD Explorations* 11 (1).

Han, J., Kamber, M., and Pei, J. 2012. *Data Mining: Concepts and Techniques*. Burlington, MA: Morgan Kaufmann.

Hawthorne, M.D. 1975. *John and Michael Banim (the "O'Hara Brothers"): A Study in the Early Development of the Anglo-Irish Novel*. Salzburg Studies in Romantic Reassessment, vol. 50. Salzburg: Institut für Englische Sprache und Literatur, Universität Salzburg.

James, G., Witten, D., Hastie, T., and Tibshirani, R. 2013. *An Introduction to Statistical Learning: with Applications in R*. New York: Springer.

Jockers, M. 2014. *Text Analysis with R for Students of Literature*. New York: Springer.

Jockers, M. Text-mining. http://www.matthewjockers. net/category/tm (accessed June 20, 2015).

Jockers, M.L. and Witten, D.M. 2010. A comparative study of machine learning methods for authorship attribution. *Literary and Linguistic Computing* 25 (2), 215–24.

Jockers, M.L. 2013. *Macroanalysis: Digital Methods and Literary History*. Urbana: University of Illinois Press.

Jones, K.S. 1972. A statistical interpretation of term specificity and its application in retrieval. *Journal of Documentation* 28 (1), 11–21.

Kilgarriff, A. 2001. Comparing corpora. *International Journal of Corpus Linguistics* 6 (1), 97–133.

Lenoir, T. 1997. *Instituting Science: The Cultural Production of Scientific Disciplines*. Writing Science. Stanford, CA: Stanford University Press.

Macdonagh, T. 1916. *Literature in Ireland: Studies Irish and Anglo-Irish*. London: T.F. Unwin.

Manning, C.D., Raghavan, P., and Schütze, H. 2008. *Introduction to Information Retrieval*. Cambridge: Cambridge University Press, 2008.

McCallum, A.K. 2002. MALLET: a Machine Learning for Language Toolkit. http://mallet. cs.umass.edu (accessed June 20, 2015).

Mendenhall, T.C. 1887. The characteristic curves of composition. *Science* n.s. 9 (214), 237–46.

Mendenhall, T.C. 1901. A mechanical solution of a literary problem. *Popular Science Monthly* 60, 97–105.

Muralidharan, A. Text mining and the digital humanities. http://mininghumanities.com (accessed June 20, 2015).

Olsen, M. 1993. Signs, symbols, and discourses: a new direction for computer-aided literature studies. *Computers and the Humanities* 27 (5–6), 309–14.

Potter, R. 1988. Literary criticism and literary computing. *Computers in the Humanities* 22 (2), 93.

Ramsay, S. 2007. Algorithmic criticism. In *A Companion to Digital Literary Studies*, ed. R.G. Siemens and S. Schreibman. Oxford: Blackwell.

Rosen, J. 2011. Combining close and distant, or the utility of genre analysis: a response to Matthew Wilkens's "Contemporary Fiction by

the Numbers". *Post* 45. http://post45.research. yale.edu/2011/12/combining-close-and-distant-or-the-utility-of-genre-analysis-a-response-to-matthew-wilkenss-contemporary-fiction-by-the-numbers (accessed December 3, 2011).

Sag, M. 2012. Orphan works as grist for the data mill. *Berkeley Technology Law Journal* 27 (4).

Shaw, R. 2012. Text-mining as a research tool in the humanities and social sciences. http:// aeshin.org/textmining (accessed June 20, 2015).

Sherman, L.A. 1893. *Analytics of Literature: A Manual for the Objective Study of English Prose and Poetry*. Boston, MA: Ginn.

Tibshirani, R., Hastie, T., Narasimham, B., and Chu, G. 2002. Diagnosis of multiple cancer types by shrunken centroids of gene expression. *Proceedings of the National Academy of Science* 99 (10), 6567–72.

Tong, X., and Evans, D.A. 1996. A statistical approach to automatic OCR error correction in context. In *Proceedings of the Fourth Workshop on Very Large Corpora*, 88–100.

Tsoumakas, G., and Katakis, I. 2007. Multilabel classification: an overview. *International Journal of Data Warehousing & Mining* 3 (3), 1–13.

Underwood, T. 2013. A half-decent OCR normalizer for English texts after 1700. *The Stone and the Shell*. http://tedunderwood.com/2013/12/10/ a-half-decent-ocr-normalizer-for-english-texts-after-1700 (accessed June 20, 2015).

Underwood, T. 2015. Where to start with text mining. http://tedunderwood.com/2012/08/14/ where-to-start-with-text-mining (accessed June 20, 2015).

Underwood, T., Black, M.L., Auvil, L., and Capitanu, B. 2013. Mapping mutable genres in structurally complex volumes. *arXiv preprint:1309.3323*. http://arxiv.org/abs/1309.3323 (accessed June 20, 2015).

Unsworth, J. 2013. Digital humanities: from 1851? Brandeis University Library and Technology Services. http://blogs.brandeis.edu/ lts/2013/05/17/digital-humanities-from-1851 (accessed June 20, 2015).

Witten, I.H., Frank, E., and Hall, M.A. 2011. *Data Mining: Practical Machine Learning Tools and Techniques*. Burlington, MA: Morgan Kaufmann.

Yang, Y. and Pederson, J.O. 1997. A comparative study on feature selection in text categorization. In *ICML '97: Proceedings of the Fourteenth International Conference on Machine Learning*.

Yeats, W.B. 1979. *Representative Irish Tales*. Atlantic Highlands, NJ: Humanities Press.

21

Textual Scholarship and Text Encoding

Elena Pierazzo

Textual Scholarship and Text Encoding: A New Theoretical Framework

For the past 25 years text encoding, particularly in the format distributed and maintained by the Text Encoding Initiative (TEI), has assumed a central role in digital editing and textual scholarship, both as a modeling and analytical tool and as an ontology for the phenomenology of the text and the page. During the same period, and most probably connected to this, a crucial shift has occurred in textual scholarship, with the role of the material support of texts – the document – taking center stage in theoretical reflection and practice, as noted by Richard Finneran (1996:x). Thanks also to the ready availability of high-definition digital facsimiles, the digital method has in fact proved to be more adequate than print in providing support for both the production and the publication of editions where the materiality of texts is central, and it has therefore been embraced by practitioners of emerging theories of textual scholarship with a strong emphasis on the so-called "bibliographic codes," such as the New Philology, the theory of the social text, and genetic criticism.[1]

The digital method referred to here has in most cases meant the use of text encoding. Text encoding is the practice by which explicit codes (or tags) are added to a text in order to make some features of the text itself explicit, with the goal of making them processable by some computerized application (Renear, 2004). In the humanities the early development of a comprehensive standard for text encoding (the one distributed by the Text Encoding Initiative) has allowed for the development of a strong community of scholar-encoders, a fact that has produced lively scholarly debates but that has not prevented the emergence of problems and issues in establishing digital scholarly editions.

A New Companion to Digital Humanities, First Edition. Edited by Susan Schreibman, Ray Siemens, and John Unsworth.
© 2016 John Wiley & Sons, Ltd. Published 2016 by John Wiley & Sons, Ltd.

The Text Encoding Initiative is an international consortium, the main purpose of which is the development and maintenance of a set of encoding practices embodied by the *TEI Guidelines for Electronic Text Encoding and Interchange* (Cummings, 2008:451). The TEI first adopted SGML as the formal language for its encoding, but since 2002 it has been expressed in XML, a widely supported markup language which has been described as the "acid-free paper" of the digital age (Price, 2008:442). The TEI is now considered the *de facto* standard for text encoding in the humanities and has become almost mandatory if a project is to be supported by major funding bodies. The reasons for this requirement are that on the one hand TEI files are based on XML, which is considered a highly sustainable technology; and on the other hand, the TEI format is considered best practice also from a scholarly point of view, being developed within a research community of practice. In fact, since the very beginning the TEI has not only provided a set of guidelines for the encoding of text but has aimed at developing a strong bond among its users, therefore developing a substantial international research community. Fotis Jannidis (2009) has declared that the TEI is three different things at once: an organization, a set of concepts and tags along with guidance on how to use them, and a research community. In fact the TEI has a strong commitment to research and scholarly applications; as stated in the TEI's Goals and Mission, the *TEI Guidelines* "seek to support discipline-specific analysis and research approaches,"[2] and they recognize the TEI's research community as one of the main assets of the TEI itself. To respond to this research vocation, the TEI launched a peer-reviewed open-access journal in 2011 (*Journal of the Text Encoding Initiative*) and has refashioned its annual members' meetings to become a scholarly conference, with selected papers published in the journal.

The TEI's main significance resides in its provision not only of a set of elements for encoding textual features, but also and more importantly of a tool for the analysis and the understanding of texts: "the TEI succeeded ... at ... the development of a new data description language that substantially *improves* our ability to describe textual features, not just our ability to exchange descriptions based on current practice" (Renear, 2004:235). With more than 500 elements and attributes, the TEI has produced a shared vocabulary, an ontology of textual features that goes beyond national and disciplinary borders.

Many in the community of textual scholarship have seen the adoption of the TEI as a way to describe the text in all its observable features, to a level of detail that was unimaginable before (Driscoll, 2006). In fact, when using TEI encoding (but also when adopting any other type of markup based on similar principles) editors add tags in order to describe some feature or other of the source they are transcribing, such as, a scribal error, a tear on the page, the presence of a date in a calendar other than the Gregorian, a variant reading present in a different source, and so on. These tags are then handled by software and transformed into a suitable format for display, in which tags may be converted into conventional scholarly markup such as, for instance, the one proposed by the Leiden convention.[3] But the key factor is that not only can one recognize and annotate many features, but that one can encode them more than once, meeting the requirements of different readerships; it is this particular characteristic that has ultimately opened new perspectives to textual scholarship, as we will see. Editors no longer have to choose between faithfully representing their sources and making their text readable beyond an audience of specialists: they can have their cake and eat it too.

Encoding and the provision of these multiform editions (also called "paradigmatic editions," for which see below) have determined a deep change in the heuristic of textual scholarship, with significant consequences from both a theoretical and a practical point of view. In fact, text encoding allows for the migration of the documentation of editorial work inside the edited text. Instead of the summative account that is normally provided explaining the criteria adopted in the edition of the text, or within the introduction, this documentation can now be placed at the exact point where the intervention takes place, making the editorial work more accountable and giving editors the possibility of returning to each intervention at leisure to verify consistency and accuracy, keeping the quality of their work under strict control. In fact, one cannot underestimate the amount of silent corrections that the editor is called on to apply to texts in order to make them "readable" for a modern audience. For example, for the preparation of the digital edition of a sixteenth-century Italian play (*Lo Stufaioulo*, by Anton Francesco Doni), expansion of abbreviations, regularization of punctuation and orthography, and so on amount to about 6652 editorial interventions out of 11,500 words, meaning that more than one every other word has been modified by the editor (Pierazzo, 2015). In a printed edition the only choice for the editor would have been to give a summative account of such interventions in the "Note to the edition." Instead, text encoding offers many more choices, with scholars being given the possibility to provide encoding – and therefore in-place documentation – for none, some, or all of the above-mentioned interventions. Furthermore, this practice also allows one to offer to the reader the same element-per-element access to the editorial work, thereby providing a much fuller and more transparent documentation of the decisions undertaken by the editor. This is one of the criteria that have been indicated by Bodard and Garcés (2009) as best practice to qualify an edition as "open source" and properly scholarly.

With so much at stake, it will not come as a surprise that a large part of the TEI community is indeed represented by textual scholars.[4] An indication of this is given by the type of messages that populate the TEI mailing list. For instance, between February 1 and 12, 2014, there were 109 messages sent to the TEI List, 79 of which were on topics directly connected to editorial issues, demonstrating how lively editorial debate is within the community.[5]

Overabundant Encoding and Paradigmatic Editions

The use of text encoding, and in particular the practice of overabundantly encoding the same textual features more than once, allows for the production of editions which can be presented to their readers in multiple ways thanks to the application of different pieces of software (and/or stylesheets). Many scholars have underlined the advantages of this approach (Rahtz, 2006; Hunter, 2007; Cummings, 2008; Rehbein, 2010; to name a few), but the consequences of such a practice may be more wide-ranging that even they might have thought. For example, let us imagine that we are to edit a medieval manuscript, the content of which is characterized by extensive use of abbreviations and peculiar spellings which may help to trace our manuscript to a particular period, geographical area, or even scriptorium. A traditional edition of such a text would have expanded the abbreviations and normalized the text according to an accepted orthography, helping the reader to appreciate the content, but losing most of the features that characterize and contextualize the manuscript. However, if the transcription is encoded in XML-TEI, it will be possible to transcribe the text with both the abbreviations and their expansions at once; with errors and without; with unconventional spellings and with regularized ones at the same time; furthermore, it is possible to record features that one may not want to display all the time, or even features which will not be displayed at all, but will instead be used to generate statistics or indexes. Let us see one example in more detail. In the hypothetical manuscript we are considering, we may see a sequence like the following

iħs

A scholar with expertise in medieval manuscripts will immediately recognize it as a standard abbreviation for the Latin word "Iesus" (Jesus). In TEI-XML one could encode this as:

```
i<choice><am>ħ</am><ex>esu</ex></choice>s
```

As one can see the element <choice> contains two elements, <am> ("abbreviation marker" in the TEI parlance) and <ex> ("editorial expansion"), where the choice indicates which one of the two we need to consider at any given time. Thanks to such an encoding it is possible to transform the text into any of the following formats:

- iħs: the abbreviated word is left as it was, a format which is characteristic of diplomatic editions.
- i[esu]s or *iesus* or i(esu)s: the abbreviation is expanded but graphically distinguished from the main text, a display which is characteristic of semi-diplomatic editions.
- iesus: the abbreviation is expanded with no graphical sign that it was once abbreviated, a display which is characteristic of reading editions.

However, an editor might also want to capitalize the word "Iesus," according to modern use; in order to achieve this result, the encoding will have to be enriched by another <choice> element, this time containing an <orig> (the "original" text as present in the source) and a <reg>, containing the regularized form:

```
<choice><orig>i</orig><reg>I</reg></choice>
<choice><am>ħ</am><ex>esu</ex></choice>s
```

In this case, outputs such as "I[esu]s" and "Iesus" will also be available. However, an editor might also think that the "h" with a stroke on top is not really a letter, but a symbol, since no letter "h" appears in the word "Iesus";[6] in this case, marking it <am> (abbreviation mark) may be considered inappropriate, and so the <choice> could instead contain the abbreviated word and the expanded one, without trying to guess which bit constitutes an abbreviation mark:

```
<choice><abbr>iħs</abbr><expan>Iesus</expan></choice>
```

With this encoding only two types of output are available:

- iħs
- Iesus

As one can see, not only one can encode the same feature in more than one way, but the markup also communicates the editor's understanding and interpretation of the letters on the page, and this will further determine the types of edition (or editions) that can be generated.

The impact of such a practice is particularly significant for documentary editions, namely editions that are based on one source at a time. Traditionally print culture has elaborated several editorial models for these editions, with differences that are both methodological (how we prepare editions) and presentational (how we publish them). These models are referred to as type-facsimile or ultra-diplomatic, diplomatic, semi-diplomatic, and reading editions, and they are distinguished primarily by different levels of editorial intervention on the text as transmitted by a primary source (Greetham, 1994:347–72). They are also differentiated by the layout and the amount of editorial comment and annotation. The choice of presenting the edition according to one of these formats pushes editors to work in certain ways: for instance, to produce a diplomatic edition editors must transcribe their sources in a much more conservative way than they would for a reading edition. The question of what to include in a transcription and how to present it, along with all the consequent methodological implications, has been at the base of harsh academic discussion, such as the one that saw historians of the Association for Documentary Editions in stark opposition to Thomas Tanselle in 1978, or the one that opposed German-style historical editions versus copy-text-based editions grounded in the Anglo-American editorial context. In the former case, Tanselle accused historians of not being consistent or conservative enough when transcribing documents (Tanselle, 1978; Kline and Perdue, 2008:19–22); in the latter, supporters of the German-style edition championed a rigid separation between recording the evidence on the page and their interpretation of that evidence, questioning editorial practices based on the establishment of authorial intention (Eggert, 2009:164–78). Editorial practices based on text encoding in some ways constitute a manner of overcoming some of issues at the heart of such disagreements. In fact, the availability of a new medium which enables the application of new sets of editorial methods allows for much clearer separation of what is medium-dependent from what is instead theoretical, restating the scholarly arguments over different grounds.

Let us consider Tanselle's criticism of the then-prevalent methodology for handling historical documents: having censured bad practices in a number of editions, his final recommendation was that "the editor's goal is to reproduce in print as many of the characteristics of the document as he can" (1978:51). This type of declaration, which merges methodological issues with the expressive capabilities of print technology, and where best practices are determined by what publishers will allow editors to express, are not isolated and reflect editors' habit of thinking in terms of the printed page. In this framework, one's methodology is shaped by what the medium allows one to do, rather than based on by what would be appropriate to do. In contrast, when using text encoding to transcribe a text, one can go beyond what print can afford, and not only encode more features more accurately, since the medium is much more flexible, but also record these features in multiple ways, as we have just seen, meeting a number of different requirements at once. In this sense, text encoding applied within a digital environment has the potential to free textual scholarship from the constraints of the medium, and has in fact enabled editors to question assumptions that were driven by factors other than scholarly preoccupation. This does not mean that digital editing is not constrained by the new medium, quite the contrary: it is the fact that the constraints of the digital environment are different than those of print that allows editors to reflect on what is best scholarly practice, distinguishing what is induced by the medium from that determined by the scholarly goals. It takes a new medium to understand the old one and the way it influenced scholarly practices.

Text encoding is thus simultaneously a different working method, which requires editors to add tags to the text while transcribing it, and a different framework-infrastructure, which requires the use of computer programs able to handle such tags according to some user-defined principles and therefore able to index, search, and display the final product. This fact then implies that we need to distinguish the data model, where the information is added (the source), from its publication, where the information is displayed (the output). In this framework, publishing models such as type-facsimile, diplomatic, or reading editions represent only some of the possible outputs of the source. This in turn raises the possibility of enriching the source with much more information than is necessary for any one single output, as the selection of what to use in any given circumstance can be made by the software upon the request of the reader. In this framework, the concept of edition splits into different levels: the source becomes a sort of data-store where the editor conflates several editions that would have been kept separated in a print framework; the software stores the intelligence on what constitutes a desirable output; the output is generated on the user's demand and represents visually the intelligence present in the software and the data-store. Such a model may remind one of computer games and cyber-literature where users select their pathways among many possibilities. And indeed such similarities have been noticed by Edward Vanhoutte (2010), who has crafted the label of "ergodic edition" (following the theoretical framework established by Aarseth, 1997) to explain and model the intrinsic user-determined dynamicity (the "egordicity") present in digital scholarly editions based on text encoding.

This mechanism, based on an overabundant, paradigmatic type of encoding, requires *de facto* that we rethink what we mean by "edition," namely a way to embody one editorial theory or another. Traditionally each type of edition (critical, diplomatic, etc.) is bound to a specific editorial theory: for instance, scholars that adopt an approach from New Philology will probably choose a diplomatic edition, while scholars adopting a copy-text theoretical approach will choose a critical edition; however, the distinction between different formats of publication becomes less meaningful once these formats no longer shape editorial methods but instead simply represent different takes on the same knowledge base. In such cases one could also say the source file may contain a diplomatic, a semi-diplomatic, a reading, and an interpretative edition – all of which are simultaneously potentially present within this source file, but with each of these editions requiring the application of different sets of scripts and styling to be actualized. In this case the traditional method of distinguishing types of editions by the quantity and quality of editorial intervention does not work anymore, since the editorial intervention is always present but not visible. Finally, this proteiform, cumulative nature of digital editions also challenges the concept of a single edited text. Which is "the text"? The redundant, paradigmatically encoded text, one of the many possible outputs, or the sum of all of them?

Similar considerations could be made for digital editions based on many witnesses, in other words, critical editions. For instance, in the case of the edition of *Achter de Schermen* edited by Peter de Bruijn, Vincent Neyt, and Dirk van Hulle (2007), readers are offered the XML source for each witness as well as a complex set of scripts able to generate multiple outputs for each of the witnesses, together with the capability of generating a combined critical and reading edition – actually, *many* critical editions, each of them based on a different copy-text which is chosen interactively by the reader. This model is groundbreaking for many reasons: not only does it challenge the definition of "critical edition," which here becomes a text generated on demand by the user, but it also blurs the distinction between documentary and critical editions, as both approaches are equally represented, and it therefore blurs also the distinctions between concurring theoretical approaches which champion different editorial formats (Vanhoutte, 2007:162–3). Print-based editorial theories are defined by various parameters: the way the edited text relates to the primary sources that transmit the text, the way variant readings are handled and combined in the final text, whether variant readings are or are not kept separated from errors, and so on. Each editorial theory requires the editor to follow one route and not another. But digital editions based on text encoding allow the luxury of not choosing, instead adopting more than one of the approaches that were traditionally kept separate. This new method therefore calls for a redefinition and a redistribution of the theoretical frameworks associated with textual scholarship.

While digital editions based on the separation of source and output seem to aim at presenting their outputs in ways that are not that dissimilar to those produced by print, they are nevertheless profoundly different in nature, and their differences need to be thoroughly assessed. I have called these "paradigmatic editions" (Pierazzo, 2014), as the choices offered to the reader are located on the axis of variation (to use the semiotic terminology introduced by Saussure and Jakobson). This is the paradigmatic axis, along which the text remains substantially syntagmatically "the same" but is presented with differences that possess different semiotic characteristics and that respond to the needs of different users or different research goals. Paradigmatic editions are not meant to be "definitive editions" in the sense that even if they may contain *many* editions, they will never contain *all* possible editions, an aspiration against which both Michael Sperberg-McQueen (2009) and Peter Shillingsburg (2006) warn their readers.

Text Encoding, the TEI, and Textual Scholarship: Open Issues

The disciplinary impact of the use of text encoding for the preparation and publication of a digital edition is likely to be enormous, as some of the earlier thoughts suggest. In addition, one should also consider the potentials of interdisciplinarity and internationality offered by TEI encoding, and the impact of these on textual scholarship. In fact, one could use TEI markup to encode historical documents of the eleventh century, modern draft manuscripts of the twenty-first century, and Greek and Latin inscriptions of the second century BCE, for instance: text encoding has indeed been used in all these cases, making this method a unique point of convergence of a form of textual scholarship which is both truly multi- and super-disciplinary.

However, in spite of the many advantages offered by encoding with the TEI, since its inception there has been a steady series of criticisms over the use of this format and the philosophy it represents. The issues expressed are threefold: (1) access, (2) flexibility, and (3) overlapping hierarchies.

The Editor as Encoder: A Revolution or an Evolution?

Learning to use the TEI requires commitment and dedication and is felt by some scholars as too technical to fall within their area of interest. Yet, in spite of such fears, learning the TEI is less arduous than one might expect. Most learners, and in particular most editors, seem to enjoy the experience, and in fact the main feedback I have collected in over 12 years of teaching the TEI is that by encoding features editors are likely to "see" more of the text than if they had done it in the traditional way (Mahony and Pierazzo, 2012; Rehbein and Fritze, 2012). This should not come as a surprise. On the one hand, editing has always had a technical component, and so editors are well positioned to adopt the new techniques here. Furthermore, however, the technique is a means, not an end, and so the interest is not in the technique itself but in the under-standing which it conveys, whether digital or pre-digital. This dual nature has been emphasized by David Greetham:

> [I]t must be emphasized that editing and textual scholarship are not simply technical skills, which once learned can be easily transferred from one field or period to another, without the editor's having developed any historical training in the new area. Editing depends upon textual scholarship, but textual scholarship is not merely method or tech-nique; it is judgment and criticism, evaluation and discrimination, encompassing histor-ical and cultural learning as well. (Greetham, 1994:5)

The acquisition of computational skills should then not been seen as outside editorial practice, nor as a revolution of such practice, but as an evolution. If learning XML and the TEI is not that difficult, it does not mean that it is completely immune from difficulties. The *TEI Guidelines* are an impressive publication: the latest version (v. 2.6.0) runs to new fewer than 1588 pages in A4 format. For both beginners and devel-opers to find one's way through such a large publication is a demanding and offputting task (Burghart and Rehbein, 2012). Simplified versions of the TEI, such as TEI Lite, do not solve the issue, as simplification often means that some of the real advantages of using the TEI are left out, particularly those in support of advanced research. Most of the available teaching material is fragmentary and is not intended for self-learning, with the remarkable, but isolated, counter-example of the *TEI by Example* project (Van den Branden *et al.*, 2010); it also stops at a level that is too low for most scholarly pur-poses or for the TEI to show its true potential. Many scholars find learning the TEI to be unappealing, especially because they soon realize that TEI-XML alone is not enough: to produce any meaningful output or analyze the encoded data, one must also become proficient in a number of programming and markup languages.

    At the time of writing, the provision of tools to process TEI-encoded files is scarce, and most of those that are available often require sophisticated computational skills to be usable. To be fair, a small number of user-friendly tools exist (Juxta and the Versioning Machine, for instance),[7] and others are under development, but for an almost 30-year-old standard the yield seems rather meager. The reasons for this scarcity of tools are complex and are not easy to tackle (though see below for a discussion of the topic), but the consequences of such a scarcity are that in order to produce a digital edition editors must either acquire a high level of computational literacy themselves or call on the support of specialized IT centers; both conditions prevent the development of a diffused practice of text encoding. Furthermore, the publication and maintenance of digital editions on the web requires adequate infrastructure, and this again is beyond the resources of most editors. A close collaboration between the communities of textual scholarship and digital humanities is therefore required in order to produce meaningful and sustainable editorial work and workflow models which encompass a reasonable amount of computational literacy without losing the empowerment brought by text encoding. The difficulty is to establish where to draw the line regarding which skills and expertise are to be expected from the editor alone (which in turn means knowing what to teach to young scholars) and what instead should be handled by tools. As we will see below, the expectation that tools may be able to handle considerable chunks of the editorial work may be not only too optimistic, but also too risky. On the other hand, it is also unreasonable to expect editors to become computationally self-sufficient; a difficult and delicate balance between these two expectations still needs to be found.

The transformation of the editor into an encoder can be seen as a way to improve one's capability of representing the material to be edited, but it can also be an unwelcome and unsettling change,[8] or even beyond the realm of editorial care. Bree and McLaverty, in fact, complain about the fact that in digital editing "the scholar is also likely to have to acquire skills which may well be useful and interesting in themselves but which stray a long way from what could be regarded as making a direct contribution to scholarly research" (Bree and McLaverty, 2009:127). Is this perception a generational one which will fade when a new digitally trained army of young scholars takes the lead? Possibly; yet the lack of supporting tools and infrastructures, and of a more widespread academic acceptance of digital outcomes, is preventing young scholars from engaging with digital editing. The provision of an environment that makes it easier for young scholars to access the new methodologies will necessarily play a fundamental role in the next few years.

When Flexibility is too Much: Building tools for Textual Scholars

Those tools for editorial work that have been (and are being) developed, with various degrees of success, are intended to support a range of scholarly tasks: transcription, facsimile analysis and segmentation, collation, building of critical apparatuses and stemmas, comparison, linguistic analysis, and a combination of two or more of the above. However, in spite of the relatively large number of tools available, these are rarely fit for the job and still have had little impact beyond the environment that produced them.

One of the biggest pros of the TEI as a modeling and research tool is its richness and flexibility. As we have seen, the TEI offers more than one way to encode what may appear to be the same phenomenon, with only slightly different nuances of meaning associated with the different encodings. This may be looked upon as one of the features that have determined the establishment of the TEI as the most-used framework for the encoding of primary sources and the creation of digital editions, as it offers scholars the possibility of being as true as possible to their research aims. However, this same feature makes it extremely difficult to develop generic tools that could help to reduce the steep learning curve required of learners of the TEI. In fact, in order to build tools that textual scholars might use for their editorial work, developers need to be able to foresee the tasks that scholars wish to perform; in other words, developers must model the work of scholars. However, this is easier said than done. While it is (relatively) simple to model the way one scholar works, or even a small group, it is much more complicated to model the working methods of a large community, owing in no small part to the different theoretical approaches at the base of their workflow, the different types of editorial product they aim to produce, and their national and disciplinary habits and idiosyncrasies. To make scholars across disciplines agree on a set of standards seems far from achievable, as admitted by Tara Andrews when she declares how "flexibility and customizability is currently much more important to textual scholars than the sort of standardization that would allow for true progress toward digital critical editions" (Andrews, 2013:63).

The flexibility of the encoding model is not the only issue when it comes to the provision of tools. The development and adoption of tools for the support of textual scholarship is a delicate operation which itself risks leading to profound changes in future scholarship. This is because, in a circular pattern, to produce a tool developers have to model editors' behaviors, but, once that the tool is produced, the tool will itself determine future behaviors as editors will probably try to model their data and their work in a way that is compatible with the tool's expectations. Of course this is not new: the same can be said for print, as discussed above, and also for the TEI itself: its development has been determined by analysis and modeling of editorial work; on the other hand, the very existence of the TEI now influences the way editors work. It is therefore essential that the scholarly community engages with the development of tools and models, and that these are elaborated from within the community, to ensure that these developments will respond to the needs of editors and not force them into constraints that limit the evolution of the discipline. A separation between editorial work and tool development is to some extent necessary, given the different roles and specialism required by the two activities; nevertheless, they must also be collaborative in order to produce long-lasting results.

Overlapping Hierarchies, Standoff Markup, and Interpretation

One of the main difficulties with text encoding based on XML (and many other languages that obey similar principles) is that this language is unable to handle so-called overlapping hierarchies. According to the rules of XML, if one wishes to encode lines of verse and syntactic boundaries, one must choose whether to privilege the verse structure over the syntactic structures, or vice versa. One cannot do both, as the boundaries of versification and syntax coincide only occasionally, whereas XML requires that one is always contained within the other. For example, if one considers the first four lines of T.S. Eliot's *Waste Land*, it would be impossible to encode both lines and clauses in XML, given the systematic use of enjambment in this part of the poem (commas mark the boundaries of the clauses):

> April is the cruellest month, breeding
> lilacs out of the dead land, mixing
> memory and desire, stirring
> dull roots with spring rain.

The same problem occurs when one attempts to encode, say, an underlining that begins within but continues beyond a deletion, or variant readings that affect overlapping sections of the text, or many other cases; as a matter of fact all texts overlap in one way or the other. The necessity of structuring every XML file within a single ordered hierarchy lies at the base of the development of the so-called OHCO model (ordered hierarchy of content object: DeRose *et al.*, 1990). This states that each text can be reduced to a single hierarchy, the components of which are perfectly contained within each other. However, the reality of texts demonstrates that this is almost never the case, since multiple points of view can be adopted simultaneously. James Cummings lists a series of possible highly sophisticated approaches that may help to circumvent the problem, namely:

- redundantly encoding the same information in multiple forms
- remodeling the document structure to merge the competing hierarchies into a non-TEI form
- element fragmentation and virtual re-creation of single elements into multiple parts, with each properly nested
- boundary marking of starting and ending element locations using milestones to form a non-nesting structure
- standoff markup, where the text is separated from the annotation and virtual re-creation of elements
- a number of competing non-XML solutions (Cummings, 2008:463).

The existence of so many possible solutions demonstrates that no single one is entirely appropriate to solve the problem; furthermore their complexity is beyond the ability of most scholar-encoders. Indeed, the issue of overlapping hierarchies has dominated scholarly debates for many years, with scholars having developed strong opinions about it. Jerome McGann (2010) has in fact declared that the main contribution of the TEI to textual scholarship is in demonstrating that the OHCO model is wrong, and by this he means that the TEI's main contribution lies precisely in its failure as a format for the encoding of scholarly editions of texts. One can sympathize with this position, and indeed the intrinsic limitations of XML are severe; as a ready solution does not exist, scholars have attempted to tackle the issue by limiting themselves to what is possible, instead of freely pursuing their research aims, and this solution is far from ideal. Yet, it is also to be noted that there is more to TEI and to text encoding than OHCO; in particular, as demonstrated by the previous discussion, the main significance of the TEI can be traced to the provision of a taxonomy for describing and accounting for the editorial work, as well as to the establishment of an international research community that uses and maintains it.

Among the possible "workarounds" listed by Cummings, one in particular has collected a large degree of consensus, namely the adoption of "standoff" annotation (Eggert, 2005; Cummings, 2009; Schmidt, 2010). According to this approach, one is to maintain a "low-density" XML source file (say, a text with only minimal markup) and to keep all complex and conflicting layers of markup in separate files which refer back to the source file and which are to be instantiated by the user on request (or just-in-time as in Berrie *et al.*, 2006). An even more radical approach is the one that sees plain text files on the one hand, and non-XML standoff markup on the other. This solution is championed in particular by

Schmidt (2010), who maintains that embedding XML markup into a text is practically and methodologically unsuitable for cultural heritage materials, whereas standoff annotation allows for a better management of knowledge and for interoperability. In his vision embedded markup makes sharing files impossible, as they are inevitably blemished by editorial interpretation. The underlying assumption is that a text "stripped out" of its markup is a text that is free of interpretation (Eggert, 2005; Berrie *et al.*, 2006; Schmidt, 2010).

Unfortunately this assumption is not sustainable: an allegedly "plain text" (that is, a text without visible codes such as XML encoding) is not a text without interpretation, but a text where interpretation is conveyed by writing conventions and implicit assumptions instead of explicit markup such as in XML. The use of a computer markup system allows for the clear and accountable documentation of editorial work, which is often silently masked by the provision of clean reading texts. In fact, most of the paragraphematic symbols (punctuation, dashes, brackets, accents, apostrophes, etc.) and conventions (capital letters, spacing, line breaks, etc.) that we now take for granted as natural and neutral parts of the text are the result of millennia of evolution of writing conventions; furthermore, in most cases they are not born with the text but are introduced by editors according to their own interpretation in order to make the text more easily accessible to modern readers. In fact, if a text was written in Antiquity, the Middle Ages, the Early Modern or Modern periods, it is very likely that at least some part of the punctuation (if not all) with which it now circulates was not an original part of the authorial text but has been deliberately inserted into the text at some point, whether by an editor, typesetter, or copyist.

If we look at the text of Shakespeare as presented by any modern edition, for instance, almost the entire paragraphematic system is the product of one or more editors, representing thereby their interpretation of the text. The fact that such a system is part of modern writing and therefore seems "natural" to a modern reader does not change its interpretative nature, which is demonstrated, for instance, by observation that no two editors of Shakespeare present the same punctuation. These symbols and conventions could themselves be considered a sort of markup, since they are added by editors to most cultural heritage texts in order to indicate many of the same things that the TEI does (verses, clauses, proper nouns, and so on), but this time with the purpose of making the texts more readable. Of this opinion is Charlotte Rouché (2012), who traces a deeply insightful history of markup, from Antiquity to today, and from *scriptio continua*, which characterizes Ancient Greek and most Latin texts of Antiquity that where written without spaces or punctuation and in capital letters only, to XML, discussing how the introduction of markers such as word spacing and paragraphematic signs were progressively (but not linearly) adopted to support different forms of reading and literacies.[9] She then discusses the introduction of scholarly markup, such as the Leiden conventions, which brings us smoothly to text encoding, where markup serves both as help for reading (by the human as well as by the computer) and as scholarly convention.

A second and perhaps more dangerous implication in the assumption that a text without (XML-type) markup is a text without interpretation is the idea that an objective text can and does exist outside the negotiation and cultural dialectic of editorial mediation which is in turn, by definition, interpretative. To consider an extreme counter-example to this assumption, in what we conventionally call Homer's *Odyssey* every single word, its location, its belonging to a structure such as the verse, for instance, is the result of millennia of stratified editorial conventions and compromises, as its most ancient witnesses are a few hundred years more recent than the supposed date of creation, and so only hypotheses can be used to postulate what happened in that temporal gap – hypotheses which are fascinating but largely unsupported.

Standoff markup may represent a practical and clever solution to a serious problem (that of overlapping hierarchies), and it enables the coexistence of different levels of encoding, but it has, or should have, nothing to do with interpretation or the lack thereof. Even when looking at a clean reading text, we must not forget its essentially interpretative nature. Scholars may decide to agree on a specific version of the text, but this can only be seen for what it is, namely a pragmatic compromise, a working hypothesis. The use of markup in textual scholarship certainly has drawbacks, but one cannot easily overlook its indubitable advantages from a scholarly and methodological point of view, the most important of which is the possibility not of avoiding editorial interpretation, but of making it explicit and accountable.

Conclusions

Digital editing is a consolidated reality. One could even say that all editing is already digital, since all modern editions are prepared with the support of computers, if only as type setter and word processor. However, only a small proportion of editions are prepared in a way that takes advantage of the possibilities and advantages that are offered to those editors who adopt text encoding as their working method. A lot of work remains to be done in order to ease access to this method and the empowerment that it entails. In this scenario, collaboration between scholars and developers remains crucial. Such a collaboration is not new: editors have always collaborated with professionals coming from the publishing industry. However, the changed technological infrastructure now requires new types of collaboration to be established, and while the change may be unsettling and even unwelcome, it is as urgent as it is necessary.

The last few years have seen the establishment of digital publications mainly in the form of e-books, a tendency that is undoubtedly destined to increase. These products barely mask the attempt to present themselves as surrogates of printed books, with the page-like metaphor as one of their defining characteristics. But since such page-like representation is resizable, it follows that complex and controlled layouts like the ones required by scholarly editions are not achievable. Furthermore, e-book formats fall very short when it comes to the functionalities that are offered by web-based scholarly editions; in fact e-books have been designed with a highly simplified model of the book in mind, namely one that is appropriate for modern novels and essays. Without a strong engagement of the editorial community with the digital medium (in the same way that the scholarly community engaged with print in its early days), the risk is that we will be left to work with inadequate models for representation which do not take into account the needs of culturally complex products such as scholarly edited texts. In the same way that Pietro Bembo and Erasmus of Rotterdam collaborated with Aldus Manutius in sixteenth-century Venice, textual scholars should feel the importance of collaboration with developers and the digital world in general in order to develop models and tools which adequately support their scholarly activities. Only in this way might we be able to establish a welcoming and productive environment for editors to work and prosper.

Notes

1 Jerome McGann claims the existence and the importance of the "bibliographical codes" of a work beside its "linguistic codes", that is, factors such as typesetting, layout, orthography, binding are to be considered together with the actual verbal content of any given text (McGann, 1991:57).

2 See The TEI website, and in particular http://www.tei-c.org/About/mission.xml.

3 On the Leiden conventions and their significance for editorial practice in Classics, see, for example Panciera (1991). The mapping of the Leiden convention into XML-TEI is at the base of the creation of the EpiDoc encoding format (Elliot *et al.*, 2011–2013).

4 The TEI Special Interest Group on Manuscripts is by far the largest of the TEI SIGs, counting over 150 subscriptions to the mailing list (January 2014). Certainly not all of them are textual scholars, but a large number are. To them one has probably to add the members of the SIG on Correspondence as well.

5 The data analysis is mine. The TEI-L online archives are freely accessible on the web: http://listserv.brown.edu/archives/cgi-bin/wa?A0=tei-l.

6 The presumed letter "h" is in fact the result of a misunderstanding of the original capital Greek form of the (abbreviated) word "ΙΗΣ", where the capital eta indeed looks like a capital H. Once the word was put in lower case, the capital eta was transcribed as a lowercase "h." I am grateful to Peter Stokes for the formulation of this explanation.

7 See respectively http://www.juxtasoftware.org/ and http://v-machine.org/. Juxta is a project developed within the NINES framework (http://www.nines.org/), while the Versioning Machine is developed by a team lead by Susan Schreibman.

8 See, for instance, an article by Tim McLoughlin (2010) where the experience of learning the TEI and using it for encoding a series of documents has led to a vivid account of the type of difficulties that such an experience entails. Rehbein (2010) answers him point-by-point in an equally vivid article.

9 On the "invention" of punctuation, the most important contribution is of course Parkes (1992), often cited by Rouché (2012). Schmidt (2010:338) thinks instead that markup and paragraphematic system are two distinct entities and should not be conflated.

References and Further Reading

Aarseth, E. 1997. *Cybertext. Perspectives on Ergotic Literature Cybertext. Perspectives on Ergotic Literature*. Baltimore: Johns Hopkins University Press.

Andrews, T.L. 2013. The third way: philology and critical edition in the digital age. *Variants* 10, 61–76.

Bree, L., and McLaverty, J. 2009. The Cambridge Edition of the works of Jonathan Swift and the future of the scholarly edition. In *Text Editing, Print and the Digital World*, ed. M. Deegan and K. Sutherland. Aldershot: Ashgate, 127–36.

Berrie, P., Eggert, P., Tiffin, C., *et al.* 2006. Authenticating electronic editions. In *Electronic Textual Editing*, ed. L. Burnard, K. O'Brien O'Keeffe, and J. Unsworth. New York: Modern Language Association, 269–76.

Bodard, G., and Garcés, J. 2009. Open source critical editions: a rationale. In *Text Editing, Print and the Digital World*, ed. M. Deegan and K. Sutherland. Aldershot: Ashgate, 83–98.

Burghart, M., and Rehbein, M. 2012. The present and future of the TEI Community for Manuscript Encoding. *Journal of the Text Encoding Initiative* 2. http://jtei.revues.org/372 (accessed February 12, 2014).

Cummings, J. 2008. The Text Encoding Initiative and the study of literature. In *A Companion to Digital Literary Studies*, ed. R.G. Siemens and S. Schreibman. Oxford: Blackwell, 451–76.

Cummings, J. 2009. Converting Saint Paul: a new TEI P5 edition of "The Conversion of Saint Paul" using stand-off methodology. *Literary and Linguistic Computing* 24 (3), 307–17.

DeRose, S.J., Durand, D.G., Mylonas, E., *et al.* 1990. What is text, really? *Journal of Computing in Higher Education* 1 (2), 3–26.

Driscoll, M.J. 2006. Levels of transcription. In *Electronic Textual Editing*, ed. L. Burnard, K. O'Brien O'Keeffe, and J. Unsworth. New York: Modern Language Association, 254–61.

Eggert, P. 2005. Text-encoding, theories of the text, and the "work-site". *Literary and Linguistic Computing* 20 (4), 425–35.

Eggert, P. 2009. *Securing the Past: Conservation in Art, Architecture and Literature*. Cambridge: Cambridge University Press.

Elliot, T., Bodard, G., Mylonas, E., *et al.* 2011–2013. EpiDoc guidelines: ancient documents in TEI XML. http://www.stoa.org/epidoc/gl/latest/index.html (accessed February 12, 2014).

Elsschot, W. 2007. *Achter de Schermen*, ed. V. Neyt, P. de Bruijn, and D. van Hulle. Antwerp and The Hague: Universiteit Antwerpen, and Huygens Instituut.

Finneran R.J., ed. 1996. *The Literary Text in the Digital Age*. Ann Arbor: University of Michigan Press.

Greetham, D.C. 1994. *Textual Scholarship: An Introduction*. New York: Garland.

Hunter, M. 2007. *Editing Early Modern Texts: An Introduction to Principles and Practice*. New York: Palgrave Macmillan.

Kline, M.-J., and Perdue, S.H. 2008. *A Guide to Documentary Editing*. Charlottesville: University of Virginia Press.

Jannidis, F. 2009. TEI in a crystal ball. *Literary and Linguistic Computing* 24 (3), 253–65.

Mahony, S., and Pierazzo, E. 2012. Teaching skills or teaching methodology? In *Digital Humanities Pedagogy: Practices, Principles and Politics*, ed. B.D. Hirsch. Cambridge: OpenBook, 215–25. http://www.openbookpublishers.com/htmlreader/DHP/chap08.html#ch08 (accessed February 12, 2014).

McGann, J. 1991. *The Textual Condition*. Princeton, NJ: Princeton University Press.

McGann, J. 2010. Electronic Archives and Critical Editing. *Literature Compass* 7(2), 37–42.

McLoughlin, T. 2010. Bridging the gap. In *Jahrbruch für Computerphilologie*, ed. M. Rehbein and S. Ryder, 10, 37–54.

Panciera, S. 1991. Struttura dei supplementi e segni diacritici dieci anni dopo. *Supplementa Italica* 8, 9–21.

Parkes, M.B. 1992. *Pause and Effect: An Introduction to the History of Punctuation in the West*. Aldershot: Ashgate.

Pierazzo, E. 2014. Digital documentary editions and the others. *Scholarly Editing*, 35.

Pierazzo, E. 2015. Lo 'Stufaiuolo' by Anton Francesco Doni. A Scholarly Edition. *Scholarly Editing*, 36. http://www.scholarlyediting.org/2015/editions/intro.stufaiuolo.html.

Price, K.M. 2008. Electronic scholarly editions. In *A Companion to Digital Literary Studies*, ed. R.G. Siemens and S. Schreibman. Oxford: Blackwell, 434–50.

Rahtz, S. 2006. Storage, retrieval, and rendering. In *Electronic Textual Editing*, ed. L. Burnard, K. O'Brien O'Keeffe, and J. Unsworth. New York: Modern Language Association, 310–33.

Rehbein, M. 2010. The transition from classical to digital thinking: reflections on Tim McLoughlin, James Barry and collaborative work. In *Jahrbruch für Computerphilologie*, ed. M. Rehbein and S. Ryder, 10, 55–67.

Rehbein, M., and Fritze, C. 2012. Hands-on teaching digital humanities. In *Digital Humanities Pedagogy: Practices, Principles and Politics*, ed. B.D. Hirsch. Cambridge: OpenBook. http://www.openbookpublishers.com/htmlreader/DHP/chap02.html#ch02 (accessed February 12, 2014).

Renear, A. 2004. Text encoding. In *A Companion to Digital Humanities*, ed. S. Schreibman, R. Siemens, and J. Unsworth. Oxford: Blackwell, 218–39. http://www.digitalhumanities.org/companion (accessed February 12, 2014).

Rouché, C. 2012. Why do we mark up texts? In *Collaborative Research in the Digital Humanities*, ed. M. Deegan and W. McCarty. Farnham: Ashgate, 155–62.

Schmidt, D. 2010. The inadequacy of embedded markup for cultural heritage texts. *Literary and Linguistic Computing* 25 (3), 337–56.

Shillingsburg, P.L. 2006. *From Gutenberg to Google*. Cambridge: Cambridge University Press.

Sperberg-McQueen, C.M. 2009. How to teach your edition how to swim. *Literary and Linguistic Computing* 24 (1), 27–52.

Tanselle, G.T. 1978. The editing of historical documents. *Studies in Bibliography* 31, 1–56.

TEI Consortium. 2009. *TEI P5: Guidelines for Electronic Text Encoding and Interchange*. http://www.tei-c.org/Guidelines/P5 (accessed February 12, 2014).

Van den Branden, R., Terras, M., and Vanhoutte, E. 2010. *TEI by Example*. http://www.teibyexample.org (accessed February 12, 2014).

Vanhoutte, E. 2007. Traditional editorial standards and the digital edition. In *Learned Love: Proceedings of the Emblem Project Utrecht Conference on Dutch Love Emblems and the Internet (November 2006)*, ed. E. Stronks and P. Boot. The Hague: DANS – Data Archiving and Networked Services, 157–74.

Vanhoutte, E. 2010. Defining electronic editions: a historical and functional perspective. In *Text and Genre in Reconstruction: Effects of Digitalization on Ideas, Behaviours, Products and Institutions*, ed. W. McCarty. Cambridge: OpenBook, 119–44.

22
Digital Materiality

Sydney J. Shep

Paul Erickson once argued that book historians "are poised to make tremendous contributions to our understanding of new electronic media" (Erickson, 2003:110). An awareness that communication is always already a mediated experience combined with the skills of forensic analysis and bibliographic imagination are as relevant to books as to any other material form, including electronic records. At the heart of the critical enterprise is an understanding of digital materiality, not framed as the intangibility of cyberspace using the superficial distinction between physical, surrogate, and virtual, but as the palpable bits and bytes of electronic hardware and software that are ubiquitous, that leave traces, and that can be read as evidence of the creation, dissemination, reception, and preservation of these new communication forms. In this era of digital incunabula, physical ("hard") and electronic ("soft") publications coexist, often in hybrid forms. Mark Z. Danielewski's *House of Leaves* (2000) and *Only Revolutions* (2006) bridge the worlds of print and digital culture and construct highly interactive, self-reflexive works. William Gibson's early electronic text *Agrippa* (1992) performs its materiality as both a computer disk and a limited-edition artist's book: on screen, the encrypted 300-line poetic codework self-erases once read; the book version's photosensitized pages fade upon exposure to light. This chapter explores the concept of digital materiality and how it is captured in metadata, in interfaces, in time and date-stamped information processing, and in the multivariate interactions of users and forms in the contemporary multiverse.

In his discussion of the Giller Prize winning novel, *The Sentimentalists*, digital humanist, book historian, and media archaeographer Alan Galey (2012) posed an ostensibly simple question: what is the difference between a fine-press limited-edition work, a mass-market paperback, and an e-book? At first glance the answer might

A New Companion to Digital Humanities, First Edition. Edited by Susan Schreibman, Ray Siemens, and John Unsworth.
© 2016 John Wiley & Sons, Ltd. Published 2016 by John Wiley & Sons, Ltd.

reside in the obvious distinction between the physical and the digital, the material and the virtual: one is an exercise in extreme physical creation from hand-setting metal types to hand-printing formes on dampened hand-made paper, to hand-binding the final product; the other two are manufactured from digital files, the commercial paperback digitally printed on machine-made paper and machine-bound, the e-book version encoded and delivered via proprietary software to, in this case, a Kobo reading device. By focusing on the bibliographic codes embodied in the title page, type, and epigraphs, however, Galey demonstrated that not only is contemporary publishing always already digital, but that the very materiality of the digital is exposed through deliberate acts of linguistic transgression: exposing and reading computer code; identifying anomalies in metadata; breaching the security walls of Kobo's digital rights management system. New media forensics, part of the digital humanists' intellectual toolkit, depends on recognizing the fundamental materiality of digital forms, extracting evidence of its existence, and interpreting its individual, unique manifestations.

Until scientists identified the nanoscale as the precise threshold between the material and the immaterial (Kirschenbaum, 2008:2), cyberspace and its world of electronic bits and bytes was popularly construed as intangible, invisible, ephemeral, unstable, and virtual. The capacity for human intervention was deemed magical and the affordances of digital objects were considered mysterious, arcane, and open only to the technologically initiated. This rhetoric contrasted sharply with that of the physical world, whose tangible, fungible, visible existence adhered to the normal, observable laws of traditional physics and remained both predictable and dependable. Since the early 2000s, however, the idea that digital objects should be reconceptualized as material, rather than virtual, has been the subject of considerable scholarly investigation in the humanities (McGann, 2001; Hayles, 2002; Drucker, 2003; Lavagnino *et al.*, 2007); it has also attracted attention in both the social sciences (Hindmarsh *et al.*, 2006; Hand, 2008) and in information science (Orlikowski, 2006; Leonardi, 2010). Scholars increasingly acknowledge that digital materiality, whether of digitized or born-digital objects, is not a contradiction in terms, but rather, a phrase that succinctly encapsulates a process of meaning making and knowledge production that emphasizes technology-in-practice rather than a technological artifact.

Textual scholarship, electronic editing, and new-media historiography have all generated substantial and significant discussions about the relationship between print and digital forms, the analog–digital continuum, and digital materiality. From the prescient work of D.F. McKenzie (1986/1999, 2002) who posited a sociology of texts that embraced all communication media, including the digital, to Jerome McGann's concept of the "socialization of texts" (1991) that underwrites current discussions of the social edition (Siemens *et al.*, 2010), and from Johanna Drucker's early research on artists' books, visible typography, and graphic forms (1994, 2003), to Alan Liu's (1994) problematization of digital media's claims to transcendence in the face of encoding practices and the imperatives of network transmission, materiality is configured as part of a "sustainable dialectic" (Drucker, 1994:43) whose phenomenological existence is inseparable from the process of interpretation. Lisa Gitelman's (2006) examination of "new" media from the early eighteenth century to the present day enriches our understanding of the interpenetration of analog and digital forms (Gitelman, 2006:95–6). N. Katherine Hayles (2012) continues to respond provocatively to the challenges and opportunities inherent in positing this communication continuum, understanding human-techno hybridity, and exploring technogenesis, the coevolution of the human and technological. Book historian Roger Chartier reminds us that material instantiation is also an act of engagement: "reading is not a solely abstract intellectual operation; it involves the body, is inscribed within a space, and implies a relationship to oneself or to others" (Chartier and Cavallo, 1999:4). Even across media forms, as Paul Eggert suggests, "whether the textual carrier be the physical page, a computational capacity, or the sound waves that transmit orally declaimed verse, there is always a material condition for the existence of text" (Eggert, 2005:428). Scholars of media archaeology and proponents of new materialism such as Wolfgang Ernst (2011) and Jussi Parikka (2012a, 2012b) also highlight the centrality of the material in their study of the hardware and software of culture.

In exploding the tactile fallacy of digital immateriality, Matthew Kirschenbaum (2008) distinguishes between two types of digital materiality: forensic and formal. Forensic materiality consists of the physical evidence of production, distribution, reception, and preservation which can be detected through the identification and analysis of various traces, residues, marks, and inscriptions visible to human sight or accessible through instrumentation. On the one hand, chips, touch screens, terminals, cables, keyboards, and mice are all capable of recording human and machine interactions. On the other hand, nanotechnology's magnetic-force microscopy can reveal the bit pattern cut into a computer disk and expose recoverable areas of corruption whether through chemical degradation of the physical substrate or multiple overwritings. Digital forensics is analogous to the activities of book historians and bibliographers working in the domain of manuscript and print artifacts who analyze, amongst other material manifestations, the physical characteristics of paper composition and manufacture, handwriting styles and inks, printmaking, illustration, and bookbinding techniques. Both embrace a kind of "crime scene investigation" process using extant material evidence and inductive reasoning to argue for patterns of textual transmission, licit or illicit interventions, or artifactual legacies of the publishing process. Galey's case study of *The Sentimentalists* which opens this chapter demonstrates how an analysis of the file names and formats for the Kobo e-book cover illustration were repurposed by the publisher from the digital file that generated the photopolymer which was handprinted in the original letterpress edition, thus complicating the simple binary of mutually exclusive print and digital forms.

Formal materiality engages with the architecture of digital media and their symbolic forms, whether the structure of individual software programs, embedded data standards and metadata encoding, or operating-system configurations. Like forensic materiality, there is always a physical manifestation, but whereas the forensic is focused on attributes, formal materiality concentrates on the digital environment which Kirschenbaum (2008) defines as "an abstract projection supported and sustained by its capacity to propagate the illusion (or call it a working model) of *immaterial* behavior: identification without ambiguity, transmission without loss, repetition without originality" (Kirschenbaum, 2008:11). Despite this illusion, existing (if hidden) content can be formally exposed using built-in functionality such as "reveal source," and "show header," or by deploying encryption keys; the existence of errors discloses the Achilles heel of an imperfect system in motion. For example, in determining why there was a different ordering of epigraphs in the e-book version of *The Sentimentalists*, Galey drilled down to the SQL database driving the publication and discovered a coding transposition that delivered the wrong information and corrupted the logical sequence of the original text.

Johanna Drucker (2013) has recently proposed that two forms of materiality be added to the lexicon of forensic and formal: distributed and performative. Each of them usefully complements and extends Kirschenbaum's distinction and draws on a wide range of philosophies and approaches. Distributed materiality, based on the work of informatics and encryption specialist Jean-François Blanchette, relates to "the complex of interdependencies on which any digital artifact depends for its basic existence"; that is, the "co-dependent, layered contingencies on which the functions of drive, storage, software, hardware, systems, and networks depend" (Drucker, 2013: paras.21, 6). Performative materiality, drawn from studies in cognition, perception, reader-response, textual hermeneutics, and interface design, further emphasizes the functional dimension of materiality, its existence defined by and interdependent upon use, interactivity, process; that is, "what something *is* has to be understood in terms of what it *does*, how it works within machinic, systemic, and cultural domains" (Drucker, 2013: para 4). As Drucker explains:

> The many dimensions of performative materiality, then, touch on each layer of digital media – in an analysis of the co-dependencies and contingencies of the material substrate, in a description of the production of display from code through processing as a performative act, in the engagement of users with the generative experience of viewing, and in the mutability and reinscribability of files in the mutable substrate of digital technology. While such a description sounds like a characterization of the essential qualities of digital media, it is meant as a description of the ways these qualities are always operating within contingent fields, flows, and relations that reconstitute them. (Drucker, 2013: para.13)

Almost three decades after the launch of the World Wide Web, it is easy for us to recognize ubiquitous computer hardware such as smartphones, tablets, laptops, or e-readers to be as physical as chairs, desks, coffee mugs, or teacups. Even software and its users leave tangible, recoverable traces on hard drives, servers and in the so-called "cloud." Data structures and file formats are equally tangible and equally recoverable; we know that computer hackers are experts at both exposing the architecture of information and identifying the wormholes to dislodge and disrupt its systems. So while we can agree that the digital world is as full of stuff as the physical world, what if that stuff is only meaningful when it interacts with a sentient being, like ourselves? Many scholars, Drucker included, argue that materiality only exists in acts of perception, in performance, in use, in practice. As Paul Leonardi suggests in the context of information systems and organizational management:

> "material" would refer not to inherent properties of the artifact, but instead to the way that the artifact exists in relationship to the people who create and use it. These alternative, relational definitions move materiality "out of the artifact" and into the space of interaction between people and artifacts. No matter whether those artifacts are physical or digital, their "materiality" is determined, to a substantial degree, by when, how, and

why they are used. These definitions imply that materiality is not a property of artifacts, but a product of the relationships between artifacts and the people who produce and consume them. (Leonardi, 2010)

In order for the instrumentality of materiality to be re-conceptualized, Hayles (2012) argues for a necessary decoupling of physicality from materiality: the former being an ontologically discrete entity, the latter being an emergent property that comes into existence through an act of engagement or, as she terms it, "attention" which identifies and isolates one or more specific, physical attributes (Hayles, 2012:91). As she notes, "materiality emerges from the dynamic interplay between the richness of a physically robust world and human intelligence as it crafts this physicality to create meaning" (Hayles, 2002:33). The work of Haidy Geismar (2013) on the relationship between materiality and metadata in the world of object management, museum curation, and digital repatriation is apposite here. She argues that the digital should be defined as a form and process rather than a fixed material or medium. The characteristics of digital objects often described as editable, interactive, open, and distributed are, according to Geismar, the result of affective relationships rather than qualities inherent to the digital technologies themselves. Drawing on Horst and Miller's anthropological perspective that "locates the digital *within* the study of social relationships and cultural difference" (Geismar, 2013), she suggests that materiality and sociality are mutually constitutive, being a fluid, interconnected, hybrid landscape of objects and practices. In this view, metadata becomes another word for epistemology; it registers not the specious value-free or neutral description of information, but a socially implicated act of construction that is situated in both time and space. In current debates about distant, machine, or hyper-reading and its relation to traditions of close reading, for instance, literary scholars have recuperated these notions of attention and affect to register the embodied, socially and politically implicated processes of surface or deep reading (Price, 2009; Ramsay, 2011; Nuttall, 2011; Hayles, 2012). Again, responsiveness to the sustained dialectic of materiality underwrites these new directions.

If metadata signals the sociological dimension of digital materiality, then paradata, a term recently coined to describe the automatic and semantic process of capture and documentation of all facets of digital humanities project decision making, exposes its ontological bases and biases, if not metaphysics. Paradata or "processual *scholia*" is a form of intellectual transparency that legitimates "computer-based visualization of cultural heritage ... as a valid scholarly method for studying and presenting cultures of the past" (Bentkowska-Kafel *et al.*, 2012:245). Like forensic, formal, distributed, and performative materiality, it is recorded in physical traces that reflect, as Willard McCarty points out in relation to computational models, "temporary states in a process of coming to know rather than fixed structures of knowledge" (in Bentkowska-Kafel *et al.*, 2012:248). Paradata exposes the nature of what we know but, equally, in conjunction with metadata, can reveal how we know what we know.

Building on Frank Upward's modeling of the records continuum, Australian archives and record-keeping practitioner Sue McKemmish (1996) refers to records and archives as always in "a process of becoming" and claims that they contain both "evidence of me" and "evidence of us," a kind of social contract that changes over time and space. How do we identify and analyze these relationships between purportedly inanimate and animate objects? One way is through a deep understanding of what, following Gibson (1979), are called "affordances"; that is, a fluid and contingent set of capabilities which define how objects can be used, even as those capabilities differ from user to user and across the spacetime continuum. Affordances are the ways in which nonhuman things or stuff become actors or agents in the construction of knowledge, or what has been termed, in the field of social semiotics, a "dialectical dance" (Sewell, 2005:92). In arguing for a new understanding of the technological shaping of social action rather than an overly simplified and reductive notion of the social shaping of technology, Ian Hutchby (2001) contends that "affordances are not exclusively prop-erties of people or of artifacts – they are constituted in relationships between people and the materiality of the things with which they come in contact … the affordances of an artifact can change across different contexts even though its materiality does not" (Hutchby, in Leonardi, 2010). Perhaps more simply, then, "when those researchers describe digital artifacts as having 'material' properties, aspects, or features, we might safely say that what makes them 'material' is that they provide capabilities that afford or constrain action" (Leonardi, 2010).

The existence of such capabilities or affordances has led to considerable debate about both the materiality and instrumentality of objects, artifacts, and things. Bruno Latour's development of actor–network theory depends on an expansive definition of things to embrace and embody physical objects, animate life-forms, digital objects, concepts, words, bodies of knowledge, and practices as well as a network model of dynamic intersections and translations that register and record the fundamentally "im/mutable mobile" nature of things as actors (Latour, 2005:196). Deleuze and Guattari's (1987) a-linear, non-arboreal concept of rhizomatous networks populated by instanti-ations of vagabond or nomadic things, constantly mutating and morphing, might model society and culture, but it is also a powerful analogy for objects in a world of digital materiality. The cultural heritage or GLAM sector, composed of galleries, libraries, archives, and museums, deals with objects, whether physical, digitized, or born-digital, all the time. The intellectual frameworks, approaches, and activities of information professionals frequently cross over and, as Kaetrena Davis Kendrick (2013) notes, are surprisingly familiar to digital humanists. Given that many digital humanities projects are located in these public institutions, tracking how the GLAM sector responds to the challenges of digital materiality can offer valuable insights. For example, public outreach has recently taken the form of object biographies that expose the rich, human-inflected stories associated with things through pictorial, textual, and audio narratives. This development offers a contemporary twist on eighteenth-century "it-narratives" with their tales of "babbling banknotes, canting coins, prosing pocket watches and soliloquizing snuffboxes" which gave way in the nineteenth century to fictionalized autobiographies of anthropomorphized talking books traveling, often tragicomically, from one owner and one *mise-en-scène* to the next (Price, 2012:108). In order to animate these objects, Neil MacGregor (2010), director of the British Museum and author of *A History of the World in 100 Objects*, talks about the need for "powerful poetic imagining" resulting in the "necessary poetry of things" (MacGregor, 2010: xv–xvi, xxiii). The lives of everyday objects are coupled with a process of revivification that turns the mundane into the extraordinary.

Museum and data curation specialist Costis Dallas captures the ways in which objects and cultures intersect by using the term "thingformation" to describe "a field of activity-laden, material entanglement" in which digital media are defined "as continuity of thing cultures across digital and physical domains." He suggests that a holistic notion of "thing cultures" might serve as a theoretical foundation for epistemically-adequate digital heritage curation (Dallas, 2011: lecture 4) and proposes a radical rethinking not only of what constitutes the "things" that are the object of curation, but of the very cultures in which they are embedded. For digital objects, these might include "digital infrastructures in cultural heritage – collection management systems, databases, digital collections, research repositories, [and] virtual museums – which unfold material things as loci of culturally situated activity" (Dallas, in Sanderson, 2014). Likewise, Sanderson (2014) is concerned with the performative materiality of heritage objects and the systems which mediate between such objects and the researcher community. She draws attention to the close parallels between Dallas's "thingformation" and Upward's' "continuum theory" and argues that the development of knowledge-enabling systems across the GLAM sector would be better served by theory and practice that recognizes the inherently complex nature of objects.

Such a sociological perspective on the interpenetration of things and cultures is shared by philosopher Jane Bennett (2010), who discusses what she terms "thing-power" in the context of vibrant matter and the political ecology of things. Marshaling figures as diverse as Lucretius, Spinoza, Darwin, and Latour, she argues for a vital materialism that works against the grain of anthropocentrism and historical materialism. She contends that "we need to cultivate a bit of anthropomorphism – the idea that human agency has some echoes in nonhuman nature – to counter the narcissism of humans in charge of the world" (Bennett, 2010:xvi). However, like many scholars faced with essentializing materiality, she acknowledges the challenges of trying to describe the self-sufficiency of the object–subject/human–nonhuman relationship. It might very well be, then, that in place of virtuality, magic has become the new space for imagining the digital. Literary scholar Steven Connor's *Paraphernalia: The Curious Lives of Magical Things* (2013) places "enchantment" at the forefront of material culture. Evoking the specific experience rather than the generic type, Connor offers a forensic analysis of personal, material engagements with the once-new: things that impart what he calls "the shock of the newly old." As he remarks:

> such things inhabit space, but are a kind of temporizing with it, a refracting of the white noon of the now into a chronic rainbow of times, with their twilight tints and hues. Such things hum with hint and import because they are there without being fully present; to hand, but not exactly *here-and-now*. (Connor, 2013:8)

From flickering screens to human-techno hybrids, digital materiality is central to the concepts, methods, and practices in and of the digital humanities. Using a toolkit that ranges from the forensic and formal, to distributed and performative materiality, we can reflect on the emergent, yet always historically situated, properties of the here and now. In his short essay "Excavation and memory," Walter Benjamin (1932/2005) posits that it is not the object itself or the inventory of the archaeologist's findings that is important, but rather, the act of marking the precise location where it is found

(Benjamin, 2005:576). In recording such acts of engagement and enchantment, digital humanists inhabit a world of reflective practice shared by media archaeography, and at the heart of which reside key questions about digital materiality. If Jonathan Franzen's *Freedom* (2010) exists as a wireless Kindle download, a torrent-released pirate, a corrupt UK recall, 45 Amazon formats and editions, and a multiverse of social-media engagements generated by Franzen's fan-atics, the history of this work is already complex: even more so if the author's creative process resides in an outmoded Dell machine with its digital palimpsests that may or may not be collected as part of his literary archive (Kirschenbaum and Werner, 2014:423–5). As Ian Hutchby (2001) proposes, "rather than restricting the analytic gaze to the construction of accounts and representations or the technology, we need to pay more attention to the material substratum which underpins the very possibility of different courses of action in relation to an artifact; and which frames the practices through which technologies come to be involved in the weave of ordinary conduct" (Hutchby, 2001:450).

References and Further Reading

Benjamin, W. 2005. *Selected Writings, Vol. 2, part 2 (1931–1934), "Ibizan Sequence" 1932*, ed. M.P. Bullock, M.W. Jennings, H. Eiland, and G. Smith. Cambridge, MA: Belknap Press, 576.

Bennett, J. 2010. Thing-power. In *Political Matter: Technoscience, Semocracy, and Public Life*, ed. S. Whatmore and B. Braun. Minneapolis: University of Minnesota Press.

Bentkowska-Kafel, A., Denard, H., and Baker, D., eds. 2012. *Paradata and Transparency in Virtual Heritage*. Farnham: Ashgate.

Berry, D. 2012. Introduction: understanding digital humanities. In *Understanding Digital Humanities*, ed. D. Berry. London: Palgrave Macmillan, 1–20.

Chandler, J., Davidson, A.I., and Johns, A. 2004. Arts of transmission: an introduction. *Critical Inquiry* 31 (1), 1–6.

Chartier, R., and Cavallo, G. 1999. Introduction. In *A History of Reading in the West*. Amherst: University of Massachusetts Press.

Connor, S. 2013. *Paraphernalia: The Curious Lives of Magical Things*. London: Profile Books.

Dallas, C. 2011. Thingformation: informing thing cultures, curating digital heritage, Lecture series 22 March – 5 April 2011. Digital Curation Institute, Faculty of Information, University of Toronto. http://entopia.org/costisdallas/2011/04/05/spring-lecture-series-at-the-digital-curation-institute-university-of-toronto (accessed January 15, 2014).

Deleuze, G., and Guattari, F. 1987. *A Thousand Plateaus: Capitalism and Schizophrenia*. Trans.

Brian Massumi. Minneapolis: University of Minnesota Press.

Drucker, J. 1994. *The Visible Word: Experimental Typography and Modern Art, 1909–1923*. Chicago: University of Chicago Press.

Drucker, J. 2003. The virtual codex from page space to e-space. http://www.philobiblon.com/drucker (accessed January 15, 2014).

Drucker, J. 2013. Performative materiality and theoretical approaches to interface. *DHQ: Digital Humanities Quarterly* 7 (1). http://digitalhumanities.org:8080/dhq/vol/7/1/000143/000143.html (accessed January 15, 2014).

Eggert, P. 2005. Text-encoding, theories of the text, and the "work-site". *Literary and Linguistic Computing* 20 (4), 425–35.

Erickson, P. 2003. Help or hindrance? The history of the book and electronic media. In *Rethinking Media Change: The Aesthetics of Transition*, ed. D. Thorburn and H. Jenkins. Cambridge, MA: MIT Press, 95–116.

Ernst, W. 2011. Media archaeography: method and machine versus history and narrative of media. In *Media Archaeology. Approaches, Applications, and Implications*, ed. E. Huhtamo and J. Parikka. Berkeley: University of California Press, 239–55.

Galey, A. 2012. "The enkindling reciter": e-books in the bibliographic imagination. *Book History* 15, 210–47.

Geismar, H. 2013. Defining the digital: a comment. *Museum Anthropology Review* 7 (1–2), 254–63. http://scholarworks.iu.edu/journals/index.php/mar (accessed January 15, 2014).

Gibson, J.J. 1979. *The Ecological Approach to Visual Perception*. London: Houghton Mifflin.

Gitelman, L. 2006. *Always Already New. Media, History, and the Data of Culture*. Cambridge, MA: MIT Press.

Hand, M. 2008. *Making Digital Cultures: Access, Interactivity, and Authenticity*. Aldershot: Ashgate.

Hayles, N.K. 2002. *Writing Machines*. Cambridge, MA: MIT Press.

Hayles, N.K. 2012. *How We Think: Digital Media and Contemporary Technogenisis*. Chicago: The University of Chicago Press.

Hindmarsh, J., Heath, C., and Fraser, M. 2006 (Im) materiality, virtual reality and interaction: grounding the "virtual" in studies of technology in action. *The Sociological Review*, 54 (4), 795–817.

Hutchby, I. 2001. Technologies, texts and affordances. *Sociology* 35 (2), 441–56.

Kendrick, K.D. 2013. Keeping the "L" in digital: applying LIS core competencies to digital humanities work. *Journal of Creative Library Practice*. http://creativelibrarypractice.org/2013/09/06/keeping-the-l-in-digital-applying-lis-core-competencies-to-digital-humanities-work (accessed January 15, 2014).

Kirschenbaum, M.G. 2008. *Mechanisms: New Media and the Forensic Imagination*. Cambridge, MA: MIT Press.

Kirschenbaum, M.G., and Werner, S. 2014. Digital scholarship and digital studies: the state of the discipline. *Book History* 17, 406–58.

Latour, B. 2005. *Reassembling the Social: An Introduction to Actor–Network Theory*. Oxford: Oxford University Press.

Lavagnino, J., McCarty, W., and Schreibman, S. 2007. Digital representation and the Hyper Real. http://www.digitalhumanities.org/dh2007/abstracts/xhtml.xq?id=219 (accessed January 15, 2014).

Leonardi, P.M. 2010. Digital materiality? How artefacts without matter, matter. *First Monday* 15, 6–7. http://www.uic.edu/htbin/cgiwrap/bin/ojs/index.php/fm/article/view/3036/2567 (accessed January 15, 2014).

Liu, A. 2004. Transcendental data: toward a cultural history and aesthetics of the new encoded discourse. *Critical Inquiry* 31 (1), 49–84.

MacGregor, N. 2010. *A History of the World in 100 Objects*. New York: Viking. http://www.britishmuseum.org/explore/a_history_of_the_world.aspx (accessed January 15, 2014).

Manoff, M. 2006. The materiality of digital collections: theoretical and historical perspectives. *portal: Libraries and the Academy* 6 (3), 311–25.

McGann, J. 1991. The socialization of texts. In *The Textual Condition*. Princeton, NJ: Princeton University Press, 69–83.

McGann, J. 2001. Visible and invisible books in *n*-dimensional space. In *Radiant Textuality: Literature after the World Wide Web*. London: Palgrave Macmillan, 167–91.

McKemmish, S. 1996. Evidence of me. *Archives and Manuscripts* 24 (1), 28–45. http://www.infotech.monash.edu.au/research/groups/rcrg/publications/recordscontinuum-smckp1.html (accessed January 15, 2014).

McKenzie, D.F. 1999. *Bibliography and the Sociology of Texts*. The Panizzi Lectures (1986). Cambridge: Cambridge University Press.

McKenzie, D.F. 2002. "What's past is prologue": the Bibliographical Society and the history of the book. In *Making Meaning: "Printers of the Mind" and Other Essays*, ed. P.D. McDonald and M.F. Suarez. Amherst: University of Massachusetts Press, 259–75.

Nuttall, S. 2011. The way we read now. http://slipnet.co.za/view/blog/sarah-nuttall/the-way-we-read-now/ (accessed January 15, 2014).

Orlikowski, W. 2006. Material knowing: the scaffolding of human knowledgeability. *European Journal of Information Systems*, 15 (5), 460–6.

Parikka, J. 2012a. New materialism as media theory. medianatures and dirty matter. *Communication and Critical/Cultural Studies* 9 (1), 95–100.

Parikka, J. 2012b. *What is Media Archaeology?* Cambridge: Polity Press.

Price, L. 2009. From the history of a book to a "history of the book". *Representations* 108, 120–38.

Price, L. 2012. *How to Do Things with Books in Victorian Britain*. Princeton and Oxford: Princeton University Press.

Ramsay, S. 2011. *Reading Machines: Toward an Algorithmic Criticism*. Urbana: University of Illinois Press.

Sanderson, K. 2014. Digital materiality, heritage objects, the emergence of evidence, and the design of knowledge enabling systems. PhD thesis, Victoria University of Wellington.

Sewell, W.H.J. 2005. The concept(s) of culture. In *Practicing History: New Directions in Historical Writing after the Linguistic Turn*, ed. G.M. Spiegel. New York: Routledge, 76–95.

Siemens, R., Elkink, M., McColl, A., *et al.* 2010. Underpinnings of the social edition. In *Online Humanities Scholarship: The Shape of Things to Come*, ed. J. McGann. http://cnx.org/content/m34335/1.2 (accessed January 15, 2014).

23

Screwmeneutics and Hermenumericals: The Computationality of Hermeneutics

Joris J. van Zundert

> But as one of my colleagues was fond of saying, humanists came into those conversations as relativists and left as positivists out of pragmatic recognition that certain tenets of critical theory could not be sustained in that environment. (Johanna Drucker, 2012)

Can the computer be a hermeneutical instrument? This question is trivial, for obviously the computer can be. As long as there is a human interpreter any object can be interpreted and can therefore be an instrument of hermeneutical activity. So the question is not if, but how. How can the computer be applied as a hermeneutical instrument of humanities? That question is less trivial, but passes over a number of important precursory questions. First of all: Must the computer be a hermeneutical instrument to humanities? Which again leads to the question: What is the role of hermeneutics in humanities? If we can – at least tentatively – answer that last question, we may progress to evaluate whether digital humanities can and must have a hermeneutics. And if so, the question becomes, how?

On Hermeneutics

Hermeneutics is the theory of text interpretation. The very root (Greek ἑρμηνεύω, *hermeneuō*) means to interpret or to translate. According to folk etymology its origin derives from Hermes, the Greek god-messenger. It is in the nature of Hermes not just to use language as a means of communication, but also to be a corrupter of words, relishing in the confusing power of his messages. He is a god of transitions and boundaries. An apt eponym for hermeneutics, thus – interpretation is the transition of knowledge that happens on the boundary between text and reader. Hermeneutics is

A New Companion to Digital Humanities, First Edition. Edited by Susan Schreibman, Ray Siemens, and John Unsworth.

already referred to in various ways by classic philosophers, but it is Philo of Alexandria who pulls together a first systematic theory which is aimed at uncovering the deeper allegorical meaning of sacred scripture (Ramberg and Gjesdal, 2013). Methodologically connected to the pivotal issue of interpreting the texts of the Bible, hermeneutics plays a central role throughout the history of philosophy, humanistic theory, philology, and literary criticism. There are numerous key works in the development of hermeneutic thinking, but one that should in any case be mentioned is *De Doctrina Christiana* of St. Augustine of Hippo (*c.*400 CE). In his work Augustine unfolds a methodology to interpret the scriptures. But more importantly, in his methodology he connects semiotics – the theory of signs and symbols – to language, and he connects the inter- pretation of language to a deeper existential meaning (cf. Green, 2008). In his theory words are signs that impart cognitive concepts to an interpreter. Just as a natural sign such as smoke signals "fire" to the interpreter, so do words convey meaning as "given" signs of language. The problem is however that this meaning may be literal or meta- phorical. The sun may stand for light of day or for light of vision. The existential aspect is raised when Augustine argues that it is the will and intention of the reader that allows her to address the deeper allegorical interpretation.

From Augustine we take a huge leap through humanistic history and we pass over Thomas Aquinas, Dante, Petrarch, Luther, Spinoza, and many other philosophers and scholars whose names and works stand witness to the profound influence of Augustine's thinking, and of the central role of hermeneutics in the humanistic disciplines (Barolini, 2007; Marchesi, 2011; Ramberg and Gjesdal, 2013). We turn to the early nineteenth century and Friedrich Schleiermacher's contribution to hermeneutic methodology. Schleiermacher points to an important aspect of interpretation, which is that it is in part emphatic in nature. A reader is able to understand a text not just because of a linguistic code shared with the author, but essentially also by sharing a human nature. Thus, a part of the interpretation and part of the meaning of a text is not based on what is in the text, but on what is external to the text. Following, broadening, and formal- izing Schleiermacher's work, Wilhelm Dilthey theorized that works are constructed from the vantage point of a particular worldview held by an author. The interpretation and understanding of a text therefore involves relating the text to the biographic and historical circumstances of its author. For both Dilthey and Schleiermacher a basic assumption is that the meaning of texts is grounded in the intentions and histories of their authors (Mallery, 1986). But more importantly, they believed that these intentions were knowable to later interpreters through reconstruction. Dilthey however recog- nized that this reconstruction would be tainted by the interpreter's present worldview. Interpretation therefore could in his opinion not be objective in a scientific sense of establishing facts empirically. But he argued that aggregation of multiple interpreta- tions could lead to valid and more generalized interpretations.

Both Schleiermacher and Dilthey point us to the fact that any interpretation necessarily involves information that is not in the data itself. This may be information that is available elsewhere in the form of other explicit data, texts, and so on. But inter- pretation also involves the unique cognition of the interpreter, which is tacit. Acknowledging the partly tacit nature of interpretation sets hermeneutics apart from other frames of interpretation such as the probabilistic model of information theory inspired by Claude Shannon.

Around the time of Dilthey's life and work hermeneutics was still tightly connected to philology, which at the start of the twentieth century was very much geared towards establishing texts according to what was perceived as the intent and ideal of the original author. With Heidegger, that was about to change. For the philosopher Martin Heidegger, the hermeneutic process is not a philological tool. Instead hermeneutics scales to an ontological level and becomes philosophical in nature. Interpretation and understanding pertain to all of us as the interplay between our self-understanding and our understanding of the world (Ramberg and Gjesdal, 2013). Heidegger holds that interpretation and understanding are to a great extent intuitive operations. Our understanding of the world is largely an immediate and unreflective grasp of what we sense, based on *a priori* knowledge accumulated from experience. Heidegger believed that this understanding is uniquely subjective. We can only "read ourselves" into a text. A few decades later, philosopher Hans-Georg Gadamer would be less pessimistic and would suggest that a human can transcend his own horizon by being exposed to the discourse and linguistics of others. Even later, Jürgen Habermas and Karl-Otto Apel added pragmatics into the equation – that is, a theory of interpretation and understanding must also take into account the intentionality of linguistics.

Hermeneutics, then, turned from a theory of the interpretation of text into an ontological theory of understanding. It can now be understood broadly as the theory of the processes that turn information into knowledge. As such, the role of hermeneutics in humanities cannot be overestimated: humanities practice is primarily hermeneutic, its main theoretical frame is hermeneutics. Consequently, the way that hermeneutics developed over time has significant ramifications for the epistemology of humanities. Humanities:

> is hermeneutic, intertextual, participatory, value-laden, context dependent, and relatively indeterminate; there are no hierarchical structures of information, no obvious causal explanations and no undisputable truths of any significance to be found. (Chambers, 2000).

The highly relativistic nature of poststructuralist hermeneutics problematizes factuality as veritably factitious. This poses problems for those realms of humanities that are concerned with establishing the concrete humanistic record – for instance in the case of philology, ironically a humanistic pursuit most intimately connected to hermeneutics. Jerome McGann rejects the poststructuralist project of, *inter alia*, Lyotard and Derrida, informed by Heidegger's philosophy, to replace "traditional science with a science of the unknown" (McGann, 2013). McGann reasons that philosophy is rather a subroutine of philology concerned with testing, reconstructing, or falsifying its subjects of attention. The primary concern of philology then is with establishing the archive of what is known or has been known: "Philology is the fundamental science of human memory". McGann reduces the impact of poststructuralist hermeneutics to an "after the fact" reinterpretation of established sources:

> For the philologian, materials are preserved because their simple existence testifies that they once had value, though what that was we can never know completely or even, perhaps, at all. If our current interests supply them with certain kinds of value, these are but Derridean supplements added for ourselves. (McGann, 2013:345–6)

Philology cannot however escape problematic hermeneutics by simply stating that its aim is a factual archive. More often than not, for instance when difficult script is encountered, interpreting medieval manuscript is nontrivial. Thus, even if it poses as merely recording the words glyph by glyph, textual editing involves interpretation. Moreover, a philologist editing a historical text cannot escape actualization without betraying the pragmatics of philology that presupposes making the archive intelligible for a current audience too. A gloss is instrumental in this translation, but therefore also not ahistorical. Any "ahistoric" presupposition of philological hermeneutics is negated by historicality:

> Not only is the decision for one possible correction rather than another already interpretation, but the question of which possibilities of correction occur to the philologist, and which don't, also depends upon his own historical horizon. … The intention toward the historical meaning changes with changes in the conception of history. … Once it has become doubtful that one can experience how it really was, then it is no less doubtful that one is in the position to establish how something was meant once. (Szondi and Bahti, 1978)

This severely upsets traditional philology, which "believes itself to be independent of its own historical point of view." Fiormonte and Pusceddu (2006) problematized in a similar vain the temporal dimension of text, arguing that genetic editions also cannot escape fundamental subjectivity: "one might say that up to now we have analyzed the literary text according to the laws of the pre-Heisenbergian universe, i.e., inside a stable system, in which the observer does not modify the object observed." *Mutatis mutandis* this "hermeneutic condition" can be generalized to many subfields of humanities. The study of history, for example, being dependent on a humanistic record as well, is affected similarly.

The Hermeneutics of Digital Humanities

Does digital humanities have a hermeneutics like humanities does? Given that digital humanities is humanities too, the answer must be yes. However, there seems to be no focused program to uncover the hermeneutics of digital humanities. I want to investigate whether a call for attention to this hermeneutics, if not a specific program, is a necessity for digital humanities. Rafael Capurro (2010) seems to have come closest to calling for a programmatic approach to digital hermeneutics. Capurro states that the Internet challenges hermeneutics because of its social relevance for the creation, communication, and interpretation of knowledge. That is, the Internet makes the creation and sharing of knowledge a more open and social activity. A problem in addressing this challenge is that the last part of the twentieth century saw a pseudo-critical rejection of hermeneutics with regard to technology in general and to digital technology in particular. But it is exactly digital technology, and more particularly the Internet, that has ontological implications or implications for how we are and behave as humans: the Internet shapes important parts of human expression and experience, and conversely humans shape the Internet as a technology by expressing themselves through it. According to Capurro, a resulting problem is that humans only very partially control the network that they shape but that is importantly shaping them.

A counterargument could be that individual humans also only very partially control their physical environment, and that moreover the power of control is unevenly distributed in the virtual as well as in the physical environment. However, Capurro's more important point is that the network is shaping us in more fundamental ways than we may realize. Our lives are increasingly expressed through digital technologies that function as extensions of our minds and bodies: we are different on Facebook, and Facebook makes us different in real life too. This raises questions of a particularly humanistic nature, and Capurro concludes that current hermeneutics fails to address these questions that "go far beyond the horizon of classic hermeneutics as a theory of text interpretation as well as beyond classic philosophic hermeneutics."

If current hermeneutics is unable to address such questions, this may explain the relative lack of theory on hermeneutics we find in digital humanities. The dialog surrounding hermeneutics seems not to have developed fully yet in digital humanities – references to hermeneutics are scant and often at a concrete level of the practice of text interpretation, such as when Katherine Hayles (2012) uses the phrase "hermeneutic close reading." Yet from several paragraphs and sections in the literature the emergence of a debate seems traceable. Like Capurro, Fred Gibbs and Trevor Owens (2012) have made programmatic claims for a hermeneutics of history writing. Their argument concentrates on data. Data has always been used by historians, but the vast quantities of it that become available should mean "that 'using' signifies a much broader range of activities." Gibbs and Owens argue that using data is not the same as fully conforming to the epistemic burden of the statistician. A playful iterative approach to quantitative tools, explorative and deliberately without the complete formal mathematical rigor, can serve to use large amounts of data to discover and frame research questions. Data does not always have to be used as evidence; in a variety of forms it can provoke new questions and explorations. Data analytics need not be by definition mathematical. "Historians must treat data as text, which needs to be approached from multiple points of view and as openly as possible" (Gibbs and Owens, 2012).

Like many contributions in the theory on digital humanities, the article by Gibbs and Owens refers to the opposition between quantification and narrative as methodological means. They write about the "epistemological jitter" and "hostility to data" on the side of historians. Their solution to this conundrum is that data can be read as text. This is true, but it is also an unsatisfactory and incomplete solution to the problem. The presupposition of data-as-text reduces the hermeneutical act to a post-processing of what remains of data after the processes of curation, analysis, and visualization. However, those processes of curation, analysis, and visualization have a hermeneutics of their own. The dialog on the hermeneutics of digital humanities cannot therefore simply posit a dichotomy between the quantitative and qualitative, and relegate hermeneutics to a qualitative aspect of interpretation of given data as if this data would not be value-laden and interpreted already. It is along these lines too that Federica Frabetti – like Capurro – has argued that new technologies affect cultural understanding. She proposes a re-conceptualization of digital humanities that indeed transcends an assumed dichotomy between the technical and the cultural aspects. Such "must be pursued through a close, even intimate, engagement with digitality and with software itself" (Frabetti, 2012). Thus part of the hermeneutics of digital humanities relates to the hermeneutics of code, computation, and quantification.

A close or even intimate engagement between digitality and hermeneutics has however not been a main concern of digital humanities. Rather, the opposite has been stressed. In a 1995 issue of *Literary and Linguistic Computing* Lisa Lena Opas-Hänninen writes: "Only where indexing and sampling are concerned does the computer offer useful help in computer-assisted literary studies. So the impact of computer-assisted techniques sets in before the interpretation and evaluation of the text begins." Looking back, Opas-Hänninen's introduction reads like a very careful attempt to avoid stating that computational analysis in the realm of literary studies can go beyond anything but a pre-hermeneutical support tool. Jan Christoph Meister in the same volume – carefully? – formulates that:

> an intelligent and well-balanced application of literary computing tools allows us to reconcile the two paradigms by measuring and mapping difference in literary structures, and then forwarding them to the ultimate hermeneutic machine, the human mind. (Meister, 1995)

Both Opas-Hänninen and Meister at the time argued that the hermeneutical potential of digital technology is limited by the fact that "only questions that can be formalized are open to electronic analysis in literary studies and this is why computer-assisted techniques can cover only part of the work of the literary critic in certain, clearly defined areas of application" (Opas-Hänninen, 1995). Meister draws a very strong opposition between the numerical and semantic paradigms: the first is connected to computing, the second to hermeneutics. His argument is basically that semantics do not apply in the computational paradigm. Algorithms can manipulate or process objects, but only insofar as they can be formalized and quantified. Computational operations are strictly and unambiguously transformative: "results are effectively nothing but a more or less sophisticated re-formulation … of the original data input." But these transparent repetitions and permutations of data are redundant in the semantic paradigm. When it comes to hermeneutics, "only those results that are different, that happen to question the validity or confinements of the procedures which produced them, will ultimately be found to be relevant and noteworthy." In retrospect it is intriguing that Meister did not consider at the time a distinctly hermeneutic conse- quence of this argument. Algorithmic transformations can in fact lead to identification of results that are different, and thus not "hermeneutically" neutral. Firstly, even a rudimentary indexing algorithm can transform the full text of a book into a list of terms used more than average per chapter, and can subsequently single out the chapter that shows the least terminological overlap. Is this not a hermeneutics expressed through the algorithm? Secondly, we can consider the breakdown of software. As long as the algorithm only transforms data, it may not be a hermeneutical thing. But it may become so when it falters over some input and breaks down or spews inconsistent and unexpected results. This is akin to what we find in Heidegger's work, which holds that only a breakdown in practice leads to theoretical knowledge (Froesse, 2006). As long as a hammer is a hammer, it is a hammer; only when it is broken do we consider its function and how it works.

Twenty years on, the consideration of hermeneutics in the digital humanities does not seem to have moved beyond a basic opposition between patterns and narrative, or quantification versus interpretation, that can already be discerned in Meister's strong binary opposition between the numerical and the semantic. This opposition often surfaces as an apparent ideological or political opposition between humanities and digital humanities. Stanley Fish for example has qualified digital humanities as just another fad answering to a crisis of legitimization of the humanities (Fish, 2010, 2011). Others point to the ideologies and institutional motivations of innovation, which certainly are not neutral (e.g., Piersma and Ribbens, 2013). These crises or ideologies, even if they exist, do not relieve us from critically evaluating the ramifications of emerging digital technologies for hermeneutics. In the first place, these technologies are increasingly used to create the humanistic artifacts that are the objects of study in the humanities. In the second place, we are applying these technologies for the capture and analysis of research data. Both of these processes, motivated by digital technologies, affect our modes of interpretation in nontrivial ways. Piersma and Ribbens argue that evaluation of these digital technologies is "even more urgent in view of the frequently implicit claims ... that technological progress also implies a new historical-scientific paradigm" – a paradigm based on quantified approaches, on computational analysis of big data, and subsequent serendipitous finds in such big data.

From the perspective of hermeneutics, however, the literature in digital humanities does not seem to justify presupposing an implicit turn to a scientific paradigm. Geoffrey Rockwell (2003), writing on the hermeneutics of text analysis, refers to the French eighteenth-century philosopher Étienne Bonnot de Condillac: analysis merely consists of composing and decomposing our ideas to create new combinations and to discover, by this means, their mutual relations and the new ideas they can produce. Rockwell argues that there is no *a priori* privilege of any procedure for deconstruction and reconfiguration. But a potential *a priori* for coherence and homogeneity in computational data analysis may have been inadvertently introduced at the very onset of automated text analysis, which is tied to the computationally constructed concordance by Roberto Busa that was commenced in the late 1940s. Concordancing aims to discover patterns of coherence in a text or corpus – in a hermeneutically naive way because it assumes that a word will have the same meaning and weight wherever it occurs. Yet even the algorithmic creation of concordances shows how deconstruction of a text and subsequent reconfiguration leads to a new text, namely the very concordance. But that is just one method of reconfiguration. To escape naive biases we should shed habitual practices and any axiomatic primacy of unity and coherence. To this end Rockwell – following Gadamer and Huizinga – suggests a hermeneutics of disciplined play that privileges experimentation and modeling, rather than a narrow quantified empirics.

Stephen Ramsay, even more than Rockwell, emphatically denies a scientific paradigm for hermeneutics.

> For decades the dominant assumption within humanities computing ... has been that if the computer is to be useful to the humanist, its efficacy must necessarily lie in the aptness of the scientific metaphor for humanistic study. (Ramsay, 2011)

Ramsay takes the contrary view, and proposes that the scientific method and metaphor are, for the most part, incompatible with the terms of humanistic endeavor and only lead to a distorted epistemology called "scientism." Ramsay follows Gadamer by stating that the hermeneutic phenomenon is basically not a problem of method at all. Hermeneutics is simply not concerned with amassing verified knowledge of the sort that would satisfy the methodological idea of science. Rather, literary criticism operates within a hermeneutical framework in which the specifically scientific meaning of fact, metric, verification, and evidence do not apply. Yet humanities too is concerned with knowledge and with truth, just of a different kind than that of science. Ramsay has also argued that the availability of vastly more digital data essentially does not change the hermeneutic assumptions of humanities. The fact is that there has always been too much information available to synthesize individually in full; the digital age just makes this condition more apparent. But now as ever hermeneutics involves finding a purposely selective and subjective path through too much information. This is the basic assumption underlying what Ramsay (2010) calls the hermeneutics of screwing around. For Ramsay the "screwmeneutical imperative" is nothing more or less than the realization of Roland Barthes' concept of "writerly text," which is the text a reader constructs by reducing all possible meanings of a text to one that is his own interpretation of it.

In the realm of markup, in the digital humanities predominantly represented by the Text Encoding Initiative (TEI), possible scientism seems not to be a very relevant issue either. This may be partly due to the descriptive rather than analytic nature of markup. The hermeneutic dialog within this domain concerns itself more with the issue of multi-perspectivity. Like Ramsay, Lou Burnard points to poststructuralist ideas:

> Texts, and other artifacts alike, are invested with meaning by our use of them, and it is therefore interpretation alone which confers value on them. Small wonder that Derrida, citing Montaigne, takes it as self-evident that "We need to interpret interpretations more than to interpret things." (Burnard, 1998)

Authorial intention, reconstruction, and original reading are concepts that have become unfashionable, Burnard admits, but he follows Dilthey by saying that there "is ample evidence that not all interpretations are equally useful or have equal explanatory force." He suggests that canonicity is in this sense a hermeneutics of aggregation. Burnard also embraces the poststructuralist idea of intertextuality: the reading and the meaning of a text is in part constructed by the references made to other texts. The rationale for markup then is that it provides a single formalized semiotic system that is able to function as an interlingua for the sharing of the multitude of individual interpretations that through aggregation can lead to a critical consensus. The claim that a single all-encompassing semiotic system is possible, and that technologies such as SGML/ XML and DTDs could be an implementation of it, has since been severely contested. Many theorists and practitioners (e.g., Buzzetti and McGann, 2006; Fiormonte and Pusceddu, 2006; Schmidt and Colomb, 2009) find that the single-hierarchy approach to text structuring that the TEI enforces does not fit well with a multitude of possible structural and semantic interpretations. In itself this dialog testifies to the fact that the approach to text encoding within the textual scholarship and digital humanities communities is primarily hermeneutically oriented.

Thus a computational turn does not automatically imply a turn to empiricism and scientism, or a disregard for hermeneutic tradition. Stylometry and the "school" of distant reading (Moretti, 2005; Jockers, 2013) may lean in their approaches more towards an empiricist or scientistic attitude. This is mainly to be attributed to the intensive use of quantification and – more importantly – statistics in those avenues of research. The work of researchers such as David Hoover (2013), Ted Underwood (2010), Karina van Dalen-Oskam (2011), Matthew Jockers, and Franco Moretti is methodologically strongly based in statistics, corpus linguistics, and natural language processing. Those methodologies are numerically inclined indeed, but this does not preclude hermeneutics – numbers of course allow interpretation too. Quantification does however introduce the problem of reduction. Current statistic approaches to stylometry, for example, are based predominantly on word frequencies and co-occurrence analyses of the surface structures of text. But aggregating words based solely on their form usually blinds these methods to more subtle semantic relations such as homonymy, metaphors, anaphors, and so on, that are also hermeneutically important. This does not however discredit numerical approaches as hermeneutical instruments. In fact they may contribute very strong hermeneutical support.

For instance, Mike Kestemont (2012) has shown using statistical means such as principal component analysis that the medieval Dutch Arthurian novel *Moriaen* stylistically stands out from the medieval compilation of Arthurian texts that it is a member of. The text forms a much closer stylistic unit with two other texts, one of which is not even an Arthurian novel but a story in the realm of the so-called *matière de France* pertaining to the culture, court, and principal personae during the reign of Charlemagne. Based on all we know about medieval Dutch genre and literary history this claim would be outrageous, were it not for a 1970s posthumously published work by a Dutch philologist that had already alluded to these possibilities. Most interestingly, that philologist and poet, Klaas Heeroma, based his conjecture on a fundamentally hermeneutic principle: he claimed he "heard" the kinship between the novels. Somewhat ironically, what is now often perceived of as one of the least hermeneutical instruments – number-crunching-based principle component analysis – indicates that Heeroma's hermeneutical "sixth sense" was right.

The example above draws our attention to another problem inherent in current quantified approaches in digital humanities. As Gibbs and Owens (2012) also point out, neighbor joining, maximum-parsimony phylogenetic trees, z-scores and such probabilistic methods that are used in stemma reconstruction, authorship attribution, and various other computational approaches seem foremost to be used as instruments of reaffirmation. They verify authorship, and they confirm canonicity and genre. They do not answer new questions, but rather solidify existing answers. This may very well be a simple sign of a field in development, of relatively immature application. However, if this confirmation bias were a genuine trait of a specific angle on quantified approaches by digital humanities, then again this would set it apart from the scientific paradigm of falsification rather than import it wholesale into the humanities. So far, quantified approaches in the digital humanities also show a relative lack of explanatory power. Stylometry, for example, can tell us – or rather indicate to us – that there are two authors of a certain text (Dalen-Oskam and Zundert, 2007). But it tells us unsatisfactorily little about how and why the individual styles differ. Engaging and uncovering the "black box" effect of such methods could in due course turn the practice of stylometry into the pursuit of a literary hermeneutics – like conventional hermeneutics but with different means.

The Computationality of Hermeneutics

Quantified approaches and distant reading currently have good press. But we should be careful not to identify digital humanities solely with these approaches. The field is decidedly broader (cf. for instance Alvarado, 2012). There is a tendency in debates to reduce the potential of computation to a methodology of quantification. The nature of digital humanities is hybrid, however, and there is not an *a priori* discontinuity with the hermeneutic traditions. We still maintain that knowledge has an interpretative character – that the state of an object is determined by its context and is dependent on the observer's interpretation. Computer-mediated text turned text into something computationally tractable. Starting with the work of Father Busa, this made the application of quantified approaches to text feasible and practical. Computational tractability, however, does not dictate quantification and a probabilistic approach. These approaches have been inspired by their success in computational linguistics, a field informed substantially by a positivist and structuralist tradition. This tradition holds that knowledge has a causal deterministic character so that the state of any given object is necessarily determined by its prior states. Probabilistics and, for instance, the Markov models that underpin many natural language processing algorithms derive ultimately from such a positivist deterministic philosophy (cf. Vandoulakis, 2011). Johanna Drucker unequivocally denied the applicability of deterministic computational methods to problems of humanistic nature:

> Positivistic, strictly quantitative, mechanistic, reductive and literal, these visualization and processing techniques preclude humanistic methods from their operations because of the very assumptions on which they are designed: that objects of knowledge can be understood as self-identical, self-evident, ahistorical, and autonomous. (Drucker, 2012)

This summarizes quite succinctly the problems inherent in probabilistic approach that can only lead to "naive empiricism" (Drucker, 2010).

Grounding the bulk of digital humanities methodology in quantification and deterministic reasoning may have far-reaching disruptive implications. Katherine Hayles pointed out that digital humanities as a field may converge towards traditional humanities or diverge from it as its own field, depending on how digital humanities articulates itself with respect to conventional humanities.

> The kinds of articulation that emerge have strong implications for the future: will the digital humanities become a separate field whose interests are increasingly remote from the traditional humanities, or will it on the contrary become so deeply entwined with questions of hermeneutic interpretation that no self-respecting traditional scholar could remain ignorant of its results? (Hayles, 2012)

Thus Hayles ties a successful interaction of digital humanities with the traditional humanities to the question of how well digital humanities will be able to cater to hermeneutics. The extent to which the hermeneutic approach is fundamental to the humanities is, however, not always well understood. In his recent history of the humanities, Rens Bod dedicates a mere two pages to the concept and history of hermeneutics, in a section titled "Hermeneutics and the anticipatory 'method'" (Bod, 2013:333–4). He disposes of the "method" as being based on guesswork and premonitions. This dismissal might be cast aside as anecdotal were it not for Bod's position as professor of computational and digital humanities, investigating the humanities from both a computational and a historical perspective. Within the dichotomy between patterns and narrative, Bod has decidedly opted for patterns as a primary principle of investigation. Leaning strongly towards a deterministic paradigm, he concludes that inferences can only be valid based on patterns to be discovered in the researched data. Another example of a dialog between the realms of computation and humanities reveals an interesting "computational" perspective on the fundamental importance of the concept of context to hermeneutics:

> We do not exclude the possibility that there may be other relationships that can constitute a valid narrative. ... However, such examples are context-dependent, and not easily generalizable, we therefore ... limit our focus to the prototypical narrative structures described. (Akker *et al.*, 2011)

This quote derives from a project whose particular aim was to find a suitable formalization for (historic) events and to build narratives – i.e., historical accounts – from these. The statement reveals the clear tension between hermeneutic context-dependency and the thrust towards the generalization needed for computational tractability. The generalization requires events to be formalized or modeled so they can be computationally traced and quantified. Researchers try to escape the problematic hermeneutics by reducing the number and type of relations that events can maintain. But the problem stubbornly persists, because formalizations and patterns are not hermeneutics-free. Just as philological practice cannot escape a certain hermeneutics, neither modeling nor quantification can escape the hermeneutics involved in choosing the basic assumptions onto which the formalizations are founded. Pasanek and Sculley, in their article on "Mining millions of metaphors," point out that in this respect there is no such a thing as a free lunch:

> It is important to avoid the illusion that automated analysis is somehow more objective or less biased than traditional methods. There is no new infallible science of literature forthcoming. As the "No Free Lunch" Theorem states, every machine learning method requires the acceptance of base level assumptions, such as the appropriate choice of distance metric or the shape of the probability distribution underlying the data. These assumptions must, at some level, be taken on faith, and influence the results of automated analysis, just as cultural and theoretical biases influence traditional analysis. (Pasanek and Sculley, 2008)

As with quantified approaches, there is a hermeneutics to any formalization. Textual scholars from Bernard Cerquiglini (1999) to Peter Shillingsburg (2013) hold that an edition of a text is not that text itself, but an intellectual argument about it. A digital edition is an interpretation, and in exactly the same sense formalizations and models are interpretations. A simple example for this is a database field, which is nothing more or less than a category label. Category labels, databases, and data models: all are models, necessarily narrow representations of aspects of reality. Confronting any database with reality, one will encounter observations that will not fit to any of the defined database fields. Therefore most data models exclude certain properties of data, which poses problems in a field such as humanities that works primarily with highly complex, heterogeneous, and nonconcrete data. To fit the observations to the chosen categories or properties of the model is to fit a subjectively observed reality to the interpretation expressed by the model. The effect is that the chosen formalization imposes a particular interpretation on a set of data that does not really fit, reducing to a certain extent the richness and complexity of the body of information. The quantitative model or data model is an impressionistic primer onto which more interpretation is painted. Thus statistics and models inform interpretative narrative on the basis of formalized reductive interpretations.

If formalizations, models, and quantifications have hermeneutics too, we can concur with Katherine Hayles (2012) when she states that the tension between algorithmic analysis and hermeneutic close reading should not be overstated. Hayles argues that often there is not an opposition but a synergetic interaction between algorithmic analysis and close interpretative reading. She points to the example of what Matthew Kirschenbaum has called "rapid shuttling," which involves a repetitive switching between the modes of close reading and of interpretation of big data analysis results, comparing the interpretations those different modes yield. Ramsay (2011), when talking about "algorithmic criticism," also points to this recursive interaction between corpus analytics and close reading that can inform humanistic inquiry of texts. What these views share is that the act of interpretation is postponed to a post-algorithmic phase. Only when the computation has been done and the algorithms and number crunching produce visualizations does the interpretative act come to the fore. This type of digital humanities hermeneutics therefore faces outward and away from the computational model, the math, and the code. It interprets only the results of the algorithmic or quantitative phase. But if it is true that algorithms and models have hermeneutics too, then should these not somehow be taken into account in establishing the validity of interpretations done in algorithmic analysis?

David Berry, like Katherine Hayles, does not:

> want to overplay the distinction between pattern and narrative as differing modes of analysis. Indeed, patterns implicitly require narrative in order to be understood, and it can be argued that code itself consists of a narrative form that allows databases, collections and archives to function at all. (Berry, 2012)

Instead of dismissing code and algorithm as hermeneutic domains, Berry is arguing for a more intertwined articulation of humanities and computer science in this respect. He proposes that digital humanities in part should also concentrate on the underlying computationality of the forms held within a computational medium: "[T]o understand the contemporary born-digital culture and the everyday practices that populate it … we need a corresponding focus on the computer code that is entangled with all aspects of our lives." According to Berry there is an "undeniable" cultural dimension to computation as well, which points to the importance of engaging with and understanding code: "Understanding digital humanities is in some sense then understanding code." Berry argues that computational techniques are not merely an instrument wielded by traditional methods. Rather, they have profound effects on all aspects of the disciplines because the computational logic is entangled with the digital representations of physical objects, texts and "born-digital" artifacts. But the way in which the digital archive is deeply computational and the ramifications of that computationality are currently not well understood, and cannot be understood without a deep dialog between humanities and computer science. Federica Frabetti (2012), reasoning along similar lines, concludes that such "an understanding must be pursued through a close, even intimate, engagement with digitality and with software itself" – which is not without problems, as digital humanities and computer science have no readily available mutually informed way of examining software, and because it is:

> especially difficult for those not active in the field of the digital humanities to see how the creation of digital surrogates of analog materials, the development of tools to support visualization and analysis, and the contribution of high-end computing skills ... constitute research. (Schreibman *et al.*, 2011)

In the domain of textual scholarship Elena Pierazzo has drawn attention to a similar need to understand coding intimately. Like others, she holds that editing a text is "interpretative and irreversible." She follows Claus Huitfeldt and Michael Sperberg-McQueen in stating that a transcription of a text consists of "a systematic program of selective alteration." Thus it is very unlikely that two scholars, even given the same transcriptional criteria, will produce the same transcription of the same exemplar (Pierazzo, 2011). As scholarly editing moves into a digital environment, computational approaches and programming acquire substantial roles and responsibilities in the creation of digital scholarly editions. Pierazzo therefore argues that this role of programming should not be underestimated, and, more importantly, "neither [should] its implicit scholarly content." Coming from a different angle but reaching a similar conclusion, Alan Galey and Stan Ruecker (2010) call attention to the design of artifacts as a critical and hermeneutical act. They argue that digital humanities must not lose sight of design as an act that shapes the meanings of artifacts, and that is no less vital to the interpretative potential of digital artifacts. Galey and Ruecker draw an analogy between software design and the textual and material design involved in book production: "By understanding how fields like book history take the design decisions embedded in physical artifacts as interpretive objects, we can begin to see digital humanists' creation of new digital artifacts as interpretive acts." Digital humanities as yet lacks a deep understanding of digital text production and software design, whereas we have a well-defined understanding of the roles of non-authorial agents in print and manuscript book production, such as scribes, binders, typographers, compositors, correctors, and illustrators (Galey and Ruecker, 2010).

The choices and methods involved in software design do shape the hermeneutics of digital humanities. Modeling encompasses the worldview of the model designer, her context, and her subjective decisions. Data models are anything but neutral – on the contrary, they are a purposefully specific selection of semantic categories and properties. Programming languages have paradigms that affect hermeneutics. Moreover, the reciprocal shaping of the hermeneutics of digital humanities by the methods of computer science extends beyond software design. The choices made in the analytical conception of any given digital humanities project affect its hermeneutic makeup. The choices of what properties to quantify, what probability distribution functions are chosen, which statistical tests are used, are in essence hermeneutically informed. Arguably these choices are currently in large part left implicitly to the experts and professionals of software design and computer science. Computer science as a field, however, is grounded not in a problematizing paradigm but in a problem-solving one. Computer scientists and software engineers have a strong generalizing proclivity. Their reasoning tends toward the inductive: solve a specific problem in a specific context and then scale the solution to general applicability. This propensity invites positivistic reasoning and reductive determinism that favors patterns and relegates the exception to the status of "corner case." These characteristics fit poorly with a humanities that is accustomed to reasoning from heterogeneous information, that favors multi-perspectivity, and that problematizes as a means to create knowledge, perspectives, and understanding. The eventual articulation of digital humanities with respect to conventional humanities – and the implications for the future that Katherine Hayles described – will depend to a great extent on how well the intimate dialog between humanities and computer science as discussed by Frabetti and Berry is established. As Galey and Ruecker showed, little attention is currently paid to the hermeneutical implications of the software design aspect. Similarly little attention is given to the hermeneutical implications of data modeling and of analytical models applied in computer science and other fields that inform the digital humanities, such as mathematics and artificial intelligence. Thus at a very fundamental level and in a substantial part of its research chain the hermeneutics of digital humanities is driven by software designers and computer scientists. This means that in practice the hermeneutic choices of digital humanities are made substantially by software designers and computer scientists. Failure to reflect critically on these choices may all too easily lead to a naive scientism permeating the digital humanities, born from the generalizing and problem-solving nature of computer science and software engineering.

Stephen Ramsay (2011) argues that it is possible to make algorithmic procedures conform to the hermeneutical methodology of humanistic critical inquiry without transforming the nature of computation. Be that as it may, this conformity will not come about without a fundamental dialog between humanities and computer science – a dialog that is not part of Ramsay's hermeneutics for digital humanities, focused as this is on post-algorithmic acts of interpretation. However, a substantial part of the specific nature of digital humanities hermeneutics arises exactly from the nature of computation. This nature need not be reductive, deterministic, absolute, and quantified, as is so often implied. Rather, we have here a rationale for exploring "hermenumericals," a hermeneutics of computation that could complement Ramsay's post-algorithmic "screwmeneutics." Computation need not be a domain of absolute numbers and binary logic. In the field of artificial intelligence, non-binary reasoning and expression of uncertainty has progressed considerably (cf. Russell and Norvig, 2009). There are subtler computing logics than the first-order logic that currently makes up the bulk of commonly used computer languages (cf. Forbus, 2008; Pratt, 1976). Some are concerned, for example, with modeling intuitive notions of truth and validity. Their nature may be a much closer fit for the hermeneutics of humanities. Exploration of the hermeneutic potential of computation is a challenge that digital humanities could pose, to itself and to computer science on behalf of the humanities. This need not imply transforming the nature of computation, but it must involve remediating the nature of hermeneutics through computational logic and design informed strongly by a dialog with humanities. It is apparent that scientific methods deriving from the humanities would be more appropriate than scientism for artificial intelligence and computer science when interacting with the humanities (cf. Mallery, 1986).

Conclusion

Unquestionably there is a role for hermeneutics in digital humanities. Thus the question becomes: What does such a hermeneutics look like? Capurro has shown how profound the ontological implications of digitality are for cultural dynamics and for the creation of humanistic artifacts. From this it follows that humanities must consider the extent and characteristics of a hermeneutics that takes the digital into consideration. Current practice shows, if it was not already self-evident, that conventional hermeneutics in its form of "post-algorithmic" interpretation takes up a large and undeniable part. At the same time, as we apply algorithms, models, and quantification, there arises an urgent need to understand the effect of these analytic methods on our hermeneutics. We have seen that the design of analytic methods is not free of its own hermeneutics. The effects and ramifications of these implicit hermeneutics on humanistic interpretation and reasoning are nevertheless unclear, poorly understood, and hardly studied. To understand these effects more fully – that is, to understand the hermeneutics of algorithmic and quantified approaches – we need a constructive and intimate dialog with the domains of computer science and software design. We cannot simply face outward after the algorithmic fact and interpret its results without implicitly but unconscientiously being a proxy to its hermeneutics. The profound effects of the digital on human culture and the humanities demands that we fully grasp its potential for hermeneutics.

REFERENCES AND FURTHER READING

Akker, C. van den, Legêne, S., Erp, M. van, *et al.* 2011. Digital hermeneutics: agora and the online understanding of cultural heritage. *Proceedings of the ACM WebSci'11.* Koblenz: ACM WebSci'11, 1–7. http://www.websci11.org/fileadmin/websci/Papers/116_paper.pdf (accessed June 20, 2015).

Alvarado, R.C. 2012. The digital humanities situation. In *Debates in the Digital Humanities,* ed. M.K. Gold. Minneapolis: University of Minnesota Press, 50–5. http://dhdebates.gc.cuny.edu/debates/text/50 (accessed February 12, 2014).

Barolini, T. 2007. Introduction. In *Petrarch and the Textual Origins of Interpretation,* ed. T. Barolini,

and H.W. Storey. Columbia Studies in the Classical Tradition. Leiden, Boston: Brill, 1–12.

Bod, R. 2013. *A New History of the Humanities: The Search for Principles and Patterns from Antiquity to the Present.* Oxford: Oxford University Press.

Burnard, L. 1998. On the hermeneutic implications of text encoding. In *New Media in the Humanities: Research and Applications: Proceedings of the first seminar on Computers, Literature and Philology,* ed. D. Fiormonte and J. Usher. Edinburgh: New Media in the Humanities: Research and Applications, 39–45. http://users.ox.ac.uk/~lou/wip/herman.htm (accessed February 12, 2014).

Buzzetti, D., and McGann, J. 2006. Critical editing in a digital horizon. In *Electronic Textual Editing*, ed. L. Burnard, K. O'Brien O'Keeffe, and J. Unsworth. New York: Modern Language Association, 53–73. http://www.tei-c.org/Activities/ETE/Preview (accessed February 12, 2014).

Capurro, R. 2010. Digital hermeneutics: an outline. *AI & Society* 35 (1), 35–42.

Cerquiglini, B. 1999. *In Praise of the Variant: A Critical History of Philology*. Baltimore: Johns Hopkins University Press.

Chambers, E. 2000. Editorial: Computers in humanities teaching and research. *Computers and the Humanities* 34 (3), 245–54.

Dalen-Oskam, K. van. 2011. Karina van Dalen-Oskam. http://www.huygens.knaw.nl/en/vandalen (accessed January 17, 2014).

Dalen-Oskam, K. van, and Zundert, J.J. van. 2007. Delta for middle Dutch: author and copyist distinction in "Walewein". *Literary and Linguistic Computing* 22 (3), 345–62.

Drucker, J. 2010. Graphesis: visual knowledge production and representation. *Poetess Archive Journal* 2 (1). http://journals.tdl.org/paj/index. php/paj/article/view/4 (accessed February 12, 2014).

Drucker, J. 2012. Humanistic theory and digital scholarship. In *Debates in the Digital Humanities*, ed. M.K. Gold. Minneapolis: University of Minnesota Press. http://dhdebates.gc.cuny.edu/ debates/text/34 (accessed February 12, 2014).

Fiormonte, D., and Pusceddu, C. 2006. The text as a product and as a process: history, genesis, experiments. In *Manuscript, Variant, Genese – Genesis*, ed. E. Vanhoutte, M. de Smedt. Gent: KANTL, 109–28. http://www.academia. edu/618689/The_Text_As_a_Product_and_ As_a_Process._History_Genesis_Experiments (accessed February 12, 2014).

Fish, S. 2010. The crisis of the humanities officially arrives. http://opinionator.blogs.nytimes. com/2010/10/11/the-crisis-of-the-humanities- officially–arrives (accessed January 12, 2014).

Fish, S. 2011. The old order changeth. *New York Times: Opinionator*. http://opinionator.blogs. nytimes.com/2011/12/26/the-old-order-changeth (accessed February 26, 2014).

Forbus, K.D. 2008. Qualitative modeling. In *Handbook of Knowledge Representation: Foundations of Artificial Intelligence*, ed. F. van Harmelen, V. Lifschitz, and B. Porter. Amsterdam: Elsevier, 361–94.

Frabetti, F. 2012. Have the humanities always been digital? In *Understanding Digital Humanities*, ed. D. Berry. London: Palgrave Macmillan, 161–71.

Froesse, K. 2006. *Nietzsche, Heidegger, and Daoist Thought: Crossing Paths In-Between*. Albany: State University of New York Press.

Galey, A., and Ruecker, S. 2010. How a prototype argues. *Literary and Linguistic Computing* 25 (4), 405–24.

Gibbs, F., and Owens, T. 2012. The hermeneutics of data and historical writing. In *Writing History in the Digital Age*, ed. J. Dougherty and K. Nawrotzki. http://writinghistory.trincoll. edu/data/gibbs-owens-2012-spring (accessed January 17, 2014).

Gleick, J. 2011. *The Information: A History, A Theory, A Flood*. New York: Pantheon.

Green, R.P.H., ed. 2008. St. Augustine of Hippo, *On Christian Teaching*. First published 1997, reissued 1999, 2008. Oxford: Oxford University Press.

Hayles, K.N. 2012. *How We Think: Digital Media and Contemporary Technogenesis*. Chicago: University of Chicago Press.

Hoover, D. 2013. Selected print and web publications, https://files.nyu.edu/dh3/public/ SelectedPublications.html (accessed January 17, 2014).

Jockers, M.L. 2013. *Macroanalysis: Digital Methods and Literary History*. Urbana: University of Illinois Press.

Kestemont, M. 2012. *Het Gewicht van de Auteur: Een onderzoek naar Stylometrische Auteursherkenning in de Middelnederlandse Epiek*. Antwerpen: Universiteit Antwerpen, Faculteit Letteren en Wijsbegeerte, Departementen Taal- en Letterkunde.

Mallery, J.C., Hurwitz, R., and Duffy, G. 1986. Hermeneutics: from textual explanation to computer understanding? *AI Memos*, Memo AIM-871. http://hdl.handle.net/1721.1/6438http://hdl. handle.net/1721.1/6438 (accessed January 17, 2014).

Marchesi, S. 2011. *Dante and Augustine: Linguistics, Poetics, Hermeneutics*. Toronto: University of Toronto Press.

McGann, J. 2013. Philology in a new key. *Critical Inquiry* 39 (2), 327–46.

Meister, J.C. 1995. Consensus ex machina? Consensus qua machina! *Literary and Linguistic Computing* 10 (4), 263–70.

Moretti, F. 2005. *Graphs, Maps, Trees: Abstract Models for a Literary History*. London: Verso.

Opas-Hänninen, L.L. 1995. Special section: New approaches to computer applications in literary studies. *Literary and Linguistic Computing* 10 (4), 261–2.

Pasanek, B., and Sculley, D. 2008. Mining millions of metaphors. *Literary and Linguistic Computing* 23 (3), 345–60.

Pierazzo, E. 2011. A rationale of digital documentary editions. *Literary and Linguistic Computing* 26 (4), 463–77.

Piersma, H., and Ribbens, K. 2013. Digital historical research: context, concepts and the need for reflection. *BMGN – Low Countries Historical Review* 128 (4), 78–102.

Pratt, V.R. 1976. Semantical considerations on Floyd-Hoare logic. In *Proceedings of the 17th Annual IEEE Symposium on the Foundations of Computer Science*. 17th Annual IEEE Symposium on the Foundations of Computer Science, 109–21.

Ramberg, B., and Gjesdal, K. 2013. *Hermeneutics*. http://plato.stanford.edu/archives/sum2013/entries/hermeneutics (accessed December 6, 2013).

Ramsay, S. 2010. The hermeneutics of screwing around: or what you do with a million books. http://www.playingwithhistory.com/wp-content/uploads/2010/04/hermeneutics.pdf (accessed January 12, 2014).

Ramsay, S. 2011. *Reading Machines: Toward an Algorithmic Criticism*. Urbana: University of Illinois Press.

Rockwell, G. 2003. What is text analysis, really? *Literary and Linguistic Computing* 18 (2), 209–19.

Russell, S., and Norvig, P. 2009. *Artificial Intelligence: A Modern Approach*, 3rd edition. Upper Saddle River: Prentice Hall.

Schmidt, D., and Colomb, R. 2009. A data structure for representing multi-version texts online. *International Journal of Human–Computer Studies* 67 (6), 497–514.

Schreibman, S., Mandell, L., and Olsen, S. 2011. Evaluating digital scholarship: Introduction. *Profession*, 123–201. http://www.mlajournals.org/doi/pdf/10.1632/prof.2011.2011.1.123 (accessed January 17, 2014).

Shillingsburg, P. 2013. Is reliable social scholarly editing an oxymoron? In *Social, Digital, Scholarly Editing*. Saskatoon: University of Saskatchewan. http://ecommons.luc.edu/ctsdh_pubs/1 (accessed January 17, 2014).

Szondi, P., and Bahti, T. 1978. Introduction to literary hermeneutics. *New Literary History* 10 (1), 17–29.

Underwood, T. 2010. Historical questions raised by a quantitative approach to language. *The Stone and the Shell*. http://tedunderwood.com (accessed January 17, 2014).

Vandoulakis, I.M. 2011. On A.A. Markov's attitude towards Brouwer's intuitionism. In *Extended Abstracts of the 14th Congress of Logic, Methodology and Philosophy of Science*. Nancy: 14th Congress of Logic, Methodology and Philosophy of Science. Available at: http://www.mendeley.com/download/public/8335063/5498343341/25aa151120b0b290b513266d49ae52c92b66da61/dl.pdf (accessed January 17, 2014).

24

When Texts of Study are Audio Files: Digital Tools for Sound Studies in Digital Humanities

Tanya E. Clement

In 2010, the Council on Library and Information Resources (CLIR) and the Library of Congress (LC) issued *The State of Recorded Sound Preservation in the United States: A National Legacy at Risk in the Digital Age*, which suggests that if we do not use sound archives, our cultural heritage institutions will not preserve or create access to them. The report concludes that users want unfettered access and better discovery tools for "deep listening" or "listening for content, in note, performance, mood, texture, and technology," but a general sense of what that means in a digital context is absent (CLIR and LC, 2010:157). In digital humanities (DH), infrastructure, resource, and tool production has primarily been centered on the examination, teaching, publication, and dissemination of textual and visual cultural artifacts. At the same time, the quiet surrounding sound studies is not simply a reflection of DH; the hush reflects a bias at the root of humanistic inquiry in general. This bias is due in part to copyright restrictions but also to the difficulties of accessing, archiving, and sharing audio formats, all of which result in a lack of models for researching, writing, and teaching with sound. It is a typical DH problem: without a better understanding of what "deep" or "close" listening entails, we cannot produce tools that afford, enhance, or dismantle and question such activities; yet, because we lack the models that proliferate work with text and images, we struggle to imagine how to describe access to sound and the research or teaching with sound we might hope to engage.

Access: Sounds, Sounds, Everywhere There's Sounds

In archives all over the world, there are millions of hours of important sound recordings dating back to the nineteenth century and up to the present day. In the USA alone, for example, the LC's American Folk Life Center has 200,000 hours of recordings in its

A New Companion to Digital Humanities, First Edition. Edited by Susan Schreibman, Ray Siemens, and John Unsworth.
© 2016 John Wiley & Sons, Ltd. Published 2016 by John Wiley & Sons, Ltd.

vaults including rich collections from all over the United States. The *Rodgers and Hammerstein Archives of Recorded Sound* of the New York Public Library has over 700,000 recordings including Broadway musicals, classical and popular music, presidential speeches, radio dramas, and television specials. *StoryCorps* has 30,000 hours of 50,000 oral histories created in just the last decade by at least 80,000 participants from a vast range of communities. Further, many collections have been digitized and are freely accessible online. At launch, the LC's *National Jukebox* project has made 10,000 recordings made by the Victor Talking Machine Company between 1901 and 1925 available from the collections of the LC Packard Campus for Audio Visual Conservation. *PennSound* at the University of Pennsylvania has 30,000 sound files online including poetry performances, and interviews and lectures with and by prominent authors from Guillame Apollinaire (1913) to Gertrude Stein (1934–1935), Ezra Pound (1939), and William Carlos Williams (1942), through the beat poets and the language poets, to poets of the present day. As well, there are over a million audio recordings in the *Internet Archive* (https://archive.org) including historical radio broadcasts, public and private presidential events, as well as musical and oral history recordings. As with the physical collections, there are an even greater number of recordings across smaller caches at libraries and archives everywhere, and in many cases these are the only texts of study for trying to understand present and bygone oral traditions of our cultures: to hear, to consider, and to teach voices both past and present. It is true that digitization is essential for sound heritage that continues to deteriorate on legacy formats (wax cylinders, aluminum discs, and electromagnetic tapes) that will become unreadable by increasingly rare legacy machines (phonographs and reel-to-reel players), but preservation and access cannot be solved through digitization alone.

Even in a time of data deluge when audio collections are being digitized constantly, cultural heritage professionals, scholars, and teachers continue to experience limited access to audio. Often, modes of access to sound collections include basic functionality such as pressing "play" and "stop," and sometimes, the juxtaposition of audio with accompanying textual transcripts and metadata affords a few free and open-source means to do what John Unsworth calls the "primitives" of humanities scholarly inquiry – "discovering, annotating, comparing, referring, sampling, illustrating, and representing" (Unsworth, 2000). For example, the *Avalon Media System* at Indiana and Northwestern and the *Oral History Metadata Synchronization* project (OHMS) out of the University of Kentucky are free, open-source content management systems designed specifically for audio and video that enhance access for end users in well-designed environments that also work well with repository infrastructures. Unlike a CMS such as Omeka or Wordpress, these systems include audio-synchronization with transcripts. Scalar, an open-source multimedia scholarly publishing platform developed in coordination with the Alliance for Networking Visual Culture and the creators of the *Vectors* journal, provides means for juxtaposing text with multimedia objects, including enabling different interpretive paths and visualizations of those paths. Finally, the *Pop Up Archive* focuses on the creation of transcriptions through speech-to-text technologies, working primarily with broadcast recordings. These tools provide a means to link a single audio or video event together with transcripts in order to facilitate scholarly primitives *with* text or the textual metadata or transcripts accompanying the multimedia event.

That there are not greater (or different) means of facilitating access and analysis with sound itself is surprising, since computer performance – in terms of speed, storage capacity, and advances in machine learning and visualization – has increased to the point where it is now entirely possible to automate some aspects of how we discover audio. The very popular *Digging into Data Challenge*, supported by funding agencies representing Canada, the Netherlands, the United Kingdom, and the United States, is a testament to the wide array of perspectives and methodologies digital projects can encompass. While most of the projects analyze image and text, others provide new methods for discovery with audio files such as the *Structural Analysis of Large Amounts of Music* (SALAMI) and the *Electronic Locator of Vertical Interval Successions* (ELVIS) projects, both of which seek to analyze music, or the *Mining a Year of Speech* and the *Harvesting Speech Datasets for Linguistic Research on the Web* projects, which seek to analyze natural language usage.

Still, software development for accessing and analyzing sonic features is underdeveloped. Some open-source software works with different aspects of the sound file itself, including *SoundCloud* for sharing annotated sound clips; the *Stories Matter* project at Concordia University for segmenting or clipping audio and making playlists; *Audacity* for visualizing and editing audio; and *Praat* for the visualization and annotation of sound features for queries and statistical analysis. At this time, however, even though we have digitized so many culturally significant audio artifacts and have developed increasingly sophisticated systems for analyzing sound, scholars interested in spoken-word texts produced at poetry performances, speeches, and storytelling gatherings have very little means to use or to understand how to use low- or high-performance audio tools that would allow for pattern recognition across multiple files or a whole collection. As a result, sound artifacts remain almost completely inaccessible for new forms of analysis and instruction in the digital age. And yet it is also our inability to conceive of and to express what we want to do with sound –what Jerome McGann (2001) calls "imagining what you don't know" – that precludes us from leveraging existing computational resources and profoundly inhibits DH technical and theoretical development in sound studies.

Analysis: Do this, Don't do that; Can't you Read the Sounds?

Humanists from a wide range of fields including (but not limited to) folk, historical, literary, music, and performance studies, linguistics and communications, historical and cultural studies hold a range of perspectives and theories on studying sound. Poet and scholar Charles Bernstein, who calls sound hermeneutics "close listening," maintains that this mode of interpretation should comprise a focus on "sound as material, where sound is neither arbitrary nor secondary but constitutive" of meaning (Bernstein, 1998:4). Jonathan Sterne defines "sound studies" as using sound to ask "big questions about the cultural moments and crises and problems of [the] time;" he and others argue that new cultural critiques are needed to combat preconceived notions concerning the "audiovisual litany" of clichés that have prevailed and restricted our understandings of sound within cultural studies (Sterne, 2012a:3; Chow and Steintrager, 2011). Sterne argues that there is a prevailing notion that the visual somehow presents an outside or objective "view" on an event or object while the auditory is an embodied, subjective immersion; or that hearing is about emotion and temporality while seeing is about intellect and spatiality (Sterne, 2012a:9). Finally, while Walter J. Ong once announced that recording technologies have heralded a new age in the study of the "voice, muted by script and print" (Ong, 1967:88), others have argued that "there is something about speech that defies theory" (Gunn, 2008:343). Certainly, theories on the nature of studying sound that are framed within the context of technologies and methodologies of production, reproduction, and representation would form a particularly fruitful conjunction of cultural and sonic studies for discussion in digital humanities.

First, work in sound and new media studies demonstrates that sociotechnical histories form an essential aspect of critically examining sound. As the well-worn Marshall McLuhan phrase reminds us: the medium is the message in the age of mass media (McLuhan, 1965). Theories based on studies of the gramophone, the phonograph, magnetic tape, and digital audio reflect this perspective. Friedrich Kittler, for example, asserts that the gramophone, as a register of the "spectrum of noise" and the "unarticulated," provokes inquiry: it "subverts both literature and music (because it reproduces the unimaginable real they are both based on)" (Kittler, 1999:22). Further, Lisa Gitelman situates the phonograph within a history of writing and reading in relation to speaking, not "according to the practices or commodification of musical notation, composition, and performance" (Gitelman, 2006:25). Instead, this speaking technology, as an inscription device widely exhibited at public fairs, raises question about how the masses "participate together in the enactment of cultural hierarchy" (35). From another perspective, Alexander G. Weheliye's work (2005) seeks to place the phonograph within a sound recording and reproduction continuum that reaches to the one-time ubiquitous Sony Walkman and coincides with (and helps us reconsider) Afro-diaspora cultural production. Work on sound technologies is further expanded with Kristen Haring's look at the hobbyist culture engendered (and gendered) around ham radios (2008) and Jentery Sayers' cultural history of magnetic recordings (2011). Finally, Jonathan Sterne's work is seminal in establishing sociotechnical cultural critiques of telephony, phonography, and radio in *The Audible Past: Cultural Origins of Sound Reproduction* (2003), while in his later book, *MP3* (2012b), he calls for "format studies" to study digital audio within this context. Other significant studies focus on histories of aurality (Smith 2001, 2006; Moten, 2003; Mills, 2010), soundscapes (Thompson, 2002; Toop, 2010; LaBelle, 2010;), and ethnographic modernities and acoustemologies (Hirschkind, 2006; Ochoa, 2006).

Second, a large part of the conversation on sound in literary study has been focused on modern and experimental poetics and how increased access to taped recordings representing the sound archive of a poet or a community of poets affects interpretations of a poem's aesthetic dimensions (Morris, 1998; Perloff and Dworkin, 2009). As the ability to easily tape live recordings began to flourish in the 1970s so did the opportunity to rethink how poems could be studied. Michael Davidson notes in an early consideration of sound and interpretation that there are a number of topics to reconsider. Davidson asserts that "the poet 'hears' as much as 'thinks' (or to phrase it more accurately ... he hears his thinking)" a poem through performance. As a result, "what any poet 'has in mind' will hardly be solved by listening to a reading any more than by reading a page. The 'text' is a more complex fact than this, and is made even more complex by the oral record" (Davidson, 1981). As such, access to the sound version becomes another artifact within the constellation of artifacts that afford how we may study the "text" of a poem and all its versions.

Beyond or alongside new questions concerning intentionality, performance, and the nature of "text," access to sounded experimental poetry lends to conversations in literary study about the constructed nature of language in general. Certainly, the structures of Henri Chopin's audio-poems and John Cage's performed pieces have long been at the center of conversations about non-representational "technological assaults on the word" (McCaffery, 1998:158). In particular, McCaffery is interested in the "new nonsemantic lexicon" represented by avant-garde sound pieces that ask the listener to go "beyond the sonic complexities" in order to question "the cultural constructedness of the phoneme and syllables themselves" (160, 162). Katherine Hayles considers experimental recordings that work to deconstruct the nature of the recording medium itself. She looks at Samuel Beckett's focus on the tape recording as an early representation of self in his one-act play *Krapp's Last Tape* and at William S. Burroughs's work "inching tape" (rubbing it against the head at different speeds), recording his voice by holding the microphone to his throat, or splicing radio snippets he had recorded himself, which can be considered another example of his text-based "cut-up method" (Hayles, 1998:90).

Third, language theories that concern sound recordings often turn to theoretical perspectives on "the voice" and the role sonic features play in theories about identity construction and meaning making with sound. Roland Barthes identifies two aspects of the voice in vocal music that contribute to meaning: the *pheno-song* or the structured elements of a piece, such as speech or melody ("everything in the performance which is in the service of communication, representation, expression"), and the *geno-song* or the material or corporal aspect of the voice (the "volume of the singing and speaking voice, the space where significations germinate") (Barthes, 1978:182). Maintaining that the "grain" of the voice is its "soul" rather than its "body," Barthes asserts that the hermeneutics of close listening requires a concert of the pheno-song (the "soul") with the geno-song (the "body") to communicate meaning.

While Barthes labels sonic vocal feature nonexpressive, Michael Chion asserts that these features do have meaning but that it is our lack of a descriptive system that precludes our ability to listen to and speak critically of these features. Chion approaches sound study by considering a hermeneutics of listening in the form of causal, semantic, and reduced listening (Chion, 2012), a tripartite that seems related to Roland Barthes's three distinct types of listening in his essay "Listening" (Barthes, 1985). In *causal listening*, the listener seeks to find out more about the source of the sound, whether the source is a tuba, a man, or a female child, while in *semantic listening* one listens to "interpret a message" (50). Chion describes listening to the sonic traits of a sound "independent of the sound's cause or comprehension of its meaning" as *reduced listening* (Chion, 2012:51). Such listening precludes description, he argues, for two reasons. First, the "fixity" of sonic features through recording is necessary for close listening, since to perceive sonic traits one must listen repeatedly. Chion, however, dismisses fixed sounds as "veritable objects" and as "physical data" that do not, he argues, represent what was actually spoken or heard within real time. Second, our "present everyday language as well as specialized musical terminology are totally inadequate to describe the sonic traits" (Chion, 2012:51).

However, this argument, that the voice is only meaningful in the context of speech that transmits a message, is a logocentric theoretical stance that has been readily contested. Adriana Cavarero, who seeks to "understand speech from the perspective of the voice instead of from the perspective of language," wants to "pull speech itself from the deadly grip of logocentrism" (Caravero, 2012:530,531). Arguing that the "voice" as understood from this perspective privileges articulated speech and a disembodied "unique" voice, Caravero asserts that "logocentrism radically denies to the voice a meaning of its own that is not always already destined to speech" (529). Caravero critiques the viewpoint of Chion (2012), McLuhan (1988), and Ong (1967), who at once essentialize the voice as "presence" and disembody and myth- (as well as myst-)icize orality. Reflecting literary scholars who study experimental poetry to understand where the avant garde pushes against and comments on culturally constructed language norms, Caravero asserts that a much more productive stance is to understand speech as "the point of tension between the uniqueness of the voice and the system of language" (Caravero, 2012:530). Similarly, Mladen Dolar argues that "It is not that our vocabulary is scanty and its deficiency should be remedied: faced with the voice, words structurally fail" (Dolar, 2012:539). Entertaining the notion of a "linguistics of non-voices" including coughing, hiccups, babbling, screaming, laughing, and singing, Dolar places these sounds outside of the phonemic structure yet not outside of the linguistic structure (Dolar, 2012:552). Finding possibilities for study in aspects of the voice such as accent, intonation, and timbre, Dolar asks the question at the heart of all of these queries: "how can we pursue this dimension of the voice?" (Dolar, 2012:544).

Finally, other cultural inquiries in sound have focused on the intersections of sound production and critical play. Tara Rodgers' *Pink Noises* (2010), for example, includes a history of women who have worked creatively and critically with electronic sound to play with time, space, and language in order to question the cultural and social contexts within which women make and have made electronic music. The *SoundBox* project from the Franklin Humanities Institute at Duke University is publishing a collection of digital "provocations" about sound that are both critical and playful. The project asks, "What if it were possible to make arguments about sound using *sound itself?*" (SoundBox, 2013) These provocations include Kenneth David Stewart's development of a "sonically inspired electric guitar," a critical-making project that provides "a cultural critique of the history of signal processing by embedding that history in the instrument" (Mueller, 2013), as well as experimental soundscapes based on field recordings, sonifications of texts and photographs, and reflective pieces that use sound to comment on other cultural artifacts.

Critical play also includes links between experimental contemporary sound art and video gaming as they are enacted in the creation of audio-based digital games. Examples include Aaron Oldenburg's work (2013) and *AudioGames.net*, an initiative shepherded by Richard van Tol and Sander Huiberts, which includes an archive of audio-based and blind-accessible games, descriptions, reviews, and articles, and an active forum. Well-known and award-winning audio game examples include *Square Waves*, in which the "Seeing Player" must collaborate with the "Hearing Player" who is only afforded headphones; *Swamp*, an online, cooperative first-person shooter in which the player is oriented with soundscapes that represent different settings; *Terraformers*, which enacts a space colony using 3D binaural recordings; and *Papa Sangre II*, which uses similar technology to guide the player through the land of the dead.

Conclusion: Sound Futures in DH

The sheer number of analog and digital sound collections indicates that musical and radio recordings and spoken texts including poetry readings and theatrical performances, oral histories and field recordings, presidential speeches and phone calls, or stories told by long-ago and present-day elders from indigenous communities are significant cultural artifacts that must be made more accessible for study. The work briefly sketched out above also suggests that sound studies has much to offer DH theories, models, tools, and pedagogies that have been developed primarily in the study of text and images, and vice versa. As this chapter shows, technologies that record, transmit, reproduce, and broadcast the voice – such as the telegraph, radio, telephone, and phonograph – have been developed within a sociotechnical history in which the goal and the process for pursuing the "meaning" of sound are both highly contested. The significance of debates concerning how spoken texts might be studied (in terms of sonic features or language content) is well expressed by Sterne, who places special emphasis on a section entitled "Voices" in the *Sound Studies Reader*, which he asserts includes pieces of which the primary concern is the "most basic of human faculties" or "what it means to be human" (Sterne, 2012a:11). To be sure, discovering convergences in seemingly divergent (technologic vs. humanistic) theories could provide a framework for thinking through how to build information infrastructures that facilitate cultural studies with digital audio collections.

Some DH projects have begun to think through the implications of infrastructure development for the study of audio in the humanities. SALAMI investigator Stephen Downie, for example, identifies 10 major research issues that must be addressed when developing music information retrieval systems, including determining effective procedures and evaluation techniques for (1) indexing, (2) retrieval queries, (3) user interface design for access and analysis, (4) audio compression for efficient processing, (5) audio feature detection that yields productive analyses, (6) machine learning algorithms, (7) classification techniques, (8) security measures for sensitive materials, (9) accessibility procedures for a range of user communities, and (10) sufficient computing and storage infrastructure development for data-intensive techniques (Downie, 2008; Downie *et al.*, 2010). Further, the HiPSTAS (*High Performance Sound Technologies for Access and Scholarship*) project out of the School of Information at the Universty of Texas at Austin and the Illinois Informatics Institute at the University of Illinois, Urbana–Champaign attempts to address the lack of infrastructures for better accessing sound in part by introducing humanists to ARLO, an application which has been developed to perform spectral visualization, matching, classification, and clustering on large collections of bird calls. Implementing ARLO for HiPSTAS on a supercomputer system at the Texas Advanced Computing Center has yielded three significant results for future uses of audio big data in the humanities: (1) an assessment of user requirements for large-scale computational analysis of spoken-word collections of keen interest to the humanities; (2) an assessment of infrastructure needed for short-term (sandbox) and long-term (sustainable) access and deployment of supercomputing resources for visualizing and mining large audio collections for humanities users; and (3) preliminary project results using these supercomputing resources to detect repetition and to find sonic features of interest such as applause and laughter (Clement *et al.*, 2014).

Finally, a new collaboration at the School of Information at the University of Maryland, College Park aims to recover temporal data concerning when a recording was made based on analysis of incidentally captured traces of small variations (electric network frequency signatures) in the electric power supply at the time of recording and comparing them to known provenance information (Su *et al.*, 2013; Oard *et al.*, 2014).

Certainly, understanding how we interpret "the voice" is productive in helping us consider how to model these activities with computational systems, but there are many areas of new inquiry which could be productive for digital humanities in general. Some include the critical study of technological transduction, reproduction, and transmission of sound; of sonic environments (comprising the contextualized clicks and hums of recording technologies, the car-alarms of a city night, or the applauding, baby-crying, coughing, dog-barking, laughing, whirring acoustemologies of soundspaces and recording spaces); as well as critically modeling the act of audition (as listening, hearing, or deafness); and critiquing aesthetics, sonic arts, and voices (both as linguistic and para-linguistic). Further, CLIR's *Survey of the State of Audio Collections in Academic Libraries* (Smith *et al.*, 2004) and the *Library of Congress National Recording Preservation Plan* (Nelson-Strauss *et al.*, 2012) cite copyright legislation reform, organizational initiatives for shared preservation networks, and improvements in the processes of discovery and cataloging as the areas where research and development for increasing access are most needed. In order to relieve backlogs of undescribed audio collections, they call for "new technologies for audio capture and automatic metadata extraction" (Smith *et al.*, 2004:11) with a "focus on developing, testing, and enhancing science-based approaches to all areas that affect audio preservation" (Nelson-Strauss *et al.*, 2012:15). The apparent need for more inquiry into infrastructure development for access and discovery as well as preservation and sustainability in sound studies should strike a resonant chord in digital humanities, and DH scholars versed in sound studies are well poised to take on these challenges.

REFERENCES AND FURTHER READING

Barthes, R. 1978. *Image–Music–Text*. New York: Hill and Wang.

Barthes, R. 1985. *The Responsibility of Forms*. Trans. Richard Howard. New York: Hill and Wang.

Bernstein, C. 1998. *Close Listening: Poetry and the Performed Word*. New York: Oxford University Press.

Caravero, A. 2012. Multiple voices. In *The Sound Studies Reader*, ed. J. Sterne. New York: Routledge, 520–32.

Chion, M. 2012. The three modes of listening. In *The Sound Studies Reader*, ed. J. Sterne. New York: Routledge, 48–53.

Chow, R., and Steintrager, J.A. 2011. In pursuit of the object of sound: an introduction. *differences*, 22 (2–3), 1–9.

Clement, T., Tcheng, D., Auvil, L., and Borries, T. 2014. High Performance Sound Technologies for Access and Scholarship (HiPSTAS) in the digital humanities. *Proceedings of the 77th Annual ASIST Conference*, Seattle, WA.

Council on Library and Information Resources (CLIR) and the Library of Congress (LC). 2010. *The State of Recorded Sound Preservation in the United States: A National Legacy at Risk in the Digital Age*. Washington DC: National Recording Preservation Board of the Library of Congress.

Davidson, M. 1981. "By ear, he sd": audio-tapes and contemporary criticism, *Credences* 1 (1), 105–20. http://www.audibleword.org/poetics/Davidson-By_Ear_He_Sd.htm (accessed February 28, 2010).

Dolar, M. 2012. The linguistics of the voice. In *The Sound Studies Reader*, ed. J. Sterne. New York: Routledge, 539–54.

Downie, J.S. 2008. The Music Information Retrieval Evaluation Exchange (2005–2007): a window into music information retrieval research. *Acoustical Science and Technology* 29 (4), 247–55.

Downie, J.S., Ehmann, A.F., Bay, M., and Jones, M.C. 2010. The Music Information Retrieval Evaluation eXchange: some observations and insights. In *Advances in Music Information Retrieval*, ed. Z.W. Rás and A.A. Wieczorkowska. Berlin: Springer, 93–115.

Gitelman, L. 2006. *Always Already New: Media, History and the Data of Culture*. Cambridge, MA: MIT Press.

Gunn, J. 2008. Speech is dead; long live speech. *Quarterly Journal of Speech* 94 (3), 343–64.

Haring, K. 2008. *Ham Radio's Technical Culture*. Cambridge, MA: MIT Press.

Hayles, N.K. 1998. Voices of out bodies, bodies out of voices: audiotape and the production of subjectivity. In *Sound States: Innovative Poetics and Acoustical Technologies*, ed. A. Morris. Chapel Hill: University of North Carolina Press, 74–96.

Hirschkind, C. 2006. *The Ethical Soundscape: Cassette Sermons and Islamic Counterpublics*. New York: Columbia University Press.

Kittler, F. 1999. *Gramophone, Film, Typewriter*. Writing Science. Stanford, CA: Stanford University Press.

LaBelle, B. 2010. *Acoustic Territories: Sound Culture and Everyday Life*. New York: Continuum.

MacKay, D. 1969. *Information, Mechanism and Meaning*. Cambridge, MA: MIT Press.

McCaffery, S. 1998. From phonic to sonic: the emergence of the audio-poem. In *Sound States: Innovative Poetics and Acoustical Technologies*, ed. A. Morris. Chapel Hill: University of North Carolina Press, 149–68.

McGann, J. 2001. *Radiant Textuality: Literature After the World Wide Web*. New York: Palgrave.

McLuhan, M. 1965. *Understanding Media: The Extensions of Man*. New York: McGraw-Hill.

McLuhan, M. 1988. *Laws of Media: The New Science*. Toronto: University of Toronto Press.

Mills, M. 2010. Deaf Jam: from inscription to reproduction to information. *Social Text* 28 (1) (102), 35–58.

Morris, A., ed. 1998. *Sound States: Innovative Poetics and Acoustical Technologies*. Chapel Hill: University of North Carolina Press.

Moten, F. 2003. *In the Break: The Aesthetics of the Black Radical Tradition*. Minneapolis: University of Minnesota Press.

Mueller, D. 2013. A sonically inspired electric guitar (in progress). SoundBox Project. http://sites.fhi.duke.edu/soundbox/2013/09/12/a-sonically-inspired-electric-guitar-in-progress (accessed December 11, 2014).

Nelson-Strauss, B., Gevinson, A., and Brylawski, S. 2012. *The Library of Congress National Recording Preservation Plan*. Washington, DC: Library of Congress.

Oard, D., Wu, M., Kraus, K., *et al.* 2014. It's about time: projecting temporal metadata for historically significant recordings. *Proceedings of the 2014 iConference*. Berlin, Germany. *ACM Digital Library*. https://www.ideals.illinois.edu/handle/2142/47262 (accessed June 20, 2015).

Ochoa, A.M. 2006. Sonic transculturation, epistemologies of purification and the aural public sphere in Latin America. *Social Identities* 12 (6), 803–25.

Oldenburg, A. 2013. Sonic mechanics: audio as gameplay. *Game Studies* 13 (1).

Ong, W.J. 1967. *The Presence of the Word: Some Prolegomena for Cultural and Religious History*. New Haven: Yale University Press.

Perloff, M., and Dworkin C.D. 2009. *The Sound of Poetry, the Poetry of Sound*. Chicago: University of Chicago Press.

Rodgers, T. 2010. *Pink Noises: Women on Electronic Music and Sound*. Durham: Duke University Press.

Sayers, J. 2011. *How text lost its source: magnetic recording cultures*. PhD thesis, University of Washington.

Sayers, J. 2013. Making the perfect record. *American Literature* 85 (4), 817–18.

SoundBox Project. 2013. http://sites.fhi.duke.edu/soundbox (accessed December 11, 2014).

Smith, A., Allen, D.R., and Allen, K. 2004. *Survey of the State of Audio Collections in Academic Libraries*. Washington, DC: Council on Library and Information Resources.

Smith, M.M. 2001. *Listening to Nineteenth-Century America*. Chapel Hill: University of North Carolina Press.

Smith, M.M. 2006. *How Race Is Made: Slavery, Segregation, and the Senses*. Chapel Hill: University of North Carolina Press.

Sterne, J. 2003. *The Audible Past: Cultural Origins of Sound Reproduction*. Durham: Duke University Press.

Sterne, J. 2012a. Sonic imaginations. In *The Sound Studies Reader*, ed. J. Sterne. New York: Routledge, 1–18.

Sterne, J. 2012b. *MP3: The Meaning of a Format*. Durham: Duke University Press.

Su, H., Garg, R., Hajj-Ahmad, A., Wu, M. 2013. ENF analysis on recaptured audio recordings. *Proceedings of the 2013 IEEE International Conference on Acoustics, Speech, and Signal Processing (ICASSP)*. Vancouver, May 26–31, 2013. 3018–3022.

Thompson, E.A. 2002. *The Soundscape of Modernity: Architectural Acoustics and the Culture of Listening in America, 1900–1933*. Cambridge, MA: MIT Press.

Toop, D. 2010. *Sinister Resonance: The Mediumship of the Listener*. New York: Continuum.

Unsworth, J. 2000. Scholarly primitives: what methods do humanities researchers have in common, and how might our tools reflect this? Paper presented at *Humanities Computing: Formal Methods and Experimental Practice*, King's College, London. http://people.brandeis.edu/~unsworth/Kings.5-00/primitives.html (accessed October 2014).

Weheliye, A.G. 2005. *Phonographies: Grooves in Sonic Afro-Modernity*. Durham, NC: Duke University Press.

25
Marking Texts of Many Dimensions

Jerome McGann

A sign is something by knowing which we know something more. (C.S. Peirce)

What is Text?

Although "text" has been a "keyword" in clerical and even popular discourse for well over fifty years, it did not find a place in Raymond Williams' important book *Keywords* (1976). This strange omission may perhaps be explained by the word's cultural ubiquity and power. In that lexicon of modernity Williams called the "Vocabulary of Culture and Society," "text" has been the "one word to rule them all." Indeed, the word "text" became so shapeshifting and meaning-malleable that we should probably label it with Tolkein's full rubrication: "text" has been, and still is, the "one word to rule them all and in the darkness bind them."

We want to keep in mind that general context when we address the issues of digitized texts, text markup, and electronic editing. Although these are the specialized concerns of this chapter, they have important bearings on all aspects of literary and philological studies. As we lay foundations for translating our inherited archive of cultural materials, including vast corpora of paper-based materials, into digital depositories and forms, we are called to a clarity of thought about textuality that most people, even most scholars, rarely undertake.

Consider the phrase "marked text," for instance. How many recognize it as a redundancy? All text is marked text, as you may see by reflecting on the very text you are now reading. As you follow this conceptual exposition, watch the physical

A New Companion to Digital Humanities, First Edition. Edited by Susan Schreibman, Ray Siemens, and John Unsworth.

embodiments that shape the ideas and the process of thought. Do you see the typeface, do you recognize it? Does it *mean* anything to you, and if not, why not? Now scan away (as you keep reading) and take a quick measure of the general page layout: the font sizes, the characters per line, the lines per page, the leading, the headers, footers, margins. And there is so much more to be seen, registered, understood simply at the documentary level of your reading: paper, ink, book design, or the markup that controls not the documentary status of the text but its linguistic status. What would you be seeing and reading if I were addressing you in Chinese, Arabic, Hebrew – even Spanish or German? What would you be seeing and reading if this text had been printed, like Shakespeare's sonnets, in 1609?

We all know the ideal reader of these kinds of traditional documents. She is an actual person, like the texts this person reads and studies. He writes about her readings and studies under different names, including Randall McLeod, Randy Clod, Random Cloud, etc. She is the Dupin of the textual mysteries of our exquisite and sophisticated bibliographical age.

Most important to realize, for our present purposes, is that digital markup schemes do not easily – perhaps do not even *naturally* – map to the markup that pervades paper-based texts. Certainly this is the case for every kind of electronic markup currently in use: from simple ASCII, to any inline SGML derivatives, to the recent approaches of standoff markup (Thompson and McKelvie, 1997). The symptoms of this discrepancy are exemplified in the AI community's struggles to simulate the complex processes of natural language and communicative exchange. Stymied of success in achieving that goal, these efforts have nonetheless been singularly fruitful for giving us a clearer view of the richness and flexibility of traditional textual machineries.

How, then, are traditional texts marked? If we could give an exhaustive answer to that question we would be able to simulate them in digital forms. We cannot complete an answer for two related reasons: first, the answer would have to be framed from within the discourse field of textuality itself; and second, that framework is dynamic, a continually emerging function of its own operations, including its explicitly self-reflexive operations. This is not to say that markup and theories of markup must be "subjective." (It is also not to say – see below – that they must *not be* subjective.) It *is* to say that they are and must be social, historical, and dialectical, and that some forms have greater range and power than others, and that some are useful exactly because they seek to limit and restrict their range for certain special purposes.

Autopoietic Systems and Co-dependency

Describing the problems of electronic texts in her book *Electronic Texts in the Humanities* (2000), Susan Hockey laconically observes that "There is no obvious unit of language" (20). Hockey is reflecting critically on the ordinary assumption that this unit is the word. Language scholars know better. Words can be usefully broken down into more primitive parts and therefore understood as constructs of a second or even higher order. The view is not unlike the one continually encountered by physicists who search out basic units of matter. Our analytic tradition inclines us to understand that forms of all kinds are "built up" from "smaller" and more primitive units, and hence to take the self-identity and integrity of these parts, and the whole that they comprise, for objective reality.

Hockey glances at this problem of the text-unit in order to clarify the difficulties of creating electronic texts. To achieve that, we instruct the computer to identify (the) basic elements of natural language text and we try to ensure that the identification has no ambiguities. In natural language, however, the basic unit – indeed, all divisioning of any kind – is only procedurally determinate. The units are arbitrary. More, the arbitrary units themselves can have no absolute self-identity. Natural language is rife with redundancy and ambiguity at every unit and level and throughout its operating relations. A long history of analytic procedures has evolved certain sets of best practices in the study of language and communicative action, but even in a short run, terms and relations of analysis have changed.

Print and manuscript technology represent efforts to mark natural language so that it can be preserved and transmitted. It is a technology that constrains the shapeshiftings of language, which is itself a special-purpose system for coding human communication. Exactly the same can be said of electronic encoding systems. In each case constraints are installed in order to facilitate operations that would otherwise be difficult or impossible. In the case of a system like TEI, the system is designed to "disambiguate" the materials to be encoded.

The output of TEI's markup constraints differs radically from the output generated by the constraints of manuscript and print technology. Whereas redundancy and ambiguity are expelled from TEI, they are preserved – are *marked* – in manuscript and print. While print and manuscript markups don't "copy" the redundancies of natural language, they do construct systems that are sufficiently robust to develop and generate equivalent types of redundancy. This capacity is what makes manuscript and print encoding systems so much more resourceful than any electronic encoding systems currently in use ("Natural language" is the most complex and powerful reflexive coding system that we know of" (Maturana and Varela, 1992).

Like biological forms and all living systems, not least of all language itself, print and manuscript encoding systems are organized under a horizon of co-dependent relations. That is to say, print technology – I will henceforth use that term as shorthand for both print and manuscript technologies – is a system that codes (or simulates) what are known as autopoietic systems. These are classically described in the following terms:

> If one says that there is a machine M in which there is a feedback loop through the environment so that the effects of its output affect its input, one is in fact talking about a larger machine M^1 which includes the environment and the feedback loop in its defining organization. (Maturana and Varela, 1980:78)

Such a system constitutes a closed topological space that "continuously generates and specifies its own organization through its operation as a system of production of its own components, and does this in an endless turnover of components" (Maturana and Varela, 1980:79). Autopoietic systems are thus distinguished from allopoietic systems, which are Cartesian and which "have as the product of their functioning something different from themselves" (Maturana and Varela, 1980:80).

In this context, all coding systems appear to occupy a peculiar position. Because "coding ... represents the interactions of [an] observer" with a given system, the mapping stands apart from "the observed domain" (Maturana and Varela, 1980:135). Coding is a function of "the space of human design" operations, or what is classically called "heteropoietic" space. Positioned thus, coding and markup appear allopoietic.

As machines of simulation, however, coding and markup (print or electronic) are not like most allopoietic systems (cars, flashlights, a road network, economics). Coding functions emerge *as code* only within an autopoietic system that has evolved those functions as essential to the maintenance of its life (its dynamic operations). Language and print technology (and electronic technology) are second- and third-order autopoietic systems – what McLuhan famously, expressively, if also somewhat misleadingly, called "extensions of man." Coding mechanisms – proteins, print technology – are generative components of the topological space they serve to maintain. They are folded within the autopoietic system like membranes in living organisms, where distinct components realize and execute their extensions of themselves.

This general frame of reference is what makes Maturana and Varela (1980:95) equate the "origin" of such systems with their "constitution." This equation means that co-dependency pervades an autopoietic structure of relations.

All components of the system arise (so to speak) simultaneously and they perform integrated functions. The system's life is a morphogenetic passage characterized by various dynamic mutations and transformations of the local system components. The purpose or goal of these processes is autopoietic – self-maintenance through self-transformation – and their basic element is not a system component but the relation (co-dependence) that holds the mutating components in changing states of dynamic stability. The states generate measurable co-dependency functions both in their periods (or basins) of stability and in their unique moments of catastrophic change.

Marking the Text: A Necessary Distinction

At the 2002 Extreme Markup Languages conference, Michael Sperberg-McQueen offered these observations on the problem of overlapping structures for SGML-based markup systems:

> It is an interesting problem because it is the biggest problem remaining in the residue. If we have a set of quantitative observations, and we try to fit a line to them, it is good practice to look systematically at the difference between the values predicted by our equation (our theory) and the values actually observed; the set of these differences is the residue. ... In the context of SGML and XML, overlap is a residual problem. (Sperberg-McQueen, 2002)

But in any context *other than* SGML and XML, this formulation is a play of wit, a kind of joke – as if one were now to say that the statistical deviations produced by Newtonian mathematical calculations left a "residue" of "interesting" matters to be cleared up by further, deeper calculations. But those matters are not *residual*, they are the hem of a quantum garment.

My own comparison is itself a kind of joke, of course, for an SGML/TEI model of the world of textualities pales in comprehensiveness before the Newtonian model of the physical world. But the outrageousness of the comparison in each case helps to clarify the situation. No autopoietic process or form can be simulated under the horizon of a structural model like SGML, not even topic maps. We see this very clearly when we observe the inability of a derivative model like TEI to render the forms and functions of traditional textual documents. The latter, which deploy markup codes themselves, supply us with simulations of language as well as of many other kinds of semeiotic processes, as Peirce called them. Textualized documents restrict and modify, for various kinds of reflexive purposes, the larger semeiotic field in which they participate. Nonetheless, the procedural constraints that traditional textualities lay upon the larger semeiotic field that they model and simulate are far more pragmatic, in a full Peircean sense, than the electronic models that we are currently deploying.

Understanding how traditional textual devices function is especially important now when we are trying to imagine how to optimize our new digital tools. Manuscript and print technologies – graphical design in general – provide arresting models for information technology tools, especially in the context of traditional humanities research and education needs. To that end we may usefully begin by making an elementary distinction between the archiving and the simulating functions of textual (and, in general, semeiotic) systems. Like gene codes, traditional textualities possess the following as one of their essential characteristics: that as part of their simulation and generative processes, they make (of) themselves a record of those processes. Simulating and record keeping, which are co-dependent features of any autopoietic or semeiotic system, can be distinguished for various reasons and purposes. A library processes traditional texts by treating them strictly as records. It saves things and makes them accessible. A poem, by contrast, processes textual records as a field of dynamic simulations. The one is a machine of information, the other a machine of reflection. Each may be taken as an index of a polarity that characterizes all semeiotic or autopoietic systems. Most texts – for instance, the chapter you are reading now – are fields that draw upon the influence of both of those polarities.

The power of traditional textualities lies exactly in their ability to integrate those different functions within the same set of coding elements and procedures.

SGML and its derivatives are largely, if not strictly, coding systems for storing and accessing records. They possess as well certain analytic functions that are based in the premise that text is an "ordered hierarchy of context objects" (the "OHCO thesis"; Renear *et al.*, 1993). This conception of textuality is plainly noncomprehensive. Indeed, its specialized understanding of "text" reflects the pragmatic goal of such a markup code: to store objects (in the case of TEI, textual objects) so that they can be quickly accessed and searched for their informational content – or, more strictly, for certain parts of that informational content (the parts that fall into a hierarchical order modeled on a linguistic analysis of the structure of a book).

These limitations of electronic markup codes are not to be lamented, but for humanist scholars they are to be clearly understood. A markup code like TEI creates a record of a traditional text in a certain form. Especially important to see is that, unlike the textual fields it was designed to mark up, TEI is an allopoietic system. Its elements are unambiguously delimited and identified *a priori*, its structure of relations is precisely fixed, it is non-dynamical, and it is focused on objects that stand apart from itself. Indeed, it defines what it marks not only *as* objective, but as objective in exactly the unambiguous terms of the system's *a priori* categories. This kind of machinery will therefore serve only certain, very specific, purposes. The autopoietic operations of textual fields – operations especially pertinent to the texts that interest humanities scholars – lie completely outside the range of an order like the TEI.

For certain archival purposes, then, structured markup will serve. It does not unduly interfere with, or forbid implementing, some of the searching and linking capacities that make digital technology so useful for different types of comparative analysis. Its strict formality is abstract enough to permit implementation within higher-order formalizations. In these respects it has greater flexibility than a standoff approach to text markup, which is more difficult to integrate into a dispersed online network of different kinds of materials (Caton, 2000). All that having been recognized and said, however, these allopoietic text-processing systems cannot access or display the autopoietic character of textual fields. Digital tools have yet to develop models for displaying and replicating the self-reflexive operations of bibliographical tools, which alone are operations for thinking and communicating – which is to say, for transforming storage into memory, and data into knowledge.

We have to design and build digital environments for those purposes. A measure of their capacity and realization will be whether they can integrate data-function mechanisms like TEI into their higher-order operations. To achieve that will entail, I believe, the deployment of dynamic, topological models for mapping the space of digital operations (see the classic study by René Thom, 1975). But these models will have to be reconceived, as one can see by reflecting on a remark about textual interpretation that Stanley Fish liked to make years ago in his lectures about interpretation. He would point out that he was able to treat even the simplest text – road signage, for example – as a poem and thus develop his own "response" and commentary on its autopoietic potential. The remark underscores a basic and almost entirely neglected (undertheorized) feature of discourse fields: that to "read" them – to read "in" them at any point – one must regard what we call "the text" and "the reader" as co-dependent agents in the field. You can't have one without the other.

Fish's observation, therefore, while true, signals a widespread theoretical and methodological weakness in our conceptions of textuality, traditional or otherwise. This approach figures "text" as a heuristic abstraction drawn from the larger field of discourse. The word "text" is used in various ways by different people – Barthes' understanding is not the same as a TEI understanding – but in any case the term frames attention on the linguistic dimension of a discourse field. Books and literary works, however, organize themselves along multiple dimensions of which the linguistic is only one.

Modeling digital simulations of a discourse field requires that a formal set of dimensions be specified for the field. This is what TEI provides *a priori*, though the provision, as we know, is minimal. Our received scholarly traditions have in fact passed down to us an understanding of such fields that is both far more complex and reasonably stable. Discourse fields, our textual condition, regularly get mapped along six dimensions (see below). Most important of all in the present context, however, are the implications of cognizing a discourse field as autopoietic. In that case the field measurements will be taken by "observers" positioned within the field itself. That intramural location of the field interpreter is in truth a logical consequence of the co-dependent character of the field and its components. "Interpretation" is not undertaken from a position outside the field, it is an essential part of a field's emergence and of any state that its emergence might assume.

This matter is crucial to understand when we are reaching for an adequate formalizing process for textual events like poetry or other types of orderly but discontinuous phenomena. René Thom explains very clearly why topological models are preferable to linear ones in dynamic systems:

> [I]t must not be thought that a linear structure is necessary for storing or transmitting information (or, more precisely, significance); it is possible that a language, a semantic model, consisting of topological forms could have considerable advantages from the point of view of deduction, over the linear language that we use, although this idea is unfamiliar to us. Topological forms lend themselves to a much richer range of combinations ... than the mere juxtaposition of two linear sequences. (Thom, 1975:145)

These comments distinctly recall Peirce's exploration of existential graphs as sites of logical thinking. But Thom's presentation of topological models does not conceive fieldspaces that are autopoietic, which seems to have been Peirce's view.[1] Although Thom's approach generally eschews practical considerations in favor of theoretical clarity, his models assume that they will operate on data carried into the system from some external source. If Thom's "data" comes into his studies in a theoretical form, then, it has been theorized in traditional empirical terms. The topological model of a storm may therefore be taken either as the description of the storm and/or as a prediction of its future behavior. But when a model's data is taken to arise co-dependently with all the other components of its system, a very different "result" ensues. Imagined as applied to textual autopoiesis, a topological approach carries itself past an analytic description or prediction over to a form of demonstration or enactment.

The view taken here is that no textual field can exist as such without "including" in itself the reading or measurement of the field, which specifies the field's dataset from within. The composition of a poem is the work's first reading, which *in that event* makes a call upon others. An extrinsic analysis designed to specify or locate a poetic field's self-reflexiveness commonly begins from the vantage of the rhetorical or the social dimension of the text, where the field's human agencies (efficient causes) are most apparent. The past century's fascination with structuralist approaches to cultural phenomena produced, as we know, a host of analytic procedures that chose to begin from a consideration of formal causation, and hence from either a linguistic or a semiotic vantage. Both procedures are analytic conventions based in empirical models.

Traditional textuality provides us with autopoietic models that have been engineered as effective analytic tools. The codex is the greatest and most famous of these. Our problem is imagining ways to recode them for digital space. To do that we have to conceive formal models for autopoietic processes that can be written as computer software programs.

Field Autopoiesis: From *IVANHOE* to 'Patacriticism

Let's recapitulate the differences between book markup and TEI markup. TEI defines itself as a two-dimensional generative space mapped as (1) a set of defined "content objects" (2) organized within a nested tree structure. The formality is clearly derived from an elementary structuralist model of language (a vocabulary + a syntax, or a semantic + a syntagmatic dimension). In the SGML/TEI extrusion, both dimensions are fixed and their relation to each other is defined as arbitrary rather than co-dependent. The output of such a system is thus necessarily symmetrical with the input. Input and output in a field of traditional textuality works differently. Even in quite restricted views, as we know, the operations of natural language and communicative exchange generate incommensurable effects. The operations exhibit behavior that topologists track as bifurcation or even generalized catastrophe, whereby an initial set of structural stabilities produces morphogenetic behaviors and conditions that are unpredictable. This essential feature of "natural language" – which is to say, of the discourse fields of communicative exchange – is what makes it so powerful, on one hand, and so difficult to model and formalize on the other.

In these circumstances, models like TEI commend themselves because they can be classically quantified for empirical – numerable – results. But as Thom observed long ago, there is no such thing as "a quantitative theory of catastrophes of a dynamical system" like natural language. To achieve such a theory, he went on to say, "it would be necessary to have a good theory of integration on function spaces" (Thom, 1975:321), something that Thom could not conceive.

That limitation of qualitative mathematical models did not prevent Thom from vigorously recommending their study and exploration. He particularly criticized the widespread scientific habit of "tak[ing] the main divisions of science, the[ir] taxonomy ... as given *a priori*" rather than trying to re-theorize taxonomics as such (1975:322). In this frame of reference we can see (1) that textualization in print technology is a qualitative (rather than a taxonomic) function of natural language, and (2) that textualization integrates function spaces through demonstrations and enactments rather than descriptions. This crucial understanding – that print textuality is not language but an operational (praxis-based) theory of language – has stared us in the face for a long time, but seeing we have not seen. It has taken the emergence of electronic textualities, and in particular operational theories of natural language like TEI, to expose the deeper truth about print and manuscript texts. SGML and its derivatives freeze (rather than integrate) the function spaces of discourse fields by reducing the field components to abstract forms – what Coleridge in the *Biographia Literaria* called "fixities and definites." This approach will serve when the object is to mark textual fields for storage and access.

Integration of dynamic functions will not emerge through such abstract reductions, however. To develop an effective model of an autopoietic system requires an analysis that is built and executed "in the same spirit that the author writ." That formulation by Alexander Pope expresses, in an older dialect, what we have called in this century "the uncertainty principle," or the co-dependent relation between measurements and phenomena. An agent defines and interprets a system from within the system itself – at what Dante Gabriel Rossetti called "an inner standing point.. What we call "scientific objectivity" is in one sense a mathematical function; in another, it is a useful method for controlling variables. We use it when we study texts as if they were objective things rather than dynamic autopoietic fields.

Traditional textual conditions facilitate textual study at an inner standing point because all the activities can be carried out – can be represented – in the same fieldspace – typically, in a bibliographical field. Subject and object meet and interact in the same dimensional space – a situation that gets reified for us when we read books or write about them. Digital operations, however, introduce a new and more abstract space of relations into the study-field of textuality. This abstract space brings the possibility of new and in certain respects greater analytic power to the study of traditional texts. On the downside, however, digitization – at least to date, and typically – situates the critical agent outside the field to be mapped and re-displayed. Or – to put this crucial point more precisely (since no measurement has anything more than a relative condition of objectivity) – digitization situates the critical agent within levels of the textual field's dimensionalities that are difficult to formalize bibliographically.

To exploit the power of those new formalizations, a digital environment has to expose its subjective status and operation (Like all scientific formalities, digital procedures are "objective" only in relative terms.) In the present case – the digital marking of textual fields – this means that we will want to build tools that foreground the subjectivity of any measurements that are taken and displayed. Only in this way will the autopoietic character of the textual field be accurately realized. The great gain that comes with such a tool is the ability to specify – to measure, display, and eventually compute and trans-form – an autopoietic structure at what would be, in effect, quantum levels.

A series of related projects to explore such tools were taken up some 10 years ago at University of Virginia's Speculative Computing Laboratory (SpecLab) (Drucker, 2009). The first of these, *IVANHOE*, was an online gamespace built for the imaginative recon-struction of traditional texts and discourse fields (*Text Technology*, 2003). Players enter these works through a digital display space that encourages them to alter and transform the textual field. The game rules require that transformations be made as part of a discourse field that emerges dynamically through the changes made to a specified initial set of materials.

As the *IVANHOE* project was going forward, a second, related project called *Temporal Modelling* was being taken up by Johanna Drucker and Bethany Nowviskie. The project sought "to bring visualization and interface design into the early content modeling phase" of projects like *IVANHOE*, which pursue interpretation through transformational and even deformative interactions with the primary data.[2] *IVANHOE*'s computer is designed to store the game players' performative interpretational moves and it then produces algorithmically generated analyses of the moves after the fact. The chief critical function thus emerges after-the-fact, in a set of human reflections on the differential patterns that the computerized analyses expose. In the *Temporal Modelling* device, however, the performative and the critical actions are much more closely integrated because the human is actively involved in a deliberated set of digital transformations. The *Temporal Modelling* device gives users a set of design functions for reconstructing a given lineated timeline of events in terms that are subjective and hypothetical. The specified field of event-related data is brought forward for transfor-mation through editing and display mechanisms that emphasize the malleability of the initial set of field relations. The project stands, conceptually, somewhere between design programs (with their sets of tools for making things) and complex websites like *The Rossetti Archive* (with their hypertextual datasets organized for on-the-fly search and analysis). It is a set of editing and display tools that allows users to design their own hypothetical (re)formulations of a given dataset.

The frankly experimental character of *Temporal Modelling*'s data (re)constructions led to an important reimagining of the original *IVANHOE* project. From the outset of that project we intended to situate the "interpreter" within the discourse field that was the subject of interpretive transformation. Our initial conception was toward what we called "Ultimate *IVANHOE*," that is, toward a playspace that would be controlled by emergent consciousness software. With the computer an active agent in an *IVANHOE* session, players could measure and compare their own understandings of their actions against a set of computer generated views. This prospect for *IVANHOE*'s development remains, but the example of *Temporal Modelling* exposed another way to situate the human interpreter at an inner standing point of an autpoietic system.

If 'pataphysics is, in the words of its originator, "the science of exceptions," the project here is to reconceive *IVANHOE* under the rubric of 'patacriticism, or the theory of subjective interpretation. The theory is implemented through what is here called the "dementianal" method, which is a procedure for marking the autopoietic features of textual fields. The method works on the assumption that such features characterize what topologists call a field of general catastrophe. The dementianal method marks the dynamic changes in autopoietic fields much as Thom's topological models allow one to map forms of catastrophic behavior. The 'patacritical model differs from Thom's models because the measurements of the autopoietic field's behaviors are generated from within the field itself, which only emerges as a field through the action of the person interpreting – that is to say, marking and displaying – a specific set of elements and relations for the field. The field arises co-dependently with the acts that mark and measure it. In this respect we characterize its structure as dementianal rather than dimensional.

As the device was originally conceived, readers engage autopoietic fields along three behavior dementians: *transaction, connection, resonance*. A common *transaction* of a page space moves diagonally down the page, with regular deviations for horizontal line transactions from left to right margin, from the top at upper left to the bottom at lower right. Readers regularly violate that pattern in indefinite numbers of ways, often being called to deviance by how the field appears marked by earlier agencies. *Connections* assume, in the same way, multiple forms. Indeed, the primal act of autopoietic connection is the identification or location of a textual element to be "read." In this sense, the *transaction* of an autopoietic field is a function of the marking of connections of various kinds, on one hand, and of resonances on the other. *Resonances* are signals that call attention to a textual element as having a field value – a potential for connectivity – that appears *and* appears unrealized.

Note that all of these behavior dementians exhibit co-dependent relations. The field is transacted as connections and resonances are marked; the connections and resonances are emergent functions of each other; and the marking of dementians immediately reorders the space of the field, which itself keeps re-emerging under the sign of the marked alteration of the dynamic fieldspace and its various elements.

These behavioral dementians locate an autopoietic syntax, which is based in an elementary act or agenting event: G. Spencer-Brown's "law of calling" (1969), which declares that a distinction can be made. From that law comes the possibility that elements of identities can be defined. They emerge with the co-dependent emergence of the textual field's control dimensions, which are the field's autopoietic semantics.

Writing and Reading in Autopoietic Fields

This 'patacritical approach to textual dementians is a meta-theory of textual fields, a pragmatistic conception of how to expose discontinuous textual behaviors ("natural language" so called, or what Habermas has better called "communicative action"). Integration of the dynamic functions begins not by abstracting the theory away from a target object – that is the method of a taxonomic methodology – but by integrating the meta-theoretical functions within the discourse space itself.

Informational discourse fields function well precisely by working to limit redundancy and concurrent textual relations. Because poetry – or imaginative textuality broadly conceived – postulates much greater freedom of expressive exchange, it exhibits a special attraction for anyone wishing to study the dynamics of textuality. Aristotle's studies of semiotic systems preserve their foundational character because they direct their attention to autopoietic rather than allopoietic discourse fields. His studies pursue a taxonomy for the dynamic process of making and exchanging (remaking) simulations.

Plato's *Dialogues*, by contrast, situate – or, more precisely, generate – their critical reflections at a standing point inside the textualities they are themselves unfolding. In this respect they have much in common with Wittgenstein's critical colloquies in the *Philosophical Investigations* or with Montaigne's *Essais*. But the dynamic play of even these textual fields remains, from the point of view of their readers, an exemplary exercise. This situation prevails in all modes of critical reflection that assume to preserve the integrity and self-identity of the textual fields they study. Two forms of critical reflection regularly violate the sanctity of such self-contained textual spaces: translation and editing. The idea that an object of criticism like a textual field *is* an object can be maintained either as an heuristic procedure or as an ontological illusion. Consequently, acts of translation and editing are especially useful forms of critical reflection because they so clearly invade and change their subjects in material ways. To undertake either, you can scarcely *not* realize the performative – even the *deformative* – character of your critical agency.

At this point let me exemplify the general markup model for autopoietic textualities. This comes in the form of the following hypothetical passage through an early poem by Robert Creeley, "The Innocence." Because imaginative textuality is, in this view, an exemplary kind of autopoietic process, any poetical work would do for a narrative demonstration. I choose "The Innocence" because it illustrates what Creeley and others called "field poetics." As such, it is especially apt for clarifying the conception of the autopoietic model of textuality being offered here. "Composition by field" poetics has been much discussed, but for present purposes it suffices to say that it conceives poetry as a self-unfolding discourse. "The poem" is the "field" of action and energy generated in the poetic transaction of the field that the poem itself exhibits. "Composition by field," whose theoretical foundations may be usefully studied through Charles Olson's engagements with contemporary philosophy and science, comprised both a method for understanding (rethinking) the entire inheritance of poetry, and a program for contemporary and future poetic discourse (its writing and its reading).

The text chosen is taken from Donald Allen's famous anthology *The New American Poetry* (first published in 1960) in its 1999 University of California Press reprinting.

The Innocence

Looking to the sea, it is a line
of unbroken mountains.

It is the sky.
It is the ground. There
we live, on it.

It is a mist
now tangent to another
quiet. Here the leaves
come, there
is the rock in evidence

or evidence.
What I come to do
is partial, partially kept

Before tracing a model for this poetic field we want to bear two matters in mind. First, the field we are transacting is localized in relation to this documentary instance of "the text." One of the most persistent and misleading procedures in traditional hermeneutics is to take the object of study as something not only abstract and disembodied, but as something lying outside the fieldspace – itself specific and material – of the act of critical representation. Second, the sequence of readings (below) consciously assumes a set of previous readings whereby certain elementary forms of order – by no means insignificant forms – have been integrated into the respective textual dementians. All such forms are extrusions from the elementary semiotic move, which is Spencer-Brown's basic law of form: that a distinction can be drawn (*as* a dementian, or within and between dementians). Thus the readings below assume that each dementian is oriented to a set of established formal objects which get called and then crossed (transformed) in the transaction of the field.

That said, let me transact the poetic field through the initial textual model supplied above.

A First Reading

I mark the following elements in the first line group (and in that act I mark as well the presence of (a) lines and (b) line groups): "Looking" as a dangling participle; "it" (line 1) as ambiguously pronominal; "line" as a word play referencing (first) this line of verse I am transacting, and (second) a landscape of "unbroken mountains" (to be marked as such only with the marking of the final line in the group). All of these are defined (connected to the fieldspace) as textual elements with marked resonances (anticipations and clear if inchoate recollections) as well as several manifest, second-order connections (e.g., "sea," "line," and "mountains" as objects in a landscape).

Line group 2 emerges to connect a network of "it" words as well as to settle the dominance of a linguistic gravity field centered in the initially marked "landscape" (a linguistic demention subdomain). As line group 3 continues to elaborate the "landscape field," several distinctly new elements emerge and get marked. They center in the words "tangent," "quiet," "evidence," the notable enjambment at the end of the line group, and the deictics "Here" and "there." The first four resonate by the differences they make with the previous elements I had defined in my transaction of the field. The deictics connect back to the second linguistic demention subdomain (the self-reflexive set of textual elements marked in line 1 as the dangling participle and the final word "line"). The fourth and last line group is itself marked as strongly resonant in itself because of the emergence within it of the unique "I" and the startling repetitions ("evidence," "partial"/"partially").

So the field transaction is marked geometrically as a complete and continuous passage from upper left to lower right and proceeding line by line left to right. That passage of the textspace marks out two control dementians, linguistic and graphical, as well as several distinct basins of order within them. In the graphical demention we see an array of marked letters, words, lines, and line groups. In the linguistic demention I have marked two distinct subdomains, one referential (the set of "landscape" semantics), one a subdomain of pure signifiers (proliferating from line 1 through the deictic markers "Here" and "there".

A Second Reading

I mark the title as strongly resonant and I find myself scanning the poem rather than reading it linearly, and marking elements unnoticed in the first reading. I re-mark the array of "it" words and connect all of them to the title, marking thereby another linguistic subdomain. I mark as resonant the striking idea of "a mist/now tangent to another/quiet," and I mark a distinction in the linguistic subdomain (of "landscape") between different sensory aspects of a "landscape." I mark as resonant the equally striking final sentence and the phrase "the rock in evidence//or evidence."

A Third Reading

This is a sequential transaction through the poem as in the first reading. It is largely devoted to marking connections between the various elements already marked with resonance values. The wordplay in "line" is marked as a strongly resonant locus of field-space connections across the several linguistic subdomains. This connective fieldspace is especially resonant as the connection between the words "line" and "tangent." I mark all of the previously marked textual elements as connected to each other in a broadly dispersed semiotic demention because I am seeing that elements in different fieldspace dementians and domains (e.g., "mist" and "quiet") are connected to each other.

A Fourth Reading

A sequential reading leads to marking the final sentence as a dramatic locus of a rhetorical demention in the fieldspace. The construction of the textspace is "What I come to do." The emergence of this idea allows me to mark the poem as a deliberated sequential organization that exposes itself in certain telling (marked) moments and textual elements: "Looking," "line," "tangent," the deictic words, the previously unmarked "we" (line 5), the enjambment between the third and fourth line groups. In all these I mark a rhetorical organization tied most centrally to the phrase "What I come to do." I mark that these marks unfold as a relation that must be seen as sequenced: "I" in the present tense here is always the present tense in the linguistic dementian of this work. Marking the verb tense in that way immediately produces the first, remarkable emergence in this reading process of the work's social dementian. "I" comes to write this poem, which is marked thereby as an event in the world and as objective as any material thing (these material things, the "landscape" things, first marked in the linguistic dementian). In that rhetorical dementian I mark as well a key element of this work's social dementian first marked in the linguistic dementian: the relation between the "we" and the "I." The phrase "is partial, partially kept" is marked now as an element in the social dementian of the textspace – as if one were to say, interpretively, that the "doing" of the poem is only one event in a larger field that the poem is part of and points toward. My acts of marking the poem fall into both the local fieldspace and the larger discourse field marked by this local poetical field. And I further mark the social space by connecting the textspace to the book in which the text is printed – for that book (the polemic it made) marks this specific text in the strongest way. At this point the sixth dementian of the fieldspace begins to get marked, the material dementian. I mark three documentary features in particular: the placement of the text in the book, the organ of publication, the date of publication. I mark as well the fact that these material features of the work are, like the word "line," double-meaninged (or double-dementianed), having a clear placement in the work's social dementian as well.

A Fifth Reading

I mark new elements in the six marked dementians that emerge in a widespread process of subdividing and proliferating. Elements defined in one dementian or subdomain get marked in another (for instance, "I" began in the rhetorical, reappeared in the social, and now gets marked in all the other dementians as well); unmarked textual features, like the letter "t," get marked as resonant; the shape of the textspace from word to line to word group is marked as a linked set of spare elements. These additional markings lead to other, previously unseen and unmarked relations and elements. The spare graphical dementian gets linked to the linguistic dementian ("The Innocence") and to the social and rhetorical dementians (the graphical spareness is only markable in relation to the absent/present discourse field in which this poetical work stands and declares its comparative allegiance).

A Sixth Reading

This is a reading that poses significant theoretical and practical issues. Time-stamped two weeks after the previous readings, this reading was negotiated in my mind as I recalled the history of my readings of the poem. It is thus a reading to be digitally marked after-the-fact. Focused on the final line group, it also marks the entirety of the autopoietic field. The reading marks the "I" as a figure in the social dementian, the poet (Creeley) who composed the poem. In that linking, however, I as reader become linked to the linguistic "I" that is also a social "I." This linkage gets enforced by marking a set of "partial" agents who "come to do" part of the continuous making of the autopoietic field (Creeley does what he does, I do what I do, and we both inhabit a space resonant with other, as yet unspecified, agents.)

Conclusion

What I theorize here and propose for a digital practice is a science of exceptions, a science of imaginary (subjective) solutions. The markup technology of the codex has evolved an exceedingly successful instrument for that purpose. Digital technology ought to be similarly developed. Organizing our received humanities materials as if they were simply information depositories, computer markup as currently imagined handicaps or even baffles altogether our moves to engage with the well-known dynamic functions of textual works. An alternative approach to these matters through a formal reconception of textspace as topological offers distinct advantages. Because this space is autopoietic, however, it does not have what mathematicians would normally call dimensionality. As autopoietic, the model we propose establishes and measures its own dimensions autotelically, as part of its self-generative processes. Furthermore, space defined by pervasive co-dependencies means that any dimension specified for the system might be formally related to any other. This metamorphic capacity is what translates the concept of a dimension into the concept of a dementian.

This model of text processing is open-ended, discontinuous, and nonhierarchical. It takes place in a fieldspace that is exposed when it is mapped by a process of "reading." A digital processing program is to be imagined and built that allows one to mark and store these maps of the textual fields and then to study the ways they develop and unfold and how they compare with other textual mappings and transactions. Constructing textualities as fieldspaces of these kinds short-circuits a number of critical predilections that inhibit our received, common-sense wisdom about our textual condition. First of all, it escapes crippling interpretive dichotomies like text and reader, or textual "subjectivity" and "objectivity." Reader-response criticism, so-called, intervened in that space of problems but only succeeded in reifying even further the primary distinctions. In this view of the matter, however, one sees that the distinctions are purely heuristic. The "text" we "read" is, in this view, an autopoietic event with which we interact and to which we make our own contributions. Every textual event is an emergence imbedded in and comprising a set of complex histories, some of which individual readers each partially realize when they participate in those textual histories. Interestingly, these histories, in this view, have to be grasped as fields of action rather than as linear unfoldings. The fields are topological, with various emergent and dynamic basins of order, some of them linear and hierarchical, others not.

Appendix A   The 'Pataphysics of Text and Field Markup

Texts and their field spaces are autopoietic scenes of co-dependent emergence. As such, their primal state is dynamic and has been best characterized by G. Spencer-Brown's *Laws of Form* (1969), where "the form of distinction" – the act of making indications by drawing a distinction – is taken as "given" and primal. This means that the elementary law is not the law of identity but the law of non-identity (so that we must say that "*a* equals *a* if and only if *a* does not equal *a*"). Identities emerge as distinctions are drawn and redrawn, and the acts of drawing out distinctions emerge as co-dependent responses to the field identities that the form of distinction calls to attention.

Spencer-Brown supplies a formal demonstration of what Alfred Jarry called 'pataphysics and that he and his OULIPian inheritors demonstrated in forms of traditional textual practice (i.e., in forms of "literature"). 'Pataphysics is a general theory of autopoietic systems (i.e., a general theory of what we traditionally call "imaginative literature"), and *Laws of Form* is a specifically *'pataphysical* event because it clearly gives logical priority to the unique act and practice of its own theoretical thought. The fifth "Chant" of Lautréamont's *Les chants de Maldoror*, Jarry's *Gestes et opinions du docteur Faustroll,'pataphysicien*, and all the descendants of those self-conscious works – Laura Riding's stories are the earliest English-language examples – are the "literary" equivalents of Spencer-Brown's *Laws of Form*.

In this view of any systematics, the taxonomy of a system is a derivation of what Peirce called an initial abduction. The abduction is a hypothesis of the total semeiotic integrity of the system. The hypothesis is tested and transformed (internally as well as externally) in a dialectical process – ultimately endless – of representation and reflection.

Appendix B   Control Dementians for a 'Patacriticism
of Textualities

The transaction of textual fields proceeds by a series of moves (field behaviors) that proliferate from an elementary modal distinction between what have been specified (above) as *connections* and *resonances*, which are the elementary behavioral forms of the textual *transaction*. These modes correspond to what traditional grammarians define as an indicative and a subjunctive verbal mood. (In this view, interrogative and interjective moods are derivatives of these two primary categories.) Emerging co-dependently with these behavioral dementians is an elementary taxonomy of control dementians that are called into form and then internally elaborated.

The history of textual studies has evolved a standard set of field formalities that may be usefully analyzed in six distinct parts. These correspond to an elemental set of dimensions for textual fields (or, in fields conceived as autopoietic systems, an elemental set of six dementians). These control dementians locate what grammarians designate as the semantics of a language.

Let it be said here that these behavioral and control dementians, like their allopoietic dimensions, comprise a set of categories that recommend themselves through an evolved history of previous use. Other dimensions (and dementians) might be proposed or imagined. However, since the proposals being advanced here are all conceived within a pragmatistic frame of reference, the categories bring with them the strong authority of a habitual usefulness.

The Linguistic Dimension/Dementian

This aspect of the textual condition has been the principal focus of attention in the West. It represents a high-order framework of conceptual markers or distinctions that unfold and multiply from an initial pair of categories, the semantic and the grammatical. The former is an elemental category, the latter is a relational one, and the two together epitomize the structure of co-dependency that pervades and in a sense defines all textual processes at every dimension. That is to say, neither marker or category has conceptual priority over the other, they generate meaning together in a co-dependent and dialectical process. However, to specify their co-dependence requires that one adopt a pragmatistic or performative approach such as we see in Maturana, Spencer-Brown, and Peirce.

The Graphical/Auditional Dimension/Dementian

Some kind of graphical and/or auditional state of affairs is a prerequisite for any appearance or functional operation of a linguistic dimension, and that state must be formally constrained. In Western attempts to clarify language and textuality, these forms are defined in the systematic descriptors of morphology and phonology, which are co-dependent subcategories of the linguistic dimension.

This graphical/auditional dimension comprises the set of a text's codes of materiality (as opposed to the specific material state of a particular document). In print and manuscript states, the dimension includes various subsets of bibliographical codes and paratexts: typography, layout, book design, and the vehicular components of those forms. (If we are considering oral texts, the material assumes auditional forms, which can have visual components as well.)

The Documentary Dimension/Dementian

This comprises the physical incarnation – the "real presence," so to speak – of all the formal possibilities of the textual process. We recognize it as a bibliographical or paleographical description of some specific object, or as a library or archival record of an object's historical passage (transmission history).

Note that this dimension does not simply constitute some brute chemical or physical thing – what Coleridge referred to when he spoke of the "object as object," which he called "fixed and dead." Coleridge's "object as object" is a negative abstraction – that is to say, a certain formal conception of the documentary dimension that sets it apart (*a priori*) from any place in a study or interpretation of textuality. A document can and – in any comprehensive approach to textuality – should be maintained as an integral function of the textual process.

A document is a particular object that incarnates and constrains a specific textual process. In terms of print and manuscript texts, it is a specific actualized state of the graphical/auditional dimension.

The Semiotic Dimension/Dementian

This dimension defines the limit state of any text's formal possibilities. It postulates the idea of the complete integration of all the elements and dynamic relations in a field of discourse. In this dimension we thus cognize a textual process in holistic terms. It is a purely formal perspective, however, and as such stands as the mirrored antithesis of the document per se, whose integrity is realized as a phenomenal event. The document is the image of the hypothesis of total form; it appears at (or as) a closure of the dynamic process set in perpetual motion by the hypothesis at the outset.

We register the semiotic dimension as a pervasiveness of patterned relations throughout the textual system – both within each part of the system and among the parts. The relations emerge in distinct types or modes: elements begin and end; they can be accumulated, partitioned, and replicated; they can be anchored somewhere, linked to other elements, and relayed through the system.

The first of those late systems of analysis called by Herbert Simon "sciences of the artificial," the science of semiotics, labels itself as a heuristic mechanism. The pervasive order of a textual process's semiotic dimension thus emerges as a function of the formal categories, both system elements and system processes, that are consciously specified by the system's agents. Order is constructed from the systemic demand for order. As a result, the forms of order can be of any type – hierarchical or non-hierarchical, continuous or discontinuous.

The Rhetorical Dimension/Dementian

The dominant form of this dimension is genre, which is a second-order set of textual forms. Genre calls into play poems, mathematical proofs, novels, essays, speeches, dramas, and so forth. The function of this dimension is to establish forms of readerly attention – to select and arrange textual materials of every kind in order to focus the interest of the reader (audience, user, listener) and establish a ground for response.

Readers and writers (speakers and listeners) are rhetorical functions. (Writers' first readers are themselves in their act of composition.) Bakhtin's celebrated studies of textual polyvalence and heteroglossia exemplify the operative presence of this textual dimension.

The Social Dimension/Dementian

This is the dimension of a textual production and of reception histories. It is the dimension of the object as subject: that is to say, of a determinate set of textual elements arrayed under names like "writer," "printer," "publisher," "reader," "audience," "user." It is the dimension that exposes the temporality function which is an inalienable feature of all the dimensions of the textual condition.

The social dimension of textuality unfolds a schedule of the uses to which its works are put beyond what New Critics liked to call "the poem itself." It is the dimension in which the dynamic and non-self-identical character of textual works is most plainly disclosed.

In most traditional theories of textuality, the social dimension is not considered an intrinsic textual feature or function. Framed under the sign "context," it is seen as the environment in which texts and documents stand. Until the recent emergence of more holistic views of environments – notably in the work of Donald McKenzie – this way of seeing textuality's social dimension forced severe restrictions on our ability to comprehend and study the dynamic character of textual processes.

NOTES

1   Peirce's seminal statement on existential graphs was given in the so-called MS 514 (published online with commentary by John F. Sowa: http://www.jfsowa.com/peirce/ms514.htm).
2   The project came out of McGann and Drucker's SpecLab: see Bethany Nowviskie's online 2003 report on the project: http://www2.iath.virginia.edu/time/time.html. That frankly experimental project is now being practically pursued by Nowviskie and her collaborators at the University of Virginia's Scholar's Lab as the Neatline Project: http://neatline.org/

REFERENCES AND FURTHER READING

Allen, D., ed. 1999. *The New American Poetry, 1945–1960*. Berkeley: University of California Press.

Caton, M. 2000. Markup's current imbalance. *Markup Languages* 3 (1), 1–13.

Drucker, J. 2009. *SpecLab: Digital Aesthetics and Speculative Computing*. Chicago: University of Chicago Press.

Hockey, S. 2000. *Electronic Texts in the Humanities*. Oxford: Oxford University Press.

Maturana, H.R., and Varela, F.J. 1980. *Autopoiesis and Cognition: The Realization of Living*. Boston: D. Reidel.

Maturana, H.R., and Varela, F.J. 1992. *The Tree of Knowledge: The Biological Roots of Human Understanding*. New York: Random House.

McGann, J. 2014. *A New Republic of Letters: Memory and Scholarship in the Age of Digital Reproduction*. Cambridge, MA: Harvard University Press.

McKenzie, D.F. 1986. *Bibliography and the Sociology of Texts: The Panizzi Lectures, 1985*. London: British Library.

Renear, A., Mylonas, E., and Durand, D. 1993. Refining our notion of what text really is: the problem of overlapping hierarchies. Final version, 1993. http://cds.library.brown.edu/resources/stg/monographs/ohco.html (accessed June 20, 2015).

Simon, H. 1981. *The Sciences of the Artificial*, 2nd edition. Cambridge, MA: MIT Press.

Spencer-Brown, G. 1969. *Laws of Form*. London: George Allen and Unwin.

Sperberg-McQueen, C.M. 2002. What matters? *Extreme Markup Languages, Montreal*. http://cmsmcq.com/2002/whatmatters.html (accessed June 20, 2015).

Text Technology. 2003. [Special issue devoted to *IVANHOE*.] *Text Technology* 12 (2).

Thom, R. 1975. *Structural Stability and Morphogenesis: An Outline of a General Theory of Models*. Trans. D.H. Fowler, Reading MA: W.A. Benjamin.

Thompson, H., and McKelvie, D. 1997. Hyperlink semantics for standoff markup of read-only documents. In *SGML Europe 97, Barcelona*. Graphical Communications Association.

Williams, R. 1976. *Keywords: A Vocabulary of Culture and Society*. London: Fontana.

26
Classification and its Structures

C. M. Sperberg-McQueen

Classification is, strictly speaking, the assignment of some thing to a class; more generally, it is the grouping together of objects into classes. A *class*, in turn, is a collection (formally, a set) of objects which share some property.

For example, a historian preparing an analysis of demographic data transcribed from census books, parish records, and city directories might classify individuals by sex, age, occupation, and place of birth. Places of birth might in turn be classified as large or small cities, towns, villages, or rural parishes. A linguist might classify each running word of a text according to its part of speech, or each sentence according to its structure. Linguists, literary scholars, or social scientists might classify words by semantic category, organizing them into semantic nets. Classification serves two purposes, each important: by grouping together objects which share properties, it brings like objects together into a class; by separating objects with unlike properties into separate classes, it distinguishes between things which are different in ways relevant to the purpose of the classification. The classification scheme itself, by identifying properties relevant for such judgments of similarity and dissimilarity, can make explicit a particular view concerning the nature of the objects being classified.

Scope

Since a classification may be based on any set of properties that can be attributed to the objects being classified, classification in the broad sense involves the identification of the properties of the objects of study, and can hardly be dispensed with in any coherent discourse. (Classification too rigidly insisted on can descend into pedantry, however, and faulty classifications can hinder understanding instead of aiding it.) Information

A New Companion to Digital Humanities, First Edition. Edited by Susan Schreibman, Ray Siemens, and John Unsworth.
© 2016 John Wiley & Sons, Ltd. Published 2016 by John Wiley & Sons, Ltd.

retrieval systems may be regarded, and are often described, as classifying records into the classes "relevant" and "not relevant" each time a user issues a query. Norms and standards such as the XML 1.0 specification or Unicode may be understood as classification schemes which assign any data stream or program either to the class "conforming" or to the class "nonconforming." Laws may be interpreted as classifying acts as legal or illegal, censors as classifying books, records, performances, and so on. Any characteristic of any kind of thing, using any set of concepts, may be viewed as classifying things of that kind into classes corresponding to those concepts. In the extreme case, the property associated with a class may be vacuous: the members may share only the property of membership in the class. In general, classification schemes are felt more useful if the classes are organized around properties relevant to the purpose of the classification. Details of the concepts, categories, and mechanisms used in various acts of classification may be found in other chapters in this collection.

In the narrower sense, for computer applications in the humanities, classification most often involves either the application of pre-existing classification schemes to, or the *post hoc* identification of clusters among, a sample of objects. The objects may be texts (e.g., the samples in language corpora), parts of texts (e.g., the structural constituents or nonstructural features of a text), bibliography entries (for subject description in enumerative bibliographies or specialized libraries), words (for semantic characterization of texts), or extra-textual events or individuals (e.g., for historical work). The classifications most familiar to the readers of this work are perhaps the classification systems used in libraries and bibliographies for classifying books and articles by subject; in what follows, examples drawn from these will be used where possible to illustrate important points, but the points are by no means relevant only to subject classification.

Since classification relies on identifying properties of the object being classified, perfect classification would require, and a perfect classification scheme would exhibit, perfect knowledge of the object. Because a perfect subject classification, for example, locates each topic in a field in an n-dimensional space near other related topics and distant from unrelated topics, a perfect subject classification represents a perfect map of the intellectual terrain covered in the area being classified. For this reason, classification schemes can carry a great deal of purely theoretical interest, in addition to their practical utility. Classification schemes necessarily involve some theory of the objects being classified, if only in asserting that the objects possess certain properties. Every ontology can be interpreted as providing the basis for a classification of the entities it describes. And conversely, every classification scheme can be interpreted with more or less ease as the expression of a particular ontology. In practice, most classification schemes intended for general use content themselves with representing something less than a perfect image of the intellectual structure of their subject area, and attempt with varying success to limit their theoretical assumptions to those to which most expected users can be expected to assent. At the extreme, the assumptions underlying a classification scheme may become effectively invisible and thus no longer subject to challenge or rethinking; for purposes of scholarly work, such invisibility is dangerous and should be avoided.

This chapter first describes the abstract structures most often used in classification, and describes some rules often thought to encourage useful classification schemes. It then gives a purely formal account of classification in terms of set theory, in order to establish that no single classification scheme can be exhaustive, and indeed that there are infinitely more ways of classifying objects than can be described in any language. Finally, it turns to various practical questions involved in the development and use of classification systems.

One-dimensional Classifications

Very simple classification schemes (sometimes referred to as *nominal* classifications, because the class labels used are typically nouns or adjectives) consist simply of a set of categories: male and female; French, German, English, and other; noun, verb, article, adjective, adverb, etc. In cases like these, some characteristic of the object classified may take any one of a number of discrete values; formally, the property associated with the class is that of having some one particular value for the given characteristic. The different classes in the scheme are not ordered with respect to each other; they are merely discrete classes which, taken together, subdivide the set of things being classified.

In some classifications (sometimes termed *ordinal*), the classes used fall into some sort of sequencing or ordering with respect to each other: first-year, second-year, third-year student; folio, quarto, octavo, duodecimo; upper-class, middle-class, lower-class.

In still other cases, the underlying characteristic may take a large or even infinite number of values, which have definite quantitative relations to each other: age, height, number of seats in parliament, number of pages, price, etc. For analytic purposes, it may be convenient or necessary to clump (or *aggregate*) sets of distinct values into single classes, as when age given in years is reduced to the categories infant, child, adult, or to under 18, 18–25, 25–35, over 35.

All of the cases described so far classify objects based on the value of a single characteristic attributed to the object. In the ideal case, the characteristic can be readily and reliably evaluated, and the values it can take are discrete. The more borderline cases there are, the harder it is likely to be to apply the classification scheme, and the more information is likely to be lost by analyses which rely on the classified data rather than the original data.

Classification Schemes as *n*-dimensional Spaces

In less simple classification schemes, multiple characteristics may be appealed to. These may often be described as involving a hierarchy of increasingly fine distinctions. The *Dewey Decimal Classification*, for example, assigns class numbers in the 800s to literary works. Within the 800s, it assigns numbers in the 820s to English literature, in the 830s to German literature, the 840s to French, etc. Within the 820s, the number 821 denotes English poetry, 822 English drama, 823 English fiction, and so on. Further digits after the third make even finer distinctions; as a whole, then, the classification scheme may be regarded as presenting the classifier and the user with a tree-like hierarchy of classes and subclasses, with smaller classes branching off from larger ones.

In the case of the Dewey classification of literature, however, the second and third digits are (almost) wholly independent of each other: a third digit 3 denotes fiction whether the second digit is 1 (American), 2 (English), 3 (German), 4 (French), 5 (Italian), 6 (Spanish), 7 (Latin), or 8 (Classical Greek), and 2 as a third digit similarly denotes drama, independent of language.

We can imagine the literature classification of the Dewey system as describing a plane, with the second digit of the Dewey number denoting positions on the x-axis, and the third digit denoting values along the y-axis. Note that neither the sequence and values of the genre numbers, nor those of the language numbers, have any quantitative significance, although the sequence of values is in fact carefully chosen.

Generalizing this idea, classification schemes are often regarded as identifying locations in an n-dimensional space. Each dimension is associated with an *axis*, and the set of possible values along any one axis is sometimes referred to as an *array*. Many salient characteristics of classification schemes may be described in terms of this n-dimensional spatial model.

It should be noted that, unlike the dimensions of a Cartesian space, the different characteristics appealed to in a classification scheme are not always wholly independent of each other. A medical classification, for example, may well subdivide illnesses or treatments both by the organ or biological system involved and by the age, sex, or other salient properties of the patient. Since some illnesses afflict only certain age groups or one sex or the other, the two axes are not wholly independent. A classification of dialects based on the pronunciation of a given lexical item can only apply to dialects in which that lexical item exists. A distinction in a social classification between hereditary and nonhereditary titles is relevant only to that part of the population which bears titles, and only in countries with a nobility. The digits 2 for drama and 3 for fiction have these meanings in the Dewey classification for literature, but not in the 900s (history) or the 100s (philosophy). And so on.

The idea of a classification as describing an n-dimensional Cartesian space is thus in many cases a dramatic simplification. It is nonetheless convenient to describe each characteristic or property appealed to in a classification as determining a position along an axis, even if that axis has no meaning for many classes in the scheme. Those offended by this inexactitude in the metaphor may amuse themselves by thinking of the logical space defined by such a classification not as a Cartesian or Newtonian one but as a relativistic space with a non-Euclidean geometry.

Some Distinctions among Classification Schemes

When the axes of the logical space are explicitly identified in the description of the classification scheme, the scheme is commonly referred to as a *faceted* classification, and each axis (or the representation of a given class's value along a specific axis) as a *facet*. The concept of facets in classification schemes was first systematized by S.R. Ranganathan, though the basic phenomena are visible in earlier systems, as the example from the Dewey classification given above illustrates.

Faceted schemes are typically contrasted with *enumerative* schemes, in which all classes in the system are exhaustively enumerated in the classification handbook or *schedule.* In a typical faceted scheme, a separate schedule is provided for each facet and the facets are combined by the classifier according to specified rules; because the classifier must create or *synthesize* the class number, rather than looking it up in an enumeration, faceted schemes are sometimes also called *synthetic* (or, to emphasize that the task of synthesis must be preceded by analysis of the relevant properties of the object, *analytico-synthetic*) schemes. Both because of their intellectual clarity and because they can readily exploit the strengths of electronic database management systems, faceted classification schemes have become increasingly popular in recent years.

Some classification schemes provide single expressions denoting regions of the logical space; in what follows these are referred to as *(class) formulas.* Formulas are convenient when the objects classified must be listed in a single one-dimensional list, as on the shelves of a library or the pages of a classified bibliography. In such schemes, the order in which axes are represented may take on great importance, and a great deal of inge-nuity can be devoted to deciding whether a classification scheme ought to arrange items first by language, then by genre, and finally by period, or in some other order.

In computerized systems, however, it is normally easier to vary the order of axes and often unnecessary to list every object in the collection in a single sequence, and so the order of axes has tended to become somewhat less important in multidimensional classification schemes intended for computer use. The provision of unique class formulas for each point in the scheme's logical space has correspondingly declined in importance, and much of the discussion of notation in pre-electronic literature on classification has taken on a distinctly quaint air. For those who need to devise compact symbolic formulas for the classes of a scheme, however, the discussions of notation in Ranganathan's *Prolegomena* (1967) are still to be recommended.

When each axis of the logical space can be associated with a particular part of the formula denoting a class, and vice versa, the notation is *expressive* (as in the portion of the Dewey system mentioned above). Fully expressive notations tend to be longer than would otherwise be necessary, so some classification schemes intentionally use inexpressive or incompletely expressive notation, as in most parts of the *Library of Congress* classification system. Expressive notations are advantageous in computer-based applications, since they make it easy to perform searches in the logical space by means of searches against class symbols. A search for dramas in any language, for example, can be performed by searching for items with a Dewey class number matching the regular expression "8.2." No similarly simple search is possible in inexpressive notations.

Some classification systems describe classes using natural-language phrases, rather than by assigning them to specific locations in a class hierarchy; library subject headings are a well-known example, but there are many others (Some classification theorists distinguish such alphabetical systems as *indexing systems*, as opposed to *classification systems* in the strict sense, restricting the latter term to systems that provide a formal notation other than natural language for their class formulas.) Typically, such systems arrange topics in alphabetical order, rather than a systematic order imposed by the structure of the classification scheme. At one extreme, such a system may use free-form textual descriptions of objects to "classify" them. Most alphabetically organized classification systems, however, differ from wholly free-form indices in one or more ways. First, in order to avoid or minimize the inconsistencies caused by the use of different but synonymous descriptions, such systems normally use *controlled vocabularies* rather than unconstrained natural-language prose: descriptors other than proper nouns must be chosen from a closed list. In the ideal case, the controlled vocabulary has exactly one representative from any set of synonyms in the scope of the classification scheme. Second, as part of the vocabulary control alphabetic systems often stipulate that certain kinds of phrases should be "inverted," so that the alphabetical listing will place them near other entries. In some schemes, particular types of descriptors may be subdivided by other descriptors in a hierarchical fashion. Thus the Library of Congress subject heading for *Beowulf* will be followed by "*Beowulf* – Adaptations," "*Beowulf* – Bibliography," "*Beowulf* – Criticism, textual," "*Beowulf* – Study and teaching," "*Beowulf* – Translations – Bibliographies," "*Beowulf* – Translations – History and criticism," and so on. The phrases after the dashes are, in effect, an array of possible subdivisions for anonymous literary works; the *Library of Congress Subject Headings* (LCSH) provide a prescribed set of such expansions for a variety of different kinds of object: anonymous literary works, individuals of various kinds, theological topics, legislative bodies, sports, industries, chemicals, and so on. Third, most systems which use controlled vocabularies also provide a more or less systematic set of cross-references among terms. At a minimum, these cross-references will include *see* references from unused terms to preferred synonyms. In more elaborate cases, *see-also* references will be provided to broader terms, narrower terms, coordinate terms (i.e., other terms with the same broader term), partial synonyms, genus/species terms, and so on. The links to broader and narrower terms allow the alphabetically arranged scheme to provide at least some of the same information as a strictly hierarchical scheme. Like the LCSH, the *New York Times Thesaurus of Descriptors* described by Mills (1983) provides a useful model for work of this kind.

The fineness of distinction carried by the classification – that is, the size of the regions in the logical space that the classification allows us to distinguish – is called (mixing metaphors) the *depth* of the classification scheme. Some classification schemes provide a fixed and unvarying depth; others allow variable depth. Depth may be added either by adding more axes to the classification, as when a library using the Dewey system subdivides 822 (English drama) by period, or by adding more detail to the specification of the value along an axis already present. Faceted classification schemes often allow facets to vary in length, so as to allow the depth of classification to be increased by providing a more precise value for any facet. Notations with fixed-length facets, by contrast, like the part of Dewey described above, cannot increase the specificity of facets other than the last without creating ambiguity.

Whether they use expressive notation or not, some classification schemes provide notations for each node in their hierarchy (e.g., one formula for "literature" and another for "English literature," and so on); in such cases, the categories of the classification are not, strictly speaking, disjoint: the broader classes necessarily subsume the narrower classes arranged below them. One advantage of expressive notation is that it makes this relationship explicit. Other schemes provide notations only for the most fully specified nodes of the hierarchy: the hierarchical arrangement may be made explicit in the description of the scheme, but is collapsed in the definition of the notation, so that the classification gives the impression of providing only a single array of values. Commonly used part-of-speech classification systems often collapse their hierarchies in this way: each tag used to denote word-class and morphological information denotes a complete packet of such information; there is no notation for referring to more general classes like "noun, without regard for its specific morphology." Markup languages similarly often provide names only for the "leaves" of their tree-like hierarchies of element types; even when a hierarchy of classes is an explicit part of the design, as in the Text Encoding Initiative (TEI), there may be no element types which correspond directly to classes in the hierarchy.

When combinations of terms from different axes are specified in advance, as part of the process of classifying or indexing an object, we speak of a *pre-coordinate* system. When a classification system limits itself to identifying the appropriate values along the various axes, and values may be combined at will during a search of the classification scheme, we speak of a *post-coordinate* system. Printed indices that list all the subject descriptors applied to the items in a bibliography, in a fixed order of axes, for example, present a kind of pre-coordinate classification scheme. Online indices that allow searches to be conducted along arbitrary combinations of axes, by contrast, provide a post-coordinate scheme. It is possible for printed indices to provide free combination of terms, but post-coordinate indexing is easier in computer systems. Post-coordinate indexing allows greater flexibility and places greater demands on the intelligence of the user of the index.

Often, classifications are defined in terms of *necessary and sufficient conditions* associated with each class, so that the assignment of some item I to some class C amounts to a claim that I satisfies all of the necessary and at least one of the sufficient conditions of C. This has an obvious translation into logical terms and is convenient for reasoning about the classes and the items classified.

In other cases, classifications are based not on necessary and sufficient conditions but on a set of *paradigmatic examples* for each class; items are assigned to one class or another based on their resemblance to the classes' paradigmatic examples. Here the assignment of an item I to a class C amounts to a claim that I is more similar, in relevant ways, to the paradigmatic examples of C than to those of other classes. The nature of the similarity measure to be used is not always clear or explicit, and even when explicit may be the subject of heated debate within a field. For a given finite population thus classified it may be possible to identify (*a posteriori*) sets of necessary and sufficient conditions for the classes, but when the classification is based on examination of a finite subset of a potentially infinite population, such empirical generalizations must tend to be provisional and may need revision when further samples of the population are examined (The classic division of life forms into the two kingdoms of plants and animals is a well-known example. The development of microscopy led to the discovery of the protists, which fall clearly into neither category and necessitated the establishment of a third kingdom. Further discoveries have followed; different authorities now identify five kingdoms, six, or more, where Linnaeus identified only two.)

When the axes and the values along each axis or the paradigmatic examples of classes are specified in advance, we can speak of an *a priori* system. When the paradigmatic examples or the axes and their values are derived *post hoc* from the items encountered in the collection of objects being classified, we may speak of an *a posteriori* or *data-driven* system. Author-specified keywords and free-text searching are simple examples of data-driven classification. Citation analysis, and in particular the study of co-citation patterns in scholarly literature, as described by Garfield (1979), is another.

In some cases, the identification of axes in a data-driven system involves statistical analysis of data. The technique of latent semantic analysis is an example: initially, the occurrence or non-occurrence of each word in the vocabulary of all the documents in the collection being indexed is treated as an axis, and a statistical analysis is performed to collapse as many of these axes together as possible and identify a useful set of axes which are as nearly orthogonal to each other as the data allow. In a typical application, latent-semantic analysis will identify documents in a space of 200 or so dimensions. It is sometimes possible to examine the dimensions and associate meaning with them individually, but for the most part data-driven statistical methods do not attempt to interpret the different axes of their space individually. Instead, they rely on conventional measures of distance in *n*-dimensional spaces to identify items which are near each other; when the classification has been successful, items which are near each other are similar in ways useful for the application, and items which are distant from each other are dissimilar.

A priori systems may also be interpreted as providing some measure of similarity among items, but it is seldom given a numerical value.

Some data-driven systems work by being given samples of pre-classified training material and inducing some scheme of properties which enables them to match, more or less well, the classifications given for the training material. Other data-driven systems work without overt supervision, inducing classifications based solely on the observed data.

A priori systems require more effort in advance than data-driven systems, both in the definition of the classification scheme and in its application by skilled classifiers. The costs of data-driven systems are concentrated later in the history of the classification effort, and tend to involve less human effort and more strictly computational effort. Data-driven classification schemes may also appeal to scholars because they are free of many of the obvious opportunities for bias exhibited by *a priori* schemes and thus appear more nearly theory-neutral. It must be stressed, therefore, that while the theoretical assumptions of data-driven systems may be less obvious and less accessible to inspection by those without a deep knowledge of statistical techniques, they are nonetheless necessarily present.

Rules for Classification

Some principles for constructing classification schemes have evolved over the centuries; they are not always followed, but are generally to be recommended as leading to more useful classification schemes.

The first of these is to avoid *cross-classification:* a one-dimensional classification should normally depend on the value of a single characteristic of the object classified, should provide for discrete (non-overlapping) values, and should allow for all values which will be encountered: perhaps the best-known illustration of this rule lies in its violation in the fictional Chinese encyclopedia imagined by Jorge Luis Borges, in which

> it is written that animals are divided into: (a) those that belong to the Emperor, (b) embalmed ones, (c) those that are trained, (d) suckling pigs, (e) mermaids, (f) fabulous ones, (g) stray dogs, (h) those that are included in this classification, (i) those that tremble

as if they were mad, (j) innumerable ones, (k) those drawn with a very fine camel's-hair brush, (l) others, (m) those that have just broken a flower vase, (n) those that resemble flies from a distance. (Borges, 1981)

One apparent exception to this rule is often found in schemes which seek to minimize the length of their class formulas: often two characteristics are collapsed into a single step in the classification hierarchy, as when a demographic classification has the classes infant (sex unspecified), infant male, infant female, child (sex unspecified), boy, girl, adult (sex unspecified), man, woman.

Other desirable attributes of a classification scheme may be summarized briefly (I abbreviate here the "canons" defined by Ranganathan). Each characteristic used as the basis for an axis in the logical space should:

1. distinguish some objects from others: that is, it should give rise to at least two subclasses;
2. be relevant to the purpose of the classification scheme (every classification scheme has a purpose; no scheme can be understood fully without reference to that purpose);
3. be definite and ascertainable; this means that a classification scheme cannot be successfully designed or deployed without taking into account the conditions under which the work of classification is to be performed;
4. be permanent, so as to avoid the need for constant reclassification;
5. have an enumerable list of possible values which exhausts all possibilities. Provision should normally be made for cases where the value is not ascertainable after all: it is often wise to allow values like *unknown* or *not specified.* In many cases several distinct special values are needed; among those sometimes used are: *unknown* (but applicable), *does-not-apply*, *any* (data compatible with all possible values for the field), *approximate* (estimated with some degree of imprecision), *disputed*, *uncertain* (classifier is not certain whether this axis is applicable; if it is applicable, the value is unknown).

In classification schemes which provide explicit class symbols, it is useful to provide a consistent sequence of axes in the construction of the class symbol (if the subject classification for literature divides first by country or language and then by period, it is probably wise for the subject classification for history to divide first by country and then by period, rather than vice versa). The sequence of values within an array of values for a given axis should also be made helpful, and consistent in different applications. Patterns sometimes suggested include arranging the sequence for increasing concreteness, increasing artificiality, increasing complexity, increasing quantity, chronological sequence, arrangement by spatial contiguity, from bottom to top, from left to right, clockwise sequence, arrangement following a traditional canonical sequence, arrangement by frequency of values (in bibliographic contexts this is called *literary warrant*), or as a last resort alphabetical sequence.

Many classification schemes appeal, at some point, to one of a number of common characteristics in order to subdivide a class which otherwise threatens to become too large (in bibliographic practice, it is sometimes advised to subdivide a class if it would otherwise contain more than 20 items). Subdivision by chronology, by geographic location, or by alphabetization are all commonly used; schedules for subdivision on chronological, geographic, linguistic, genre, and other grounds can be found in standard classification schemes and can usefully be studied, or adopted wholesale, in the creation of new schemes.

Classification schemes intended for use by others do well to allow for variation in the depth of classification practiced. Library classification schemes often achieve this by allowing class numbers to be truncated (for coarser classification) or extended (for finer); markup languages may allow for variable depth of markup by making some markup optional and by providing element types of varying degrees of specificity.

For many applications of classification, the assignment of an object to a class should depend only upon the object and the classification scheme, and not (for example) on the identity of the classifier. In some fields (e.g., part-of-speech tagging), classification schemes are often tested by measuring the consistency with which different classifiers trained in the scheme classify the same data in the same way (referred to in computational linguistics as *inter-annotator agreement*); higher scores indicate more reliable repeatability of classification. Inter-annotator agreement is often used to set a target for machine classification of input; when an automatic process agrees with human annotators as often as they agree among themselves, then classification can be automated with no perceptible drop in quality (In practice, machine classification is often deployed even when it does not quite reach this standard, the drop in quality being made up for by dramatic increases in quantity of data.) Inter-annotator agreement can also be used as a quality measure for classification schemes and their documentation.

It is also desirable, in schemes intended for general use, to provide for semantic extension and the addition of new concepts; this is not always easy. Library classification schemes often attempt to achieve this by providing standard schedules for subdividing classes by chronology, geographic distribution, and so on, to be applied according to the judgment of the classifier; the *Colon Classification* goes further by defining an array of abstract semantic concepts which can be used when subdivision by other standard axes is not feasible or appropriate. It provides a good illustration of the difficulty of providing useful guidance in areas not foreseen by the devisers of the classification scheme:

1. unity, God, world, first in evolution or time, one-dimension, line, solid state, …
2. two dimensions, plane, cones, form, structure, anatomy, morphology, sources of knowledge, physiography, constitution, physical anthropology, …
3. three dimensions, space, cubics, analysis, function, physiology, syntax, method, social anthropology, …
4. heat, pathology, disease, transport, interlinking, synthesis, hybrid, salt, …
5. energy, light, radiation, organic, liquid, water, ocean, foreign land, alien, external, environment, ecology, public controlled plan, emotion, foliage, aesthetics, woman, sex, crime, …
6. dimensions, subtle, mysticism, money, finance, abnormal, phylogeny, evolution, …
7. personality, ontogeny, integrated, holism, value, public finance, …
8. travel, organization, fitness.

In markup languages, a simple semantic extension takes the form of allowing *class* or *type* attributes on elements: for any element type *e*, an element instance labeled with a *class* or *type* attribute can be regarded as having a specialized meaning. In some markup languages, elements with extremely general semantics are provided (such as the TEI *div*, *ab*, or *seg* elements, or the HTML *div* and *span* elements), in order to allow the greatest possible flexibility for the use of the specialization attributes.

Any new classification scheme, whether intended for general use or for use only by a single project, will benefit from clear documentation of its purpose and (as far as they can be made explicit) its assumptions. For each class in the scheme, the scope of the class should be clear; sometimes the scope is sufficiently clear from the name, but very often it is essential to provide *scope notes* describing rules for determining whether objects fall into the class or not. Experience is the best teacher here; some projects, like many large libraries, keep master copies of their classification schemes and add annotations or additional scope notes whenever a doubtful case arises and is resolved.

A Formal View

From a purely formal point of view, classification may be regarded as the partition of some set of objects (let us call this set *O*) into some set of classes (let us call this set of classes *C*, or the *classification scheme*).

In simple cases (nominal classifications), the classes of *C* have no identified relation to each other but serve merely as bins into which the objects in *O* are sorted. For any finite *O*, there is a finite number of possible partitions of *O* into non-empty pairwise disjoint subsets of *O*. As a consequence, there is at most a finite number of extensionally distinct ways to classify any finite set *O* into classes; after that number is reached, any new classification must reconstitute a grouping already made by some other classification and thus be extensionally equivalent to it. Such extensionally equivalent classifications need not be intentionally equivalent: if we classify the four letters *a*, *b*, *l*, *e* according to their phonological values, we might put *a* and *e* together as vowels, and *b* and *l* as consonants. If we classed them according to whether their letter forms have ascenders or not, we would produce the same grouping; the two classifications are thus extensionally equivalent, though very different in intention. In practice, the extensional equivalence of two classifications may often suggest some relation among the properties appealed to, as when classifying the syllables of German according to their lexicality and according to their stress.

In some cases, the classes of *C* can be related by a proximity measure of some kind. In such a classification, any two adjacent classes are more similar to each other than, say, a pair of non-adjacent classes. If such a classification scheme relies on a single scalar property, its classes may be imagined as corresponding to positions on, or regions of, a line. If the classification schema relies on two independent properties, the classes will correspond to points or regions in a plane. In practice, practical classification schemes often involve arbitrary numbers of independent properties; if *n* properties are used by a classification scheme, individual classes may be identified with positions in an *n*-dimensional space. The rules of Cartesian geometry may then be applied to test similarity between classes; this is simplest if the axes are quantitative, or at least ordered, but suitably modified distance measures can be used for purely nominal (unordered, unquantitative) classifications as well: the distance along the axis may be 0, for example, if two items have the same value for that axis, and 1 otherwise.

If we imagine some finite number of classes, and conceive of a classification scheme as being defined by some finite-length description (say, in English or any other natural language) of how to apply those classes to some infinite set of objects, then it may be noted that there is an infinite number of possible groupings which will not be generated by any classification scheme described in our list. The argument is as follows:

1. Let us label the classes with the numbers 1 to n, where n is the number of classes.
2. Let us assume that the objects to be classified can be placed in some definite order; the means by which we do this need not concern us here.
3. Then let us place the descriptions of possible classifications also into a definite order; it is easy to see that the list of descriptions is likely to be infinite, but we can nevertheless place them into a definite order. Since we imagine the descriptions as being in English or some other natural language, we can imagine sorting them first by length and then alphabetically. In practice, there might be some difficulty deciding whether a given text in English does or does not count as a description of a classification scheme, but for purposes of this exercise, we need not concern ourselves with this problem: we can list all English texts, and indeed all sequences of letters, spaces, and punctuation, in a definite sequence (If we cannot interpret the sequence of letters as defining a rule for assigning objects to classes, we can arbitrarily assign every object to class 1.)
4. Now let us imagine a table, with one row for each description of a classification scheme and one column for each object to be classified. In the cell corresponding to a given scheme and object, we write the number of the class assigned to that object by that classification scheme. Each row thus describes a grouping of the objects into classes.
5. Now, we describe a grouping of the objects into classes which differs from every grouping in our list:

    (a) Starting in the first row and the first column, we examine the number written there. If that number is less than n, we add 1 to it; if it is equal to n, we subtract $n - 1$ from it.
    (b) Next, we go to the next row and the next column, and perform the same operation.
    (c) We thus describe a diagonal sequence of cells in the table, and for each column we specify a class number different from the one written there. The result is that we have assigned each object to a class, but the resulting grouping does not correspond to any grouping listed in the table (since it differs from each row in at least one position).

We are forced, then, to conclude that even though our list of finite-length descriptions of classification schemes was assumed to be infinite, there is at least one assignment of objects to classes that does not correspond to any classification scheme in the list (The list contains only the schemes with finite-length descriptions, but the classification we have just described requires an infinitely large table for its description, so it does not appear in the list.) There are, in fact, not just the one but an infinite number of such classifications which are not in the list.

Since the list contains, by construction, every classification scheme that has a finite-length description, we must infer that the classifications described by the diagonal procedure outlined above do not have any finite-length description; let us call them, for this reason, *ineffable* classifications.

The existence of ineffable classifications is not solely of theoretical interest; it may also serve as a salutary reminder that no single classification scheme can be expected to be "complete" in the sense of capturing every imaginable distinction or common property attributable to the members of *O*. A "perfect" classification scheme, in the sense described above of a scheme that perfectly captures every imaginable similarity among the objects of *O*, is thus a purely imaginary construct; actual classification schemes necessarily capture only a subset of the imaginable properties of the objects, and we must choose among them on pragmatic grounds.

Make or Find?

Whenever systematic classification is needed, the researcher may apply an existing classification scheme or else devise a new scheme for the purpose at hand. Existing schemes may be better documented and more widely understood than an *ad hoc* scheme would be; in some cases they will have benefited from more sustained attention to technical issues in the construction of a scheme than the researcher will be able to devote to a problem encountered only incidentally in the course of a larger research project. Being based on larger bodies of material, they may well provide better coverage of unusual cases than the researcher would otherwise manage; they may thus be more likely to provide an exhaustive list of possible values for each axis. And the use of a standard classification scheme does allow more direct comparison with material prepared by others than would otherwise be possible.

On the other hand, schemes with broad coverage may often provide insufficient depth for the purposes of specialized research (just as the thousand basic categories of the Dewey Decimal system will seldom provide a useful framework for a bibliography of secondary literature on a single major work or author), and the studied theoretical neutrality of schemes intended for wide use may be uncongenial to the purpose of the research.

In the preparation of resources intended for use by others, the use of standard existing classification schemes should generally be preferred to the *ad hoc* concoction of new ones. Note that some existing classification schemes are proprietary and may be used in publicly available material only by license; before using an established classification scheme, researchers should confirm that their usage is authorized.

For work serving a particular research agenda, no general rule is possible; the closer the purpose of the classification to the central problem of the research, the more likely is a custom-made classification scheme to be necessary. Researchers should not, however, underestimate the effort needed to devise a coherent scheme for systematic classification of anything.

Some Existing Classification Schemes

Classification schemes may be needed, and existing schemes may be found, for objects of virtually any type. Those mentioned here are simply samples of some widely used kinds of classification: classification of documents by subject or language variety, classification of words by word class or semantics, classification of extra-textual entities by socioeconomic and demographic properties, and classification of images.

The best-known *subject classification* schemes are those used in libraries and in major periodical bibliographies to provide subject access to books and articles. The *Dewey Decimal Classification* (DDC) and its internationalized cousin the *Universal Decimal Classification* (UDC) are both widely used, partly for historical reasons (the Dewey system was the first widely promoted library classification scheme), partly owing to their relatively convenient decimal notation, and because their classification schedules are regularly updated. In the USA, the *Library of Congress* classification is now more widely used in research libraries, in part because its notation is slightly more compact than that of Dewey.

Less widely used, but highly thought of by some, are the *Bliss Bibliographic Classification*, originally proposed by Henry Evelyn Bliss and now thoroughly revised, and the *Colon Classification* devised by Shiyali Ramamrita Ranganathan, perhaps the most important theorist of bibliographic classification in history. Both are fully faceted classification schemes.

The controlled vocabulary of the *Library of Congress Subject Headings* may also be useful; its patterns for the subdivision of various kinds of subjects provide useful arrays for subordinate axes.

Researchers in need of specialized subject classification should also examine the subject classifications used by major periodical bibliographies in the field; Balay (1996) provides a useful source for finding such bibliographies.

The creators of *language corpora* often wish to classify their texts according to genre, register, and the demographic characteristics of the author or speaker, in order to construct a stratified sample of the language varieties being collected and to allow users to select subcorpora appropriate for various tasks. No single classification scheme appears to be in general use for this purpose. The schemes used by existing corpora are documented in their manuals; that used by the Brown and the Lancaster–Oslo/Bergen (LOB) corpora is in some ways a typical example. As can be seen, it classifies samples based on a mixture of subject matter, genre, and type of publication:

A   Press: reportage
B   Press: editorial
C   Press: reviews
D   Religion
E   Skills, trades, and hobbies
F   Popular lore
G   Belles lettres, biography, essays
H   Miscellaneous (government documents, foundation reports, industry reports, college catalog, industry house organ)
J   Learned and scientific writings
K   General fiction

L   Mystery and detective fiction
M   Science fiction
N   Adventure and western fiction
P   Romance and love story
R   Humor

Some corpus projects have produced, as a side effect, thoughtful articles on sampling issues and the classification of texts. Biber (1993) is an example. Some corpora, for example the British National Corpus, have not attempted to provide a single text classification in the style of the Brown and LOB corpora. Instead, they provide descriptions of the salient features of each text, allowing users to select subcorpora by whatever criteria they choose, in a kind of post-coordinate system.

Some language corpora provide word-by-word annotation of their texts, most usually providing a single flat classification of words according to a mixture of word-class and inflectional information (plural nouns and singular nouns, for example, thus being assigned to distinct classes). A variety of *word-class tagging* schemes is in use, but for English-language corpora the point of reference typically remains the tag set defined by the Brown Corpus of Modern American English, as refined by the Lancaster–Oslo/Bergen (LOB) Corpus, and further refined through several generations of the CLAWS (Constituent Likelihood Automatic Word-tagging System) tagger developed and maintained at the University of Lancaster (Garside and Smith, 1997). When new word-class schemes are devised, the detailed documentation of the tagged LOB corpus (Johansson *et al.*, 1986) can usefully be taken as a model.

Semantic classification of words remains a topic of research; the classifications most frequently used appear to be the venerable work of Roget's *Thesaurus* and the newer more computationally oriented work of Miller and colleagues on *WordNet* (on which see Fellbaum, 1998) and their translators, imitators, and analogs in other languages (on which see Vossen, 1998).

In *historical work*, classification is often useful to improve the consistency of data and allow more reliable analysis. When systematic classifications are applied to historical sources such as manuscript census registers, it is generally desirable to retain some account of the original data, to allow consistency checking and later reanalysis (e.g., using a different classification scheme). The alternative, *pre-coding* the information and recording only the classification assigned, rather than the information as given in the source, was widely practiced in the early years of computer applications in history, since it provides for more compact data files, but it has fallen out of favor because it makes it more difficult or impossible for later scholars to check the process of classification or to propose alternative classifications.

Historians may find the *industrial*, *economic*, and *demographic classifications* of modern governmental and other organizations useful; even where the classifications cannot be used unchanged, they may provide useful models. Census bureaus and similar governmental bodies, and archives of social science data, are good sources of information about such classification schemes. In the Anglophone world, the most prominent social science data archives may be the Inter-university Consortium for Political and Social Research (ICPSR) in Ann Arbor (www.icpsr.umich.edu) and the UK Data Archive at the University of Essex (www.data-archive.ac.uk). The Council of European

Social Science Data Archives (www.nsd.uib.no/cessda) maintains a list of data archives in various countries both inside and outside Europe.

With the increasing emphasis on image-based computing in the humanities and the creation of large electronic archives of images, there appears to be great potential utility in classification schemes for images. If the class formulas of an image classification scheme are written in conventional characters (as opposed, say, to being themselves thumbnail images), then collections of images can be made accessible to search and retrieval systems by indexing and searching the image classification formulas, and then providing access to the images themselves. Older image classification schemes typically work with controlled natural-language vocabularies; some resources use detailed descriptions of the images in a rather formulaic English designed to improve the consistency of description and make for better retrieval. The *Index of Christian Art* at Princeton University (http://ica.princeton.edu) is an example.

The difficulties of agreeing on and maintaining consistency in keyword-based classifications or descriptions of images, however, have meant that there is lively interest both in unstructured natural-language *tagging* of images by humans and in automatic recognition of similarities among graphic images; there is a great deal of proprietary technology in this area. Insofar as it is used for search and retrieval, image recognition may be thought of as a specialized form of data-driven classification, analogous to automatic statistically based classification of texts.

REFERENCES AND FURTHER READING

Anderson, J.D. 1979. Contextual indexing and faceted classification for databases in the humanities. In *Information Choices and Policies: Proceedings of the ASIS Annual Meeting, vol.* 16, ed. R.D. Tally and R.R. Deultgen. White Plains, NY: Knowledge Industry Publications, 194–201.

Balay, R., ed. 1996. *Guide to Reference Books*, 11th edition. Chicago: American Library Association.

Biber, D. 1993. Representativeness in corpus design. *Literary and Linguistic Computing* 8 (4), 243–57.

Borges, J.L. 1981. *The Analytical Language of John Wilkins*. Trans. R.L.C. Simms. In *Borges: A Reader*, ed. E.R. Monegal and A. Reid. New York: Dutton, 141–3.

Bowker, G.C., and Star, S.L. 1999. *Sorting Things Out: Classification and its Consequences*. Cambridge, MA: MIT Press.

Deerwester, S., Dumais, S.T., Furnas, G.W., Landauer, T.K., and Harshman, R. 1990. Indexing by latent semantic analysis. *Journal of the American Society for Information Science* 41 (6), 391–407.

Fellbaum, C., ed. 1998. *WordNet: An Electronic Lexical Database*. Cambridge, MA: MIT Press.

Floud, R. 1979. *An Introduction to Quantitative Methods for Historians*. London: Methuen.

Foskett, A.C. 1996. *The Subject Approach to Information*, 5th edition. London: Library Association. [first published by Linnet Books and Clive Bingley, 1969.]

Garfield, E. 1979. *Citation Indexing: Its Theory and Application in Science, Technology, and Humanities*. New York: Wiley.

Garside, R., and N. Smith, N. 1997. A Hybrid Grammatical Tagger: CLAWS4. In *Corpus Annotation: Linguistic Information from Computer Text Corpora*, ed. R. Garside, G. Leech, and A. McEnery. London: Longman, 102–21.

Johansson, S., Atwell, E., Garside, R., and Leech, G. 1986. *The Tagged LOB Corpus*. Bergen: Norwegian Computing Centre for the Humanities.

Kieft, R.H., ed. 2008. *Guide to Reference*. Chicago: American Library Association. http://www.guidetoreference.org (accessed June 20, 2015).

Kuhn T. 1977. *Second Thoughts on Paradigms*. In *The Structure of Scientific Theories*, 2nd edition, ed. F. Suppe. Urbana: University of Illinois Press, 459–82.

Library of Congress Cataloging Policy and Support Office. 1996. *Library of Congress Subject Headings,*

19th edition, 4 vols. Washington, DC: Library of Congress.

Mills, H. 1983. The *New York Times* Thesaurus of Descriptors. In *Software Productivity*. Boston: Little, Brown, 31–55.

Mills, J., and Broughton, V. 1977–. *Bliss Bibliographic Classification*, 2nd edition. London: Butterworth.

Ranganathan, S.R. 1967. *Prolegomena to Library Classification*, 3rd edition. Bombay: Asia Publishing House.

Ranganathan, S.R. 1989. *Colon Classification*, 7th edition. Basic and Depth version. Revised and edited by M.A. Gopinath. Vol. 1, Schedules for Classification. Bangalore: Sarada Ranganathan Endowment for Library Science.

Svenonius, E. 2000. *The Intellectual Foundation of Information Organization*. Cambridge, MA: MIT Press.

Vossen, P. 1998. Introduction to EuroWordNet. *Computers and the Humanities* 32, 73–89.

Part IV
Dissemination

27

Interface as Mediating Actor for Collection Access, Text Analysis, and Experimentation

Stan Ruecker

Interface design is a frequent necessity in the digital humanities, where there is a longstanding tradition of scholars producing systems both for their own use and for the use of others. While it is possible to approach the problems of designing, programming, and testing an interface from the perspective of a "naïve" reading of what an interface is and does, another core activity of digital humanists is to interrogate more deeply every aspect of scholarly activities, with the twin goals of improving our understanding and our best practices. One possibly fruitful lens for examining interface design is actor–network theory (ANT), which posits that the way to achieve a more complete understanding of the structure, and of the behaviors of people interacting with technology, is to somewhat level the playing field and treat all the parts of the system as having potential for action within the network of associations that represent one aspect of the system.

For purposes of discussion, we can identify three types of digital humanities interface projects. They focus respectively on collections, text analysis (sometimes with visualization), and design experiments. Within each type there is a range. For collections and federations of collections, the terrain is diverse, from some that are relatively "boutique" projects, sometimes dealing with a single author, to others that are dedicated to entire fields of study, or that function as general digital libraries (e.g., Figure 27.1).

On the text analysis side, the range goes from Steve Ramsay's command-line scripts to David Hoover's out-of-the-box Excel-based text analysis, to Stéfan Sinclair's series of online toolkits (the current one is *Voyant*, created collaboratively with Geoffrey Rockwell; Figure 27.2).

A New Companion to Digital Humanities, First Edition. Edited by Susan Schreibman, Ray Siemens, and John Unsworth.
© 2016 John Wiley & Sons, Ltd. Published 2016 by John Wiley & Sons, Ltd.

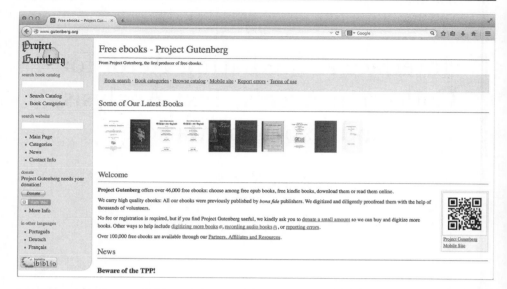

Figure 27.1   The *Project Gutenberg* collection interface provides access to tens of thousands of e-books.

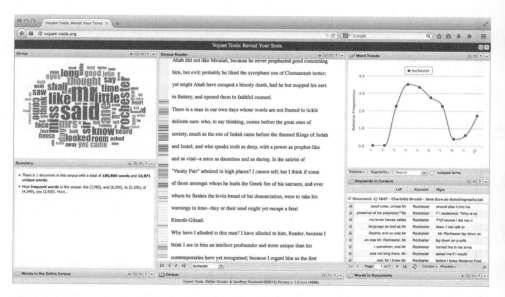

Figure 27.2   The *Voyant* text analysis interface reveals Charlotte Bronte's use of the name Rochester in *Jane Eyre*. Project led by Stéfan Sinclair and Geoffrey Rockwell.

Finally, there are projects where the design of experimental human–computer interfaces is at the heart of the scholarly activity. These prototypes are for "thinking through making" and may deal with either collection contents or analysis tools or both, but vary from those two categories in that experimental prototypes are not intended to be

Figure 27.3   A model proposing a design for a handheld conversation. Design by Liz Jernegan.

production systems: they only need to be robust enough to reify the parts of a concept that are the focus of inquiry (e.g., Figure 27.3).

That said, what all three types of interfaces (collection, text analysis, and prototype) have in common is that they are placed at the intersection of people and technology. If we adopt the lens of ANT, then the people, the underlying technology (whether a collection or an analytical process), and the interface itself all become actors in the network. The interface, however, plays a unique role in that it is a mediating actor – it exists primarily to provide a means of enhancing the communication between people, the technology, the content, and the abstract concept being experimentally investigated. Once we recognize this role for the interface, we can begin to ask questions about how well it is serving the purpose of mediating. For example, does it assume a uniformity of understanding about core concepts and terminology, or does it recognize multiple communities of practice? Does it distinguish between levels of sophistication or experience, or is it predicated on people having reached a fairly specific level of competency? What kinds of content information does it make visible or even privilege, and what kinds does it deprecate or perhaps keep invisible?

Actor–network Theory (ANT)

Although ANT is primarily a practice of sociologists, which is to say scholars studying existing social concepts, systems, and behaviors, it can also be a valuable approach for designers (e.g., Fleischmann, 2006), who are more interested in examining the evocative, the suggestive, or the speculative in order to have a better understanding for the purposes of creating. In examining human–computer interfaces through the perspective of actor–network theory, perhaps the first item to note is that the name of the perspective involves terms that are not used in their conventional senses. Bruno Latour has famously remarked that he is dissatisfied with the entire term: "There are four things that do not work with actor–network theory; the word actor, the word network, the word theory and the hyphen! Four nails in the coffin" (Latour, 1997).

The reason for his dissatisfaction relates to the misunderstandings that can arise from people who already have reasonably established ideas about what constitutes an actor, a network, and a theory. In this case, an actor is anything that pursues a program of action, a network is the perhaps fleeting associations among actors, and theory does not suggest a well-constructed set of testable hypotheses so much as a perhaps fruitful speculation. Among its principal proponents, Law and Singleton (2013) have recently described it as a sensibility. The hyphen, of course, functions to indicate a compound adjective and has been read by some people as suggesting that actors and networks might be one and the same, or at least related in a way that is problematic (e.g., Cressman, 2009).

Interfaces as Actors

What does it mean for software to be an actor? Is this a designation that will apply only to very specific kinds of software, or is it useful to consider all software, and particularly all human–computer interfaces, in this category?

In terms of specialized software, the top of the agential list are software "agents," whose purpose is to act on behalf of people. In a related category are various attempts to develop artificial intelligence through a process of training, where one of the goals of the approach is that the results are not entirely predictable. Insofar as the software "learns," perhaps through the activation and strengthening of connections between nodes, the outcome of the learning process needs to be studied in order to be understood. This stands in contradistinction to mainstream software, where the programmer has arranged for a kind of mechanical reaction to input conditions. When that predictability is compromised, we describe the software has having a bug that must be found and removed.

However, even a mechanical reaction can be understood as acting. In his well-known paper on hydraulic door closers (published under a pseudonym), Bruno Latour (1988) analyzes at some length the implications for people of offloading the responsibility for shutting the door onto a mechanical device. The mechanism usually acts predictably, but on occasions it falters, inclining people to respond to it as something that has a temperament. Its default behavior may also be at odds with the wishes of the people encountering it, who for example might want to have the door partially open to communicate to other people at a given moment that they are accessible if necessary, but are not readily available for exchanges involving casual sociality. In this respect, it is not difficult to personify the door closer as a kind of strict police, with an intransigence about its duty that requires human resistance to overcome. A door closer, however, is a relatively simple technology compared with a human–computer interface.

Assumptions of Uniformity

There are many reasons for treating a user community as having a uniformity of understanding of core concepts and vocabulary. First is that the specificity of a task can suggest that the one function will fit all – there is no need to question the assumption that everyone using a computer will be able to grasp the idea of a search box and recognize it by the word "search." Next is learnability. If it should arise that different users do not share concepts or terminology, then hopefully some will already share the ones used by the designers and programmers, and the others will just have to learn. Finally is the pragmatic argument that there are only so many resources available for interfaces, and customization to any great extent is a luxury that cannot be afforded.

However, not all tasks are simple. For example, in the *Metadata Open New Knowledge* (MONK) project (www.monkproject.org), we were attempting to make some of the state-of-the-art text-mining tools available in a form that would permit them to be useful for scholars in the humanities. MONK (Figure 27.4) is one of several projects that combined all three types of digital humanities interface. First, it was a repository of an ever-growing collection of source documents such as novels, plays, and poems, so in that sense the interface was required to provide collection access. Second, it involved some sophisticated text analysis tools with shorthand names like *Naïve Bayes* and

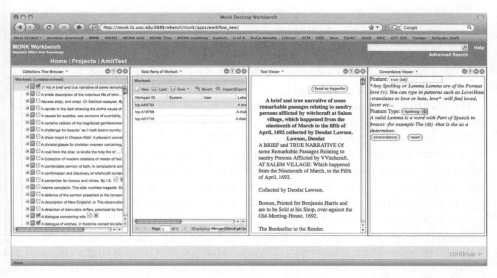

Figure 27.4 A screenshot of one of the MONK interface iterations. Design by Milena Radzikowska. Lead Programmer Amit Kumar.

Support Vector Machines. Third, although it was primarily an infrastructure project (with funding from the Mellon Foundation), the innovation of attempting to get a diverse set of complicated systems running together involved some experimentation at every level.

What seemed clear right from the start was that we would not be able to rely on a community of practice that shared core concepts and vocabulary. For example, one of the key text-mining functions of MONK was that it would allow the user to provide a collection of short text passages like sentences or paragraphs that represented some higher-level concept, and have the system search its collections to find similar passages. For some months, the members of the design team referred to this function as Search by Example. We thought it would communicate the purpose of using the tool to people who had never used a tool of this kind before.

However, from the perspective of the computer scientists, a description of this kind was unacceptable. It was simply wrong. What was running was not a search process in any conventional sense, and to call it a search was misleading. What the user was actually doing was providing training materials to a supervised (or perhaps semi-supervised) Naïve Bayes classification algorithm. A better label for the button, although not a perfectly adequate one, might therefore be Classification. The use of this term was also more accurate with respect to the task we were asking the user to do. In order for the system to work, it wasn't optimal to provide only positive examples. It was better to provide examples of several kinds, with as many of each kind as possible, so that the system could use the differences between the sets of examples to establish its classification rules. One of the most effective uses was made by Steger (2013), who was looking in detail at the sentimental novel. Her training set involved examples of various characteristically sentimental scenes, such as betrothals, the return of prodigals, deathbed recantations, and so on. One of her conclusions was that the distribution of these scenes provided a structure for the ebb and flow of the emotions of the reader.

What also became clear in designing the interfaces for MONK was that there was a well-established distinction in the text-mining community between classification and clustering. Classification implies that the user is involved in "supervising" or in our case "semi-supervising" the process by providing examples. Clustering, on the other hand, is unsupervised – the system takes the input and groups it automatically, usually into a preset number of categories.

The discussion continued into the other two reasons for making an assumption of uniformity – if people didn't know what the word classification meant, then it was probably too dangerous for them to be using MONK at all. Further, we had a budget and timeline to meet, and couldn't spend too much on these details. Be right rather than wrong, was more or less our decision, and let the chips fall where they may. To be fair, the project did provide some very well-written documentation that not only explained the terminology, but also did a credible job of describing how the processes were working under the hood. RTFM.

However, if we investigate the interface to MONK through the lens of ANT, it might be possible to more clearly understand what we were attempting to do, and to produce some improved best practices for doing it. For example, within ANT, the interface is an actor in a social network. The network also includes the algorithms and the programmers responsible for them, the collection curators and their laboriously cleaned documents, the designers, the user experience (UX) and usability experts, the various hardware devices and network protocols involved, and the wide range of potential users of the system.

The discussion then becomes one of mediation. How does the interface act in such a way that it simultaneously accommodates the core concepts and vocabulary of all the parties involved, and serves as a support for communication among them?

One answer is that it is simply impossible, which can have a variety of implications for the users. First, in order to use the system responsibly, they may need to become experts in the underlying technologies. The purpose of the interface still remains mediation, but it is a much simpler form of mediation because the other actors are on the one hand the algorithms and their implementers, and on the other hand a group of people who already speak the same language. The problem with this solution is that it does not meet the original brief of the project, which was to make these technologies accessible to scholars in the humanities, whose interest, experience, and expertise typically lies elsewhere.

A second possibility is that the users encounter the system knowing nothing about the technology they are using, much as people watching television or driving a car do not need to understand anything about the technologies "under the hood." An understanding of how to use the interface is sufficient. In fact, many theorists have proposed that the use of a system may simply be to provide patterns to help enrich subsequent interpretation. Jerome McGann (2001) calls this process "deformance," while Stéfan Sinclair (2003) and Stephen Ramsay (2011) prefer the term "play." In each case, it can be argued that the mechanism behind the transformation is less important than the resulting patterns:

> I navigate through a text with the same blend of fascination, anxiety, and excitement as I explore the streets of an unfamiliar city: I do not hesitate to venture down mysterious pathways and streets, even though they may lead to a dead end. Various things along my journey may prompt me to change directions, and although I often do not know where I am going, I know that I am somehow accumulating a broader representation of the terrain. If I were given a detailed map and a path to follow, I would be robbed of the enjoyment of exploration and serendipitous discovery. If I were given a list of the monuments and features of the city, I would still only have limited understanding of it. Similarly, lists of words and other components of a text can be very useful and informative, but to truly experience the text I need other means of exploring it. (Sinclair, 2003)

The problem with this approach is that scholarly activity involving algorithms inevitably requires some discussion of what the algorithms do. No responsible journal editors would be pleased with the answer "who cares?" The legacy of the sciences is too powerful and too closely connected to computer programming to permit what is essentially an artistic engagement that may or may not lead to further insight.

Another answer is that it is possible for an interface to function as a mediating object, or perhaps more precisely a boundary object (Star and Griesemer, 1989), that can support the translation from highly precise technical concepts and vocabulary to terminology that is sufficiently connected to the concept and vocabulary domains of the various communities of potential users from the humanities. The danger to be avoided with a boundary object is that it can become an attempt at education rather than communication, and it is generally true that people using an interface are attempting to do something rather than learn. It is sometimes possible, however, for them to learn along the way, as a kind of side effect of whatever they are doing. One underutilized strategy is to make use of tooltips that appear on rollover and contain a set of different terms to describe the same thing. Although redundant in the sense that more than one term is displayed, they can serve a boundary function by connecting for the user the different ways in which different communities discuss the same topic. To revisit our MONK example, we might, for instance, have labeled our function "Clustering" and written our tooltip to say "Provide examples in order to locate items like them." One hurdle that would need to be overcome, however, is the argument that the additional description is simply misleading or wrong from the perspective of the more precise technical community, who are using a term that doesn't communicate the benefit of the function to the user community.

Levels of Sophistication or Experience

It is often the case that interfaces are designed for the first-time user. The principle is that the factors that make a first-time experience straightforward and pleasurable will continue to operate with more experienced users: simplicity, clarity, transparency. Further, without a pleasurable first-time experience, the user is less likely to return to the software to become more experienced with it. The disadvantage of this approach is that the users who do return may want to begin trying additional functionality that was not necessary on the first visit. In the cases of some tools, like those contained in *MS Office* or the *Adobe Creative Suite*, the number of functions can become quite large, and experienced users sometimes find themselves looking in vain for a function that existed in a previous version, but has since been removed in the attempt to make the first-time user experience easier. Functions that are not removed may also be relegated to an obscure location. Worse still are interfaces where the arrangement and visual appearance of controls does not correspond to their frequency of use. Generally speaking, the controls most commonly needed should be most obvious and convenient, while less frequent functions should be lower in the hierarchy.

One alternative strategy is to provide a set of interfaces, designed respectively for the beginning, intermediate, and advanced user. Putting the choice under user control allows people to decide how they would like to deal with the system. Sapach and Saklofske (2013) have recently proposed a related strategy with a gaming metaphor, where the users of a scholarly editing environment would "level up" by gaining experience with previous levels of the interface.

From the ANT perspective, one consideration to keep in mind is that the various actors may have expertise that is not central to the use of the system, but can be acknowledged in order to improve the user experience, even in testing. In particular with experimental prototypes, it is unlikely that anyone using the system will have direct experience of anything quite like them. It is therefore necessary for the interface to mediate in some way between the existing knowledge and specialization of the people working with the prototype and the intended functionality. One way to improve

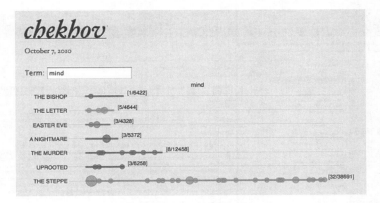

Figure 27.5 The *Bubblelines* prototype showing short stories by Chekhov, with the term "mind" as it appears in each. Design by Carlos Fiorentino. Programmer Alejandro Giacometti.

that mediation is to provide the participants in the user experience study with content that makes sense to them, that looks like the kind of materials they often use (Figure 27.5) (Giacometti *et al.*, 2012). For designers who are typically used to slapping in some "faked up" lorem ipsum content, providing this communicative advantage can sometimes seem unreasonable.

Making Visible and Concealing

There has been some attention in the digital humanities community to what we have called "rich-prospect browsing interfaces," where the approach is to make some meaningful representation of every item in the collection available to the user, who can then manipulate those representations using tools that emerge from the kinds of metadata that are available (Ruecker *et al.*, 2011).

Rich-prospect browsing works best with small collections, numbering in the hundreds or thousands of items. In the digital humanities this is quite a large number of collections, although, as the field expands, the aggregation of content is becoming increasingly common, either through amalgamation of collections under one umbrella or through federation of collections through one common portal. In these cases, it is not possible to represent all individual items simultaneously, but it is possible to subset the collection with an initial search, then treat the results as a smaller collection that can be browsed using a rich-prospect approach.

Central to the idea of rich-prospect browsing is the concept of the meaningful representation of individual collection items. Sometimes accomplished with words and sometimes with images, meaningful representation for a mediating object between different communities of practice should most likely contain either information from each community, or else some hybrid form that sits between.

However, rich-prospect browsers are not the only way of making contents visible to the user. One of the most popular of the more conventional methods consists of simply listing items, or listing items alphabetically by letter of the alphabet. While sometimes

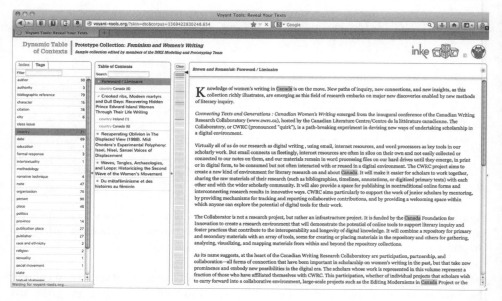

Figure 27.6 The *Dynamic Table of Contexts*, showing results for the semantic tag that has been named "country" by the document curator. Design by Jennifer Windsor. Lead programmer Andrew MacDonald.

discouragingly tedious for the user to navigate, lists at least have the virtue that the contents are being made visible rather than being hidden.

The question that arises is whether or not there are instances where the mediating function of the interface is best served by choosing to keep some things invisible. A typical example is XML tagging, where the reader is usually not interested in seeing the markup unless searching for a concept or attempting to render the text into a form that is viewable online or printable. Even in the case of XML, however, it can be necessary to make some human-readable version of the tags available so that the text can be searched more readily. For instance, in the prototype reading environment called the *Dynamic Table of Contexts* (DToC; Figure 27.6), the reader is able to see the semantic encoding in order to use it to add or subtract items from the table of contents (Ruecker *et al.*, 2014).

In order for the tagging to make sense to someone who is not familiar with the schema, the DToC has a "curator" mode that allows a person who knows the collection to both select the tags that will be displayed and rename them to a more accessible form.

Conclusions

Although it is possible to think of human–computer interfaces as a sort of mundane, utilitarian part of a system, they are often serving a much more complex role, where considering them as actors in the ANT sense is a reasonable way to improve our understanding. In the digital humanities in particular, where examining the "tools of the trade" is a core practice, ANT allows us to consider what an interface is doing from a more nuanced perspective. By studying interfaces as mediating actors, it is possible to see that some of the decisions that need to be made for all three types of digital humanities interfaces can be guided by an awareness that there are multiple actors involved, and that the interface is where the negotiation of meaning among them can take place.

REFERENCES AND FURTHER READING

Callon, M. 1986. The sociology of an actor-network: the case of the electric vehicle. In *Mapping the Dynamics of Science and Technology: Sociology of Science in the Real World*, ed. M. Callon, J. Law, and A. Rip. London: Macmillan, 19–34.

Cressman, D. 2009. A brief overview of actor-network theory: punctualization, heterogeneous engineering and translation. ACT Lab/Centre for Policy Research on Science and Technology (CPROST) School of Communication, Simon Fraser University, Canada.

Fleischmann, K. 2006. Boundary objects with agency: a method for studying the design–use interface. *Information Society* 22 (2), 77–87.

Giacometti, A., Ruecker, S., Fiorentino, C., and the INKE Research Group. 2012. Showcase browsing with Texttiles 2.0 and BubbleLines. *Scholarly and Research Communication* 3 (2).

Latour, B. 1988. [pseud. "Jim Johnson"]. Mixing humans and non-humans together: the sociology of a door-closer. *Social Problems* 35 (3), 298–310.

Latour, B. 1997. On recalling ANT. Lancaster: Department of Sociology, Lancaster University. http://www.lancaster.ac.uk/fass/sociology/research/publications/papers/latour-recalling-ant.pdf (accessed June 20, 2015).

Law, J. 1992. Notes on the theory of the actor-network: ordering, strategy, and heterogeneity. *Systems Practice* 5 (4): 3,79–93.

Law, J., and Singleton, V. 2013. ANT and politics: working in and on the world. *Qualitative Sociology* 36, 485–502.

McGann, J. 2001. *Radiant Textuality: Literature After the World Wide Web*. New York: Palgrave.

Miettinen, R. 1999. The riddle of things: activity theory and actor–network theory as approaches to studying innovations. *Mind, Culture and Activity*, 6 (3), 170–95.

Ramsay, S. 2011. *Reading Machines: Toward an Algorithmic Criticism*. Urbana: University of Illinois Press.

Ruecker, S., Radzikowska, M., and Sinclair, S. 2011. *Visual Interface Design for Cultural Heritage: a Guide to Rich-Prospect Browsing*. Farnham: Ashgate.

Ruecker, S., Adelaar, N., Brown, S., *et al.*, and the INKE Research Group. 2014. Academic prototyping as a method of knowledge production: the case of the Dynamic Table of Contexts. *Scholarly and Research Communication* 5 (2).

Sapach, S., Saklofske, J., and the INKE M&P Team. 2013. Gaming the scholarly edition: opening the private sphere of academic scholarly editing to public apprenticeship via digital game paradigms. Paper presented at Media in Transition 8. MIT, May 3–5, 2013.

Sinclair, S. 2003. Computer-assisted reading: reconceiving text analysis, *Literary and Linguistic Computing* 18 (2), 175–84.Star, S.L., and Griesemer, J. R. 1989. Institutional ecology, "translations" and boundary objects: amateurs and professionals in Berkeley's Museum of Vertebrate Zoology. *Social Studies of Science* 19, 387–420.

Steger, S. 2013. Patterns of sentimentality in Victorian novels. *Digital Studies/Le champ numérique* 3 (2). http://www.digitalstudies.org/ojs/index.php/digital_studies/article/view/238 (accessed January 15, 2014).

28
Saving the Bits: Digital Humanities Forever?

William Kilbride

Scholarship in the humanities is always to some extent historical. Research outputs remain current for long periods – longer even than the scholars who create them may realize. These long life cycles create distinctive risks of loss or decay; but while preservation of humanities research was once about the chemical and biological hazards facing physical collections, it is increasingly a digital concern too.

A series of standards has emerged in the last decade to codify best practice on the preservation of born-digital and digitized content, while a growing community has coalesced around issues of longevity, authenticity, and stewardship of digital materials. Digital preservation has progressed rapidly, borrowing promiscuously from many sectors and professions. This pace of development is increasingly a barrier to entry: the new glut of tools, standards, projects, and services can seem bewildering. As with much digital infrastructure, digital preservation has been to some extent directed to the needs of data-intensive sciences, especially space science and to a lesser extent the social sciences. Consequently there are two abiding risks for those humanities scholars trying to ensure a long-term future for their precious digital cargo: that the emerging practices of digital preservation are a poor fit to the changing needs of humanities; and that jargon and miscommunication confound thoughtful efforts to engage.

It is commonly argued that the case for digital preservation should be articulated as a case for access and use (e.g., BRTF, 2010; HLEG, 2010). Whilst this is true in a narrow sense, the prospect of persistent access to data is not necessarily appetizing, especially as volumes of data grow. Access and use, like preservation, are means to an end. The challenge is surely about enabling enduring impact by thoughtful analysis and consideration of digital collections, which in turn delivers lasting outcomes to the wider community . These are the reasons why digital preservation matters, and these are the reasons why digital humanities and digital preservation need to remain in close dialog with each other.

A New Companion to Digital Humanities, First Edition. Edited by Susan Schreibman, Ray Siemens, and John Unsworth.

This chapter introduces and reviews some of the major and familiar themes from digital preservation in the last decade. It is written to ensure that digital humanities and digital preservation remain properly engaged with each other. Frequent and clear communications are essential to ensure that digital research infrastructures are able to provide the sorts of preservation services that digital humanities require now and will likely need in the future.

Data, the Humanities, and Digital Preservation

The distinctive expectations and approaches of humanities research are debated and explored throughout this volume. Although others will comment more fully on these aspects of digital humanities, a number of terms need to be delineated within the context of digital preservation.

For example, there is a fundamental problem with the word "data" – and not just the question of singular or plural. In digital preservation "data" is (are) routinely presented to archives as "submission information packages." They are transformed into "archival information packages" and are distributed as "dissemination information packages" (see Lavoie, 2004:11–12, for an explanation of the terminology). This is not a statement about empirical value, merely a simple way to distinguish data from hardware or processes. Humanities don't have "data" in the way that sciences do: they have sources, and the constitution of sources is complicated. Sources are specific, fragmentary, and tricky, requiring a proper understanding of context and configuration before they can be deployed. Interpolation is perilous, classification is risky, and even naming things can be challenging. So while the British Library's *Electronic Beowulf* may be the earliest digitized manuscript, it is not data in the way that physical sciences might understand. The digitized surrogate is data in the sense of not being hardware or software: it is data in the sense of being a systematic series of measures of the colour of a manuscript; but it is hardly data about the "Spear Danes in days gone by."

This has implications for how the humanities proceed, including digital humanities. More radical voices notwithstanding, humanities scholarship is empirical, hermeneutic, and historically situated. Because sources do not stand up on their own, scholarship can scarcely verify conclusions by empirical means alone. The humanities proceed methodologically and with a steady reliance on consistency, economy, and efficiency. Statements of fact are always dependent on their context, to a large extent dependent on their paradigm, and only ever as meaningful as the language which contains them.

Of these issues, it is the historical constitution of sources that leads to a conclusion about the need for preservation. Interpretation changes through time. We understand the Beowulf manuscript in the British Library to be important because Grímur Jónsson Thorkelin identified it as such in the late eighteenth century (for an account of Thorkelin's "discovery" of *Beowulf* see Kiernan, 1986). His transcription of it is interesting because he was the first person to recognize its significance; before then it was simply another under-studied and fire-blackened manuscript in the Cotton collection. He only became aware of the manuscript as part of a study tour sponsored by the Danish crown with the explicit objective "to collect and record all the extant Danish and Norwegian Monuments, Deeds, and Documents ... on his promise to deliver on his homecoming to Our National Archive and the great Library all the Collections he in such manner may procure" (Kiernan, 1986), that is, as part of a nationalistic project to develop and sustain a definitive national mythology at a time of revolutionary turmoil and war across mainland Europe (Niles, 1997:4). So the manuscript's significance emerged at a given point in time, and early transcripts remain important not just for the early insights they give to a decaying manuscript but also because their reception reveals the cultural history of their production and subsequent deployment.

This example could be repeated in many different branches of the humanities. The point is that humanities research, its methods, and sources are freighted by the history they have lived through. That history, which might also be called context or provenance, cannot be recreated in a laboratory or interpolated by clever simulation. Digital scholarship, especially in the humanities, has a distinctive need for digital preservation.

Digital Preservation is about People and Opportunities, not Data and Risks

The need for digital preservation may be compelling, but that doesn't make it fun reading. Unkind critics might differentiate two literary forms: snappy premonitions of digital doom, and great mounds of dreary technical flotsam. The former is prone to exaggeration; the latter seems at times detached from real needs. But both need to be understood if we are to ensure that digital humanities has a future for the long term.

Digital preservation mostly started with a significant effort of awareness-raising, which begat a genre of reportage regarding unplanned data loss. There are many examples of this, so only three are quoted here that are immediately relevant to the humanities:

- Amanda Spencer reported in 2009 that 40% of the web links cited in answers to parliamentary questions in the period 1997–2006 no longer resolved (Spencer *et al.*, 2009; see also Pennock, 2013). It is worth supplementing Spencer's finding by observing that these are not simply occasional websites, but were being used to inform and justify the decisions of government. It may not be the great fire of 1834 (Shenton, 2013), but being able to check these references is an important way to hold government to account in the present and to reflect on the course of public policy in retrospect. Moreover, the web harvesting technology that could prevent this from happening has been in existence since at least 1996.
- In 1999 the Archaeology Data Service reviewed the fate of digital data resulting from archaeological research in the UK and Ireland (Condron *et al.*, 1999). It concluded that, not only was most data not managed in ways that could ensure functionality for future use, there was scant attention paid to maintaining the fragile physical media on which data was stored. It is worth underlining these findings by noting that the process of excavation is destructive and that in some cases the digital objects may be the only meaningful residue left after an expensive intervention which cannot be repeated. Even in 1999 the mechanisms to protect fragile physical media had been understood for many years.
- Finally, in 2010 the Digital Preservation Coalition (DPC), with Portico and the University of London Computer Centre (ULCC), published a study into the

preservation practices adopted by digitization projects funded by the Joint Information Systems Committee (JISC) of the Higher Education Funding Councils (DPC, 2009). Sixteen projects were invited to comment on how long their data would be available after the end of the project. Some gave vague, aspirational answers: "indefinitely" and "in perpetuity"; some gave carefully worked-out answers based on specific knowledge of their institutional policies (e.g., 10 years then a policy review which may result in a move to another platform); some promised only the five-year minimum required from the grant agreement; one realized that it had no specific infrastructure at all. JISC's funding for digitization was an investment in the future, the sort of infrastructure that is built in boom times to sustain and extend scholarship in leaner times. Those leaner times have come. The return on investment has never been more needed.

These are only three short examples of data loss that have a particular resonance with humanities scholarship. All too often, digital preservation reads like a sorry tale of things that could have been avoided.

This sorry tale can easily drown out the importance of digital collections. Digital data has value: this generation has embraced digital technology because of the opportunities it affords and the ways of working and interacting which were simply not available previously. Digital technology has significant implications: enabling students to see ancient manuscripts up close; speeding up the process of data sharing for archaeologists; providing evidence to support public policy. It has implications for us in the "real world." However, the deployment of digital technology depends on the configuration of software and hardware and people, three features which are constantly in motion. Consequently, access to digital collections cannot be guaranteed without some effort to manage this configuration. Data loss will almost certainly result if this is not managed, but it would not be a problem if it did not have consequences.

In short, digital preservation is not simply about data or access: it is about people and opportunities. It is not mere digital life-support: it is the custody of potential. Those getting started in digital preservation would be wise to start here and worry about data loss once they have worked out what they can't afford to lose and what they can't afford to keep.

Five Challenges and what we've Done about them

It is relatively easy to bemoan the problem; but after a decade or more it is now possible to examine solutions. Rather than try to give a comprehensive narrative of these (see Brown, 2013, for an excellent guide), the solutions can be grouped roughly into the sorts of practical challenges that the scholarly community faces.

Capturing the Configuration of Software, Hardware, and People

A basic task for digital preservation is to capture and represent the configuration of software, hardware, and user that makes digital objects meaningful. This somewhat generic challenge has typically been met by capturing and providing metadata and other associated documentation to ensure access (see Gartner and Lavoie, 2013, for a complete introduction to the topic). Different levels of representation are required and preservation metadata is not a subset of resource discovery metadata. The Open Archival Information System (OAIS) standard provides a reference model in which an information object is created out of a data object (i.e., a digital object) through the provision of representation information (Lavoie, 2004:10–14). OAIS is largely silent on the specifics of metadata, so the PREMIS working group has provided a model for preservation metadata with five entities which in turn are described by a series of semantic units (PREMIS, 2012). It makes no specific requirement for how this information is presented, simply noting that it should be recoverable in some way. One popular way of encoding this information is to use the Metadata Encoding and Transmission Standard (METS), which is itself an XML implementation of an OAIS information package (Vermaaten, 2010).

Parallel to the development of metadata standards, the digital preservation community has been active in the development of technical registries which maintain and disclose core information for preservation tasks (see for example Delve *et al.*, 2012, and Brown, 2007, for descriptions of different registry services). There has been discussion of the need for registries of representation information and their potential (Brown, 2008) but it is hard to find examples of deployment.

Change is here to Stay

Capturing representation information at the point of creation will not be sufficient to ensure long-term access. Change is here to stay, whether as changes in hardware, operating systems, software, the interdependencies of systems, standards, file format specifications, capacities of software to comply with standards, the capacity of operators, the ability to capture, store or present metadata, and so on. One might conclude wrongly that change is the problem. On the contrary, as Naughton argues, "disruption is a feature not a bug" (2012:43–110). The architecture both of IT systems and the information economy enables rapid innovation to occur at low cost in front of a global marketplace. This is why so many online services have become so successful so quickly – and also why services fall out of use. "So anyone who yearns for a period of stability – an intermission that will give us time to catch our collective breath and get a grip on things – is doomed to disappointment" (Naughton, 2012:108–9). Thus instead of trying to stem the tide of innovation, digital preservation is an active process that needs to embrace change, planning on the assumption that plans are always provisional.

This has a policy implication: agencies which engage in digital preservation will need to be (or become) learning institutions maintaining close contact with emerging trends and solutions. The practical implementation of that objective can be seen in the focus paid to preservation planning, a specific functional area of OAIS (Lavoie, 2004:9). A series of planning tools have emerged to assess institutional readiness, such as AIDA or CARDIO (Pinsent, 2009; CARDIO, 2011); practical development and testing of digital preservation plans, such as PLATO or SCOUT (Becker and Rauber, 2011); and ongoing assessment of repository functions, such as the Data Seal of Approval (www. datasealofapproval.org; see Schumann and Mauer, 2013).

Storage is not Preservation, but Storage Matters

There is a common misconception that preservation issues can be resolved with robust storage. This is a frustrating conflation, because storage is important but is not the solution per se. There is a substantial literature on storage architectures, and there is little benefit in rehearsing it here (see Petersen, 2009, for an introduction to the concepts necessary for a meaningful dialog between data-center managers and digital preservation practitioners).

Contrary to rumors, bit preservation is not a solved problem (Rosenthal, 2010). From an engineering perspective, preservation mostly follows the same trends for mainstream data storage but it tends to add a more specialist policy layer. OAIS distinguishes archiving from dissemination and submission, a split which has been replicated in many preservation services. For example the term "dark archive" has been used in the publishing industry to describe an archive which permits no public access, unless and until a pre-agreed trigger event occurs (see Beagrie, 2013:3–5, for a more complete explanation). This is an example of a broader concept of escrow in which a trusted third party provides digital preservation services on behalf of two or more clients, with the assumption that source code or data will be supplied in the event of some pre-agreed event, such as insolvency of a service provider (Hoeren et al., 2013:168–96). In both examples it is the legal arrangements, not the technology, that are distinctive. Moreover, both arrangements assume that an administrator is routinely checking that archived content remains viable even if it is not publicly accessible; in this sense no OAIS is a completely dark archive.

The technical and legal aspects of storage are aligned in the LOCKSS technology, which provides a mechanism to replicate and validate content over a distributed network. Typically deployed so that libraries can manage e-journal content, as in CLOCKSS or UK LOCKSS Alliance (Rusbridge and Ross, 2007; Beagrie, 2013:18–20), LOCKSS has been deployed to provide secure replication of other types of content such as the MetaArchive Collective. The principle that multiple copies of data should be stored in different locations, while ensuring that datasets remain synchronized underpins storage concerns in digital preservation which is increasingly understood as a distributed activity (Skinner and Schulz, 2010).

Digital Preservation Tools become Obsolete

Digital preservation has been likened to a relay race in which the information object needs to be passed on at the end of a lap (Rusbridge, 2006). This has three implications for digital preservation architectures.

Firstly, architectures which are modular and standards-based will be more attractive than monolithic black-box solutions (Abrams et al., 2010). Technology like Archivematica and Preservica offer "preservation as a service" composed not of a single product in a single repository but as a series of tools that can be configured to specific needs. In this sense the metaphor of the "trusted repository" as a place where things are placed seems increasingly redundant: it is rather more about assessing the trustworthiness of the remote tools and services which are assembled.

Secondly, systems may need to generate metadata that explains the chain of custody of a digital object – which in turn means that representation information accretes through time. PREMIS has always assumed that metadata is an open-ended commitment, while ideas of how to manage authenticity of digital records continue to evolve (Salza *et al.*, 2012). Finally, anyone looking to acquire a preservation service should be looking not only at their current offerings but also at their succession plans.

Digital Resources are Intolerant of Gaps in Preservation

The examples of data loss quoted above came about in part because technology changed faster than planning and implementation of digital infrastructure. Whereas analog preservation and archiving could happen at the end of a document's active life cycle, decisions about digital preservation need to occur much earlier.

Archivists, records managers, librarians, and publishers have long understood collections from a life-cycle perspective, even if the specific terms and approaches vary. Digital data life cycles like the Digital Curation Centre's lifecycle model (Higgins, 2008; see also Harvey, 2010) point to the need for preservation to be considered earlier not later. In part this is the logic behind emerging services such as *DMP Online* (Sallans and Donnelly, 2012). Experience with the JISC Digitization Programme suggests that preservation planning may need to be embedded in the policy and infrastructure of projects even before funding is approved (DPC, 2009).

Digital preservation is also an ongoing task, so risk management approaches have been deployed by a number of institutions and projects to provide a framework in which risks can be articulated, monitored, and passed onward to senior management for action (DRAMBORA, 2007; Barateiro *et al.*, 2010; Vermaaten *et al.*, 2012).

Risk management provides a framework in which different classes of problems can be analyzed simultaneously – environmental and financial risks as well as technical ones. Experience, like that of the Arts and Humanities Data Service, shows that sudden changes to funding impair digital preservation however thoughtfully executed. As Rosenthal drily observes, "Money turns out to be the major problem facing the future of our digital heritage" (Rosenthal, 2012). Funding for preservation is complicated by (at least) two reasons. Firstly few agencies would claim to have fully developed their digital preservation capacity, meaning that the early years of digital preservation are about capital expenditure as well as service delivery (Kilbride, 2013). Secondly, the value proposition for digital preservation can be weak. In 2010 a Blue Ribbon Task Force expressed the problem exactly that: "sustainable economics for digital preservation is not just about finding more funds. It is about building an economic activity firmly rooted in a compelling value proposition, clear incentives to act, and well-defined preservation roles and responsibilities" (BRTF, 2010:13). Knowing, expressing, and modeling the underlying costs of digital preservation has proven tricky (Kejser, 2013), and articulating the benefits of digital preservation can be hard (Beagrie *et al.*, 2010), all of which means that modeling the economics sustainability of digital resources is tricky (Lavoie and Grindley, 2013). But without a sound economic basis, everything else is provisional.

Five Emerging Trends and what they mean

It may seem that digital preservation is set to move from its early phase of anxiety to a positive future of tools, techniques, and capacity. There are grounds for optimism. Even so, continuing research is needed from which humanities scholars can benefit, and to which they can make a distinctive contribution. Five examples are presented below, to provide rhetorical symmetry with the five challenges delineated above.

Firstly, whereas technologies are emerging to deal with the "internet of documents" (e.g., Pennock, 2013) the Internet is rapidly developing into an environment of services. So instead of simple hypertext, users now routinely access a complex interaction of services in which it is hard to disentangle data from applications: as Naughton argues, "the network is now the computer" (2012:175–208). This integration means long chains of interdependence between distributed and fragmented tools and services. This creates two challenges for long-term preservation: how do we assess and manage an environment with complex and extensive dependencies; and how can we define and stabilize a canonical or authentic view of that environment at any given time.

Secondly, and related to this point, digital preservation has tended to fetishize files. This is less true of the more abstract development of standards (e.g., Lavoie, 2004:10–14) but it is certainly true of operational guidance offered to those depositing data in archives (e.g., Archaeology Data Service, undated). As long ago as 2006 Rusbridge doubted if file format obsolescence was really such a big problem, and even without considering the growing integration of data and applications, Todd observes that a critical component of file format selection is the capacity of the user community, the strategic purpose of the archive, and the available budget (Todd, 2009:2). This last point seems critical: given the costs associated with digital archaeology, given the inevitable loss associated with migration, and bearing in mind the sheer scale of the problem – the question seems rather less about data loss and rather more about workflow and capacity. And in any case, if we care about making sense of systems where files are only one component (e.g., McGarva *et al.*, 2009; Prom, 2011; Wright, 2012; Ball, 2013; Pennock, 2013), or looking for relationships between files (John, 2012), then we really should be looking beyond the file.

A third issue underlines our need to think beyond the file: the rapid growth in data volumes, whether measured in absolute numbers of files or in absolute numbers of bytes. Digital preservation needs to work at scale without adding additional costs. Rosenthal (2012) has observed three trends here: that the demand for data storage grows at around 60% per year; that bit density on disks increases at around 25% per year; and that budgets of IT centers grow at no more than 2% per annum. At face value, these three trends could point to an impending costs crisis which is amplified by three other issues – the lack of skilled practitioners to sort out the mess and the lack of training to support them (Kilbride *et al.*, 2013); the extent of public expectation for access to data; and the growing complexity of the components stored in those over-filled repositories. There are really only two practical responses to these brute economic realities and our capacity to deal with them. Either we embrace some kind of regulated neglect (Kilbride, 2010a), or we develop policies and tools that can cope with much larger volumes of data. Volumes of data present another kind of threat: that inadvertently we find ourselves serving up sensitive or dangerous data that contains unknown risks or creates unintended liabilities. This must be every data manager's worst nightmare; but if the response is simply to lock down huge volumes of material so that it cannot be accessed, or worse still to delete it in the name or public safety, then the unintended consequences could be more severe than we think. A little bit of selection, some planned deletion, and potentially a whole lot of graceful decay will help our tools target those resources that really matter and help us spot the dangers early.

Fourthly, the digital preservation literature is strewn with examples of failure, but there are fewer descriptions of success. If the demand for digital preservation is weak or diffuse (BRTF, 2010:1–23), it is also temporally dynamic and path-dependent (28–30). So while we can reasonably suppose that success depends on decisions made today, success is constantly deferred. Instead of promising success, therefore, the best that most agencies can do is offer compliance. Community standards can be invoked to demonstrate the extent to which actions confirm to current perceptions of best practice. The idea of the "trusted repository" dates back to 1996 (CPA and RLG, 1997) and can be traced through various working parties (e.g., RLG and OCLC, 2002; RLG and NARA, 2005; CRL and OCLC, 2007; nestor, 2009) to the recent release of ISO 16363 (ISO, 2011). But compliance is not as compelling as success. Perhaps digital preservation is only visible when it is not working (Kilbride, 2010b). More success stories are needed.

Finally, a very different kind of research could revolutionize digital preservation entirely. Intervention in document life cycles seems to be a holy grail among archivists and records managers – alluring but always just out of reach. Instead of trying to prevent obsolescence in digital materials, perhaps it would be preferable to build preservation-ready systems in which obsolescence simply did not occur. All most people will ever need is a software filter that can identify when an object is not supported by the current platform and which can sensibly select from the family of services that translate between the old object and the modern platform (either by emulation or by migration), reporting errors or deviations in the process. Such a solution could not be engineered by intervening early in a document's life cycle, nor even in the planning of the document; it means inserting long-term thinking into the life cycles of our digital infrastructures. The real challenge for digital preservation is to make obsolescence obsolete.

Conclusion

Slightly more than a decade ago there was precious little practical digital preservation advice on offer: one could be expert in the topic with perhaps three days' reading and a world authority by completing a single research project. That is no longer the case.

While such obvious progress is welcome, the speed of change can also inhibit practical engagement from those researchers with the greatest to gain from the new kinds of services available and most to lose should they fail. Researchers in the digital humanities are not simply beneficiaries of digital preservation; they are critical to its success. So long as digital preservation remains an "unsolved" problem, this dialog remains important; so long as the digital preservation community continues to grow, so the mechanisms for enabling that dialog will need to continue to adapt.

REFERENCES AND FURTHER READING

Abrams, S., Kunze, J., and Loy, D. 2010. An emergent micro-services approach to digital curation infrastructure. *International Journal of Digital Curation* 5 (1), 172–86. 10.2218/ijdc.v5i1.151 (accessed June 20, 2015).

Archaeology Data Service (undated). *Guides to Good Practice*. Archaeology Data Service / Digital Antiquity. http://guides.archaeologydataservice.ac.uk (accessed June 20, 2015).

Ball, A. 2013. *Preserving Computer-Aided Design (CAD)*. DPC Technology Watch Report 13-02. Digital Preservation Coalition. 10.7207/twr13-02 (accessed June 20, 2015).

Barateiro, J., Antunes, G., Freitas, F., and Borbinha J. 2010. Designing digital preservation solutions: a risk management-based approach. *International Journal of Digital Curation* 5 (1), 4–17. 10.2218/ijdc.v5i1.140 (accessed June 20, 2015).

Beagrie, N. 2013. *Preservation Trust and Continuing Access for e-Journals*. DPC Technology Watch Report 13-04. Digital Preservation Coalition. 10.7207/twr13-04 (accessed June 20, 2015).

Beagrie, N., Lavoie, B., and Woollard, M. 2010. *Keeping Research Data Safe 2*. JISC. http://www.jisc.ac.uk/media/documents/publications/reports/2010/keepingresearchdatasafe2.pdf (accessed June 20, 2015).

Becker, C., and Rauber A. 2011. Decision criteria in digital preservation: what to measure and how. *Journal of the Association for Information Science and Technology* 62, 1009–28. 10.1002/asi.21527 (accessed June 20, 2015).

Brown, A. 2007. Developing practical approaches to active preservation. *International Journal of Digital Curation* 2 (1), 3–11. 10.2218/ijdc.v2i1.10 (accessed June 20, 2015).

Brown, A. 2008. *White Paper: Representation Information Registries*, PLANETS Project D7/PC3. http://www.planets-project.eu/docs/reports/Planets_PC3-D7_RepInformationRegistries.pdf (accessed June 20, 2015).

Brown, A. 2013. *Practical Digital Preservation: A How-to Guide for Organizations of Any Size*. London: Facet.

BRTF. 2010. *Sustainable Economics for a Digital Planet: Ensuring Long-Term Access to Digital Information*. Blue Ribbon Task Force. http://brtf.sdsc.edu (accessed June 20, 2015).

CARDIO. 2011. Collaborative Assessment of Research Data Infrastructure and Objectives (CARDIO). Digital Curation Centre. http://www.dcc.ac.uk/sites/default/files/documents/Cardio_Characteristics_By_Statement.pdf (accessed June 20, 2015).

Condron, F., Richards, J., Robinson, D., and Wise, A. 1999. *Strategies for Digital Data: a Survey of User Needs*, Archaeology Data Service, University of York. http://archaeologydataservice.ac.uk/legacy/strategies (accessed June 20, 2015).

CPA (Commission on Preservation and Access) and RLG (Research Libraries Group). 1996. *Preserving Digital Information: Report of the Task Force on Archiving of Digital Information*. http://www.oclc.org/research/activities/past/rlg/digpresstudy/final-report.pdf (accessed June 20, 2015).

CRL (Center for Research Libraries) and OCLC (Online Computer Library Center). 2007. *TRAC: Trustworthy Repositories Audit & Certification: Criteria and Checklist*. http://www.crl.edu/PDF/trac.pdf (accessed June 20, 2015).

Delve, J., Puhl, J., and Cardenas, T.J. 2012. Enabling emulation as a digital preservation approach: the TOTEM technical registry. In *iPres 2012, The International Conference on the Preservation of Digital Objects*, Toronto, Canada.

DPC (Digital Preservation Coalition). 2009. *JISC Project Report: Digitisation Programme: Preservation Study April 2009*, JISC. http://www.jisc.ac.uk/media/documents/programmes/digitisation/jisc_dpp_final_public_report.pdf (accessed June 20, 2015).

DRAMBORA. 2007. *Digital Repository Audit Method Based on Risk Assessment*. http://www.repositoryaudit.eu/img/drambora_flyer.pdf (accessed June 20, 2015).

Gartner, R., and Lavoie, B. 2013. *Preservation Metadata*, 2nd edition. DPC Technology Watch Report 13-3. Digital Preservation Coalition. 10.7207/twr13-03 (accessed June 20, 2015).

Harvey, R. 2010. *Digital Curation: A How-To-Do-It Manual*. New York: Neal-Schuman.

Higgins, S. 2008. The DCC curation lifecycle model. *International Journal of Digital Curation* 3 (1), 134–40. http://ijdc.net/index.php/ijdc/article/view/69 (accessed June 20, 2015).

HLEG. 2010. *Riding the Wave: How Europe can Gain from the Rising Tide of Scientific Data*. Final Report of the High Level Expert Group on Scientific Data. European Union. http://cordis.europa.eu/fp7/ict/e-infrastructure/docs/hlg-sdi-report.pdf (accessed June 20, 2015).

Hoeren, T., Kolany-Raiser, B., Yankova, S., Hecheltjen, M., and Hobel, K. 2013. *Legal*

Aspects of Digital Preservation, Cheltenham: Edward Elgar Publishing.

ISO. 2011. Audit and certification of trustworthy digital repositories. ISO 16363:2011 (International Organization for Standardization).

John, J.L. 2012. *Digital Forensics and Preservation*. DPC Technology Watch Report 12-02. Digital Preservation Coalition. 10.7207/twr12-03 (accessed June 20, 2015).

Kejser, U. 2013. *Evaluation of Cost Models and Needs & Gaps Analysis (Draft)*. 4C Project D3.1. http://4cproject.eu/component/docman/doc_download/30-d3-1-evaluation-of-cost-models-and-needs-gaps-analysis-ms12-draft (accessed June 20, 2015).

Kiernan, K. 1986. Part one: Thorkelin's discovery of *Beowulf*. In *The Thorkelin Transcripts of "Beowulf"*. Anglistica XXV. Copenhagen: Rosenkilde and Bagger, 1–41. http://www.uky.edu/~kiernan/Thorkelin/Th_1 (accessed June 20, 2015).

Kilbride, W. 2010a. Here comes the tide. *What's New* 31. http://www.dpconline.org/newsroom/whats-new/651-whats-new-issue-31-november-2010#Editorial31 (accessed June 20, 2015).

Kilbride, W. 2010b. We are the people but who exactly are we? *What's New* 26. http://www.dpconline.org/newsroom/whats-new/610-whats-new-issue-26-june (accessed June 20, 2015).

Kilbride, W. 2013. What's what: capital revenue and the great Post-it note crisis of 2006. *What's New* 53. http://www.dpconline.org/newsroom/whats-new/981-whats-new-issue-53-march-2013#whatswhat (accessed June 20, 2015).

Kilbride, W., Cirinna, C., and McMeekin, S. 2013. Training in digital preservation: what we've learned and what we're going to do about it. http://www.rinascimento-digitale.it/conference2012/paper_ic_2012/kilbride_paper.pdf (accessed June 20, 2015).

Lavoie, B. 2004. *The Open Archival Information System Reference Model: An Introductory Guide*. DPC Technology Watch Report 04-01. Digital Preservation Coalition. http://www.dpconline.org/component/docman/doc_download/91-introduction-to-oais (accessed June 20, 2015).

Lavoie, B., and Grindley, N., 2013. *A Draft Economic Sustainability Reference Model*. 4C Project. http://www.4cproject.eu/ms9-draft-esrm (accessed June 20, 2015).

McGarva, G., Morris, S., and Janee, G. 2009. *Preserving Geospatial Data*. DPC Technology Watch Report 0901. Digital Preservation Coalition. http://www.dpconline.org/component/docman/doc_download/363-preserving-geospatial-data-by-guy-mcgarva-steve-morris-and-gred-greg-janee (accessed June 20, 2015).

Naughton, J. 2012. *From Gutenberg to Zuckerberg: What You Really Need to Know About the Internet*. London: Quercus.

nestor. 2009. *Catalogue of Criteria for Trusted Digital Repositories, Version 2*. nestor Working Group Trusted Repositories Certification. http://files.d-nb.de/nestor/materialien/nestor_mat_08_eng.pdf (accessed June 20, 2015).

Niles, J.D. 1997. Introduction: Beowulf truth and meaning. In *A Beowulf Handbook*, ed. R.E. Bjork and J.D. Niles. Lincoln: University of Nebraska Press, 1–12.

Pennock, M. 2013. *Web Archiving,*. DPC Technology Watch Report 13-01. Digital Preservation Coalition. 10.7207/twr13-01 (accessed June 20, 2015).

Petersen, M. 2009. *Building a Terminology Bridge for Digital Information Retention and Preservation Practices*. Storage Network Industry Association Data Management Forum White Papers. http://www.snia.org/sites/default/files/SNIA-DMF_Building-a-Terminology-Bridge_20090515.pdf (accessed June 20, 2015).

Pinsent, E. 2009. *Assessing Institutional Digital Assets: The AIDA Self-Assessment Toolkit Mark II*. University of London Computer Centre. http://aida.jiscinvolve.org/wp/files/2009/05/self_assessment_toolkit_ii.doc (accessed June 20, 2015).

PREMIS. 2012. *PREMIS Data Dictionary for Preservation Metadata. Version 2.2*. http://www.loc.gov/standards/premis/v2/premis-2-2.pdf (accessed June 20, 2015).

Prom, C. 2011. *Preserving Email*. DPC Technology Watch Report 11-01. Digital Preservation Coalition. 10.7207/twr11-01 (accessed June 20, 2015).

RLG (Research Libraries Group) and NARA (National Archives and Records Administration). 2005. *Draft Audit Checklist for Certifying Digital Repositories*. Task Force on Digital Repository Certification. Mountain View, CA: RLG. http://web.archive.org/web/20050922172830/http://www.rlg.org/en/pdfs/rlgnara-repositorieschecklist.pdf (accessed June 20, 2015).

RLG (Research Libraries Group) and OCLC (Online Computer Library Center). 2002. *Trusted Digital Repositories: Attributes and Responsibilities*. Working Group on Digital Archive Attributes. Mountain View, CA: RLG. http://www.oclc.org/research/activities/past/rlg/trustedrep/repositories.pdf (accessed June 20, 2015).

Rosenthal, D. 2010. Bit preservation: a solved problem? *International Journal of Digital Curation* 5 (1), 134–48. 10.2218/ijdc.v5i1.148 (accessed June 20, 2015).

Rosenthal, D. 2012. Storage will be a lot less free than it used to be. http://blog.dshr.org/2012/10/storage-will-be-lot-less-free-than-it.html (accessed June 20, 2015).

Rusbridge, A., and Ross, S. 2007. The UK LOCKSS pilot programme: a perspective from the LOCKSS Technical Support Service. *International Journal of Digital Curation* 2 (2), 111–22. 10.2218/ijdc.v2i2.34 (accessed June 20, 2015).

Rusbridge, C. 2006. Excuse me? Some digital preservation fallacies. *Aridane* 46. http://www.ariadne.ac.uk/issue46/rusbridge (accessed June 20, 2015).

Sallans, A. and Donnelly, M. 2012. DMP Online and DMPTool: different strategies towards a shared goal. *International Journal of Digital Curation* 7 (2), 123–9. 10.2218/ijdc.v7i2.235 (accessed June 20, 2015).

Salza, S., Guercio, M., Grossi, M., *et al.* 2012. *Report on Authenticity and Plan for Interoperable Authenticity Evaluation System.* APARSEN FP7 Project.

Schumann, N., and Mauer, R. 2013. The GESIS Data Archive for the Social Sciences: a widely recognised data archive on its way. *International Journal of Digital Curation* 8 (2), 215–22. http://www.ijdc.net/index.php/ijdc/article/viewFile/8.2.215/329 (accessed June 20, 2015).

Shenton, C. 2013. *The Day Parliament Burned Down.* Oxford: Oxford University Press.

Skinner, K., and Schulz, M., eds. 2010. *A Guide to Distributed Digital Preservation.* Atlanta, GA: Educopia Institute. http://www.metaarchive.org/sites/metaarchive.org/files/GDDP_Educopia.pdf (accessed June 20, 2015).

Spencer, A. Sheridan, J., Thomas, D., and Pullinger, D. 2009. UK government web continuity: persisting access through aligning infrastructures. *International Journal of Digital Curation* 4 (1), 107–24. http://www.ijdc.net/index.php/ijdc/article/view/106/81 (accessed June 20, 2015).

Todd, M. 2009. *File Formats for Preservation.* DPC Technology Watch Report 09-02. Digital Preservation Coalition. http://www.dpconline.org/component/docman/doc_download/375-file-formats-for-preservation (accessed June 20, 2015).

Vermaaten, S. 2010. A checklist and a case for documenting PREMIS-METS decisions in a METS profile. *D-Lib Magazine* 16 (9/10). http://dlib.org/dlib/september10/vermaaten/09vermaaten.html (accessed June 20, 2015).

Vermaaten, S., Lavoie, B., and Caplan, P. 2012. Identifying threats to successful digital preservation: the SPOT *Model for Risk Assessment. D-Lib Magazine* 18. http://www.dlib.org/dlib/september12/vermaaten/09vermaaten.html (accessed June 20, 2015).

Wright, R. 2012. *Preserving Moving Pictures and Sound.* DPC Technology Watch Report 12-01. Digital Preservation Coalition. 10.7207/twr12-01 (accessed June 20, 2015).

29

Crowdsourcing in the Digital Humanities

Melissa Terras

As Web 2.0 technologies changed the World Wide Web from a read-only to a co-creative digital experience, a range of commercial and noncommercial platforms emerged to allow online users to contribute to discussions and use their knowledge, experience, and time to build online content. Alongside the widespread success of collaboratively produced resources such as *Wikipedia* came a movement in the cultural and heritage sectors to trial crowdsourcing – the harnessing of online activities and behavior to aid in large-scale ventures such as tagging, commenting, rating, reviewing, text correcting, and the creation and uploading of content in a methodical, task-based fashion (Holley, 2010) – to improve the quality of, and widen access to, online collections. Building on this, within digital humanities there have been attempts to crowdsource more complex tasks traditionally assumed to be carried out by academic scholars, such as the accurate transcription of manuscript material.

This chapter aims to survey the growth and uptake of crowdsourcing for culture and heritage, and more specifically within digital humanities. It raises issues of public engagement and asks how the use of technology to involve and engage a wider audience with tasks that have been the traditional purview of academics can broaden the scope and appreciation of humanistic inquiry. Finally, it asks what this increasingly common public-facing activity means for digital humanities itself, as the success of these projects demonstrates the effectiveness of building projects for, and involving, a wide online audience.

Crowdsourcing: an Introduction

Crowdsourcing – the practice of using contributions from a large online community to undertake a specific task, create content, or gather ideas – is a product of a critical cultural shift in Internet technologies. The first generation of the World Wide Web

A New Companion to Digital Humanities, First Edition. Edited by Susan Schreibman, Ray Siemens, and John Unsworth.

had been dominated by static websites, facilitated by search engines which only allowed information-seeking behavior. However, the development of online platforms which allowed and encouraged a two-way dialog rather than a broadcast mentality fostered public participation, the co-creation of knowledge, and community-building, in a phase which is commonly referred to as "Web 2.0" (O'Reilly, 2005; Flew, 2008). In 2005, an article in *Wired* magazine discussed how businesses were beginning to use these new platforms to outsource work to individuals, coining the term "crowdsourcing" as a portmanteau of "outsourcing" and "crowd":

> Technological advances in everything from product design software to digital video cameras are breaking down the cost barriers that once separated amateurs from professionals. Hobbyists, part-timers, and dabblers suddenly have a market for their efforts, as smart companies in industries as disparate as pharmaceuticals and television discover ways to tap the latent talent of the crowd. The labor isn't always free, but it costs a lot less than paying traditional employees. It's not outsourcing; it's crowdsourcing. (Howe, 2006a)

The term was quickly adopted online to refer to

> the act of a company or institution taking a function once performed by employees and outsourcing it to an undefined (and generally large) network of people in the form of an open call. This can take the form of peer-production (when the job is performed collaboratively), but is also often undertaken by sole individuals. The crucial prerequisite is the use of the open call format and the large network of potential laborers. (Howe, 2006b)

Within a week of the term being coined, 182,000 other websites were using it (Howe, 2006c) and it rapidly became the word used to describe a wide range of online activities from contributing to online encyclopedias such as *Wikipedia*, to tagging images on image-sharing websites such as *Flickr*, to writing comments on blogs, to proofreading out-of-copyright texts on *Project Gutenberg*, or contributing to open-source software (an analagous term to crowdsourcing, citizen science, has also been used where the small-scale tasks carried out online contribute to scientific projects; Silvertown, 2009).

It is important to note here that the use of distributed (generally volunteer) labor to undertake small portions of much larger tasks, gather information, contribute to a larger project, or solve problems, is not new. There is a long history of scientific prizes, architectural competitions, genealogical research, scientific observation and recording, and linguistic study (to name but a few applications) that have relied on the contribution of large numbers of individuals to undertake a centrally managed task, or solve a complex problem (see Finnegan, 2005, for an overview). For example, the *Mass-Observation Project* was a social research organization in the United Kingdom between 1937 and the 1960s, which relied on a network of 500 volunteer correspondents to record everyday life in Britain, including conversation, culture, and behavior (Hubble, 2006). The difference between these projects and the modern phenomenon of crowdsourcing identified by Howe is, of course, the use of the Internet, the World Wide Web, and interactive web platforms as the mechanism for distributing information, collecting responses, building solutions, and communicating around a specified task or topic. There was an intermediary phase, however, between offline volunteer labor and the post-2006 "crowdsourcing" swell, where volunteer labor was used in conjunction with computers and online mechanisms to collect data. Brumfield (2013a) identifies at least seven genealogy projects, such as *Free Births, Marriages and Deaths* (FreeBMD, http://freebmd.org.uk), *Free Registers* (FreeREG, http://www.freereg.org. uk), and *Free Census* (FreeCEN, http://www.freecen.org.uk), that emerged in the 1990s:

> out of an (at least) one hundred year old tradition of creating print indexes to manuscript sources which were then published. Once the web came online, the idea of publishing these on the web [instead] became obvious. But the tools that were used to create these were spreadsheets that people would use on their home computers. Then they would put CD ROMs or floppy disks in the post and send them off to be published online. (Brumfield, 2013a)

The recent phenomenon of crowdsourcing, or citizen science, can thus be seen as a continuation of the use of available platforms and communications networks to distribute tasks amongst large numbers of interested individuals, working towards a common goal.

What types of web-related activities are now described as "crowdsourcing"? Daren Brabham (2013:45) proposes a useful typology, looking at the mostly commercial projects which exist in the crowdsourcing space, suggesting that there are two types of problems which can be best solved using this approach: information management issues and ideation problems. Information management issues occur where information needs to be located, created, assembled, sorted, or analyzed. Brabham suggests that knowledge discovery and management techniques can be used for crowdsourced information management, as they are ideal for gathering sources or reporting problems: an example of this would be *SeeClickFix* (http://en.seeclickfix.com), which encourages people to "*report* neighborhood issues and see them get *fixed*" (SeeClickFix, 2013). An alternative crowdsourcing approach to information management is what Brahbam calls "distributed human intelligence tasking": when "a corpus of data is known and the problem is not to produce designs, find information, or develop solutions, but to process data" (Brabham, 2013:50). In the least creative and intellectually demanding of the crowdsourcing techniques, users can be encouraged to undertake repetitive "micro-tasks," often for monetary compensation, if the task is for a commercial entity. An example of this would be Amazon's *Mechanical Turk* (https://www.mturk.com), which "gives businesses and developers access to an on-demand, scalable workforce. Workers select from thousands of tasks and work whenever it's convenient" (Amazon Mechanical Turk, 2014) – although *Amazon Turk* has been criticized for its "unethical" business model, with a large proportion of its workers living in developing countries, working on tasks for very little payment (Cushing, 2013).

The second type of task that Brabham identified as suited to crowdsourcing consists of ideation problems: where creative solutions need to be proposed, that are either empirically true, or a matter of taste or market support (Brabham, 2013:48–51). Brabham suggests that crowdsourcing is commonly used as a form of "broadcast search" to locate individuals who can provide the answer to specific problems, or provide the solution to a challenge, sometimes with pecuniary rewards. An example of an online platform using this approach is InnoCentive.com, which is predominantly geared towards the scientific community to generate ideas or reach solutions, for research and development, sometimes with very large financial prizes: at time of writing, there were three awards worth $100,000 on offer. Brabham suggests that an alternative crowd-sourcing solution to ideation problems is "peer-vetted creative production" (Brabham, 2013:49), where a creative phase is opened up to an online audience, who submit a large number of submissions, and voting mechanisms are then put in place to help sort through the proposals, hoping to identify superior suggestions. An example of this approach would be Threadless.com, a creative community that designs, sorts, creates, and provides a mechanism to purchase various fashion items (the website started with t-shirts, but has since expanded to offer other products).

Since its introduction in 2006, the term "crowdsourcing" is now used to cover a wide variety of activities across a large number of sectors:

> Businesses, non-profit organizations, and government agencies regularly integrate the creative energies of online communities into day-to-day operations, and many organiza-tions have been built entirely from these arrangements. (Brabham, 2013:xv)

Brabham's overall typology is a useful tool, as it provides a framework in which to think about both the type of problem that is being addressed by the online platform, and the specific crowdsourcing mechanism that is being used to propose a solution. Given the prevalence of the use of crowdsourcing in online communities for a range of both commercial and not-for-profit tasks, it is hardly surprising that various implementations of crowdsourcing activities have emerged in the cultural and heritage sector at large, and the digital humanities in particular.

The Growth of Crowdsourcing in Cultural and Heritage Applications

There are many aspects of crowdsourcing that are useful to those working in history, cultural and heritage, particularly within galleries, libraries, archives, and museums (GLAMs), which have a long history of participating with members of the public and generally have institutional aims to promote their collections and engage with as wide an audience as possible. However, "Crowdsourcing is a concept that was invented and defined in the business world and it is important that we recast it and think through what changes when we bring it into cultural heritage" (Owens, 2012a). The most obvious difference is that payment to those who undertake tasks is generally not an option for host institutions, but also that "a clearly ethical approach to inviting the public to help in the collection, description, presentation, and use of the cultural record" needs to be identified and pursued. Owens (2012a) sketches out a range of dif-ferences between the mass crowdsourcing model harnessed by the commercial sector and the use of online volunteer labor in cultural and heritage organizations, stressing that "many of the projects that end up falling under the heading of crowdsourcing in libraries, archives and museums have not involved large and massive crowds and they have very little to do with outsourcing labor." Heritage crowdsourcing projects are not about anonymous masses of people, they are about inviting participation from those who are interested and engaged, and generally involve a small cohort of enthusiasts to use digital tools to contribute (in the same way as they may have volunteered offline to organize and add value to collections in the past). The work is not "labor" but a meaningful way in which individuals can interact with, explore, and understand the historical record. It is often highly motivated and skilled individuals that offer to help, rather than those who can be described with the derogatory term "amateurs." Owens (2012a) suggests that crowdsourcing within this sector is then a complex interplay between understanding the potentials for human computation, adopting tools and software as scaffolding to aid this process, and understanding human motivation.

No chronological history of the growth of crowdsourcing in culture and heritage exists, but the earliest large-scale project which adopted this model of interaction with users was the *Australian Newspaper Digitisation Program* (http://www.nla.gov.au/content/newspaper-digitisation-program), which in August 2008 asked the general public to correct the OCR (optical character recognition) text of 8.4 million articles generated from their digitized historic Australian newspapers. This has been a phenomenally successful project, and by July 2015 over 166 million individual lines of newspaper articles had been proofread and corrected by volunteer labour. The resulting transcriptions can aid others not only in reading, but also in finding, text in the digitized archive. After the success of this project, and the rise of commercial crowdsourcing, other projects began to adopt crowdsourcing techniques to help digitize, sort, and correct heritage materials. In 2009 one of the earliest citizen science projects that is based on historical data, the *North American Bird Phenology Program* (www.pwrc.usgs.gov/bpp) was launched to transcribe 6 million migration-card obser-vations collected by a network of volunteers "who recorded information of first arrival dates, maximum abundance, and departure dates of migratory birds across North America" between 1880 and 1970 (*North American Bird Phenology Program*, undated). At time of writing, over a million cards have been transcribed by volunteers, allowing a range of scientific research to be carried out on the resulting data.

Crowdsourcing in the heritage sector began to gather speed around 2010 with a range of projects being launched that asked the general public for various types of help via an online interface. One of the most successful of these is another combination of historical crowdsourcing and citizen science, called *Old Weather* (www.oldweather.org), which invites the general public to transcribe weather observations that were noted in ships' logbooks dating from the mid-nineteenth century to the present day in order to "contribute to climate model projections and ... improve our knowledge of past environmental conditions" (Old Weather, 2013a). *Old Weather* launched in October 2010 as part of the *Zooniverse* (www.zooniverse.org) portal of 15 different citizen science projects (which had started with the popular gallery classification tool, *Galaxy Zoo* (www.galaxyzoo.org), in 2009). The *Old Weather* project is a collaboration of a diverse range of archival and scientific institutions and museums and universities in both the UK and the USA (*Old Weather*, 2013b), showing how a common digital platform can bring together physically dispersed information for analysis by users. At time of writing, over 34,000 logs and seven voyages have been transcribed (three times, by different users, to ensure quality control, meaning that over 1,000,000 individual pages have been transcribed by users; Brohan, 2012), and the resulting data are now being used by both scientists and historians to understand both climate patterns and naval history (with their blog regularly updated with findings: http://blog.oldweather.org).

A range of other notable crowdsourcing projects launched in the 2010–2011 period, showing the breadth and scope of the application of online effort to cultural heritage. These include (but are not limited to): *Transcribe Bentham*, which is discussed in more detail below; the Victoria and Albert Museum's tool to get users to improve the cropping of their photos in the collection (http://collections.vam.ac.uk/crowdsourcing); the United States Holocaust Museum's "Remember Me" project, which aims to identify children in photographs taken by relief workers during the immediate aftermath of the Second World War, to facilitate connections amongst survivors (http://rememberme. ushmm.org); New York Public Library's *What's on the Menu?* project (http://menus. nypl.org), in which users can transcribe their collection of historical restaurant menus; and the National Library of Finland's *DigitalKoot* project (www.digitalkoot.fi/index_ en.html), which allowed users to play games that helped improve the metadata of their Historical Newspaper Library. The range and spread of websites that come under the crowdsourcing umbrella in the cultural and heritage sector continues to increase, and it is now a relatively established, if evolving, method used for galleries, libraries, archives, and museums. A list of nonprofit crowdsourcing projects in GLAM institutions is maintained at www.digitalglam.org/crowdsourcing/projects. Considering this activity in light of Brabham's typology, above, it is clear that most projects fall into the "information management" category (Brabham, 2013), where an organization (or collaborative project between a range of organizations) tasks the crowd with helping to gather, organize, and collect information into a common source or format.

What is the relationship of these projects to those working in digital humanities? Obviously, many crowdsourcing projects depend on having information – or things – to comment on, transcribe, analyze, or sort, and therefore GLAM institutions, who are custodians of such historical material, often partner with university researchers who have an interest in using digital techniques to answer their humanities or heritage-based research question. There is often much sharing of expertise and technical infrastructure between different projects and institutions: for example, the *Galaxy Zoo* platform which underpins *Old Weather* also is used by *Ancient Lives* (http://ancientlives. org) to help crowdsource transcription of papyri, and *Operation War Diary* (http://www. operationwardiary.org) to help transcribe First World War unit diaries. Furthermore, those working in digital humanities can often advise and assist colleagues in partner institutions and scholarly departments: *Transcribe Bentham* is a collaboration between University College London's Library Services (including UCL's Special Collections), the *Bentham Project* (based in the Faculty of Laws), UCL Centre for Digital Humanities, the British Library, and the University of London Computing Centre, with the role of the Digital Humanities Centre being to provide guidance and advice with online activities, best practice, and public engagement. Another example of collaboration can be seen in events such as the CITSCribe Hackathon in December 2013, which "brought together over 30 programmers and researchers from the areas of biodiversity research and digital humanities for a week to further enable public participation in the transcription of biodiversity specimen labels" (iDigBio, 2013).

Crowdsourcing in the digital humanities can also be used to sort and improve incomplete datasets, such as a corpus of 493 non-Shakespearean plays written between 1576 and 1642 in which 32,000 partially transcribed words were corrected by students over the course of an eight-week period using an online tool (http://annolex.at.

northwestern.edu; see Mueller, 2014), indicating how we can use crowdsourcing to involve humanities students in the gathering and curating of corpora relevant to the wider humanities community. Scholars in the digital humanities are well placed to research, scope, and theorize crowdsourcing activities across a wider sector: for example, the *Modeling Crowdsourcing for Cultural Heritage* project (http://cdh.uva.nl/projects-2013-2014/m.o.c.c.a.html) based at the Centre for Digital Humanities and Creative Research Industries Amsterdam, both at the University of Amsterdam, is aiming to determine a comprehensive model for "determining which types and methods of crowdsourcing are relevant for which specific purposes" (Amsterdam Centre for Digital Humanities, 2013).

As we shall see, below, digital humanities scholars and centers are investigating and building new platforms for crowdsourcing activities – particularly in the transcription of historical texts. In addition, digital humanities academics can help with suggestions on what we can do with crowdsourced information once collected; we are now moving into a next phase of crowdsourcing, where understanding data mining and visualization techniques to query the volume of data collected by volunteer labor is necessary. Finally, there is the beginnings of a body of literature on the wider area of crowdsourcing, both across the digital humanities and in the GLAM sector, and taken together these can inform those who are contemplating undertaking a crowdsourcing project for a related area. It should be stressed that it is often hard to make a distinction between what should be labeled a "GLAM sector" project and what should be labeled "digital humanities" in the area of crowdsourcing, as many projects are using crowdsourcing not only to sort or label or format historical information, but to provide the raw materials and methodologies for creating and understanding novel information about our past, our cultural inheritance, or our society.

Following on from the success of the *Australian Newspapers Digitisation Program* which she managed, Holley (2010) brought issues of "Crowdsourcing: how and why should libraries do it" to light, in a seminal discussion that much subsequent research and project implementation has benefited from. Holley proposes that there are several potential benefits in using crowdsourcing within a library context (which we can also extrapolate to cover those working across the GLAM sector, and in digital humanities). The benefits of crowdsourcing noted are that it can help to: achieve goals the institution would not have the resources (temporal, financial, or staffing) to accomplish itself; achieve these goals more quickly than if working alone; build new user groups and communities; actively engage the community with the institution and its systems and collections; utilize external knowledge, expertise, and interest; improve the quality of data, which improves subsequent user search experiences; add value to data; improve and expand the ways in which data can be discovered; gain an insight into user opinions and desires by building up a relationship with the crowd; show the relevance and importance of the institution (and its collections) by the high level of public interest in the project; build trust and encourage loyalty to the institution; and encourage a sense of public ownership and responsibility towards cultural heritage collections (Holley, 2010).

Holley also asks what the normal profile of a crowdsourcing volunteer in the cultural, heritage, and humanities sector is, stressing that from even early pilot projects the same makeup emerges: although there may be a large number of volunteers who originally sign up, the majority of the work is done by a small cohort of super-users, who achieve significantly larger amounts of work than anyone else. They tend to be committed to the project for the long term, appreciate that it is a learning experience, which gives them purpose and is personally rewarding, perhaps because they are interested in it, or see it as a good cause. Volunteers often talk of becoming addicted to the activities, and the amount of work undertaken often exceeds the expectations of the project. Holley (2010) argues that "the factors that motivate digital volunteers are really no different to factors that motivate anyone to do anything," saying that interest, passion, a worthy cause, giving back to the community, helping to achieve a group goal, and contributing to the discovery of new information in an important area are often reasons that volunteers contribute. Observations and surveys of volunteers by site managers noted various techniques that can improve user motivation, such as adding more content regularly, increasing challenges, creating a camaraderie, building relationships with the project, acknowledging the volunteer's help, providing rewards, and making goals and progress transparent. The reward and acknowledgment process is often linked to progress reports, with volunteers being named, high achievers being ranked in publicly available tables, and promotional gifts.

Holley provides various tips that have provided guidance for a variety of crowdsourcing projects, and are worth following by those considering using this method. The project should have a clear goal that presents a big challenge, report regularly on progress, and showcase results. The system should be easy and fun, reliable and quick, intuitive, and provide options to users so they can choose what they work on (to a certain extent). The volunteers should be acknowledged, rewarded, supported by the project team, and trusted. The content should be interesting, novel, focused on history or science, and there should be lots of it (Holley, 2010).

Holley's paper was written just before many of the projects outlined above came on-stream, stressing the potential for institutions, and challenging institutional structures to be brave enough to attempt to engage individuals in this manner. By 2012, with various projects in full swing, reports and papers began to appear about the nuances of crowdsourcing in this area, although "there is relatively little academic literature dealing with its application and outcomes to allow any firm judgements to be made about its potential to produce academically credible knowledge" (Dunn and Hedges, 2012:4).

Ridge (2012) explores the "frequently asked questions about crowdsourcing in cultural heritage," noting various misconceptions and apprehensions surrounding the topic. Ridge agrees with Owens (2012b) that the industry definition of crowdsourcing is problematic, suggesting instead that it should be defined as

> an emerging form of engagement with cultural heritage that contributes towards a shared, significant goal or research area by asking the public to undertake tasks that cannot be done automatically, in an environment where the tasks, goals (or both) provide inherent rewards for participation. (Ridge, 2012)

Ridge draws attention to the importance of the relationships built between individuals and organizations, and that projects should be mindful of the motivations for participating. Institutional nervousness around crowdsourcing is caused by worries that malicious or deliberately bad information will be provided by difficult, obstructive users, although Ridge maintains this is seldom the case, and that a good crowdsourcing project should have inbuilt mechanisms to highlight problematic data or users, and validate the content created by its users. Ridge returns again to the ethics of using volunteer labor, allaying fears about the type of exploitation seen in the commercial sector exploitation by explaining that

> Museums, galleries, libraries, archives and academic projects are in the fortunate position of having interesting work that involves an element of social good, and they also have hugely varied work, from microtasks to co-curated research projects. Crowdsourcing is part of a long tradition of volunteering and altruistic participation. (Ridge, 2012)

In a further 2013 post, Ridge also highlights the advantages of digital engagement via crowdsourcing, suggesting that digital platforms can allow smaller institutions to engage with users just as well as large institutions, can generate new relationships with different organizations in order to work together around a similar topic in a collaborative project, and can provide great potential for audience participation and engagement (Ridge, 2013). In fact, Owens (2012b) suggests that our thinking around crowdsourcing in culture and heritage is the wrong way round: rather than thinking of the end product and the better data that volunteers are helping us create, institutions should focus on the fact that crowdsourcing marks a fulfillment of the mission of putting digital collections online:

> What crowdsourcing does, that most digital collection platforms fail to do, is offers [*sic*] an opportunity for someone to do something more than consume information … Far from being an instrument which enables us to ultimately better deliver content to end users, crowdsourcing is the best way to actually engage our users in the fundamental reason that these digital collections exist in the first place … At its best, crowdsourcing is not about getting someone to do work for you, it is about offering your users the opportunity to participate in public memory. (Owens, 2012b)

The lessons learned from these museum- and library-based projects are important starting points for those in the digital humanities who wish to undertake crowdsourcing themselves.

Crowdsourcing and Digital Humanities

In a 2012 scoping study of the use of crowdsourcing particularly applied to humanities research, 54 academic publications were identified that were of direct relevance to the field, and a further 51 individual projects, activities, or websites were found which documented or presented some aspect, application, or use of crowdsourcing within humanities scholarship (Dunn and Hedges, 2012). Many of these projects have cross-overs with libraries, archives, museums, and galleries, as partners who provide content or expertise, or who host projects themselves, and many of them are yet to produce a tangible academic outcome. As Dunn and Hedges point out, at a time when the web is simultaneously transforming the way in which people collaborate and communicate, and merging the spaces which the academic and non-academic communities inhabit, it has never been more important to consider the role which public communities – connected or otherwise – have come to play in academic humanities research. (Dunn and Hedges, 2012:3).

Dunn and Hedges (2012:7) identify four factors that define crowdsourcing used within humanities research. These are: a clearly defined core research question and direction within the humanities; the potential for an online group to add to, transform, or interpret data that is important to the humanities; a definable task which is broken down into an achievable workflow; and the setting up of a scalable activity which can be undertaken with different levels of participation. Very similar to the work done in the GLAM sector, the theme and research question of the project are therefore the main distinguishing factors from other types of crowdsourcing, with digital humanities projects learning from other domains such as successful projects in citizen science or industry.

An example of such a project fitting into this humanities crowdsourcing definition, given its purview, is *Transcribe Bentham* (http://blogs.ucl.ac.uk/transcribe-bentham), a manuscript transcription initiative that intends to engage students, researchers, and the general public with the thought and life of the philosopher and reformer, Jeremy Bentham (1748–1832), by making available digital images of his manuscripts for anyone, anywhere in the world, to transcribe. The fundamental research question driving this project is to understand the thought and writings of Bentham more completely – a topic of fundamental importance to those engaged in eighteenth- or nineteenth-century studies – given that 40,000 folios of his writings remain untranscribed "and their contents largely unknown, rendering our understanding of Bentham's thought – together with its historical significance and continuing philosophical importance – at best provisional, and at worst a caricature" (Causer and Terras, 2014a). The objectives of the project are clear, with the benefit to humanities (and law, and social science) research evident from the research objectives.

Dunn and Hedges (2012:18–19) list the types of knowledge that may be usefully created in digital humanities crowdsourcing activities, resulting in new understanding of humanities research questions. These digital humanities crowdsourcing projects are involved in: making ephemera available that would otherwise not be; opening up information that would normally be accessible to distinct groups; giving a wider audience to specific information held in little-known written documentation; circulation of personal histories and diaries; giving personal links to historical processes and events; identifying links between objects; summarizing and circulating datasets; synthesizing new data from existing sources; and recording ephemeral knowledge before it dissipates. Dunn and Hedges stress that an important point in these crowdsourcing projects is that they enable the building up of knowledge of the process of how to conduct collaborative research in this area, while creating communities with a shared purpose, which often carry out research work that goes beyond the expectations of the project (19). However, they are keen to also point out that

> most humanities scholars who have used crowd-sourcing in its various forms now agree that it is not simply a form of cheap labour for the creation or digitization of content; indeed in a cost-benefit sense it does not always compare well with more conventional

means of digitization and processing. In this sense, it has truly left its roots, as defined by Howe (2006) behind. The creativity, enthusiasm and alternative foci that communities outside that academy can bring to academic projects is a resource which is now ripe for tapping in to. (Dunn and Hedges, 2012:40).

As with Owens' thoughts on crowdsourcing in the GLAM sector (2012), we can see that crowdsourcing in the humanities is about engagement, and encouraging a wide, and different, audience to engage in processes of humanistic inquiry, rather than merely being a cheap way to encourage people to get a necessary job done.

Crowdsourcing and Document Transcription

The most high-profile area of crowdsourcing carried out within the humanities is in the area of document transcription. Although commercial optical character recognition (OCR) technology has been available for over 50 years (Schantz, 1982), it still cannot generate high-quality transcripts of handwritten material. Work with texts and textual data is still the major topic of most digital humanities research: see the analysis by Scott Weingart of submissions to the Digital Humanities Conference 2014, which showed that of the 600 abstracts, 21.5% dealt with some form of text analysis, 19% were about literary studies, and 19% were about text mining (Weingart, 2013). It is therefore no surprise that most digital humanities crowdsourcing activities – or at least those emanating from digital humanities centers and/or associated in some sense with the digital humanities community – have been involved in the creation of tools which help transcribe important handwritten documents into machine-processable form.

Ben Brumfield, in a talk presented in 2013, demonstrated that there were 30 collaborative transcription tools developed since 2005 (Brumfield, 2013a), situating the genealogical sites, and those such as *Old Weather* and *Transcribe Bentham*, in a trajectory which leads to the creation of tools and platforms which people can use to upload their own documents, and manage their own crowdsourcing projects (reviews of these different platforms are available on Brumfield's blog at http://manus cripttranscription.blogspot.co.uk, and at time of writing there are now 37 collaborative tools for crowdsourcing document transcription, listed by Brumfield at http:// tinyurl.com/TranscriptionToolGDoc). The first of these customizable tools was Scripto (http://scripto.org), a freely available, open-source platform for community transcription developed in 2011 by the Center for History and New Media (CHNM) at George Mason University alongside their Papers of the United States War Department project (http://wardepartmentpapers.org). Another web-based tool, specifically designed for Transcription for Paleographical and Editorial Notation (T-PEN) (http://t-pen.org/TPEN), coordinated by the Center for Digital Theology at Saint-Louis University, provides a web-based interface for working with images of manuscripts. *Transcribe Bentham* has also released a customizable, open-source version of its Mediawiki-based platform (https://github.com/onothimagen/cbp-transcription-desk), which has since been used by the Public Record Office of Victoria, Australia (http:// wiki.prov.vic.gov.au/index.php/Category:PROV_Transcription_Pilot_Project). The toolbar developed for *Transcribe Bentham*, which helps people encode various aspects of transcription such as dates, people, deletions, etc., has been integrated into the *Letters of 1916* project at Trinity College Dublin (http://dh.tcd.ie/letters1916). The platform *Letters of 1916* uses is the *DIYHistory* suite, built by the University of Iowa, which itself is based on CHNM's *Scripto* tool. Links between crowdsourcing projects are common.

There is now a range of transcription projects online, ranging from those created, hosted, and managed by scholarly or memory institutions, to those entirely organized by amateurs with no scholarly training or association. A prime example of the latter would be *Soldier Studies* (www.soldierstudies.org), a website dedicated to preserving the content of American Civil War correspondence bought and sold on eBay, to allow access to the contents of this ephemera before it resides in private collections, which, although laudable, uses no transcription conventions at all in cataloging or transcribing the documents it finds (Brumfield, 2013a).

The movement towards collaborative online document transcription by volunteers not only uncovers new, important historical primary source material, but it also "can open up activities that were traditionally viewed as academic endeavors to a wider audience interested in history" (Causer and Terras, 2014a). Brumfield points out that there are issues which come with this:

> There's an institutional tension, in that editing of documents has historically been done by professionals, and amateur editions have very bad reputations. Well now we're asking volunteers to transcribe. And there's a big tension between, well how do volunteers deal with this [process], do we trust volunteers? Wouldn't it be better just to give us more money to hire more professionals? So there's a tension there. (Brumfield, 2013a)

Brumfield further explores this in another blog post, where he asks:

> what is the qualitative difference between the activities we ask amateurs to do and the activities performed by scholars ... we're not asking "citizen scholars" to do real scholarly work, and then labeling their activity scholarship – a concern I share with regard to editing. If most crowdsourcing projects ask amateurs to do little more than wash test tubes, where are the projects that solicit scholarly interpretation? (Brumfield, 2013b)

There is therefore a fear that without adequate guidance and moderation, the products of crowdsourced transcription will be what Shillingsburg referred to as "a dank cellar of electronic texts" where "the world is overwhelmed by texts of unknown provenance, with unknown corruptions, representing unidentified or misidentified versions" (2006:139). Brumfield (2013c) points out that Peter Robinson describes both the utopia and the dystopia of crowdsourcing transcription: utopia in which textual scholars train the world in how to read documents, and a dystopia in which hordes of "well-meaning but ill-informed enthusiasts will strew the web willy-nilly with error-filled transcripts and annotations, burying good scholarship in rubbish" (Robinson, quoted in Brumfield, 2013c). To avoid this, Brumfield suggests that partnerships and dialog between volunteers and professionals is essential, to make methodologies for approaching texts visible, and to allow volunteers to become advocates "not just for the material and the materials they are working on through crowdsourcing project, but for editing as a discipline" (Brumfield, 2013c).

Care needs to be taken, then, when setting up a crowdsourcing transcription project, to ensure that the quality of the resulting transcription is suitable to be used as the basis for further scholarly humanistic inquiry, if the project is to be useful over a longer term and for a variety of research. The methods and approaches in assuring transcription quality of *content* need to be ascertained: whether the project uses double-keying (where two or more people enter the same text to ensure its veracity), or moderation (where an expert in the field signs off the text into a database, agreeing that its content meets benchmarked standards). However, in addition to this the *format* that the data is stored in needs to be structured to ensure that complex representational issues are preserved, and that any resulting data created can be easily reused and textual models can be understood, repurposed, or integrated with other collections. As Brumfield (2013a) points out, digital humanities already has a standard for documentary scholarly editing in the Text Encoding Initiative guidelines (2014), which have been available since 1990 and provide a flexible but robust framework within which to model, analyze, and present textual data. However, only seven of the crowdsourcing manuscript transcription tools (out of the 30 then available) attempted to integrate TEI compliant XML encoding into their workflow (Brumfield, 2013a). Projects which have used TEI markup as part of the manuscript transcription process, such as Transcribe Bentham, have demonstrated that users can easily learn the processes of encoding texts with XML if clear guidance and instruction is given to them, and it is explained why they should make the effort to do it (Brumfield, 2013a; Causer and Terras, 2014a, 2014b). Brumfield (2013a) stresses that is it the responsibility of those involved in academic scholarly editing within the digital humanities to ensure that their work on establishing methods and guidelines for academic transcription is felt within the development of public-facing transcription tools, and if we are engaging users so that they can built their own skillsets, we need to use our digital platforms to train them according to pedagogical and scholarly standards: "Crowdsourcing is a school. Programs are the teachers. We have to get it right" (Brumfield, 2013d). Brumfield (2013c) also highlights that it is the responsibility of those working in document editing, and the digital humanities, to release guides to editing and transcribing that are accessible to those with no academic training in this area, such as computer programmers building transcriptions tools, if we wish for the resulting interfaces to allow community-led transcription to result in high-quality textual material.

Future Issues in Digital Humanities Crowdsourcing

We are now at a stage where crowdsourcing has joined the ranks of established digital methods for gathering and classifying data for use in answering the types of questions of interest to humanities scholars, although there is much research that still needs to be done about user response to crowdsourcing requests, and how best to build and deliver projects. There are also issues about data management, given that crowdsourcing is now reaching a mature phase where a variety of successful projects have amassed large amounts of data, often from different sources within individual projects: the million pages from *Old Weather* from different archives; over 3 million words transcribed by volunteer labor in the *Transcribe Bentham* project (Grint, 2013) from both UCL and the British Library; approximately 1500 letters transcribed in *Soldier Studies* (2014), which at a conservative estimate must give at least half a million words of correspondence from the American Civil War. Issues are therefore arising about sustainability: what will happen to all this data, particularly with regard to projects that do not have institutional resources or affiliation for long-term backup or storage? There are also future research avenues to investigate cross-project sharing and amalgamation of data: one can easily imagine either centrally managed or federated repositories of crowdsourced information that contain all the personal diaries that have been transcribed, searchable by date, place, person, etc.; or all letters and correspondence that have been sent over time, or all newspapers that were issued on a certain date worldwide. Both legal and technical issues will come into play with this, as questions of licensing (Who owns the volunteer-created data? Who does the copyright belong to?) and cross-repository searching will have to be negotiated, with related costs for delivering mechanisms and platforms covered. The question of the ethics of crowdsourcing is one that also underlies much of this effort in the humanities and the cultural and heritage sector, and projects have to be careful to work with volunteers, rather than exploit them, when building up these repositories and reusing and repurposing data in the future. Ethical issues come sharply into focus when projects start to pay (usually very little) for the labor involved, particularly when using online crowdsourcing labor brokers such as Amazon's *Mechanical Turk*, which has been criticized as a

> digital sweatshop ... critics have emerged from all corners of the labor, law, and tech communities. Labor activists have decried it as an unconscionable abuse of workers' rights, lawyers have questioned its legal validity, and academics and other observers have probed its implications for the future of work and of technology. (Cushing, 2013)

The relationship between commerce and volunteers, payment and cultural heritage, resources and outputs, online culture and the online workforce, is complex. A project such as Emoji-Dick (www.kickstarter.com/projects/fred/emoji-dick) – which translated *Moby-Dick* into Japanese Emoji icons using Amazon's *Mechanical Turk* – is a prime example of what emerges when the lines of public engagement, culture, art, fun, low-paid crowdsourced labor, crowdfunding, and an internet meme, collide. Institutions and scholars planning on tapping into the potential labor force crowdsourcing offers have to be aware of the problems in outsourcing such labor, often very cheaply, to low-paid workers, often in developing countries (Cushing, 2013).

Returning to Brabham's typology on crowdsourcing projects, we can also see that although most projects that have used crowdsourcing in the humanities are information management tasks in that they ask volunteers to help enter, collate, sort, organize, and format information, there is also the possibility that crowdsourcing can be used within the humanities for ideation tasks: asking big questions, and proposing solutions. This area is undocumented within digital humanities, although the Association for Computers and the Humanities (ACH) and the 4Humanities.org initiative have both used an open-source platform, All Our Ideas (www.allourideas.org), to help scope out future initiatives (ACH, 2012; Rockwell, 2012). ACH also hosts and supports *DH Questions and Answers* (http://digitalhumanities.org/answers), a successful community-based questions and answers board for digital humanities issues, which falls within the ideation category of crowdsourcing. There is much scope within the humanities in general to explore this methodology and ideation mechanism further, and to engage the crowd in both proposing and solving questions about the humanities, rather than using it only to self-organize digital humanities initiatives.

Crowdfunding is another relatively new area allied to crowdsourcing, which could be of great future benefit to digital humanities, and humanities projects in general. Only a few projects have been started to date within the GLAM sector, both for traditional collections acquisition and for digital projects. The British Library is attempting to crowdfund for the digitization of historical London maps (British Library, 2014); the Naturalis Biodiversity Centre in Leiden is raising funds via crowdfunding to purchase a *Tyrannosaurus rex* skeleton (http://tientjevoortrex. naturalis.nl); the Archiefbank or the Stadarcheif Amsterdam has raised €30,000 to digitize and catalog the Amsterdam death registers between 1892 and 1920 (Stadsarchief Amsterdam, 2012); and a campaign to crowdfund the £520,000 needed to buy the cottage on the Sussex coast where William Blake wrote "England's green and pleasant land" was launched in 2014 (Flood, 2014). A project called *Micropasts* (http://micropasts.org), funded by the UK's Arts and Humanities Research Council based at UCL and the British Museum, has developed a community platform for conducting, designing, and funding research into the human past, testing opportunities in crowdfunding: over the next few years this will be an area which has much potential for involving those outside the academy with core issues within humanities scholarship.

Crowdsourcing also offers a relatively agile mechanism for those working in digital humanities to respond immediately to important contemporary events, preserving and collating evidence, ephemera, and archive material for future scholarship and community use. For example, the *September 11th Digital Archive* (http://911digitalarchive. org), which "uses electronic media to collect, preserve, and present the history of the September 11, 2001 attacks in New York, Virginia, and Pennsylvania and the public responses to them" (*September 11 Digital Archive*, 2011), began as a collaboration between the American Social History Project at the City University of New York Graduate Center, and the Center for History and New Media at George Mason University, immediately after the terrorist attacks. Likewise, the *Our Marathon* archive (http://marathon.neu.edu), led by Northeastern University, provides an archival and community space to crowdsource an archive of "pictures, videos, stories, and even social media related to the Boston Marathon; the bombing on April 15, 2013; the subsequent search, capture, and trial of the individuals who planted the bombs; and the city's healing process" (*Our Marathon*, 2013). There is clearly a role here for those within the digital humanities with technical and archival expertise to respond to contemporary events by building digital platforms that will keep records for the future, while at the same time engaging with a community – and often a society – in need of sustained dialog to process the ramifications of such events.

There is also potential for more sustained and careful use of crowdsourcing within both the university and the school classroom, to promote and integrate ongoing humanities research aims, but also to "meet essential learning outcomes of liberal education like gaining knowledge of culture, global engagement, and applied learning" (Frost Davis, 2012). There are opportunities for motivated students to become more involved and engaged with projects that digitize, preserve, study, and analyze resources, encouraging them to gain first-hand knowledge of humanities issues and methods, but also to understand the role that digital methods can play in public engagement:

> Essential learning outcomes aim at producing students with transferrable skills; in the globally networked world, being able to produce knowledge in and with the network is a vital skill for students. Students also benefit from exposure to how experts approach a project. While these tasks may seem basic, they lay the groundwork for developing deeper expertise with practice so that participation in crowdsourcing projects may be the beginning of a pipeline that leads students on to more sophisticated digital humanities research projects. Even if students don't go on to become digital humanists, crowdsourced projects can help them develop a habit of engagement with the (digital) humanities, something that is just as important for the survival of the humanities. Indeed, a major motivation for humanities crowdsourcing is that involving the public in a project increases public support for that project. (Frost Davis, 2012)

Crowdsourcing within the humanities will then continue to evolve, and offers much scope for using public interest in the past to bring together data and build projects which can benefit humanities research:

> Public involvement in the humanities can take many forms – transcribing handwritten text into digital form; tagging photographs to facilitate discovery and preservation; entering structured or semi-structured data; commenting on content or participating in discussions, or recording one's own experiences and memories in the form of oral history – and the relationship between the public and the humanities is convoluted and poorly understood. (Dunn and Hedges, 2012:4)

By systematically applying, building, evaluating, and understanding the uses of crowdsourcing within culture, heritage, and the humanities, by helping develop the standards and mechanisms to do so, and by ensuring that the data created will be usable for future scholarship, the digital humanities can aid in creating stronger links between the public and humanities research, which, in turn, means that crowdsourcing becomes a method of advocacy for the importance of humanities scholarship, involving and integrating non-academic sectors of society into areas of humanistic endeavor.

Conclusion

This chapter has surveyed the phenomenon of using digital crowdsourcing activities to further our understanding of culture, heritage, and history, rather than simply identifying the activities of digital humanities centers, or self-identified digital humanities scholars. This is an important distinction about the nature of digital humanities research, its home, and its purview. Much of the crowdsourcing activity identified in the GLAM sector comfortably fits under the digital humanities umbrella, even if those involved did not self-identify with that classification: there is a distinction to be made between projects which operate within the type of area which is of interest to digital humanities, and those run by digital humanities centers and scholars.

With that in mind, this chapter has highlighted various ways in which those working in digital humanities can help advise, create, and build crowdsourcing projects working in the area of culture and heritage, both to add to our understanding of crowdsourcing as a methodology for humanities research and to build up resulting datasets which will allow further humanities research questions to be answered. Given the current pace of development in the area of crowdsourcing within this sector, there is much that can be contributed from the digital humanities community to ensure that the resulting methods and datasets are useful, and reusable, particularly within the arena of document transcription and encoding. In addition, crowdsourcing affords vast opportunities for those working within the digital humanities to provide accessible demonstrators of the kind of digital tools and projects which are able to forward our understanding of culture and history, and also offers outreach and public engagement opportunities to show that humanities research, in its widest sense, is a relevant and important part of the scholarly canon to as wide an audience as possible. In many ways, crowdsourcing within the cultural and heritage sectors is digital humanities writ large: indicating an easily accessible way in which we can harness computational platforms and methods to engage a wide audience to contribute to our understanding of society and our cultural inheritance.

References and Further Reading

ACH. 2014. ACH agenda setting: next steps. Association for Computers and the Humanities blog. http://ach.org/2012/06/04/ach-agenda-setting-next-steps (accessed January 29, 2014).

Amazon Mechanical Turk. 2014. Amazon Mechanical Turk, Welcome. https://www.mturk.com/mturk/welcome (accessed January 16, 2014).

Amsterdam Centre for Digital Humanities. 2013. Modeling crowdsourcing for cultural heritage. http://cdh.uva.nl/projects-2013-2014/m.o.c.c.a.html (accessed January 17, 2013).

Brabham, D.C. 2013. *Crowdsourcing.* MIT Press Essential Knowledge Series. Cambridge, MA: MIT Press.

British Library. 2014. Unlock London maps and views. http://support.bl.uk/Page/Unlock-London-Maps (accessed January 29, 2014).

Brohan, P. 2012. New uses for old weather. Position paper, AHRC Crowdsourcing Study Workshop, May 2012. http://crowds.cerch.kcl.ac.uk/wp-content/uploads/2012/04/Brohan.pdf (accessed January 29, 2014).

Brumfield, B. 2013a. Itinera nova in the world(s) of crowdsourcing and TEI. Collaborative Manuscript Transcription blog. http://manuscripttranscription.blogspot.co.uk/2013/04/itinera-nova-in-worlds-of-crowdsourcing.html (accessed January 29, 2014).

Brumfield, B. 2013b. A Gresham's law for crowdsourcing and scholarship. Collaborative Manuscript Transcription blog. http://manuscripttranscription.blogspot.co.uk/2013/10/a-greshams-law-for-crowdsouring-and.html (accessed January 29, 2014).

Brumfield, B. 2013c. The collaborative future of amateur editions. Collaborative Manuscript Transcription blog. http://manuscripttranscription.blogspot.co.uk/2013/07/the-collaborative-future-of-amateur.html (accessed January 29, 2014).

Brumfield, B. 2013d. In *Text Theory, Digital Documents, and the Practice of Digital Editions*, ed. J.J. van Zundert, C. van den Heuvel, B. Brumfield, *et al.* Panel session, Digital Humanities 2013, University of Nebraska, Lincoln. July 2013.

Causer, T., and Terras, M. 2014a. Crowdsourcing Bentham: beyond the traditional boundaries of academic history. *International Journal of Humanities and Arts Computing* 8 (1), 46–64.

Causer, T., and Terras, M. 2014b."Many hands make light work. Many hands together make merry work": Transcribe Bentham and crowdsourcing manuscript collections. In *Crowdsourcing our Cultural Heritage*, ed, M. Ridge. London: Ashgate, 57–88.

Cushing, E. 2013. Amazon Mechanical Turk: the digital sweatshop. UTNE. http://www.utne.com/

science-and-technology/amazon-mechanical-turk-zm0z13jfzlin.aspx#axzz3DNzILSHI (accessed Januaary 29, 2014).

Dunn, S., and Hedges, M. 2012. *Crowd-Sourcing Scoping Study: Engaging the Crowd with Humanities Research*. Arts and Humanities Research Council. http://crowds.cerch.kcl.ac.uk/wp-content/uploads/2012/12/Crowdsourcing-connected-communities.pdf (accessed January 16, 2014).

Finnegan, R. 2005. *Participating in the Knowledge Society: Research beyond University Walls*. Basingstoke: Palgrave Macmillan.

Flew, T. 2008. *New Media: An Introduction*, 3rd edition. Melbourne: Oxford University Press.

Flood, A. 2014. Crowdfunding campaign hopes to save William Blake's cottage for nation. *The Guardian*, September 11, http://www.theguardian.com/culture/2014/sep/11/crowdfunding-campaign-william-blake-cottage (accessed June 20, 2015).

Frost Davis, R. 2012. Crowdsourcing, undergraduates, and digital humanities projects. http://rebeccafrostdavis.wordpress.com/2012/09/03/crowdsourcing-undergraduates-and-digital-humanities-projects (accessed January 29, 2014).

Grint, K. 2013. Progress update, 24 to 30 August 2013. Transcribe Bentham blog. http://blogs.ucl.ac.uk/transcribe-bentham/2013/08 (accessed January 29, 2014).

Holley, R. 2010. Crowdsourcing: how and why should libraries do it? *D-Lib Magazine* 16 (3/4). http://www.dlib.org/dlib/march10/holley/03holley.html (accessed January 29, 2014).

Howe, J. 2006a. The rise of crowdsourcing. *Wired*, June 2006. http://www.wired.com/wired/archive/14.06/crowds.html (accessed January 17, 2014).

Howe, J. 2006b. Crowdsourcing: a definition. Crowdsourcing blog. http://crowdsourcing.typepad.com/cs/2006/06/crowdsourcing_a.html (accessed January 17, 2014).

Howe, J. 2006c. Birth of a meme. Crowdsourcing blog. http://www.crowdsourcing.com/cs/2006/05/birth_of_a_meme.html (accessed January 17, 2014).

Hubble, N. 2006. *Mass-Observation and Everyday Life*. Basingstoke: Palgrave Macmillan.

iDigBio. 2013. CITScribe Hackathon. https://www.idigbio.org/content/citscribe-hackathon (accessed January 30, 2014).

Mueller, M. 2014. Shakespeare his contemporaries: collaborative curation and exploration of Early Modern drama in a digital environment. *DHQ: Digital Humanities Quarterly* 8 (3). http://www.digitalhumanities.org/dhq/vol/8/3/000183/000183.html (accessed January 30, 2014).

North American Bird Phenology Program (undated). About BPP. http://www.pwrc.usgs.gov/bpp/AboutBPP2.cfm (accessed February 9, 2014).

Old Weather. 2013a. Old Weather: our weather's past, the climate's future. http://www.oldweather.org (accessed January 17, 2014).

Old Weather. 2013b. Old Weather, About. http://www.oldweather.org/about (accessed January 17, 2014).

O'Reilly, T. 2005. What is Web 2.0? http://www.oreilly.com/pub/a/oreilly/tim/news/2005/09/30/what-is-web-20.html (accessed Januaary 16, 2014).

Our Marathon. 2013. About the Our Marathon archive. http://marathon.neu.edu/about (accessed January 28, 2014).

Owens, T. 2012a. The crowd and the library. http://www.trevorowens.org/2012/05/the-crowd-and-the-library (accessed January 16, 2014).

Owens, T. 2012b. Crowdsourcing cultural heritage: the objectives are upside down. http://www.trevorowens.org/2012/03/crowdsourcing-cultural-heritage-the-objectives-are-upside-down (accessed January 17, 2014).

Ridge, M. 2012. Frequently asked questions about crowdsourcing in cultural heritage. Open Objects blog. http://openobjects.blogspot.co.uk/2012/06/frequently-asked-questions-about.html (accessed January 18, 2014).

Ridge, M. 2013. Digital participation, engagement, and crowdsourcing in museums. London Museums Group blog. http://www.londonmuseumsgroup.org/2013/08/15/digital-participation-engagement-and-crowdsourcing-in-museums (accessed January 18, 2014).

Rockwell, G. 2012. All our ideas: the value of the humanities. 4Humanities. http://4humanities.org/2012/10/all-our-ideas-the-value-of-the-humanities (accessed January 28, 2014).

Schantz, H.F. 1982. *The History of OCR, Optical Character Recognition*. Manchester Center, VT: Recognition Technologies Users Association.

SeeClickFix. 2013. Report non-emergency issues, receive alerts in your neighbourhood, http://en.seeclickfix.com (accessed January 16, 2014).

Silvertown, J. 2009. A new dawn for citizen science. *Trends in Ecology & Evolution* 24 (9), 467–71.

September 11 Digital Archive. 2011. About the September 11 Digital Archive. http://911digitalarchive.org/about (accessed January 29, 2014).

Shillingsburg, P.L. 2006. *From Gutenberg to Google: Electronic Representations of Literary Texts.* Cambridge: Cambridge University Press.

Soldier Studies. 2014. Civil War Voices. http://www. soldierstudies.org (accessed January 29, 2014).

Stadsarchief Amsterdam. 2012. Actie Overgenomen Delen. https://stadsarchief. amsterdam.nl/archieven/archiefbank/actie_ overgenomen_delen (accessed June 20, 2015).

Text Encoding Initiative. 2014. P5: Guidelines for Electronic Text Encoding and Interchange. http://www.tei-c.org/release/doc/tei-p5-doc/en/ html (accessed January 29, 2014).

Weingart, S.B. 2013. Submissions to Digital Humanities 2014. The Scottbot irregular. http://www.scottbot.net/HIAL/?p=39588 (accessed January 28, 2014).

30
Peer Review

Kathleen Fitzpatrick

Peer review – the assessment of scholarly work by experts in the field – is of paramount importance in the life of academic research and scholarship. In fact, it may be the genre's *sine qua non*, the singular element – beyond research, beyond method – that separates it from other public modes of investigation and publishing. Academic researchers encounter peer review in almost every aspect of the ways that they work: funding proposals are evaluated by peer bodies; employment, retention, and promotion applications are accompanied by evaluative letters from more highly placed peers and are reviewed by committees; and of course publications rely on the evaluations of external reviewers. At every step along the way, the process of peer review enables us to say that the work in question has been considered by authorities in the field, thus allowing us to place some kind of confidence in the quality of the work itself.

That there are problems with the conventional form of peer review as practiced by many contemporary publishers is likely to come as no surprise. The literature is rife with studies of peer review's flaws, especially in the sciences and social sciences,[1] and recent years have seen some quite public failures of the peer review process.[2] As a result, many researchers today are raising questions about whether the modes of peer review that we employ need to be significantly improved. This chapter will explore a few studies and experiments that focus on reinventing the peer-review process for the increasingly digital world of journal publishing, but this volume's focus on the digital humanities requires an additional angle on the question of peer review: the optimal structure and organization of review processes for work that is not shaped like a traditional journal article, but that is rather web-native, that must be produced directly on the network in order to be produced at all, and that therefore cannot always have its "writing" phase separated from its "publication" phase, with a review period carefully nestled between.

A New Companion to Digital Humanities, First Edition. Edited by Susan Schreibman, Ray Siemens, and John Unsworth.
© 2016 John Wiley & Sons, Ltd. Published 2016 by John Wiley & Sons, Ltd.

Peer review as it is conventionally practiced, that is to say, is a bad fit for many of the ways that scholars in the digital humanities work today, as the projects they develop frequently can only be reviewed before their production is complete or after they are published – and yet we still need robust modes of evaluation for digital work. Such evaluation is necessary in no small part because peer review is not a process whose importance ends with publication; rather, the results of that peer review, the fact of its having successfully transpired, becomes the input in a range of other forms of assessment, including most significantly those used in personnel-oriented processes like hiring, retention, and promotion. In other words, we cannot simply conduct peer review within a field like the digital humanities in ways that work only for us; we must create processes that serve the needs of our own community of practice while remaining fully legible to scholars from other such communities, including most especially those committee members and administrators whose disciplinary homes may lie far outside our field.

Peer review thus presents the digital humanities with a particularly challenging and useful sort of design problem and a productive terrain for experimentation. What might happen if practitioners within the field were to develop research projects that began with an examination of the goals and purposes of peer review and that imagined new systems that might better meet those goals? If we were inventing peer review today directly for the web – peer review as a service – what might we want it to do for us, and how best might it be structured?

The history of peer review reveals the complexity of the purposes to which it is put.[3] Conventional wisdom locates the origins of peer review in the mid-eighteenth century establishment of the "committee on papers," which was charged with evaluating and approving material to be published in the Royal Society's journal, *Philosophical Transactions* (Kronick, 1990). This point of origin indicates peer review's basis as a mechanism of selection, designed to winnow submissions into the best set of papers for the publication. Such a gatekeeping process is made necessary by the structure and economics of print publishing: the journal, which provides the best possible means of getting work in front of readers, can only distribute so many articles in so many issues per year, and so there is a premium on ensuring that the work so distributed is the best available.

There is, however, an alternative story of the origins of peer review, which locates its birth not in the mid-eighteenth-century processes of journal publication but in the sixteenth- and seventeenth-century scene of book publishing in England (Biagioli, 2002). In order to be licensed by the crown to print books – to receive the royal imprimatur – one had to attest that one would not publish anything heretical or seditious. Printers were thus required to serve not just as distributors of knowledge but as censors of it as well, determining what was and was not appropriate for publication. When the royal societies were established, bearing the royal imprimatur, they took on this responsibility for any work they distributed. In this history, then, the earliest form of peer review was focused not on determining the scientific merit of papers to be distributed but rather on ensuring that there was nothing in them that could be deemed dangerous to the church or the state. This mode of peer review as censorship gradually shifted its emphasis to focus instead on issues of quality and technical accuracy, but there nonetheless lingers in our uses of peer review a mode of evaluation that is not just about the determination of merit but rather about the regulation of the borders of appropriate discourse.

External peer review, perhaps surprisingly, did not become a generally accepted practice among scientific journals until the middle of the twentieth century.[4] And the modes of peer review that are now most identified with it – most notably, double-blind peer review, in which the identities of both authors and reviewers are anonymized – are even more recent practices. Double-blind peer review was developed in order to ensure the best possible objectivity and is intended to keep the focus of the evaluation on the work, and not on the identity or affiliation of the work's author. The rise of double-blind peer review, in fact, is generally credited with facilitating a significant increase in the diversity of voices represented in major scholarly and scientific publications; female authors, authors of color, and authors from less prestigious institutions were assisted in getting work into key journals when those journals worked to minimize the role of *ad hominem* reviewer bias in the process. The effects, overall, have been salutary, but questions nonetheless remain about how anonymous a piece of writing – or a review of that writing – can ever really be, especially in a small field of experts.[5] And further concerns exist about the kinds of ungenerous, if not downright unethical, behaviors that anonymity can inadvertently promote.[6]

So, on the one hand, peer review is meant to serve the goals of increasing the quality of the available research by selecting the best work for distribution. And, of course, peer review's recursive elements – especially the "revise and resubmit" – reveal the desire (very frequently successfully achieved) of those engaged in the process to improve the work under review. On the other hand, peer review is also used, if only incidentally and unconsciously, as a means of policing the boundaries of scholarship, of determining the edges of the thinkable, and keeping that which is not approved as knowledge out. Peer review can become as much a mechanism of exclusion as of selection. This tendency is most visible today in the ways that scholars and review committees rank the prestige of journals: a crucial factor in determining that prestige is often not what the journals publish, but what they do not. Selectivity, after all, is a factor of rejection rate; the more work that is excluded, the better.

The significance of exclusivity only holds, however, in an ecology in which it can be enforced. The web presents a quite different ecology. Zones of exclusion can be carved out online – publications can be created that benefit from the same workflows for selection and editorial control as have long existed in print – but the general tendency is toward proliferation. An increasing quantity of work is simply published directly to the web, without the intermediate stages of editorial selection and review so fundamental to print-based publishing. Researchers create websites themselves, or they participate in publishing collectives, and through these structures their work finds its way directly to its audience. However, though there is no need in this publishing workflow for selection, there remains a need for evaluation, both to improve the quality of the researchers' future work and to serve as the input for those personnel evaluations and other assessment rubrics that will follow. There remains, in other words, a need to develop post-publication means of review that can demonstrate to those outside the community of practice that work that has not followed the conventional means of editorial selection and pre-publication peer review is nonetheless *good*.

Beyond this specific need for assessment in the lives of researchers, however, there is another crucial reason for the development of post-publication review mechanisms: to help readers, including future researchers, cope with the internet's overwhelming abundance. So much is published online that it can be impossible for anyone to figure out what they should be reading, or what projects they should be exploring, or what resources are out there for their own work. A post-publication mode of peer review can help with this problem, by shifting the key action involved in review, as Clay Shirky (2008) has suggested, from gatekeeping to filtering, from determining what gets published to determining what ought to be read. Or, put another way, post-publication peer review has the potential to turn its attention from filtering out the bad to what Dan Cohen (2012) has referred to as catching the good, directing attention to texts and projects that readers within a community ought to know about.

This is a profound transformation, and one whose implications for the hierarchical structures of academic life should not go unremarked. In conventional scholarly publishing, a successful peer review process results in the work being published. The mark of distinction is therefore conferred at the moment of publication: that this book or journal article *exists* is the sign that someone, or a few someones (at minimum an editor, and usually at least a couple of reviewers, most of whose identities remain unknown to the reader) have determined that it is worth the reader's time. In born-digital publishing processes, however, distinction is not conferred at publication; that the project exists means only that the author or project team thought it worthwhile. Distinction instead becomes conferred through *reception*, through the uses and reuses made of the text or project, through the responses of its readers or users, and through the company that the work keeps. Distinction is produced, in other words, by the community, and it is conveyed through that community's interactions: a reader comes to know that a text or project is worth the time that will be spent on it when someone he or she knows and trusts recommends it. That recommendation may come in the form of a traditional citation, or it may come as reference embedded within another online text, or it may simply be offered as a link on a social media site. The key factor in following that link to the recommended text is a desire to engage, both with the text and the recommender.

Recommendations such as these, and the inbound links that they create, are only one form of the many possible traces of post-publication peer review. Other evidence of such review might include a range of quantitative metrics including page hits or downloads, indicating the frequency with which a community is interacting with the text or project, as well as more properly qualitative measures such as comment and discussion at a range of levels of formality. Other evidence might include post-publication project reviews published in other venues, indexing and related forms of inclusion in other projects, and so forth. The dispersal of such evidence of reception (as opposed to the concentrated evidence of the successful pre-publication review in the very existence of the text) suggests that post-publication review bears an ambient aspect. It surrounds the text or project, seemingly becoming a part of the environment in which it is used. In order for such review to be understood *as review*, it cannot simply be taken as given, as can conventional review methods; instead, the evidence of review must itself be gathered, evaluated, and interpreted. Admittedly, this creates more work, both for authors or project directors and for future evaluators; simply knowing, in the print regime, that peer review had occurred was a convenient shorthand for quality control, without which more time must be spent in assessing a project's impact on its field. Several projects are under way, however, in scientific communication circles, exploring alternative metrics that might be gathered at the article level; among these projects, *Altmetric* (http://www.altmetric.com) and *ImpactStory* (http:// impactstory.org) are working to gather and present the ambient data that accretes around publications, giving readers and authors a picture of the citations, comments, inbound links, Twitter references, and other means through which an article has circulated within its community. These projects, however, while compelling, do not solve the problems surrounding peer review for the digital humanities, as they focus exclusively on work published as articles (and articles contained within a narrow range of repositories at that), and the information they gather on those articles is almost entirely quantitative. For the digital humanities to benefit from such alternative metrics, significant work will need to be done to adapt altmetric tools for use with a range of kinds of projects, as well as to develop similar tools to gather and analyze qualitative forms of interaction.

Such analysis is required of open, online, post-publication review not just because it is new, or different, but precisely *because we can see it*. Critics raise a range of questions about open review processes: Who were the reviewers? Were they the "right" readers? Were there enough readers? Did they leave enough comments? Were the comments sufficiently rigorous or critical? These are important questions to ask, but it's equally important to note that we've almost never been led to ask such questions about our existing review processes, precisely because of their invisibility. We haven't much wondered, for instance, whether the reviewers in a traditional journal review process were the right reviewers, or whether their comments were good enough, or substantial enough, or whether those reviews have in fact had a positive effect on the final published text. All we have known is that a reliable editor is in charge, that some kind of fairly standard process occurred, and that the resulting work is good. In post-publication review, we have all of those markers except the standard process; in its place, there is a wealth of data available that might help us decide for ourselves whether the project has been reviewed critically enough and by the right people. The hitch is that we have to evaluate the data in order to get the answer.

The very openness of the review data, both to evaluation and to creation, points to one of the aspects of open review (and of the Internet more generally) that makes many scholars nervous: the changing definition that it implies of the "peer." There is a good deal of discomfort – and not at all without reason – with the sense that *anyone* could say *anything* online. Opening work up to critique from those who do not understand the scholarly or scientific enterprise, or to those with a political ax to grind, can produce a particularly destructive form of discourse.[7] It is for this reason important to indicate that though the status of "peer" is opening up in the era of Internet communication, there are nonetheless still some limits to that openness. The rise of peer-to-peer technologies has resulted in an understanding of the peer as any node connected to a network, and this suggestion that the peer could be devolving from the academic sense of "credentialed colleague" to "just anybody" is understandably a difficult one to swallow.[8] There are two things to consider here, however: first, the importance of knowing that the peers we rely upon in peer review are credentialed colleagues derives in no small part from their anonymity; if we know who the participants in a review process are, we can perhaps become a little less reliant on a strict definition of the pool. And second, opening up the notion of the peer need not lead to a review environment in which the voice of "just anybody" carries as much weight as the voice of an expert. In fact, the crucial change is not that the status of peer has been radically democratized; it is rather that the status of peer is not conferred based on pre-existing credentials, but is rather earned based upon participation in a review process. One *becomes* a peer through the quality of one's interactions with a community of practice.[9]

That post-publication review processes might be understood as ambient, however, is not to suggest that they will simply *happen* in the absence of any guidance or direction. New review processes require careful planning and steering. Review plans should in fact be written into the specifications for new digital projects. In designing these review plans, communities of practice should make their expectations transparent, defining processes, modes of participation, norms for communication, and so forth.[10]

Many examples of such new review models are currently available, ranging from very lightweight, minimal practices to intensive processes. At the former end of the scale is the longest-running of these new review models, *arXiv*, a pre-print server hosting papers in high-energy physics, mathematics, and other related fields. *arXiv* was not intended to be an intervention into the practices of peer review, but rather a means for scientists in high-stakes fields to get working papers into circulation in a far more timely fashion than journal publishing processes permitted. Moreover, most of the papers hosted on *arXiv* go on to be published in a traditionally peer-reviewed journal. However, several of *arXiv*'s practices constitute what might be thought of as a proto-review of sorts. First, in order for an author to post a paper within one of *arXiv*'s subfields for the first time, an existing member of that subfield must vouch for him or her; this basic declaration that the author is indeed a member of our community of practice, and that his or her work should be considered part of our sphere of interest, constitutes peer review at its most basic. Moreover, *arXiv* provides both means for readers to comment on posted articles and means for authors to obtain a range of metrics about an article's use. Again, the authors do typically go on to publish these articles in journals that add their own layer of selection-oriented review. However, while *arXiv*'s community processes and usage metrics may not be intended to stand alone as post-publication peer review, they nonetheless point the way toward understanding how new work interacts with its community of practice.[11]

At the other end of the scale may be the review process employed by the journal *Kairos*. *Kairos* numbers among the longest-standing electronic journals, publishing "web texts" focused on exploiting the affordances of computer and network technologies for expressive composition and communication. These web texts are interactive and design-oriented, and as such they cannot be captured in print or PDF format. They must be interacted with online in order to be read. *Kairos*'s editorial team has developed a three-tiered review process that works with such interaction. The first tier of review for submitted projects is conducted by the editorial board, which determines whether the project is appropriate and of sufficient merit to pursue. The second tier involves a lengthy discussion among all members of the *Kairos* editorial board, who collectively produce a response for the project authors. The majority of submissions that make it through this stage of the process do so with a "revise and resubmit." In the third tier of review, a member of the editorial team is assigned to work directly with the authors, providing extensive feedback and working closely (and, obviously, non-anonymously) with the authors to help facilitate the revision process. The cycle repeats when the revised text is resubmitted, with the editorial board determining collectively when the project is "ready" for publication. *Kairos*'s review process thus retains its pre-publication selection function while eschewing anonymity and shifting its emphasis to focus intensively on improving the work under review (*Kairos*, undated).

Many new review experiments are popping up in and around scientific publications: Faculty of 1000, for instance, publishes several projects that intervene in the review process. *F1000Research*, for instance, describes itself as an "open science journal," offering swift publication after an editorial check, with post-publication peer review offered via both open refereeing (insofar as is possible, *F1000Research* promises at least two qualified reviewers for every article) and reader commenting. Authors are then able to revise and republish based upon those reviews and comments, and articles that pass peer review are deposited into PubMed Central and indexed in the relevant databases. The result is that the time to publication is shrunk to just a few days, and the articles are made available (with any accompanying data) in a fully open-access format while nonetheless reaching the official channels through which scientists conduct their research (*F1000Research*, undated). Another Faculty of 1000 project, *F1000Prime*, is a database listing articles published in other venues that have been recommended by over 5000 experts in biological and medical sciences; this secondary layer of post-publication review enables a form of community-based information gathering and filtering that helps bring important work to the attention of others in the field (*F1000Prime*, undated).

PeerJ presents two further experiments in communication for the biological and medical sciences: *PeerJ Pre-prints*, a distribution and feedback mechanism for pre-publication work, and *PeerJ* itself, a peer-reviewed journal. As with many open-access journals in the sciences, authors with work accepted in *PeerJ* are required to pay publication fees; however, *PeerJ* also offers a set of comparatively inexpensive lifetime pricing plans that, paid any time before acceptance, permit publication of one, two, or an unlimited number of papers per year. Much of the peer review process looks familiar: submitted papers are handled by an academic editor who is responsible for finding peer reviewers. However, peer reviewers are encouraged to reveal their identities, and all community members are asked to contribute at least one review per year. Moreover, reviewers focus exclusively on scientific validity (rather than impact), and use review tools that enable speedy, structured response (*PeerJ*, undated).

There are numerous other examples that could be similarly explored here across the sciences. Those experiments typically retain their focus on the article as the unit of scholarly communication, however, which somewhat limits their applicability to the digital humanities. However, digital humanists have engaged in a series of experiments with other forms of scholarship as their primary focus. The edited volume *Debates in the Digital Humanities*, for instance, explored the ways that its community of authors might work together in communally reviewing a large-scale text (*Debates in the Digital Humanities*, 2013). MediaCommons Press has similarly provided a platform through which editors and authors can present edited volumes, monographs, and other such extended work to a community for open discussion and review (MediaCommons Press, undated).

To this point, however, such experimentation in the form of peer review has mostly focused on fairly traditional textual scholarly outputs. Where the scholarly object has become more genuinely multimodal, peer review has taken more traditional form. For instance, the model of peer review employed by NINES, the *Networked Infrastructure for Nineteenth-Century Electronic Scholarship*, focuses less on new ways of reviewing than on providing assessment for the kinds of projects that have not traditionally had peer review available to them. NINES aggregates the metadata surrounding digital objects produced by a range of libraries, archives, and other digital projects, providing a singular point of entry for scholars doing research in the field. Metadata collections proposed for inclusion in NINES are reviewed by experts in the field, who focus both on the intellectual content of the collection and on its technical structure. Inclusion in NINES (or in the other period-based sites that come together as part of the Advanced Research Consortium, including *18thConnect*, *Rekn*, and MESA) thus constitutes evidence of successful peer review, as well as providing a means for new digital projects to reach and interact with a community of scholars (NINES, undated).

All of these projects and experiments in the future of peer review suggest potential avenues for future exploration. All present benefits for expanding modes of digital research, but none as yet bring together the particular strengths of the digital humanities: an engagement with the problems of information and network design; an analysis of the structure and significance of networked data; an emphasis on the interpretation and communication of that data. These interests indicate the availability of peer review itself as fertile ground for future work in the digital humanities.

NOTES

1 Just a few of the many possible citations: see Zuckerman and Merton (1971), Peters and Ceci (2004), Godlee (2000), van Rooyen (2001); see also Rowland (2002) for an overview of the literature on peer review, and see *Nature*'s peer review debate (2006) for a wide-ranging exploration of the issues and alternatives.

2 While John Bohannon, writing in *Science*, presented his infamous "sting" – in which he submitted the same fake paper, authored by a nonexistent scientist from an invented institution, to over 300 open-access journals, more than 150 of which accepted it – as an indictment of author-pays OA publishing (Bohannon, 2013), Curt Rice argues that the real issue is a "meltdown" of the peer review system (Rice, 2013). Rice points to some recent and quite spectacular cases of failure in peer review, including that of Diederik Stapel, a Dutch social psychologist whose decades of fabricated data were not uncovered by reviewers. The Stapel scandal is far from an isolated incident; other recent cases include that

of German physicist Jan Hendrick Schön, the exposure of whose fraudulent work resulted in many of his papers being retracted – 8 of which had originally been published in, and have since been withdrawn by, *Science*.

3 For a more detailed exploration of this history, see Fitzpatrick (2011).

4 See Weller (2001) for a detailed history of the implementation of contemporary peer review practices in scientific publications; see also Spier (2002), who notes that *Science* and *The Journal of the American Medical Association* only began using external reviewers in the 1940s.

5 See Guédon and Siemens (2002): "Alas, anyone capable of evaluating research in a given specialty generally knows that specialty sufficiently to identify the probable author of the manuscript under review" (18).

6 See Godlee's (2000) exploration of one particularly egregious example; see also Campanario (1998).

7 One such destructive interaction between scientific research and the open web manifested until recently around climate

science; any discussion of human causality in global climate change resulted in a flood of comments from skeptics, making it appear to the casual observer that there was a debate within the community. More recently, however, climate scientists have begun using the same open tools to debunk the denials; see, for instance "Skeptical Science" (undated).

8   For an example of this technological redefinition of the "peer" in the context of peer review, see Anderson (2006).

9   This is of course true in the strictly technological sense as well: a node connected to a peer-to-peer network only achieves the status of peer when it succeeds in communicating

with the network according to the correct protocols.

10 See Fitzpatrick and Santo (2012). While focused primarily on more textually oriented forms of digital publication, this report might nonetheless open some possibilities for those wishing to develop new peer review models for digital work.

11 See "The *arXiv* endorsement system" (2009). Though *arXiv* makes no claims for the status of peer-reviewed publication, the versions of papers posted on *arXiv* are frequently cited, and often far more rapidly than those published in a formal journal of record. See Larivière *et al.* (2013).

References and Further Reading

Anderson, C. 2006. Wisdom of the crowds. *Nature*. doi:10.1038/nature04992. http://www.nature.com/nature/peerreview/debate/nature04992.html (accessed June 20, 2015).

arXiv. 2009. The *arXiv* Endorsement System. http://arxiv.org/help/endorsement (accessed June 20, 2015).

Biagioli, M. 2002. From book censorship to academic peer review. *Emergences* 12 (1), 11–45.

Bohannon, J. 2013. Who's afraid of peer review? *Science* 342 (6154), 60–5. http://www.sciencemag.org/content/342/6154/60.full (accessed June 20, 2015).

Campanario, J.M. 1998. Peer review for journals as it stands today, part 2. *Science Communication* 19 (4), 277–306.

Cohen, D. 2012. Catching the good. *Dan Cohen*. http://www.dancohen.org/2012/03/30/catching-the-good (accessed June 20, 2015).

Debates in the Digital Humanities. 2013. About *Debates in the Digital Humanities*. Accessed December 27. http://dhdebates.gc.cuny.edu/about (accessed June 20, 2015).

F1000Prime (undated). What is *F1000Prime?* http://f1000.com/prime/about/whatis (accessed June 20, 2015).

F1000Research (undated). About. http://f1000research.com/about (accessed June 20, 2015).

Fitzpatrick, K. 2011. *Planned Obsolescence: Publishing, Technology, and the Future of the Academy*. New York: New York University Press.

Fitzpatrick, K., and Santo, A. 2012. Open review: a study of contexts and practices. *MediaCommons*. http://mcpress.media-commons.org/open-review (accessed June 20, 2015).

Godlee, F. 2000. The ethics of peer review. In *Ethical Issues in Biomedical Publication*, ed. A.H. Jones and F. McLellan. Baltimore: Johns Hopkins University Press, 59–84.

Guédon, J.-C., and Siemens, R. 2002. The credibility of electronic publishing: peer review and imprint. *TEXT Technology* 11 (1), 17–35.

Kairos (undated). Editorial board and review process. http://kairos.technorhetoric.net/board.html (accessed June 20, 2015).

Kronick, D.A. 1990. Peer review in 18th-century scientific journalism. *JAMA: Journal of the American Medical Association* 263 (10), 1321–2.

Larivière, V., Sugimoto, C.R., Macaluso, B., *et al.* 2013. arXiv e-prints and the journal of record: an analysis of roles and relationships. *arXiv* 1306.3261 [cs.DL] (June 13). http://arxiv.org/abs/1306.3261 (accessed June 20, 2015).

MediaCommons Press (undated). *MediaCommons*. http://mcpress.media-commons.org (accessed June 20, 2015).

Nature. 2006. Peer review: debate. http://www.nature.com/nature/peerreview/debate (accessed June 20, 2015).

NINES (undated). Peer review. http://www.nines.org/about/scholarship/peer-review (accessed June 20, 2015).

PeerJ (undated). *PeerJ*: how it works. https://peerj.com/about/how-it-works (accessed June 20, 2015).

Peters, D.P., and Ceci, S.J. 2004. Peer review practices of psychological journals: the fate of published articles, submitted again. In *Peer Review: A Critical Inquiry*, D. Shatz. Lanham, MD: Rowman & Littlefield, 191–214.

Rice, C. 2013. Open access publishing hoax: what *Science* magazine got wrong. *The Guardian*. http://www.theguardian.com/higher-education-network/blog/2013/oct/04/science-hoax-peer-review-open-access (accessed June 20, 2015).

Rowland, F. 2002. The peer-review process. *Learned Publishing* 15 (4), 247–58.

Shirky, C. 2008. *Here Comes Everybody: The Power of Organizing Without Organizations*. New York: Penguin.

Skeptical Science (undated) http://www.skepticalscience.com (accessed June 20, 2015).

Spier, R. 2002. The history of the peer-review process. *TRENDS in Biotechnology* 20 (8), 357–8.

Van Rooyen, S. 2001. The evaluation of peer-review quality. *Learned Publishing* 14 (2), 85–91. doi:10.1087/095315101300059413.

Weller, A.C. 2001. *Editorial Peer Review: Its Strengths and Weaknesses*. Medford, NJ: Information Today.

Zuckerman, H., and Merton, R.K. 1971. Patterns of evaluation in science: institutionalization, structure, and functions of the referee system. *Minerva* 9 (1), 66–100. doi:10.1007/BF01553188.

31

Hard Constraints: Designing Software in the Digital Humanities

Stephen Ramsay

We call it "media," because, as the oldest meaning of this word would suggest, it lies somewhere in the middle: between the author and the reader, the voice and the ear, the artist and "the work." Yet this particular meaning – this way of talking about painting or newspapers – dates only to the middle of the nineteenth century. That the term also, around this time, came to designate those who could speak to the dead only emphasizes its liminal nature. What's more, a medium (to add yet another association) is the substance in which something is "cultured." Even in our present moment of relative maturity with respect to media studies, it sometimes seems as if there is no obvious platform upon which one may stand outside the object we are considering.

Lev Manovich, in a recent book, casts light on the vexing question of digital media by noting that Nicklaus Wirth had it right back in 1976: "medium = algorithms + a data structure" (Manovich, 2013:207). This is a useful re-intervention on a number of counts. It rejects (as a medium might put it) the "as above, so below" account in which it all comes down to "bits" or "zeros and ones" – a description that, however technically accurate, avoids meaningful distinction. It addresses, also, the confusing multiplicity of digital representations. Describing the computer – or even just the screen – as a medium would seem to admit an infinity of possible classifications. This, in turn, leads to the conceptual rabbithole of notions like "remediation," in which media are defined recursively in terms of what they "contain." Speaking in terms of algorithms and data structures – things that do lie almost literally between the chip and, say, the image – sets a boundary condition on the entire discussion, since both can be clearly identified and enumerated. The painter is constrained by the nature of oil paint; the photographer is constrained by the nature of film; the programmer is constrained by the ways in which data can be tractably arranged and manipulated.

A New Companion to Digital Humanities, First Edition. Edited by Susan Schreibman, Ray Siemens, and John Unsworth.

The constraints under which an artist works are potentially productive. The French experimental arts collective known as the Oulipo, as I and others have noted,[1] understands this fact more deeply than most, but all artists work within systems of constraint (even if the point is to transcend those constraints). When Anselm Kiefer glues sticks and ashes to his canvases or Piero's Jordan meanders convincingly toward the distant hills, we might say (with Edward Tufte) that they are trying to "escape flatland" (Tufte, 1990:12) – escape, that is, the constraints of the medium using the medium itself. Thus George Bernard Shaw, in *Mrs. Warren's Profession*, contrives an offstage kitchen that can accommodate all but two of the characters (who must, perforce, stay on stage). Shakespeare "cram[s] within this wooden O the very casques / That did affright the air at Agincourt" (*Henry V*: I.i.131–5). Schoenberg demands that all 12 notes be sounded; Scarlatti restricts the ensemble to four players. Nothing explains the endurance of the sonnet as a verse form in English – a language without the abundant rhymes or the regular rhythms of Italian – except the constraints it introduces, and over which poets continue to seek transcendence. You can be ingenious inside or outside "the rules," but either way, the rules are what enable the idea to come forth.

But the emphasis must be placed on the word "potential." If constraints can be productive, they can just as easily be stifling and oppressive. A forced confession is hardly "productive" for being constrained, and the history of art is full of instances in which state censorship succeeded in creating deadened, politically lifeless work. Defective musical instruments, toys and games with missing pieces, broken tools, and the like are seldom liberating, and are sometimes dangerous. In these and in many other similar cases, constraints *frustrate* plans, aspirations, ideas, visions.

Computers, though, thrive on constraints, and it is precisely at the level of data structures and algorithms that the constraints appear most stringent. There are perhaps upwards of 50 billion web pages in existence at the time of this writing, on subjects ranging from Irish politics to elephant funerals; every one of those web page consists of a tree data structure traversed using one of only a handful of well-known algorithms (depth first or breadth first, pre-order, in-order, post-order …). All digital images – no matter what their subject – are square matrices of numbers; making any one of them look like they were taken using a Polaroid SX-70 in 1975 requires a filtering algorithm, and there aren't that many different types of them. Nearly every database in existence uses a model (algorithm + data structure) first specified by E.F. Codd in 1970; cutting-edge "NoSQL" databases, ironically, return to a data model that is *older*. The digital representation of the letters that make up the most common characters in European (and many non-European) writing systems have had the same internal numeric codes since the 1960s.

It would be a mistake, though, to imagine that the relationship between data structure and screen is merely that of form and content. In describing a painting, we may say, crudely, that it is made up of various pigments possessing certain properties (hue, saturation, viscosity, etc.), and that the painter has combined these materials into an image. Whenever we try to say that of computational representations, we are in danger of not really describing what's going on. The screen is indeed made up of pixels possessing certain properties – hue, saturation, and, allowing for refresh speed, viscosity – but those pixels rest atop a chain of abstractions that, in the normative case, shield *both* programmer and user from the most basic elements of the material.

A programmer who creates a simple image viewer very likely used the functions already made available by the operating system – say, a PNG library along with the widget set for the operating system's user interface. PNG is a data structure; operations on the data contained within PNG images (like compression) involve algorithms. The authors of the PNG library were able to draw upon a set of algorithms and data structures provided by other libraries (e.g., zlib) and the programming language in which it was written (C).[2] Languages, of course, are abstractions; even a fairly low-level language like C is providing not only a set of convenient functions for generating assembly language, but providing a comparatively simplified view of the memory system of a modern computer (while also allowing the programmer to behave as if all microprocessor hardware is more or less the same). Assembly language is an abstraction on top of the machine code. At the level of machine code, the distance between program and what lies beneath is almost as yawning a gulf as that between image viewer and C code; clocks, flip-flops, and registers on top of arithmetic logic units on top of half-adders on top of NAND-gates …

But unlike NAND-gates (or, for that matter, images), algorithms and data structures are to be found in most layers of this system. At the very bottom, those structures are "baked in" to the hardware and not normally subject to reconfiguration by the programmer, and yet at this level the field of possibilities is at its widest. With each layer of abstraction – each arrangement of the data and concomitant narrowing of the field of possible procedures – the environment is further constrained. At the level of a programming language, the freedom remains palpable (though languages can and do restrict what can be done with the underlying hardware). The greatest restrictions are imposed upon the user of the software.

Here, I believe it is necessary that we speak not of medium, but of genre. "Genre" is what happens when we turn from the artist to the viewer, who, in the most simplistic case, expects (at least once upon a time) the painting to be a "picture," the unities to be observed, and the symphony to finish. These expectations, as Carolyn Miller noted, "acquire meaning from situations," and serve to connect "the private with the public, the singular with the recurrent" (Miller, 1984:163). Taxonomy can only ever be provisional, in the sense that Wittgenstein put forward with the notion of games.[3] Audience expectation defines the regime of artistic flexibility (since an artist is also an audience) while the artist defines, provokes, or reinforces audience expectation (which is to say, with Barthes, that the audience is always an artist). Ezra Pound said "Make it new." One might also profitably, cleverly, and with great ingenuity make it old. Still, our conventional – and mostly casual – notions of genre with respect to digital formations are badly flawed.

We imagine, to start with, that the relationship between medium and genre in digital environments is more or less as it is with non-digital environments. There are codex books, and then countless types of content (sci-fi novels, spy thrillers, coming-of-age stories). There is oil painting, and then there are certain styles of painting with oils (Mannerism, Fauvism, Abstract Expressionism). This is implicitly to put forth distinctions between hard constraints that can't easily be changed (the physical constraints of codex bookmaking involving paper, ink, fixity, length) and soft constraints that evolve over time (prefaces, introductions, chapters, indices). When the soft constraints extend into matters of plot, character, and subject, we begin to use terms like "genre fiction" or "genre painting" – which is merely to point out that the constraints have become rigid and deterministic (though not always to bad effect).

Digital representations not only blur these distinctions, but surface the role of the person constraining the medium. When we ask, "Who is the author of this book?" or "Who took that photograph?" we mean the person who created the "content" using the medium. In neither case do we mean to designate the person who invented the codex or the reflex camera. We are aware, of course, that whoever did create these things defined the regime of what is possible with those media, but that form of "authorship" seems entirely separate – a matter of merely historical interest for the novelist or the landscape photographer. With software, however, that person or group of people – *even if not known to the author* – plays a far more active, present, and fluid role.

As usual, the difference made by the digital is largely a matter of speed and scale. Artists have played with media in the past – experimenting, in the case of book arts and visual media, with every manner of surface, pigment, shape, durability, and size. Programming languages and general-purpose computing hardware render the process of constraining the engagement of subsequent interactors approximately as fluid as using software itself to create image, text, or video, while also making it so that the resulting constraints are easily offered to other users, authors, and creators. The result is a creative environment in which the tools and media one works in come to determine the generic nature of the outcome – as if Fauvism had developed not through imitation, but through the distribution of new paints and brushes that were only capable of creating certain kinds of paintings. Hard constraints become as cheap as soft ones.

Text messaging, for example, would appear to have a number of hard constraints; no message can be over 160 characters, messages are dispatched in the order in which they are received, and (assuming SMS) the messages can only contain text. There also appear to be soft constraints; emoticons and abbreviations are conventional, though no more required than introductions are required in books. Upon close inspection, though, it becomes clear that the distinction between hard and soft constraints is mostly a matter of perspective. There is, in fact, no technical reason for the 160-character constraint;[4] there is nothing about a computer or any of the algorithms one might impose upon its data structures that require messages to be received in the order in which they are sent; there is no physical limit that prohibits the use of images or video. One could design a system that allowed for more text (Instant Messaging) or less text (Twitter). One could build a (possibly hilarious) message system in which the phenomenon by which messages appear out of order is made a virtue; in this system, the order in which messages is sent is random. Less boldly, one might propose a "real-time" messaging system in which *words* appear in the order they are received. Finally, there is no particular reason to have text at all (Vine, Snapchat, etc.).

This fluidity hangs over many, if not most, engagements with digital tools and frameworks. Ultimately, the user is aware that most apparently hard constraints are in fact soft, and that that softness is the result of someone else's authorial agency. However, the degree to which those constraints "come forward" in a digital engagement varies widely.

In a first-person shooter, the constraints are part of the game. Lines of sight are fixed, the various properties of weapons are predetermined, and goals large and small are set by the designer. Victory occurs despite the constraints, and in fact victory is generally less meaningful when constraints are lifted (using the obligatory cheat codes). But since the constraints are what enable gameplay, the software tends to manufacture desire for the sort of capabilities that would require re-engineering the constraints themselves (via programming). When game companies release software for creating mods, the sensation for the user is of a welcome loosening of soft constraints; the hard constraints can remain. One might contrast this, however, with a modern flight simulator in which exact verisimilitude is highly prized. Such software is touted for its realism and the fact that one can "do anything" the real plane can do. However, when the paint on a nacelle is off or the yoke fails to have the feel of the real thing, users complain loudly. One might say that they are demanding realism, but they are more properly demanding a reconfiguration of hard constraints over which they are usually powerless.

Word-processing software putatively allows one to "do anything" with text. The experience is mostly of a constraint-less environment, even though it is in fact (like its antecedent, the typewriter) a quite rigidly constrained environment. As soon as one finds it difficult to start numbering with page 10, or to change the leading of a paragraph, or to have text run sideways down the page, the constraints suddenly seem distinctly unproductive. WordPerfect's much-beloved "reveal codes" feature had the effect of allowing people to believe that the hard constraints could be manipulated (softened) and therefore placed under their control (the "codes," of course, were not those of the programming language in which WordPerfect was written).

The World Wide Web is one of the more stunning examples of the complex interplay of hard and soft constraints. Ordinary Web development (of the sort that confines itself to HTML and CSS) is tightly constrained by the Document Object Model (DOM). Complete control over the DOM only becomes possible with JavaScript, and yet JavaScript's capabilities within the browser are entirely circumscribed by the browser platform itself. In recent years, browsers have afforded the user the option to create plugins or extensions (usually also in JavaScript) that can alter the appearance and behavior of the browser, but within limits. The browser itself is written (in the case of the major browsers) on top of a "toolkit" – a a set of software libraries that are essentially designed for the task of creating browsers and browser-like applications. There are, in other words, half-a-dozen places one might stand as an "author" (or a user) when it comes to Web browsers, and dozens and dozens of ways to reshape the medium.

Any new system we propose will involve some combination of a finite set of algorithms and data structures. This is the "stuff" from which any imaginable software system can be made. As with paint or photographic film, there is no hard mapping between data structure and content or subject. That is to say, common data structures like linked lists and b-trees lead to certain types of software only to the degree that grades of graphite lead to certain kinds of drawings. There is a relationship: b-trees are far more suited to hierarchical than linear data, just as graphite is more suited to work with complex shading effects. But these constraints tend not to predetermine genre. For this reason, it makes sense to speak of "the digital medium" exactly to the degree that it makes sense to speak of "the visual medium." At this level, the set of possible constraints is so wide that it hardly merits any notice.

The development of software lies, rather, in a complex set of decisions involving systems of constraint. It will not do to say, "The user shouldn't be constrained at all." That is an argument that may be relevant to discussions of software licensing, open access, and other sociopolitical aspects of technology, but it makes no sense as a guiding principle for software development itself. What's more, "programming," as such, is only one – and perhaps not even the most significant – aspect of the process of creating computational systems.[5]

Whatever one might say about the old media, it tended not to lie to its users. This is not to say that one couldn't plant ghosts in photographs or saw women in half. Even perspective is a sort of lie. But in most cases, the viewer is willingly suspending disbelief (or better, willingly activating faith), and the creator is seldom if ever being deceived. Our present situation is different. Privacy options are hidden. Constraints are lifted for a fee that was never mentioned up front. We speak (in gaming) of "level grinding," "farming," and "catassing" to describe enforced pathologies that are at best deceptive, and at worst mentally damaging to the participants. Key facilities are confined to an "expert mode" that requires a completely different set of user competencies. Jails are broken at the cost of warranties. Every open port is an attack vector.

Stated baldly, all of these are bad. But the actual situation is more nuanced. In a world saturated with software, matters such as privacy, time, and attention are fully reified – we trade privacy for affordance, time for pleasure, and attention for reward, and often do so willingly and knowingly. Sometimes this arrangment is so that the creators of the software can make a living (or a fortune) doing it, but it is also often the case that privacy, time, and attention are necessary in order to provide the set of constraints under which the user can flourish. The ethical questions (and there are many) almost always involve coercion and secrecy, not the fact that transactions occur.

All of this might seem a bit distant from the normative concerns of digital humanities, which mainly pertain to presenting humanities content digitally or analyzing humanistic data. But I would argue that the stakes are just as high if not higher than they are with platforms like Google and Facebook. Every re-presentation of the human record is a condensation and reframing of that record. Typically, we conceive our responsibility in this realm as having to do with context and interpretation. The idea is that if we are fully transparent about our own subjectivity, we will have discharged our duty to the user. The concern, therefore, is how to find the space between allowing unfettered access to everything (no context) and carefully guided, heavily curated tours of data (which may constrain so much that interpretative possibilities are eliminated). Data analysis represents a like situation. No humanist needs to be told that maps, graphs, trees, and charts can purvey falsehood or that they are essentially interpretative in nature, and yet we are very often concerned to outpace the viewer's ability to locate bias – as if admitting to bias magically removes it.

The question, rather, is whether a given representation constrains the user's view in a way that leads to further thought and discussion. The key element here is that thoughts and discussions are the result of the constraints, not something that happens as a side effect. In the case of thematic research archives, it is not fundamentally a question of interpreting more or less, but of defining the set of constraints under which the user will operate, and making those constraints not just plain or accessible, but *commensurable* (in the sense of creating the right fit between the creators and the users). The creator of a visualization is likewise trying to constrain the user's view by *limiting* possible interpretations, so that some other feature can be more easily seen.

But once again, hard constraints in digital systems will eventually reveal themselves as soft. In some cases, the ability to "re-constrain" can be built into a system, but it is in the nature of software to allow for more radical transformations. Because software is built from algorithms and data structures, software systems can be refactored and rebuilt, re-formed and re-released, frozen, rejected, or abandoned with far less friction than most other media. "I was using Scrivener, but I switched to Ghost." "I don't think I could use Word without the macros I've been building for 10 years." "Version 2 of Cocoon is a ground-up rewrite of Version 1." "C11 attempts to improve support for Unicode in C." "Tiling window managers represent a break with the traditional desktop metaphor." "Minecraft is more fun with the Aether mod." "I'm done with Facebook." It is hard to find precise analogs to such statements in non-digital media, and yet this is the daily speech of software users.

The preceding considerations give rise to five principles (there are undoubtedly more) for those developing software systems in the humanities:

- *Conceive of what the user can and cannot do as one of the principal questions in the development of a software system.* "The user can ..." is a constant refrain. What the user cannot do, though, is less likely to be an object of explicit concern.[6] Considering what the user cannot see, or move, or interact with, though, will likely serve to define not just the "user experience," but the kind of thoughts and connections that are made with the material (this is as true of research archives as it is of data analysis and visualization projects).

- *Avoid substituting transparency for the harder questions of affordance.* There is a natural tendency to counterbalance highly curated views of data with a "here's everything" backend: all the code, all the data, perhaps even all the design documents for the user to do with as they please. The existence of such open backend archives is laudable – it is, indeed, one step toward good librarianship in most cases. The problem occurs when we imagine that making these kinds of context-free collections available excuses us from the responsibility we have to make curated data fully active and engaging. "Verifying the results," for example, shouldn't require the user to rebuild the system itself.

- *Build like Plato, but think like Heraclitus.* Ideally, software systems should be modular, extensible, and highly fault-tolerant, which means paying attention to the ideals embodied in standards and best practices. In reality, "everything flows" (as Heraclitus purportedly said); all software systems – including the standards upon which so much future hope rests – degrade, transform, and are eventually replaced by entirely new approaches and frameworks. This is not "planned obsolescence," so much as a recognition that the algorithms and data structures of software systems resemble Lego bricks (or better, the sand paintings of Tibetan Buddhism) more than stress-tested, durable building materials. This fragility is part of what makes it possible for hard constraints to be rendered soft.

- *Avoid punishing users for attempting to render hard constraints soft.* Rendering hard constraints soft is almost the literal definition of hacking, but it can occur in less explicit and intentional ways. Rocket jumping in the original *Doom* is a classic example, and so is the infamous trick whereby a student increases the number of pages in a document by changing only the size of the periods.[7] Security issues aside, it is a mistake to plug up these kinds of holes when they're discovered, since they represent the emergent properties of constraint.

• *Treat developers no different from users.* The above principles extend all the way down the stack. The design of application programming interfaces (APIs) can and should be the art of defining what cannot be done. "Read the source" is an absurd substitution for documentation. Endless backwards compatibility crushes any emergent properties a software ecosystem might possess. A library that can't be used for unforeseen purposes probably isn't worth writing in the first place.

We call it "media" because it's not the main thing. The medium is the carrier, the underdrawing, the locus of storage and memory. The main things are the human actors creating, learning, interacting, reconfiguring, and being reconfigured. Nonetheless, since digital tools and frameworks are based upon a fundamental set of primitives (algorithms and data structures), they allow those human actors to build and tear down quickly. We can imagine this process as being akin to engineering or writing, but it might more profitably be imagined as a set of game tokens (balls, chips, dice, cards, boundary markers), which, when combined with agreements, constraints, rules, and good will, can lead to thought, creativity, and conversation. Leonardo famously (though perhaps spuriously) said that "art breathes from containment and suffocates from freedom." He might also have added that it thrives under conditions in which we enter into containment willingly and with purpose.

NOTES

1 See, especially in the context of digital humanities, articles by Stéfan Sinclair and Mark Wolff, as well as Ramsay.

2 libpng was written by Guy Eric Schalnat, Andreas Dilger, John Bowler, Glenn Randers-Pehrson, and others.

3 Ludwig Wittgenstein, in a famous passage in *Philosophical Investigations*, observes, "Consider, for examples, the activities that we call 'games'. I mean board-games, card-games, ball-games, and so on. What is common to them all? – Don't say: 'They "must" have something in common, or they would not be called "games"' – but *look and see* whether there is anything common at all." (Wittgenstein, 2009:36).

4 The 160-character limit is usually attributed to the communications researcher Friedhelm Hillebrand, who established the number as "perfectly sufficient" by "tapping out random sentences and questions on a sheet of paper." See Milian (2009).

5 This is one of many reasons why calls for universal "code-literacy" may be misguided. Conceptual understanding of computation might well have much to recommend it as a compulsory subject, but this sort of knowledge stands to the development of software systems as elementary calculus stands to space rocketry – one component of a complex system determined at every stage by concerns that range from the practical to the political.

6 One notable exception is game design, since it is in the very nature of game mechanics to define explicitly what the player is not allowed to do (hold two objects at once, pass through walls, rotate an object past 90 degrees, etc.).

7 This trick is widely documented on the Web at sites like *Instructables* and *Wikihow*. The more dramatic illustrations of the technique are on *YouTube* (e.g., InternetJordan, 2007).

REFERENCES AND FURTHER READING

Barthes, R. 1975. *The Pleasure of the Text*. Trans. R. Miller. New York: Farrar-Noonday.

Codd, E.F. 1970. A relational model of data for large shared data banks. *Communications of the ACM* 13 (6), 377–87. DOI:10.1145/362384.362685.

InternetJordan. 2007. How to make an essay look longer on paper trick. https://www.youtube.com/watch?v=tt3ac0inzbM (accessed June 20, 2015).

Manovich, L. 2013. *Software Takes Command*. New York: Bloomsbury Academic.

Milian, M. 2009. Why text messages are limited to 160 characters. *Los Angeles Times*, May 3, 2009.

Miller, C.R. 1984. Genre as social action. *Quarterly Journal of Speech* 70, 151–67. DOI:10.1080/00335638409383686

Pound, E. 1934. *Make It New*. London: Faber.

Ramsay, S. 2011. *Reading Machines: Toward an Algorithmic Criticism*. Urbana: University of Illinois Press.

Shakespeare, W. 1995. *King Henry V*. Ed. T.W. Craik. 3rd series. London: Thompson-Arden.

Tufte, E.R. 1990. *Envisioning Information*. Cheshire, CT: Graphics Press.

Wirth, N. 1976. *Algorithms + Data Structures = Programs*. Englewood Cliffs, NJ: Prentice-Hall.

Wittgenstein, L. 2009. *Philosophical Investigations*. Ed. and trans. G.E.M. Anscombe, P.M.S. Hacker, and Joachim Schulte. Malden, MA: Wiley-Blackwell.

Part V

Past, Present, Future of
Digital Humanities

32

Beyond the Digital Humanities Center: The Administrative Landscapes of the Digital Humanities

Andrew Prescott

I recently took part in an "awayday" meeting to develop a strategic plan for the Department of Digital Humanities at King's College London. Among the suggestions for improvement of the department made on a sticky note was "NO MORE SPREADSHEETS." It was a fair comment. No one becomes involved with digital humanities in order to ensure that digital humanities projects are more accurately costed or their management made more streamlined. Digital humanities is about creativity and experimentation; they should be a disorganized play space, not a model of managerial propriety. I became interested in digital humanities because I am fascinated by archives and manuscripts, and want to see how digital technologies provide new perspectives on them. Anything that distracts me from that is a waste of time and energy. I do not want to write strategy documents or prepare Gantt charts. I find bureaucratic processes such as research assessment or teaching reviews soul-destroying. I am very bad with money and not a good person to be in charge of budgets, and I am too distracted by research and writing to be a good manager. I do digital humanities because I want to do cool things. But if I want to get the money and resources to do cool things, I need to write carefully costed grant applications, to prepare project plans, and to persuade the university's managers that digital humanities work is worthwhile. To achieve that, I need to fill out spreadsheets, and get others to complete them as well. The spreadsheets are an inescapable part of our condition.

In 1993, Kevin Kiernan and I undertook some digital imaging of a burnt Cotton manuscript at the British Library. Kevin wrote that the experiment seemed "to portend the start of something really big, expensive, and earth-shattering" (Kiernan, 1994). Digital humanities is potentially (but not necessarily) expensive. We have equipment requirements which can go beyond those of conventional humanities departments,

A New Companion to Digital Humanities, First Edition. Edited by Susan Schreibman, Ray Siemens, and John Unsworth.
© 2016 John Wiley & Sons, Ltd. Published 2016 by John Wiley & Sons, Ltd.

as recent use of synchrotron light sources to examine ancient manuscripts illustrates (Morton *et al.*, 2004; Fleming and Highfield, 2007). We generate data which requires a storage infrastructure and specialist staff to manage the data. Ensuring that digital scholarship is preserved and made sustainable over a long period of time requires resources to undertake the curatorial activities of selection, maintenance, and updating. However, the main expense in digital humanities work is not the capital cost of equipment and buildings. If all we needed was specialist digital equipment, we could probably persuade university administrators and funding bodies to buy it for us, as capital expenditure is a nice containable one-off. What makes digital humanities expensive is the people.

Conventional humanities research is still frequently undertaken by the "lone scholar," digging into books, manuscripts, and other cultural artifacts in libraries, archives, and museums. Such research can be fitted into regular research days and university vacations. Many assumptions of university management about scholarly publication patterns and career paths in the humanities are still predicated on a "lone scholar" model, even in newer disciplines such as media and cultural studies. One characteristic of digital humanities is that much of its scholarship is team-based and does not easily fit into such historic administrative structures. Of course, this does not mean that digital humanities research cannot be undertaken by lone scholars. Some of the most important reflexive discussion of how engagement with technology is transforming understanding of history, culture, and society continues to be undertaken in these traditional ways. As the volume of digital materials grows, such critical commentary will become more, not less, important. But digital humanities also involves the creation of digital resources ranging from online editions to 3D reconstructions, and at the heart of the digital humanities is the idea that humanities scholarship can be carried out and expressed in a digital environment, that the humanities need no longer be bound by the technological restrictions of the printed codex. The conventional academic structures of humanities scholarship are geared to the production of books and articles. As humanities scholarship moves away from the production of scholarship in book or article form, so different administrative structures will be required.

In order to engage in such digital scholarship, teamwork is essential. The principal investigators who inspired and directed the creation of *The Proceedings of the Old Bailey, 1674–1913* (www.oldbaileyonline.org) were legal historians but they needed to enlist many other people to bring their vision to fruition. They required advice from project analysts with experience in the creation of digital resources as to how to approach the material. They used a digitization team to scan the original printed proceedings. These images were turned into machine-readable text by teams of keyboarders. The structure of the XML tags which control the display and search of the digitized text was defined by specialist XML designers. Automated software was used for some of the tagging, but other tagging had to be undertaken by experienced editors with an understanding of the way the XML was structured. A high degree of computer expertise was required for the design of the search engine, the indexing of the data, the creation of the interface, and the mounting of the resource on servers. Again, these various activities were often best undertaken by a team. This complex network of activity had to be tied together with strong project management. Four separate funding agencies provided funding for the development of *The Proceedings of the Old Bailey,* as well as the three universities in which the project was based. The project web pages list 22 people who were involved in its development. The administrative infrastructure required for the creation of groundbreaking digital scholarship has more in common with filmmaking than old-style academic publishing.

It is a commonplace that success in the digital economy depends as much on successful business models as on technological innovation. T. Michel Nevens (2000:81) has observed that "Although Silicon Valley is justly famous for technological innova-tion, innovations in management approaches, policies and investment strategies – in short, business models – are equally responsible for the Valley's extraordinary economic performance." As is well known, the success of Google depends on its highly targeted advertising, while the resurgence of Apple reflects the success of the business models associated with iTunes. Amazon's initial focus on book selling reflected the fact that books are suitable commodities for online ordering and dispatch, while the Amazon fulfillment service, in which third parties undertake warehousing and dispatch while Amazon provides the ordering platform, is a good example of an innovative business model in online retailing. Just as with Google, Amazon, or Microsoft, the ability of digital humanities to establish itself as a significant force driving forward the academic world's development of digital scholarship depends on its ability to create innovative business models within the academy. According to Nevens, successful Silicon Valley business models are:

> flexible. They are highly focused ... They are talent driven. Technical, marketing and managerial talent are in short supply, and Silicon Valley firms have devised ways to leverage other people's talent as well as develop their own. Finally, Silicon Valley business models are open and fluid. (Nevens, 2000:81–2)

Notwithstanding the importance of Stanford University in fostering the development of Silicon Valley, universities are generally conservative bureaucratic environments which are far removed from the open and flexible environment of Silicon Valley. If flexibility and openness are preconditions for success in the digital world, can this be achieved by digital humanities units in a university environment?

In recent years, utopian claims as to the way in which digital humanities might reshape the academy (usually the American academy) have become commonplace. The *Digital Humanities Manifesto 2.0* (2009) envisages the emergence of a new institutional topography: "not just disciplinary, but one involving alternative configurations to producing knowledge – open-ended, global in scope, designed to attract new audiences, and to establish novel institutional models." The manifesto imagines the disappear-ance of the traditional academic department and its transformation into a temporary pop-up phenomenon of "finite knowledge problematics" which "comes into existence for a limited period, only to mutate or cease as the research questions upon which it is founded become stable and their explanatory power wanes." Among the kind of transient departments imagined by the manifesto are a Department of Print Culture Studies, an Institute of Vocal Studies, and a Department of Erasure Studies. This is an attractive vision, but the reality would probably prove less appealing: arbitrarily defined subject areas reflecting whatever the university's marketing department thinks is the best choice, taught by adjunct staff on short-term contracts. Utopian visions of the sort found in the *Digital Humanities Manifesto* are helpful insofar as they encourage debate about the nature and character of humanities scholarship, but are less useful as a blueprint for the exploitation of the potential of digital technologies to stimulate the production of innovative forms of scholarship.

Commentators have acknowledged the importance of developing appropriate institutional structures to support the digital humanities, but there is little detailed discussion of what these structures might look like. Thus, while Willard McCarty in 2008 surveyed the different types of practice within digital humanities and urged that "the institutional structures we build for the digital humanities should reflect the nature of the practice as it has emerged in the last few decades" (McCarty, 2008:259), he did not develop further what this meant, beyond a recognition that digital humanities was more than a "support" activity. Similarly, Christine Borgman (2009) argued passionately that the digital humanities were at a critical moment of transition from a niche area to a fully fledged community, and stressed the importance of arguing for the development of infrastructure to support this, but was again vague as to exactly what this structure might consist of. The potential contribution of particular areas of the academy to the development of digital humanities has occasionally been stressed. Kirschenbaum (2010) has stressed the particular affinity between English departments and the digital humanities, while Sula (2013) points out that digital humanities also embraces materials and methods of interest to many other disciplines apart from English, and argues that libraries are particularly well placed to develop networks of expertise in the digital humanities.

The administrative landscape of the digital humanities is filled with what McGann (2014:131) has vividly described as "a haphazard, inefficient, and often jerry-built arrangement of intramural instruments – freestanding centers, labs, enterprises, and institutes, or special digital groups set up outside the traditional departmental structure of the university." The directory of digital humanities centers maintained by the international umbrella organization centerNet (http://digitalhumanities.org/center net) listed in August 2014 nearly 200 separate digital humanities centers across every continent. Similarly, the Humanities, Arts, Science, and Technology Alliance and Collaboratory (HASTAC: www.hastac.org) has over 400 affiliated organizations. The digital humanities center has provided the main engine for the growth of digital humanities over the past 25 years, and there can be no doubt that digital humanities centers will continue to play a leading role in shaping digital scholarship. This is apparent from two recent reports, a survey of digital humanities in the United States produced in November 2008 for the Council on Library and Information Resources by Diane M. Zorich (2008), and *Sustaining Digital Humanities: Host Institution Support Beyond the Start-Up Phase* by Nancy L. Maron and Sarah Pickle (2014). These works provide the most detailed accounts of the administrative framework of the digital humanities, but most of the examples discussed in them are from the United States of America. To provide a more international perspective, it is also essential to refer to the remarkable series of articles by Patrik Svensson (2009, 2010, 2011, 2012) reviewing the emerging landscape of the digital humanities. Svensson addresses many aspects of the intellectual formation of the digital humanities, but his emphasis on the way in which various digital humanities units function as spaces allowing new forms of intellectual contact and collaboration is vital in understanding the success of the center as a means of promoting digital humanities. John Bradley (2012) has also provided important insights into the philosophy underpinning the development of digital humanities centers in his description of the way in which the Department of Digital Humanities at King's College London was conceived as a unit for the pursuit of collaborative research in which the computing specialist works hand-in-hand with the humanities researcher as an intellectual peer, with none of the distinction between academic and professional staff which so frequently bedevils collaborative work.

The digital humanities center is helpfully defined by Diane Zorich as "an entity where new media and technologies are used for humanities-based research, teaching, and intellectual engagement and experimentation. The goals of the center are to further humanities scholarship, create new forms of knowledge, and explore technology's impact on humanities-based disciplines" (Zorich, 2008:4). Among the characteristic activities of a digital humanities center are the creation of digital resources, the production of digital tools for humanities work, the organization of lectures and seminars, the provision of digital humanities training in a variety of forms ranging from workshops to academic degree programs, and collaborative work in developing digital skills, expertise, and projects in other departments. While the digital humanities center is not a necessary precondition of digital humanities activity, nevertheless many of the hopes and dreams of digital humanities have in recent years been bound up with the work of such centers. The funding and advocacy of the digital humanities offered by bodies such as the National Endowment for the Humanities (NEH) and the Mellon Foundation has encouraged universities to invest in the creation of digital humanities centers, many of which have quickly built up imposing portfolios of projects. One of the oldest and most celebrated of such centers is the Institute for Advanced Technology in the Humanities at the University of Virginia (www.iath. virginia.edu), which since 1992 has built up a portfolio of over 50 collaborative research projects by faculty from both humanities and computer science departments in subjects ranging from Tibetan literature in the Nyingma tradition to the circus in America. One of the attractions of such centers for university management is that they are often very successful in attracting large quantities of research income. The Department of Digital Humanities at King's College London secured over £8 million in research grants for about 30 projects between 2008 and 2013.

While there is a strong family resemblance between digital humanities centers, almost every center differs in its formal character, with a plethora of ingenious administrative and institutional solutions used by different universities and colleges to create, develop, and maintain their centers. Some are freestanding institutes, administered at faculty or university level; others form parts of existing academic departments, in disciplines ranging from literature to library studies; some are academic departments in their own right; others are treated as support services and are part of the library or computing services; some just consist of loose alliances of local enthusiasts. The disciplinary relationships of digital humanities centers are equally complex: some are avowedly interdisciplinary and float above faculty or school level; others are placed under disciplinary umbrellas. Most longstanding digital humanities centers have undertaken a bewildering institutional journey of change, development and uncertainty in their funding and governance. The Humanities Research Institute (HRI) at the

University of Sheffield, for example, arose from the shared location of a number of early humanities computing projects in office space provided by the University Library. The Arts and Humanities Graduate School provided the HRI with a more formal governance structure through a management committee, leading the HRI to acquire an additional role in promoting interdisciplinary activity. The HRI eventually became one of a number of overarching "supercenters" and was funded directly by the Faculty. However, growing emphasis on its digital services saw it subsequently formally defined as a support service within the Faculty. Many older digital humanities centers can tell similar tales of administrative improvization and adjustment, reflecting a consensus among university administrators that, while it was important that there was digital expertise in the humanities, no one was sure exactly where it fitted in.

The digital humanities center offers many advantages. It provides a clear focus of expertise within the university, a place where academic researchers can easily find authoritative and trustworthy advice on digital humanities. The way in which digital humanities centers develop portfolios of projects covering a wide range of disciplines, countries and periods illustrates to academic colleagues the potential scope of digital humanities and promotes the cross-fertilization of digital humanities approaches across different disciplines. The digital humanities center helps assure the long-term sustainability of digital scholarship by ensuring that standards and technical approaches used by projects are open and sustainable. For Mark Sample (2010), a digital human-ities center can be "the chance to work with programmers who speak the language of humanities as well as PERL, Python, or PHP," to share notes with "colleagues who routinely navigate grant applications and budget deadlines, who are paid to know about the latest digital tools and trends - but who'd know about them and share their knowledge even if they weren't paid a dime." In Sample's view, a center is valuable as "an institutional advocate on campus who can speak within a single voice to adminis-trators, to students, to donors, to publishers, to communities about the value of the digital humanities." Digital humanities centers often act as "interdisciplinary 'third places' – a term sociologist Ray Oldenburg has used to identify a social space, district from home and workplace" (Zorich, 2008:vi). Within this "third place," projects and ideas can cross-pollinate, so that the musicologist can see how the approach of (say) classicists to the digital markup and presentation of material is relevant to her. One of the most valuable roles of a digital humanities center is in providing a neutral space for shared discussion, programming, making and sharing of ideas. Patrik Svensson has described how this interest in creating new spaces of scholarship (an interest shared with librarians) has influenced the development of the Swedish HumLab. There is perhaps a tendency to want to assign fixed functions to a digital humanities center, and a feeling that it should perform a readily defined and well understood role, just like a library or archive. However, as Sula (2013) has illustrated in his thoughtful discussion of a conceptual model to define the relationship between digital humanities and libraries, the boundaries between the digital humanities center and other institutional components of the academy are usually fluid, reflecting not only local institutional structures and strengths but also the evolution of technology and scholarly methods.

The digital humanities center has been the major institutional vehicle of the digital humanities, and this will probably continue to be the case. However, it would be mistaken to assume that the self-funded digital humanities center is the indispensable *sine qua non* of digital humanities. The potential value of funding and infrastructural development by national government or regional agencies is illustrated by the European experience. In the UK, the Joint Information Systems Committee (JISC) of the Higher Education Funding Councils has been very active since the 1970s in promoting many digital initiatives in a variety of disciplines and has been the main architect of the cyberinfrastructure of UK higher education, while the Arts and Humanities Research Council has funded a series of initiatives including the Arts and Humanities Data Service and an ICT Methods Network (although funding for these was withdrawn in 2008). In France, the national service for funding and carrying out academic research, the *Centre National de la Recherche Scientifique*, has supported the development of *Le centre pour l'édition électronique ouverte* (Cléo) which has developed a highly integrated platform for open access academic publishing in the arts and humanities. There have been some major European Union initiatives, such as for example NeDiMAH (the Network for Digital Methods in the Arts and Humanities: www.nedimah.eu), which is mapping the use of digital research across Europe and promoting its coordination by creating an integrated ontology and online forum, and the ambitious DARIAH (Digital Research Infrastructure for the Arts and Humanities: www.dariah.eu), which seeks to build an integrated cooperative network of people, information, and tools to facilitate long-term access and use of research data across Europe. DARIAH has recently established a formal legal consortium to allow members from fifteen European countries to collaborate together in developing a shared European research infrastructure. The international federation, centerNet, a constituent organization of the Alliance of Digital Humanities Organizations, is also seeking to build links between digital humanities centers internationally. The way in which these various international networks and initiatives develop will be fundamental to the future development of cyberinfrastructures for digital scholarship in the arts and humanities.

It is easy to create a digital humanities center; on the centerNet web pages, Lynne Siemens provides a guide as to how to set up a digital humanities center which suggests that the main requirements are enthusiasm and support (ideally in the form of some seed corn funding) from the university's management (Siemens, 2012). The difficult trick with a digital humanities center is to keep it going ten or twenty years down the road. Most digital humanities centers are established following some successful research grants, and "soft" research funding is generally the lifeblood of the center. Consequently, digital humanities is a land populated by projects. Anne Burdick and colleagues, in their book *Digital Humanities* (2012), see the project as the basic unit of digital humanities: "Projects are both nouns and verbs. A project is a kind of scholarship that requires design, management, negotiation, and collaboration" (Burdick *et al.*, 2012:124). In the view of these authors, the project is the main means by which digital humanities is shaping post-print scholarship and exploding the conventions associated with a book- and article-bound academy. This is perhaps an exaggerated view: projects are equally important in many other types of academic activity, as the large number of non-digital projects including activities ranging from performances to research networks funded by research councils illustrate. The growth of the project in the arts and humanities is perhaps due more to changes in the funding opportunities available to scholars than to the rise of digital media. This raises an important point: the extent to which digital humanities centers pursue research because of its inherent intellectual interest or simply in order to raise the research income necessary to keep the center in business. As a center grows, securing sufficient new research projects and income to retain all the staff can become increasingly difficult and demanding, and may discourage risk taking. All those who have been involved in developing a digital humanities center will be familiar with the difficult decision as to whether to pursue a project which is not technically or intellectually rewarding but might offer some funding to keep a member of staff in post. For many digital humanities centers, the pressing issues of sustainability are not technical ones but the rather more prosaic ones of securing reliable long-term funding to keep the center's staff in place.

The dependence of centers on soft funding from research grants is both a blessing and a curse. Digital humanities centers are often among the most successful humanities units in grant capture, but their desperation to keep the money flowing can mean that the center and its staff end up on a treadmill, putting in grant applications in which they are not terribly interested just to raise money, thereby losing control of the intellectual agenda of the center. Bethany Nowviskie (2012) in a perceptive lecture reviewing the evolution of provision in the digital humanities at the University of Virginia, perhaps historically the leading institution in the field, has described how the Scholars' Lab stemmed from previous facilities in the library and IT service. As a result, the Scholars' Lab has stable funding provided by the library and IT service, and Nowviskie considers this a major factor in explaining its success. Likewise, the Maryland Institute for Technology in the Humanities, another of the most successful US centers, is jointly supported by Maryland University's College of Arts and Humanities and the University of Maryland Libraries. It is possible that, in our anxiety to affirm the intellectual credentials of digital humanities and demonstrate its parity with longstanding humanities disciplines, we too quickly distance ourselves from libraries and IT services. In funding terms, if nothing else, there is a great deal to say for digital humanities centers having a closer relationship with libraries and IT services.

Another means of creating a mixed economy and reducing financial risk is to develop teaching income. Teaching has been an important component of digital humanities centers since their inception. For example, the early workshops organized by Harold Short and Willard McCarty at King's College London were fundamental to developing institutional support for the development of digital humanities there. More recently, the organization of summer workshops and institutes has been a major means of spreading the gospel of digital humanities. The Digital Humanities Summer Institute, a week-long program held at the University of Victoria in Canada, attracts annually over 600 participants. Many centers offer full Masters' programs and a number are now offering undergraduate programs. But while teaching can provide a means of ensuring the financial sustainability of the center, it creates its own difficulties and dilemmas. In designing a digital humanities teaching program, it can be difficult to ensure the right balance of practical skills and reflective analysis. A program that simply engages in a highly theorized form of "digital studies" will not give sufficient weight to the aspiration of digital humanities to transform scholarly practice and communication. On the other hand, teaching that focuses on, say, programming and technical skills runs the risk of overlooking the potential of the humanities to provide new critical insights into our digital praxis. Above all, there is the problem of who undertakes this teaching. For most university courses, a doctoral qualification is an essential qualification for teaching. However, the staff in digital humanities centers with the deepest technical understanding and awareness of digital humanities practice often may not have doctorates. How far and in what way do they get involved in the teaching program? Is a doctorate an essential qualification to being a fully paid-up member of the digital humanities community?

These tensions around staffing and career structures are at the heart of the dynamics shaping the institutional infrastructure of the digital humanities. For Jerome McGann (2014:130–1), the very existence of the various digital humanities centers, labs, and institutes represents (paradoxically) a rejection by humanities academics of digital scholarship, a wish to keep at arm's length the different types of people and skills required for digital work. He points out how:

> The emergence of digital technology has brought a new and crucial populace into the university. So far as the university's political and social structure is concerned, they are employees hired to serve the faculties. I leave aside the fact that these people are often scholars of distinction in their own right. (McGann, 2014:130)

Although the skills of these staff are essential for digital humanities scholarship, the structure of the institution separates them from regular faculty. McGann points out that, to make matters even more difficult, these staff "are an expensive population to support, commanding high salaries, often higher than the faculty persons they might be working with" (2014:130). These tensions are also explored by John Bradley (2012) in his description of the development of the Department of Digital Humanities at King's College London. Bradley rejects the idea that the vision and shape of a project should be determined by the leadership of academics from conventional humanities departments. Instead, he envisages digital humanities research as being taken forward by shared discussions involving a range of academic and technical specialists, with the modeling work undertaken in the development of digital humanities projects representing a major research activity. Bradley sees the digital humanities researcher as equivalent in status (if not in background) to the conventional humanities academic, and takes issue with Jennifer Edmond (2005), who has argued for the creation of a profession of "digital humanities intermediaries" acting as brokers between humanities researchers and technical staff. For Bradley, the process of expressing humanities scholarship in digital form is in itself an act of research just as important and equal in intellectual weight to more conventional humanities scholarship. Bradley expresses concern that in many institutions technical work is regarded as "a kind of support work – perhaps, in extreme cases, as similar to what is done to the academic's car by his garage mechanics" (Bradley, 2012:11), and deprecates the use of the term "techie" by humanities scholars "who don't know and understand the work we do." Abhorring such distinctions, Bradley declares that "innovation in the digital humanities often arises out of the pooled talents of a range of experts, and in the best environment where this happens there is recognition and support for the interlinked actions of many players" (Bradley, 2012:11).

Bradley describes a kind of institutional paradise for digital humanities; the question is the extent to which it has ever been achieved and the scale on which it is likely to be achieved. It is striking, for example, that notwithstanding the philosophy described by

Bradley, very few of the more technically oriented staff from the Department of Digital Humanities were submitted by King's College London to the British research assessment exercise in 2014, suggesting institutional pressures in another direction. In general, the ability of digital humanities centers to provide adequate career development opportunities for their staff has been patchy. Digital humanities centers are frequently created by groups of enthusiastic and charismatic academics who have realized the potential of digital technologies to transform their subject area. They use research income to recruit some students with a talent for coding, perhaps persuade some people with a professional computing background to join them or offer someone from the library or IT services a more interesting job. Everything goes well. More research income is secured, and the team grows and jells. The students had meant to go on and do a PhD, but the work in the center is more interesting and they are after all working in a university. But the more successful the research team is, the more difficult it is to secure the money to keep the team together. Some grant applications fail, and some longstanding members of the Center lose their jobs. Then the indispensable geographic information systems (GIS) specialist, conscious that his skills are in demand in industry, asks for a promotion. The university administration say that there isn't a promotion mechanism for someone on his type of contract. One of the most talented of the staff who came in as student notices a lectureship in digital humanities elsewhere. With 10 years' experience on a dozen digital humanities projects, this staff member is superbly qualified for an academic position in digital humanities, but the lectureship requires a PhD, which she never completed because she was so devoted to the work of the center. It gradually dawns on most of the staff of the center that they have become trapped there, doomed constantly to try and secure income from a dwindling stream of research income. Their commitment to the work means that they will probably stay, but their hopes that they were contributing to a new form of academic enterprise and that they might have an exciting new type of career have been betrayed.

This is the situation in far too many digital humanities centers: very talented, scholarly and knowledgeable staff with vast experience of the creation of digital humanities projects who have devoted themselves to securing the projects to keep the center afloat and have never had the opportunity to build the academic career in digital humanities they would like. To some extent, this is an unavoidable result of the way in which academic career structures have developed in recent years. One of the most unattractive features of American university life is the apartheid between "faculty" (with those holding tenure regarded as the highest point of human evolution) and other "staff." While the intellectual protections provided by tenure are undoubtedly necessary, this does not justify the effective denigration of other intellectual workers such as librarians, archivists, and IT specialists. As Bradley (2012:12) emphasizes, this leads to the unstated assumption in digital humanities that "faculty" provide the vision, while the technical staff implement it. One of the most unfortunate developments in UK higher education in recent years has been the importation of this distinction between "academic staff" and "professional services," with librarians and other cognate groups losing their longstanding "academic-related" status. In other European countries, similar academic hierarchies frequently mean that digital humanities skills are seen as secondary, and academic leadership and vision is regarded as the most important requirement. It is perhaps in challenging these antiquated power structures that the digital humanities has one of its best opportunities to transform the academy, but one must be careful not to run away with utopian enthusiasm. The adjunct crisis in the United States shows how attacks on the privileged position of academic staff can easily prove counterproductive. Yet somehow we need to find a means of moving towards a reshaping of academic structures so that it can accommodate both the writer/researcher and the programmer as intellectual equals and achieve that vision of a shared enterprise described by John Bradley.

For Jerome McGann (2014:1), the digital humanities center represents in many ways a failure of the academy adequately to engage with the way in which the whole of our cultural inheritance is being recurated and re-edited in digital forms and institutional structures. McGann points out how, in large projects like *Eighteenth Century Collections Online* and *Google Books*, the lead has been taken by large commercial publishers and libraries and there has been little involvement hitherto by scholars of the period, notwithstanding the efforts of projects such as 18thConnect to retrospectively fix the resulting problems. McGann suggests that part of the reason for this lack of scholarly involvement is the liminal position of the digital humanities center and its staff within universities. Similarly, in another powerfully argued piece, Peter Robinson (2014) notes that the growth of the digital humanities since 1995 has been largely due to the support from research funders and the resulting growth of digital humanities centers, which have produced "scores of [projects], worldwide, offering (again and again) access to outstanding scholarship and to resources otherwise inaccessible" (Robinson, 2014:245). This project work has also fed into the growth of shared tools such as TEI. However, Robinson sees this phase as having now reached the limits of its expansion and suggests that a backlash against this model is now evident. Robinson notes that even the 200 institutions belonging to centerNet represent a tiny proportion of 200,000 universities worldwide, and it is unlikely that we will ever see a situation where there is sufficient funding to allow most of these universities to have a digital humanities center. The digital humanities center was an appropriate response to a situation where there were few people with the skills, equipment, and resources to undertake digital scholarship. We are now in a different situation:

> Now we have millions of digital objects to address, as the whole body of world knowledge and culture is translated into digital form. Now we have in the Internet a medium that unites communication, collaboration, and publication into an instantaneous and fluid whole. In a moment, we can see what someone else has created, we can add to it, publish it – and in turn, another person can see, add, publish. And "anyone" is anyone with a computer, anyone with a mobile phone – more than a billion people. We are no longer pioneers for a few. The whole world is turning digital, and we are part of it. (Robinson, 2014:247)

For Robinson, the digital humanities center has fulfilled its role, and we now need to think about the type of connectivity necessary to create large-scale cyberinfrastructures. These criticisms reflect the criticisms of Diane Zorich, who notes that digital humanities centers are prone to becoming standalone silos engaging in "boutique digitization" which limit scale and connectivity:

> First, the silo-like operation of current centers favors individual projects that are not linked to larger digital resources that would make them more widely known within the

research community. When one examines the projects of the 32 surveyed centers en masse, one finds hundreds of projects of potential interest to larger communities that are little known outside the environs of the center and its partners. Moreover, in the absence of preservation plans, many of these projects risk being orphaned over time, as staff, funding, and programming priorities change. In the absence of repositories that enable greater exposure and long-term access, the current landscape of many silo-like centers results in unfettered and untethered digital production that will be detrimental to humanities scholarship.

The silo-like nature of centers also results in overlapping agendas and activities, particularly in areas of training, digitization of collections and metadata development. With centers competing for the same limited funding pool, they can ill afford to continue with redundant efforts. (Zorich, 2008:49)

Maron and Pickle (2014), building on some of these concerns, paint a picture of digital humanities work often having an uncertain place in the overall management of data and computational activity within universities. They suggest that, in order to enhance the impact and longevity of digital humanities work, it is necessary to have more integrated institutional support and methodologies.

The common thread in all these recent criticisms of the digital humanities center is the need to scale up the work of the centers and to create greater connectivity. Exactly how this can be achieved is often left unclear. The most concrete suggestions are made by Peter Robinson (2014), who argues for the development of new forms of online collaboration by scholars working with the millions of digital objects now available so that "What Google Maps and TripAdviser do for hotels and restaurants, what Orbitz and SkyScanner and Expedia do for airline schedules, we could do for books, manuscripts, texts, knowledge" (Robinson, 2014:253). Robinson sees collaboration around tools, rights, and access as essential to achieving this, and argues for a shift from content creation towards collaborative work on existing data. This is a beguiling vision. While humanities is frequently depicted as the domain of the "lone scholar," it has nevertheless always been a highly collaborative endeavor. We may gather our data separately, but we then often share and discuss it. What we need to do is to transfer this behavior into an online environment, so that we collaborate and link together our explorations of libraries and archives. However, such collaborative environments will still require some kind of technical support and focus, and the digital humanities center will continue to have a role here. If digital humanities is to have an impact on our future digital state in a world of "big digitization" by large commercial interests, increased cooperation and links will be essential. The work of centerNet will be vital in fostering such collaboration. As Robinson notes, the role of the European DARIAH project, with its explicit focus on the sharing of data and the creation of infrastructures to facilitate this, also points a way forward. The creation of large-scale research infrastructures of the type envisaged by DARIAH can be seen as representing a digital parallel to the emergence of library consortia in the twentieth century, and may prove to be equally influential in the way in which future scholars access information and disseminate their scholarship.

This still leaves uncertain the question as to how digital humanities relates to the mainstream academy. McGann sees the digital humanities labs and centers as a means of distancing academic engagement in the development of digital infrastructures.

Does this mean that we should as a community be pressing harder for the development of digital humanities centers into full-blown academic departments? There is of course a risk that by corralling digital humanities into a separate department, we provide an even more effective silo which discourages the adoption of digital methods in other disciplines. However, it is more likely that digital techniques will become so commonplace in other disciplines that the function of digital humanities as a separate activity will be questioned. Peter Webster of the British Library, for example, has remarked that "The end game for a Faculty of DH should be that the use of the tools becomes so integrated within Classics, French, and Theology that it can be disbanded, having done its job" (Webster, 2013). This is perhaps an oversimplistic view of both the nature of digital methods and the structure of humanities research. As Robinson (2014:255) observes, there will always be a need for trailblazing new developments on the intersection of humanities and information technology, and it is undoubtedly in this kind of pioneering scientific work that an important part of the future mission of digital humanities lies. But what is the most appropriate nature of the space in which such work can be taken forward? As we have seen, the center, for all its strengths, has significant drawbacks, and may have outlived its usefulness. The academic department seems too constrained by past traditions easily to cope with the mixture of skills and perspectives which the digital humanities will require. We may perhaps need to think about the development of specialist labs and units, with a more focused scientific agenda than the present digital humanities centers, perhaps analogous to the units in which systems biology is studied or the "dry labs" of bioscientists.

Digital humanities centers have played an important part in transforming the landscape of humanities scholarship, but as we seek to build and extend our digital infrastructure to cope with the new digital world, the mission will be a twofold one: first, to build greater connectivity and collaboration between and across existing centers, resources, and practitioners; and, second, to ensure that we do not lose our pioneering spirit and continue to seek out and explore technologies that will shed fresh light on our cultural heritage and inheritance. In pursuing that mission, building and creating networks is the most important activity of all. We must build alliances with coders, librarians, curators, photographers, archivists, artists, project managers, and all the range of new professions and skills. This must inherently involve restating where the academic sits into that network – wherever it is, it is not automatically at the top of the tree. Those engaged in digital humanities work in universities also need to forge alliances with those bodies outside the academy that shape our digital and cultural landscape: libraries, archives, galleries, opera houses, theatres, orchestras, dance companies, broadcasters, as well as digital artists, and startups of all kinds. The digital humanist should be an explorer in this new cultural landscape, and in doing so should be constantly seeking to create new cross-connections and new links.

As Mark Sample has eloquently stated:

> don't sit around waiting for a digital humanities center to pop up on your campus or make you a primary investigator on a grant. Act as if there's no such thing as a digital humanities center. Instead, create your own network of possible collaborators. Don't hope for or rely upon institutional support or recognition. To survive and thrive, digital

humanists must be agile, mobile, insurgent. Decentralized and nonhierarchical. Stop forming committees and begin creating coalitions. Seek affinities over affiliations, networks over institutes. (Sample, 2010)

The existing infrastructure has provided a very effective means of building digital humanities in its first phase, but we must be wary of putting all our energy into preserving that infrastructure. The institutional landscape of the digital humanities must evolve and change as the digital world changes, and the watchwords will always be flexibility and nimbleness. The digital humanities has always been pragmatic and effective at building alliances and connections, and it needs to draw on these strengths in developing its next phase.

REFERENCES AND FURTHER READING

Borgman, C. 2009. The digital future is now: a call to action for the humanities. *DHQ: Digital Humanities Quarterly* 3 (4).

Bradley, J. 2012. No job for techies: technical contributions to research in the digital humanities. In *Collaborative Research in the Digital Humanities*, ed. M. Deegan and W. McCarty. Farnham: Ashgate, 11–26.

Burdick, A., Drucker J., Lunenfeld, P., Presner, T., and Schnapp, J. 2012. *Digital Humanities*. Cambridge, MA: MIT Press.

Digital Humanities Manifesto 2.0. 2009. http://www.humanitiesblast.com/manifesto/Manifesto_V2.pdf (accessed August 1, 2014).

Edmond, J. 2005. The role of the professional intermediary in expanding the humanities computing base. *Literary and Linguistic Computing* 20 (3), 367–80.

Fleming, N., and Highfield, R. 2007. Diamond Synchotron to use x-rays to examine Dead Sea Scrolls. *Daily Telegraph*, 12 September. http://www.telegraph.co.uk/science/science-news/3306654/Diamond-synchrotron-to-use-x-rays-to-examine-Dead-Sea-Scrolls.html (accessed August 1, 2014).

Fraistat, N. 2012. The function of digital humanities centers at the present time. In *Debates in the Digital Humanities*, ed. M.K. Gold. Minneapolis: University of Minnesota Press, 281–91.

Kiernan, K.S. 1994. Digital preservation, restoration, and dissemination of medieval manuscripts. In *Scholarly Publishing on the Electronic Networks, Proceedings of the Third Symposium*, ed. A. Okerson. Washington DC: ARL Publications. http://www.uky.edu/~kiernan/eBeo_archives/#A (accessed August 1, 2014).

Kirschenbaum, M.G. 2010. What is digital humanities and what's it doing in English departments? *ADE Bulletin* 150, 55–61. http://www.ade.org/bulletin (accessed August 1, 2014).

Maron, N.L. and Pickle, S. 2014. *Sustaining the Digital Humanities: Host Institution Support Beyond the Start-up Phase*. Ithaka S+R. http://www.sr.ithaka.org/research-publications/sustaining-digital-humanities (accessed August 1, 2014).

McCarty, W. 2008. What's going on? *Literary and Linguistic Computing* 23 (3), 253–61.

McCarty, W., and Kirschenbaum, M. 2003. Institutional models for humanities computing. *Literary and Linguistic Computing* 18 (4), 465–89.

McGann, J. 2014. *A New Republic of Letters: Memory and Scholarship in the Age of Digital Reproduction*. Cambridge, MA: Harvard University Press.

Morton, R.W., Gislason J.J., Hall, G.S., Bergman, U., and Noel, W. 2004. Preliminary investigations for x-ray imaging the Archimedes palimpsest using elemental x-ray area maps and stereoview elemental x-ray imaging. http://www.archimedespalimpsest.org/pdf/archimedes_g.pdf (accessed 1 August 2014)

Nevens, T.M. 2000. Innovation in business models. In *The Silicon Valley Edge: A Habitat for Innovation and Entrepreneurship*, ed. C.-M. Lee, W.F. Miller, M.G.Hancock, and H.S. Rowen. Stanford, CA: Stanford University Press.

Nowviskie, B. 2012. Too small to fail: keynote lecture to the Japanese Association for Digital Humanities. http://nowviskie.org/2012/too-small-to-fail (accessed August 1, 2014).

Robinson, P. 2014. Digital humanities: is bigger better? In *Advancing Digital Humanities: Research,*

Methods, Theories, ed. P.L. Arthur and K. Bode. Basingstoke: Palgrave Macmillan, 243–7.

Sample, M. 2010. On the death of the digital humanities center. http://www.samplereality. com/2010/03/26/on-the-death-of-the-digital-humanities-center (accessed August 1, 2014).

Siemens, L. 2012. *Formation of a DH Lab*. THATCamp Caribe, November 2012. http:// lynnesiemens.files.wordpress.com/2012/06/dh-centres-final.mov (accessed August 1, 2014).

Sula, C.A. 2013. Digital humanities and libraries: a conceptual model. *Journal of Library Administration* 53 (1), 10–26.

Svensson, P. 2009. Humanities computing as digital humanities. *DHQ: Digital Humanities Quarterly* 3 (3). http://www.digitalhumanities. org/dhq/vol/3/3/000065/000065.html (accessed June 20, 2015).

Svensson, P. 2010. The landscape of the digital humanities. *DHQ: Digital Humanities Quarterly* 4 (1).

Svensson, P. 2011. From optical fiber to conceptual infrastructure. *DHQ: Digital Humanities Quarterly* 5 (1).

Svensson, P. 2012. The digital humanities as a humanities project. *Arts and Humanities in Higher Education* 11 (1–2), 42–60.

Webster, P. 2013. Where should the digital humanities live? http://peterwebster. me/2013/05/10/where-should-the-digital-humanities-live (accessed August 1, 2014).

Zorich, D. 2008. *A Survey of Digital Humanities Centers in the United States*. Washington, DC: Council on Library and Information Resources. http://www.clir.org/pubs/reports/pub143/con tents.html (accessed August 1, 2014).

33
Sorting Out the Digital Humanities

Patrik Svensson

It is appropriate to start a chapter on sorting the digital humanities out with questioning whether we really need to sort it out at all. This is a warranted question, given all the time and effort that has gone into defining, consolidating, expanding, questioning, and institutionalizing the field (Gold, 2012; Terras *et al.*, 2013). In a workshop held at Umeå University in December 2013 about the future of the field, one of the participant groups suggested that the questions we will ask in five to seven years will be the same, but we will have different tools with which to answer them. There is a suggestion of circularity here, and looking at the history of humanities computing and the digital humanities, it is quite clear that many of the arguments resurface over time. It is almost comforting to read Martin Wynne's *Humanist* list comment (2013) on the reorganization of digital humanities at Oxford, and relate it to Lou Burnard's text (2002) on the reorganization of the same unit about 10 years earlier. They both relate to institutional placement and the perils and advantages of having a servile function within the university system. There are a number of issues like this one that can be traced over time, including reward systems, alternative careers, the value of the scholarship produced, and disciplinary boundary making. It may well be that some of these often inward-looking issues will never be sorted out, and that there are other issues that do not surface in the discussion about the field. In this chapter, I suggest that we need to revitalize the discussion.

Geoffrey Bowker and Susan Leigh Star (1999) demonstrate how classificatory systems have meaning in a very material sense and how categories can be invisible and be made visible. The digital humanities clearly does not consist of numerous discrete blocks that can be sorted out, and there is no way of solving the puzzle of digital humanities in any definite fashion. However, the notion of sorting out helps to frame the question

A New Companion to Digital Humanities, First Edition. Edited by Susan Schreibman, Ray Siemens, and John Unsworth.
© 2016 John Wiley & Sons, Ltd. Published 2016 by John Wiley & Sons, Ltd.

of the future of the field in a way that indicates that a solution is possible. The main argument of this chapter is that this solution does exist, not a one-size-fits-all or a complete solution, but a way of thinking about the digital humanities that brings together the humanistic and the digital through embracing a non-territorial and liminal zone. Furthermore, the idea of sorting out the field draws our attention to its structures and classifications and forces us to think about the building blocks, categories, and issues that comprise the field.

This sorting out is intimately related to different epistemic traditions, disciplinary perspectives, and epistemologically situated technologies associated with the digital humanities as an intersectional field. There is a great deal of negotiating going on in such zones, and I argue that there has to be a willingness to understand other traditions without necessarily giving up disciplinary integrity (cf. Ratto, 2012). Furthermore, epistemic technologies can play a central role in challenging knowledge traditions and developing new knowledge, which requires us to be reflective of our own practices and assumptions and be willing to engage with other epistemic positions.

This chapter starts with a discussion of the status of the digital humanities and the common assumption that it is a field in disarray. I maintain that making the digital humanities into an institutionalized discipline can be counterproductive, in giving away some of the distinct advantages of a liminal position. This discussion is followed by a provisional analysis of the current situation that indicates that there is an opportunity for moving ahead productively, but that there are a number of issues and stances that need to be addressed. I argue that the territorial ambitions of some of the digital humanities organizations can be problematic at a time when the field is being negotiated and expanded. The second part of the chapter responds to a call for action by Melissa Terras from the perspective of the work going on in the Alliance of Digital Humanities Organizations (ADHO) and suggests possible actions and strategies required to move forward. These are embedded in a model of digital humanities that I will present. I posit that the institutional instability that has often been identified as a problem in the history of the digital humanities can be a key factor for developing the field. The chapter ends with a proposal for a code of conduct for the field and a list of actionable suggestions for the digital humanities.

The Ever-emerging Field of Digital Humanities

It is often assumed that the digital humanities is in flux and not particularly stable as an institutional construct. While this might be true to some degree, there are obviously constants to the field. For instance, there is almost always a relationship to traditional humanities disciplines such as English and history, some sort of technological infrastructure, and a degree of perceived incompatibility with the system of higher education (whether it be reward systems, the view of the humanities, or allowances for alternative careers).

Furthermore, this instability has probably been influenced by there being an open, visible, and lively discussion about the field. While this is not a situation unique to the digital humanities, it seems more likely with interdisciplinary fields and fields undergoing change, such as art history in the 1980s and 1990s (Klein, 2005:113) and

American studies in the late 1990s (Klein, 2005:168). However, the extent to which the debate has taken place online is likely to be unique to the digital humanities. Many of the best-known people in the field debate on Twitter together with others, including graduate students and officers at funding agencies such as the National Endowment for the Humanities. Online forums are often active, and when the Postcolonial Digital Humanities initiative hosted an open thread on "The digital humanities as a historical 'refuge' from race/class/gender/sexuality/disability?" (Koh and Risam, 2013), there were 165 comments, most of them quite substantial, over five days. As the history of the field shows, there has been a longstanding solid online engagement, with the *Humanist* list being one of the first academic email lists when it was started in 1987 by list curator Willard McCarty. This relative openness and outspokenness has undoubtedly contributed to the sense of the field as fractured and unstable, as polemic discussions have taken place live in public. Furthermore, the public and repeated preoccupation with the organization, history, and future of the field across media can come across as inward-looking and self-referential. The argument here is not necessarily that this is not true, but that we have to be sensitive to the ways in which the field is constructed, projected, and enacted across media and communication channels.

The stability of a given knowledge domain is among other things linked to how it is categorized in the academic system, its disciplinary heterogeneity, and the discourse about the area. The descriptor "discipline" is normally taken to denote a more static and less interdisciplinary area than "field" or "studies." What gives disciplines a certain degree of stability is that they are associated with an epistemic tradition, objects of inquiry, assumptions, theories, methods, ways of sharing research, and career paths (Repko, 2008:4–5). There is a certain sense of unity associated with disciplines, although that does not mean that disciplines are static and unchanging (Klein, 2005:50). Disciplines and fields change over time, and while it might not be productive to suggest a developmental or evolutionary trajectory, there are patterns to disciplinary changes (Becher and Trowler, 2001:43). A common movement has been towards specialization, although this does not always lead to the formation of new disciplines (Weingart, 2010:11). There are also multiple possible trajectories of different kinds of interdisciplinary formations (Klein, 2010:22). Undergoing a formational stage or remaining in an interdisciplinary state is not unique to the digital humanities, but the field has certainly been trapped for a long time in an uncertain state without becoming a discipline or getting reasonably established as an interdiscipline or an academic area (such as American studies). I suggest that there are at least three reasons for this elongated status.

Firstly, there has been an incompatibility between the digital humanities and the institutional expectations of academia. When looking at the history of the field (as humanities computing), it is clear that in many cases the digital humanities could not secure an institutional position that easily accommodated a line of work that was different to most other areas in the humanities. Such work included operating between traditional university structures such as departments and disciplines, engaging with technological infrastructure, and needing to engage a variety of professional competencies for carrying out the work. That humanities computing partly was institutionalized as service centers (with varying degrees of autonomy) and institutes (maybe more akin to humanities centers than anything else) has probably added to the incompatibility. It should also be pointed out, however, that we are concerned with different types of incompatibilities, and that over the years a discourse of dissatisfaction has developed within the digital humanities about the humanities as a whole and the academy.

Secondly, having an institutional position outside the traditional structures of academia can be central for carrying out certain kinds of work. Traditionally, many digital humanities centers and platforms have operated fairly broadly across the humanities. It is easier to engage with other humanities disciplines without being seen as a competing discipline or as affiliated with a specific discipline such as English. There are thus benefits to this liminal position. Furthermore, the digital humanities has more recently become a platform for engaging with the future of the humanities more broadly. This is an activity that speaks to all of the humanities, not least junior scholars, and which can be easier to organize from a position outside of traditional departments or disciplines. If there is interest in renewing the humanities at large, it simply makes more sense working with the traditional disciplines from an in-between position, rather than from a distinct disciplinary position.

Thirdly, the digital humanities currently brings together a range of epistemic traditions, disciplines, and perspectives. The lively dialog in and about the field is partly a consequence of this multivocal situation, and the variety of positions makes institutionalizing efforts difficult. Bringing together different traditions requires a great deal of negotiation, and the formation of a new discipline normally leads to a decentering of particular disciplinary identities and eventually to the establishment of a distinct epistemic regime. There can actually be a considerable strength in an unresolved situation, as it is easier for different knowledge communities to gather around boundary objects such as the digital without having to become institutionalized as a discipline. Arguably, this will also produce stronger scholarship than if the digital humanities attempts to operate from a more closed-off position.

It is not surprising that there would be an interest in turning the digital humanities into a discipline, given the history of the field and the institutional template of academia. This is one way of sorting out the field, but not the only one, and while there is no single solution, I argue that the very reasons why the digital humanities may be seen as unstable are actually good reasons for not moving in the direction of becoming an institutionalized discipline.

A Provisional Analysis of the Current State of Affairs

A major development over the last couple of years has been a substantial expansion of the field, larger institutional support, many more actors, and a range of new expectations. This has led to a substantial pressure on the field as traditionally conceived, which is unsurprising given the history of the field as a fairly narrow (but important) enterprise and given the current visibility and attraction. This pressure comes from humanistic traditions with a digital engagement that have not been seen as a major part of digital humanities (such as new media studies and rhetoric and composition), from incoming scholars in fields such as gender studies and media studies, and from humanistic and institutional leadership. There are also alternative digital humanities platforms with different notions of what the field can be, such as the Postcolonial Digital Humanities movement and the Humanities, Arts, Science, and Technology Alliance and Collaboratory (HASTAC).

The part of the digital humanities community that identifies with a 40- or 50-year-long tradition sometimes makes the point that their past struggles, often related to being institutionally marginalized, are not acknowledged and that there is a risk of giving away what the field has achieved at a point when there is finally leverage and support for the digital humanities. In a provocative *Humanist* post, Craig Bellamy (2013) opines that:

> Sure I am being a gadfly, but if anyone can use the term "digital humanities" for what ever purpose (and others will believe them), then the past 40 odd years of work in this field will be wasted.

While this is almost certainly not a representative standpoint of the community, it is important to acknowledge that a tension does exist here, and that this tension is not only about institutional prestige or resources, but also about epistemology and different epistemic traditions.

It would be wrong to assume, however, that this expanded variety of digital humanities is mainly a result of interested parties coming to the field at a time when it has considerable traction. Rather, the digital humanities organizations, mainly coming out of humanities computing, were part of taking on this new role for the digital humanities. In particular, a group of key members of the humanities computing community worked towards forming the Alliance of Digital Humanities Organizations in the early 2000s, publishing the Blackwell *Companion to Digital Humanities* (Schreibman *et al.*, 2004), renaming the annual conference series (from the joint annual conference of the Association for Computers and the Humanities and the Association for Literary and Linguistic Computing to Digital Humanities Conference) and were also influential when the National Endowment for the Humanities created its Initiative for Digital Humanities in 2006. There was apparently a realization that humanities computing would not be the flavor of the 2000s and that another scope and packaging were needed. An intriguing question is to what extent humanities computing leadership realized that they were also staking out a pathway that would eventually decenter their own community. There was resistance inside and outside the leadership group and, at times, fairly heated discussions (Svensson, 2016). In any case, at least parts of the larger community did not embrace this reorientation, or more likely it was simply not clear that a shift in names would be more than exactly that. It would also seem that much of the institutional groundwork did not actually change, and that the grounding in the epistemic tradition of humanities computing prevailed.

The pressure described at the beginning of this section has stimulated, and even forced, some more considerable change. This is partly a result of the digital humanities now being a more diverse set of communities, but also because of discursive changes and actual reorientations. The uptake of the idea of big-tent digital humanities is an example of this shift, but arguably with minor impact. As I have argued elsewhere, the tent is still largely made of the same kind of epistemic fabric and is seen as exclusionary and territorial (Svensson, 2012). Indeed, some of the moves by the digital humanities organizations can be seen as aggressive at a time when it is more important to focus on discussing the core values and directions of the field. While the big tent is not overly aggressive as a discursive construction, the global territorialization of the field is more noteworthy in this regard. Again, this concerns a series of name changes and also new territories being added to the map. Examples include the renaming of the Association for Literary and Linguistic Computing to the European Association for Digital Humanities in 2011, and the recent addition of Australasian and Japanese associations.

I am not arguing that there is anything wrong with this territorial reconfiguration and expansion, but given the tension and pressure already indicated, these moves can be seen as challenging. An illumining example is centerNet, which describes itself as "an international network of digital humanities centers." It assumes that the center is a key building block for the digital humanities. Furthermore, it is clearly embedded within the traditional digital humanities organizations, and thus cannot be said to represent the digital humanities outside these traditions, although it can be seen as attempting to spread this model throughout the world (essentially exporting a specific model of digital humanities). Additionally, centerNet strives to represent the digital humanities in a number of strategic contexts such as the Consortium of Humanities Centers and Institutes and several European-level initiatives. While each of these points is part of the seemingly successful and defendable institutional strategy of centerNet, a central question is whether this strategy is the best given the ongoing negotiation and reorientation of the field. However, it may be that center-Net is currently moving towards a less territorial stance. The composition of the newly appointed editorial board for *DHCommons*, a centerNet publication, is diverse and fairly inclusive.

The digital humanities is obviously much more than the tradition of humanities computing and the associations that descend from this tradition, but this particular tradition is institutionally significant. It is understandable that it did not automatically embrace large-scale changes that might not be compatible with what was seen as the core orientation of the field. One point of tension deals with the discourse associated with some of the other actors, including organizations such as HASTAC, which partly focus on the reformation of the university and the digital humanities as a transformative agent. Such discourses sometimes do not touch ground and can be a way of using the field as a tool in an institutional fight to leverage the humanities. These are important goals and sentiments, but there can be a real gap between on-the-ground computational work and far-away institutional visions. Similarly, initiatives such as Postcolonial Digital Humanities take for granted a critical (and important) vocabulary of power, postcolonialism, genealogy, discourse, gender, and globalization. This vocabulary may not feel familiar to a community not normally engaged with this kind of discourse. This is not just a matter of the actual issues at stake, but the penetrability or impenetrability of discourse and practices surrounding different epistemic traditions. Interestingly, the working definition of digital humanities employed by the Postcolonial Digital Humanities website is "a set of methodologies engaged by humanists to use, produce, teach, and analyze culture and technology" (Risam and Koh, undated). This definition could be said to be imposing a methodology reading on the digital humanities as a field that is more akin to the humanities computing of the past than present-day digital humanities, and hence locking digital humanities in a form that is arguably by definition less susceptible to their reformational agenda.

I argue that all the perspectives discussed up to this point are important to the digital humanities, and that the coming together of these and other epistemic traditions is critical to the further development of the field. This does not mean that the integrity of such traditions should necessarily be challenged, but rather that everyone will have to adapt to some degree and there have to be sites and affordances for this exchange to actually take place. Such processes will be looked at in more detail in a later section, but for now it is worth pointing out that such adaptive work requires a common purpose, willingness to engage, and some degree of humbleness.

Accepting the Challenge

Critiquing, historicizing, and contextualizing the digital humanities is important, and there is a growing literature contributing to this understanding. There is a risk, however, that this work does not actually impact the field in that it does not necessarily go from critique to any suggestions on how to move forward in any comprehensive and sophisticated way. There is also a risk of getting caught up in binaries and specific epistemic positions, not least when debates are quick and heated.

This is not to suggest that the community (to the extent that there is a single community) is incapable of handling the situation, or that there is an easy solution (to the extent that there is anything to solve), but that the digital humanities composes a complex and intriguing construct with considerable potential and leverage. Needless to say, the digital humanities is not the only complex institutional formation. Another example is the development of American studies from the 1920s onwards, which has been characterized by a series of debates and institutional strategies (Klein, 2005: Chapter 7). Lucy Maddox argues that because of the uncertain status of American studies over time, there has been a critical examination not least from within about "its methods of inquiry, its aims, its intellectual coherence, its relationship to other disciplines and fields of study" (1999:viii). This description resonates with the situation of digital humanities. There are certain factors, however, that contribute to the potential for the field not to get as fully mobilized as other fields, including institutional incompatibility, a large epistemic range, epistemic technologies, the epistemologically aggressive stance of some individuals and some institutional actors, and substantial internal and external pressure.

Melissa Terras poses an interesting challenge in a text on critiques of the digital humanities and how to be constructive about solutions (from the point of view of her work in ADHO):

> Most people "within" Digital Humanities ... are people who want Digital Humanities to be as open and as great as possible. This whole field has been built on the hard work of many academics who have given up their free time to try and entrench the use of computing in humanistic study into an academic field of enquiry, and it wouldn't exist without them, even if the form it exists in is currently imperfect. I would say, from where

I sit on various committees, that people want to keep DH growing, and growing healthily. So if there are things wrong with DH, then do give concrete examples, or propose concrete solutions, so they can be taken forward. They're listening – we're listening. (Terras, 2013)

While this is a laudable attitude, the argument is also embedded in the institutional frame of digital humanities and its history. It is not as simple as everyone wanting the field to be "as open and as great as possible," since "open" and "great" are keyed to one's epistemological position. This is why the big tent of digital humanities is not as open as it may seem at first glance. Regardless, Terras's challenge is a worthy one, and the rest of this chapter will be an attempt to respond to this challenge. One point of departure is that the best and most effective way to develop and renew the field is to work with the ADHO. While it would have been possible to propose a wholly new organization or framework, the ADHO seems like the best possible platform (at least at this point). Also, it would make little sense and show little respect to respond to Terras's challenge through choosing not to engage with the ADHO.

The response will be on different levels of concretion. An initial discussion of epistemology will lead to a contoured model of the digital humanities. This model will then be used to discuss specific issues, and whenever possible, solutions will be suggested. Again, as I have argued, there has to be an awareness that there is not one solution, and that some of the problems may not actually be problematic. The solutions suggested, or any attempt at comprehensively renewing the digital humanities, will need be embedded in a set of strategies to actually make such renewal possible. A number of such strategies are proposed in the code of conduct and list of action points that end the chapter.

On the Epistemology of the Digital Humanities

In a study of archaeological research with a strong technological component, Matt Ratto (2012) investigated situations where multiple epistemic traditions come together, and when technology plays a significant role. The research carried out by the archaeologist in the study was refuted by three communities for three different reasons, and Ratto uses the term "epistemic double-binds" to describe this situation. The concept of epistemic double-binds describes the inability to fulfill the simultaneous requirements of several knowledge communities (2012:579). Ratto's case study concerned the technology-rich reconstruction of pre-Roman temples with a particular focus on the terra cotta roofs, where a key concern was to challenge the standard explanation of images on the façades of such temples. They had been seen as propaganda for cultural elites, but this view was challenged through a virtual-reality construction, which seemed to demonstrate that the elite could not actually see the images. The traditional classical and terra cotta archaeologists were hesitant to see the reconstruction as a legitimate statement about the past, while more technologically oriented archaeologists argued that the reconstructions were not realistic enough. A third community, computer programmers and scientists, did not find the reconstruction innovative on a technological level. However, it could be argued that the refutations are also in fact an indication of success in the sense that the investigated project apparently challenged three traditions at the same time. While this is not necessarily a guarantee of the quality of the work, the response demonstrates engagement across epistemic traditions (including the "home" discipline).

Ratto usefully points to the difficulty of bridging between technically inflected and humanities-inflected epistemological conditions. Modeling, visualization, and simulation technologies can be said to be epistemic technologies. Through their epistemological embeddedness, such technologies can point to fractures between and within humanities disciplines, and they can also reinforce and develop positions within scholarly domains (2012:568). Since the digital humanities is a technologically embedded field, epistemic technologies are bound to play a significant role. For instance, markup and encoding technologies impose certain ways of seeing and interpreting the world, resulting in clashes between the computational expertise associated with making such structures and some disciplinary scholars who find incompatibility between their work and standardized encoding schemas. And digital humanists coming from gender or postcolonial studies may oppose the computational paradigm and the encoding structures because they see little recognition of the structures of power and oppression built into encoding schemas. Similarly, computationally driven enterprises such as cultural analytics and maker labs are deeply embedded in terms of their epistemology. A traditional art historian encountering a video wall visualization of a subset of artwork may not accept the argument that the visualization will allow open-ended critical explorations of art. Activities such as maker labs, hackathons, and that-camps embed ideas about technologies and the world that do not often seem to be steeped in the real world. As Mattern (2013) points out:

> not only does the hackathon reify the dataset, but the whole form of such events – which emphasize efficiency and presume that the end result, regardless of the challenge at hand, will be an app or another software product – upholds the algorithmic ethos.

A fair degree of work produced in the digital humanities does not get to the point of double-binds, as there is too little in-depth critique across knowledge communities. There may therefore not be a constructive way of preventing or resolving such binds if they were to occur. There is often critical and epistemic engagement coming from only one position, and often this is not the "home" discipline or area (outside the digital humanities). By and large, the humanities as a whole has had little interest in engaging deeply on a critical level with the work produced within the digital humanities. Overall, the critique tends to be shallow as a result of being caught up in binary oppositions, structural issues, and institutional parameters. Also, it would seem that there are other factors restricting in-depth critique. The communal sensibility and sometimes defensive stance of digital humanities (in particular as humanities computing) can restrict a more nuanced critique from that group, and a lack of engagement with the materiality of the digital in traditional disciplines may preclude a knowledgeable engagement with such work (or elicit a blanket negative response), even if it is based in the discipline. If a project or argument based in a humanities discipline gets a blanket rejection from both the discipline and the digital humanities (as humanities computing), we are concerned with an epistemic double-bind, but one that probably does not show the depth of the critique presented in Ratto's case study. It is also possible that the digital humanities more broadly (not humanities computing) would reject the project or argument as too disciplinary or too technological, and then there would be a three-part refutation. An interesting question is whether resolving the double-bind is always the most productive strategy. Not ending up with epistemic double-binds may be an advantageous goal, but if the critique is too bland and unitary, there might be a lack of interpretative and conceptual depth. Ultimately, however, going through a process of establishing epistemic double-binds and then resolving them would seem most transformative.

Where does this lead us? For one thing, the field always seems to fail to deliver on at least some level, whether it be intellectual robustness and citations in top journals; degree of openness; technological, theoretical, or material engagement; disciplinary recognition; institutional status; public engagement; or possibly quality of the work produced. While there will never be – nor should there be – a full solution, the response could be to dig deeper epistemologically and cherish the differences, rather than to institutionalize the field as a more unitary discipline. In many ways, the digital humanities is already a place for this kind of work, but the lockups described earlier seem to block some of the potential of this position. Becoming a discipline might result in an avoidance of double-binds and epistemic challenges, but such a development appears unrealistic and is not the best way to develop the field. It seems that the different traditions are just too dissimilar and institutionally unlikely to come together in a tight disciplinary formation. I argue that the coming together of different disciplines, traditions, and modes of engagement in a looser configuration can be quite productive. Furthermore, a liminal position is also useful for being able to challenge different actors and to be engaged in a renewal of the humanities.

I advocate an epistemologically open field that has an institutional core with integrity and an ideational foundation, and works with the whole of the humanities and outside actors. It accommodates several overlapping modes of engagement between the humanities and the digital (study object, tool, medium of expression). Many members of the community are affiliated with both the digital humanities and a field, whereas others are based mainly in the digital humanities. Importantly, this institutional core incorporates members coming from the tradition of humanities computing as well as humanities disciplines and other traditions and specialties. While much work is placed between different traditions, there is acceptance for both specialized humanities computing work and monograph writing as well as many other practices, and these ideally engage with each other through a shared platform and identity.

The field is thus simultaneously a place for disciplinary engagement and for intersectional epistemic work. As noted previously, many of the tensions and institutional challenges associated with the digital humanities can be related to this intermediate position. I have argued that instead of abandoning such a position, we need to embrace and develop it. The epistemic tension demonstrated by Ratto's work can indeed be useful or even necessary to carry out some work between the humanities and the digital.

There are some frameworks that can be useful when exploring this intermediate position. Work on trading zones can illuminate how epistemological boundary work is carried out (Galison, 1999). According to Galison's work on physicists from different paradigms, knowledge communities can be coordinated around objects of study, even if they disagree as to their understanding of the objects under study and the exchange process. One important point here is that agreement is not always possible or necessary. However, the transactional metaphor at play here can seem to underplay the dynamic, critical, and emergent qualities of such operations. The concept of temporary autonomous zones is very different in this sense (Bey, 1991), as it stresses zones of free culture at the fault lines of controlled systems (often political). Emergent creativity and work on the boundary lines are key parameters, and the work on temporary autonomous zones can inform the digital humanities about the importance of agility and not being institutionally too stable. However, the digital humanities will always be more institutionalized than such zones. Indeed, it would seem advantageous for the digital humanities to embody both systematic epistemic work around shared objects and some of the dynamic and creative qualities associated with temporary autonomous zones. The work done by language and power structures in intersectional work is further explicated by research carried out on contact zones (Pratt, 1991). There is a sensitivity required to facilitate such zones and, in particular, the framework stresses the importance of being sensitive to cultural, social, and linguistic identity and context. There is also a realization in Pratt's work that there is a need for social and intellectual spaces for sub-communities. She says that such spaces can be used to "construct shared understandings, knowledges, claims on the world that they can then bring into the contact zone" (1991:40). This finds echoes in Ratto's argument that we need to overcome differences without removing them fully (2012:582).

Towards a Code of Conduct for the Digital Humanities

Overcoming differences without removing them takes work and sensitivity. All of the frameworks for intersectional work described in the previous section draw on the notion of a community with shared values and sentiments. This does not imply that all issues are resolved, but that there are guidelines for how to work together. One way of formalizing such guidelines is through having a code of conduct for the digital humanities. Such codes can be powerful in that they ideally capture and define modes of engagement, common sentiment, and rules that are accepted by a community and are necessary for being a member of that community. It is not a matter of single statements so much as a number of statements that together constitute the code of conduct. At times, individual statements can seem to be simple, taken for granted, or just naïve, but the job of a code of conduct is exactly to make transparent what is expected. Sometimes the things about ourselves that we take for granted may not actually carry over into action or personal and institutional awareness, and a code of conduct can remind us of shared values even when we overstep. I suggest that the following list can be the beginning of a code of conduct for **ADHO** and for the digital humanities more generally:

1. Attempt to enact an open, inviting, and largely non-territorial field, while also demonstrating integrity, sharpness, and a willingness to push on epistemological boundaries.
2. Acknowledge the different levels at which scholarly, technological, and institutional work has to be carried out, and encourage the digital humanities to operate between these levels.

3.   Engage with technology practically, creatively, and critically.
4.   Do not assume that there is only one model of the digital humanities, or that the digital humanities is only one tradition.
5.   Do not attack arguments or positions without having attempted to understand the position or argument under attack.
6.   Be reflective about the discursive and intellectual framing provided by your own epistemic tradition (or traditions).
7.   Recognize the embeddedness of epistemic traditions, and that they relate to practice, expressive modalities, and materiality, as well as ideas, theories, and methods.
8.   Humbleness and constructiveness are useful qualities in negotiating different epistemic traditions and positions.
9.   Be aware that there are certain issues that are epistemologically loaded, and try to acquire a good sense of their context and history before bringing them up in interdisciplinary exchange.
10. Be prepared to be pushed out of your comfort zone, but also to work within your comfort zone in a diverse and constructive setting.
11. Harassment, intimidation, or discrimination based on race, religion, ethnicity, language, gender identity or expression, sexual orientation, physical or cognitive ability, age, appearance, or any group status is unacceptable.

Actionable Suggestions for the Digital Humanities

While the code of conduct provides an important foundation, it does not address Terras's challenge sufficiently. In the following, I aim to provide conceptually grounded and actionable suggestions as a response. While these are a response to the challenge, they are also a more general attempt at outlining a path forward for the digital humanities in an intermediate time perspective.

1.   Embrace a notion of the digital humanities as a contact zone with integrity that can host a variety of epistemic traditions, modes of engagement with the digital, infrastructures, and institutional models. This is essentially a non-territorial model by which the digital humanities has integrity as well as a close, multilevel collaboration with humanities disciplines and other actors. This requires curatorial qualities, deep intellectual–technological interchange, an openness to other traditions, and a willingness to go beyond the big-tent idea of the digital humanities. Curatorship is needed to maximize the benefits of the coming together of many traditions and epistemic positions. Intellectual work involves the profound interweaving of the critical and the technological. There has to be an openness to other perspectives and no expectations that specific traditions should abandon their epistemic core, but there will be adaptation. The big tent has to be replaced by something that is not steeped predominantly in one tradition.
2.   Tone down the aggressive and territorial rhetoric and action (in all camps). This does not mean that there should not be sharp and engaging dialog, but hopefully the interaction can be characterized by first trying to understand the other

position before engaging in critique, and by seeing the digital humanities as a place for different epistemic positions. This also implies understanding your own position and the particular situatedness of concepts and ideas (such as "collabora-tion," "nice," "making," "genealogy," and "criticality"). Critically, this is not about always being "nice," although niceness is important, but about facilitating mean-ingful and constructive dialog. Concretely, a code of conduct can support such a development (see the previous section). The goal is not epistemological merging, but coming together from different traditions and engaging richly across these. In any case, it probably makes sense not to start with the most unresolvable issues.

3.   Instead of building a new platform for the digital humanities, it would be advan-tageous to draw on the rich infrastructure, history, and political competence of the largest digital humanities organization. ADHO has a strong institutional position and is responsible for some of the main infrastructures of the field (the annual conference series, journals, etc.). As part of the renewal, half the positions on the board could come from outside the core constituencies and traditions. This would be a major change, of course, and it will have to be carried out sensibly and with respect. The field would have to retain integrity, which means that the new orga-nization would have to draw on people and partners that are sympathetic to the idea of a renewed digital humanities.

4.   Use the annual Digital Humanities Conference as a platform and testing ground for renewal, and consider making an upcoming conference into a primary testing ground. The experimental stance of digital humanities can be enacted through the format of the conference too, exemplifying the ways in which the digital humanities can manifest ideas, infrastructures, and expressions. Ideally, the conference following this one would be a good time to announce the implementation of a new charter for ADHO.

5.   Work with other organizations and fields in order to manifest and sustain digital humanities as a key platform for engaging with the humanities and the digital: memory institutions, all humanities disciplines, other platforms for the human-ities (such as humanities centers and the 4humanities initiative), some interpreta-tive social science institutions, technology and science fields, intersectional fields such as gender studies, and organizations such as HASTAC. Double or triple affiliation can be a very useful institutional strategy. People are not restricted to one identity in any context. For instance, HASTAC scholars (graduate students supported by HASTAC and their local institution) so inclined could have an extra affiliation with ADHO. A professor at a humanities department can have a secondary affiliation with a digital humanities institution. Actual institutional configurations and possibilities vary considerably, but the basic idea of multiple affiliations and being a contact zone can be implemented in very different ways. Also, there can be a rich collaboration with individuals who are based elsewhere, but do not have a formal affiliation with a digital humanities initiative.

6.   See the digital humanities as a platform for the humanities. This does not mean that every digital humanist or digital humanities institution has to engage with the long-term future of the humanities, but rather that they should acknowledge and embrace the fact that the digital humanities can have this function. It is an opportunity and responsibility that comes out of seeing the digital human-ities as a liminal zone. This function cannot be forced on any institution, but

through empowering others and being open to dialog, the digital humanities can secure this place. Obviously, there can also be other institutions that function as platforms for the humanities.

7. Engage with infrastructure critically and creatively. There is a need for a humanistic framing of academic infrastructure, and despite several attempts, there is a great deal of work to be done for the infrastructural vision to match the notion of an open, inclusive, and intellectually driven digital humanities. Infrastructure is also an example of where the digital humanities can help the humanities as a whole, and where there can be significant mutual benefits. Humanists need better ways of understanding and packaging infrastructure, but also need to mobilize the critical potential of their own work to situate and problematize their own infrastructure. In this way, academic infrastructure can become an example of where critical perspectives and concrete building come together. This would seem a worthy challenge for the digital humanities.

8. Engage with space. We are spatially situated beings, and while academic space is often a precious commodity, it can help channel and situate the digital humanities. Well-designed spaces with humanistic infrastructure and digital presence can help bring epistemic traditions together and provide a means of engaging critically and technologically. Such spaces do not need to be large or look a certain way. What is important is that they map onto the ideational foundation of the digital humanities initiative in question. Furthermore, while we may not want to talk about digital space, some operations would simply not lend themselves to be physically spatialized. Networked communities, publication platforms, and distributed research environments can also play a significant role.

9. Be sensitive to the importance of institutional specificity. Different institutions are configured, enabled, and constrained differently, and there are significant national differences. For instance, tenure-track systems are not universal and not all institutions of higher education are traditional comprehensive universities, and there is a marked difference between creating a digital humanities platform at a technical university college and creating one at a liberal arts college or a comprehensive university. And the very sense that there should be a center or a platform is built on certain kinds of institutions and available resources. In any case, the field will probably have to think more in terms of national and international infrastructure in the long run, and resources will have to be centralized to some extent, as well as distributed, and there will have to be ways of sharing costs and resources. At the same time, there must be room for institutional and intellectual dissimilarity. Paying attention to the specificity of the local condition is likely to give better return on investment than adopting a generic model of the digital humanities by default. It is therefore important that there is a range of models and examples, and that ADHO does not impose an imprint model on aspiring institutions, whether in the Anglo-American world or outside.

10. Acknowledge the multiple genealogies of the digital humanities. There are many trajectories that have led to present-day digital humanities, and some of these are not part of the official foundational narrative. With the current situation, there are also other fields and disciplines that have a vested interest in the field. Even with an essentially non-territorial model, there will always be some institutional

tension, but through not excluding anyone or any tradition, this tension can be productive. The scalability of such a model depends on many actors and interests, and academia is not a zero-sum game. Furthermore, with a development towards increasing specialization in the field, an open model can better allow and empower subgroups within the context of the digital humanities as a whole.

Most of these points relate to the necessity of having a real awareness of differences in perspectives and epistemic traditions. We tend to take certain aspects of our own traditions for granted, and taking a step back is not necessarily easy. Language and discourse play a vital role here in assigning frames to our epistemic traditions. Let me illustrate this with two examples.

The digital humanities is often described as inherently collaborative, not just the field, but also its technologies, projects, and people. Collaboration is an active and visible parameter in the narrative and framing of digital humanities. Not working collaboratively is often construed as an exception. Lisa Spiro states that the digital humanities community sees collaboration as an ethos necessary for its mission and work, and adds parenthetically, "even as it recognizes that some work is better done in solitude" (2012:25). Similarly, Bethany Nowviskie classifies situations "in which digital humanities practitioners work without explicit assistance or collaborative action" as "edge cases" (2011:170). Also, the kind of collaboration seen as central to the digital humanities is epistemologically flavored. It is not any collaboration, but one compatible with the project-based and technology-rich work processes associated with the tradition of digital humanities. It is unlikely that a standard seminar situation would be seen as highly collaborative in the same fashion. Furthermore, the focus on collaboration in the digital humanities also means that much individual work within the field is made invisible. This is reinforced by an often oppositional scheme between the digital humanities and the traditional humanities, by which the digital humanities is seen as collaborative, while the humanities is seen as being anchored in a highly individualistic model.

Another example is the inclusion or non-inclusion of gender, power, postcolonial, and environmental perspectives in digital humanities work. Adeline Koh and Roopika Risam (2013) argue that such categories tend to be blanketed out in computationally driven work in the digital humanities. According to their analysis, these categories have been largely invisible. This claim can be problematized, but it is certainly true that the field has not been heavily inflected along these axes. This situation is changing, however, which is partly a result of intersectional work and a broader scope for the digital humanities. An interesting example is the connection between environmental humanities and digital humanities, where there are many potential synergies. For instance, the digital humanities interest in "making" and intellectual middleware aligns well with the exploration of offering alternative narratives of "nature" in the environmental humanities (cf. Galison, 2014). And through the influx of scholars from areas such as gender studies, and the consequential epistemic negotiation, it is likely that there will be a stronger engagement for such perspectives within the community of digital humanities. At the same time, such traditions – when in contact with the digital humanities – will likely have to negotiate their relation to matters such as technological infrastructure, language, materiality, and making.

Conclusion

It seems likely that the next five years will be critical for the shaping of the digital humanities. There are multiple possible pathways ahead, and while there is no definite way of sorting the digital humanities out, I have suggested in this chapter that we need to embrace and develop the liminal position of the field rather than move away from being in between. The big tent will never be big enough, and we need to give up some of the old binaries and move forward as an epistemologically open, intellectually curious, and technologically engaged enterprise. We need to be aware of our own epistemic commitments and be generous enough to try to understand others' before critiquing them on epistemological grounds. This does not mean giving up one's own disciplinary anchorage or sense of sharpness, but rather being willing to learn and negotiate. Having a code of conduct can help us identify and foster shared community values.

We need to take time to constitute the field before we attempt to use one particular model of digital humanities as a template to develop the digital humanities internationally. However, it may well be that what we find out is that it will never be appropriate to simply advocate one model. Furthermore, as a humanities-wide enterprise, the digital humanities can represent the humanities in certain contexts and be an experimental platform for enacting and imagining the future of the humanities. The digital humanities can never be strong enough without working with the rest of the humanities. This does not mean, though, that the field should not have integrity or that digital humanities always has to reach out to the rest of the humanities.

A point about humility too. As a young graduate student in English linguistics, I had learned that the archaeologist Sir Colin Renfrew was coming to my university to receive a scholarly prize. One of my primary interests at the time was the history of languages, and I was quite interested in Professor Renfrew's work and him approaching linguistics from the point of view of archaeology. I contacted him and asked him whether he would be willing to give me an interview during his visit. I was happy he accepted, and I had a wonderful conversation with him. He must have been about 60 years old at the time and was generous with his time. He told me how his interest in historical linguistics and archaeology had made him realize that he needed to have a better grasp of molecular biology. He started to go to molecular biology conferences, and for a long time he would sit at the very back, listening and learning. He said that he had to devote time to getting a sense of the field and current research. After a year or two, he told me, he was actually invited to sit up front and be an active part of the dialog. This taught me about the importance of intellectual humility. Renfew showed respect through taking the time to learn the "language" and more about the field, although he could probably have imposed himself in a much more direct way. There is a lot to be said for such generosity and humility in the context of the digital humanities. And even if we cannot sort the digital humanities out, let's at least try!

REFERENCES AND FURTHER READING

ADHO (undated). ADHO conference code of conduct.http://adho.org/administration/conference-coordinating-program-committee/adho-conference-code-conduct (accessed February 8, 2014).

Becher, T. and Trowler, P. 2001. *Academic Tribes and Territories: Intellectual Enquiry and the Cultures of Disciplines*, 2nd edition. Buckingham: Open University Press/SRHE.

Bellamy, C. 2013. *Humanist* mailing list. August 2013. http://lists.digitalhumanities.org/piper mail/humanist/2013-August/011183.html (accessed February 8, 2014).

Bey, H. 1991. *T.A.Z.: The Temporary Autonomous Zone, Ontological Anarchy, Poetic Terrorism: Anarchy and Terrorism*. Brooklyn, NY: Autonomedia.

Bowker, G.C. and Star, S.L. 1999. *Sorting Things Out: Classification and its Consequences*. Cambridge, MA: MIT Press.

Burnard, L. 2002. Humanities computing in Oxford: a retrospective. http://users.ox.ac.uk/~lou/wip/hcu-obit.txt (accessed February 8, 2014).

CenterNet (undated). An international network of digital humanities centers. http://digitalhuman ities.org/centernet (accessed February 8, 2014).

Galison, P. 1999. Trading zone: coordinating action and belief. In *The Science Studies Reader*, ed. M. Biagioli. New York: Routledge, 137–60.

Galison, P. 2014. Visual STS. In *Visualization in the Age of Computerization*, ed, A. Carusi, A.S. Hoel, T. Webmoor, and S. Woolgar. New York: Routledge, 197–225.

Gold, M.K., ed. 2012. *Debates in the Digital Humanities*. Minneapolis: University of Minnesota Press.

Klein, J.T. 2005. *Humanities, Culture, and Interdisciplinarity: The Changing American Academy*. Albany, NY: State University of New York Press.

Klein, J.T. 2010. *Creating Interdisciplinary Campus Cultures: A Model for Strength and Sustainability*. San Francisco: Jossey-Bass.

Koh, A., and Risam, R. 2013. Open thread: the digital humanities as a historical "refuge" from race/class/gender/sexuality/disability? http://dhpoco.org/blog/2013/05/10/open-thread-the-digital-humanities-as-a-historical-refuge-from-raceclassgendersexualitydisability (accessed February 8, 2014).

Maddox, L., ed. 1999. *Locating American Studies: The Evolution of a Discipline*. Baltimore: Johns Hopkins University Press.

Mattern, S. 2013. Methodolatry and the art of measure. http://places.designobserver.com/fea ture/methodolatry-in-urban-data-sci ence/38174 (accessed February 8, 2014).

Nowviskie, B. 2011. Where credit is due: precon-ditions for the evaluation of collaborative digital scholarship. *Profession* 2011, 169–81.

Pratt, M.L. 1991. Arts of the contact zone. *Profession* 1991, 33–40.

Ratto, M. 2012. CSE as epistemic technologies: computer modeling and disciplinary difference in the humanities. In *Handbook of Research on Computational Science and Engineering: Theory and Practice*, ed. J. Leng and W. Sharrock. Hershey, PA: IGI Global, 567–86.

Repko, A.F. 2008. *Interdisciplinary Research: Process and Theory*. Los Angeles: SAGE.

Risam, R., and Koh, A. (undated). Postcolonial digital humanities: mission statement. http://dhpoco.org/mission-statement-postcolonial-digital-humanities (accessed February 8, 2014).

Schreibman, S., Siemens, R., and Unsworth, J., eds. 2004. *A Companion to Digital Humanities*. Oxford: Blackwell.

Spiro, L. 2012. "This is why we fight": defining the values of the digital humanities. In M.K. Gold, *Debates in the Digital Humanities*. Minneapolis: University of Minnesota Press, 16–34.

Svensson, P. 2012. The digital humanities as a humanities project. *Arts and Humanities in Higher Education* 11 (1–2), 42–60.

Svensson, P. 2016. *Big Digital Humanities: Imagining a Meeting Place for the Humanities and the Digital*. Ann Arbor: University of Michigan Press.

Terras, M. 2013. On changing the rules of digital humanities from the inside. http://melissaterras.blogspot.se/2013/05/on-changing-rules-of-digital-humanities.html (accessed February 8, 2014).

Terras, M., Nyhan, J., and Vanhoutte, E., eds. 2013. *Defining Digital Humanities: A Reader*. Farnham: Ashgate.

Weingart, P. 2010. A short history of knowledge for-mations. In *The Oxford Handbook of Interdisciplinarity*, ed. R. Frodeman, J.T. Klein, and C. Mitcham. Oxford: Oxford University Press, 3–14.

Wynne, M. 2013. *Humanist* mailing list. September 2013. http://lists.digitalhumanities.org/piper mail/humanist/2013-September/011275.html (accessed February 8, 2014).

34

Only Connect: The Globalization of the Digital Humanities

Daniel Paul O'Donnell, Katherine L. Walter, Alex Gil, and Neil Fraistat

Figure 34.1 is from Melissa Terras's infographic, *Quantifying the Digital Humanities* (Terras, 2012). The map shows the distribution of physical centers in the digital humanities, as defined by members of the Alliance of Digital Humanities Organizations (ADHO), across the globe (see also Dacos, 2014). As Domenico Fiormonte has argued, it can also serve as a proxy for other types of activity in the field, including, broadly speaking, the residency of members of ADHO-affiliated digital humanities societies (Fiormonte, 2012).

But, as Fiormonte also points out, the "blank" areas on Terras's map can serve as an inverse proxy for other data. Linguistic diversity, for example, or relative poverty: they include most of the world's low-, lower-middle-, and middle-income economies (Ahlenius and UNEP, 2012). In other words, while practitioners of the digital humanities tend to define their discipline as being both highly collaborative and highly international (Siemens, 2009; Scheinfeldt, 2010; Siemens and Burr, 2013), it is for the most part the case that our international and collaborative activity is conducted along a primarily east–west axis among a relatively small number of mostly contiguous high-income economies in the northern hemisphere: Japan, Taiwan, South Korea, Canada, the United States, the countries of western and central Europe, and, in the South, Australia and New Zealand (for a survey of the digital humanities in a global context, focusing particularly on this question, see Fiormonte *et al.*, forthcoming; also Galina, 2013a; and especially Dacos, 2014).

This lack of connection between researchers in high-income economies and the rest of the world is the more surprising because the digital revolution that makes our field possible is also having a very pronounced effect on these lower-income regions. While Internet penetration in "the Global South" is often quite low (Internet World Stats,

A New Companion to Digital Humanities, First Edition. Edited by Susan Schreibman, Ray Siemens, and John Unsworth.
© 2016 John Wiley & Sons, Ltd. Published 2016 by John Wiley & Sons, Ltd.

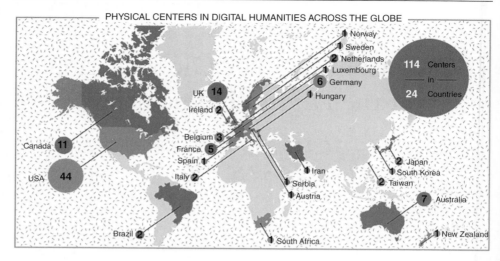

Figure 34.1 Physical digital humanities centers (Terras, 2012). Used by permission is Melissa Terras. Data from Centernet.

2014), its growth, especially in the form of mobile broadband subscriptions, massively outpaces that in the high-income world (International Telecommunication Union, 2011). Moreover, these rates rise considerably when you consider the demographic from which digital humanities researchers are typically drawn: citizens with a tertiary education. Among this population group, many middle-, lower-middle-, and low-income economies have Internet penetration rates that rival or exceed those found in high-income regions: Senegal, for example, outranks in this demographic both Israel and the United States, while Turkey, Uruguay, Costa Rica, Brazil, Macedonia, Ecuador, Mexico, Thailand, Serbia, and Honduras all have penetration rates well above 60% for citizens with a tertiary education (International Telecommunication Union 2011, chart 5.5).

In other words, while the distribution of physical digital humanities centers on Terras's map closely reflects both the distribution of high-income versus middle-, lower-middle-, and low-income economies and the distribution of Internet penetration among the general population in such regions, it does not reflect either the geographic spread of Internet penetration among the tertiary-educated or the rate of change in various forms of ICT connectivity across the globe. Maps showing these figures would have far fewer and much smaller "blank" spots. They would suggest the possibilities for a community of digital humanities researchers that is far wider than it currently seems to be.

As Titilola Babalola and others have noted, however, Internet penetration and rapidly increasing broadband access are not the only factors that affect one's ability to carry out digital humanities research. Other factors that can affect such work – and especially inhibit collaboration across economic divides – include lack of infrastructure (especially lack of access to consistently available electricity or bandwidth), lack of training, lack of access to international research (Babalola, 2013), and different disciplinary self-definitions (Galina, 2013b; Babalola, 2013). The domination of English as the language of communication within the digital humanities can lead to a largely unacknowledged valorization of Anglo-American research norms, genres, and interests over those of other traditions and regions (Fiormonte, 2013; Fiormonte *et al.*, forthcoming). The gaps these disparities and differences create are such that digitally active researchers in middle-, lower-middle-, and low-income economies can simply fail to see themselves or what they do in the English-language-dominated research carried out by digital humanists in the high-income economies (Galina, 2013b; Babalola, 2013; Dacos, 2014).

So what does it take to engage across this divide? Fiormonte, Numerico, and Tomasi have described the globalization of the digital humanities as "the true innovation of the next decade," beyond even "Big Data, mega-platforms and the mass archivisation of data," because of its ability to provoke

> a series of discussions on previously neglected topics: ... the linguistic-cultural problem, ... cross-cultural representation within ... international organizations, ... English-speaking dominance in the processes of discussion and factual evaluation, ... the hierarchical structure of the management and ownership of major archives and repositories, ... the relationship of DH to colonial and subaltern studies,... and the need for a critical approach in connection with the social sciences. (Fiormonte *et al.*, forthcoming)

Galina, likewise, has discussed the power that comes from collaboration between what she describes as "the center" and "the periphery," while noting the potential for "spectacular" failure:

> It is important that we understand that we sometimes unconsciously incorporate assumptions into our proposals and initiatives that do indeed affect inclusiveness or representation. We must be careful to avoid playing "catch up" or initiatives that automatically assume that the objective is to "help" countries currently on the periphery to become just like the model DH centre. We can all learn and benefit from each other and collaboration should work in both directions. Methods that have worked effectively in one cultural setting may fail spectacularly in another (and vice versa) and certain reasoning of how things should work does not apply similarly to other frameworks. Models, surveys, truisms should be placed in context. Periphery countries can contribute by framing and stating more explicitly how and in what ways true collaboration can be achieved. (Galina, 2013b)

This chapter looks at what happens when digital humanities researchers do attempt to extend their collaborations across traditional regional, economic, and linguistic boundaries. Its authors have been responsible for establishing several of the more prominent efforts in recent years to reconfigure the digital humanities in a global context – efforts that have been inspired in large part, indeed, by Terras's map. What we have discovered is that such collaborations are about more than simply building infrastructure or encouraging people to collaborate across these traditional boundaries (though, as Gil points out, simply encouraging people to "start collaborating with someone who lives very far away from you" can represent an important first step; see Gil and Priego, 2013). Perhaps especially in the case of interregional and interlinguistic collaborations, infrastructural, linguistic, financial, and conceptual differences can create barriers to communication and collaboration that cannot be disguised. Successful collaboration in such an environment requires us to recognize, validate, and accommodate such differences rather than see them as obstacles that can (or should) be overcome.

While it is tempting to see globalization as an opportunity for transferring knowledge, experience, and access to infrastructure from a developed North to an underdeveloped South, our experience suggests that successful collaboration in this context is far more about developing understanding than merging practice. Equitable and effective networks of association respect national, cultural, and linguistic divides and indeed profit from them. As we have discovered, the process of learning about these divides improves disciplinary practice and knowledge on all sides. In a field that is famously "nice" (Scheinfeldt, 2010), it can be invigorating (and useful) to discover just how much can be learned from disagreement and lack of common experience – from discovering that it may be *less* "easy for us to 'call bullshit'" than we first thought (Scheinfeldt, 2010) to learning that methodological disputes can be every bit as difficult to resolve as theoretical ones when researchers approach problems from different starting points in terms of infrastructure and the institutional, disciplinary, economic, and societal contexts of their work (cf. Scheinfeldt, 2010, who is speaking primarily of a North American context).

And finally, we have also discovered that (supra)-network building is itself a form of praxis within the digital humanities – a third form that is neither clearly "hack" nor "yack" but combines elements of both (see Nowviskie, 2014, on the origins and problems with these currently popular terms for the intersection of coding and theory in the digital humanities). As O'Donnell has argued, the digital humanities can perhaps best be understood as a paradiscipline, that is to say a "set of approaches, skills, interests, and beliefs that gain meaning from their association with other kinds of work":

> Becoming a Digital Humanist does not necessarily require abandoning previous understandings of the things that interest you, though it will almost certainly change how you approach your subject. It is entirely possible to be *both* a Digital Humanist *and* a "Big Theorist," just as it is possible to be a Digital Humanist and a textual critic, philologist, historian, or archaeologist. (O'Donnell, 2012a)

In this context, the construction of supra-networks that transcend national, linguistic, regional, and economic boundaries contributes to the development of the digital humanities as a research field as surely as does the publication of a specific work of digital theory or the development of a new standard or approach to a methodological problem. Although our efforts are still very much in their initial phases, we believe that the discipline as a whole is already richer for the diversity of problems we have been able to bring to the fore and the breadth of solutions and accommodations we have been able to discover collectively.

The rest of this chapter looks at the lessons we have learned through our efforts with two recent projects that have been established to address the problem of the "blank" areas on Terras's map: centerNet, an international network of digital humanities centers, and Global Outlook::Digital Humanities (GO::DH), a special interest group (SIG) for researchers interested in promoting supra-regional and linguistic collaboration and contact. These two initiatives tackle the problem of internationalization and globalization from different perspectives: institutional in the case of centerNet and individual in the case of GO::DH. In each case, however, the issues that have arisen and the lessons that have been learned are quite similar: successful collaboration across traditional national, regional, linguistic, economic, and political boundaries requires, above all, an ability to recognize differences as something to be recognized and validated rather than solved.

The approach we take in this chapter is frankly and deliberately anecdotal. In doing so, we recognize that this imposes several limits on our analysis. By reporting on the experiences of a limited number of people and organizations as they tackle a few specific problems in the globalization of digital humanities research and teaching, for example, we necessarily exclude other perspectives, experiences, and problems. Thus, we do not discuss, except in passing, recent European experience in the development of large international, multilingual collaborations among participants in, for the most part, high-income economies. In a similar way, we do not discuss, again except in passing, efforts by scholars within middle-, lower-middle-, and low-income economies to organize on a "South–South" and/or linguistic basis (as, for example, within La Red de Humanidades Digitales [RedHD]).

Likewise, by focusing on the recent experiences of two specific organizations, we tie our work to the discussion of a particular moment in time and, as a result, may appear to run the risk of obsolescence in a handbook covering a discipline that is famously future-oriented.

At the same time, however, we believe that this personal and historically focused approach brings with it several advantages over a broader or more theoretical study. If there is one thing the authors have learned from their recent experiences in the globalization of the digital humanities, it is that an openness to experience and interactive learning is a *sine qua non* of successful global collaborations. Our most important discoveries have proceeded from exigencies of the moment and have often been unanticipated. The GO::DH approach to *ad hoc* translation (see below), for example, arose from a challenge by one of the non-Anglophone members of its executive when this issue of the cost of a more formal translation policy first arose – and it was the success of this unplanned approach that allowed the organization to have the confidence to accept submissions in "any language" for its inaugural essay prize.

Moreover, we also believe with Fiormonte, Numerico, and Tomasi that the current moment represents an inflection point in the history of our discipline. Just as the essays in the original Blackwell *Companion to Digital Humanities* (Schreibman *et al.*, 2004) captured (and indeed helped shape) an important moment in the transition from "humanities computing" to a more widely conceived field of study, so too, we believe, the essays in this particular collection are appearing at a similarly transitional moment. As recently as 2012, Matthew Gold could publish a well-received collection of essays on *Debates in the Digital Humanities* without any contribution on globalization or the practice of the digital humanities outside of its traditional home in the high-income economies – an omission that would be unthinkable in a similar collection today. Since then, interest in supporting and exploring connections outside Europe, North America, Australia, New Zealand, and Japan has become a more and more central concern. In 2013 and 2014, ADHO introduced balance among regions, including those outside the high-income economic areas, as an explicit criterion for the choice of both keynote speakers at and the location of its flagship conference, Digital Humanities. At DH 2014 (Lausanne), a third plenary spot was added to ensure representation from outside "the Global North," and the choice of Australia for DH 2015 (the first time the conference was held outside of Europe and North America) was motivated in part by a desire to bring the conference closer to participants in Asia. In early 2014, indeed, ADHO adopted a protocol that explicitly encourages the participation of hosts for its conference outside of Europe and North America as part of its annual rotation.

And finally, this chapter is about the human practice of the digital humanities rather than its technological development – a practice which, as Fiormonte (2012) has argued, necessarily involves an understanding of the individuals and organizations involved. Technological problems and solutions, even those with a considerable theoretical component, are subject to unavoidable obsolescence: even theoretical articles about the practice of and possibilities for "electronic editing" published in the late 1990s and early 2000s have now, for the most part, been passed by subsequent developments in mobile, collaborative, and other technologies and the theoretical reconception this technology has brought with it. The principle of collaboration across economic and regional divides derived from our experience working in the early days of the globalization of the digital humanities, however, is unlikely to age as quickly. Technologies will change, individual countries and regions may become richer or poorer, and we can expect the "blank" areas or Terras's map to become better integrated into the global practice of our discipline. But the problems of collaborating across economic, technological, and linguistic divides will remain. In this sense, we believe that our experiences in establishing two early and influential mechanisms for the discovery and development of such collaborations will remain an important and hopefully useful example for those developing similar collaborations across such boundaries in the future.

centerNet

centerNet is an an international network of digital humanities centers and a constituent organization of the ADHO. Its primary mission is the promotion of digital humanities centers as a cyberinfrastructure in the humanities, providing support and guidance to center directors, and the creation and distribution of educational programming and other initiatives that support the work of digital humanities centers. Centers are important to the development of the digital humanities because they provide a sustainable infrastructure: the centerNet charter defines a center as an organization that is engaged in more than one project and has continuing institutional recognition and support, as opposed to individual scholars and research projects, which depend primarily on grants for their day-to-day funding and, as a result, provide far less sustainable infrastructure.

centerNet was born at a North American summit meeting of digital humanities centers and funders in April 2007 co-hosted by the National Endowment for the Humanities (NEH) and the Maryland Institute for the Humanities (MITH). Soon after it was up and running, steering committee members began to realize that center-Net's mission and goals might create opportunities for expanding the organization internationally. Could we for example promote exchanges of scholars or students among centers? Could we reach agreements and form "sister centers" in different parts of the world? When the humanities or humanities funding is under attack, can we provide a social networks to aid one another in some way? With funding from the

NEH, the University of Nebraska–Lincoln's Center for Digital Research in the Humanities (CDRH), and MITH, centerNet held its first international summit meeting in London in 2010. Center directors Katherine Walter (CDRH) and Neil Fraistat (MITH) invited 60 centers and funders to attend, and it was there that international discussion and action began to take shape. At the summit, general consensus among invitees was that collaboration would lead to increased focus on the importance and need for cyberinfrastructure for the digital humanities; the potential for new opportunities for research; improved advocacy for centers and funding in the humanities; and opportunities to promote education, training, and other collaborative efforts among centers.

One assumption of the organizers was that centers in other parts of the world were similar to those in North America. This proved to be somewhat naïve. Although much effort was made in advance of our initial meeting to identify centers throughout the world (indeed, centerNet was the primary source for Terras's 2012 map) and to learn something about them, we were unable to discover many outside the northern hemisphere with the exception of those in the high-income economies of Australia and New Zealand. There is, to be sure, a variety of different kinds of centers within North America itself. As Neil Fraistat has noted:

> some are primarily service units, some primarily research, some a mixture of both. Some centers focus explicitly on digital humanities, some engage the humanities but are organized around media studies, or code studies – disciplines that are increasingly converging with digital humanities. North American centers tend to arise from the bottom up; European and Asian centers from the top down. North American centers tend to focus exclusively on humanities and, sometimes, the interpretive social sciences. European and Asian centers are more likely to be dispersed through the disciplines, or to be organized as virtual rather than physically located centers. (Fraistat, 2012:283)

Yet the concept of a "center" as we were understanding it still had connotations to North Americans that were often unknown in other parts of the world: even beyond the basic distinctions Fraistat describes above, centers around the world can be quite different from one another in their characteristics, mission, and funding, and certainly not all are built on the North American model. As subsequent studies and articles have confirmed, there are significant differences between those in high-income and middle- and low-income regions. This has led us to take a slower approach and to depend upon nascent groups in low-income regions for information and advice.

Before discussing further the important issue of disparate income regions, a few words about centerNet's experience with regional chapters. The formation of regional chapters involves, to greater or lesser extents, navigating political, linguistic, and cultural differences. Initial regional affiliates or chapters were developed in Asia/Pacific, Europe, North America, and the UK and Ireland. To give some examples of issues within regions: centerNet Europe deals with significant differences in language and culture that can lead to misunderstanding or impatience. In Asia/Pacific, centers rely upon English as a lingua franca for communicating and may be in relative proximity. But some Asia/Pacific countries have stronger cultural affiliations with other regions of the world. For example, Australia and New Zealand, as part of the

Commonwealth, might have been as logically placed in centerNet UK and Ireland (now part of centerNet Europe) as in centerNet Asia/Pacific. Also, there may be political barriers to cooperation, as for example is the case between the People's Republic of China and surrounding countries.

Moreover, there is no guarantee that proximity will make things easier: while Mexico is, with Canada and the United States, part of the North American economic block, there was initially very little contact between researchers and institutions in Mexico and the other two countries – in part because Mexican academic organization is somewhat dissimilar to that of its northern neighbors (the digital humanities in Mexico is largely supported through libraries rather than centers) and, perhaps even more importantly, because there have been until very recently so few personal connections between digital humanities researchers in Mexico and those in Canada, the USA, and other high-income economies.

In the last several years, centerNet has begun to seek members outside the high-income economic regions, beginning in Central and South America thanks to the efforts of La Red de Humanidades Digitales (RedHD), a consortium of scholars, primarily in Mexico, who are affiliated with Global Outlook::Digital Humanities (GO::DH). As centers develop in these regions, centerNet is available to advise center directors as needed and to provide opportunities for collaboration among centers in other parts of the world. Developing the network has been a slow process, hampered in part by the disparity in infrastructure between developed nations and developing nations.

Moreover, the institutional organization particularly in Central and South America and in Africa can be quite different from that found in high-income economies in North America, Europe, and Asia/Pacific. While growth of centerNet may have been quite gradual, in part because of linguistic and cultural barriers and difficulties in identifying relevant networks in developing nations or in having introductions to such networks, we have come to value these as opportunities for understanding, and in that light many centerNet initiatives are aimed at creating international networks where possible – networks that may be social as well as more concrete. centerNet has become a member organization of ADHO – the only constituent organization, indeed that has a membership consisting of institutions rather than individuals. The centerNet inter-national executive council expanded in 2015 from two representatives per region to 25 center directors representing gender, linguistic, and geographic diversity. This is a step forward, we hope, to greater involvement and understanding at the highest levels of the organization. We have discovered that, at least as far as centers are concerned, region is less important than other forms of constituency as an organizing principle for our board, and for the organization as a whole.

Global Outlook::Digital Humanities

If centerNet represents an institutional approach to the construction of a supra-network, the experience of Global Outlook::Digital Humanities (GO::DH) represents a personal one.

The goal of GO::DH is to connect individuals and groups working on digital schol-arship or preservation around the world, with a focus on areas outside of the regions represented by the constituent organizations that make up ADHO (all of which are currently led by and principally serve researchers living in high-income economies). The group has its origins in discussions among Marcus Bingenheimer (Taiwan and USA), Peter K. Bol (USA), Neil Fraistat (USA), Jenjou Hung (Taiwan), Jieh Hsiang (Taiwan), Daniel Paul O'Donnell (Canada), Harold Short (UK), Ray Siemens (Canada), and Christian Wittern (Japan) at the 2013 Digital Humanities conference in Hamburg concerning the state of digital humanities research in mainland China and the difficulty of developing contacts – even among researchers with similar disciplinary interests – across economic boundaries.

The initiative began to take on concrete shape in November 2012 at a meeting on the digital humanities in Havana organized by Ray Siemens and the *Investigating New Knowledge Environments* (INKE) project (INKE is funded by the Social Sciences and Humanities Research Council of Canada). The discussions in Hamburg involved researchers (primarily Sinologists) from high-income economies discussing the difficulties they had in finding and engaging with researchers from middle-, lower-middle-, and lower-income economic regions in their for the most part common discipline. The INKE-organized meeting in Havana, however, brought together researchers from different regions, economies, and humanities disciplines, whose common interests revolved around the broader topic of the impact of digital technology on the representation and dissemination of knowledge.

Tours of the National Library of Cuba, meetings with administration and researchers at the Casa de los Americas cultural institute, and lectures by participants in the seminar all highlighted the extent to which problems pursued across regional, economic, and disciplinary barriers were, in fact, often quite complementary. While no North American national or university library, for example, faces infrastructure difficulties similar to that faced by the National Library of Cuba, the problems the library is attempting to solve are relatively common: digitizing, cataloging, and disseminating metadata and digital replicas of its often unique holdings. At the same time, the differences which divide researchers in high-, middle-, lower-middle-, and low-income economies also resulted in a broadening of our understanding of the field. Researchers from high-income economies thinking about questions of sustainable computing or new models of scholarly dissemination, for example, found themselves learning much from the efforts and example of their Cuban colleagues: academic discourse in Cuba involves a broader spectrum of participants than is common in the more university-focused high-income economies, and Cuban efforts to overcome often severe infrastructure deficits have led to the development of novel forms of low-bandwidth and no-bandwidth publication and dissemination.

Perhaps the most important lesson from the INKE workshop in Havana, however, involved the politics of international collaboration. In part because of its origins as an ADHO-sponsored initiative, the original GO::DH proposal had a strong focus on discovery and development (O'Donnell, 2012b, contains a slightly modified version of the original proposal, but one that still retains much of its original character and point of view). The project saw itself as a way of encouraging researchers in high-income economies to seek out researchers in middle-, lower-middle-, and low-income economies and provide assistance in the form of access to research moneys, collaboration, and, perhaps, expertize, surplus equipment, and other forms of material aid: a project, in other words, that was about expanding the network already inhabited by researchers from high-income economies to include more projects and people from middle-, lower-middle-, and low-income regions.

The idea that GO::DH would work better as a supra-network – or in this case as an organization that saw its job as being to bring already-existing networks in different regions and contexts together – came out of a final workshop on globalization on the last day of the Havana meeting. A translation error during one of the presentations resulted in a reference to differences between the "first" and "third" worlds. A lively discussion about the implications of this ordination followed – a discussion that ended up going far beyond the original time limit and developed into an *ad hoc* plenary session – and helped establish a sense that globalization in the digital humanities meant paying attention to the intersection of existing practices and networks rather than the expansion or superior valorization of any one network or set of practices. The differences between researchers, research practices, and research projects in different types of economies, in other words, were not problems to be solved. A collaboration that would succeed across economic and other barriers would have to be a collaboration that was able to accommodate different approaches, experiences, and contexts.

The extent to which this new approach changed the focus of GO::DH can be seen by comparing the original proposal for the special interest group mentioned above to the description of the organization's goals in the "about" section of its own website (Global Outlook::Digital Humanities, 2013a). The original proposal focused on outreach, development, recruitment, and assistance. It discussed the need for "engaging with digital humanities researchers and institutions in geographical areas not currently involved with ADHO," for "bringing people, projects, and institutions together and fostering engagement with and by ADHO and other members and institutions in our community" (both O'Donnell, 2012b:2). It saw the new SIG as being most closely aligned with the ADHO committee responsible for recruiting new member organizations (O'Donnell, 2012b:2–3). The emphasis throughout was on the need to create a network by which ADHO members could come into contact with "others" working outside of the high-income economies and to foster collaboration with "others" who might or might not define themselves as digital humanists.

The "about" section of the GO::DH website, on the other hand, reflects the SIG's post-Cuba sense of its mission. While still clearly identifying itself as a Special Interest Group of the ADHO, the project's self-definition explicitly rules out outreach and recruitment as goals, focusing instead on the groups bridging, or supra-networking, functions:

> The purpose of GO::DH is to help break down barriers that hinder communication and collaboration among researchers and students of the Digital Arts, Humanities, and Cultural Heritage sectors in high, mid, and low income economies.
>
> GO::DH is not an aid or an outreach programme. Participants come from all over the world, and we all recognize that excellent work is being done in the Digital Arts, Humanities, and Cultural Heritage around the world; furthermore, we know that students, researchers, and institutions in all geographic regions and types of economies all have much to contribute to the development of digitally enabled work in the arts, humanities, and cultural heritage sector.

What GO::DH does instead is leverage the complementary strengths, interests, abilities and experiences of participants through special projects and events, profile and publicity activity, and by encouraging collaboration among individual projects, institutions, and researchers. Its core activities are **Discovery**, **Community-Building**, **Research**, and **Advocacy**. It helps its members learn more about digital work in the Arts, Humanities, and Cultural Heritage sectors; it acts to foster collaboration and cooperation across regions and economies; it coordinates research on and in support of the use of technology in these areas across the globe; and it advocates for a global perspective on work in this sector. (Global Outlook::Digital Humanities, 2013a)

Linguistic Issues

GO::DH is a multichannel community. It operates a mailing list (globaloutlookdh-l@uleth.ca), a website/blog (http://globaloutlookdh.org/), and other social media feeds (https://www.facebook.com/GlobalOutlookDH and https://twitter.com/Global OutlookDH), and organizes face-to-face events (THATCamp Caribe 2013 and 2° encuentro humanistas digitales mexico 2014) and competitions (Global Outlook::Digital Humanities, 2013b).

Given this range of activities and the makeup of our community, language use is an important topic. Part of the mission of GO::DH is to advocate for localized digital humanities – that is to say digital humanities done in individuals' own languages and using cultural artifacts and examples drawn from their own culture. As a result, the community encourages members to write and speak in whatever language they feel most comfortable or effective in. GO::DH itself does not have an official language and its website is capable of supporting multiple translations of its content.

This is an area in which we have had some success. Although most of GO::DH's administration and the majority of its members' communication is conducted in English, the digital humanities' lingua franca, a not inconsiderable part of list traffic is in other languages (primarily Spanish). Several key pages on the website, likewise, have been translated into more than one language (including Chinese, Japanese, and Spanish). Since 40% of the steering committee was Spanish-speaking, and since the first GO::DH conference was co-organized with the Spanish-language digital humanities organization RedHD, a much larger than usual share of its administration is also carried out in a language other than English.

Our success in this matter comes in part from the approach we have taken to handling multilingual matters. Translation is, of course, very expensive if done well and (often) quite poor if done automatically. Although GO::DH was given a small startup grant from the University of Lethbridge, this money ($5000) was not nearly enough to pay for systematic translation of the community's website, let alone the traffic on its mailing list. What we have done instead is to encourage community members to treat linguistic knowledge like any other skill that can be leveraged to help colleagues: users are encouraged to translate or even just paraphrase postings and web pages into their own language, whenever they feel this would be useful for increasing exposure or reducing opportunities for confusion among members of their speech community. This provides community-responsive approach to multilingual communication. Different web pages on the site have been translated into different languages: the page describing our essay prize is found in English, Spanish, and Italian; the page describing the working groups is found in English and Spanish; other entries have been translated into Chinese, French, Arabic, Nepali, and Portuguese. Email discussions, likewise, often include several languages as individuals with a reading knowledge of one language respond in whatever they feel more comfortable writing in.

Our largest experiment in this approach to language use came with the GO::DH essay prize (Global Outlook::Digital Humanities, 2013b). Launched in the summer of 2013, this prize was for "research papers looking at some aspect of the national, regional, or international practice of the digital humanities." After some debate, and recognizing that it had expertize in a considerable number of languages among its members, the adjudication panel decided to experiment with accepting submissions in any language.

In the end, the competition received 53 submissions in seven languages, five of which languages could be read well by members of the committee (English, Chinese, Spanish, French, and German); for the remaining two, Polish and Korean, the panel was able to recruit with relative ease native and near-native speakers with relevant experience to assist them in their evaluation (to ensure consistency, the additional readers were integrated into the pool of readers and assigned more than one paper to read). The adjudication process – which followed the "two reader" system used by many granting agencies – was able to reach a consensus on the final ranking with relative ease. Approximately 30% of the submissions to the competition and 44% of the winning entries were written in languages other than English. A special issue of the journal *Digital Studies/Le champ numérique* is being devoted to these winning entries, with each paper published in its original language and French or English, the two official languages of the journal.

Cultural Differences

GO::DH's experience shows how the language skills of a community can be leveraged with relative ease to encourage the development of multilingual and localized disciplinary practice. Indeed, the most serious problems we have had with language use has involved the one most members of our community share: English. Because English is a lingua franca with native speakers, its use in the digital humanities unavoidably privileges those who were born to it or who have mastered it from years of exposure and practice (for digital humanities, see Clavert, 2013; and postings by Dacos, Fiormonte, Gigliozzi, McCarty, O'Donnell, and others on the Humanist and GlobalOutlookDH-l mailing lists). An important early discussion on the list involved rhetorical pitfalls native speakers of English could fall into that made it more difficult for non-speakers to follow. Dacos, discussing proposals for multilingual sessions at the discipline's main international conference, DH, argued that we should adopt "Globish" for our sessions (as is common in an informal medium like email, the following quotations contain various shorthand forms and solipsisms; these have not been marked with *sic*):

> I don't think that we have to fight English a common language. But I would defend
> Globish as a common language, because there are few non English native speakers that are
> able to speak/write with a very elegant and subtlety language in English. For this reason,

I would recommend to revamp the organization of our DH international events. They should be held in Globish, with a lot of respect for non-native speakers. Some propositions:

- when an English native speaker is speaking, all non native would have a "green card" that they could rise at any time during the conference. This would be used to say "I don't understand, you speak too fast, or you are making references to cultural anglo-american knowledge"
- international conferences should take care of the quality of the sound in the rooms used for conferences. For example, the quality of the sound during the introducing conference of Claudine Moulin in Hambourg was not good, and it was difficult to understand 100% of her talk, which was very interesting.
- during the expertise process of DH conferences, we have to encourage non native speakers by any possible ways. The goal should be to reach parity. We should consider that perfection of the English language SHOULD NOT BE ANYMORE a criteria of selection. That will take time. We should consider that this change won't occur in less than 5 or 10 years. But we should involve in this process. Affirmative action could be one way. Other ways could be to put money in translation processes. We could also ask to English native speakers to submit their article in Spanish or in French … They would discover how difficult it is for us, and that they should become more indulgent in the selection process. Or both (Dacos, 2013).

Later, these ideas came to be formulated as some list "rules," aimed primarily at native speakers of English:

1. Be really careful about humour, especially humour that could be misread as being dismissive, insulting, or mockery. One reason for this is because, as is well known, email doesn't convey tone well at all. But in the case of this specific list, we are also dealing with a variety of different academic cultures – what comes across as normal bantering in a more free-rolling academic culture may appear to be extremely aggressive in another.
2. Be careful about allusions to pop culture, and national history and politics. Many people may not get them. But more importantly, allusions and inside jokes shared among a small group of people can quickly create a sense of exclusion among those who don't know the references being made.
3. Since this is an academic list, we will find ourselves disagreeing with each other, attempting to correct or improve each other's ideas, and so on. In keeping with (1), be careful about how you phrase these disagreements: again, what may seem like relatively light criticism in one academic culture may seem crushing in another; and especially if there are language issues involved, it can be difficult to clear things up. This doesn't mean that we can't criticize each other's ideas, but rather that we should always try to phrase this disagreement as constructively and supportively as possible.
4. Generally, try to write in short sentences and using common words (this is true, BTW, of all languages on the list): you are being read by people who are not as strong in your language as you are.
5. Always try to provide context for people: use more links to external sites than you might normally (e.g., to explain ideas and give examples). (O'Donnell, 2013a)

Infrastructure and Administration

Our final issue involved infrastructure and administration. Although GO::DH strives to recognize rather than try to resolve differences in language, practice, and resources among its members, we have found this most difficult in practice with regard to our administration. Although our membership and executive includes people from a much larger number of countries than is represented on Terras's map, all but one of the members of our administration are currently located in high-income economies: the great majority of our founding executive are resident in Canada, the United States, and Western Europe, while our current five-person steering committee consists of individuals from Canada (three), the United States (one), and Nigeria (one).

This distribution, even down to the relative over-representation of Canada-based scholars, closely reflects Fiormonte's analysis of the leadership of more traditional organizations in the digital humanities (see Table 1 in Fiormonte, 2012, with the qualifications in O'Donnell, 2013b) – though, in as much as 40% of our steering committee are native speakers of Spanish and only 20% are native speakers of English, we show considerably more linguistic diversity. In part, this may be a function either of the self-selecting nature of the founding executive (most of whom were part of common previous informal networks), or a legacy of the SIG's origins as an "outreach" initiative.

But it may also be a function of the difference in resources between high-income and middle-, lower-middle-, and low-income economies: because they have less access to cheap and reliable Internet bandwidth, researchers outside of high-income economies may be both less willing to put themselves forward for participation in the organization's administration and less able to participate in the leadership opportunities that exist. The relative cost and difficulty of participation in steering committee activities by our member in Nigeria, for example, is considerably higher than that of the other members based in the United States and Canada. Applications and channels of communication that are (in essence) free and reliable to researchers based in high-income economies (including chat and VOIP applications like Google Plus and Skype) are difficult and can be expensive to use in some lower-middle- and low-income economies. Despite several attempts through the year, for example, the GO::DH steering group has simply never been able to hold a synchronous meeting of the entire committee due to infrastructure difficulties in Nigeria. A potential member of the SIG administration from Cuba would find it even more difficult to participate in meetings held using any of the synchronous communication tools taken for granted by researchers in high-income economies, given that country's very limited bandwidth, and internal and externally imposed restrictions on access to common telecommunications applications and infrastructure.

We have, as of yet, been unable to solve this problem satisfactorily. Our attempts at asynchronous meetings (e.g., by email or other forms of messaging) have not been been very satisfactory and we have, as a result, tended instead to delegate research, decision, and execution of specific tasks to individuals on the steering committee – vitiating, in some sense, the advantage of a collective decision-making process. It is possible, of course, that this is an artifact of an executive that is primarily resident in high-income economies: a larger board with more experience working with less reliable and cheap infrastructure may also have better ideas – or more patience – for the administration of a virtual organization such as GO::DH using less bandwidth-intensive methods.

Conclusion

centerNet and Global Outlook::Digital Humanities are only two organizations that have contributed to the development of the digital humanities' recent sense of itself as a global discipline. And even then, their main contribution may be that they have helped establish a framework for activity that was already well under way within the community. centerNet is an organization that encourages collaboration among already existing institutions as well as the development of new centers by (generally quite experienced) digital humanities researchers. GO::DH, for its part, owes much of its initial success to the willingness of researchers to bring already existing globalization efforts (such as the World of DH and the conference of RedHD) under its umbrella. While both can claim some responsibility for raising issues of globalization and inter-regional collaboration to prominence within the discipline, neither can claim primary responsibility for the original development of this interest.

At the same time, however, the two were developed explicitly as ways of formally encouraging the development of networks among researchers and institutions in a global context. In both cases, the organizations began with researchers resident in high-income economies who, inspired in part by Terras's map, were interested in working with researchers and institutions across linguistic, regional, and economic boundaries – perhaps especially those located in Terras's "blank" areas. And while both initiatives were aware of the dangers involved, both nevertheless – perhaps unavoidably, given their initial composition – began with at least some sense of their mission as involving out-reach from "us" to "them": the expansion of the digital humanities as this was practiced among our collaborators in high-income economic regions to a broader group of poten-tial colleagues and collaborators in middle- and low-income economies.

Not surprisingly, in actual practice, we have found the "blank" areas to be anything but blank. While it remains the case that researchers active in the use of computation in the humanities less often self-identify as "digital humanists" outside of the high-income economic regions, this often has less to do with lack of interest or knowledge of the field than differences in definition, institutional structures, and, at times, a sense that they are less welcome or less able to participate in a field dominated organization-ally by researchers from high-income economies, and linguistically by English speakers.

The result is that both organizations have had to change their focus and assump-tions about what they were attempting to do and how the new collaborations they were proposing would work. And in both cases, one of the most important realizations has been that their work is less about building networks of common interest among disparate participants than about establishing supra-networks that are able to recog-nize and accept infrastructural, linguistic, financial, and conceptual differences among their constituents. At a relatively easy level, this means, for example, accepting that different regions of the world have, for a variety of institutional, historical, and economic reasons, different concepts of what a digital humanities "center" does and where it might be located. At a more difficult level, however, it might also mean

recognizing that differences in access to and the reliability of computational infrastructure also must be accepted and accommodated if collaboration between economic
regions is going to take place. Researchers working in middle-, and especially lower-
middle- and low-income economies, work in an environment that is simply different
from that of researchers in high-income economies – a fact that affects how each
group works, the types of problems they are interested in, the solutions they come up
with, and the nature of their contribution to the collaborations they participate in.
While we suspect there are few researchers anywhere, including in high-income economies, who do not wish that they had access to better, faster, cheaper, and more envi-
ronmentally friendly technology, the fact that some researchers have better access to
such infrastructure than others means that their work is different, not necessarily
better or normative.

All lessons we have learned from our (supra)-network-building activities extend
from this observation. Although we do not believe that the digital humanities' famous
"niceness" is a bad attribute, we have discovered that collaboration across boundaries
requires acknowledging the existence of differences of situation, opinion, and practice
that cannot always be resolved. Thus in the case of linguistic differences, GO::DH has
found that its most powerful solution to the problem of translation lies in accepting
that only the most important texts *must* be translated, and that translation and paraphrasing in such contexts is something members can donate as a contribution to the
community. Similarly, in the case of its management, centerNet realized that the benefits of a large board that adequately represents the diversity of its global constituency
outweigh those of a more focused but less diverse executive. The difficulties that arise
from this approach, however, are illustrated by the problems GO::DH has been having
in expanding the regional diversity of its current executive or working with the varying
access to cheap and reliable infrastructure among its current membership.

Finally, we find ourselves in agreement with Galina (2013a, 2013b) and Fiormonte
and colleagues (forthcoming) when they argue that this kind of work represents an
important disciplinary praxis. While the issues we discuss in this chapter are largely
organizational and focused on the processes rather than results of research collaboration, we believe that the digital humanities as a discipline is the better, in concrete
ways, for such efforts. Bringing researchers with different experiences, problems, and
solutions into contact with each other not only makes our work lives more pleasant, it
changes our understanding of the discipline by forcing us to recognize its contingent
nature: in a field that is often focused on standards, solutions, and methodology, it can
be useful to realize the extent to which the best solution or standard can vary depending
on the economic, geographical, linguistic, or institutional situation of the researcher
and his or her audience.

REFERENCES AND FURTHER READING

Ahlenius, H., and UNEP. 2012. Country income
groups (World Bank classification) | UNEP/
GRID-Arendal. Maps & Graphics Library. http://
www.grida.no/graphicslib/detail/country-

income-groups-world-bank-classification_1394
(accessed June 20, 2015).

Babalola, T. 2013. Factors hindering the absorption
of digital humanities in developing countries:

a focus on Nigeria. Presented at the CSDH-SCHN Congress 2013, June 5, Victoria.

Clavert, F. 2013. The digital humanities multicultural revolution did not happen yet. *L'histoire contemporaine à l'ère numérique*, April 26. http://www.clavert.net/the-digital-humanities-multicultural-revolution-did-not-happen-yet (accessed June 20, 2015).

Dacos, M. 2013. [globaloutlookDH-L] Presentation and concrete propositions. January 27. http://listserv.uleth.ca/pipermail/globaloutlookdh-l/2013-January/000188.html (accessed June 20, 2015).

Dacos, M. 2014. La stratégie du sauna finlandais. *Blogo Numericus*. http://blog.homo-numericus.net/article11138.html (accessed January 28, 2014).

Fiormonte, D. 2012. Towards and cultural critique of the digital humanities. In *Controversies around the Digital Humanities*, ed. M. Thaller. Historical Social Research / Historische Sozialforschung 37.1. Köln: QUANTUM and Zentrum für Historische Sozialforschung, 59–76.

Fiormonte, D. 2013. [globaloutlookDH-L] Waiting for God(o)h, January 20. http://listserv.uleth.ca/pipermail/globaloutlookdh-l/2013-January/000163.html (accessed June 20, 2015).

Fiormonte, D., Numerico, T., and Tomasi, F (forthcoming). Digital humanities from a global perspective. In *The Digital Humanist: A Critical Inquiry*. https://docs.google.com/document/d/1Us2BeEVuvadlZa87qeCMgHdtVwK8E5muQb34i0iU4Fk/edit.

Fraistat, N. 2012. The function of digital humanities centers at the present time. In *Debates in the Digital Humanities*, ed. M.K. Gold. Minneapolis: University of Minnesota Press, 281–91.

Galina, I. 2013a. Las humanidades digitales globales. *Humanidades Digitales: Blog colectivo de la Red de Humanidades Digitales de México*, November 8. http://humanidadesdigitales.net/blog/2013/11/08/las-humanidades-digitales-globales (accessed June 20, 2015).

Galina, I. 2013b. Is there anybody out there? building a global digital humanities community. *Humanidades Digitales: Blog colectivo de la Red de Humanidades Digitales de México*, July 19. http://humanidadesdigitales.net/blog/2013/07/19/is-there-anybody-out-there-building-a-global-digital-humanities-community (accessed June 20, 2015).

Gil, A., and Priego, E. 2013. Global perspectives: interview with Alex Gil. *4Humanities*. http://4humanities.org/2013/01/interview-with-alex-gil (accessed June 20, 2015).

Global Outlook::Digital Humanities. 2013a. About. *Global Outlook::Digital Humanities*. http://www.globaloutlookdh.org/about (accessed June 20, 2015).

Global Outlook::Digital Humanities. 2013b. Global Digital Humanities Essay Prize. *Global Outlook::Digital Humanities*. http://www.globaloutlookdh.org/global-outlookdigital-humanities-global-digital-humanities-essay-prize (accessed June 20, 2015).

Gold, M.K., ed. 2012. *Debates in the Digital Humanities*. Minneapolis: University of Minnesota Press.

International Telecommunication Union. 2011. *Measuring the Information Society 2011*. Geneva: International Telecommunication Union. http://www.itu.int/net/pressoffice/backgrounders/general/pdf/5.pdf (accessed June 20, 2015).

Internet World Stats. 2014. Internet users in Africa 2014-Q2. Internet World Stats. http://www.internetworldstats.com/stats1.htm (accessed June 20, 2015).

Nowviskie, B. 2014. On the origin of "hack" and "yack." Bethany Nowviskie. http://nowviskie.org/2014/on-the-origin-of-hack-and-yack (accessed June 20, 2015).

O'Donnell, D.P. 2012a. "There's no next about it": Stanley Fish, William Pannapacker, and the digital humanities as paradiscipline. *dpod Blog*, June 22. http://dpod.kakelbont.ca/2012/06/22/theres-no-next-about-it-stanley-fish-william-pannapacker-and-the-digital-humanities-as-paradiscipline (accessed June 20, 2015).

O'Donnell, D.P. 2012b. Global Outlook::Digital Humanities. Lethbridge: Alliance of Digital Humanities Organizations. https://www.dropbox.com/s/2mnbaqub6avxyr9/globaloutlookDigitalHumanities2.pdf?dl=0 (accessed June 20, 2015).

O'Donnell, D.P. 2013a. [globaloutlookDH-L] A revolution yet to happen, April 30. http://listserv.uleth.ca/pipermail/globaloutlookdh-l/2013-April/000319.html (accessed June 20, 2015).

O'Donnell, D.P. 2013b. The true north strong and hegemonic: or, why do Canadians seem to run DH. *dpod Blog*, March 7. http://dpod.kakelbont.ca/2013/03/07/the-true-north-strong-and-hegemonic-or-why-do-canadians-seem-to-run-dh (accessed June 20, 2015).

Scheinfeldt, T. 2010. Why digital humanities is "nice." *Found History*, May 26. http://www.foundhistory.org/2010/05/26 (accessed June 20, 2015).

Schreibman, S., Siemens, R., and Unsworth, J., eds. 2004. *A Companion to Digital Humanities*. Oxford: Blackwell.

Siemens, L. 2009. It's a team if you use "reply all": an exploration of research teams in digital humanities environments. *Literary and Linguistic Computing* 24 (2), 225–33. doi:10.1093/llc/fqp009.

Siemens, L., and Burr, E. 2013. A trip around the world: accommodating geographical, linguistic and cultural diversity in academic research teams. *Literary and Linguistic Computing* 28 (2), 331–43. doi:10.1093/llc/fqs018.

Terras, M. 2012. Quantifying digital humanities. Melissa Terras' blog. http://melissaterras.blogspot.ca/2012/01/infographic-quanitifying-digital.html (accessed June 20, 2015).

35

Gendering Digital Literary History: What Counts for Digital Humanities

Laura C. Mandell

> In many cutting-edge critical discourses – e.g., globalization theory – the speed with which women can drop off the map takes my breath away. (Susan Friedman, in Cvetkovich *et al.*, 2010:242)

Ever since Anne Snitow's "A Gender Diary" was published in 1990, we have noticed that feminist activists confront numerous double-binds and paradoxes. In the forum discussing whether the term "woman" can be used "as a sponsoring category" from which the epigraph comes, Susan Friedman uncovers such a double-bind with which I'll grapple here. In order to be published in print, the forum concluded, a feminist critique cannot pose as a recovery project alone, but instead must address multiple discourses. That is, as to "what counts" (per the title of this chapter), one needs to count higher, adding to the numbers of minorities addressed and theoretical approaches deployed. However, the minute one adds other critical discourses to feminism, women tend to disappear from the discussion, rendering recovery projects even more necessary. To repeat Freidman's insight once again, women stop counting as significant so easily that "it takes [your] breath away" (Cvetkovich *et al.*, 2010:242).

Two principles inform my analysis of the problem of the disappearance of women writers from systems of valuation via paradoxical necessity. First, an approach that is beneficially required of any literary criticism is what N. Katherine Hayles named "media-specific analysis, … a kind of criticism that pays attention to the material apparatus producing the literary work as a physical artifact":

> Lulled into somnolence by five hundred years of print, literary studies have been slow to wake up to the importance of MSA. Literary criticism and theory are shot through with

A New Companion to Digital Humanities, First Edition. Edited by Susan Schreibman, Ray Siemens, and John Unsworth.

unrecognized assumptions specific to print. Only now, as the new medium of electronic
textuality vibrantly asserts its presence, are these assumptions clearly coming into view.
(Hayles, 2002:29–30)

My second principle is that, while new media make it possible for these "unrecognized
assumptions" stemming from print culture to come into view, gender analysis makes
them salient. That is, print culture has absorbed and materialized earlier forms of
misogyny, putting it to its own uses, so that combining feminist with media-specific
analysis can provide a powerful tool for analyzing our own "somnolence" in order to
wakefully invent digital forms.

After showing that women writers are being recovered and forgotten in cycles,
both in print and potentially in digital media, I will investigate how print media
obfuscated itself as a medium, pretending to transfer intentions from one mind to
another, once and for all, by deploying the figure of woman as a scapegoat for the
material, ephemeral, and historically imbricated. Next, I'll examine two digital
projects that are aimed at recovering women writers which do more than give us
new content: they perform structural work, attempting to combat that paradoxical
feminist necessity to produce a high count of women writers while simultaneously
valuing them individually. Finally, I'll argue for the thick contextualization of
women writers even amidst the push to analyze big data, but will also add my hope
that feminists make major interventions in data mining and topic modeling. Taken
as a whole, this chapter demonstrates that feminist digital literary history needs
to perform media as well as gender analysis, as called for by Susan Brown and
colleagues (2006:320).

Cycles of Forgetting

In 1989, Roger Lonsdale published his Oxford collection, *Eighteenth-Century Women's
Poetry*, introducing it by not only remarking how little was known among English
professors about the topic, but also pointing to an earlier moment, the end of the
eighteenth century, when there were so many publishing women poets that no one
thought they would ever disappear from our literary purview:

> Reviewing [one of over thirty collections] of verse [written by women in the 1790s],
> Ralph Griffiths ... felt able to [pronounce,] "it is no longer a question, whether woman
> *is* or *is not* inferior to man in natural ability, or less capable of excelling in mental accom-
> plishments." (*Monthly Review*, 1798, quoted in Lonsdale, 1989:xxi)

"In retrospect," Lonsdale adds, "Griffith's complacency ... must seem ludicrously
unjustified. ... Anyone admitting to an interest in eighteenth-century women poets
will soon learn to live with the politely sceptical question, 'Were there any?'" (Lonsdale,
1989:xxi). Despite the fact that there were hundreds of them – the Cardiff Corvey
Women Writers on the Web database lists 1065 works by women published between
1790 and 1835[1] – at some point in the evolution of literary history, these women
writers ceased to count.

In 1998, Cathy Davidson made a claim very similar to the one made by Ralph Giffiths in 1798. Describing publications around 1985, she was confident enough to assert that the publishing of women writers had triumphed; they would not be forgotten again:

[Nina Baym and Jane Tomkins] worked to make visible a woman's tradition in American literature ... Series at Beacon Press, the Feminist Press, Oxford University Press (notably The Schomburg Library of Nineteenth-Century Black Women Writers), and Rutgers University Press – to name just a few – changed the canon of American literature. (Davidson, 1998:447–8)

Yet despite this celebration of a changed canon, performing data-mining techniques to count the writers in anthologies that have been published over the last decades reveals that women writers have not yet made significant inroads (Levy and Perry, 2015). And feminists were even after 1985 still engaged in recovering forgotten women writers, especially early modern women writers who had "published" in manuscript form, not print (Ezell, 1993). Writing in the 1990s, Kathryn Sutherland expressed hope for bringing women's work to light via digital media, based on her perception that print had failed to do so:

[I]f computers do not substitute for books, they may substitute for the absence of books; and this is what concerns me as a scholar working to rehabilitate women's writings. (Sutherland, 1993:53)

But many of the projects undertaken in the 1990s fell by the wayside, like Sutherland's own Project Electra, assimilated by the Oxford Text Archive with, as far as I can tell, its origins as a feminist project unmarked.

Many digital recovery projects of women's writing have, like *Project Electra*, never realized their ambitions: the *Perdita Project* has been commercialized – it is now sold by Adam Matthew Digital – and *Chawton House Novels Online*, including so many women writers, has been taken down since Pickering & Chatto began publishing it as a printed series. Some digital anthologies do exist and persist: the *Women Writers Online* project (http://www.wwp.northeastern.edu/wwo), discussed in more detail below; Mary Mark Ockerbloom's *Celebration of Women Writers* (http://digital.library.upenn. edu/women/writers.html), the *Victorian Women Writers Project* (http://webapp1.dlib. indiana.edu/vwwp/welcome.do), recently revitalized thanks to the efforts of Michelle Dalmau; my own *Poetess Archive* (http://www.poetessarchive.org), its revitalization under way. But several have not been updated since sometime between 2000 and 2005: the Emory *Women Writers Project* (http://womenwriters.library.emory.edu), *British Romantic Women Writers at Davis* (http://digital.lib.ucdavis.edu/projects/bwrp). *Voices from the Gaps: Women Writers and Artists of Color* (http://voices.cla.umn.edu) was last updated in 2009 – these are not living projects. We have sites giving us diaries and letters by women writers,[2] and many individual women writers exist at http://www. luminarium.org, an anthology; we have a good Emily Dickinson site, despite the fact that her works themselves are put up on separate sites by Amherst and Harvard (http:// www.emilydickinson.org); *Woolf Online* houses only one novel (http://www.woolfonline. com); an Elizabeth Barrett Browning site (http://ebbarchive.org/index.php) is as yet rather small in scope; and a site about the relatively unknown Baroness Elsa von

Freytag-Loringhoven (http://digital.lib.umd.edu/transition?pid=umd:50580) gives us many versions of her poems, but her oeuvre is quite small. With the exception of the *Willa Cather Archive* (http://cather.unl.edu) and a very promising *Jane Austen's Fiction Manuscripts* site (http://www.janeausten.ac.uk/index.html), currently under way, we have nothing as yet on the scale of the Whitman, Blake, or Rossetti archives, or the sites for Shakespeare, Thomas Gray, Herman Melville, to name a few more – no sites, that is, which focus on bringing us a woman's entire oeuvre, through many editions and revisions, along with all her letters, diaries, and other writings.

Many do-it-yourself (DIY) 1990s-looking sites have disappeared, as evinced by all the dead links bedeviling a 2001 article by Georgianna Ziegler called "Women writers online: an annotated bibliography of web resources" (http://extra.shu.ac.uk/emls/06-3/ziegbib.htm) and the minority pages at Alan Liu's *Voice of the Shuttle* (http://vos.ucsb.edu/browse.asp?id=2746). Some persist without having been completed in any way, currently out of date: for Julian of Norwich, Margery Kempe, Mary Leapor, Ann Yearsley, Anna Barbauld, Mary Hays, Jean Toomer, and Zora Neale Hurston. Amy Earhart talks about early hopes for opening the canon via the web and the gradual disappearance of those DIY projects as well as the sheer dwarfing of them in relation to the big well-funded projects that simply reiterated the masculinist canon:

> While many early digitizers of texts believed in the web as a space in which the canon might be broken … , [w]ith limited exceptions, a majority of early projects reinforced canonical bias. (Earhart, 2012:312–13)

Thus, while scholars from 1798 to 1998 have declared that the absence of women writers is a condition that we can or have already overcome, this absence threatens to persist, in both print anthologies and the Web taken as a whole, as if it were one great anthology.

And recovery projects are not in great demand. In the forum quoted in the epigraph to this chapter, "Women as the sponsoring category," Ann Cvetkovich, Susan Fraiman, Susan Stanford Friedman, and Miranda M. Yaggi seem to agree that, as Cvetkovitch puts it, "projects that focus exclusively on women writers are limited if they presume that a history of women's writing is sufficient justification for the project" (Cvetkovich *et al.*, 2010:248). For, Yaggi adds:

> while we could once justify grouping women writers together under the rubric "women's writing" by a sense of their shared oppression, such a justification no longer works. We need to seek other, more broadly based frameworks … (Cvetkovich *et al.*, 2010:236)

The category "woman" can't underwrite scholarship anymore. Dealing with women's oppression is not enough. Though working to bring the history of women's writing to the fore is important, it is only really justified if it is digital: Yaggi adds, "Even the word 'recovery' can elicit knee-jerk distaste or disinterest if not immediately qualified as 'digital' and disassociated from earlier [print] modes of recovery" (Cvetkovich *et al.*, 2010:248). Such "disassociation" involves, again, broadening one's interests to other "fields of inquiry such as the history of print culture, science and technology, or transatlantic studies" (Cvetkovich *et al.*, 2010:248). However, if there are, as I have suggested, cycles of forgetting women writers, we disassociate from recovery at our peril. Moreover, two different speakers at this forum in two different contexts insist that it is only by expanding to include other fields that feminist work becomes "publishable" (Cvetkovich *et al.*, 2010:247,249). Why do they privilege producing a published book, so much so that they are encouraging feminists to forgo participating in the unpopular task of recovering women writers and to publish a printed book instead?

A printed book is a thing, enabling it to be a monument, but, when formed into a disciplinary monument, it is a decontextualized and decontextualizing thing. Print offers a soundless, supposedly bodiless, and allegedly eternal venue for articulation, and, as Pierre Bourdieu puts it, "eternal life is one of the most sought-after social privileges" of any class, intellectual or otherwise (1979:72). Transcendental ambitions, borne and bred by the book, I would argue, lead these thinkers away from recovery projects onto attempts at monumentalizing. But even though the participants in the forum want eternal life for feminism, the attempt to achieve eternal life via the printed book, is, I will now demonstrate, intrinsically inimical to women writers. (A century from now, will there be anthologies of twenty-first-century criticism that include as many women writers as men, some valued as major?) It is precisely the desire for transcendence as it is fed by the printed book, I will now show, that denigrates women writers, demotes them to the merely ephemeral and minor.

Forgotten by Print

In the process of mediation, when one is writing and publishing a book, there is never a moment without concern for one's own particular immortality in, via, and through the act of mediation. In a chapter of my 1999 book *Misogynous Economies*, I argued that the desire for immortality through print has motivated the systematic erasure of women's literary history from anthologies and textbooks (Mandell, 1999:107–28). So, for example, during the time that disciplinary anthologies were coming into existence, creating with their tables of contents the monuments of literature strewn around the field of English Studies, Robert Southey published two different anthologies. One, the three-volume collection called *Specimens of the Later English Poets, with preliminary notices*, lists 213 authors, many women among them, in an index that doubles as his table of contents, listing the volume in which they appear and the date of their death. In a passage playing upon the meaning of the greek word *anthologia*, "a collection of flowers,"[3] Southey introduces his *Specimens* by explaining that he is simply collecting authors of various periods so that people can see what ordinary, or even bad, writing was like during older periods of time:

> Many worthless versifyers are admitted among the English Poets, by ... charity towards the dead. ... There were other reasons for including here the reprobate, as well as the elect. My business was to collect specimens as for a *hortus siccus*; not to cull flowers as for an anthology. ... The taste of the publick [in previous generations] may better be estimated from indifferent Poets than from good ones; because the former write for their contemporaries, the latter for posterity. (Southey, 1807:iv–v)

This is not an anthology of living but a collection of dead flowers, specimens of what was once popular but is definitively not timeless literature. For that, one must go to Southey's 1831 collection of poets, *Select Works of the British Poets, from Chaucer to Jonson, with Biographical Sketches*, containing 21 male poets, whose genuine, enduring fame "has no present tense" because it extends now and forever. Ripped out of the womb of historical context, which is itself dead and withered, the great writers become part of a tradition, transcendent, immortal. The anthologizers Southey and also William Hazlitt constituted the discipline of English literature as transcendent traditions, and they accomplished this task by turning women writers into mere historical context, "the reprobate" in relation to the canon, never "the elect" (Southey, 1807:iv).

In a related argument, Julia Flanders points out another way that print culture embodies women writers in contrast to transcendentalizing men. Early modern women writers have not been edited in the way that men have, many only ever having been printed once, during their lifetimes. There simply are not printed editions that can be compared in an apparatus. In contrast, works by men have been published and republished. Consequently, the editing which canonical male authors typically undergo – editors listing "accidents" of local, contemporaneous publishing, and variants among various witnesses – transforms the material document into a timeless text containing the author's immortal intention, having sloughed off all contingent meanings. The historical context of each individual edition is cleared away, relegated to notes that elucidate meaning (Flanders, 1997:133–4). Again, women writers only appear in the materiality of the single print run. Because of the way that, in masculinist editing theory, "the text of the author" is conceived as "universalized and disembodied textuality," any "physical document" in which it was originally embodied is conceived as "corruption and debasement" and placed firmly "in the realm of the monstrous and the deviant"; it is seen as "an unchaste female body" that can be "chastise[d]" in order to produce a text reflecting pure, disembodied authorial intent (Flanders, 1997:129). Women's writing conveniently falls into the category of the monstrous and unchaste, the reprobate.

What Southey's anthologizing activity demonstrates is that saving male writers in disciplinary anthologies and authoritative editions is not enough by itself to establish their work as eternal: there must be concomitantly a production of collections containing works of merely historical interest and facsimile editions. Sexism is served by the media of mass-printed anthologies and anthological textbooks as well as "authoritative" editions – not the medium of print per se, but the medium in the forms that we have constructed it in order to ground the discipline of literary history. This sexism makes women writers, whose writings are coded as mere historical ephemera and purely physical, disappear habitually, regularly, and cyclically (Ezell, 1990; Woods, 1994; Mandell, 1999). In reviewing the Brown *Women Writers Project*, Susanne Woods asks, "how can we recover early women's writing in English once and for all?" (Woods, 1994:19).

Is it in fact the case that women's writings must come, in the end, not to count after publication, only ever recovered and re-recovered, whether digitally or in print? Do we have to keep re-finding it? This question is crucial to digital literary historians because answering it will suggest, I hope, how to make feminist digital recovery projects that actually achieve what they set out to do: recover women writers for literary history, if not once and for all, then more permanently than has so far been accomplished. Can the creators of historical digital archives make women count, and, if so, how?

Digital De-contextualization

A print book's ambition to exist as an eternal monument problematizes its capacity to recover women writers "once and for all," since women must be defined as ephemera in order to provide a necessary contrast and contain the threatened return of materiality. Does the same structure arise in digital media? Though not rock-solid in the matter of monuments, the "flickering signifiers" of digital media nonetheless live in an allegedly disembodied sphere (Hayles, 1999). Encoding digital editions in eXtensible Markup Language (XML), and particularly in the set of tags offered by the Text Encoding Initiative Consortium (http://www.tei-c.org), does entail a level of abstraction away from the physical and from presentation of text on the screen: this too, as Alan Liu has successfully argued, entails the ambition to achieve transcendence (2004), the very same ambition, I would argue, that prompted coding women's writing as of merely historical interest in print.

Additionally, the notion of gathering a "grand" archive of materials – on a digital scale – participates in a kind of "monumental logic," as Wernimont suggests (2013:5–6). Like Ellen Rooney, Wernimont condemns merely additive projects whereby the goal is to produce the highest number of women writers published online. Clearly she is right: discriminatory sexual difference informs ways of counting, given that male monuments are built by adding numbers of text to a single man's oeuvre, whereas the monumentality of feminist archives consists in increasing the number of authors, adding to women writers continuously and making it difficult for users to know how much attention to give to any individual writer. After all, too much information is as bad as too little if you cannot tell what counts as meaningful, or how to account for significance in a way that isn't about numbers. A recent critic has spoken of digital media (databases, Callahan offers) as providing "gardens of history" (Hatfield, 2006, quoted in Callahan, 2010:4), indicating that we may not have come very far from the anthological model: we can say about both databases and anthologies that we have a few great men in a database/anthology, each with many works, and many women in a database/print collection, each one with few works. Wernimont insists that digital projects of women writers must "facilitate access by helping users sort through an abundance of data and push against monumentalism in some way" (2013:6).

What way? How can we push against monumentalism? And if we push against it partly by recovering numbers of women writers, what place is left for a field of literature in which each woman writer can count? Flanders notices a paradox connected to the placing of women's writing: if we insist on its materiality and presence by putting forward a high number of women authors, thwarting transcendental ambitions by refusing to edit these writers in an authoritative, disembodied way, then we feed into the norm according to which women's writing is material and men's is not, but if we edit them according to the standards of authoritative editions, we perpetuate the set of standards according to which most women writers are denigrated as merely ephemeral, counting not as literature but as historically interesting (Flanders, 1997:137,140–1).

Re-contextualizing

The problem of valuing women writers is as follows: for women writers to be counted, one must create for them the authoritative editions of writing that denigrate the material body, disregarding the specificity of gender, or worse, abjecting it, scapegoating it as if it were to blame for mortality, for materiality as such. Susan Belasco helpfully designates the apparatus of authoritative editions an "infrastructure," demonstrating that, without such an infrastructure, women writers are not discussed by literary critics anywhere near as often as canonical male writers, despite the wealth of literary criticism that already exists for their works (Belasco, 2009:332). Changing our focus from "authoritative edition," a print hangover, to "infrastructure" more broadly allows us to think of alternatives to an apparatus that necessitates a disembodied text or "the work," as editorial theory designates it.[4] It also enables us to think digitally. Two feminist digital projects reconceive the infrastructure of women's writing: (1) *Orlando: Women's Writing in the British Isles from the Beginning to the Present* (http://orlando.cambridge.org), and (2) the *Women Writers Project*, formerly at Brown and currently at Northeastern University (http://www.northeastern.edu/nulab/women-writers-project-2).

The *Orlando* project effectively dismantles the canon and makes women count by virtue of its infrastructure, both socioeconomic and digital. Because it was generously funded, the *Orlando* project was able to hire many able researchers to deeply contextualize 1139 women writers. They are deeply contextualized via

> two distinct types of documents. The first type consists of sometimes extensive biocritical articles on individual writers (primarily British women writers but also a selection of male and international women writers), which are deeply tagged for structure (e.g., paragraphs, document divisions), content (e.g., names, organizations), and interpretive material (e.g., political affiliations, sexual identity, occupation; authorship issues, intertextuality, landmark texts). The second type consists of briefer records of related material, of the historical landmarks, and minutiae that contextualize our view of literary history. (Grundy *et al.*, 2000:269)

In terms of chronology, women authors writing at the same time as Maria Abdy, for instance, would share all the contextual events that are listed when one generates a chronology for her (Figure 35.1).

Thus Abdy's world is given a thick description, but that description applies to many others of her era as well as to all the women writers comprising her context. The intertextuality tag is arguably the most interesting tag in *Orlando*'s semantic markup: here women's writing is connected to the writings of others, male and female, who are quoted, addressed, or to whom each writer alludes (Brown *et al.*, 2004). *Orlando* is not a collection of writings by women but rather an apparatus for women writers. The infrastructure of *Orlando*, I would suggest, is specifically designed to make a high number of women writers count.

The textbase of the *Women Writers Project* (WWP), called *Women Writers Online* (WWO), presents women's writing: currently 150 texts, and it is averaging 15 new texts per year. In the WWO the materiality of the texts is preserved – the long s, for instance, as well as original spellings. But it does not merely offer facsimile editions.

Figure 35.1 Chronology of Maria Abdy from *Orlando*.

The texts are typed and so are analyzable via the visualization tools now available at WWO. They are also deeply encoded using a variant of the TEI specific to the WWO. This means that a great deal of care has been taken to present each text; in fact, the editors are paid for their work, and Oxford University Press occasionally publishes a volume to meet the demand of classes and researchers. In addition to the care with which each individual writer is treated, the WWP has been awarded several important grants. Grants typically de-privilege the work of archiving women writers because the National Endowment for the Humanities (NEH) Office of Digital Humanities supports tool building but not archive building, innovation but not sustenance (Earhart, 2012:314). As Susan Brown and colleagues point out, "serving" or "delivering" women's writing (or indeed any kind of writing) in digital media is coded a feminine task, such service bordering on the servile (Brown *et al.*, 2008:37). It is by virtue of code development and tool building that the WWP has been funded by grants (Wernimont, 2013:15,18).

We now have these two exemplary projects, *Orlando* and *Women Writers Online*. So now what? "Is the mere presence," Wernimont asks, " – the fact of being there, of having women's work exist in digital archives – enough to address the continued marginalization of women's writing?" (2013:4). It is not enough: as every good digital humanist knows, "build it and they will come" is a dangerous philosophy. But *Orlando* in particular, with its interpretive tagset, does more than simply proffer digital biographies of women: it participates in "the politics of knowledge representation" (Brown *et al.*, 2006:323); it provides what Wernimont (2013:8) calls "a feminist response to the elisions at the heart of sorting and editing". In fact, Brown, Clements, and Grundy say, "we were trying to devise a tagset that would make visible what previous literary historical methods had made invisible or excluded":

> In contrast to the sorting out of women in older literary histories which excluded them, we were trying to sort women into the version of literary history we were constructing. (Brown *et al.*, 2006:321)

The intertextuality tag mentioned above provides just one example of rewriting women's literary history such that women are not seen as forming a tradition, given each writer's intertextual connections with men's writing as much or more so than with other women (Brown *et al.*, 2004:197). Both *Orlando* and the *Women Writers Project* have been able to pay their contributors, and doing so has made it necessary for both archives to charge subscription fees. It is up to us now, as a community of scholars who care about the future shape of literature, to insist that our libraries subscribe, to pay the fees that make possible this new kind of infrastructure, crucial to recuperating literary history. In this respect, consumption is a form of production: we are co-designing the archive constituted by the Internet as consumers who insist upon the presence of these projects.

Big Data Versus Encoded Data

I wish to conclude by discussing countlessness, a new type of monumentalism – digital, this time – which threatens once again to devalue women writers. Why? 1139 in *Orlando* + 150 in WWO = 1289. When marshaled in huge numbers, women writers are not countless enough: in the absolute biggest datasets, the number of women is dwarfed in comparison to every man who ever wrote and becomes a small if not insignificant subset of the data stream. Margaret Ezell has successfully argued that twentieth-century anthologies erased early modern women writers by focusing on print culture. But the digital has similar problems, she suggests. "The electronic 'archive' model" of digital publishing – online editions which are successful "because of their size, scope, and ability to be all inclusive" – that publishing model threatens to erase a substantial portion of women's literary history just as twentieth-century anthologies recovering women writers had done insofar as they privileged print. Early modern women writers, she has shown, published in manuscript, and sometimes wrote domestic volumes not meant for circulation at all. These manuscripts should not on that account be designated either non-literary or uninteresting:

> Because of this easy transference of older critical terms and textual conceptualizations into a new editorial media, I would argue that editors of electronic projects ... need to be more aware of the significance of the materiality of texts, of the social conventions of handwritten culture as they may differ from print cultures, and the multiple ways in which these unique, single copy-texts are of interest and value to scholars. (Ezell, 2010:108)

For Ezell, refusing to "'edit' out the richness and complexity" of these manuscripts' "way of communicating" is a means for "positive feminist interrogation of editorial principles" – again, essential to making women writers count in literary history by paying attention to medium.

However, we confront here another double-bind – this time between the monumentality of countlessness and careful editing. Neither careful editing nor even producing large numbers of women writers will avoid replicating the print invisibility of women as we transfer the archive of women's writing and history to the Internet insofar as digital humanists focus their attention on algorithmically exploring big data. Bethany Nowviskie has noticed in comments on a blog posting by Miriam Posner (2012) about women encoders the small number of women who are involved in topic modeling, data mining, and highly mathematical, computational work in general. If feminists only create archives and do not then take the further step of doing cutting-edge research by learning how to use new tools for exploring them, we risk seeming only to *serve* in the ways that editorial work itself is feminized and denigrated as service in the field of literary studies. As we code innumerable documents in the archive of women's history, coding them in ways that make them theoretically interesting, let us also perform cutting-edge digital research on these very sites, for then, in order to talk about significant results, the world will have to talk about Felicia Hemans instead of Herman Melville. Rich encoding of a high count of women's texts is crucially important at our moment and can work to shape the literary history that is constituted by the Web. But so is trying out algorithms and innovative design on the resulting archives, no matter how relatively small.

There is a kind of misogyny accompanying the printed book that perpetuates this double-bind which insists that, to overcome sexism, feminists must count higher and lower at the same time. We continuously find ourselves caught in the paradoxical necessity to bring us many to make women significant, and yet focus on one or two lest significance is lost. The very same misogynist economy threatens us in the digital realm as well. Most recovery projects give us large numbers of women writers without caring about and enhancing the significance of each one, a problem confronted by *Orlando* and *Women Writers Online*, through thick contextualization and careful editing, respectively. But the digital adds a new threat to render women writers invisible: its valuation of countlessness. Big data threatens to eradicate the history of women writers altogether, given that women originally published in small print runs and via manuscript circulation. The answer is not to do nothing in despair: it is both/and. Just as the paradoxical need to bring us many women and yet focus on them all was a feat that has been accomplished by *Orlando* through mechanical means for individuation, we can confront the new double-bind as well. No matter how much or how many, data can be infinitely atomized and analyzed: we need to perform cutting-edge research on archives of women writers, even if those archives do not offer the countlessness of big data. Then, a scholar looking back from the year 3000, summarizing important research results, will notice that women's history was exceedingly important to the world of the twenty-first century. "The most important theoretical and technical advances," she will say, "were discovered in exploring women's literary history."

NOTES

1 The CW3 database is freely searchable on the web: https://www2.shu.ac.uk/corvey/CW3/. Some of the works listed in this database are available via the Nebraska Corvey Novels Project: http://english.unl.edu/corvey/html/Projects/CorveyNovels/CorveyNovels Index.htm.

2 There are excellent sites for the letters of Lady Mary Wortley Montagu (http://andromeda.rutgers.edu/~jlynch/Texts/montagu-letters.html), Elizabeth Barrett Browning (http://digitalcollections.baylor.edu/cdm/landingpage/collection/ab-letters), and George Eliot (http://www.warwickshire.gov.uk/georgeeliot), as well as diaries for the Irish writers Dorothy Stopford Price (http://dh.tcd.ie/pricediary) and Mary Martin (http://dh.tcd.ie/martindiary).

3 "Collection of flowers" is the first definition of the term "anthology" in its list of meanings in Samuel Johnson's *Dictionary* of 1755.

4 Such a move resembles arguments against seeking authorial intent as an editing practice by Jerome McGann, D.F. MacKenzie, and others (Flanders, 1997:132).

REFERENCES AND FURTHER READING

Belasco, S. 2009. The responsibility is ours: the failure of infrastructure and the limits of scholarship. *Legacy* 26 (2), 329–36.

Bourdieu, P. 1979. *Distinction: A Social Critique of the Judgement of Taste*. Trans. Richard Nice (1984). Cambridge, MA: Harvard University Press.

Brown, S., Clements, P., and Grundy, I. 2004. Intertextual encoding in the writing of women's literary history. *Computers and the Humanities* 38, 191–206.

Brown, S., Clements, P., and Grundy, I. 2006. Sorting things in: feminist knowledge representation and changing modes of scholarly production. *Women's Studies International Forum* 29, 317–25.

Brown, S., Clements, P., and Grundy, I. 2007a. An introduction to the Orlando project. *Tulsa Studies in Women's Literature* 26, 127–34.

Brown, S., Clements, P., Grundy, I., Balzas, S., and Antoniuk, J. 2007b. The story of the Orlando project: personal reflections. *Tulsa Studies in Women's Literature*, 26 (1), 135–43.

Brown, S., Smith, M.N., Mandell, L., et al. 2008. Agora.techno.phobia.phila2: feminist critical inquiry, knowledge building, digital humanities. *Digital Humanities 2008: Book of Abstracts*. University of Oulu. http://www.ekl.oulu.fi/dh2008/Digital%20Humanities%202008%20Book%20of%20Abstracts.pdf (accessed March 28, 2014).

Callahan, V. 2010. *Reclaiming the Archive: Feminism and Film History*. Detroit: Wayne State University Press.

Cohoon, J.M., and Aspray, W. 2006. *Women and Information Technology: Research on Underrepresentation*. Cambridge, MA: MIT Press.

Cvetkovich, A., Fraiman, S., Friedman, S.S., and Yaggi, M.M. 2010. Woman as the sponsoring category: a forum on academic feminism and British women's writing. *Partial Answers* 8 (2), 235–54.

Davidson, C. 1998. Preface: no more separate spheres! *American Literature* 70 (3), 443–63.

Dryden, A. 2014. Dissent unheard of. *Model View Culture: Technology, Culture, and Diversity Media*, Mythology Issue (4), 17 March 2014. http://modelviewculture.com/pieces/dissent-unheard-of (accessed March 24, 2014).

Earhart, A. 2012. Can information be unfettered? Race and the new digital humanities canon. In *Debates in the Digital Humanities*, ed. M.K. Gold. Minneapolis: University of Minnesota Press, 309–18. http://dhdebates.gc.cuny.edu/debates (accessed March 28, 2014).

Ezell, M.J.M. 1990. The myth of Judith Shakespeare: creating the canon of women's literature. *New Literary History* 21 (3), 579–92.

Ezell, M.J.M. 1993. *Writing Women's Literary History*. Baltimore: Johns Hopkins University Press.

Ezell, M.J.M. 1999. *Social Authorship and the Advent of Print*. Baltimore: Johns Hopkins University Press.

Ezell, M.J.M. 2010. Editing early modern Women's manuscripts: theory, electronic editions, and the accidental copy-text. *Literature Compass* 7 (2), 102–9, http://onlinelibrary.wiley.com/doi/10.1111/j.1741-4113.2009.00682.x/full (accessed March 29, 2014).

Flanders, J. 1997. The body encoded: questions of gender and the electronic text. In *Electronic Text: Investigations in Method and Theory*, ed. K. Sutherland. Oxford: Clarendon Press, 127–44.

Grundy, I., Clements, P., Brown, S., et al. 2000. Dates and chronstructures: dynamic chronology in the Orlando project. *Literary and Linguistic Computing*, 15 (3), 265–89.

Hatfield, J. 2006. Imagining future gardens of history. *Camera Obscura* 21 (2/62), 185–9.

Hayles, N.K. 1999. *How We Became Posthuman: Virtual Bodies in Cyberspace*. Chicago: University of Chicago Press.

Hayles, N.K. 2002. *Writing Machines*. Cambridge, MA: MIT Press.

Haynes, D.J., Keyek-Franssen, D., and Molinaro, N. 2005. *Frontiers: A Journal of Womens Studies*, 26 (1). Special Issue: Gender, race, and information technology.

Lerman, N., Mohun, A.P., and Oldenziel, R. 1997. *Technology and Culture*, 38 (1). Special Issue: Gender analysis and the history of technology.

Levy, M., and Perry, M. 2015. Distantly reading the Romantic canon: quantifying gender in current anthologies. *Women's Writing* 22 (2), 132–55.

Liu, A. 2004. Transcendental data: toward a cultural history and aesthetics of the new encoded discourse. *Critical Inquiry* 31 (1), 49–84.

Lonsdale, R., ed. 1989. *Eighteenth Century Women Poets: An Oxford Anthology*. New York: Oxford University Press.

Mandell, L. 1999. *Misogynous Economies: The Business of Literature in Eighteenth-Century Britain*. Lexington: University Press of Kentucky.

Posner, M. 2012. Some things to think about before you exhort everyone to code. Miriam Posner: Blog, 29 February 2012. http://miriamposner.com/blog/some-things-to-think-about-before-you-exhort-everyone-to-code (accessed March 28, 2014).

Snitow, A. 1990. A gender diary. In *Conflicts in Feminism*, ed. M. Hirsch and E.F. Keller. New York: Routledge.

Southey, R. 1807. *Specimens of the Later English Poets, with preliminary notices*. London: Longman, Hurst, Rees, and Orme. http://reader.digitale-sammlungen.de/resolve/display/bsb10750264.html (accessed March 27, 2014).

Sutherland, K. 1993. Challenging assumptions: women writers and new technology. In *The Politics of the Electronic Text*, ed. W. Chernaik, C. Davis, and M. Deegan. London: University of London Centre for English Studies, 53–67.

Wajcman, J. 2004. *TechnoFeminism*. Malden, MA: Polity Press.

Wernimont, J. 2013. Whence feminism? Assessing feminist interventions in digital literary archives. *DHQ: Digital Humanities Quarterly*, 7 (1). http://digitalhumanities.org:8080/dhq/vol/7/1/000156/000156.html (accessed March 11, 2014).

Wernimont, J., and Flanders, J. 2010. Feminism in the age of digital archives: the Women Writers Project. *Tulsa Studies in Women's Literature* 29 (2), 425–35.

Woods, S. 1994. Recovering the past, discovering the future: the Brown University Women Writers Project. *South Central Review* 11 (2), 17–23.

36

The Promise of the Digital Humanities and the Contested Nature of Digital Scholarship

William G. Thomas III

Whether engaged in history, literary criticism, philosophy, or philology, scholars in the digital humanities have been concerned with reshaping their scholarly activity and their institutional structures for a natively digital world. They have been open to multiple forms of analysis, to sharing sources and materials (data), and to adopting large-scale, distributed models of scholarship. They have proceeded from an important recognition: that we are now in an era of capaciousness, of ubiquitous storage, of networked information, and of unprecedented access. Rather than orienting scholarship around a model of scarce materials, limited access, and expert gatekeeping, the digital humanities at its most vibrant has been about widening the scope of the humanities, opening access to sources, and broadening definitions of scholarly activity.

As an example, in 2011, the University of Nebraska–Lincoln started an experimental project called the *History Harvest*. Its main objective was to digitize, collect, curate, and interpret family and community history. Every year students, working with expert faculty, select a community to engage with and undertake a "harvest" of family letters, photographs, stories, and objects. In 2012, the *History Harvest* focused on North Omaha, birthplace of Malcolm X, a jazz hub in the twenties, and a terminal point for much of the Great Migration. The students invited anyone to bring their family records for discussion and digitization. Dozens of North Omaha residents brought their history: church records, military records, jazz albums, photographs, and homestead titles. These records were shared, discussed, documented, and digitized.

One individual, Warren Taylor, brought his great-great-grandmother's pewter folding cup that she carried as a slave in the fields. He also brought her penny, an 1840 "Liberty" penny that she carried with her, a symbol of eventual freedom. Both had been passed down for generations in the family.

A New Companion to Digital Humanities, First Edition. Edited by Susan Schreibman, Ray Siemens, and John Unsworth.
© 2016 John Wiley & Sons, Ltd. Published 2016 by John Wiley & Sons, Ltd.

The animating premise of the *History Harvest*, like many digital humanities research projects, is that our digital heritage is fundamentally skewed toward government and elite sources. The base research being conducted in the *History Harvest* is, therefore, aimed at archival first-order work of digital capture, encoding, and sharing. Building a publicly accessible collection, the project can provide a foundation for the generation of future scholarship on a range of subjects, places, and periods. But, like the digital humanities writ large, the *History Harvest* will reach fruition when the larger community takes advantage of the specifically digital nature of the collection in order to create new forms of historical discovery and argument. Like many other digital projects, the first-order effort at digitization, collection, and assembly of materials serves multiple worthy purposes. If successful, the project might open up digital humanities methods to smaller partnering institutions, sustain a robust hub of scholars, and expose fresh archives for inquiry at multiple scales of analysis. Although promising and opportunistic, such projects should lead ultimately *toward* digitally native interpretive scholarship.

Yet, paradoxically, the 20-year surge in the digital humanities – from 1993 to 2013 – has produced relatively little interpretive or argumentative scholarship. In this first phase of the digital humanities, scholars produced innovative and sophisticated hybrid works of scholarship, blending archives, tools, commentaries, data collections, and visualizations. For the most part in the disciplines, however, few of these works have been reviewed or critiqued. Because the disciplines expect interpretation, argument, and criticism, it could be argued that digital humanists have not produced enough digital interpretive scholarship, and what we have produced has not been absorbed into the scholarly disciplines.

At the core of this matter of concern lies a twofold contest over the nature of scholarship. Between the core disciplines and the digital humanities there is a difference in kind over whether digital works constitute scholarship. Within the digital humanities, there is a difference in degree over what constitutes digital scholarship. In the next phase of the digital humanities, the contested nature of this twofold problem deserves our attention. Scholars might build bridges to the core disciplines in ways that define their works and give shape to digital scholarship. We might ask what forms of scholarly expression and communication are suited to the digital environment and what qualities and properties do digital works possess. What components characterize digital scholarship? What types of data do digital works feature and how are they arranged? What is the nature of their interpretive salience? How do they function?

Rather than explain the self-evident ways that digital scholarship differs from or extends traditional print scholarship, a question I wish to bracket, we might explore the nature of digital scholarship and the variation it takes. In the digital humanities we have experienced two decades of unfettered experimentation in the form of scholarship. Although such experimentation should continue, genres that can be circulated, reviewed, and critiqued would afford colleagues in the disciplines ways to recognize and validate this scholarship. Properly focused but broadly defined, such genres might alter the disciplinary conversation and appear in venues that provide a foundation for future scholarship in the disciplines. In the next phase of the digital humanities, then, scholars have the opportunity to debate, and perhaps clarify, the qualities and characteristics of digital scholarship.

***

The uncertain and contested nature of digital scholarship can be seen in two reports published in 2013 on the state of the humanities in American higher education: Harvard University's *Mapping the Future* report and the American Academy of Arts and Sciences' *The Heart of the Matter*. Each of these reports made extensive recommendations, but neither the Harvard report nor *The Heart of the Matter* explored in detail the impact of the digital humanities on the disciplinary modes of scholarly research and communication. Harvard's report was telling – it included just a single reference to digital humanities in one footnote in its 53-page document. *The Heart of the Matter* report directly acknowledged "the digital age" but mostly focused on two developments: the rise of open online learning environments and the opportunities that digital projects create for lifelong learning and the preservation of cultural texts and documents.

Citing a handful of digital initiatives, such as the Perseus Digital Library, *The Heart of the Matter* offered just one, highly instrumental and deterministic, statement on the possibilities of the digital age:

> Online resources offer unprecedented opportunities for scholars to frame topics of public interest, to participate in a wider community of public intellectuals, and to reach general audiences. The digital world offers vast new possibilities, not only for delivering instruction, but also for facilitating research and for making the past and future possibilities come alive to students of all ages: historic buildings are reconstructed; family trees can be traced; classic texts and manuscripts are made accessible. (National Commission on the Humanities & Social Sciences, 2013:52)

From the beginning of the 1990s, however, as the networked possibilities of the World Wide Web became more and more robust, Edward Ayers, Jerome McGann, and others repeatedly argued that we have the entire human record (cultural, written, spoken, performed) to digitize, organize, prepare, interconnect, analyze, and *interpret*, and we have the digital capacities (memory, networks, and protocols) to do so in ways we were only beginning to realize (McGann, 1997, 2001; Ayers, 1999). The work of digital scholars, therefore, would not be a simple operation of migration of data from analog to digital, as envisioned in *The Heart of the Matter*. This effort would be a humanistic scholarly endeavor, a process of assembling, encoding, editing, and interpreting. It would demand that we consider anew how we represent knowledge, and it would require newly trained scholars and practitioners who had fluency in the hardware and software technologies of the digital medium. These digital scholars would attempt unexpected, non-traditional forms of scholarship, and their work would not fit within the well-established confines of the monograph or the academic journal. Instead of merely facilitating research, digital technologies would shift the definition of scholarship and digital scholars would invent new modes of interpretive argument and criticism. "A major goal of mature hypertextual history," Ayers wrote in 1999, "will be to embody complexity as well as to describe it."

Many scholars in the digital humanities began to see themselves as, and to act as, an open community of practice, including anyone whose energy, expertise, and enthusiasm aligned with theirs. Rather than conceiving of their project as necessitating a separate discipline or field, digital humanists worked within the disciplines from a loosely defined set of common methods, all concerned with a broad recognition: that humanistic understanding and inquiry were being reconstituted in digital form through digital technologies.

The first 20 years of the digital humanities, then, saw widespread experimentation around three orders of scholarly activity, each building on and in relation to the other, each sometimes pursued within the other:

1. reassembling the human record in digital form;
2. shaping the affordances of humanistic materials in digital form; and
3. creating discipline-based interpretive scholarship in digital form.[1]

These scholarly activities could be understood as sequential, and yet each could be independently pursued. Scholars built digital archives, layered them with affordances that were premised on interpretive decisions, then wove interpretive scholarship into a digital project. So interwoven were these activities that non-digital scholars could see little that resembled their expectations for peer-reviewed scholarship. Meanwhile, digital humanists found few reasons, given the contours of the medium, to approach their work differently (Waters, 2013).

Nearly 20 years later, we might ask how far we have come on each of these three endeavors. By some measures, we have not come very far, especially toward the third. A recent overview of digital innovation in scholarly publication in the humanities found that there were few hypertextual works that embodied complexity or altered the mode of scholarly communication in ways uniquely suited to the online space. Ayers' vision, however appealing, was unfulfilled. Innovation in humanities scholarship, Alan Gross and Joseph Harmon concluded, "has been confined, for the most part to sidestream venues; mainstream publication has yet to be seriously affected." The authors found it "disturbing" that after two decades they had found "so little" Internet-based scholarship in the humanities. And even "more disturbing," the innovative scholarship they did find was mostly marginal to the careers of the scholars who produced it, funded nearly entirely through outside agencies, and produced as special projects, "not routine activities." (Gross and Harmon, "The future is already here: the internet revolution in science and scholarship." Manuscript shared with the author, May 2013).

One reason for the lack of progress toward discipline-based interpretive digital scholarship has been the continuous vitality of the monographic culture in the humanities. At least in the discipline of history, the monographic form has continued to serve as the principal means by which the profession communicates. Built on the rigorous review of evidence, argument, and narrative quality, this system has produced stunning examples of creative and exciting scholarship (Ayers, 2013a). In addition, journals often serve as the gatekeeper and record of scholarship in the humanities and social sciences, reviewing and critiquing monographs in addition to publishing scholarly articles that shape the discipline's conceptual, methodological, and theoretical frameworks. Yet most journals do not index, review, refer to, incorporate, imprint, or publish anything created solely for the digital medium. Because digital work is rarely featured or recognized in the leading journals, among other reasons, younger scholars have proven reluctant to develop born-digital scholarship, and departments have had difficulty evaluating this scholarship for promotion and tenure (Ensign, 2010; Townsend, 2010; Howard, 2012).[2]

These barriers to digital scholarship, however, are only the most visible, and they hide the larger epistemological and heuristic questions. More precisely, the problem we face, according to historian Chiel van den Akker, is that "the historical monograph no longer seems an appropriate model for historical understanding in a digital environment." In fact, the digital environment supports, indeed demands, new narrative forms that are more participatory, dialogic, procedural, reciprocal, and spatial. Akker suggests that the "dialogic process" is "what matters most" and what defines online scholarship. He argues that the process of engagement with the reader distinguishes "online narrativity" from the linear narrative forms found in monographic scholarship (Akker, 2013:107,113).

Similarly, Ann Rigney has pointed out the monograph "can no longer be taken as a given." She notes that "in the new media ecologies ... digitization and the internet offer new technologies for producing and disseminating historical knowledge and, in the process, present both opportunities and challenges." Digital humanists, she argues, have charted a "new theoretical model for viewing historical narrative in terms of its social production by multiple agents across different platforms" (Rigney, 2010:100).

If the new media ecologies Rigney refers to are indeed naturally "multimodal," then they demand new practices in scholarly production. For Rigney, the result is clear: scholarship will be characterized by "distributed authorship" and undertaken through networks or hubs of scholarly activity. Continuous flows of information and analytical procedures will unfold as scholarship. There will be no fixed final product (Rigney, 2010:117).

Recently, computer scientist Jaron Lanier has suggested a variety of ways that books, authorship, and readership might change in the digital environment. Worrying that we might lose "the pattern of what a book is in the stream of human life and thought," Lanier predicts that books of the future will be crowdsourced, will be written with the aid of artificial intelligence software, and will change between readings or between readers. "Books will be merged with apps, video games, virtual worlds, or whatever other digital format becomes prominent," he argues (Lanier, 2012:354–7).

As a second-order move, digital scholars have emphasized the need for establishing "affordances" embedded in the digital objects being assembled and digitized for humanistic inquiry and research. Affordances might include encoded metadata, enriched markup, specialized interfaces, geospatial and locational encoding, programs for sifting through data, and application programming interfaces (APIs).

The idea of affordances in the digital humanities has been borrowed from several disciplinary theories. The first is ecological psychology, building on the work of James Gibson, a leading theorist in perception, and the term is worth examining. According to Gibson, an affordance is the particular quality of an object or an environment that allows particular types of action. Affordances are also properties of an object or environment that affect the capabilities of an actor, and in this sense they are relative to the type of actor. In Gibson's well-known example, the properties of a surface, such as the ground beneath our feet, could be either "stand-on-able," affording support for heavy animals to walk or run upon, or "sink-into-able," affording no such support except for water bugs. The affordances, therefore, are relative to the actor, not just abstract physical properties. Gibson explained, "different layouts afford different behaviors for different animals, and different mechanical encounters." But Gibson also developed the theory of affordances to support his ideas of perception, arguing that affordances cut "across the dichotomy of subjective–objective" and point "both ways, to the environment and to the observer" (Gibson, 1979:127–8).

Second, human–computer interface (HCI) theorists adopted the term after Donald Norman used it in *The Psychology of Everyday Things*. Norman considered affordances to be user interfaces with properties that were perceptually salient, and in this way his use of the term went beyond Gibson's original theory. He considered affordances to be perceived by the actor and already known and familiar. They were culturally dependent and shaped by the prior experiences of the user. Norman also suggested that an affordance included the way in which the possibilities of the object are made known to, conveyed, or made "visible" to the user (Norman, 1988).

Scholars in digital humanities have loosely applied the term in both the original Gibson formulation and in the HCI derived sense popularized by Norman. Ignoring the substantial difference between the two has led to some confusion. Affordances might best be considered properties of digital objects that are relative to the reader rather than uniform. They are not linear or fixed. Indeed, much of the energy and work in the digital humanities community has been framed around building digital objects with particular properties, tools that are inflected in ways specific for humanistic inquiry, interpretive acts, and formulating hypotheses. These efforts have been substantial, and include large-scale digital editing projects, interface design for digital reading, query design, and data encoding. The shaping of affordances has been preparatory to, and vital for, further interpretive scholarship (Deegan and McCarty, 2012:166).

Janet Murray in *Inventing the Medium: Principles of Interaction Design as a Cultural Practice* (2012) explains how the digital medium exploits certain affordances. Rather than settle for remediation of old media into digital forms, Murray encourages scholars and designers to "think more radically." She describes four essential affordances of the digital medium: procedural, spatial, encyclopedic, and participatory. According to Murray, "these four properties constitute our design space, the context for all of our design choices." Every work of digital scholarship can be assessed on the degree to which it maximizes these four affordances. Some works may be more spatial than participatory, or more encyclopedic than procedural. Murray's formulation of an "affordance grid" offers a particularly helpful way to categorize digital works. By placing a digital project on the scale of its relative engagement in each affordance category, Murray suggests we can "map an existing or proposed artifact against the larger design space in order to identify opportunities for growth and to predict the direction of media innovation." Affordance mapping entails asking, "What does it do? What can I (the interactor) do? Where am I in relation to the whole? What are the boundaries of this domain?" (Murray, 2012:45,51,91).

But even within digital humanities, we are often vague about what we mean by *digital scholarship*. Unsurprisingly, given the strong emphasis on digital humanities as solely a methodological approach, some scholars consider the first- and second-order activities listed above to be *de facto* digital scholarship. Others suggest that any monographs or scholarly journal articles derived from digital modes of inquiry and research also naturally qualify as digital scholarship, even if the final publication of these results takes place in traditional formats and scholarly venues. The former position holds that the digital humanities might mke use of tools and methods divorced from the concerns, questions, and understandings in a specific discipline. The latter position appreciates the need for disciplinary grounding but does not recognize the fundamental renegotiation in the form of scholarly communication that the digital medium demands. We might therefore distinguish between second-order and third-order work in the digital humanities, and between *digitally informed* scholarship and *digital* scholarship.

Edward Ayers recently provided a useful start: *digital* scholarship is "discipline-based scholarship produced with digital tools and presented in digital form." He has suggested that we need, in fact, to innovate more aggressively and to invest in its creation. "Digital scholarship is the missing part of the cycle of productivity that we have long believed our investments in information technology would bring to institutions of higher education" (Ayers, 2013a).

Scholarship built on and from digitized sources and presented in digital form would prove appropriate to the digital environment in ways that the monograph no longer satisfies. A robust digital infrastructure for the disciplines used in the service of specific arguments, moreover, would allow the humanities scholar possibly to:

- amplify an argument within nested modules of evidence and historiography;
- simulate the worlds we are trying to reveal in multiple dimensions;
- embody the full range and complexity of the historical problem;
- reveal simultaneity of time, place, and scales; and
- situate multiple perspectives of historical participants, past scholars, and current readers and collaborators.

Although Ayers' definition of digital scholarship is explicitly "discipline-based," most historians, to take one subset of the digital humanities, have remained bystanders in the broader effort to create digital scholarship at any of the three levels. In a survey of historical scholarship for the period 2003 to 2013, compiling an index of over 1000 digital history scholarly products (blogs, projects, hypertexts, archives, conference papers, journal articles, and websites), digital activity skewed heavily toward particular institutions and formats. During this period, the American Historical Association annual meeting hosted 281 conference papers or presentations focused on digital scholarship. The number and variety of these papers were impressive, but over 75 were given at just one conference: the 2012 conference when the president of the association made a concerted effort to showcase digital scholarship. With over 200 scholar-led, and over 50 student-led digital history projects, the scope of digital history scholarship has expanded measurably in the last decade. Yet nearly all of these projects were housed in a few centers and institutes where digital history has been nurtured and sustained with institutional and social support (George Mason University, University of Virginia, University of Nebraska, Stanford University) (Thomas and Nash, 2013).[3]

In sum, the digital humanities across several disciplines has deferred substantive engagement with the third-order problem of interpretation, narrativity, and argument in digital form. Charitably, digital scholars have been concerned with creating frame-works suitable for interpretive arguments; less charitably, digital scholars have been willfully unconcerned with interpretation, argument, and criticism. While some digital humanists have regarded the first- and second-order assembly of digital resources in itself to be an act of interpretation, scholars in the disciplines by and large have resisted this view. In response, digital scholars might not only endeavor to explain the interpretive affordances they undertake but also formulate agreed-upon genres for digital scholarship.

The scholarship of the digital humanities largely resides outside the disciplines, but this precarious situation threatens to render either the disciplines irrelevant to the digital future of cultural communication or the digital humanities irrelevant to the future of the core disciplines in the humanities. If we renew our efforts to imagine genre conventions for something we would call digital scholarship, then we could create forms of scholarly communication so robust and well established that a digital work could become an essential work in the field of history or literary criticism.

In this way the digital humanities holds more promise than yet realized – to broaden its methods into the disciplines, to alter the interpretive models in the disciplines, and to shape more fully the means of disciplinary intervention. Digital humanities scholars have been especially effective at creating hubs of network-enabled scholarly activity and engaging students as collaborators. Greg Crane has recently drawn attention to the need for "a new culture of learning" not only for the field of classics, but also more broadly for the humanities. According to Crane, "we need a laboratory culture where student researchers make tangible contributions and conduct significant research." Crane argues that "the crush of data challenges us to realize higher ideals and to create a global, decentralized intellectual community where experts serve the common understanding of humanity" (Crane, 2012a, 2012b). Ayers also recently called for students to participate in a cycle of "generative scholarship." He suggested that students build their work alongside ongoing research projects so that their contri-butions are assessed, validated, and preserved (Ayers, 2013b).

In the training of graduate students, digital humanities might consider a serious effort to classify digital scholarship to provide a rough typology for those both in the field and outside of it, as a set of definitions for genres suitable to our disciplines. Although digital scholarship is often collaborative and blurs the line between archive, tool, and publica-tion, we might search for common forms of scholarly intervention, train students for these genres, and establish categories of digital scholarship for review in the disciplines. For 20 years, digital scholars have called for experimentation in the forms of scholarship, and the results have been exciting. Concentrating on a few forms, at this important juncture, would support systems of review and evaluation, provide clarity for disciplinary structures of scholarly communication, sustain a common framework for graduate training, and encourage scholars to participate in the creation of digital scholarship.

A few forms of digital scholarship have become relatively well defined and commonly pursued across the digital humanities. They are offered here not as a definitive list but as suitable categories for organizing and presenting digital scholarship.

Interactive scholarly works (ISWs). These works are hybrids of archival materials and tool components, and are situated around a historiographically significant or critical concern. These works often assert a methodological argument as well, demonstrating that the combination of tools and materials serves as a method worthy of applying to the problem. Interactive scholarly works have a limited set of relatively homogeneous data, and they might include a textual component on the scale of a brief academic journal article. They feature an API for users to access the data and programming directly. Relatively tightly defined in subject, ISWs provide users with a high degree of interactivity in a limited framework. Elijah Meeks and Karl Grossner have recently proposed a definition for these works: "a digital archive ... a tool for exploring ... , and an argument about [a subject]. Furthermore, it makes a methodological argument that its representations – its computational model and visualizations – are a useful means for reasoning about [the subject]" (Meeks and Grossner, 2012).

Digital projects or thematic research collections (TRCs). Digital projects, sometimes referred to as thematic research collections, are perhaps the most well-defined genre in digital humanities scholarship. Carole L. Palmer's 2004 review of these works emphasized several qualities, such as their heterogeneous datatypes, structured but open-ended, designs to supporting research, multi-author participation, and primary sources. Combining tools and archival materials framed around a historiographically significant or critical problem, these projects are sprawling investigations. Typically gathering thousands of objects and records from widely varying institutions and in widely varying formats, digital projects contain "digital aggregations" of primary sources that support research on a particular theme or historical question. Scholars embed interpretive affordances in the collection and use these affordances to open up new modes of inquiry and/or discovery. They are open-ended projects and often support ongoing research by multiple scholars or teams. Often traditional peer-reviewed scholarship is derived from thematic research collections. The next phase of thematic research collections might feature interpretive scholarship embedded within and in relationship to the collection (Palmer, 2004).

Digital narratives. These scholarly works are born-digital, and they primarily feature a work of scholarly interpretation or argument embedded within layers of evidence and citation. They do not and presumably cannot exist in analog form. They may be multimodal, multi-authored, and user-directed. They may change between and among readings, either through updates or algorithmic reconstitutions. Unlike the first generation of "e-books," which transferred analog books into digital formats, these nonlinear, multimodal narratives offer explicit hypertext structures. These works primarily provide multiple points of entry for readers and situate evidence and interpretation in ways that allow readers to unpack the scholarly work. They are highly configured, deeply structured, and strongly interpretive pieces of scholarship. They could be standalone self-generating web sites, cloud applications, or presented in a media-rich scholarly publishing framework such as Scalar.

Simulations constitute a new form for scholarly research and publication as well. Interpretive decisions are embedded at every level in any simulated, textured environment, and feature a range of media products, including video, audio, and 3D models and game engines. Historical simulations and humanities-oriented games possess varying degrees of interpretive strength. Some are purely representational and feature minimal interpretive or argument-driven analysis. Others offer simulated decision-trees in a game-engine environment with heavily interpretive choices (McGann and Drucker, 2000; Coltrain, 2013). Hybrid media objects that combine text, graphics, live action, and animation sequences also constitute what Lev Manovich (2013) calls "a new species" in the digital medium, and they can be evaluated using Murray's affordance grid as well as the matrix table provided here (Table 36.1). While simulations will likely become in and of themselves a category of digital scholarship with particular characteristics that set them apart from the above types of scholarly work, at this writing they are most commonly used in a supplementary fashion.

In a landmark 1997 study on the future of narrative, Janet Murray emphasized specific qualities inherent in cyberspace, and we may consider in a similar fashion what qualities characterize the above categories of digital scholarship (Murray, 1997). Assessing the types of data, components, organization, scope, interpretive nature, and character of digital works allows us to separate one category from

Table 36.1   Matrix of digital scholarship.

	Interactive scholarly works	Digital projects or thematic research collections	Digital narratives
Type of data	Homogeneous, primary	Heterogeneous, primary	Integrated, layered
Components	APIs, scripting	Schema, data models	Analysis, modules
Organization	Hypothesis	Theme or subject	Criticism
Scope	Tightly defined	Capacious	Problem-oriented
Interpretative nature	Query-based	Affordances	Multimodal
Character	Procedural inquiry	Open-ended	User-directed, hypertextual
Examples	ORBIS (orbis.stanford.edu) *Visualizing Emancipation* (dsl.richmond.edu/emancipation) *Railroaded* (railroaded.stanford.edu) *Who Killed William Robinson?* (canadianmysteries.ca/en/robinson.html) *O Say Can You See: Early Washington DC Law and Family* (earlywashingtondc.org)	*Valley of the Shadow* (valley.lib.virginia.edu) *Whitman Archive* (whitmanarchive.org) *Mapping the Republic of Letters* (republicofletters.stanford.edu) *Digital Gazetteer of the Song Dynasty* (songgis.ucmerced.edu)	*The Differences Slavery Made* (www2.vcdh.virginia.edu/AHR) *Gilded Age Plains City* (gildedage.unl.edu) *Who Shot Liberty Valance?* (mamber.filmtv.ucla.edu/LibertyValance) *Hearing the Music of the Hemispheres* (scalar.usc.edu/anvc/music-of-the-hemispheres) *Queering Slavery Working Group Tumblr* (http://qswg.tumblr.com)

another. An ISW, for example, differs from a TRC not only because its scope is more tightly defined, but also because its interpretive nature lies in the query structures it provides the reader rather than in the encoded affordances that a TRC builds into its archival materials. The ISW operates around a series of procedural inquiries, whereas the TRC offers open-ended investigatory structures. These characteristics of the categories are not meant to be exhaustive, but illustrative, as a basis for categorization and review.

***

The contested nature of digital scholarship stems in part from an unresolved tension between the digital humanities and the disciplines. Many digital humanists take the position that digital environments demand multimodal, reciprocal, nonlinear modes of scholarship. Scholars in the disciplines perceive an inherent contradiction between that form of scholarship and criticism, review, and evaluation. Because criticism has been based on fixity, the fluidity and reciprocity at the heart of the digital environment's affordances suggest that traditional mechanisms of review no longer apply. In other words, if the defining characteristic of digital scholarship is that users make their meanings alongside and in relation to the interpretive framework of the creators, then how do we encourage digital scholars to develop arguments and work critically? More fundamentally, is it possible to conduct scholarly argumentation and conversation in this environment?

In the 2004 *Companion to Digital Humanities*, Claire Warwick's essay urged scholars to take "into account the culture of long-established print scholarship" and to consider "a new way to see, and thus to perceive the complexities in the process of interpreting humanities materials" (Warwick, 2004). The genres for such scholarship were limited in 2004, but a decade later they are beginning to take shape. The majority of all humanities activity is already and will continue to take place in the digital environment.[4] It seems clear that if digital scholars do not shape the future of humanities scholarship online in the open Web, then others will. In short, the grand challenge from nearly 20 years ago is still before the digital humanities. Only now, we have the tools and networks to make progress in ways we did not then. Will humanities scholars continue to produce conventional scholarship only to deposit it online? Or will we fulfill the promise of the digital humanities and take advantage of the networks, spaces, and audiences online to create and refine new forms of our scholarship?

Bridging the gap between the digital humanities and the disciplines will require changes to institutional priorities and practices at all levels by all parties, including the digital humanities community. In the next phase of the digital humanities, scholars may be called upon to play a more purposeful role in making interpretive arguments, to establish genres of digital scholarship, to engage in meaningful critical review of digital scholarship, and to deal more forcefully and deliberately with the digital divides in our disciplines.[5]

NOTES

1 The recent controversies at the Modern Language Association over "who's in and who's out" of digital humanities and the arguments over whether coding is a necessary characteristic of digital humanists have led to numerous efforts to define digital humanities as a field. As defined here, "building" broadly includes both editing and encoding, as well as, in some cases, programming. The emphasis here is less on programming as a requirement and more on building digital infrastructures that allow interpretive modes of scholarship.

2 Indeed, Robert Townsend's 2010 survey of AHA members regarding research and teaching found that nearly half of those polled had considered publishing online, and valued digital publication as a means to reach a wider audience of historians and get their work out more quickly. He also found that those who have not yet published in an online journal, but would consider it, overwhelmingly cited the perception that online scholarship lacks the scholarly recognition and prestige of print publication as the main reason for their reluctance (Townsend, 2010).

3 The Zotero library, available under the group "DigitalHistory" (http://www.zotero.org/groups/digitalhistory), includes digital history-related projects, tools, essays, and blogs which we located by systematically surveying the websites of various digital history and humanities centers, university history departments, and classroom syllabi, and conducting Google searches for "digital history," "student projects," and variations thereof. We also consulted the CHNM Compendium of Digital Humanities for items relating to digital history. In addition, we have documented 281 papers, panels, and sessions related to digital history presented at the AHA from 2003 to 2013. This list was compiled by reading through the online programs for the aforementioned years and making note of the topic and affiliation of the speakers, sessions, or panels. Many scholarly associations, including the Organization of American Historians, do not keep past conference bulletins online, or do so only with titles. We used the AHA not only because it is the largest conference, but also because the AHA's website includes full title and abstract information for each paper, thus producing the most accurate data.

4 An indicator of the extent of humanities research activity online is *Wikipedia*, a collective effort that began in 2003. Page views in *Wikipedia* climbed to over 200 billion in 2012 worldwide. Over 100,000 new articles are created each day. Wikipedians made over 2 billion edits to the site in 2012. The Library of Congress' *Chronicling America* (chroniclingamerica.loc.gov) alone had over 30 million page views in 2012. Between 2000 and 2006 (the only years for which data are available), the Library of Congress' *American Memory* (memory.loc.gov) page views rose from 228 million to 996 million. See the Annual Reports of the Librarian of Congress, http://www.loc.gov/about/reports/annualreports (accessed January 2014).

5 The Council on Library and Information Resources (CLIR) has provided essential leadership in calling attention to the need for broader investment in digital scholarship. The Digital Public Library of America (DPLA) has begun to focus national attention on the problem of digital preservation and access.

REFERENCES AND FURTHER READING

Akker, C. van den. 2013. History as dialogue: on online narrativity. *BMGN – Low Countries Historical Review* 128 (4), 103–17.

Ayers, E.L. 1999. The pasts and futures of digital history. http://www.vcdh.virginia.edu/Pasts Futures.html (accessed January 2014).

Ayers, E.L. 2013a. Does digital scholarship have a future? *EDUCAUSE Review*, 48 (4), 24–34.

Ayers, E.L. 2013b. A more radical online revolution. *The Chronicle Review,* February 4, 2013.

Cohen, D.J., Frisch, M., Gallagher, P., *et al.* 2009. Interchange: the promise of digital history. *Journal of American History*, 95 (2), 442–51.

Coltrain, J. 2013. A 3D common ground: bringing humanities data together inside online game engines. Short paper presented at Digital

Humanities 2013, http://dh2013.unl.edu/abstracts/ab-420.html (accessed January 2014).

Crane, G. 2012a. The humanities in the digital age. Paper presented at *Big Data & Uncertainty in the Humanities*, University of Kansas. http://www.youtube.com/watch?v=sVdOaYgU7qA (accessed January 2014).

Crane, G. 2012b. Greek, Latin and a global dialogue among civilizations. Center for Hellenic Studies, Harcard University. http://chs.harvard.edu/CHS/article/display/4827 (accessed January 2014).

Darnton, R. 1999. The new age of the book. *New York Review of Books*, March 18.

Deegan, M., and McCarty, W., eds. 2012. *Collaborative Research in the Digital Humanities*. Farnam: Ashgate.

Eijnatten, J. van, Pieters, T., and Verheul, J. 2013. Big data for global history: the transformative promise of digital humanities. *BMGN – Low Countries Historical Review* 128 (4), 55–77.

Ensign, R. 2010. Historians are interested in digital scholarship but lack outlets. *Chronicle of Higher Education*. Wired Campus Blog, October 5, 2010, http://chronicle.com/blogs/wiredcampus/historians-are-interested-in-digital-scholarship-but-lack-outlets/27457 (last accessed January 2014).

Gibson, J. 1979. *The Ecological Approach to Visual Perception*. Boston, MA: Houghton Mifflin.

Harvard University. 2013. *The Teaching of the Arts and Humanities at Harvard College: Mapping the Future*. Cambridge, MA: Harvrd University. http://artsandhumanities.fas.harvard.edu/files/humanities/files/mapping_the_future_31_may_2013.pdf (accessed Januaary 2014).

Howard, J. 2012. Historians reflect on forces reshaping their profession. *Chronicle of Higher Education*, January 8. http://chronicle.com/article/Historians-Reflect-on-Forces/130262 (accessed January 2014).

Jockers, M.L. 2013. *Macroanalysis: Digital Methods and Literary History*. Urbana: University of Illinois Press.

Lanier, J. 2012. *Who Owns the Future?* New York: Simon & Schuster.

Manovich, L. 2013. *Software Takes Command*. New York: Bloomsbury Academic.

McGann, J. 1997. Imagining what you don't know: the theoretical goals of the Rossetti Archive. Institute for Advanced Technology in the Humanities. http://www2.iath.virginia.edu/jjm2f/old/chum.html (accessed January 2014).

McGann, J. 2001. *Radiant Textuality: Literature After the World Wide Web*. New York: Palgrave.

McGann, J., and Drucker, J. 2000. The Ivanhoe game: an introduction. Institute for Advanced Technology in the Humanities. http://www2.iath.virginia.edu/jjm2f/old/IGamehtm.html (accessed January 2014).

McGrenere, J., and Ho, W. 2000. Affordances: clarifying an evolving concept. *Proceedings of Graphics Interface, 2000*.

Meeks, E., and Grossner, K. 2012. ORBIS: An interactive scholarly work on the Roman world. *Journal of Digital Humanities* 1 (3). http://journalofdigitalhumanities.org/1-3/orbis-an-interactive-scholarly-work-on-the-roman-world-by-elijah-meeks-and-karl-grossner (accessed January 2014).

Moretti, F. 2007. *Graphs, Maps, Trees: Abstract Models for a Literary History*. New York: Verso.

Murray, J. 1997. *Hamlet on the Holodeck: The Future of Narrative in Cyberspace*. New York: Free Press.

Murray, J. 2012. *Inventing the Medium: Principles of Interaction Design as a Cultural Practice*. Cambridge: MIT Press.

National Commission on the Humanities & Social Sciences. 2013. *The Heart of the Matter*. Cambridge, MA: American Academy of Arts & Sciences. http://www.humanitiescommission.org/_pdf/hss_report.pdf (accessed January 2014).

Norman, D. 1988. *The Psychology of Everyday Things*. New York: Basic Books.

Palmer, C. 2004. Thematic research collections. In *A Companion to Digital Humanities*, ed. S. Schreibman, R. Siemens, and J. Unsworth. Oxford: Blackwell. http://www.digitalhumanities.org/companion (accessed February 12, 2014).

Pressner, T., Schnapp, J., and Lunenfeld, P. 2009. *The Digital Humanities Manifesto 2.0*. http://www.humanitiesblast.com/manifesto/Manifesto_V2.pdf (accessed January 2014).

Rigney, A. 2010. When the monograph is no longer the medium: historical narrative in the online age. *History and Theory*, Theme Issue 49 (December), 100–17.

Svensson, P. 2010. The landscape of digital humanities. *DHQ: Digital Humanities Quarterly* 4 (1).

Thomas, W.G., and Ayers, E.L. 2003. The differences slavery made: a close analysis of two American communities. *American Historical Review* (December 2003).

Thomas, W.G., and Nash, K. 2013. *DigitalHistory Zotero Library*. http://www.zotero.org/groups/digitalhistory (accessed January 2014).

Townsend, R.B. 2010. How is new media reshaping the work of historians? *Perspectives on History*, November 2010.

Warwick, C. 2004. Print scholarship and digital resources. In *A Companion to Digital Humanities*, ed. S. Schreibman, R. Siemens, and J. Unsworth. Oxford: Blackwell. http://www. digitalhumanities.org/companion (accessed January 12, 2014).

Waters, D. 2013. An overview of the digital humanities. *Research Library Issues* 284, 3–11.

White, R. 2011. *Railroaded: The Transcontinentals and the Making of Modern America*. New York: W.W. Norton.

37

Building Theories or Theories of Building? A Tension at the Heart of Digital Humanities

Claire Warwick

The phrase "more hack less yack" is perhaps one of the most abused and misunderstood in the history of digital humanities scholarship, and one of the most potentially injurious to the harmonious conduct of DH as a field in the future. It has been all too readily used as a Twitter-friendly portmanteau term to describe an alleged binary opposition between makers and theorists in DH and beyond. In this chapter I will examine the arguments on both sides of the debate, investigating the question of whether such a non-permeable opposition may truly be said to exist.

So where did this terminology originate, and what are the problems caused by this binary view of a digital subject? Initially the phrase comes out of the culture of the THATCamp movement in DH. These are a series of participatory unconferences which began in 2008 at George Mason University in the USA, and whose spirit is described thus on their website:

> THATCamp stands for "The Humanities and Technology Camp." It is an unconference: an open, inexpensive meeting where humanists and technologists of all skill levels learn and build together in sessions proposed on the spot. An unconference is to a conference what a seminar is to a lecture, what a party at your house is to a church wedding, what a pick-up game of Ultimate Frisbee is to an NBA game, what a jam band is to a symphony orchestra: it's more informal and more participatory. (www.thatcamp.org)

I do not mean to imply that THATCamp is a negative influence on the world of DH, and indeed it has brought many new people to our field, and opened up important areas for discussion. "More hack less yack" was coined to describe the spirit of participatory idea-sharing, and of making rather than listening passively to someone talk. In the context of such an unconference, this phrase was unproblematic, and appropriately

A New Companion to Digital Humanities, First Edition. Edited by Susan Schreibman, Ray Siemens, and John Unsworth.
© 2016 John Wiley & Sons, Ltd. Published 2016 by John Wiley & Sons, Ltd.

inspiring (Nowviskie, 2014). However, as is often the case with memorable phrases that can encapsulate a great deal in small space, it quickly leaked into other areas of DH parlance, perhaps carried on the vector of Twitter. Here it began to have a life of its own, sometimes as a hashtag: a shorthand term encapsulating the desire of some in DH to make things, as opposed to talking or writing about them.[1] As Nowviskie explains, this had the unfortunate effect of making the phrase, coined originally in a light-hearted fashion, take on a weight of communication baggage to which it was unsuited, and which has the danger of making our field look unscholarly or even gimmicky (Nowviskie, 2014).

Nevertheless, the term is evidence of a deeper debate in the field of DH: the apparent opposition between making and doing and thinking and theorizing. As Nowviskie rightly says, this can be used in two senses the question of how credit is ascribed in the Alt-Ac and in faculty communities, and the question of making versus theory. As Nowviskie argues, academic faculty and graduate students are used to gaining credit for being yackers; in other words by the quality of their thought, as evidenced by their ability to write and speak eloquently about their work. Alt-Ac DH is, however, predicated on the question of making things, primarily digital resources, for which people are then credited.

This question of what scholarly communities value and how they ascribe credit for work is vital, but we should not imagine that this is unique to DH. In this chapter I will review some of the DH debates about this and compare them to the way such ideas have been discussed as other new disciplines developed. In doing so I shall argue that there are historical precedents for what DH is experiencing; this may be the inevitable pain of developing into a mature discipline.

Critiques of Digital Humanities

In the last few years DH has been described as "the next big thing," perhaps even the savior of the humanities (Pannapacker, 2012). It is also experiencing a very rapid growth and attracting new scholars to the discipline, many of whom are relatively early in their careers. If we are experiencing the "come to DH moment" it is hardly surprising that our pleasure in so doing attracts some envy or disquiet from more traditional fields, and that DH scholars themselves should question whether the nature of DH as it has been is appropriate for the field as it will be (Pannapacker, 2012). Some of these critiques have recently been expressed in terms of the apparent opposition between making and theorizing.

One of the most prominent was by Stanley Fish, the eminent literary scholar and theorist. In two blogs for the *New York Times* he describes DH as an evangelical discipline whose adherents promise to take over the literary field, right its previous wrongs, solve the apparent crisis in the humanities, and equip students with skills that will get them jobs (Fish, 2012a). He also notes that it has taken over from postmodernism and associated theories as the most popular subject for sessions at the MLA conference (Fish, 2011). This is significant: we should remember that Fish made his name in, and remains a star of, highly theorized, postmodernist-influenced writing about literature. He seems to betray a certain level of anxiety that the next generation chooses to express an interest in a field in which he is not a central figure. It is not surprising, therefore, that he seems to be arguing that DH scholarship is overly simplistic – obsessed with finding patterns in data, whose meaning we are too unsubtle to interpret; not sure what we are looking for, or why we are looking for it, and surprised by what we find. In other words, that DH is barely worthy of the term scholarship because we do too much and think too little (Fish, 2012b). There is also a strong implication that our field does not take sufficient cognisance of theory – in effect, that we are not sufficiently expert players in the game of theory wars – and that as a result ours is not a respectable discipline.

Other, different, critiques have come from scholars who identify themselves with DH, but whose previous work has either been within, or strongly influenced by, other fields that are strongly theorized, predominantly those of literature and cultural studies of which Fish might well approve. With a strapline of "Transformative Digital Humanities: Doing Race, Ethnicity, Gender, Sexuality and Class in DH" on their website (http://transformdh.org), they describe themselves as #TransformDH, a term coined after a panel session at the American Studies Association in 2011. Philips's blog (2011) provides a very helpful overview of this process and links to other bloggers' views on what she calls the "hack versus yack debate." However, in essence #Transform DH scholars, for example Cerire (2012), have argued that DH is too optimistic, present-centered, positivist, and simplistic. They recommend a greater engagement with questions of gender, class, race, and sexuality, and agree with Liu (2012), who advocates for DH to make better linkages with literary and cultural theory.

Such arguments have often been made via the informal publication media of the blogosphere and Twitter. The nature of the media by which such ideas are spread is important, and, surprising as it may appear, also has a something of a historical precedent. Blogs are, by their nature, personal, often tending towards the polemical or even satirical, and are usually not moderated or peer-reviewed. Twitter is a medium of fast, real-time exchange, much used in DH, where arguments must be massively condensed, and may, as a result, lack nuance. It is interesting to note, therefore, that DH methodology storms often seem to be associated with Twitter, whether this is the origin of the argument or the vector for discussing it (Schuman, 2014). The original arguments may be distorted by a Twitter storm, where ideas are exchanged too fast, groundless assumptions made, friends and colleagues weigh in to support each others' opinions, or rebut attacks, and the original subtlety of the ideas is degraded. This is not necessarily a bad thing: the writers may have wanted to spark debate by being deliberately controversial.[2] But it can lead to false polarization of attitudes of the hack and yack type.

Yet if, after the immediate passion has dissipated, we look at the blogs that spark the debates, it is noticeable that writers, especially those within the DH community, are seldom seeking to create binary opposition. They may point out that certain themes have been neglected but in doing so, blog after blog (with the notable exception of those by Fish) wants to stress commonality rather than widen differences. For example, Cerire replies to a critique of her ideas and those of #TransformDH by Roger Whitson (2012). She asserts her own view that traditional DH is overly liberal, in its rhetoric of "openness, collaboration and inclusiveness," contrasting this with what she terms "little-t" activist theories of gender, disability, sexuality, etc. Yet she also strives for agreement and points of commonality between theoretical discourse and DH:

In that sense, I agree with Roger. Digital humanities doesn't need to stop doing the critical work it's already doing. But #transformDH suggests, to my mind rightly, that the jolt of the oppositional can be powerful, when it is rooted in a critical activism that builds on the little-t theories that have preceded and exist alongside it, rather than manifesting as nerdy beleagueredness. (Cerire, 2012)

Her rhetoric may be avowedly confrontational, yet in seeking common ground she is still, arguably, conforming to the collaborative, communitarian expectations of the kind of liberal DH she critiques. Could this be because as a field we are, as Scheinfeldt (2010) argues, too nice? In response to the Fish blog, Underwood cautioned that we would do well to avoid being dragged into the kind of theory wars that beset more mature disciplines:

"Literary scholars are addicted to a specific kind of methodological conflict. Fish is offering an invitation to consider ourselves worthy of joining the fight. Let's not." (Underwood, 2011)

There is a striking sense that many of the articles and blogs on the making versus theorizing debate slide away from the initial provocation and seek a middle ground of agreement; that we are all DH and this is in the end what matters. Might it be because of the Big Tent ideology? I shall go on to argue that theoretical and methodological differences may be healthy in a young field, and that big tents can become suffocating. Before doing so, it is important to look at the other side of the argument: we need to be clear what the theorizing tendency is reacting against.

Making and Building in Digital Humanities and Beyond

There has long been a strong view in digital humanities that "real humanists make tools," as the slogan for the (now apparently defunct) Text Analysis Developers Alliance (TADA) (http://tada.mcmaster.ca/blog) put it. In his reply to the Fish blog, Steve Ramsay – a maker whose theorizations Fish (2012b), uniquely, approves – sets out a deliberately controversial view that "digital humanities is about building things" and that to be a true DHer, one must be able to code – although, in typical DH fashion, even he seeks consensus, softening the more controversial statement thus:

I'm willing to entertain highly expansive definitions of what it means to build something. I also think the discipline includes and should include people who theorize about building, people who design so that others might build, and those who supervise building (the coding question is, for me, a canard, insofar as many people build without knowing how to program). I'd even include people who are working to rebuild systems like our present, irretrievably broken system of scholarly publishing. (Ramsay, 2011a)

Yet he still finishes that section by saying, "But if you are not making anything, you are not – in my less-than-three-minute opinion – a digital humanist."

But this should not be seen as evidence of support for an unintellectual stance; quite the reverse. In his fascinating book *Reading Machines* (2011b), Ramsay approaches literary criticism by way of making – he creates and employs scripts and tools to analyze language. But he makes it clear that this is in itself a critical method. Thus the activity of making and doing – not simply the analysis of the resultant data – is, inherently, intellectually meaningful. There are immediate parallels, which Ramsay recognizes (Ramsay and Rockwell, 2012), between his work and that of Galey and Ruecker (2010): that a digital prototype is, in itself, an argument. For Galey and Ruecker, the act of creating the prototype, including the critical discussion of how it is made, and what problem it is intended to address, is an important intellectual exercise. Doing and making become their own theory.

A slightly different combination of making and doing can be found in the more specialized field of critical code studies which is associated with DH, computer science and game studies. This, as the name suggests, views computer code as an object of study, in a way that is, arguably, analogous to the study of a literary text (Marino, 2006). It also insists that it is important to understand the capacities of digital tools and techniques used to create resources, because they have an important effect on the affordances of the final resource. This is not making, but, in the study of a digital artifact, it brings the expression of a critical opinion (yack) and the results of making (hack) together.

It is also arguable that we cannot fully understand digital resources until we have made them ourselves: that it is only by writing programs, building databases, digitizing material or marking up text that we fully appreciate the complexity of what might appear relatively simple in digital terms, at least to the non-maker (Turkle, 2009). This philosophy lies behind much of the teaching that we do in DH programs. We do not necessarily expect our students to be full-time digitizers, encoders, or programmers, but we teach them to do so, so that they should understand the digital objects that they will go on to work with.

Beyond DH, this is also the philosophy of the movement that urges that everyone should be taught coding, advanced by organizations such as Code Academy. This is often expressed as a way to enhance employability and equality, by giving women a way into the male-dominated IT sector (O'Dell, 2011). But its proponents also argue that understanding code is vital as a way to ensure that children think critically about the digital resources and artifacts that they use and that surround them (O'Dell, 2011). In this sense it is related to calls for more basic information and media literacy. But coding is arguably more fun than learning information skills in a library, and so seems to have achieved a higher media profile, and more popular support: indeed from 2014 coding will become compulsory for schoolchildren in the UK (Curtis, 2013). The idea that language (whether coding or not) affects young minds, and that the understanding of its mechanics is an essential tool if we are not to be prey to manipulation in the modern age, is one that has an older resonance, as we shall see.

The Critical Making movement has also provoked controversy. Critical making is discussed in more detail in Chapter 1, but its supporters assert that making something (in this case often a physical, rather than digital artifact) is indeed an intellectual endeavor (Ratto, 2011). However, the assumption that making is not clever, but thinking is, seems to be an abiding theme in academia, not simply in the humanities.

As I have argued elsewhere, humanities scholars who make things have often been sneered at by colleagues. The question of whether an edition of a text should be regarded as the intellectual equal of an analytical monograph has a long history which, in many ways, mirrors current anxieties about how scholars, especially those early in their careers, can be adequately rewarded for the creation of a digital resource (Warwick, 2011).

Johanna Drucker argues that DH must have a more theorized discourse of making so that we can prove the worth of our discipline to others from theorized fields (Drucker, 2012). But why must we do so? Why is making so ill-regarded? I suggest because it speaks to a series of questions that DH has yet to solve. How can makers show that they are as intellectually able as those who theorize? How does making a digital resource differ from what librarians do when they mount an electronic journal on a server? How can the complexity and value of something digital be recognized, if those who assess it are humanities scholars who perceive themselves as thinkers, yet, innocent of code studies, are more used to uncritical use of digital resources in their research? It is that we, as a young discipline, still don't agree on what counts; what makes one scholar greater than another or one student cleverer than another; what sort of thing gets high marks in exams, credit in tenure or promotion, or stars in the Research Excellence Framework (REF). To return to the big-tent analogy, we do not yet know how to measure the lion tamers against the clowns, or the program sellers against the hot-dog vendors.

In the process of aging we shall have to address such questions, or decide that our activities have to take place in different tents, whether in the same or different fields. Indeed, Ramsay (2013) argues that this is already happening. However, it is instructive to look at the history of how two humanities disciplines, English and History, have developed – the arguments they have had about what matters and how to count it, and their methodological debates – to determine what perspective may be gained on the current arguments within DH.

The Development of English Studies

Matt Kirschenbaum (2010) has written an excellent article entitled "What is digital humanities and what's it doing in English departments?" His aim seems to be to prove that DH is a proper field of inquiry, and explain why respectable English departments might want it. But underlying this bipartite title is the assumption that unlike DH – the exciting new discipline that requires explication – English is monolithic, venerable, and perhaps just a little old-fashioned. This is hardly surprising: most of us would share the view of English studies as one of the great backbones of the humanities. Yet it has been so for a relatively short time, in comparison, for example, to classical studies, and the birth pains and adolescent traumas of English studies surely have something to teach us in DH.

We are not alone, as DH scholars, in working in a field that has for many years lacked respect from those in older fields. Just as DH has been, and usually still is, practiced and taught in departments of a different name and nature, so was English, once. In Cambridge, the subject was initially established under the Board for

Mediaeval and Modern Languages in 1878, and the holder of the first King Edward VII chair of English, A.W. Verrall, was a classicist (Goldie, 2013). Independent English departments were established earlier in the nineteenth century within the University of London (later to become UCL) and its rival institution, King's College London (Palmer, 1965:15–28). English was initially associated with extension teaching for working men and the education of women. The study of literature was thought to be morally inspiring and to provide a guide to proper living for the lower and female classes, neither of which had access to the classical literature that was part of education of upper-class schoolboys. A facility in the mechanics of language, which could be tested in an examination, was also thought of as useful for the administration of the government at home and in the growing empire (Baldick, 1983:59–75). Thus literature in English was substituted for that in classical languages, but it was not regarded as their equal in rigor or prestige. The doubtful associations with which it had grown up, as well as the lack of prestige of the new university colleges in London, meant that it was seen as a second-class, rather marginal subject (Goldie, 2013).[3]

The two most prestigious institutions were slow to associate themselves with English studies, as a result. But when they finally did, matters became even more controversial and publicly unpleasant (was this the "come to English moment"?). By the 1880s pressure had been building for some time for the establishment of a chair in English at Oxford University. Yet there remained considerable skepticism as to whether it was a subject of real intellectual study, or whether it was "mere chatter about Shelley," as E.A. Freeman, Regius Professor of History, put it (Palmer, 1965:95). There was also a question of how matters of taste and moral value might be examined: many Oxford academics felt it was impossible at the time, and the debate continued to dog the subject for decades afterwards (Potter, 1937:134). One way to do this, championed by Freeman and D.M. Monro, the Provost of Oriel College, was to base the study of literature upon philology, and the study of the history of the English language. This was vehemently opposed, notably by John Churton Collins, who argued that it was possible to teach English literature in a rigorous fashion by means of literary criticism, rhetoric, and philosophy (Goldie, 2013:65). The debate became heated, public, personal, and unpleasant.

It is also notable that it was conducted in the most rapid publication media of the time, such as periodicals and the letters columns of daily newspapers. The initial debate about the need for an English degree had been stirred up by Churton Collins's attacks on Edmund Gosse in the *Quarterly Review*, and Gosse's replies were delivered via the *Pall Mall Gazette* and the *Oxford Magazine*. Churton Collins then wrote a letter to *The Times* criticizing the phililogists, and Freeman replied in *The Contemporary Review*. Two other Oxford professors, Edward Armstrong and Thomas Case, published their critiques of the proposals in pamphlets, and the details of the debates held in congregation at Oxford were reported in *The Times* (Palmer, 1965:78–103). The public nature of the debates and relative speed of publication of these periodicals, produced using the latest that Victorian technology could offer, suggest immediate parallels to the blogged and tweeted debates about DH. It is also noticeable that the venues ranged from relatively informal media, such as pamphlets, to a newspaper of record: again there are parallels with our current situation, where debates about DH have appeared in media ranging from tweets to the *New York Times* blog.

In the end the first professor of English at Oxford was a specialist in ancient Germanic philology, A.S. Napier, and the degree program was established with, and retains, a strong element of philology and history of language. However, there was initial anxiety that so many of the students were women: if men did not want to study this new subject, perhaps it was still not quite respectable (Palmer, 1965:116–17).

Cambridge acquired an independent school of English even later, in 1917, with the final version of the Tripos (or degree) established in 1926. The anti-German sentiments stirred up by the First World War were prejudicial to philology, a subject strongly associated with German scholarship, and to the study of the Germanic roots of English language (Collini, 1998). The newly published Newbolt Report also stressed the importance of literature in English in asserting patriotic, national values. It was also, in some ways, a reaction to the excesses of journalistic war reporting and government propaganda. The study of English seemed to promise what we might now describe as media literacy: if students understood how language worked, there was less risk of them being manipulated by it, while still being inspired by the morally uplifting aspects of literature (Baldick, 1983).

The Cambridge method of studying English was, then, from its origins, very different from that at Oxford: the instructions for the first chair in English stipulated that its holder was "required to treat his subject on literary and critical rather than on philological and linguistic lines" (Potter, 1937:216). Yet there remained the problem of establishing objective, factual criteria against which to examine students, in the absence of philology and history of language. Fortunately a young academic called I.A. Richards had begun to experiment with a way of teaching students to read poetry which he called "practical criticism" (Martin, 2000). This was sorely needed; as his book of the same name shows, most undergraduates of the day had little idea of how to analyze poetry in anything but the most banal fashion. Richards regarded this as a serious omission in their education (Fry, 2000). He too was aware of the influence that journalistic and propagandistic language could have on the way that people thought and behaved, and believed that only detailed study of the way that language worked would remedy this (Richards, 1930: e.g., 248). This has interesting contemporary parallels with the motivation of the coding for all movement, discussed above.

It is curious, however, that, as Potter (1937:254–67) has argued, neither in Cambridge nor anywhere else was it felt important that students should be taught about language by learning to write creatively. This seems odd, when compared to degrees in, for example, music, where both composition and analysis are stressed as vital to the understanding of an art form. Richards described his method as scientific, yet it did not include the kind of practice in creative writing that might be analogous to laboratory experiments. In this sense, it differs from the learning by doing method that underlies so much DH pedagogy, and movements such as maker spaces and code academies, which all stress a mixture of making and critique. However, it is intriguing to note that many of the most vocal advocates of the idea that DH should be more heavily theorized, and less focused on making, are from, or formed in, the field of literary studies, predominantly in North America. Practical Criticism remains the foundation of Cambridge English, but was far less influential on the rest of UK English than it was in North America, where, with its successor, New Criticism, it influenced undergraduate pedagogy profoundly (Martin, 2000). Could it be that the urge to privilege theorization and analysis over making and doing comes from the emphasis that Practical Criticism and the New Critics placed on thought and analysis, to the exclusion of creativity as a method of understanding the humanities? Could it be that we are still feeling the influence of Richards' methods, almost a century after he designed them?

Practical Criticism and New Criticism may have been successful because they provided an objective method for examining undergraduates. Yet arguments persisted: F.R. Leavis's assertion of the moral values of English literature, influenced by Richards and his pupil William Empson, was widely challenged, even, or perhaps especially, within Cambridge itself (Martin, 2000). This was followed by the bitter and damaging debates about critical theory, especially Structuralism, in the 1980s. Debates persist, throughout UK English studies, as to the relative value of practical criticism, critical theory and the older philological traditions: views on who is winning differ, depending on who you ask, and which department they are part of.

The above provides a brief case study in the development of English studies in the UK, although there were numerous methodological battles in the USA and elsewhere. Yet English grew into a powerful, dominant, subject despite, or perhaps even because of, fundamental divisions about the way the subject should be taught, its underlying philosophy, what ought to be stressed and what dispensed with. Ramsay (2011a) speculates about what might happen if an influential university such as Duke or Yale were to reject encoding and building as a foundation of DH, and wonders if this is tenable, or whether it matters. But this is precisely what did happen in English studies when a leading university that was a rather late adopter of a discipline dissented from a more accepted method. It is also worth noting the original reason for these methodological arguments: uncertainty about how to measure the comparative worth of those who study such a discipline. In the case of nineteenth- and twentieth-century English studies, this concerned examining students; in twenty-first-century DH we are perhaps more preoccupied with the evaluation of academic research. Nevertheless, the question of what counts and how to measure excellence in a new and developing field is still one that preoccupies us, and drives internal debates about practices and methods.

History and Questions of Method

Such debates are not, of course, limited to the field of English. As Higham argues, arguments about methods, and what to count (sometimes in a very literal sense), characterized the development of history in the nineteenth and twentieth centuries. The study of history is also often associated with that of an older field from which it diverged; for example classics or philosophy. Academic history was also influenced by the technological developments and preoccupations of the times, especially in the case of the North American school of scientific history, whose practitioners were at pains to stress their independence from philosophy (Higham, 1965:87–144). But there have also been very longstanding debates as to what constitutes history, properly done; what has value, what kind of evidence ought to be used, and what kind of a field it is.

Higham discusses the relationship between social science and history, which has been debated since the late nineteenth century (Higham, 1965:108). As with English studies, there were discussions about what constituted history and how it should be done, to the extent that an entirely different school of history developed in France: the Annales school. The Annalistes were reacting against previous scholarship, dominated by political and diplomatic history (*histoire événementielle*). They thought this was focused too narrowly on individuals and events which might be very untypical of the experience of the larger population at a given time. Instead they chose to stress the importance of studying "*structures*" and "*mentalités*" (patterns of thought) over the "*longue durée*" (long periods of time) across large geographical regions, for example in Braudel's famous work *La Méditerrannée* (1949). The aim of this method was to track patterns of behavior and consumption in a population over long periods, as opposed to the study of high-status individuals, or notable events; to look at phenomena that did not change for centuries, "*l'histoire immobile*" rather than implied progress over relatively short periods (Le Roy Ladurie, 1966). This involved collaborative, organized studies involving teams of scholars and the collection and analysis of huge amounts of data; far more akin to scientific research than that of the lone historical scholar, which had been, and arguably continues to be, more common (Hexter, 1972[4]).

The Annalistes had a huge influence on the practice of history in France, which as a result developed rather differently as a field compared to North America or the UK. Nevertheless, the question of whether the study of history should concentrate on narratives, chronology, and change over time; or whether it should be data-driven, and influenced by a social-scientific search for patterns, and statistically measurable and generalizable phenomena, is far from answered. As Cochran and Hofstadter (1973) put it, the historian "may wonder whether he is a writer or a technician, a scientist or a prophet."

Social-science-driven history often lends itself to the use of computational tools and techniques, and thus tends to be the method best known to DH scholars who are not historians. As Fogel makes clear, the most intensively computational of these methods, cliometrics, does not simply use social-scientific ideas or theories as an aid to historical thought, but relies on the rigorous testing of large sets of data (Fogel, 1983:26ff). Yet even he concludes that cliometrics and data-driven history are ideal for the study of groups but are less well suited to that of individual experience: social-scientist-influenced historians would be less interested in discussing the death of the poet Keats from tuberculosis, and more about exploring patterns of tubercular infection in nineteenth-century England (Fogel, 1983:29). Gaddis (2002), however, argues that the essence of history is the study of chronology and change over time, and that social science methods, with their stress on what is typical, often developed for the study of a group over a relatively short time period, are therefore not appropriate for the historian. He argues that if historians wish to borrow methods from outside the humanities, they would be better to look at those in science, since disciplines such as cosmology are concerned with how the universe has changed over huge sweeps of time (Gaddis, 2002:17–34).

As is evident from the writers quoted above, historians regard it as vital to discuss the theory of history and to debate methods, to the extent that this branch of the subject has its own name – historiography. Higham describes the circumstances of its growth thus:

> American historians in recent years have shown a special predilection for writing about historical writing. Although still uncomfortable in the rarefied regions of the philosophy of history, they have become addicted to the more tangible sort of commentary we call

historiography. The sheer quantity is astonishing: historians ordinarily know that their own history is too small and provincial a part of their whole jurisdiction to deserve a large share of their attention. (Higham, 1965:89)

Although written about history, in 1965, we might quite easily adapt Higham's words, replacing history with DH, and they would sound remarkably current. Perhaps we are on our way to developing a new branch of DH: digital-humanities-ography sounds very ugly indeed, but most of us would recognize the phenomenon – which is, of course, what I am indulging in here.

Higham argues that historians feel a need not only to do history, but to theorize it, and discuss how it has been done, and might be done. Undergraduate history courses usually include classes in historiography, because it is regarded as an essential part of a historian's training. The historian must be able both to articulate and to understand the theory of the discipline, and to practice the study of history. Few historians would claim that it is possible, or even desirable, to privilege or advocate for one as inherently more valuable than the other. However, as we have seen above, while they may understand the wider historiography of their field, most historians practice a certain type of history, whether that is of geographical areas, periods of time, or types of people (for example, history from below as opposed to the study of elites). They may also have a more or less strictly and clearly expressed allegiance to practicing history in a particular way, whether this is the study of patterns and structures, using large datasets, or the interrogation of change over time and the production of narrative-driven history. In other words, for this mature discipline, as with many others, doing, building, and theorizing are all important: the negotiation of the balance may differ, but balance there must be.

Conclusion

Unlike markup, tents are not infinitely extensible. To DHers of a certain age it may feel normal and desirable to be "nice" and collegial. However, the examples of English and history suggests that as disciplines develop it may become increasingly difficult for all their members to agree about how things should be done. There may be heated, sometimes public, personal, and hurtful debates about methods and theory, but they do not necessarily threaten the future of a discipline. It may be that they are inevitable and healthy in a growing field. Certain methodological stances or approaches may become, or remain, dominant, but local variations and distinctive ways of doing the subject may develop, and indeed persist. Some scholars may be more passionate in their adherence to certain methods; others may prefer to explore the potential of mixing different methods, but be more influenced by one. Yet this does not stop scholars associating themselves with the field as a whole: Annalistes were still historians, Leavisites still English scholars. Indeed it was their commitment to the development and improvement of the subject, and the education of future scholars, that motivated them to propound such methods, and which led to such passionate debates about the future of a field.

It is also important to return to the idea of measurement and judgment of relative excellence. The arguments made in the nineteenth and twentieth centuries that no one could, or should, examine students in English studies, because matters of taste and moral improvement were inherently subjective, now seem untenable. Yet these debates were as pressing and important to the scholars of the time as ours about how different types of DH scholarship should be evaluated are to us, whether that is to do with Alt-Ac versus tenure track, or the problem of how early-career scholars gain credit for digital projects in a scholarly world that overvalues the monograph. In young disciplines such debates may be inevitable, especially when their adherents feel misunderstood by their more traditional colleagues. It is to be hoped that, with the progress of time and inevitable changes in scholarship, our debates will seem equally unnecessary and incomprehensible.

It may be that DH will have to let go of our ideas of niceness and methodological agreement, and accept the likelihood that different schools and methods of doing DH will emerge. This may entail public battles, schisms, and regroupings, but it does not necessarily threaten the integrity of the discipline; it may even be a sign of strength and confidence. My own formation as a Cambridge English student has left its mark on the way that I regard literary scholarship, as will be evident if I discuss such matters with someone developed in a more philological tradition. We may also find, in future, that, for example, UCLDH students have a characteristic view of their field that is discernible when compared to, say, those from Stanford. They may even be as unrepentant, and even proud of their intellectual origins as I am of mine. It is also important to remember that any given scholar can do DH and also be interested in a particular method such as postcolonialism or the cultural turn. It is not necessary to choose between a theoretical alignment and DH, and indeed some of the most exciting future scholarship may emerge from the marriage between such theories and DH practice.

Where then does this leave hack versus yack, building versus theorizing? It may be that for a field that has long been dominated by the study of text and words, we have been guilty of not studying the much-misused statement with which I began this chapter with enough attention. Rather than focusing our attention on the nouns, we might more productively consider the qualifiers. The phrase does not imply total exclusion, simply a choice of emphasis; one which might, perfectly reasonably, be reversed according to the scholar's inclination. This is, perhaps, a way forward for DH, given all those blogs and articles that strive for consensus, even while commenting on disagreement. It would be possible to imagine flavors of DH that concentrated exclusively on making to the exclusion of commentary or theorization, or on digital-humanities-ography without the practice: but a study of how other fields develops suggests that this is unlikely.

The hack versus yack debate is polarized and not especially fruitful. However, thinking about more and less — questions of how doing and thinking may be balanced within a larger discipline — is surely a more reasonable way to proceed. It may be perfectly reasonable to protest that DH has not been sufficiently reflective, or concerned with theories and the cultural contexts for our research, in the past; but this does not mean that all of those protesting about an overly naïve and positivist research context are advocating an entirely theorized future for the field. It may be equally reasonable to insist that DHers, whether students or those later in their DH careers, should be able to master practical techniques in order to understand the complexity of digital resources; but surely only the most hard-core of hackers would suggest that such making can exist devoid of all intellectual commentary or context. The really exciting ground for debate is the question of the proportions of, and balance between, building and theorizing in DH, and an honest and intellectually nuanced debate about how such activities may be evaluated and rewarded. It is in this negotiation of more and less that the field may grow into a truly mature discipline, worthy to claim its place at the core of humanities research and teaching.

Acknowledgments

I am very grateful to Professor H.R. Woudhuysen and Dr. M. J. Sewell for advice on, and discussion about, the development of English studies and historical method, respectively.

NOTES

1 I must confess to have used it this way myself, with little thought to what trouble might be caused in future.

2 It was not until I began constructing the list of references that I noticed how many of these provocative posts about DH methods are written in early January, coinciding with the annual MLA convention, during which attention is a scarce commodity.

3 UCL was especially suspect: known as "the Godless Institution in Gower Street" (Harte and North, 2004).

4 Hexter's article is not only a very valuable source of information about the Annalistes, but a witty and subtle parody of their style of writing, including the impressive length of both text and footnotes, the handling of evidence, and the use of (in this case rather spurious) maps.

REFERENCES AND FURTHER READING

Baldick, C. 1983. *The Social Mission of English Criticism 1848–1932*. Oxford: Clarendon Press.

Braudel, F. 1949. *La Méditerranée et le Monde Méditerranéen a l'époque de Philippe II*. Paris: Colin.

Cerire, N. 2012. In defence of transforming DH. *Works Cited*, January 8. http://nataliacecire.blogspot. co.uk/2012/01/in-defense-of-transforming-dh.html (accessed June 20, 2015).

Cochran, T., and Hofstadter, R. 1973. History and the social sciences. In *The Varieties of History: From Voltaire to the Present*, 2nd edition, ed. F. Stern. London: Macmillan, 347–68.

Collini. S. 1998. Cambridge and the study of English. In *Cambridge Contributions*, ed. S.J. Ormrod. Cambridge: Cambridge University Press, 42–64.

Curtis, S. 2013. Teaching our children to code: a quiet revolution. *Daily Telegraph*, November 4. http://www.telegraph.co.uk/technology/ news/10410036/Teaching-our-children-to-code-a-quiet-revolution.html (accessed June 20, 2015).

Drucker, J. 2012. Humanistic theory and digital scholarship. In *Debates in the Digital Humanities*, ed. M.K. Gold. Minneapolis: University of Minnesota Press, 85–95.

Fish, S. 2011. The old order changeth. *New York Times: Opinionator*. http://opinionator.blogs. nytimes.com/2011/12/26/the-old-order-changeth (accessed June 20, 2015).

Fish, S. 2012a. The digital humanities and the transcending of mortality. *New York Times: Opinionator*. http://opinionator.blogs.nytimes.com/2012/01/09/ the-digital-humanities-and-the-transcending-of-mortality (accessed June 20, 2015).

Fish, S. 2012b. Mind your P's and B's: the digital humanities and interpretation. *New York Times: Opinionator*. http://opinionator.blogs.nytimes.

com/2012/01/23/mind-your-ps-and-bs-the-digital-humanities-and-interpretation (accessed June 20, 2015).

Fogel, R.W. 1983. "Scientific" history and traditional history. In *Which Route to the Past?* ed. R.W. Fogel and G.R. Elton. New Haven, CT: Yale University Press, 5–71.

Fry, P. 2000. I.A. Richards. In *The Cambridge History of Literary Criticism. Volume 7: Modernism and the New Criticism*, ed. A.W. Litz, L. Menand, and L. Rainey. Cambridge: Cambridge University Press, 179–99.

Gaddis, J.L. 2002. *The Landscape of History: How Historians Map the Past*. Oxford: Oxford University Press.

Galey, A., and Ruecker, S. 2010. How a prototype argues. *Literary and Linguistic Computing* 25 (4), 405–24.

Goldie, D. 2013. Literary studies and the academy. In *The Cambridge History of Literary Criticism. Volume 6: The Nineteenth Century, c.1830–1914*, ed. M.A.R. Habib. Cambridge: Cambridge University Press, pp. 46–71.

Harte, N., and North, J. 2004. *The World of UCL 1828–2004*. London: UCL Press.

Hexter, J. 1972. Fernand Braudel and the Monde Braudellien. *Journal of Modern History* 44, 480–539.

Higham, J. 1965. *History: Professional Scholarship in America*. Baltimore: Johns Hopkins University Press.

Hofstadter, R. 1973. History and the social sciences. In *The Varieties of History: From Voltaire to the Present*, ed. F. Stern, 2nd edition. London: Macmillan, 359–68.

Kirschenbaum, M. 2010. What is digital humanities and what's it doing in English departments? *ADE Bulletin* 150, 55–61. http://www.ade.org/bulletin (accessed June 20, 2015).

Le Roy Ladurie, E. 1966. *Les paysans de Languedoc*. Paris: SEVPEN.

Liu, A. 2012. Where is cultural criticism in the digital humanities? In *Debates in the Digital Humanities*, ed. M.K. Gold. Minneapolis: University of Minnesota Press, 490–509.

Marino, M. 2006. Critical code studies. *Electronic Book Review*, April 12. http://www.electronicbookreview.com/thread/electropoetics/codology (accessed June 20, 2015).

Martin, W. 2000. Criticism and the academy. In *The Cambridge History of Literary Criticism. Volume 7: Modernism and the New Criticism*, ed. A.W. Litz, L. Menand, and L. Rainey. Cambridge: Cambridge University Press, 267–321.

Nowviskie, B. 2014. On the origin of "hack" and "yack." Nowviskie.org. January 8. http://nowviskie.org/2014/on-the-origin-of-hack-and-yack (accessed June 20, 2015).

O'Dell, J. 2011. Teaching women to code. *Washington Post*, November 1. http://www.washingtonpost.com/business/technology/tackling-techs-gender-problem-the-right-way-teaching-women-to-code/2013/01/11/d307df2a-5b36-11e2-b8b2-0d18a64c8dfa_story.html (accessed June 20, 2015).

Palmer, D.J. 1965. *The Rise of English Studies: An account of the Study of English Language and Literature from its Origins to the Making of the Oxford English School*. Oxford: Oxford University Press

Pannapacker, W. 2012. Pannapacker at MLA: the come-to-DH-moment. *The Chronicle of Higher Education*, January 7. http://chronicle.com/blogs/brainstorm/pannapacker-at-the-mla-2-the-come-to-dh-moment/42811 (accessed June 20, 2015).

Philips, A. 2011. #transformDH: a call to action following ASA 201. HASTAC blog, October 26. http://www.hastac.org/blogs/amanda-phillips/2011/10/26/transformdh-call-action-following-asa-2011 (accessed June 20, 2015).

Potter, S. 1937. *The Muse in Chains: A Study in Education*. London: Jonathan Cape.

Ramsay, S. 2011a. Who's in and who's out. Steve Ramsay blog, January 8. http://stephenramsay.us/text/2011/01/08/whos-in-and-whos-out (accessed June 20, 2015).

Ramsay, S. 2011b. *Reading Machines: Toward an Algorithmic Criticism*. Urbana: University of Illinois Press.

Ramsay, S. 2013. DH types one and two. Steve Ramsay blog. March 3. http://stephenramsay.us/2013/05/03/dh-one-and-two (accessed June 20, 2015).

Ramsay, S., and Rockwell, G. 2012. Developing things: towards an epistemology of building in the digital humanities. In *Debates in the Digital Humanities*, ed. M.K. Gold. Minneapolis: University of Minnesota Press, 75–84.

Ratto, M. 2011. Critical making: conceptual and material studies in technology and social life. *The Information Society* 27 (4), 252–60.

Richards, I.A. 1930. *Practical Criticism: A Study of Literary Judgement*. London: Kegan Paul.

Scheinfeldt, T. 2010. Why digital humanities is "nice." *Found History*, May 26. http://www.foundhistory.org/2010/05/26 (accessed June 20, 2015).

Turkle, W. 2009. Hacking as a way of knowing. pzed.ca. http://pzed.ca/access2009pei-william-j-turkel-hacking-as-a-way-of-knowing (accessed June 20, 2015).

Underwood, T. 2011. Why digital humanities isn't actually "the next thing in literary studies." *The Stone and the Shell*, December 27. http://tedunderwood.com/2011/12/27/why-we-dont-actually-want-to-be-the-next-thing-in-literary-studies (accessed June 20, 2015).

Warwick, C. 2011. Archive 360: the Walt Whitman Archive. *Archive* 1 (1). http://www.archivejournal.net/issue/1/three-sixty (accessed June 20, 2015).

Whitson, R. 2012. Does DH really need to be transformed? My reflections on #mla12. Roger T. Whitson, PhD, blog, January 18. http://www.rogerwhitson.net/?p=1358 (accessed June 20, 2015).

Index

Figures are represented in italics

A New Companion to Digital Humanities, First Edition. Edited by Susan Schreibman, Ray Siemens, and John Unsworth.
© 2016 John Wiley & Sons, Ltd. Published 2016 by John Wiley & Sons, Ltd.